ARCHAEOLOGY
OF THE
LAND OF THE BIBLE

THE ANCHOR YALE BIBLE REFERENCE LIBRARY is designed to be a third major component of the Anchor Yale Bible group, which includes the Anchor Yale Bible commentaries on the books of the Old Testament, the New Testament, and the Apocrypha, and the Anchor Yale Bible Dictionary. While the Anchor Yale Bible commentaries and the Anchor Yale Bible Dictionary are structurally defined by their subject matter, the Anchor Yale Bible Reference Library serves as a supplement on the cutting edge of the most recent scholarship. The series is open-ended; the scope and reach are nothing less than the biblical world in its totality, and its methods and techniques the most up-to-date available or devisable. Separate volumes will deal with one or more of the following topics relating to the Bible: anthropology, archaeology, ecology, economy, geography, history, languages and literatures, philosophy, religion(s), theology.

As with the Anchor Yale Bible commentaries and the Anchor Yale Bible Dictionary, the philosophy underlying the Anchor Yale Bible Reference Library finds expression in the following: the approach is scholarly, the perspective is balanced and fair-minded, the methods are scientific, and the goal is to inform and enlighten. Contributors are chosen on the basis of their scholarly skills and achievements, and they come from a variety of religious backgrounds and communities. The books in the Anchor Yale Bible Reference Library are intended for the broadest possible readership, ranging from world-class scholars, whose qualifications match those of the authors, to general readers, who may not have special training or skill in studying the Bible but are as enthusiastic as any dedicated professional in expanding their knowledge of the Bible and its world.

David Noel Freedman
GENERAL EDITOR

THE ANCHOR YALE BIBLE REFERENCE LIBRARY

ARCHAEOLOGY
OF THE
LAND OF THE BIBLE
10,000–586 B.C.E.

by Amihai Mazar

CENTER FOR JUDAIC-CHRISTIAN STUDIES

YALE

AYBRL

Yale University Press New Haven and London

First published in 1990 by Doubleday, a division of Random House, Inc.
First paperback edition published October 1992. First Yale University Press
impression 2009.

Printed in the United States of America.

Library of Congress Cataloging-in-Publication Data
Mazar, Amihai, 1942–
    Archaeology of the land of the Bible, 10,000–586 B.C.E. / by Amihai
Mazar. — 1st pbk. ed.
        p. cm. — (The Anchor Bible reference library)
    Includes bibliographical references and indexes.
    1. Bible — Antiquities. 2. Palestine — Antiquities. I. Title. II. Series.
BS621.M39   1992
220.9'3 — dc20   92-8432
                                                              CIP

ISBN 978-0-300-14007-1 (pbk.)

A catalogue record for this book is available from the British Library.

CONTENTS

PREFACE TO THE 1992 EDITION

This paperback edition is almost identical to the hardcover edition published in 1990, except for improvements in the graphic presentation of the maps and corrections of minor typographical mistakes.

During the three years since the first edition was updated, continued archaeological research in Israel and Jordan has brought to light some interesting discoveries. Additional studies have appeared in print. Some of the main discoveries, results of other studies, and references to recent publications are presented in the updated Appendix to this edition (pp. 551–55).

AMIHAI MAZAR
April 1992

PREFACE

Palestine—the land of the Bible—has been a prime target for archaeological research for the last hundred years. The desire to understand the Bible was a motivating force behind the evolvement of biblical archaeology. Interpretation of the finds was essentially intended to illuminate the *realia* of the biblical narrative. Over the years, however, the scope of archaeology in Palestine has been greatly extended. Biblical archaeology adapted itself to universal developments in archaeological research. Currently the field covers a wide spectrum of subjects related to the cultural changes in the country studied against the broader background of the ancient Near East.

The wide-scale archaeological activity in Israel and Jordan has revealed a tremendous quantity of data, its opulence and variety out of all proportion to the small size of the country. Hundreds of archaeological projects of different character and scope are carried out each year. The digestion of the data uncovered is overwhelming even for professional archaeologists, not to mention scholars of related subjects.

It is the purpose of this volume to present a comprehensive, updated, and as objective as possible picture of the archaeological research of Palestine relating to the Old Testament period. I choose to begin the survey with the earliest permanent settlements, dating to ca. 10,000 B.C.E., and to terminate the discussion with the destruction of the first temple by the Babylonians in 586 B.C.E and the period of Babylonian domination. The Persian period, though part of the historical scope of the Old Testament, is excluded, as I view it as the beginning of the era of the second temple.

The raw material for this book was gleaned from hundreds of preliminary and final reports, short notices, and papers scattered in dozens of periodicals, monographs, and jubilee and memorial volumes. Dynamic changes and new discoveries prompt new interpretations of and approaches to essential subjects, and sometimes one is even embarrassed by the totally opposing explanations of the same phenomena. These varying opinions are presented here in the text or in the notes.

Over recent decades, considerable discussion has taken place concerning the essence of the archaeology of the Holy Land. Should this field be regarded as an individual discipline, or is it just another branch of Near Eastern archaeology? Moreover, what impact does it have on current biblical, historical, and literary studies, and what are the pitfalls to be avoided by archaeologists in correlating their findings to these fields? Although this book is written as a straightforward introduction to the archaeology of Palestine, wherever possible I discuss the implications of the discoveries for biblical history. Hopefully this work will serve to narrow the ever growing fissure between archaeologists and other scholars of disciplines relating to biblical studies.

This book would not have been written without the encouragement of R. Blizzard, Jr., and D. A. Pryor, president of the Center for Judaic Christian Studies. I am grateful to Professor D. N. Freedman for his editorial comments on the entire text, as well as to the following scholars for important comments on particular chapters: W. G. Dever (Chapters One through Six); O. Bar-Yosef (Chapter Two); T. E. Levy (Chapter Three); P. de Miroschedji (Chapter Four); T. Dothan (Chapters Seven and Eight). The initial texts of Chapters Two, Three, Eight, and Nine were translated from the Hebrew by R. Grafman; the entire text was edited and prepared for publication by Janet Amitai. Rahel Solar prepared the maps and many of the line drawings. The editorial staff of Doubleday, and particularly Ms. Theresa D'Orsogna, made special efforts to bring this book to press. Finally, the discoveries described in this book would not be available without the endless efforts of my colleagues, the "dirt archaeologists" who are dedicated to the exploration of the ancient cultures of the Land of the Bible. To all, I am truly grateful.

A. MAZAR
*Jerusalem, October 1987**

* Some updatings of the text and notes were made at the beginning of 1989.

ACKNOWLEDGMENTS AND CREDITS

The photographs and line drawings in this book are published with the kind permission of the following scholars and institutions:

Collection of the Israel Department of Antiquities and Museums, photograph supplied by the Israel Museum: 2.1; 2.5; 2.9; 3.11; 3.12; 3.14; 3.16; 3.20; 4.21; 4.22; 5.9; 5.11; 6.18; 6.20; 6.21; 6.22; 7.8; 7.10; 7.14; 7.15; 7.16; 7.17; 7.18; 7.19; 7.20; 7.22; 7.23; 8.7; 8.8; 8.15; 8.16; 8.28; 8.33; 9.7; 10.13; 10.14; 10.34A; 11.24; 11.25; 11.26; 11.27; 11.28; 11.33; 11.35; 12.4; 12.5; 12.6.

Israel Department of Antiquities: 3.8; 3.9; 3.17; 3.18; 4.18; 4.23; 4.24; 4.25; 5.8; 5.9; 5.10; 5.12; 6.5; 6.19 (partly); 7.13 (partly); 7.16; 7.25; 7.31; 8.30; 8.31; 10.35; 11.6; 12.3.

Israel Museum: 2.5; 2.6; 7.29; 10.5; 10.18; 10.27; 11.22; 11.29; 11.30; 11.32; 12.7.

R. Amiran, Israel Museum: 4.5; 4.11; 4.12; 4.20; 4.24.

N. Avigad, Institute of Archaeology, The Hebrew University of Jerusalem: 10.8; 10.9; 10.10; 11.40.

G. Barkai, Institute of Archaeology, Tel Aviv University: 11.36 left; 11.37; 11.38; 11.39.

Beer-sheba Expedition, Institute of Archaeology, Tel Aviv University: 11.2; 11.13; 11.31.

Beer-sheba Museum: 11.21.

I. Beit-Arieh, Institute of Archaeology, Tel Aviv University: 4.8; 4.9; 4.10; 10.24; 11.23.

A. Biran, Nelson Glueck School of Biblical Archaeology, Jerusalem: 6.7; 6.13; 8.26; 10.4; 10.25; 11.4; 11.7; 11.19; 11.20.

E. Braun, Israel Department of Antiquities and Museums: 4.2.

British School of Archaeology, Jerusalem (Jericho Expedition): 1.5; 2.4; 2.7; 5.6; 6.17 (partly); 6.19 (partly).

City of David Expedition, Institute of Archaeology, The Hebrew University of Jerusalem, Israel Exploration Society: 9.3; 11.15; 11.36 right.

R. Cohen, Israel Department of Antiquities and Museums: 5.3; 5.4; 9.13; 9.14; 9.15; 9.16; 10.26.

F. M. Cross, Harvard University: 8.34.

W. G. Dever, Tucson University, and R. Cohen, Israel Department of Antiquities: 5.2.

W. G. Dever and Nelson Glueck School of Biblical Archaeology, Jerusalem: 5.5; 6.10; 9.11; 9.12.

M. Dothan, Haifa University: 6.3.

T. Dothan, Institute of Archaeology, The Hebrew University of Jerusalem: 7.27; 7.28; 7.30; 7.26B.

Ecole Biblique et Archéologique Française de Jerusalem and Editions Recherche sur les Civilisations, Paris: 4.15; 9.6; 11.1; 11.11.

A. Eitan, Israel Department of Antiquities: 10.30.

C. Epstein, Israel Department of Antiquities: 3.4; 3.17; 5.7.

S. Gitin, W. F. Albright, Institute of Archaeology, Jerusalem, and T. Dothan, Hebrew University (Tel Miqne Expedition): 8.6.

Ecole Biblique et Archéologique Française de Jerusalem (Tell el-Far'ah Expedition): 4.4 (partly); 4.15.

A. N. Goring-Morris, Institute of Archaeology, The Hebrew University: 2.10.

I. Finkelstein, Bar-Ilan University, Ramat Gan: 6.11; 8.19; 8.21; 8.25.

Hazor Expedition, The Hebrew University, Israel Exploration Society: 1.4; 1.6; 6.6; 6.14; 7.5; 7.6; 7.7; 7.21; 9.8; 10.6; 11.10; 11.16; 11.17.

R. Hecht Museum, Haifa University; Photo: Israel Museum: 11.34.

Z. Herzog, Institute of Archaeology, Tel Aviv University: 6.12; 9.10; 10.12; 10.22; 11.2; 11.3; 11.12.

Institute of Archaeology, The Hebrew University: 1.3; 4.4 (partly); some pottery drawings in 4; 6.10; 10.2; 11.8.

Israel Exploration Society, illustrations reproduced from the book *The Architecture of Ancient Israel* (editors: H. Katzenstein, E. Netzer, A. Kempinski, R. Reich) 1987: 4.19; 7.2; 9.9; 10.7; 11.14; 12.8. Illustration reproduced from Y. Aharoni, *Arad Inscriptions*: 10.23. Illustration reproduced from R. Amiran, *Early Arad*: 4.20. Illustration reproduced from *EAEHL*: 7.11.

G. L. Kelm, Southwestern Baptist Theological Seminary, and A. Mazar, The Hebrew University (Tel Batash Expedition): 6.8; 7.4; 10.33; 10.34B; 11.18; 12.1; 12.2.

A. Kempinski, Institute of Archaeology, Tel Aviv University: 4.14; 8.22; 8.23; 8.24.

M. Kochavi, Institute of Archaeology, Tel Aviv University: 1.8; 6.2; 6.4 (partly); 6.15; 6.17; 7.3; 7.32.

T. E. Levy, Nelson Glueck School of Biblical Archaeology, Jerusalem: 3.6; 3.19.

A. Mazar, Institute of Archaeology, The Hebrew University of Jerusalem: 8.9; 8.10; 8.11; 8.12; 8.13; 8.14; 8.17; 8.18; 8.20; 8.27; 8.32; 10.31; 10.32.

E. Mazar, Institute of Archaeology, The Hebrew University of Jerusalem: 10.11.

Z. Meshel, Institute of Archaeology, Tel Aviv University: 2.11; 10.28; 10.29.

P. de Miroschedji, French Archaeological Mission, Jerusalem: 4.6; 4.7; 4.13; 4.17.

T. Noy, Israel Museum: 2.3.

E. D. Oren, Ben-Gurion University, Beer-sheba: 7.26A; 8.2.

The Oriental Institute, University of Chicago: 4.16; 6.17 (partly); 7.13 (partly); 8.3; 8.4.

J. Perrot, French Archaeological Mission, Jerusalem: 2.8; 2.10; 3.2; 3.5; 3.8; 3.10; 3.15; 3.21.

M. W. Prausnitz, Israel Department of Antiquities: 4.25.

B. Rothenberg, Tel Aviv: 7.31.

Samaria Expedition: 10.2; 10.3.

D. Ussishkin, Tel Aviv University Institute of Archaeology: 1.7; 10.15; 10.16; 10.17; 10.19; 10.20; 11.5.

Wellcome-Marston Expedition to Lachish: 7.24.

A. Zertal, Haifa University: 8.28; 8.29.

Drawings prepared for this book by Rahel Solar, based on various original publications: 3.7; 6.9; 6.15; 6.16; 7.3; 7.6; 7.9; 7.12; 7.26; 8.1; 9.2; 9.4; 9.5; 10.1; 11.19.

Maps prepared by Rahel Solar: 1.1; 1.2; 2.2; 3.1; 4.1; 4.3; 5.1; 6.1; 8.5; 9.1.

Scripture quotations are taken from the Holy Bible, New International Version, Copyright © 1973, 1978, 1984, International Bible Society.

Translations of the Siloam inscription and Lachish letter no. 4 are taken from *ANET* with permission of Princeton University Press.

BIBLIOGRAPHIC NOTE

The notes in this volume refer mainly to the most recent publications. The latter usually cite earlier discussions which the interested reader may wish to review. General reference books (such as *EAEHL*, Kenyon [1979], and Aharoni [1982]), except in exceptional cases, are not included in the notes, as they are pertinent to all the subject matter. Due to space considerations, I was forced to omit the full title of papers as well as references to most of the final excavation reports. References to the latter can be found at the end of each relevant entry in the *EAEHL* and in the comprehensive bibliographies (updated until 1980) prepared by Eleanor K. Vogel; see E. K. Vogel, *Bibliography of Holy Land Sites. I. Hebrew Union College Annual* 42 (1971), pp. 1–96; ibid. II, 52 (1981), pp. 1–92 (offprints of the latter have been issued).

Other general books which are not mentioned in the notes are the following:

W. F. Albright, *The Archaeology of Palestine*, revised ed., Harmondsworth 1960.

W. F. Albright, *Archaeology and the Religion of Israel*, fifth ed., New York 1969.

D. W. Thomas (editor), *Archaeology and Old Testament Study*, Oxford 1967.

K. M. Kenyon, *The Bible and Recent Archaeology* (revised by P. R. S. Moorey), London 1987.

P. R. S. Moorey, *Excavations in Palestine*, Cambridge 1981.

H. D. Lance, *The Old Testament and the Archaeologist*, London 1983.

H. Weippert, *Palästina in Vorhellenistischer Zeit, Handbuch der Archäologie, Vorderasien II*, Band I, München 1988 (an updated comprehensive synthesis).

The following are some of the excavation reports pertaining to major multistrata *tells* in Palestine. These reports are listed according to the site and in the chronological order of their publication:

Beth-Shean:
1. A. ROWE, *The Topography and History of Beth Shan*, Philadelphia 1930.
2. ———, *The Four Canaanite Temples of Beth Shan*, Philadelphia 1940.
3. F. JAMES, *The Iron Age at Beth Shan: A Study of Levels VI–IV*, Philadelphia 1966.
4. E. D. OREN, *The Northern Cemetery of Beth Shan*, Leiden 1973.

Gezer:

1. R. A. S. MACALISTER, *The Excavations of Gezer*, vols. 1–3, London 1912.
2. W. G. DEVER, H. D. LANCE, and G. E. WRIGHT, *Gezer I: Preliminary Report of the 1964–66 Seasons*, Jerusalem 1970.
3. W. G. DEVER (ed.), *Gezer*, vol. 2, Jerusalem 1974.
4. ———, *Gezer*, vol. 4, Jerusalem 1986.
5. J. D. SEGER and H. D. LANCE, *Gezer*, vol. 5, *The Field I Caves*, Jerusalem 1988.

Hazor:

1. Y. YADIN et al., *Hazor*, vol. 1, Jerusalem 1958.
2. ———, *Hazor*, vol. 2, Jerusalem 1960.
3. ———, *Hazor*, vols. 3–4 plates, Jerusalem 1961, 1989.

Jericho:

1. K. M. KENYON, *Excavations at Jericho*, vol. 1, London 1960.
2. ———, *Excavations at Jericho*, vol. 2, London 1965.
3. K. M. KENYON and T. A. HOLLAND, *Excavations at Jericho*, vols. 3–5, London 1981–1983.

Lachish:

1. O. TUFNELL et al., *Lachish II: The Fosse Temple*, London 1940.
2. O. TUFNELL, *Lachish III: The Iron Age*, London 1953.
3. ———, *Lachish IV: The Bronze Age*, London 1958.
4. Y. AHARONI, *Investigations at Lachish: The Sanctuary and the Residency (Lachish V)*, Tel Aviv 1975.

Megiddo:

1. P. L. O. GUY, *Megiddo Tombs*, Chicago 1938.
2. R. S. LAMON and G. M. SHIPTON, *Megiddo*, vol. 1, Chicago 1939.
3. G. LOUD, *Megiddo*, vol. 2, Chicago 1948.

Tell Beit Mirsim:

1. W. F. ALBRIGHT, *The Excavation of Tell Beit Mirsim in Palestine. 1. The Pottery of the First Three Campaigns. AASOR* 12 (1932).
2. ———, *The Excavation of Tell Beit Mirsim. 1A. The Bronze Age Pottery of the Fourth Campaign. AASOR* 13 (1933).
3. ———, *The Excavation of Tell Beit Mirsim. 2. The Bronze Age. AASOR* 17 (1938).
4. ———, *The Excavation of Tell Beit Mirsim. 3. The Iron Age. AASOR* 21–22 (1943).

LIST OF ABBREVIATIONS

AASOR	Annual of the American Schools of Oriental Research
ADAJ	Annual of the Department of Antiquities of Jordan
Aharoni (1979)	Y. AHARONI, The Land of the Bible: Historical Geography (rev. ed.), Philadelphia 1979
Aharoni (1982)	Y. AHARONI, The Archaeology of the Land of Israel, Philadelphia 1982
AJA	American Journal of Archaeology
Amiran (1969)	R. AMIRAN, Ancient Pottery of the Holy Land, Jerusalem 1969
Anati (1963)	E. ANATI, Palestine Before the Hebrews, New York 1963
ANET	J. B. PRITCHARD (ed.), Ancient Texts Relating to the Old Testament (3rd ed.), Princeton 1969
ANEP	J. B. PRITCHARD (ed.), The Ancient Near East in Pictures, Princeton 1954
Architecture	H. KATZENSTEIN et al. (eds.), The Architecture of Ancient Israel, Jerusalem 1987 (Hebrew; English ed. forthcoming)
'Atiqot	'Atiqot: Journal of the Israel Department of Antiquities and Museums
BA	The Biblical Archaeologist
BAR	Biblical Archaeology Review
BASOR	Bulletin of the American Schools of Archaeological Research
BAT	Biblical Archaeology Today: Proceedings of the International Congress on Biblical Archaeology, Jerusalem 1985
Bright (1981)	J. BRIGHT, A History of Israel (3rd ed.), Philadelphia 1981
CAH	I. E. S. EDWARDS, C. J. GADD, and N. G. HAMMOND (eds.), The Cambridge Ancient History (3rd ed.), vols. 1–2, Cambridge 1970–75
Callaway Festschrift	J. F. DRINKARD, G. L. MATTINGLY, J. M. MILLER (eds.), Benchmarks in Time and Culture. Essays in Honor of Joseph A. Callaway, Atlanta 1988.
COWA 2	R. W. EHRICH (ed.), Chronologies in Old World Archaeology, Chicago 1965

COWA 3	R. W. EHRICH (ed.), *Chronologies in Old World Archaeology* (rev. ed. in press)
de Vaux (1978)	R. DE VAUX, *Early History of Israel*, Philadelphia 1978
Dothan (1982)	T. DOTHAN, *The Philistines and Their Material Culture*, New Haven 1982
EAEHL	M. AVI-YONAH and E. STERN (eds.), *Encyclopedia of Archaeological Excavations in the Holy Land*, Jerusalem 1975–78
EI	*Eretz-Israel: Archaeological, Historical and Geographical Studies*
Emmaus Colloquium	P. DE MIROSCHEDJI (ed.), *L'Urbanization de la Palestine à l'Age du Bronze Ancien, Actes du Colloque d'Emmaus (20–24 Octobre 1986)*, Paris (in press)
Gibson (1971)	C. L. GIBSON, *Textbook of Syrian Semitic Inscriptions. I. Hebrew and Moabite Inscriptions*, Oxford 1973
Glueck Festschrift	J. A. SANDERS (ed.), *Near Eastern Archaeology in the Twentieth Century: Essays in Honor of Nelson Glueck*, New York 1970
Hadidi (1982)	A. HADIDI (ed.), *Studies in the History and Archaeology of Jordan*, Amman 1982
HEI	J. SHAVIT (ed.), *The History of Eretz Israel*, Jerusalem 1984 (Hebrew)
Hennessy (1967)	J. B. HENNESSY, *The Foreign Relations of Palestine During the Early Bronze Age*, London 1967
IEJ	*Israel Exploration Journal*
JBL	*Journal of Biblical Literature*
JNES	*Journal of Near Eastern Studies*
Kenyon (1979)	K. M. KENYON, *Archaeology in the Holy Land* (rev. ed.), London 1979
Kenyon Festschrift	P. R. S. MOOREY and P. PARR (eds.), *Archaeology in the Levant: Essays for Kathleen Kenyon*, London 1978
Mazar (1986)	B. MAZAR, *The Early Biblical Period: Historical Essays*, Jerusalem 1986
Mellaart (1966)	J. MELLAART, *The Chalcolithic and Early Bronze in the Near East and Anatolia*, Beirut 1966
PEQ	*Palestine Exploration Quarterly*
Qedem	*Qedem: Monographs of the Institute of Archaeology, The Hebrew University of Jerusalem*
Rose Festschrift	L. G. PERDUE, L. E. TOOMBS, and G. L. JOHNSON (eds.), *Archaeology and Biblical Interpretation: Essays in Memory of D. Glen Rose*, Atlanta 1987
Symposia	F. M. CROSS (ed.), *Symposia Celebrating the 75th Anniversary of the American Schools of*

	Oriental Research (1900–1975), Cambridge, Mass., 1979
TA	*Tel Aviv: Journal of the Tel Aviv University Institute of Archaeology*
Tufnell Festschrift	J. Tubb (ed.), *Palestine in the Bronze and Iron Ages: Papers in Honour of Olga Tufnell*, London 1985
WHJP	B. Mazar (ed.), *The World History of the Jewish People*, vol. 1, Jerusalem 1963; vol. 2, Jerusalem 1970; vol. 3, Jerusalem 1971; vols. 4–5, Jerusalem 1979
Wright (1961)	G. E. Wright "The Archaeology of Palestine," pp. 73–112 in: G. E. Wright (ed.), *The Bible and the Ancient Near East: Essays in Honor of William Foxwell Albright*, New York 1961
Wright (1965)	G. E. Wright, *Shechem: The Biography of a Biblical City*, New York and London 1965
Wright (1985)	G. R. H. Wright, *Ancient Buildings in South Syria and Palestine*, vols. 1–2, Leiden 1985
Wright Festschrift	F. M. Cross et al. (eds.), *Magnalia Dei: The Mighty Acts of God. Essays on the Bible and Archaeology in Memory of G. E. Wright*, New York 1976
Yadin (1963)	Y. Yadin, *The Art of Warfare in Biblical Lands*, Ramat-Gan 1963
Yadin (1972)	Y. Yadin, *Hazor*, London 1972
ZAW	*Zeitschrift für die alttestamentliche Wissenschaft*
ZDPV	*Zeitschrift des Deutschen Palästina-Vereins*

LIST OF TABLES

LIST OF MAPS AND ILLUSTRATIONS

List of Maps and Illustrations

PAGE

GLOSSARY OF GEOGRAPHIC TERMS

HEBREW	ARABIC	ENGLISH
Tel	Tell	Mound
Hurvah	Khirbeh	Ruin
Nahal	Nahr, Wadi	River, Brook
Har	Jebel	Mountain
'En	Ain	Spring

ARCHAEOLOGY
OF THE
LAND OF THE BIBLE

CHAPTER ONE

INTRODUCTION

THE GEOGRAPHIC SETTING

The evolution of human culture in Palestine was greatly affected by the country's geographic location,[1] topography, climate, water, and other natural resources.[2]

In spite of its small size, Palestine comprises extremes in topography, landscape, and environmental conditions. Lengthwise, the borders of the country, from Dan in the north to Elath in the south, include 410 km (256 miles), but only 220 km (140 miles) of this territory, from Dan to Beer-sheba, are adaptable to permanent settlement. To cross from the Mediterranean Sea to the Jordan River, one travels an average of 80 km (50 miles), and the inhabited land in Transjordan is no more than 40 km (25 miles) wide. In all, the fertile land in the country, including the semiarid regions of the northern Negev and Transjordan, approximates 20,000 sq km (nearly the size of New Jersey).

The geographic location of the country determined its important role in the history of the ancient Near East. On the one hand, Palestine formed a bridge between the two ends of the Fertile Crescent—Egypt on the south and Syria and Mesopotamia in the north; on the other hand, it was compressed between the Mediterranean Sea on the west and the desert to the east. This unique situation was a basic factor in Palestine's history and cultural development. More than any other country in the ancient world, Palestine was always directly or indirectly connected with other parts of the Near East and the eastern Mediterranean. Its closest ties were naturally with Egypt and Syria, but relations with Mesopo-

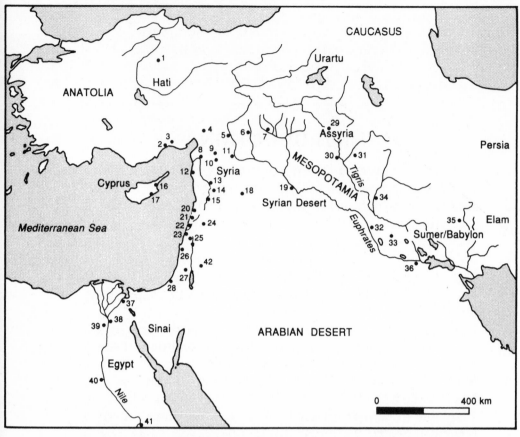

1.1 MAP OF THE ANCIENT NEAR EAST. 1: Hattusha; 2: Mersin; 3: Tarsus;
4: Sinjirli (capital of Sama'l); 5: Carchemish; 6: Haran; 7: Gozan (Tel Halaf);
8: Alalakh; 9: Aleppo; 10: Ebla (Tell Mardikh); 11: Emar (Tell Meskeneh);
12: Ugarit (Ras Shamra); 13: Hama; 14: Qatna; 15. Kadesh (Tell Nebi Mind);
16: Enkomi; 17: Kition; 18: Tadmor (Palmyra); 19: Mari; 20: Byblos;
21: Beirut; 22: Sidon; 23: Tyre; 24: Damascus; 25: Hazor; 26: Megiddo;
27: Jerusalem; 28: Gaza; 29: Nineveh; 30: Assur; 31: Nuzi; 32: Babylon;
33: Nippur; 34: Eshnunna; 35: Susa; 36: Ur; 37: Tell el-Dabʿa (Avaris, Pa-
Ramesses); 38: Memphis; 39: Saqqarah; 40: Tell el-Amarna; 41: Thebes.

tamia, Anatolia, Cyprus, the Aegean, and Arabia also had
considerable influence on its cultural history.

Palestine, in fact, should be considered part of the more
extensive region generally denoted "the Levant," including
Palestine, Lebanon, and the western half of Syria (the Orontes
Valley and the region of Aleppo), which have various common

geographic and climatic factors. The Levant's southern part, comprising Palestine, Lebanon, and southern Syria, constitutes a homogeneous unit which conforms with the biblical definition of the Land of Canaan.

Palestine's landscape today is a culmination of geological changes including sea incursions and tectonic movements, the last of which were witnessed by the earliest humans in the Jordan Valley, who lived there between one and two million years ago.

North of the Negev Desert, the country can be divided into several major longitudinal strips, the topography, breadth, and altitude of which vary: the coastal plain, the Shephelah foothills, the central mountain ridges, the Judean Desert (located east of the Judean Hills), the Rift Valley, mountains or plateaus east of the Rift Valley, and the eastern desert. East-west valleys, the most important of which is the valley of Jezreel, transect these units and create natural communication lines between the coastal plain and the inner parts of the country.

Palestine's coastline lacks natural inlets, except for the large Bay of Haifa with the port at Acre, and the coves at Jaffa, Dor, and ʿAtlit. In the south, the coastal plain is wide, and parts of it are covered by sand dunes originating from the Nile. Farther inland, in the south, the plain rises to become low hills consisting of loess soil (soft, sandy soil). North of the Yarkon River, where it is called the "Sharon Plain," the coastal plain narrows. Two north-south sandstone (*kurkar*) ridges divide the Sharon into long narrow troughs which could easily become marshes due to poor drainage. The Sharon is known to have been forested in antiquity with oaks and terebinth trees. The coastal plain narrows even more along the Carmel ridge, which descends into the sea at Haifa. In the valley of Acre and north to Rosh Haniqrah, the plain again widens. Rosh Haniqrah is a mountain ridge on the sea line which creates a natural border between Israel and Lebanon.

The coastal plain abounds in light, sandy soil (*hamra*) and water sources, and consequently it is one of the most fertile agricultural areas of the country. It is transected by several rivers, the most important of which (from north to south) are the Naaman, Kishon, Taninim, Alexander, and Yarkon. South of the Yarkon, most of the waterways, such as the Sorek, Lachish, Gerar, and Gaza brooks, are dry most of the year.

The foothills known by the biblical term "Shephelah" comprise a region of limestone hills which reach a height of 400 m above sea level. These hills lead to the Judean Hills, but farther north they are almost nonexistent. Inner alluvial valleys in the Shephelah, such as the Ajalon, Sorek, and Elah, provided land for agriculture and routes connecting the coastal plain and the inner mountains. The light gray *rendsina* soil of the Shephelah is conducive to pasture and to growing vines and olive trees.

The central mountainous ridge is divided into several different units. The northernmost is the Upper Galilee, where the topography is rigid and steep, and where the highest mountain in Israel (Har Meiron, 1,208 m above sea level) is located. The Lower Galilee, as its name implies, is lower, and its ridges are separated by inner east-west valleys such as the Netofa and Beth-Hakerem. In the east, plateaus such as the Issachar highland separate the mountains from the Jordan Valley.

The mountains of Samaria, bordered on the north by the Valley of Jezreel and on the south by the region of Shechem, are rather shallow; they are separated by wide inner valleys, such as those of Dothan and Sanur, that provide cultivable land and communication routes. The Shechem Brook and Wadi Far'ah cross the central mountains from west to east and serve as important links between the Jordan Valley and the coastal plain. South of Shechem, in the lands of Ephraim and Benjamin, the mountains become steeper, and inner valleys are sparse. The main route here is along the north-south watershed, connecting Shechem, Jerusalem, and Hebron.

The saddle of Jerusalem, about 800 m above sea level, is another important west-east pass in this region; it leads from the central coastal plain toward Jericho and the Amman area in Transjordan. The Hebron Hills recall those of the land of Ephraim in their steepness and lack of inner valleys. Both these regions reach heights of almost 1,000 m above sea level. The mountains, with an average annual rainfall of 600 mm and *terra rosa* soils, were heavily forested in antiquity. Settlement was possible only after the felling of the forest and the construction of terraces on the slopes. The border zones between the mountains and the desert to their east, and the

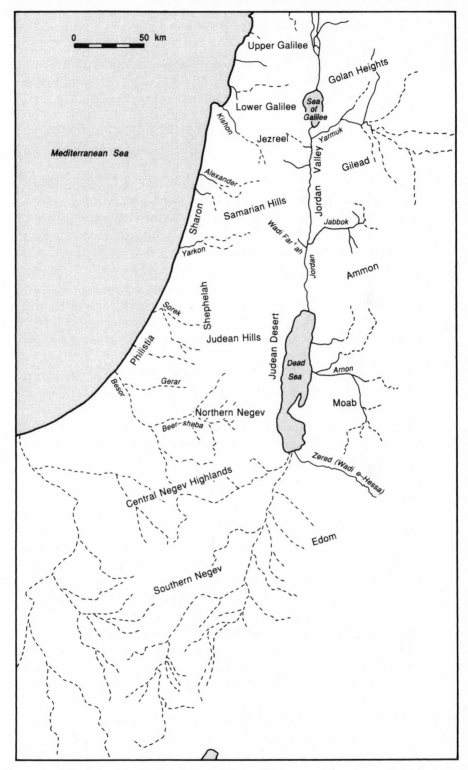

1.2   MAP OF GEOGRAPHIC REGIONS IN PALESTINE.   5

hills south of Hebron, were, however, suited to pasture and cultivation of cereals.

The valleys of Jezreel and Beth-Shean are the largest inner valleys in the country. Their abundant alluvial soil and water sources made them the natural granaries of the country, and consequently they were heavily settled in antiquity. The international route between Syria and Egypt passed through these valleys, and thus they were of particular strategic importance.

The narrow strip of land separating the mountains from the Jordan Valley becomes more and more arid as one proceeds southward from the Gilboa ridge, and south of Wadi Far'ah it becomes a desert. This desert region, south of Wadi Qelt, is called the "Judean Desert," and it played an important role in the history of the country due to its proximity to Jerusalem; it was utilized by pastoral nomads and was a natural shelter for refugees and rebels. Twenty kilometers in width, the Judean Desert is demarcated on the east by steep cliffs descending to the Jordan Valley and the Dead Sea, 400 m below sea level.

The Rift Valley, the longest and deepest natural fissure in the world, extends from northern Syria to eastern Africa and is one of the most vital geographic features in Palestine. It includes the Huleh Valley, the Lake of Galilee, the Jordan Valley, the Dead Sea, and the Arabah. The northern part of the Rift Valley, with its Mediterranean climate, played a significant role in ancient settlement and international traffic. The valleys of Beth-Shean and Succoth (the Damiah region, near the junction of the Jabbok River [Nahr ez-Zerkah] and the Jordan) were well adapted to agriculture and human habitation. The climatic conditions in the Rift Valley become worse as one proceeds south along the Jordan Valley, where settlements were established only in oases such as Jericho.

Several natural passes cross the Rift Valley to connect the western and eastern parts of Palestine. One of the most important of these is the Damiah crossing of the Jordan, where the Wadi Far'ah route connects with the valley of Succoth and leads to the Jabbok River and the Transjordan highland. Another important link is along the Yarmuk River south of the Lake of Galilee, and a third is east of Jericho.

Transjordan is divided into several subregions. In the north, it is bordered by Mount Hermon, 2,500 m above sea level, which is the most southern of the high ridges of the Anti-Lebanon. South of the Hermon are the basaltic Golan Heights, an offshoot of the vast volcanic regions of Bashan and Hauran. The Golan plateaus are divided by deep ravines, and on the south, the region is bordered by the deep gorge of the Yarmuk River. South of the Yarmuk is the Gilead ('Ajlun) highland, a fertile plateau conducive to settlement. Farther south are the plateaus of Ammon and Moab (south of Amman), which are quite arid. The Arnon River (Wadi Mujib) forms a natural obstacle to north-south traffic in the land of Moab, located east of the Dead Sea. Nahal Zered (Wadi Hesa) was also vital in antiquity, as it created the natural border between Moab and Edom. To its south, the mountains of Edom, reaching heights of over 1,600 m, extend to the Red Sea. The narrow, fertile Transjordanian plateaus are bounded on the east by the large eastern desert of Jordan, which extends to modern Iraq.

Although most of western Palestine enjoys a Mediterranean climate with sufficient rain and pleasant temperatures, conditions are more arid in the south. South of the Lachish Brook (Wadi Suchreir) is the vast region of the northern Negev, covered largely by loess soils. The average annual rainfall in the Judean Hills reaches 600 mm, but as one proceeds southward, the yearly amount decreases. In the region of the Besor and Gaza brooks it only approximates 250 mm, so farming is possible only in years of plentiful rain. In this region the southern extent of permanent settlement in the country fluctuated. Farther south and east, in the semiarid Beer-sheba and Arad valleys, the environmental conditions were even more harsh, and habitation occurred only in selected periods.

South of Beer-sheba, the Negev Desert comprises several distinct subregions. The central Negev highlands, bordered on the south by the great natural cavity of Machtesh Ramon and on the east by the cliffs of Machtesh Gadol and Nahal Zin, has an average annual rainfall of 60 mm. It is ideal for pastoralism, but agriculture was possible only by the use of sophisticated irrigation methods in exploiting winter floods. The Zin region, east of the highlands, and the southern Negev are more desolate, mountainous, and difficult to cross. Two major routes crossed the Negev from the north toward the Red Sea: that running through the Arabah Valley (the southern part of the Rift Valley), and the "Gaza Road," connecting

Gaza and the Red Sea via the important oasis of Kadesh-Barnea.

The Elath-Aqaba region at the head of the Red Sea was the important gateway to naval and caravan commerce with southern Arabia and eastern Africa. The sandstone strip north of the granite mountains of this region contained copper ores, exploited several times in antiquity.

Invading armies, trade caravans, and messengers crossed strategically situated Palestine. The Sinai Desert west of the Negev forms the natural barrier between Egypt and Palestine. The 180 km separating the eastern branch of the Nile from el-Arish could be crossed only by way of the desert route across north Sinai, where substantial water sources were lacking. This route was the land bridge between Egypt and Asia, exploited during several historical periods. Its continuation became known as the "Via Maris" (The Way of the Sea). The latter extended up the coastal plain from Gaza to Aphek, bypassing the Yarkon River; it continued along the eastern edges of the Sharon Plain, running through Wadi 'Ara to the Jezreel Valley near Megiddo. From there one branch proceeded to the Beth-Shean Valley and Transjordan, another continued northward through Hazor toward Syria, and a third passed from Megiddo or across the Carmel to the valley of Acre and the Lebanese coast.

The second main international route, known as the "King's Highway," runs close to the border between the settled area and the desert in Transjordan. It was the main north-south communication axis in this region, connecting Syria with the Red Sea and Arabia.

The Mediterranean coast of Palestine is mostly straight and not convenient for anchoring. The few bays which could serve as natural ports are those of Acre, Haifa, Dor, and Jaffa. The river mouths such as those of the Na'aman near Acre, the Kishon near Haifa, the Yarkon north of Tel-Aviv and Nahal Lachish near Ashdod provided additional safe ports. The importance of the naval connections along the eastern Mediterranean forced the ancient peoples of Palestine to build port towns also in unconvenient places, especially along the southern coast (such as at Gaza and Ashkelon). This chain of ports enabled tight naval connections during various periods between Palestine, Egypt, the coasts of the Levant, Cyprus, southern Turkey, and the Aegean. The intensity of these connections changed from one period to the other, but in most of the periods under discussion in this book the naval connections of Palestine were an important factor in its economy and cultural development.

Thus, in spite of its small dimensions, Palestine, like the Levant in general, is a heterogeneous region, divided into well-defined areas of different ecological and environmental character. This is the background to the development throughout history of separate, rival geopolitical units, each with its own regime, ethnic features, and material culture. As a bridge between the centers of civilization in Egypt and Mesopotamia, Palestine was influenced by both these powers. It was also a pawn in the continuing struggle for control of the Near East between the great powers and in their hostile designs upon each other. The proximity of the country to the sea facilitated connections with the eastern Mediterranean civilizations, while the deserts on the east and south were the source of conflict between "the desert and the sown," in which desert nomads invaded the fertile lands whenever a crisis or a collapse in government provided the opportunity.

THE TELL AND THE RUIN

The prerequisites of an ancient settlement were sufficient land, water availability, communication routes, and a defendable position. A combination of these features was found only in limited areas of Palestine, mainly close to perennial fountains and rivers. Once a site was chosen, it was obviously also suited to the needs of later generations, and the subsequent occupations in the same place created the artificial mound known as a *tell*. This phenomenon is fundamental to the archaeology of the Near East. Most of the pre-Hellenistic towns in Palestine are to be found in such *tells*. Their average area is 7–20 acres; the smallest known is half an acre, while the largest, Tel Hazor, measures 200 acres.[3] Many *tells* were settled over a period of between one and two thousand years, and their accumulated debris may include more than twenty layers of ruined cities, each forming an archaeological stratum.

In addition to *tells*, there are thousands of other sites of varying types. Many can be defined as "ruins," inhabited only during one or a few periods. They are important for the study of the country's settlement history; and for the prehistoric

1.3   Tel Beth-Shean.

and protohistoric periods (the eighth through fourth millennia B.C.E.) they are essential, as the initial occupation of most *tells* does not predate the urban age in the third millennium B.C.E. In later periods also, the smaller settlements outside the main fortified cities are major components of the settlement pattern, and in arid areas, these ruins are almost the only type of site to be found.

HISTORY OF THE RESEARCH

The history of the archaeological research of Palestine may be divided into three major phases: (1) pre–World War I; (2) the interwar period; and (3) the post-1948 period.[4]

The first attempts at surveys and scientifically controlled excavations occurred before World War I; in fact, the research of the country started with systematic surface surveys and historical-geographic studies carried out during the nineteenth century by the American scholar E. Robinson, the British Palestine Exploration Fund (the main explorers were C. Conder and H. H. Kitchener), and the Frenchman Ch. Clermont-Ganneau. But these studies were mainly concerned with visible ruins related mostly to the Roman and later periods. The main achievement concerning the Old Testament period in this early phase of research was the identification of many biblical places with ruins and sites which in many cases preserved the ancient names.

The major breakthrough in archaeological methodology concerning the early periods was made by the Englishman Sir F. Petrie, who toward the end of the last century grasped the essential nature of the ancient *tells* as well as the importance of pottery for establishing relative chronology. His excavation at Tell el-Hesi in southern Palestine (codirected by the American F. J. Bliss) between 1890 and 1894 was the first systematic archaeological project in an ancient *tell*. The title chosen for the report of this excavation—*A Mound of Many Cities*, published by Bliss in 1894—implies the basic character of the *tell*, described in this volume for the first time.

Petrie was followed by a number of archaeologists who carried out excavations at major mounds before the outbreak of World War I. Of these excavations, the most renowned were the ones performed by the Irishman R. A. S. Macalister at Gezer (1902–9); Bliss and Macalister at other mounds in the Shephelah; D. Mackenzie at Beth-Shemesh (1911–12); the Americans G. A. Reisner and C. S. Fisher at Samaria (1908–11); the Germans G. Schumacher and C. Watzinger at Megiddo (1903–5); the Austrian E. Sellin at Taanach (1902–4); and Sellin and Watzinger at Jericho (1907–8). Two expeditions worked at the City of David in Jerusalem—one under R. Weill and the other under M. B. Parker (the latter aided by the French Dominican scholar Père H. Vincent, one of the founders of systematic archaeological research in Palestine).

Though excavation techniques were in their infancy in this pioneering phase of research, several serious attempts were made to record systematically, and to publish promptly, the successive strata of building remains and the location of finds. Unfortunately, the methods employed were not suited to the complex problems facing the archaeologist in the excavation of a *tell*. Of these early enterprises, the excavation at Samaria is outstanding due to the excavators' approach to architecture and stratigraphy—an approach which greatly influenced the following generation of archaeologists.[5] The publication of large amounts of pottery and other finds from these early excavations (particularly from Gezer) was the foundation of the typological-chronological framework used in later stages of the research.

The twenty inter–world war years were productive for the archaeology of Palestine. Through the vigorous activity of American, British, German, French, and Jewish scholars and institutions, the field progressed considerably. Large-scale archaeological enterprises characterize this period. Of these, the largest were the American excavations at Beth-Shean (directed by C. S. Fisher, G. M. FitzGerald, and A. Rowe between 1921 and 1933) and at Megiddo (directed by C. S. Fisher, P. L. O. Guy and G. Loud between 1925 and 1939). Huge areas were exposed in these projects, and a large amount of data came to light. Advances in the methods of excavation and in the registration of the finds enabled better interpretation, though by modern standards these projects were far from satisfactory.

The work of W. F. Albright during these years is of special significance. With his excavations at Tell el-Ful (1922–23, 1933) Bethel (1927), and Tell Beit Mirsim (1926–32), he began the archaeological research of smaller sites chosen for research with the intention of shedding light on biblical-historical issues. He promoted the comparative study of pottery and stratigraphic observation, and he set a standard for archaeological publications in his report on the excavations at Tell Beit Mirsim. His main contribution, however, was in the integration of field work (including surface surveys) with biblical research, historical geography, and general Near Eastern studies. Albright thus shaped his concept of biblical archaeology, which had a great impact on future generations of American and Israeli scholars.[6]

During this time, various excavations were carried out by scholars who were trained mainly as theologians, and whose motivation in coming to dig in the Holy Land was religious. Several of these projects were conducted under the guidance of Albright, such as the excavations at Tell en-Nasbeh (directed by F. Badé between 1927 and 1935), Beth-Shemesh (directed by E. Grant, 1928–33), and Shiloh (directed by the Danes A. Schmidt and H. Kjaer between 1922 and 1932). The excavation of Tell el-Kheleifeh near Aqaba by N. Glueck (1938–40) is an example of a pioneering enterprise carried out by a prominent member of the Albrightian school.

British activity during these years was of special importance due to the independent approach and methods employed. Thirty-three years after his first dig at Tell el-Hesi, Petrie came back to Palestine and started a series of excavations in the southern coastal plain, which may be regarded as a pioneer attempt at a regional study. These included Tell Jemmeh (1926–27), Tell el-Farʿah (south; 1927–29), and Tell el-Ajjul (1930–34). The sun-dried mud bricks, which served as the main building material in this region, are very difficult to excavate even by modern techniques; nevertheless, Petrie's achievements were remarkable.[7] His stratigraphic observations and typological approach in the study of artifacts formed the basis for later progress in methodology. Petrie's students, J. L. Starkey and O. Tufnell, improved his methods in their work at Lachish (1932–38). Tufnell's publication of Lachish is exemplary for the archaeology of Palestine.

An important attempt at international collaboration between American institutions and British and Jewish archaeologists (E. L. Sukenik from The Hebrew University) took place at Samaria between 1930 and 1935 under the direction of J. W. Crowfoot. At Samaria, K. M. Kenyon introduced for the first time methods of stratigraphic excavation and observation of earth layers which had recently been developed in England. Other British projects between the wars were those of R. A. S. Macalister, J. G. Duncan, and J. W. Crowfoot in the City of David in Jerusalem (1923–28); of J. Garstang at Jericho (1930–36); and of R. W. Hamilton at Tell Abu Hawam near Haifa. Et-Tell, located northeast of Ramallah and identified with the biblical ʿAi, was excavated (1933–35) by the French Jewish archaeologist J. Marquet-Krause, some of the pioneers of Israeli archaeology working under her direction.

Exploration of the Stone Age and protohistoric periods started during these years. Among the various excavations, we should mention those at Teleilat Ghassul (carried out by the Jesuit fathers A. Mallon and R. Koppel), which opened the door to our knowledge of the Chalcolithic period.

In addition to excavations, the interwar years also saw the beginning of systematic surface surveys. W. F. Albright placed emphasis on historical geography, integrating surface surveys into theoretical research in this field. A systematic survey of Transjordan carried out by N. Glueck was the boldest demonstration of this approach. The German scholars A. Alt and M. Noth developed their own school of historical geography, including the results of archaeological research in a critical approach to the biblical narrative.

Varied field methods and approaches to the interpretations of the finds were prevalent at this time. The British work can be seen as opening the way to modern, near quantitative methodology in field work and in the processing of the results. The Beth-Shean and Megiddo projects resembled the large-scale works carried out in other parts of the ancient Near East at the same time. Albright and his students emphasized the meticulous study of pottery chronology and stratigraphy in addition to the integration of field work into biblical and general ancient Near Eastern research. Together, these various approaches were the seeds of future developments in the archaeology of Palestine.

The political climate between 1939 and 1949 almost brought a stop to field work. The third phase in the evolution of the archaeology of Palestine began after the 1948 Israeli War of Independence, when Palestine was divided between the states of Jordan and Israel. Subsequent developments in archaeological study in the two states did not run along parallel lines.

In Jordan, most of the initial work was carried out by foreign expeditions. These included K. M. Kenyon's excavations at Jericho (1952–58) and in Jerusalem (1961–67). At Jericho, Kenyon introduced the British methods developed by M. Wheeler and others; these methods eventually brought about a change in excavation techniques throughout the country (see later). The American expedition at Shechem, directed by G. E. Wright (1956–66), was the schoolroom for a generation of younger American archaeologists working in both Jordan and Israel. Other enterprises in Jordan were those at Tell el-Far'ah (north; directed by Père R. de Vaux between 1946 and 1960); Dothan (J. P. Free, 1953–60); Gibeon (J. B. Pritchard, 1956–62); Taanach (P. Lapp, 1963–68); 'Ai (J. A. Callaway, 1964–69); and Tell el-Ful (P. Lapp, 1964).

Since 1967, archaeological activity in Transjordan has developed, and it is now vigorous, thanks to both foreign and Jordanian scholars. Among the excavations in Transjordan, we should mention Dibon (F. V. Winnett and A. D. Tushingham, 1950–56); Tell Deir Alla (H. J. Franken, 1960–64; M. M. Ibrahim and G. Van der Kooij, 1979–); Tell es-Sa'idiyeh (J. B. Pritchard, 1964–67; J. Tubb, 1985–); Bab edh-Dhra' (P. Lapp, 1965–67; W. E. Rast and R. T. Schaub,

1975–   ); Pella (R. H. Smith, 1967–   ; J. B. Hennessy, 1979–   ); Heshbon (S. H. Horn and L. T. Geraty, 1968–78); Buseirah (C. M. Bennett, 1971–74); Sahab (M. M. Ibrahim, 1972–75); Jawa (S. W. Helms, 1973–75); Teleilat Ghassul (J. B. Hennessy, 1968–77); Tell el-Mazar (H. Yassin); Tell el-Umeiri (L. T. Geraty and L. G. Herr, 1980–   ). In addition, various surveys have been carried out by teams working in different parts of Jordan. These projects in the last two decades have revolutionized our knowledge of the history and archaeology of Transjordan.[8]

In Israel, archaeological activity started just after the foundation of the state in 1948. The first excavation was directed by B. Mazar at Tell Qasile (1948–51, 1956) on the outskirts of Tel Aviv. Thenceforth, the field developed rapidly, mainly due to the work of Israeli archaeologists, but also under the impetus of foreign expeditions. The Israeli founders of biblical archaeology—scholars such as B. Mazar, Sh. Yeivin, Y. Yadin, N. Avigad, and Y. Aharoni—were to a great extent followers of W. F. Albright in their approach to the role of archaeology in relation to biblical history and historical geography as integrated disciplines.

1.4 Members of the Hazor expedition, 1958 season. Among those in the first row (sitting) are (from right to left) A. Volk; I. Dunayevsky; Y. Aharoni; R. Amiran; Y. Yadin; T. Dothan; M. Dothan; A. Rosen.

The extensive excavations at Hazor between 1955 and 1958, directed by Y. Yadin together with Y. Aharoni, R. Amiran, M. Dothan, T. Dothan, C. Epstein, J. Perrot, and the architect I. Dunayevsky, were a workshop for a whole generation of young Israeli archaeologists. The latter have been largely responsible for the progress in archaeology since the early sixties. Dozens of major projects have been carried out by archaeologists working in five universities in Israel, in the Department of Antiquities, in the Israel Museum, and in other local museums and institutions. Aside from the Israeli expeditions, various foreign scholars—American, French, German, and Japanese—conducted excavations in the ancient sites of Israel. Among these excavations, the expedition at Gezer gained a particular importance as the field school for a group of American archaeologists, some of whom later developed projects of their own. Cooperation between Israelis and foreign scholars in joint projects became a common feature, leading to the merging of different traditions in the methodology of field work. The list of most of the archaeological excavations carried out in Israel between 1948 and 1988 is to be found in Table 1.

Table 1:   Main Archaeological Excavations Carried Out in Israel Since 1948

(Sites Arranged from North to South)

Site	Director(s)	Years	Main Sponsoring Institution(s)
Dan	A. Biran	1966–	Department of Antiquities and NGSBAJ[†]
Hazor	Y. Yadin	1955–58, 1968	The Hebrew University
Achzib	M. W. Prausnitz	1958–64	Department of Antiquities, University of Rome
	E. Mazar	1988–	The Hebrew University
Kabri	A. Kempinski		Tel Aviv University
Acre	M. Dothan	1973–	Haifa University
Tell Keisan	J. Briend, J. B. Humbert	1971–79	École Biblique et Archéologique Française de Jerusalem

Site	Director(s)	Years	Main Sponsoring Institution(s)
Tell Abu Hawam	J. Balensi	1985–	French Archaeological Mission, Jerusalem, and Haifa University
Shiqmona	Y. Elgavish	1962–79	Haifa Museum
Golan Heights	C. Epstein	1974–	Department of Antiquities
	M. Kochavi, P. Beck	1987–	Tel Aviv University
Tel Kinrot	F. Fritz	1980–	University of Mainz
Tel Yin'am	H. Liebovits	1976–	Univ. of Texas, Austin
Beth-Yerah	P. Delougaz, H. Kantor	1953, 1963–66	The Oriental Institute, University of Chicago
	P. Bar-Adon	1953–55	Department of Antiquities
	D. Ussishkin	1968	Department of Antiquities
	D. Bahat, E. Eisenberg, O. Yogev	1970–	Department of Antiquities
Tell Qiri	A. Ben-Tor	1975–78	The Hebrew University
Yoqneam	A. Ben-Tor	1977–	The Hebrew University*
Tel Qashish	A. Ben-Tor	1979–	The Hebrew University
Megiddo	Y. Yadin	1960–71	The Hebrew University
Beth-Shean	Y. Yadin, S. Geva	1983	The Hebrew University
	A. Mazar	1989–	The Hebrew University
Tel Kitan	E. Eisenberg	1975–77	Department of Antiquities
Dor	E. Stern	1980–	The Hebrew University*
Tel Mevorakh	E. Stern	1973–76	The Hebrew University
Tel Zeror	K. Ohata	1964–66, 1974	Society of Near Eastern Studies in Japan
"Tel Hefer"	S. Palei, Y. Porath	1979–	Department of Antiquities and State University of New York, Buffalo
Tel Poleg	R. Gophna	1959, 1962	Department of Antiquities
Tel Michal	Z. Herzog	1977–80	Tel Aviv University
Tell Qasile	B. Mazar	1948–51, 1956	The Hebrew University and Museum Eretz Israel*
	A. Mazar	1971–74, 1982–	
Jaffa	Y. and H. Kaplan	1955–74	Museum Eretz Israel
Tel Gerisa	Z. Herzog	1981–	Tel Aviv University
Aphek	M. Kochavi, P. Beck	1972–85	Tel Aviv University
'Izbet Sartah	M. Kochavi, I. Finkelstein	1976–78	Tel Aviv University and Bar-Ilan University

Site	Director(s)	Years	Main Sponsoring Institution(s)
Tel Dalit	B. Cresson, R. Gophna	1978–80	Tel Aviv University and Baylor University
Shiloh	I. Finkelstein	1981–84	Bar-Ilan University
Yavneh-Yam	Y. Kaplan	1966–69	Museum Eretz Israel
Gezer	G. E. Wright, W. G. Dever	1964–71	Nelson Glueck School of Biblical Archaeology, Jerusalem
	J. D. Seger	1972	
Jerusalem			
Temple Mount, "Ophel"	B. Mazar E. Mazar	1968–79 1985–87	The Hebrew University The Hebrew University
Jewish Quarter	N. Avigad	1969–82	The Hebrew University
Citadel	R. Amiran, A. Eitan, H. Geva	Various	Israel Museum and Jerusalem City Museum
City of David	Y. Shiloh	1978–83	The Hebrew University
Hinnom cemeteries	G. Barkai	1979–88	Tel Aviv University
Giloh	A. Mazar	1977–81	The Hebrew University and Department of Antiquities
Ramat Rahel	Y. Aharoni G. Barkai	1959–62 1984	The Hebrew University Tel Aviv University
Valley of Rephaim	G. Edelstein, E. Eisenberg	1982–	Department of Antiquities
Tel Batash (Timnah)	G. L. Kelm, A. Mazar	1977–	Southwestern Baptist Theological Seminary and The Hebrew University
Tel Miqne (Ekron)	S. Gitin, T. Dothan	1981–	W. F. Albright Institute of Archaeological Research and The Hebrew University
Beth-Shemesh (Givat Sharet)	C. Epstein, D. Bahat	1971–73	Department of Antiquities
Hartuv	A. Mazar, P. de Miroscedji	1985–88	Hebrew University and French Archaeological Mission Jerusalem
Yarmuth	A. Ben-Tor	1970	The Hebrew University
	P. de Miroschedji	1980–	French Archaeological Mission, Jerusalem
Ashdod	M. Dothan, D. N. Freedman	1962–72	Department of Antiquities

Site	Director(s)	Years	Main Sponsoring Institution(s)
Ashkelon	L. E. Stager	1985–	The Oriental Institute, University of Chicago, and Harvard University
Lachish	Y. Aharoni	1966	The Hebrew University
	D. Ussishkin	1973–	Tel Aviv University*
Tel Erani	S. Yeivin	1956–61	Department of Antiquities
	A. Kempinski	1985–	Ben Gurion University
Tell el-Hesi	L. E. Toombs, D. G. Rose, V. M. Fargo	1970–83	American Schools of Oriental Research
Tel Nagila	R. Amiran, A. Eitan, R. A. Mitchell	1962–63	Institute for Mediterranean Studies*
Tel Halif	J. D. Seger	1977–	American Schools of Oriental Research
Tel Seraʿ	E. D. Oren	1973–76	Ben Gurion University
Tel Haror	E. D. Oren	1982–	Ben Gurion University
En Gedi	B. Mazar	1961–65	The Hebrew University
Deir el-Balah	T. Dothan	1972–81	The Hebrew University
Arad			
Iron Age	Y. Aharoni	1962–64	The Hebrew University
Early Bronze Age	R. Amiran	1964–	Israel Museum
Bir Abu Matar, Bir Safadi	J. Perrot	1952–59	French Archaeological Mission, Jerusalem
Beer-sheba	Y. Aharoni	1969–74	Tel Aviv University
Tel Malhata	M. Kochavi	1967	The Hebrew University*
	M. Kochavi	1971	Tel Aviv University
Tel Masos	Y. Aharoni, F. Fritz, A. Kempinski	1972–75	Tel Aviv University and University of Mainz
	A. Kempinski	1979	Tel Aviv University
Tel ʿIra	I. Beit-Arieh	1977–81	Tel Aviv University
	A. Biran	1979	NGSBAJ
ʿAroer	A. Biran, R. Cohen	1976–81	Department of Antiquities and NGSBAJ
Tel Esdar	M. Kochavi	1963–64	Department of Antiquities
Hurvat Uza	B. Cresson, I. Beit-Arieh	1982–	Tel Aviv University and Baylor University
Kadesh-Barnea	R. Cohen	1975–82	Department of Antiquities

Site	Director(s)	Years	Main Sponsoring Institution(s)
Negev Highlands			
Iron Age sites	R. Cohen, Z. Meshel	Various	Department of Antiquities Tel Aviv University
Beer Resisim	W. G. Dever, R. Cohen	1978–80	Department of Antiquities and Univ. of Arizona
Kuntillet 'Ajrud	Z. Meshel	1975–76	Tel Aviv University and Department of Antiquities
Timna'	B. Rothenberg	1964–	Museum Eretz Israel
Har Yeruham	M. Kochavi, R. Cohen	1963, 1973	Department of Antiquities

*Sponsored also by the Israel Exploration Society
(included are sites ranging in time from the Chalcolithic until the end of the Iron Age)
† Nelson Glueck School of Biblical Archaeology, Jerusalem

The excavations at major *tells* are only one aspect of this archaeological activity. Hundreds of salvage digs and small-scale excavations have been carried out at smaller sites such as fortresses, rural settlements, cemeteries, and so forth. The finds from the latter complement those from the multiperiod mounds and throw light on important aspects of the settlement history of the country. Another aspect of field research in Israel are systematic surface surveys carried out by the Israel Survey and other teams since the early sixties. Thousands of archaeological sites have been located, mapped, and described, enabling spatial analysis of settlement phenomena in the various periods.

The main institutions involved in archaeological research in Palestine are the universities of Israel and Jordan; the departments of antiquities of both states; the Israel Exploration Society; the American Schools of Oriental Research with its branches at Jerusalem (The Albright Institute of Archaeological Research) and at Amman (the American Center of Oriental Research); the French Archaeological Mission in Jerusalem; École Biblique et Archéologique Française; The Nelson Glueck School of Biblical Archaeology in Jerusalem (an offshoot of the Hebrew Union College); and the British School of Archaeology in Jerusalem. Another important aspect of the archaeological activity in Israel is the involvement of volunteers in excavations, making these excavations field schools where thousands of students can study biblical archaeology and history.

The number of archaeological projects in Israel and now also in Jordan is overwhelming and unprecedented compared with other countries, making the archaeology of Palestine a vivid, dynamic, and constantly changing field of study.

STRATIGRAPHY

Deciphering the stratigraphy of multileveled *tells* is not an easy task. Settlement activity was always accompanied by various earthworks such as leveling and the construction of retaining walls and fills composed of previous occupation debris. Digging of foundation trenches for new walls, garbage and storage pits, graves, cisterns, and drainage canals caused interruptions in the horizontal accumulation of occupation debris; "robbers' trenches" employing available building materials caused damage to remains. Such operations often resulted in older finds' being intermixed with more recent ones.

Another problem facing the archaeologist is inconsistencies in the history of occupation in the various parts of the same site. A city wall, gate, and temple might have been in use for several generations, while the dwellings from the same time were changed and rebuilt, and the floors of streets and courtyards raised. Partial settlement of a site in certain periods results in considerable differences in the number of occupation levels in the site's different areas. The establishment of thorough intersite stratigraphy is the first step on the way to ascertaining the comparative stratigraphy of a region or of the country as a whole. Though such problems are faced by archaeologists worldwide, they are even more pronounced when dealing with ancient Near Eastern *tells*, and the digging methods we employ must take into consideration such complicated situations.

EXCAVATION METHODS

Two opposing approaches to field methodology have developed in Palestine since 1948. The traditional method of Near Eastern archaeology was based on wide-scale exposure of complete architectural units. Stratigraphy was analyzed mainly

1.5 Hazor, Area A (1958). The area exemplifies the wide-scale "architectural" approach. The Solomonic six-chamber gate is seen in the lower part of the picture (see Chapter Nine).

on the basis of the relation between different architectural components such as walls and floor levels. Assemblages of pottery and other finds found on floors of structures represented the last phase of occupation in their findspots, while assemblages from tombs signified the duration of occupation. This approach, prevalent during most of the interwar period, was maintained by Israeli, French, and other archaeologists until late in the sixties.

The second approach was introduced by K. M. Kenyon at Jericho.[9] Rooted in the British tradition, her methodology

1.6   Jericho, Area A. The deep section excavated by K. Kenyon.

emphasized the vertical dimension by analyzing the various earth layers and their contents. It was presumed that each level had significance in the history of the site. By tracing these strata, Kenyon believed, the archaeologist would be able to detect many stratigraphic features which could not be defined by wide-scale exposure employed by the "architectural" school. The techniques developed, known as the "Wheeler-Kenyon method," were intended to enable consistent verification of the earth layers and to analyze their contents. The method was quickly adopted by G. E. Wright at Shechem, and subsequently at most American excavations, such as ʿAi, Taanach, Gezer, Tell Jemmeh, and Tell el-Hesi.[10]

The advantages of the Wheeler-Kenyon method were recognized in Israel, and the technical aspects of the method were adopted by Israeli archaeologists in the late fifties and early sixties (at Tell Qasile [1959], Ramat Rahel [1960], Ashdod, and others). Since then these technical aspects have become standard procedure in this country. A grid of squares of 5 × 5 m is the framework for the excavation; balks left between the squares form sections of the earth layers, and examination of these levels during excavation enables more precise stratigraphic observation. However, Kenyon's concepts

1.7 Lachish, Area S (1982–85). The stratigraphy of the mound is studied by digging a 10-m-wide section divided into 5 × 5 m squares.

appeared to many Israelis too constraining; their main deficiency seemed to be the lack of comprehensive horizontal exposure. To most Israeli archaeologists, narrow and deep sections, even if excavated meticulously, appeared to be insufficient for understanding the complex process of occupation at Near Eastern sites, and such sections were thought to possibly lead to incorrect conclusions. A good example is Jerusalem, where several Israeli expeditions have shown that Kenyon's interpretations with regard to basic features in the history of the city were mistaken due to her preoccupation with painstaking excavation in limited trenches. As settlement in all parts of an ancient site is not homogeneous, the Israeli "architectural" approach believes that only widespread exposure and comparison of the results from the various areas will ascertain the occupational history of a site.

Current field work in Israel and Jordan incorporates a compromise between the "architectural" and the "earth layers analysis" approaches. As much as possible of the area of the site is exposed with the intention of uncovering complete architectural units and studying their layout. Cross-examination of the occupational history is achieved by excavating at several different points. Analysis of the earth layers is not neglected: sections are examined and in many cases recorded by drawing and photography. The integration of the two approaches eventually leads to a balanced method of digging; such a method is now utilized by many field archaeologists in the country.[11] Archaeological field work, however, is to a great extent an art as well as a combination of training and professional skill. No rigid methodology can ensure success, and flexibility and creative thought by field directors are mandatory. The character, talent, and common sense of the archaeologist are no less important than his training and the resources available to him.

Archaeological excavation is destructive; once excavated, an area is essentially closed to further research. Consequently, the documentation, registration, and publication of all phenomena and finds in the field are vital. The methods of registration vary. In most Israeli excavations, for example, the registration is based on a daily graphic description of each area of excavation. Pottery and other finds are numbered in sequence with a "basket number." A locus number is given to every defined feature in the excavation. A daily "basket

1.8 Aphek: view of the acropolis and the Turkish citadel. To the left: area where remains of a Middle Bronze IIA palace were discovered; the area inside the citadel includes remains of a Middle Bronze IIB–C palace and a Late Bronze II residency. The picture illustrates the most common current approach to field work in Israel: combining the "architectural" outlook, which advocates the exposure of large areas, with the Wheeler-Kenyon stratigraphic method.

list" comprises the baskets allocated each day in that particular area, their findspot (grid number and locus number), a description of their contents, and the stratum. Other forms are used to record the daily excavation diary and the description of each locus. Computers serve as a technical tool facilitating registration and the processing of results.[12]

COPING WITH THE FINDS

The variety of finds from settlement sites includes architectural remains and burials which contain large quantities of pottery, metal objects, and stone objects, as well as inscriptions, artworks of various kinds (seals, pottery and metal figurines, jewelry, ivory works, and so forth), animal bones, and plant remains. In rare cases, mainly in arid zones, wood, leather, basketry, and textiles are preserved. All these finds comprise the raw material for reconstructing cultural changes. Their study, processing, and integration into a comprehensive picture is comparable to constructing a huge jigsaw puzzle; the cooperation of specialists for various types of finds is essential. Modern archaeology, therefore, is based on an interdisciplinary approach, involving architects, physicists, chemists, physical anthropologists, social anthropologists, osteologists, paleobotanists, paleoenvironmentalists, geologists, potters, metallurgists, paleographers, philologists, historians, art historians, computer programmers, and statisticians. Only full-scale cooperation among scholars in these different fields of research can bring about a comprehensive interpretation of the finds.

Pottery is the most abundant find in excavations and is the best tool for analyzing chronological, regional, and ethnic changes, as well as foreign relations. Great efforts are made in the study of ancient pottery: pottery experts study technical aspects of manufacture; petrography (microscopic examination of transparent thin sections of pottery) provides an insight into the physical composition of the clay; neutron activation analysis provides an exact breakdown of the chemical composition of clays, making possible a determination of their place of origin. Morphological, typological, and comparative studies of ceramics have increased our knowledge of the relative chronology of the pottery in each site, region, and period. Quantitative analysis enables scholars to refine the conclusions and to identify minute chronological and regional developments. Aspects of pottery making serve as criteria for defining regional cultures in the various periods. Imported ceramics evidence trade relations between various parts of the country and with its neighbors.

Similar typological and laboratory studies are carried out on other classes of finds and materials, such as metal objects. Faunal, botanical, and environmental studies are intended to illuminate the impact of ecology on human cultural history, and they provide an insight into ancient agriculture, diet, and economy. When combined with historical investigation, they allow a reconstruction of the cultural history of the country.

REGIONAL STUDIES

Only a wide regional approach can provide a comprehensive picture of settlement and cultural change in a certain area. Several projects in Israel and Jordan are based on this outlook. The best example is perhaps the study of the Arad–Beer-sheba region initiated by Y. Aharoni nearly thirty years ago. It started with sporadic surveys and culminated in the excavation of six sites, achieving a complete archaeological picture of the entire region. Other such projects are being carried out in the Negev highlands (by R. Cohen and staff from the Israel Survey); in the Shephelah (integration of the work of surveys and of separate expeditions at Lachish, Ekron, Tel Batash, Gezer, and Yarmuth); in the Yarkon Basin; in the mountains of Samaria (by A. Zertal); in the land of Ephraim (by I. Finkelstein); in the western valley of Jezreel (by A. Ben-Tor); in the northwestern Negev and northern Sinai (by E. D. Oren); in the Golan Heights (by M. Kochavi and P. Beck); in the Baqʿah Valley of Transjordan (by P. McGovern); and elsewhere. This comprehensive regional view has become dominant in the archaeology of Palestine.

CHRONOLOGY

Relative chronology is ascertained by typological sequences of objects, particularly of pottery, established by comparative studies of stratified assemblages from various sites in a certain region. Comparison of assemblages within the regions enables us to define a relative sequence in each area, and to establish a chronological order for the entire country.

Once the relative sequences have been obtained, absolute chronology can be established. For the earlier periods, carbon 14 tests are the basis for dating. There are, however, serious problems in utilizing these tests. Such problems mainly concern the validity of C 14 calibration based on dendrochronology; calibrated dates in the fourth and third millennia B.C.E. appear to be too early when compared to dates ascertained through Egyptian chronology.[13] From ca. 3000 B.C.E. the absolute chronology of Palestine is based to a large exent on that of Egypt. Egyptian objects found in Palestine—including royal inscriptions, scarab seals, and others—and artifacts exported from Palestine to Egypt and found in dated contexts provide the basis for a chronological framework. The dependence on Egyptian chronology is so strong that any change in the latter necessitates a parallel shift concerning Palestine. The Egyptian finds may, however, be misleading, as scarabs, statues, and other Egyptian artifacts were considered precious or sacred objects and may have been kept as heirlooms for generations.

While the correlation with Egypt is based on direct export and import of objects, Mesopotamian chronology is less important, since in most periods the relations with Mesopotamia were indirect through the mediation of Syria. Imported pottery and other artifacts from Cyprus and Greece also play a significant role in chronological studies, but sometimes one forgets that absolute dates in these countries are based to a large extent on those in Egypt and the Levant, making the danger of circular argumentation great. For the period of the Israelite monarchy, correlations between archaeological phenomena and historical data known from the Bible and from Assyrian and Babylonian documents are of particular importance for dating, but such correlations must be carried out with care, as several serious mistakes have been made in this realm in the past.

TERMINOLOGY AND PERIODIZATION

Terminology for the early periods in Palestine is based upon worldwide periodization maintained since the 1819 work of the Danish archaeologist Ch. J. Thomsen. This is the Three Age System, which divides the early periods into three major units: the Stone Age, the Bronze Age, and the Iron Age. For Palestine, this terminology was accepted, but it underwent several changes and adaptations. Thus, it has been recognized that between the Stone and the Bronze ages there is an additional "Copper Age," denoted "Chalcolithic." Some Israeli archaeologists tend to use terms with ethnic connotations—"Canaanite period" and "Israelite period"—instead of the terms "Bronze Age" and "Iron Age."[14] In this book, however, we will maintain the widely accepted Three Age division.

Another terminological problem relates to two transitional periods: that between the Chalcolithic period and the Early

Bronze Age, and that between the Early Bronze and Middle Bronze ages. These were given special names by scholars, intended to emphasize their uniqueness, but the result was only chaos. In Table 2, the terminological and chronological "skeleton" used in this book is presented. The subdivisions and alternative terms will be found in the relevant chapters.

Table 2:   The Archaeological Periods of Palestine (Neolithic until Iron Age)

Pre-Pottery Neolithic A	ca. 8500–7500 B.C.E.
Pre-Pottery Neolithic B	7500–6000 B.C.E.
Pottery Neolithic A	6000–5000 B.C.E.
Pottery Neolithic B	5000–4300 B.C.E.
Chalcolithic	4300–3300 B.C.E.
Early Bronze I	3300–3050 B.C.E.
Early Bronze II–III	3050–2300 B.C.E.
Early Bronze IV/Middle Bronze I	2300–2000 B.C.E.
Middle Bronze IIA	2000–1800/1750 B.C.E.
Middle Bronze IIB–C	1800/1750–1550 B.C.E.
Late Bronze I	1550–1400 B.C.E.
Late Bronze IIA–B	1400–1200 B.C.E.
Iron IA	1200–1150 B.C.E.
Iron IB	1150–1000 B.C.E.
Iron IIA	1000–925 B.C.E.
Iron IIB	925–720 B.C.E.
Iron IIC	720–586 B.C.E.

PUBLICATIONS

One of the major problems facing the archaeological profession worldwide is the great time gap between the completion of the field work and the publication of its results. The meticulous work required to prepare the publication sometimes takes more than a decade. Numerous excavations remain unpublished, and the achievements of field work often remain inaccessible to the scholarly world. This "professional disease" has been recognized as a major obstacle to the progress of archaeology, and most institutes involved in the archaeology of Palestine are now investing special efforts to overcome the deficiency. Periodicals, monograph series, and various collections of papers provide a framework for preliminary and final reports, in addition to the hundreds of synthesis papers. The situation is improving, but a gap of at least ten years between excavation and publication seems to be unavoidable, and the results of too many projects still remain out of public reach.

IDEOLOGY AND INTERPRETATION

Archaeology in Palestine in the past, and to a large extent even today, has been motivated by interest in the Bible. Many of the archaeologists working in the country had a background in biblical research and thus tended to interpret the archaeological finds from a historical and biblical viewpoint. Tendencies in biblical studies sometimes appear to overshadow objectivity in interpretation, and the fundamentalist approach has also had its impact. On such background some major mistakes were made in the interpretation of archaeological discoveries in Palestine; examples are the identification of "King Solomon's mines" at Timnaᶜ, the location of Ezion-Geber, the interpretation of the "Warren Shaft" in Jerusalem as the Jebusite "Sinnor," and more. Today there is a continuous intellectual effort by archaeologists and by biblical and ancient Near Eastern historians to integrate their studies and to fertilize each other's field of research.

Though utilizing the various techniques and applied sciences of modern archaeology, the approach of most scholars working in Palestine essentially remained rooted in the historical, humanistic tradition of Near Eastern archaeology and biblical studies. The philosophy of the British-American "new archaeology" and its jargon, based on anthropology and looking upon archaeology as part of the social sciences, is utilized only on a limited scale. Yet the influence of the anthropological approach is seen in modern research goals. Subjects such as demographic changes, settlement patterns, detection of seminomadic pastoral cultures, studies of transitional periods and of cultural changes are demonstrative. Utilization of ethnoarchaeology also finds expression in current work carried out in Israel and Jordan. When combined with the traditional historical view, the above-mentioned fields of research are gradually changing the face of the archaeology of Palestine.[15]

The new trends in world archaeology raised questions and controversy concerning the basic nature of the discipline. In America, traditional biblical archaeology as understood by W. F. Albright and G. E. Wright was based on a very specific approach to the relationship between archaeology and biblical studies.[16] Interpretation of archaeological data was sometimes interlocked with theological concepts. This was particularly clear concerning some of the most questionable historical issues related to biblical history, such as the historical framework to the period of the patriarchs and to the conquest of Canaan by the Israelites. The answers of traditional biblical archaeologists to such issues tended to be simplistic and fundamental.

Current archaeological research in Palestine tends to be professional, secular, and free from theological prejudices. It tends to acquire the objective data from field work by utilizing the best methods available today in world archaeology. The new trend has motivated scholars to redefine this field of research. Thus W. G. Dever called for the abandonment of the term "biblical archaeology" in favor of the term "Syro-Palestinian archaeology." This suggestion reflects the tendency to abandon the theological approach of traditional biblical archaeology in favor of a secular, professional approach which defines the archaeology of the Levant as a specific branch of world archaeology with its own methods and goals.[17] One can fully agree with Dever's analysis of the past nature of biblical archaeology and the changes that passed over this field of research during the last decades. The call for a professional approach to archaeological reseach is fully justified, as archaeological research today is a strict discipline with developed techniques and methodology. Furthermore, the archaeology of the Levant must be studied against the wider background of Near Eastern studies. However, as Dever himself admits, the mutual relationship between biblical studies and the archaeology of the Land of the Bible continues to inspire scholars in both fields. The implications of archaeological reseach for biblical studies and history are sometimes of prime importance. The new questions and subjects raised by modern archaeological research of the Bronze and Iron ages in Palestine gain a special flavor and interest when studied in relation to the biblical text and extrabiblical documents. In that sense, "biblical archaeology" is still a justified term for this field of inquiry. Whatever term will be used for defining the discipline, the archaeology of Palestine and that of the related countries are unique and ever increasing resources for reconstructing the social, environmental, and cultural background from which the Hebrew Bible emerged. Thus biblical archaeology, like many branches of knowledge, lends itself to changes and new contents.

NOTES

1. Some Israeli scholars avoid the use of the term "Palestine" because of its modern political connotations. Thus Aharoni (1982) denotes the country "the Land of Israel" or uses the transliteration "Eretz-Israel" (see the note by the translator, A. F. Rainey, on p. xiii). Like the editors of *IEJ*, I find the name "Palestine" the most suitable geographical term denoting the modern states of Israel and Jordan.

2. E. Orni and E. Efrat, *Geography of Israel,* Jerusalem 1966; de Vaux (1978), pp. 3–25; Aharoni (1979), pp. 3–63.

3. The word *tell* is used in both Arabic and Hebrew. The Arabic transliteration is written *tell*, while the Hebrew form is spelled *tel*.

4. For a survey of the history of research until 1918, see N. A. Silberman, *Digging for God and Country,* New York 1982. For general surveys of the history of the research, see the contributions of P. J. King, G. I. Davis, P. Benoit, M. and H. Weippert and A. Mazar in *Callaway Festschrift,* pp. 15–128. See also P. J. King, *American Archaeology in the Mideast,* Philadelphia 1983; W. G. Dever in: G. A. Knight and G. M. Tucker, eds., *The Hebrew Bible and Its Modern Interpretation,* Philadelphia 1985, pp. 31–74; G. A. M. Broshi, *The Israel Museum Journal* 6 (1987), pp. 17–32.

5. Wright in: *Glueck Festschrift,* pp. 3–40; idem, *EI* 9 (1969), pp. 25*–29*.

6. L. Running and D. N. Freedman, *William Foxwell Albright: A Twentieth Century Genius,* New York 1975.

7. W. M. F. Petrie, *Seventy Years in Archaeology,* London 1931.

8. For a comprehensive bibliography, see J. A. Sauer, *BASOR* 263 (1986), pp. 1–25. See also the three volumes of essays on the archaeology of Jordan: A. Hadidi (editor). *Studies in the History and Archaeology of Jordan,* vol. 1, Amman 1982; vol. 2, Amman 1985; vol. 3, Amman 1987; and R. H. Dorneman, *The Archaeology of the Transjordan,* Milwaukee 1983.

9. K. M. Kenyon, *Beginning in Archaeology,* New York 1952.

10. W. G. Dever and H. D. Lance, *A Manual of Field Excavation,* Cincinnati 1978; W. G. Dever, *BA* 43 (1980), pp. 41–48. For updated surveys of excavation methods, see the contributions of G. W. Van Beek, J. McRay, and J. J. Davis in *Callaway Festschrift* pp. 131–222.

11. For the differences between Israeli and American methods during the early seventies, see W. G. Dever, *EI* 11 (1973), pp. 2*–8*; idem (see note 10); Y. Aharoni, *EI* 11 (1973), pp. 48–53 (Hebrew). This debate now is somewhat anachronistic.

12. For a description of the Israeli method of registration, see Y. Aharoni (ed.), *Beer Sheba*, vol. 1, Tel Aviv 1973, pp. 119–33. A computerized variation of this method was used for the first time at Tel Batash (Timnah) in 1977. See also: J. F. Strange, *Callaway Festschrift*, pp. 307–24.

13. J. M. Weinstein, *Radiocarbon* 26 (1984), pp. 297–366; idem, *Callaway Festschrift*, pp. 235–60.

14. M. Dothan in: *BAT*, pp. 136–41.

15. For the evaluation of the impact of the "new archaeology" on "Syro-Palestinian archaeology," see W. G. Dever, *BASOR* 242 (1981), pp. 15–29; L. E. Toombs in: *Rose Festschrift*, pp. 41–52; idem, *Callaway Festschrift*, pp. 337–52.

16. W. F. Albright in: D. N. Freedman and J. C. Greenfield (eds.), *New Directions in Biblical Archaeology*, New York 1971, pp. 1–16; G. E. Wright in: ibid., pp. 167–86; F. M. Cross, *BA* 36 (1973), pp. 2–5.

17. W. G. Dever, *Harvard Theological Review* 73 (1980), pp. 1–15; idem, *BA* 45 (1982), pp. 103–7. For the most comprehensive presentation of Dever's view see his paper cited in note 4 to this chapter. Opposing his view, see H. D. Lance, *BA* 45 (1982), pp. 97–101; Y. Yadin in: *BAT*, pp. 21–27; H. Shanks, *BAR* 13:2 (1987), pp. 54–57. See also J. A. Sauer, *BA* 45 (1982), pp. 201–9; G. Rose in: *Rose Festschrift*, pp. 53–64.

CHAPTER TWO

THE FIRST AGRICULTURAL COMMUNITIES:
The Neolithic Period (ca. 8500–4300 B.C.E.)

BEFORE AGRICULTURE

The earliest known remains of any human culture, dated to between one and two million years ago, were discovered along the great Syro-African Rift at several sites—including Olduai Gorge in East Africa, and Ubeidiya in the Jordan Valley south of the Lake of Galilee. The reconstruction of human physical and cultural evolution from this early beginning to the onset of the historical era is the task of prehistorians, and in this field of research the discoveries in the Near East, and particularly those in Israel, are vital.[1]

Our survey will begin just before one of the major transformations in human's way of life: the transition from subsistence based on food gathering and hunting to food producing. The transition from the food-gathering phase to fully developed agriculture and pastoralism was a long process which began in the Near East around 10,500 B.C.E. and lasted several thousands of years. It was accompanied by changes in social organization and economic activity which expressed themselves in the establishment of settled communities and the eventual birth of the ancient Near Eastern civilizations. Some of the most important steps in this development can be traced in Palestine.

THE NATUFIAN CULTURE

During the last two thousand years of the Epi-Paleolithic period, from ca. 10,500–8500 B.C.E. (radiocarbon dates), specific local cultures emerged in the Levant with a more developed social organization, subsistence economy, and religious beliefs. The best known is the Natufian culture, which was widespread throughout Palestine and Syria as far as the Euphrates River.[2] The Natufian form of life, which probably developed from that of the Kebaran which preceded it, was in its floruit at the time when climatic fluctuations marked the end of the glacial age. The melting of the glaciers brought about a rise in sea level. The coastal line was reduced, rainfall was more excessive than in our own day, and large parts of the country were covered with forests. Hunters abounded in the Negev and Sinai, which were rich in vegetation.

The Natufians remained basically food gatherers and hunters, but their social organization was more complex than that of their predecessors. They lived in communities which are estimated to have included up to 150 individuals; their permanent base sites were located near major water sources and where wild grain could easily be found. From here groups of hunters set out for more distant regions for seasonal sojourns. In their base settlements, the Natufians built some of the earliest known dwellings: round huts were for a family of about 3 persons; clusters of such huts perhaps belonged to extended families.

A variety of flint tools and bone and stone implements are indicative of significant technological developments in this period. Most of the flints are tiny microliths, typical throughout the Epi-Paleolithic period, which served as spearheads and arrowheads for hunting. There were, however, also flint sickle blades fastened to bone hafts; these were used for harvesting wild grain, canes, and straw. Other flint tools were employed in the preparation of leather goods and in carving wood. Bone tools included points, harpoons, and hooks for hunting and fishing. Mortars and pestles served to grind flour from wild grain and from acorns collected in the country's oak forests.

Burials found at Natufian sites comprise valuable evidence for the study of the physical structure of the people, their belief in afterlife, and their art. Many of the skeletons were of children under sixteen years; the adult mortality age ranged between twenty and thirty, only few reaching fifty. Some of the burials were contracted and articulated, but others were disarticulated and secondary, perhaps belonging to the hunters at seasonal sites who were reburied at the base settlement. Some of the skeletons were ornamented with carefully fashioned jewelry made of tubular dentalium shells, animal bones,

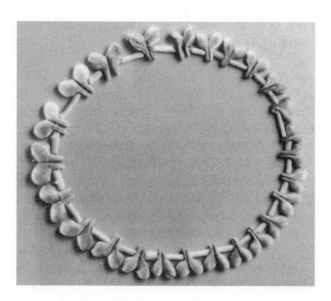

2.1 A Natufian necklace made of bone and dentalia, found in the el-Wad cave, Mount Carmel.

and various stones. A unique burial form was discovered at the site of Nahal Oren on Mount Carmel: pierced elongated limestone mortars symbolized a sort of conduit between the living and the dead; the upper part of the stones protruded above the surface, while their base was level with the corpse. A stone pillar 1.2 m high, found at a Negev site, may have symbolized a divinity, like later examples. Carved Natufian bone and stone objects mainly represented game animals; a unique specimen depicts a human couple having intercourse, and one of a dog may support the osteological evidence that canine domestication had been introduced.

During the closing phases of the Natufian culture, regional cultures developed in Palestine, such as the Harifian in the Negev and northern Sinai and the Khiamian of northern Palestine. The latter is considered already an early Neolithic culture.

THE NEOLITHIC AGE
(8500–4300 B.C.E.)

INTRODUCTION

The four millennia of the Neolithic period (New Stone Age) in the ancient Near East saw numerous changes and developments of far-reaching consequence.[3] The basis of human subsistence changed from food gathering to food production, a revolution introducing agriculture and, later, herding as principal economic factors. There were also important technological innovations, such as the development of building techniques, sophistication in the preparation of stone, bone, leather, and wood artifacts, and finally the appearance of pottery in domestic use. New features in the realm of spiritual life were expressed in burial customs and art. As in the previous Epi-Paleolithic era, the culture of the Levant as a whole—from the Euphrates to Palestine—was largely homogeneous, though there were regional differentiations.

The beginning of the Neolithic overlaps with the end of the Pleistocene and beginning of the Holocene geological periods. Temperatures were reaching the levels of today, but annual precipitation was greater. Rainy periods, mainly during the seventh and sixth millennia B.C.E., allowed settlement in present-day arid or semiarid regions such as the Sinai Peninsula and the Negev.

The Neolithic period is commonly divided into two main parts, each further subdivided into two major subperiods. The following terminology was first suggested by K. M. Kenyon and is still widely used today, though other terms have also been proposed.[4] The dates are based on uncalibrated carbon 14 readings.[5]

Pre-Pottery Neolithic A	(henceforth PPNA)	8500–7500 B.C.E.
Pre-Pottery Neolithic B	(henceforth PPNB)	7500–6000 B.C.E.
Pottery Neolithic A	(henceforth PNA)	6000–5000 B.C.E.
Pottery Neolithic B	(henceforth PNB)	5000–4300 B.C.E.

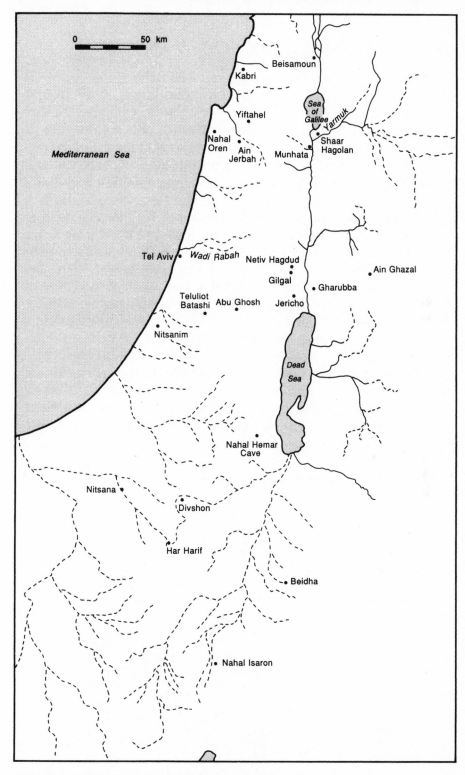

2.2   MAP OF MAJOR EXCAVATED NEOLITHIC SITES.

PRE-POTTERY NEOLITHIC A (PPNA)

The first stage of the Pre-Pottery Neolithic is not very well documented. Given this fact, the concentration of several sites in the Jordan Valley is of particular importance. The key site is Jericho (Tell es-Sultan), and north of it are the sites of Gilgal, Netiv Hagdud, and Gesher (near Munhata). Other sites from this period are Nahal Oren on Mount Carmel, Hatoula in the northern Shephelah, and a site in southern Sinai near St. Catherine Monastery.

Tell es-Sultan, ancient Jericho, was first settled by the bearers of the Natufian culture. The Neolithic levels are spread over the entire 6.5 acres (2.5 hectares) of the mound west of the local spring. If all this area was settled, the community probably numbered up to about one thousand people (Kenyon's estimate of two thousand seems exaggerated). The accumulation of the Pre-Pottery Neolithic debris alone reached an unprecedented depth of 9–10 m, 6 of which dated to PPNA and 3–4 to PPNB. This accumulation represents a continuous occupation of over two thousand years.[6]

Round or oval dwellings, 4–6 m in diameter, are characteristic of this period.[7] At Jericho the structures were made out of hog-backed mud bricks (bricks with flat bottoms and convex

2.3 Nahal Oren: Pre-Pottery Neolithic A dwellings (plan, section, and reconstruction).

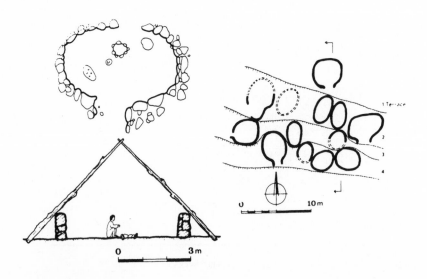

backs); the upper part of these dwellings was perhaps dome shaped and constructed of reeds and clay. The floors were made of stone bedding and clay plaster.

At the western edge of the mound of Jericho, Kenyon discovered a succession of massive protective walls, used and rebuilt throughout the PPNA and PPNB periods. In one of the PPNA stages, the wall stood at a height of almost 6 m, and it was partially constructed of huge stones. On the outer side of the wall, a broad trench or fosse hewn into the rock was discovered. A massive round tower within the wall was amazingly well constructed. The tower measured 8.5 m in diameter and is preserved to a height of 7.7 m; it was built with a solid stone core, and a steep stairway led to its top. The walls and tower of PPNA Jericho are a most surprising discovery from a period when almost no public architecture is known elsewhere. They were explained by Kenyon as a fortification system, and they led her to define Jericho as the earliest urban community known. An alternative suggestion,

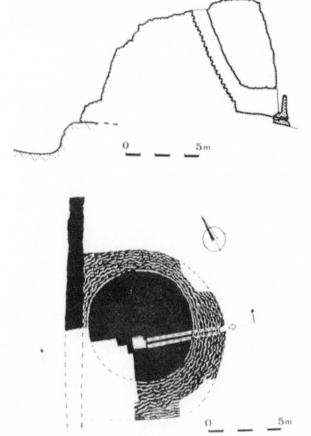

2.4 Jericho: plan and section of the outer wall and tower.

offered by O. Bar-Yosef, is that the massive walls were intended to protect the settlement from the thrust of silt and eroded debris from the wadi to the west.[8] The round tower remains unexplained by this theory, but it could not have had a defensive purpose due to its location on the inner side of the wall. Perhaps it had some ritual function.

The massive structures at Jericho reflect the existence of social organization and central authority which could recruit, for the first time in human history, the necessary means and manpower for such building operations. Technical skill, planning, and construction ability at Jericho must have been at a level only slightly inferior to that in later, Bronze Age periods. Jericho, whether it should be defined as a large village or an urban community, undoubtedly reflects a revolution in terms of social organization and technical knowledge.

The emergence of agriculture is the essence of the Neolithic revolution. Seeds collected at PPNA sites show that for the first time, cultured barley, single-corn wheat (*Einkorn*), lentils, and legumes were cultivated. The subsistence economy of Jericho was probably based on irrigation farming—exploiting the water of the nearby spring through canals, as is done today at this oasis.

The flint industry of the PPNA people to a minor extent continued the Natufian tradition of shaping microliths, but many new forms appeared and provide information on a wide variety of crafts and means of livelihood. Flint adzes and hoes, polished stone celts and sickle blades were used for farming; numerous aerodynamically shaped arrowheads indicate that hunting was still prevalent; borers, burins, and scrapers were needed for leather and wood work; and for the first time, typical wide flat querns were employed to prepare flour.

Burials were found in contracted position inside the settlement, as in the preceding period. At the end of PPNA an extraordinary custom was introduced and is well exemplified at Jericho: skulls, without jaws were removed and kept in groups in the house, while the bodies were buried under the house floor and in open spaces.

The Neolithic communities of Palestine are part of a widespread development which took place throughout the Levant. Early Neolithic sites in Syria, such as Tell Aswad near Damascus and Tell Mureybat on the Middle Euphrates, are evidence of a material culture which was very close to

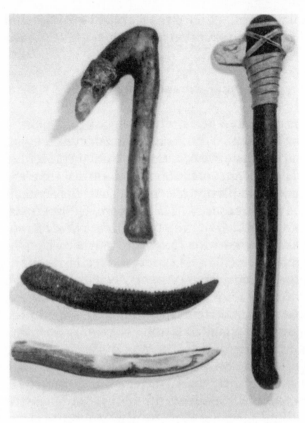

2.5 Reconstructed Neolithic agricultural tools (axe, adze, and sickles) made of flint, wood, and bone.

that of Palestine, though there were some regional distinctions.[9] Evidence of contemporary sites of hunter-gatherers was found in the Negev and Sinai. Commercial transactions were carried out between these communities. The most prominent expression of such commerce is the trade in obsidian—a volcanic glass which originated in Anatolia and has been found at PPNA sites in Palestine and Syria. Laboratory examinations have succeeded in locating the exact source of the obsidian in Anatolia.[10] The barter offered by the people of Palestine was perhaps produce from the Dead Sea (bitumen, salt) or materials from Sinai and the Negev (such as special stones and marine shells).

Thus, the PPNA period saw the emergence of agriculture and the beginning of herding. The settled communities comprised more complex societies and some sort of central authority capable of organizing public works and utilizing advanced technology. This period was a crucial step forward in the history of human civilization in the ancient Near East.

PRE-POTTERY NEOLITHIC B (PPNB)

The second part of the Pre-Pottery Neolithic period, mainly in the seventh millennium B.C.E., saw a considerable population increase and expansion of settlement. Kenyon presented this culture as alien to its predecessor, claiming that the PPNB people immigrated from the north; but the current view (J. Mellaart, P. Mortensen, A. M. T. Moore, O. Bar-Yosef) is that this culture essentially developed from its predecessor while acquiring some innovations from the northern Levant.

PPNB sites were located in a variety of regions: in the Mediterranean vegetational belt (Yiftahel, Nahal Oren, Abu Ghosh), in the Jordan Valley (Jericho, Munhata, Beisamoun), in the Judean Desert (Nahal Hemar), in the Negev and in the Arabah (Nahal Divshon, Nahal Isaron, Nitsana, and other sites), in Transjordan (Ain Ghazal, Beidha and Basta), and in the eastern and southern desert belt such as in southern Sinai. Settlement in the areas mentioned—areas which are today arid or semiarid—supports evidence from other studies that during the seventh millennium B.C.E. rainfall was more abundant than at present, and probably even heavier than in the PPNA period. Even dry regions such as the Transjordanian plateaus are thought to have been covered by oak forests.

The superb achievements of the PPNB people were not limited to Palestine. Large Neolithic sites with similar cultural phenomena are known throughout the Levant, both in southern Syria (Tell Ramad) and in the Upper and Middle Euphrates (Tell Mureybat, Abu Hureyra, and Tell Bouqras). They demonstrate the homogeneous culture of the area and the relations between the subregions. As in the previous period, the cultural milieu of the entire Levant was to a large extent homogeneous.

Settlements in Palestine were extraordinarily large for this period, and they can be compared only to some sites in Syria and Anatolia. The largest known PPNB site is Ain Ghazal, a 30-acre site north of Amman in Transjordan. Beisamoun is second in size (10 acres), and Jericho is third with 6 acres. The socioeconomic factors which led to their growth are not entirely clear. Was it the trade of minerals and bitumen of the Dead Sea which caused Jericho to flourish, as E. Anati has suggested?[11] It is more plausible that Jericho's good fortune derived from the possibilities inherent in the agricultural exploitation of its vicinity. A large community such as Ain Ghazal may have developed as a result of the interactions between farmers and hunters in Transjordan. Anyway, the location of the large sites of this period in the Jordan Valley and in Transjordan emphasizes the importance of the eastern part of Palestine.

Agriculture greatly progressed in PPNB. The cultivation of species of cereals over hundreds of years culminated in the harvest of two-row barley (*Hordeum distichum*) and double-row emmer wheat (*Triticum dicoccum*). The wild wheat with a soft spikelet (*Triticum dicoccoides*), still found today in the Levant, is the ancestor of the cultivated wheat with a hard spikelet. Legumes were also grown, though fruits were still gathered from the wild. Goats became the principal "farmyard" animals, but the rearing of sheep (probably originating from the Zagros Mountains of western Iran) and cattle (represented in clay figurines) also seem to have been introduced.

A new domestic architecture developed in the PPNB with the introduction of rectangular-shaped dwellings. At Jericho the houses are 3×7 m and were constructed of elongated mudbricks. The floors, and occasionally even the walls, were covered with a thick layer of clay plaster polished to a luster, a technique known also at other Neolithic sites located as far north as Anatolia. Imprints of platted mats found on the floors are evidence of straw weaving; basins sunk into the floor and thickly coated with clay plaster served as fireplaces. This early use of clay led eventually to the discovery of pottery making. At Ain Ghazal, Yiftahel in the western Galilee, and the site of Abu Hureyra on the Upper Euphrates, large rectangular buildings have thick lime floors which exemplify advanced knowledge in preparing lime in large quantities from burnt limestones.[12] A unique house plan of the period was discovered at Beidha in Transjordan, where stone dwellings consisted of several rectangular rooms arranged in a row, one behind the other.[13]

The outer "defensive" wall at Jericho which served as a terrace wall was rebuilt twice in this period, though the round tower had gone out of use already during the PPNA period. As at Jericho, a similar outer wall found at Beidha was perhaps intended to stop silt and eroded materials which endangered the settlement.

The PPNB flint industry included a variety of tools, such as sickle blades, axes (the latter used in agriculture, and for wood cutting and carving), long-bladed knives, scrapers, borers, and superbly made tanged arrowheads. Many of these tools were manufactured by a technique known as "pressure flaking," carried out after heating the flint. Stone querns were saddle shaped, and polished stone bowls evidence a developed stone industry. A variety of bone tools were used for sewing, weaving, basketry, fishing, and other works. At Ain Ghazal fragments of coarse pottery from this period give witness to the first experiments in pottery making in Palestine.

A unique collection of finds at the remote Nahal Hemar cave in the Judean Desert provides abundant data on otherwise unknown crafts from this period, such as weaving and preparation of bone and wood implements.[14] Textiles made of flax were found in this cave; they not only show that this plant was cultivated, but are astounding evidence of the technological knowledge of twining. Ropes were prepared from palm fibers. Containers from cords made of vegetal material were lined with bitumen. The long-distance trade in raw materials, evident in the PPNA, continued in the PPNB.

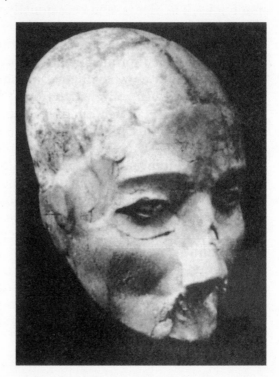

2.6 Plastered skull from Jericho (Pre-Pottery Neolithic B).

The spiritual and artistic world of the PPNB can be pictured from burial customs and several other finds of the period. The practice of skull removal known in the PPNA now became common, and in several cases the skulls were modeled with plaster as if to give them a lifelike appearance. Such plastered skulls were discovered at Jericho, Ain Ghazal, Beisamoun (in the northern Jordan Valley), and Tell Ramad near Damascus.[15] The most outstanding group is a cache of seven skulls uncovered at Jericho; some of these are naturalistically rendered with emphasis on the outline of cheeks, brows, and lips. The eyes were marked with seashells. The decoration of a skull found at the Nahal Hemar cave was created by the application of bitumen from the nearby Dead Sea and probably was meant to represent the hairdo. This practice of plastering and decorating skulls must express a belief in an afterlife and probably represents an ancestor cult in which it was believed that the soul abided within the skull. Similar rites can be found among tribes in the Pacific, where skulls of relatives as well as of captives are also "given life" through modeling and painting.

Depictions of the human face and body were also sculptured, in full or in mask form. Plaster statues of human figures were discovered at Jericho and at Ain Ghazal, and fragments were found in the Nahal Hemar cave. The Jericho group comprised a man, a woman, and a child. The man's head was made in flat relief with a narrow mouth, thin lips, seashells as eyes, protruding eyebrows, and hair and beard depicted in red paint. Two large groups of such statues, one including thirty-seven figures, were discovered at Ain Ghazal.[16] Ten of them are about 0.9 m tall and were molded from plaster on a core of reeds and grass. Resembling those from Jericho, they represent somewhat squat humans with oversize flat heads. One figure is of a nude female holding her breasts. Twelve of the statues are only about 0.45 m high and have a schematic torso to which the molded head and shoulders are attached. Their eyes are outlined in blue-green paint, and their faces are sometimes painted red. These smaller figures were found at the feet of the larger statues and may represent children. The plaster statues were perhaps also related to an ancestor cult or represented a pantheon of deities. The custom of depicting large human figures in clay is peculiar to this period; it may suggest a belief that man was created by being molded in clay—an idea that finds expression in the creation story in the Book of Genesis, and that is to be found in the ancient myths of the Sumerians and Egyptians.[17]

Other artistic representations of the human face are in the form of stone masks, found south of Hebron and in the cave of Nahal Hemar.[18] The Nahal Hemar masks are painted with red and green lines. The masks were perhaps also related to the ancestor cult, or used in magic rites of the shamanistic type.

2.7 A ritual stone mask found south of Hebron (Pre-Pottery Neolithic B).

Additional Neolithic works of art are small clay and stone statuettes of human figures or animals (goat, sheep, and cattle) with a possible apotropaic function. One of the earliest examples of a standing stone with cultic significance was found in a niche in a Jericho room and was perhaps a symbol of a deity.

It thus appears that the PPNB was a time of settlement expansion and population growth. Agriculture and herding now provided the economic basis for a more complex society; craftsmen developed new techniques and modes of expression to meet the demands of the contemporary ritual and burial practices.

The end of the period was accompanied by a great decline

in settlement activity. Large sites such as Ain Ghazal and Yiftahel were abandoned, and at Jericho there may have been an occupation gap. The reasons for the crisis are uncertain. Some scholars have suggested that drier climatic conditions prevailed; others suppose that extensive exploitation of land and deforestation brought about crucial environmental changes.

THE POTTERY NEOLITHIC PERIOD (PN)

Our knowledge of both the cultural history and the climatic and environmental conditions in Palestine in the sixth and fifth millennia B.C.E. is rather sparse.[19] Few excavations have been carried out at sites dating from this period, and there is only one site where a continuous stratigraphic series has been revealed (Hurvat Minhah). Certain scholars (such as J. Perrot and A. M. T. Moore) maintain that there was an occupation gap of close to a millennium between PPNB and the following PN period in Palestine. Others tend to see continuity between the two, mainly on the basis of the flint industry. In Syria such a continuation is demonstrated at sites such as Abu Hureyra, Tell Bouqras, and Tell Ramad.[20]

The most significant innovation of this period is pottery. Its invention most probably resulted from the earlier uses of clay for plastering floors and sunken basins; a chance or intentional fire in such a basin would have transformed the clay into hard and durable material. Once human beings learned to add tempering materials such as straw or pieces of stone to the clay, they could produce portable containers. From this point pottery vessels were to become one of the most important components of the material culture. The earliest attempts at pottery making already occurred late in the seventh millennium B.C.E., as some finds at Ain Ghazal have shown.

From the beginnings of pottery making, each population group, differentiated by its ethnic, tribal, or geopolitical character, developed its preferred shapes, decoration techniques, and motifs. Nonetheless, there were considerable interrelationships between contemporary groups. Thus, from the PN onward, pottery becomes one of the major tools of the archaeologist for defining the geographic sphere, chronological developments, and correlations of ancient cultures.

The Neolithic pottery comprises mainly simple, crude,

handmade vessels, made on mats and fired at low temperature. The range of shapes is limited: bowls, deep kraters, storage jars, and small closed jars. The vessels have simple flat bases; the rims are plain and unmolded; handles are small knobs or rounded lugs. The details of decoration vary according to the region, but there are some prevalent designs—such as triangular motifs, zigzag lines, and herringbone pattern—which were applied either by paint or by incisions.

Apart from the invention of pottery, however, the PN was a period of major change in settlement pattern from that of the PPNB. The sites were small, and their location limited to the fertile plains. The fringe areas and the deserts appear to have been either uninhabited or settled by hunters and pastoralists who were not part of the mainstream of cultural development in the fertile areas.

PN cultures in Syria greatly resembled those of Palestine, yet they appear to have been more varied and affluent. Sites such as Byblos and Ras Shamra along the coast, Tell Judeidah in the Amuq Valley, and dozens of settlements in inland Syria (mainly along the Litani, Orontes, and Queiq rivers and in the Upper Euphrates Valley) have produced rich finds from this period. It appears that in Syria there was a greater continuity from the PPNB period to the early PN. The settlements—concentrated in the fertile regions—based their economy on agriculture and stock, including the beginnings of cattle breeding. After 5500 B.C.E., northern Syria became part of the larger Tell Halaf civilization of northern Mesopotamia, while southern Syria, Lebanon, and Palestine developed their own PN cultures, to a large extent interrelated with each other.

The key site for southern Palestine in this period is again Jericho. People lived there in sunken shallow pit dwellings; some rectilinear structures were constructed at the end of the period. The crude pottery was sometimes decorated in combined techniques—such as reserved slip, which created patterns of light-colored triangles and chevrons on a red slipped background; incised herringbone pattern; and bands of red paint creating zigzag designs. Convex jar rims (known as "bow rims") were common to Jericho and to other late PN cultures throughout Palestine and southern Syria. The flint tools included many sickle blades and tanged arrowheads, as well as chisels, axes, and knives. Kenyon suggested a separation of the PN at Jericho into two subphases (PNA and PNB). Other sites, in the Shephelah (Teluliot Batashi) and in the coastal plain, demonstrate the spread of this PN culture throughout the southern part of Palestine. However, we still lack sufficient data as to the chronological correlation between these southern cultures and the PN cultures of northern Palestine.

The most important culture in the north of the country during the earlier half of the PN period is the Yarmukian, named after the Yarmuk River.[21] The key sites are near Kibbutz Shaar Hagolan and at nearby Hurvat Minhah (Munhata), both in the Jordan Valley. At Hurvat Minhah this culture was found in Level 2B2, above PPN levels and below

2.8 Excavations at the Pottery Neolithic site of Hurvat Minhah (Munhata) in the Jordan Valley. The stone structures on the left are from the Wadi Rabah phase (early fifth millennium B.C.E.). The pits in the center and on the right are from the Yarmukian phase (sixth millennium B.C.E.).

later PN phases. The Yarmukian culture spread throughout the valley of Jezreel and along the coastal plain as far as the area of Tel Aviv (at Habashan Street). In Transjordan it is represented in the upper levels at Ain Ghazal. The dwellings at Shaar Hagolan were in shallow pits as at Jericho. Typical flint tool kits were composed of adzes and axes with polished cutting edges, knives, arrowheads, and serrated sickle blades. The pottery was decorated with horizontal bands and zigzag patterns, both created by incising a frame of two parallel lines filled with incised herringbone pattern; strips of red paint were applied along the line bordering the incised bands; sometimes, the entire vessel was covered with reddish paint, except for the reserved incised decoration band.

A peculiar type of pottery figurine most probably depicts the Yarmukian fertility goddess. Its head is elongated and pointed, and the eyes resemble kernels of grain. The only complete example of such a figurine, found at Hurvat Minhah, is shown seated, holding her breasts; she is depicted with exaggerated hips. Images of the mother goddess were worshiped by various Neolithic communities—such as that of the fifth millennium B.C.E. at Hacilar in Anatolia, where a

2.9 A clay figurine showing a seated woman, probably a fertility goddess. Found at Munhata; from the Yarmukian phase (sixth millennium B.C.E.).

unique collection was found. Schematic incisions of human faces and female sexual organs on pebbles are another Yarmukian form of art related to a fertility cult.

The Yarmukian culture was replaced by the Wadi Rabah culture. Like the Yarmukian, this new culture expanded in northern Palestine and along the coastal plain. Key sites are Ain Jerbah and nearby Hazorea (in the valley of Jezreel), and the Wadi Rabah site, near Rosh Haayin (close to the sources of the Yarkon River). The discovery of the Wadi Rabah culture in the lowest occupation levels of some major *tells* in the north—such as Megiddo, Beth-Shean, Shechem (Tell Balatah), and Tell el-Farʿah (north)—signifies that culture's role in the settlement history of the country.[22] There is evidence that the Wadi Rabah culture, or a very similar cultural form, also spread in southern Lebanon and Syria.

In the Wadi Rabah culture rectangular structures with stone foundations were built for the first time. The flint tools were mainly manufactured for agricultural needs: adzes, axes, and sickle blades were common, while arrowheads became rare, reflecting a decline in hunting. The pottery is better made, and a richer variety of forms appear. The vessels were decorated with incised and impressed patterns made with pointed tools, and some were covered with well-burnished dark red, brown, or black slip; the latter pottery is known in Syria as "Dark-Faced Burnished Ware." This ware reflects the cultural relations between the two parts of the Levant—relations which are further substantiated by bow rims of jars. Some evidence for ties with the Tell Halaf civilization of northern Syria have also been detected.

Did this well-developed Wadi Rabah culture emerge locally, or was it the result of an emigration from Syria? It did, undoubtedly, differ to a large extent from its Yarmukian predecessor, and it closely resembles finds in Byblos on the coast of Lebanon and at the Baqʿah of Lebanon. In fact, northern Palestine and Lebanon may have been part of one cultural entity. But the transition from the Yarmukian to the Wadi Rabah phase and the origins of the latter are not entirely clear—as there might have been other, interim cultural phases, as seen at Hurvat Minhah.[23]

There is evidence for the existence of additional regional cultures in Neolithic Palestine—such as at the site of Gharubba in the central Jordan Valley, which produced a unique assemblage of delicately painted pottery, unparalleled elsewhere.[24]

The basic relative sequence of the regional cultures can be determined, though a lot of data is still missing. Few carbon 14 datings for this period exist, and the absolute chronology is still vague. It appears that the earlier part of the PN period, represented by Jericho PNA in the south and the Yarmukian culture in the north, extended through the late sixth and the first half of the fifth millennium B.C.E., while the later phase, represented in the south by Jericho PNB and in the north by the Wadi Rabah culture, developed during the mid–fifth millennium B.C.E.

The subsistence economy did not change much during this period, except that domesticated animals (goats, sheep, cattle, and pigs) appear to have outnumbered wild game.

A group of outstanding finds from Kabri, in the northern part of the Acre Valley, is possible evidence for long-range trade relations in the mid–fifth millennium B.C.E. A stone jar with a bow rim in this group recalls pottery jars of the late PN phase. The group includes an exceptionally large and unique obsidian core, 38 cm long; an elaborate, superbly made obsidian mirror; and several stone vessels of admirable workmanship. The objects seem to have originated in Syria— except the obsidian core, which came from Anatolia.[25]

No PN remains were found in the Negev, Sinai, and the deserts of Transjordan. One view holds that the climate after the PPNB period became drier, causing desertion of the arid zones throughout the Levant.[26] It is more probable that groups of Neolithic hunters continued to survive throughout the period in these regions. They would have retained their older traditions but did not develop pottery.

DESERT REGIONS IN THE NEOLITHIC PERIOD

Alongside the sedentary settlements of the Neolithic period, there were other communities in which hunting remained the basis for subsistence. The latter thrived in the Judean Desert, in the southern Negev, in Sinai, and along the desert fringes in Transjordan. Neolithic sites in these regions include groups of rounded huts, perhaps used as seasonal dwellings. A most prominent feature in these regions are hunting installations known, due to their kitelike shape, as "desert

2.10 Har Harif
(central Negev):
remains of round
dwelling from the
Harifian culture
(eighth millennium
B.C.E.).

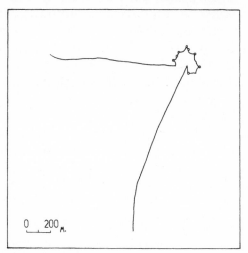

2.11 Plan of a
"desert kite."

0 200 M.

kites." Hundreds of these have been first identified by air
reconnaissance in Transjordan as well as in the Syrian Desert.
Some smaller examples have been noted in the Elath region
and in Sinai.[27] The kites were constructed of stone; each
included two long arms (sometimes as long as 2.5 km)
converging into a kind of funnel and leading into a killing

area surrounded by walls and shooting positions. These huge traps were used most probably for hunting gazelles, which were driven in herds into the wide openings of the kites until they reached the narrow killing area. The dating of the kites to the Neolithic period is based on excavations at one of them, as well as on the discovery of nearby settlements. The total length of kite walls in Transjordan alone is estimated at having been several thousand kilometers, entailing huge, long-term construction efforts which may have extended from the seventh to the fourth millennium B.C.E.

In the Elath region, in addition to several desert kites, a number of settlements and isolated shrines can be dated to the seventh through fifth millennia B.C.E. A shrine at Biqat Uvda, comprised a courtyard and a Holy of Holies in which a row of standing stones was found. Nearby, animals, perhaps panthers, were depicted by means of grouping stones; these depictions are evidence of a peculiar Neolithic desert art.[28]

The groups of hunters who lived on the fringes of fertile country must have been in mutual economic relations with the sedentary communities. The hunters probably supplied the meat and leather to the villagers, while the barter of the latter may have been grain. This may explain the plethora of Neolithic sites in the Transjordan desert fringes, such as Ain Ghazal (which ironically means "the spring of the gazelle") and Beidha. Perhaps communities of hunters existed beside those of farmers; at times, conflicts may have broken out. It thus was the Neolithic period that saw the beginning of the symbiosis and periodic rivalry between the dwellers of the desert and those of the sown—a relationship which was to remain a fundamental of human society in the ancient Near East.

NOTES

1. For a general survey of the prehistoric period in Palestine, see O. Bar-Yosef, *Annual Review of Anthropology* 9 (1980), pp. 101–33.

2. D. A. E. Garrod, *Proceedings of the British Academy* 43 (1957), pp. 211–27; F. R. Valla, *Le Natufien: Une Culture préhistorique en Palestine,* Paris, 1975; O. Bar-Yosef in: J. Cauvin and P. Sanlaville (eds.), *Préhistoire du Levant,* Paris 1981, pp. 389–408 (English); O. Bar-Yosef in: T. C. Young and P. E. L. Smith (eds.), *The Hilly Flanks: Essays on the Prehistory of Southwestern Asia,* Chicago 1983, pp. 11–42.

3. J. Mellaart, *The Neolithic of the Near East,* London 1975, particularly pp. 16–69, 227–43; A. M. T. Moore, *BASOR* 246 (1982), pp. 1–34; Bar-Yosef in: Cauvin and Sanlaville (see note 2), pp. 555–69.

4. Moore (see note 3) suggests the following terminology and dates:

> *Archaic Neolithic:*
> Neolithic 1: 8500–7600 B.C.E.
> Neolithic 2: 7600–6000 B.C.E.
> *Developed Neolithic:*
> Neolithic 3: 6000–5000 B.C.E.
> Neolithic 4: 5000–3750 B.C.E.

5. J. M. Weinstein, *Radiocarbon* 26 (1984), pp. 297–366. The date 7600 B.C.E. for the transition from PPNA to PPNB is based on carbon 14 readings in Syria; see Moore (note 3), p. 8. (The date 3750 B.C.E. proposed by Moore for the end of the Neolithic period is based on only one carbon 14 reading, from Ain Gharuba in the Jezreel Valley.) See also Y. Garfinkel et al., *IEJ* 37 (1987), pp. 40–42, where a date of 6840 B.C.E. (plus or minus fifty years) is given for seeds from PPNB occupation levels at Yiftahel.

6. K. M. Kenyon and T. A. Holland, *Excavations at Jericho,* vol. 3, London 1981, passim; ibid., vol. 5, London 1983, pp. 639–705; Kenyon (1979), pp. 19–40; K. M. Kenyon, *Digging Up Jericho,* London 1957, pp. 51–76.

7. O. Bar-Yosef, A. Gopher, and A. N. Goring-Morris, *Paleorient* 6 (1980), pp. 201–6; T. Noy, *Israel Museum News* 3 (1968), pp. 22–27; T. Noy et al., *Proceedings of the Prehistoric Society* 39 (1973), pp. 75–99.

8. O. Bar-Yosef, *Current Anthropology* 27 (1986), pp. 157–62.

9. J. Cauvin, *AASOR* 44 (1977), pp. 19–48.

10. C. Renfrew et al., *Proceedings of the Prehistoric Society* 32 (1966), pp. 30–72; ibid., 34 (1968), pp. 319–31.

11. E. Anati, *BASOR* 167 (1962), pp. 25–31.

12. E. B. Banning and B. F. Bird, *BASOR* 255 (1984), pp. 15–20; O. G. Rollefson and A. H. Simons, *BASOR Supplement* 23 (1985), pp. 35–52; Y. Garfinkel, *Journal of Field Archaeology* 14 (1987), pp. 199–212.

13. D. Kirkbride, *PEQ* 98 (1966), pp. 8–72.

14. O. Bar-Yosef, *A Cave in the Desert: Nahal Hemar.* Israel Museum Catalogue No. 258, Jerusalem 1985. D. Alon and O. Bar-Yosef, Nahal Hemar Cave ʿAtiqot 18 (1988).

15. D. Ferembach and M. Lechevallier, *Paleorient* 1 (1973), pp. 223–30; D. Lechevallier, *Abou Ghosh et Beisamoun,* Paris 1978; H. de Contenson, *Archaeology* 24 (1971), pp. 278–85.

16. Rollefson and Simons (see note 12). For a color picture, see the front cover of *BAR* 13:2 (1987).

17. R. Amiran, *BASOR* 167 (1962), pp. 23–25.

18. For the mask from the Hebron area, see T. Ornan, *Man and His Country: A Selection of the Dayan Collection.* Israel Museum Catalogue No. 270, Jerusalem 1986, pp. 18–19; for Nahal Hemar, see note 14.

19. Moore (see note 3); idem, *Levant* 5 (1973), pp. 36–68; L. E. Stager in: *COWA* 3.

20. For a summary and bibliography, see H. Weiss (ed.), *Ebla to Damascus,* Washington 1985, pp. 50–64.

21. M. Stekelis, *The Yarmukian Culture,* Jerusalem 1973. For a Yarmukian site in Transjordan, see Z. Kafafi, *ADAJ* 29 (1985), pp. 31–34.

22. Y. Kaplan, *IEJ* 8 (1958), pp. 149–60; idem, *BASOR* 194 (1969), pp. 2–38; idem, *EI* 5 (1958), pp. 9–24 (Hebrew); A. Ben-Tor, '*Atiqot* 3 (1966), pp. 1–26 (Hebrew).

23. Some scholars designate the Wadi Rabah phase "Early Chalcolithic" (see Y. Kaplan in the publications referred to in the preceding note; R. Gophna in: *HEI,* vol. 1, pp. 77–80 [Hebrew]). Such terminology can hardly be accepted, since the use of metal appears to be a fundamental part of a Chalcolithic culture, while in the case of the Wadi Rabah stage no metal was evident. Furthermore, the contemporary and closely related cultures in Syria and Lebanon are universally termed "Neolithic."

24. J. Mellaart, *ADAJ* 3 (1956), pp. 24–33.

25. M. Stekelis, *EI* 8 (1967), pp. 35–37 (Hebrew); M. W. Prausnitz, *EI* 9 (1969), pp. 122–29 (Hebrew).

26. Moore (see note 3), p. 25.

27. Z. Meshel, *TA* 1 (1974), pp. 129–43; A. Betts, *Levant* 15 (1983), pp. 1–10; ibid. 16 (1984), pp. 25–34.

28. U. Avner, *TA* 11 (1984), pp. 115–31; O. Yogev, *Qadmoniot* 16 (1983), pp. 118–22 (Hebrew).

CHAPTER THREE

INNOVATIVE COMMUNITIES OF THE FOURTH MILLENNIUM:
The Chalcolithic Period
(ca. 4300–3300 B.C.E.)

INTRODUCTION

The term "Chalcolithic" (based on the Greek *chalcos*, "copper," and *lithos*, "stone") marks the appearance of copper—the first metal used by man—although stone implements continued in use. The Chalcolithic period extended over the late fifth and most of the fourth millennia B.C.E., and it saw the appearance of unique related cultures in Palestine with extraordinary settlement patterns, economy, social structure, and spiritual life.[1]

In the history of archaeological research in Palestine, various cultures have been named "Chalcolithic," confusing its designation. In this book, we shall not use ambiguous terms such as "Early Chalcolithic" or "Late Chalcolithic." The main culture of the Chalcolithic period is the Ghassulian culture; this latter term will be used here in its most comprehensive framework—including regional variations such as that found along the Beer-sheba Brook and farther north, as well as that evidenced by the burial caves with ossuaries found in the coastal plain. Related Chalcolithic cultures include that of the Golan Heights and the still almost unknown culture in the Galilee and the northern valleys.

The key site for the study of this period is Teleilat Ghassul, 50 acres in area, located on a slope overlooking the northeastern shore of the Dead Sea. The excavation of the uppermost occupation levels of Teleilat Ghassul, carried out during the thirties, provided the basis for the definition of the term "Ghassulian culture." A sequence of ten occupation phases uncovered in more recent excavations was estimated by J. B. Hennessy (on the basis of carbon 14 tests) as spanning a period of approximately one thousand years.[2] The earliest stratum was described as containing remains similar to those found in the PNB at other sites, but the transitional stages from this early phase to the developed Ghassulian culture are yet to be published. When they are, Teleilat Ghassul will possibly reveal the origins of the Chalcolithic culture. At most other sites, the Chalcolithic cultures are generally found only in their most developed stage.

SETTLEMENT PATTERN

The distribution of Chalcolithic settlements differs to a large extent from that of both the preceding and succeeding periods. Clusters of sites have been found along wadi banks in peripheral areas of Palestine. The best example is perhaps the northern Negev, where a comprehensive survey and excavations have revealed over seventy Chalcolithic settlements over a distance of 110 km along the banks of the Beersheba Brook and its continuation, the Besor Brook.[3] Another concentration is to be found farther northward, on the banks of the Gerar Brook. This is a region of loess soil, in which winter floods have carved deep wadi courses. The floodwaters comprised a periodic source of water, which was made available year-round by digging shallow pits in the wadi beds. The region was entirely uninhabited in Neolithic times, and the Chalcolithic inhabitants found here a primeval land that was ideal for widespread settlement based on herding and agriculture. The sites are of various sizes; many are very small, while others are 10–20 acres in area (such as Gilat, Shiqmim, and Bir Safadi). This regional study makes possible a tentative reconstruction of the social and political structure in the Chalcolithic period. A model based on "chiefdoms," with central settlements dominating smaller sites within the sphere of their territory, has been suggested by T. E. Levy.

In the Judean Desert, evidence of a seminomadic, pastoral Chalcolithic population came to light in the exploration of

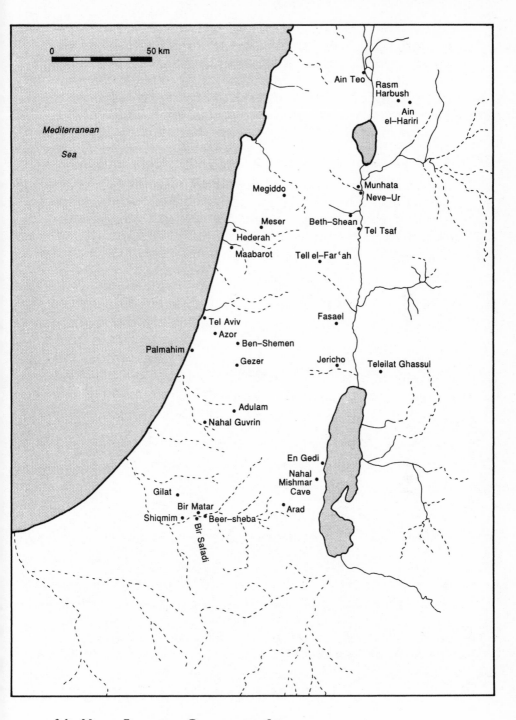

3.1 Map of Excavated Chalcolithic Sites.

3.2 Looking south at Beer-sheba Brook and the sites of Bir Safadi (A) and Bir Matar (B).

caves in the desert canyons. The oasis at En Gedi may have served a community as a cultic center, as is indicated by the temple discovered there on the spur overlooking the spring.

A chain of Chalcolithic settlements has been detected along the Jordan Valley. Teleilat Ghassul, overlooking the south-eastern end of the valley, was probably, considering its size and long occupation, the main administrative and economic center for the area. Surprisingly, no Chalcolithic settlement is known to have existed at the tell of Jericho, which was of major importance in the previous period. Yet large Chalco-lithic sites are known farther north in the Jordan Valley, mainly near alluvial fans, along wadi courses (such as Nahal Fasael and Wadi Far'ah), and in the Beth-Shean Valley (where a large site is known near Kibbutz Neve-Ur).

The distribution of Chalcolithic settlements in the Medi-terranean climate zone of central and northern Palestine is still unclear. Some are known along the wadis of the foothills.[4] The impression is that, in these regions convenient for habitation in the Mediterranean climatic zones of the country, the number of Chalcolithic sites and their size fall short of those sites known in the peripheral zones of the northern Negev and the Jordan Valley. This is a strange phenomenon to which no satisfactory explanation has yet been given. Perhaps the Chalcolithic sites in the alluvial plains are covered by thick silt deposits which make their detection difficult.

A peculiar concentration of about twenty sites was explored by C. Epstein in a limited basaltic area in the central Golan Heights.[5] This region, only sparsely inhabited prior to the Chalcolithic period, became the focus of an independent culture slightly different from the Ghassulian.

The settlement pattern of the Chalcolithic period was thus rather exceptional in the history of Palestine. In contrast to the situation in the preceding and succeeding periods, the Chalcolithic pattern emphasized the peripheral, semiarid re-gions as opposed to the more convenient fertile regions of Mediterranean climate. The desert fringes, the Judean Desert, and the Golan Heights suited an economy based on herding; this fact is suggested in the motifs of the ritual objects from the period, which often illustrate horned animals. It appears, however, that agriculture was also developed. Olive trees were grown for the first time (particularly in the Golan Heights), suggesting that olive oil, which was to be one of the major products of the country for centuries to come, was first produced in this period.

SETTLEMENT PLANNING AND ARCHITECTURE

Plans of Chalcolithic villages are known only from a few sites. Teleilat Ghassul and Shiqmim indicate that there was some degree of planning. They were both densely built, large, unfortified villages, composed of groups of dwelling units constructed along streets and dead-end alleys. The only public buildings known at these sites are temples found at Teleilat Ghassul. A unique plan was worked out on the Golan Heights,

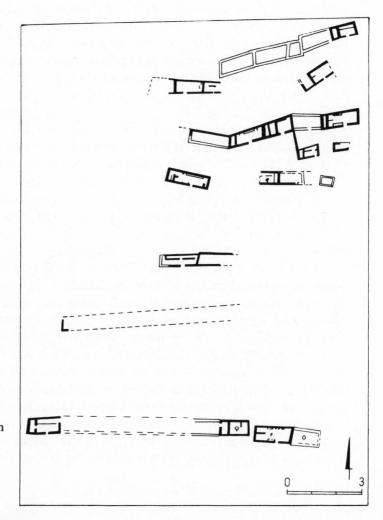

3.3 Plan of the Chalcolithic settlement at Ain el-Hariri, in the Golan Heights.

0   3

where rectangular houses were attached to one another at their narrow sides to create several parallel chains of houses with open spaces between the chains. Twenty to fifty houses were counted in the largest settlements of this region. The chains are explained by Epstein as units serving extended families, each rectangular unit serving one nuclear family.

The Chalcolithic houses encompassed a single rectangular large space, sometimes accompanied by a side chamber. At Teleilat Ghassul, the houses generally measured about 3.5 × 12 m. They were "broad houses," with the entrance in the middle of one of the long walls. Large adjacent courtyards included silos and probably served as sheep pens. A well-preserved Chalcolithic farmhouse complex at Fasael in the Jordan Valley includes a large fenced courtyard and a dwelling unit comprising a "broad room" and two square chambers.[6]

The architectural tradition of "broad houses" is especially evident on the Golan Heights. The chains of abutting dwellings there comprised rectangular buildings measuring 6 × 15 m on the average, massively built of large basalt stones, and paved with stone slabs. The entrance was in the center of one of the long walls; in most cases there was a bench opposite

3.4 Chalcolithic house at Rasm Harbush, the Golan Heights. The house is 6 × 15 m in size and is one in a chain of similar houses.

the opening, a cultic niche containing a stone statue, and an additional, small room at the far narrow side of the house.

A unique type of subterranean architecture is found in the Beer-sheba region. The Chalcolithic settlers took advantage of the soft loess soil to carve out a series of burrows and subterranean dwellings, storage and work rooms.[7] These underground quarters, which resemble ant nests in plan, were suited to the regional climate and are a good example of the creativity characteristic of the Chalcolithic people and their adaptation to the environment. At Bir Safadi and Bir Abu Matar, where J. Perrot discovered such burrows, it was suggested that they represent the earliest phase of settlement there, and that after they had begun to collapse, partially built rectangular houses were sunk into the pits which had been formed. In the final phase, rectangular stone structures were wholly constructed on the surface, as at Teleilat Ghassul. But this evolution was probably not a general feature, and some of the freestanding houses may well have been erected contemporaneously with the subterranean systems. At Shiqmim, the largest of the Chalcolithic settlements in the northern Negev, the dwellings resemble those of Teleilat Ghassul, and no subterranean installations were found.

The Temple at En Gedi An isolated Chalcolithic temple complex, unrelated to any settlement, was discovered on a high spur above the oasis of En Gedi, on the western shore of the Dead Sea.[8] The complex comprised a large courtyard surrounded by a stone fence and entered through a well-planned, double-doored gatehouse with benches along its walls. A round structure in the center of the courtyard was explained by the excavators as a ceremonial water basin. At one side of the courtyard, there was a rectangular auxiliary room, and next to it, a second, simpler entrance to the complex. The temple itself was a rectangular "broad room," measuring about 5 × 20 m, with the entrance in the long wall facing the courtyard. Similar to other dwellings from this period, the temple represented the home of the god. A Holy of Holies— a horseshoe-shaped installation with a polished standing stone—was placed opposite the doorway. Animal bones and ash found in circular pits were the remains of the sacrifices made here, and benches in the temple served for offerings. The "broad room" concept in the En Gedi temple was the

3.5 Bir Safadi: an underground dwelling.

3.6 Shiqmim: a Chalcolithic dwelling comprising a rectangular courtyard and a large rectangular room.

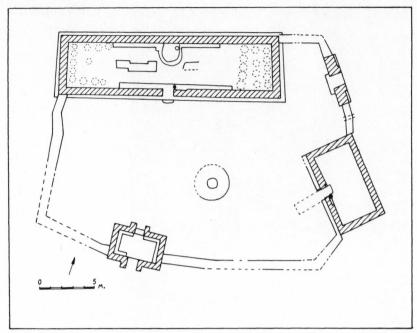

3.7 Plan of the temple at En Gedi.

beginning of a tradition of religious architecture in Palestine which was to continue throughout the third millennium B.C.E. until the end of the Early Bronze Age.

The temple probably served seminomadic pastoralists who lived in the Judean Desert, but it can also be explained as a sanctuary and focus for pilgrimage of distant Chalcolithic communities, such as Teleilat Ghassul. The temple was abandoned at the end of the Chalcolithic period, and its entrance was blocked. Although it was found almost empty of finds, the opulence of the ritual objects which must have belonged to this temple can be pictured from the extraordinary treasure of copper and ivory artifacts discovered in the "Cave of the Treasure" in Nahal Mishmar to the south. The treasure most probably belonged to the temple and was hidden in this remote cave by its priests (see p. 75).

The En Gedi temple probably reflects the religious architecture of the Ghassulian culture, as two unpublished temples at Teleilat Ghassul are reported to be of a similar plan. No other public buildings are known from the Chalcolithic period, so it would appear that the religious institutions played a leading role in the social and economic life of the time.

POTTERY

The wealth of daily objects discovered at Chalcolithic sites is indicative of the significant progress made in this period in comparison to its predecessor. Pottery is found in large quantities and is generally better made. Most vessels were handmade, but some of the smaller ones were produced on a simple form of potter's wheel. Large jars were made on mats, which could be turned during the shaping of the clay. The mat impressions on the bases of such vessels (as well as an actual mat found at Nahal Mishmar) reveal a high standard of weaving technology.

The variety of pottery shapes is quite broad in comparison to the preceding Neolithic period. Typical are large storage jars in which agricultural produce and liquids were kept. The huge pithoi of the period are among the largest ever made in Palestine. There is also a wide variety of smaller closed vessels, large kraters, and numerous bowls with flat bases and straight, oblique sides. Such bowls with high fenestrated foot perhaps had cultic use. The cornet, a V-shaped cup with a long pointed base, is a vessel type common at Teleilat Ghassul and at sites in central Palestine, but rare in the Beer-sheba region and absent on the Golan Heights. The churn, used for churning milk to obtain butter, is characteristic of a society where herding was an important economic factor. It is common in the Beer-sheba region, but rare at Teleilat Ghassul and absent from the Golan sites. The significance of the cornet and churn in the Chalcolithic environment is demonstrated by the fact that they feature on two pottery cultic figures found at Gilat.

Lug handles, often in the form of a long, narrow cylinder longitudinally pierced, are a hallmark of Chalcolithic pottery throughout the country. Ropelike decoration, made of clay bands with finger impressions, is often found on jars, particularly in the Golan culture. Simple painted decoration, mainly broad bands in red, is common at Teleilat Ghassul and Beer-sheba, and delicately painted geometric designs such as triangles, nets, and stripes are occasionally found on some of the smaller vessels at the former site.

Features of the pottery common to most of the country appear to be predominant over regional variability. These

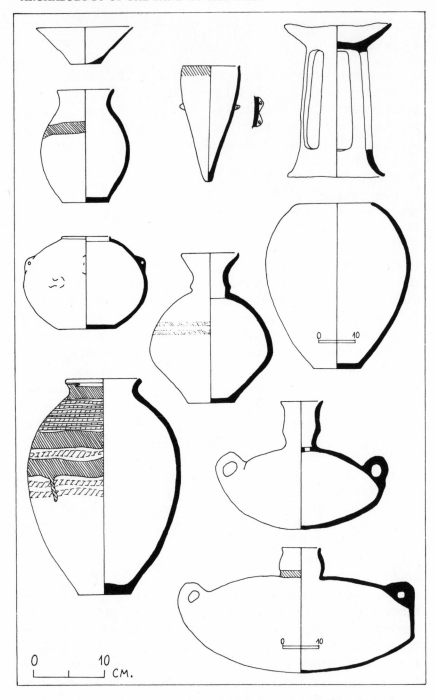

3.8 Selected Chalcolithic pottery from Azor and Beer-sheba.

3.9 Storage jar from the Golan Heights.

3.10 Pottery churn from Beersheba.

mutual characteristics in the realm of pottery, as well as in other aspects of the material culture, enable us to group all the regional variants in the central and southern parts of the country under one general term, "Ghassulian culture."

The long duration of the Ghassulian pottery assemblage can be deduced from Hennessy's renewed excavations at Teleilat Ghassul, where the assemblage appears with slight changes throughout the nine settlement phases there (except in the earliest, which is said to be close to PNB).

STONE IMPLEMENTS

The Flint Industry A new inventory of flint implements characterizes the Chalcolithic period. Especially common are axes and adzes used for turning the soil and possibly also for chopping and working wood. Flat tabular scrapers and various borers and awls were employed in leather work, and sickle blades—attached in groups to a handle—were used for harvesting. Studies of the flint industry have led to the identification of certain production centers and of a trade in flint tools between different parts of the country.[9]

Stone Vessels and Shell Objects A sophisticated, labor-intensive industry producing basalt vessels operated in the northern part of the country (the Golan Heights or eastern Galilee) and in Transjordan. Its beautifully made products were apparently considered precious objects, as they were marketed to southern Chalcolithic communities such as those in the Beer-sheba region. Especially common are large bowls and bowls on a high pedestal resembling pottery forms and occasionally ornamented with incised motifs.

Objects made of a variety of hard stones which originated outside Palestine are evidence of a trade over an even greater distance. Examples are hematite used for making mace-heads and apparently originating in Sinai, as well as obsidian which continued to be imported from Anatolia. Typical agricultural implements of this period are the so-called hoeing stones: round, crudely worked stones which were pierced in the center. These may have been used as weights for digging sticks, a major agricultural tool in a period when animal-driven plows were not yet known.

Bone and shell objects, including a particular type of trapezoidal pendant, are common among Chalcolithic assemblages.

THE COPPER INDUSTRY AND THE "CAVE OF THE TREASURE"

The most significant innovation of the Chalcolithic period is the appearance of a sophisticated copper industry. Various objects made from this metal have been discovered in settlements: some simple axeheads at Teleilat Ghassul, and several mace-heads and other artifacts in the Beer-sheba region. Our knowledge of the copper industry in this period, however, was revolutionized with the discovery in 1961 (by P. Bar-Adon) of the metal hoard in the "Cave of the Treasure" in Nahal Mishmar, a remote cave on a cliff face in the Judean Desert (north of Masada).[10] The well-hidden cache included 436 copper objects, wrapped in a mat. They were exceptionally well preserved due to the extremely dry weather conditions. Accompanying them were typical Chalcolithic potsherds, stone vessels, flint tools, ivory objects, and shell pendants. A large number of perishable materials was also found in an excellent state of preservation. These included linen and woolen textiles (the only examples known from this period), fragments of a wooden and bone loom, loom weights, implements for spinning thread, remnants of worked leather (of a sandal and of a garment), various basketry (mats, baskets, a sieve, ropes), as well as food remains. The latter are particularly in.ormative in regard to the agriculture and diet of the Chalcolithic era (see p. pp. 85–86).

The copper objects of the cache were very well made and illustrated a sophisticated technology of casting metal, including the earliest appearance of the "lost wax" (*cire perdue*) process. The metal in this group was an alloy of copper with a small amount of arsenic and other rare trace elements. This material could not have originated in the Arabah mines or in Cyprus; the closest source probably lies in the mountains of Armenia, near the Russo-Turkish border. The arsenic imparted

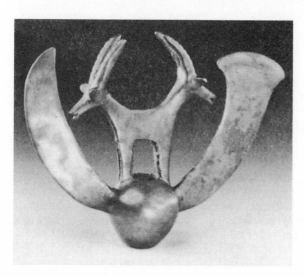

3.11 Nahal Mishmar hoard: a copper ritual object composed of a mace-head, two blades, and a double-headed horned animal. Height 11 cm.

several important properties to the copper: it became strong and easily poured during casting, facilitating precise casting of complex objects in the "lost wax" technique. The cult objects include peculiar ceremonial artifacts—mainly hollow, ornamented rods which apparently served in processions as standards mounted on wooden staves. There were also "crowns," decorated with a variety of symbolic and geometric shapes; as well as copper vessels and some ornamented, ceremonial weapons (for the artistic motives, see p. 81).

3.12 Nahal Mishmar hoard: a copper ritual object in the form of a crown. The two projected parts probably represent temple facades; they are decorated with horns of mountain goat and knobs representing constructional beams. Diameter 16.8 cm.

The knowledge and skill of the smiths are quite astonishing for the fourth millennium B.C.E. It has been suggested (by J. Perrot) that the sophisticated ritual objects were imported from Anatolia; an alternative is that just the arsenic ore was brought from the north, the artifacts themselves being locally made. The only fourth millennium B.C.E. copper-industry installations known from the Levant were found in the Beer-sheba region. They were discovered together with mace-heads and some fragmentary copper scepters similar to those of the Nahal Mishmar treasure, raising the possibility that the Nahal Mishmar objects were produced by professional metalsmiths living in this area. These artisans may have used imported arsenic ores; they may even have alloyed them with local ores coming from the Arabah mines; the artisans' highly specialized metal industry may have been a significant eco-nomic factor contributing to the wealth of the Chalcolithic settlement of the northern Negev.

Who brought this quantity of splendid artifacts to the remote cave in the Judean Desert? It is tempting to assume (following D. Ussishkins' suggestion) that the hoard was originally the equipment of the temple at En Gedi. If indeed the hoard belonged to that temple, it means that there was no proportion between the wealth accumulated in the temple and the economic strength of the desert dwellers during the Chalcolithic age. It thus can be assumed that the temple at En Gedi was sacred to Chalcolithic communities located far away, such as those of Teleilat Ghassul and the Beer-sheba region.

RITUAL ART

The Chalcolithic period is noteworthy for its abundance of art objects, which comprise an invaluable source for the study of ritual art, symbolism, and artistic expression.[11] This artistic oeuvre is of particular significance in the light of the paucity of such art in the succeeding Early Bronze Age.

The wall paintings found at Teleilat Ghassul are some of the most outstanding works of ancient art from Palestine. The paintings were executed on the white plastered walls of certain buildings, which may have been chapels serving a cluster of houses. The walls had numerous coats of plaster (twenty in one case), each painted layer covering a previous painting. The best-preserved painting depicts a large, eight-

3.13   Fresco from Teleilat Ghassul showing an eight-pointed star (1.84 m in diameter); to the star's left are two ritual masks and mythological creatures (?). On the right, the depiction is possibly of a fragmentary temple facade. Painted in red, black, gray, and white.

pointed star (1.84 m in diameter) painted in red, black, and white, probably symbolizing the sun. On its left are various creatures—including two monstrous heads, perhaps ritual masks representing mythological creatures. On the right is a fragmentary depiction, possibly of a building facade (a temple?). Two paintings depict ceremonial processions. One of these, almost entirely defaced, probably portrays worshipers proceeding toward two gods shown on a dais. The other painting is a colorful illustration of three figures walking hand in hand; the first figure is holding a sickle in its right hand. On other walls, depictions of large birds, a kneeling leopard, and various monsters are painted. This artistic mode is peculiar to Teleilat Ghassul and is indicative of the importance of that site. The skill displayed by the painters is evidence of a crystallized, local artistic tradition developed by professional artists for ritual uses. Wall paintings in buildings are known

in the Neolithic period in Anatolia (Çatal Huyük) and Mesopotamia (Umm Dabaghiyah), but the latter are much earlier,
and we lack any link to prove the continuity of this tradition.

In the Beer-sheba region, ivory figurines were produced in
an original, unique style.[12] They were made locally, as is
indicated by ivory waste and cutting tools uncovered at the
site of Bir Safadi. The raw material may have been local
hippopotamus ivory; or perhaps elephant tusk imported from
Africa via Egypt, or from northern Syria, where there were
still elephants as late as the second millennium B.C.E. Several

3.14 Ivory
statuettes from the
Beer-sheba culture.
Right: male figure
from Bir Safadi,
height 33 cm. Left:
female figure, un-
known provenance,
height 29 cm.

of these works of art depict nude males and females standing in frontal posture, with hands on their thighs or beside the body; the largest, a male figure, is 33 cm high. Other works show birds, and heads of men and women; all are carved in a peculiar, highly stylized fashion. On the upper part of the males' heads is a depression which may have held offerings (such as grain); this feature recalls similar depressions on the heads of basalt statues from the Golan Heights (see later). A pregnant female statuette with emphasized sexual organs is undoubtedly a fertility goddess, possibly the mother goddess so common since Neolithic times. The male figures probably also depict deities. The Beer-sheba statuettes are unique; the only possible parallel are contemporary ivory figurines of the

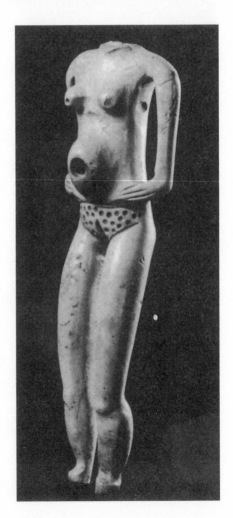

3.15 "Venus from Beer-sheba." An ivory statuette from Bir Safadi, representing a naked, pregnant female, most probably a fertility goddess. Height 12 cm.

Badarian and Amratian cultures of the Chalcolithic period in Egypt, which have some common technological and stylistic features. Two stone statuettes from the fourth millennium B.C.E. site of Tepe Yahya in Iran somewhat resemble the Beer-sheba statuettes. They are one of several parallels between Chalcolithic finds in Palestine and finds at Tepe Yahya, implying the existence of remote connections between fara-way cultures in this period.[13]

Two sculptured vessels from Gilat, north of Beer-sheba, are illustrative of the iconography of the Beer-sheba culture.[14] One of them depicts, in a rather grotesque style, a seated nude female holding a cylindrical object under one arm and supporting a churn on her head with her other hand. The

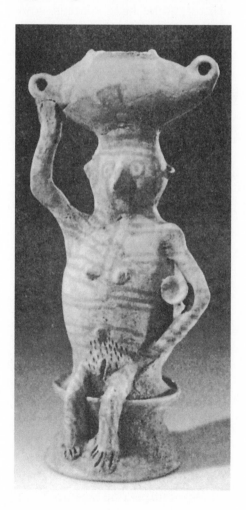

3.16 Gilat: a red painted pottery statuette representing a seated, naked female (goddess?) holding a churn on her head and a vessel under her arm. Height 30 cm.

body and facial details are painted in red, and the vagina is emphasized. The second, complementary vessel depicts a ram bearing three cornets on his back; cornets may have had some cultic use related to milk products or may even have been used for milking. Thus, the two objects were probably related to rituals connected with herds and dairy production; the female figure probably represented the fertility goddess.

On the Golan Heights, basalt figures (defined by C. Epstein as "household idols") were found in almost every Chalcolithic house.[15] These are cylindrical blocks of stone that were fashioned, seemingly by master craftsmen, in the form of a human head with a depression in its upper part probably for offerings (as in the male ivory figurines from Beer-sheba). Each statue has an individual character; some have goatees, some are horned. They probably represent personified fertility divinities.

3.17   A basalt idol from the Golan Heights, height 20 cm.

The design and decoration of the Chalcolithic pottery ossuaries (see p. 84) also reflect the artistic and religious world of the period. Various motifs connect the ossuaries with other Chalcolithic art objects: the prominent "nose" on the facade of some, the large eyes painted on one example, and their very form, a stylized house or animal. These elements give expression to a belief in an afterlife and are typical of the rich Ghassulian artistic mode of expression.

The copper objects from the Nahal Mishmar hoard (see p. 73) are a beautiful illustration of Chalcolithic art. Animal heads, mainly of ibexes and rams, appear in several cases and are probably an expression of a belief in magic protection sought from gods for the flocks. One of the standards depicts four ibex heads alongside a ram's head with twisted horns— an interesting combination of wild and domesticated animals. Human faces and various birds are featured, and there is also a wealth of stylized geometric ornamentation: incised herringbone and zigzag patterns, spiral ridges, and various knobs. The extent of stylization and the wish to achieve artistic harmony is demonstrated by a mace-head to which two opposing blades are attached. Between the blades, two ibex heads with a single common body are depicted. Motifs similar to those on the copper objects are found on the pottery ossuaries and on the basalt figures from the Golan; such motifs are representative of the iconographic and stylistic traditions common to various regions of the country, although the technical details of their production may have varied.

The considerable stylization prevalent in Ghassulian art is exemplified by the "violin-shaped" stone figurines, which are

3.18 A stone "violin-shaped" figurine from Gilat, probably depicting a schematized human torso.

schematic depictions of the human torso and apparently symbolize a fertility god or goddess. These have interesting parallels from western Anatolia, the Cycladic Islands, and Crete, though in those regions they appear several centuries later.

The artistic tendency of the Ghassulian people is also evident in their daily objects. At the Beer-sheba sites, floors are paved with pebbles decorated with red marks; on various objects there are incised combinations of lines and symbols of unknown significance (such as a five-pointed star, possibly a solar symbol, incised on flint scrapers); and pottery is often ornamented with signs of religious significance, such as snakes and a tree.

Thus, Chalcolithic art in Palestine is extraordinarily opulent. It presents a world of widespread faith in fertility deities, whose function was to protect and ensure the fertility of man, animal, and field, and in heavenly bodies—the sun and possibly the stars as depicted in the wall paintings. Birds and monstrous (or mythological) figures also were featured in the iconographic world of the period.

BURIAL CUSTOMS

Cemeteries outside settlements appeared for the first time during the Chalcolithic period. At Adeimeh, 2 km distant from Teleilat Ghassul, a necropolis consisted of three types of tombs: dolmens (tablelike tombs, built of three large stone slabs), *tumuli* (circular cairns), and simple cist graves dug into the ground where the burial was secondary (after the bones were collected). In spite of the distance between the Adeimeh necropolis and Teleilat Ghassul, the former probably served the latter settlement. The cemetery of Shiqmim in the northern Negev comprises built-up tombs with rounded stone foundations (1–3.5 m in diameter) which may have had a brick superstructure. Each structure contained several disarticulated corpses of adults and children in secondary burials. The varying sizes of the circles led Levy to infer the existence of a hierarchy in the Chalcolithic society.[16] A related burial form are the *nawamis*: fields of constructed, circular, stone burial chambers known from southern Sinai. These perhaps belonged to pastoralists or copper miners who lived in south-

3.19 Foundations of a round burial structure in a cemetery near Shiqmim, with bones *in situ*.

ern Sinai during the last centuries of the fourth millennium
B.C.E. (see pp. 96, 100).

In the central coastal plain between Hederah in the north
and Azor in the south, the bones were placed in ossuaries—
special pottery containers—which were placed in caves. Some
ossuaries are shaped like buildings, occasionally with gabled
roofs. Four small feet may represent a form of construction
in the swampy areas of the coastal plain, where wooden
houses would have to be raised above their surroundings. The
facades of the ossuaries are decorated, most commonly with
a human nose. Occasionally eyes are also shown, and in
several cases, work tools are depicted; the decorations of the
ossuaries indicate belief in life after death. Other ossuaries
have the stylized shape of an animal (possibly a sheep) or are
formed like jars.[17]

3.20 A group of pottery ossuaries from Azor.

The practice of burial inside the settlements, which was
predominant during the Neolithic period, is also occasionally
found at Chalcolithic sites in the form of simple articulated
burials below floors. Thus, heterogeneous burial customs
prevailed during this period; secondary burial appears to have
been common, but it was executed in various ways.

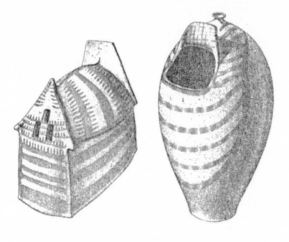
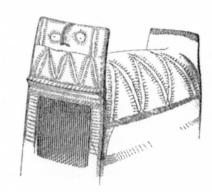

3.21   Three ossuaries from Azor.

SUBSISTENCE ECONOMY

The abundance of sites in what are at present semiarid regions calls for explanation. Paleoenvironmental studies for Palestine seem to show a heavier precipitation during the Chalcolithic period; a slightly higher average rainfall than today—some 100–150 mm a year—would have allowed cultivation and pasturage in these semiarid regions. At Teleilat Ghassul, located in what is now a dry region, evidence of the past existence of marshes has been found.

Levy assumes that agriculture in the Beer-sheba region was carried out mainly in the riverbeds, and that it relied on winter floods. In the central and northern parts of the country, where cultivation conditions were better than those of Beer-sheba, various crops were grown. Food remains in the Nahal Mishmar cave as well as at other sites point to a developed agriculture including wheat, barley, olives, dates, garlic, onions, pomegranates, lentils, nuts, and the use of acorns. Intensive palm and olive cultivation probably began in this period and was to become one of the sources of wealth for the country in later periods. Linen found in the "Cave of the Treasure" evidences the growing of flax and the sophisticated technological knowledge required in this textile manufacture.

Some of the food remains in the "Cave of the Treasure" possibly indicate trade in agricultural products within the country, since some of the crops represented in the cave (such as olives) could not be grown in the desert. Pastoralism and herding were perhaps of great importance during the Chalcolithic period. There is abundant evidence of the exploitation of animals, mainly sheep and goats but also some cattle and pigs. Pigs would provide a good livelihood for permanent settlers in a moist climate, and their remains are found at Chalcolithic sites, except in those at the southeastern extremity of the Beer-sheba region. The extent of animal husbandry is evidenced by studies of the bones, from the suitability of the areas where sites are located, and from the abundance of Chalcolithic churns, cornets, and works of art related to animal fertility.[18]

The custom of secondary burial that prevailed in the Chalcolithic ossuary cemeteries was believed by J. Perrot and others to reflect the lifestyle of seminomadic societies practicing transhumance. This might be the case concerning the peripheral areas of the country, such as the Judean Desert. In dry seasons and in years of drought, herders would move to the Mediterranean climatic zone of the country. But more current studies emphasize the sedentary, agricultural way of life even in the peripheral areas such as the Beer-sheba region, where nonsecondary burials prevailed.

THE ORIGINS OF THE GHASSULIAN CULTURE AND ITS CHRONOLOGY

The peculiar nature of the Ghassulian culture is characterized by its extraordinary settlement pattern, pottery, stone tools, advanced copper technology, utilization of art to express religious beliefs, and burial customs. All of these have no precedent in the previous period and are only to a limited extent continued in the succeeding one. It has to be asked, therefore, whether this culture was intrusive—introduced by immigrants to Palestine—or whether it developed locally from the preceding PN. Furthermore, its significance in the overall scheme of ancient Near Eastern cultures of the fifth and fourth millennia B.C.E. and its exact time span must be ascertained.

Carbon 14 tests from the early phases of the Chalcolithic

settlement at Teleilat Ghassul yielded a date in the mid–fifth millennium B.C.E. (according to the conventional, uncalibrated dating method). Testing of the finds from the Judean Desert and Beer-sheba region—finds probably from the end of the period—have given a date in the second half of the fourth millennium B.C.E.[19]

If the Ghassulian culture indeed did continue over such a long time, it would have overlapped most of what is known as the "Ubeid," and the beginning of the "Uruk," periods in Mesopotamia. During the latter period the crystallization of the Sumerian culture began, and toward its end the Sumerian script made its appearance. In Syria and in Egypt, Chalcolithic cultures flourished—the most outstanding of which was that of Tell Halaf, which spread in northern Mesopotamia and north Syria. Several parallels between the cultures of Palestine and those in neighboring lands can be cited, but they do not as yet provide a decisive solution to the origin of the Ghassulian culture. The closest comparisons come from Syria, especially from the coastal sites of Byblos and Ras Shamra (Ugarit) and from the 'Amuq region farther north. There are also ties with more distant regions, such as the parallels with Iran cited earlier. Indications of connections between the Ghassulian culture and the 4th millennium B.C.E. cultures of Egypt are exhibited in details of the potter's craft, flint working, art (in the ivory figurines), and trade (the import of such materials as haematite, granite, and alabaster). These far distant connections possibly resulted from complex trade relations and cultural influence between various parts of the ancient Near East.

Several scholars viewed the Ghassulian culture as intrusive in Palestine. Thus J. Mellaart claimed that brachycephalic skulls found in Chalcolithic burials in Palestine pointed to the Armenia-Caucasus region as the origin of the culture. But according to P. Smith this argument is no longer considered valid. Other scholars have proposed that the Ghassulian culture evolved in the Syrian Desert (J. Perrot), or that it was part of a broader movement of people from the east which also led to the rise of the contemporary Ubeid culture in Mesopotamia and the cultures of northern Syria (J. B. Hennessy). These suggestions, however, were not based on any substantial evidence. The alternative approach (suggested by A. M. T. Moore and T. E. Levy) infers an indigenous development.[20] Such a possibility gained strength after Hennessy's excavations at Teleilat Ghassul, where the earliest occupation phase was seen as similar to late PN, developing into the Ghassulian culture in the following phases.

A synthesis of the two approaches has been suggested by C. Elliott. In her opinion, the Ghassulian culture was a local development of the Neolithic blended with influence of Mesopotamian Ubeid elements that arrived via Syria around 4000 B.C.E. This latter influence finds expression in certain pottery forms, and in the copper working, which may have originated in Iran, reaching the west via Mesopotamia. This combinative theory, perhaps in a slightly amended form, appears to be the most feasible. A major difficulty in solving the problem of Ghassulian origins is the gap in our knowledge concerning southern Syria, and the limited data concerning northern Palestine, where perhaps the missing link between the latest PN and the Ghassulian cultures can be found. It is reasonable to assume that the Ghassulian culture crystallized among an ethnic group (or groups) which reached Palestine during the fifth millennium B.C.E.; such immigrants would have introduced and developed their own traditions in the realm of art and technology, while at the same time undergoing assimilation into the indigenous population, who preserved certain traditions of their own. A complex process of this sort would explain the aspects peculiar to the Chalcolithic culture in Palestine, as well as the regional divergencies.

THE COLLAPSE OF THE GHASSULIAN CULTURE

Around 3300 B.C.E., the Ghassulian culture came to an end under enigmatic circumstances. The most important centers were abandoned, and they remained unoccupied in subsequent times. This is the case at Teleilat Ghassul, at the Beer-sheba sites, in the Judean Desert, and on the Golan Heights. The abandonment of the En Gedi temple and the blocking of its entrance, as well as the hiding of the metal treasure in the Nahal Mishmar cave, imply some traumatic event. But no evidence of violence has been found in the last Chalcolithic occupation levels, and the reasons for the desertion remain to be determined. Various explanations have been offered, including the suggestion that the new migrants, bearing the culture of the succeeding Early Bronze Age I, brought an end to the Chalcolithic settlements in Palestine. Some scholars (Perrot, Hennessy, Kempinski) even hold that the new culture became entrenched in the northern and central parts of the country, while the Chalcolithic people still lived in the south.[21] Another external cause may have been an Egyptian invasion, and subsequent colonization, of southern Palestine during the beginning of the Dynastic Period in Egypt (see p. 107). Continuous years of drought, and perhaps epidemics or other natural catastrophes, should also be taken into account. As in other transitional periods, the heritage of the Chalcolithic culture was retained and absorbed in the following period. The extent of this continuity is, however, a matter of opinion.

NOTES

1. Anati (1963), pp. 285–314; Mellaart (1966), pp. 20–37; J. Perrot, *Supplement au dictionnaire de la Bible* 8 (1968), pp. 286–446; R. de Vaux in: *CAH*, vol. 1, part 1, pp. 520–38; Kenyon (1979), pp. 50–65; Aharoni (1982), pp. 35–47; C. Elliott, *Levant* 10 (1978), pp. 37–54; T. E. Levy, *BA* 49 (1986), pp. 82–108; R. Gophna in: *HEI*, vol. 1, pp. 83–94; I. Gilead, *Journal of World Prehistory* 2 (1988), pp. 397–443.

2. According to Hennessy, from ca. 4600 until at least 3600 B.C.E., and probably even later; see J. B. Hennessy in: Hadidi (1982), pp. 55–58.

3. D. Alon and T. E. Levy, *IEJ* 30 (1980), pp. 140–47; idem, *Current Anthropology* 24 (1983), pp. 105–7; T. E. Levy, *Michmanim* 3 (1986), pp. 5–20; idem (editor), *Shiqmim* I (BAR International Series 356 I–II), Oxford 1987.

4. These settlements include the large site of "Gat-Guvrin" (near Kibbutz Gat); an eight-acre site adjacent to Tel Adulam; three settlements along the Sorek Brook and several sites in the coastal plain. The sites near Adulam and in the Sorek Valley (between Beth-Shemesh and Tel Batash) were surveyed by the author in 1977–78.

5. C. Epstein, *BASOR* 229 (1978), pp. 27–45; idem, *IEJ* 33 (1983), pp. 255–57; idem, *BA* 40 (1977), pp. 57–62; idem, *Michmanim* 3 (1986), pp. 5–16 (Hebrew).

6. Y. Porath, *'Atiqot* 17 (1985), pp. 1–19 (includes a general discussion of Chalcolithic houses). Unlike the excavators, Porath interprets the main rectangular spaces in the houses at Teleilat Ghassul, the Golan Heights, and other sites as unroofed courtyards. This interpretation was considered but rejected by C. Epstein concerning the Golan houses.

7. J. Perrot, *Paleorient* 10 (1984), pp. 75–96.

8. D. Ussishkin, *TA* 7 (1980), pp. 1–44.

9. S. A. Rosen, *Michmanim* 3 (1986), pp. 21–32.

10. P. Bar-Adon, *The Cave of Treasure: The Finds from the Caves in Nahal Mishmar*, Jerusalem 1980.

11. C. Elliott, *PEQ* 109 (1977), pp. 4–25; C. Epstein in: *Kenyon Festschrift*, pp. 23–35; D. O. Cameron, *The Ghassulian Wall Paintings*, London 1981.

12. J. Perrot, *Syria* 36 (1959), pp. 8–19; idem, *EI* 7 (1964), pp. 92*–93*; ibid. 9 (1969), pp. 100*–1*; idem, *Syria-Palestine*, Archeologia Mundi, Geneva 1979, vol. 1, pp. 159–61, pls. 49–61; R. Amiran and M. Tadmor, *IEJ* 30 (1980), pp. 137–39; M. Tadmor in: *Treasures of the Holy Land*, New York 1986, pp. 59–84, where other art objects discussed in this section are illustrated and discussed.

13. R. Amiran, *Iran* 11 (1973), p. 184; idem, *IEJ* 26 (1976), pp. 157–62.

14. D. Alon, *'Atiqot* 11 (1976), pp. 116–18; R. Amiran, *'Atiqot* 11 (1976), pp. 119–20; M. Tadmor in: *Treasures of the Holy Land* (see note 12), pp. 62–66 (with color illustrations).

15. C. Epstein, *IEJ* 25 (1975), pp. 193–201; 38 (1988), pp. 205–23.

16. T. E. Levy and D. Alon, *BASOR* 248 (1982), pp. 37–59 (includes extensive survey of Chalcolithic burial customs); idem, *BASOR Supplement* 23 (1985), pp. 121–35.

17. J. Perrot and D. Ladiray, *Tombes à ossuaires de la région cotière Palestiniènne au IVe millenaire avant l'ère chrétienne*, Paris 1980.

18. T. E. Levy, *World Archaeology* 15 (1983), pp. 15–36; I. Gilead, *Michmanim* 3 (1986), pp. 17–28 (Hebrew).

19. J. M. Weinstein, *Radiocarbon* 26 (1984), pp. 297–366. Dendrochronological calibration of the carbon 14 readings may necessitate raising these figures by several hundred years. This will complicate matters in regard to the chronology of the succeeding period, for which we have several good correlations to Egyptian chronology (see discussion in Chapter Four, p. 108).

20. A. M. T. Moore, *Levant* 5 (1973), pp. 64–68; Levy (see note 1), p. 86.

21. Hennessy (1967), p. 85.

CHAPTER FOUR

THE EMERGENCE OF CITIES:
The Early Bronze Age
(ca. 3300–2300 B.C.E.)

INTRODUCTION

During the last centuries of the fourth millennium B.C.E. far-reaching changes occurred throughout the ancient Near East. In both pharaonic Egypt and Sumerian Mesopotamia literary civilizations developed, characterized by complex systems of government and by religious, administrative, and social hierarchies. These two great civilizations succeeded, for the first time in the history of mankind, in organizing masses of people to carry out large-scale public works exploiting for irrigation the Nile, Tigris, and Euphrates rivers. Both civilizations developed a system of writing, as well as monumental architecture and art.

In Mesopotamia this progress was gradual; its origins can be detected in the fifth and fourth millennia B.C.E. (Ubeid period). During what is known as the "Proto-literate" age (Uruk and Jemdet Nasr periods, 3500–3000 B.C.E.),[1] the Sumerian culture was consolidated. During the early third millennium B.C.E., Uruk, the city of Gilgamesh, was, in the terms of the time, a megalopolis, having an area of no less than 400 acres. Monumental temple architecture was a manifestation of the central role of the religious institutions in the Sumerian society. The Sumerian city-states of the following Early Dynastic Period (ca. 3000–2400 B.C.E.) are well known to us both from written documents and from elaborate archaeological finds. During this era, which corresponds to most of the Early Bronze Age in Palestine, Sumerian culture reached a zenith, and the basic concepts of Mesopotamian civilization were established. Many of these concepts found their way to northern Syria, where a parallel literate civilization, centered at Ebla, was evolving. About 2370 B.C.E., the Semitic dynasty of Sargon established the empire of Akkad which included all Mesopotamia and northern Syria. Sargon's grandson, Naram Sin, destroyed the great palace of Ebla.

The pharaonic civilization of Egypt emerged ca. 3100 B.C.E. The Archaic Period (Dynasties 0–II) and the Old Kingdom (Dynasties III–VI) lasted throughout most of the third millennium B.C.E. until the First Intermediate Period (ca. 2160 B.C.E.), when Egypt entered a period of decline. The basic concepts of Egyptian civilization were created during the Old Kingdom, and they found their expression in elaborate art and architecture. The Pyramids, the vivid wall reliefs in built-up tombs, and the lively sculpture of this period evidence the scope and richness of Egyptian capability in the third millennium B.C.E. From the very beginnings of their history, the Egyptians looked beyond their isolated country; their lack of timber, agricultural products, and other raw materials urged them to establish relations with the Levant.

Thus, during the third millennium B.C.E., Palestine and Syria felt the impact of the two great civilizations which emerged at either end of the Fertile Crescent. Northern Syria was under the direct cultural influence of Mesopotamia—so much so that the evolving literate culture of Ebla utilized the Sumerian script. In southern Syria, Lebanon, and Palestine, connections with Egypt had a certain effect, and some Mesopotamian and Anatolian influence also permeated via northern Syria. This region was the arena for the appearance of a local urban culture which developed in the Early Bronze Age II–III from the Early Bronze I sedentary agrarian society.

THE EARLY BRONZE I PERIOD
(ca. 3300–3050 B.C.E.)

TERMINOLOGY

During the first phase of the Early Bronze Age (henceforth EB I), new cultural factors appeared in Palestine. Some may have been introduced by new population groups, while others developed from the previous period. As a result, independent regional cultural traditions appeared simultaneously in various parts of the country. Certain common features and overlappings between these cultures, however, make tracing their chronological development difficult. Studies devoted to EB I since the pioneer work of G. E. Wright in 1937 have produced a variety of opinions concerning major questions, such as the degree of continuity from the preceding period, the classification of the finds, the origin of the population, and the inner cultural development.[2] To make things even more complicated, different terms have been used for the same archaeological phenomena.[3] G. E. Wright, and later R. de Vaux, attributed some of the assemblages under discussion here to "Late Chalcolithic." But the excavation of the cemetery at Tell el-Farʾah (north) in the early fifties has shown that some of the pottery assemblages which were designated "Late Chalcolithic" are in fact contemporary with other pottery groups which were designated "Early Bronze I." In an article published in 1958, Wright suggested to include the groups he had previously designated as "Late Chalcolithic" (such as the "Gray Burnished Ware") in the EB I period. He also suggested a subdivision of the period into three subphases: EB IA, EB IB and EB IC. This division was based mainly on the development of certain pottery groups, such as the "Gray Burnished Ware" and other pottery groups of the period. During the same years K. M. Kenyon, following her excavations at Jericho, suggested the term "Proto-Urban" to denote the phases which Wright called EB IA and EB IB. She also designated three main contemporary pottery groups of the period with the terms Proto-Urban A, B, and C. A phase called EB I by Kenyon came after the Proto-Urban period and is parallel to Wright's EB IC. Later studies have shown that the diversity of the pottery groups in this period is even greater than thought before. The differentiation between the EB IA and EB IB of Wright is not entirely clear, and Kenyon's classification of pottery groups does not cover all the varied assemblages known from this period. Thus P. de Miroschedji suggested to add another group—Proto-Urban D—to Kenyon's method; the excavators of Bab edh-Dhraʿ near the Dead Sea used the term IB IA to denote an early phase of EB I in this site, with pottery that is almost uncomparable anywhere else in the country. More recent excavations of EB I sites and cemeteries show that there was a great regional diversity in this period, and that it is almost impossible to suggest a subdivision of the period that will be valid to the entire country. Furthermore, D. L. Esse has shown that the phase denoted "EB IC" by Wright (as well as by his followers P. Lapp and J. Callaway) and "EBI" by Kenyon (and by her followers such as B. Hennessy) appears to lack any true contents, and those terms should be abandoned; the material ascribed to them is in fact related to the onset of urbanization in Palestine in the following, EB II period. In our opinion, the term EB I should include all the preurban assemblages of the Early Bronze Age; early and late assemblages of this period can be defined in certain regions of the country, but the regional diversity does not allow a general terminology which will be valid for the inner division of the period in the entire country.

SETTLEMENT PATTERN

The settlement pattern of EB I Palestine shows an interesting combination of continuation and change in relation to the preceding Chalcolithic period. On the one hand, the EB I sites to a large extent portray Chalcolithic features, as most of them were modest unfortified agricultural villages. On the other hand, their location shows a great shift from the preceding pattern. Areas which were densely settled in the Chalcolithic period—such as the Golan Heights, the Judean Desert, and the Teleilat Ghassul and Beer-sheba regions—were either totally or partially deserted. The few EB I sites found in these parts of the country were usually situated in different spots from their Chalcolithic predecessors (as in the vicinity of Beer-sheba); in fact, R. Gophna has shown that only about 30 percent of EB I settlements were established on Chalcolithic sites.

Numerous EB I settlements were established in the fertile regions of the country: the coastal plain, the northern plains, the central hill country, the Shephelah, and the Jordan Valley. Many of the sites were established near land and water resources and close to important roads—the three basic requirements for continuous settlement. In many cases the sites developed, in the following EB II period, into urban

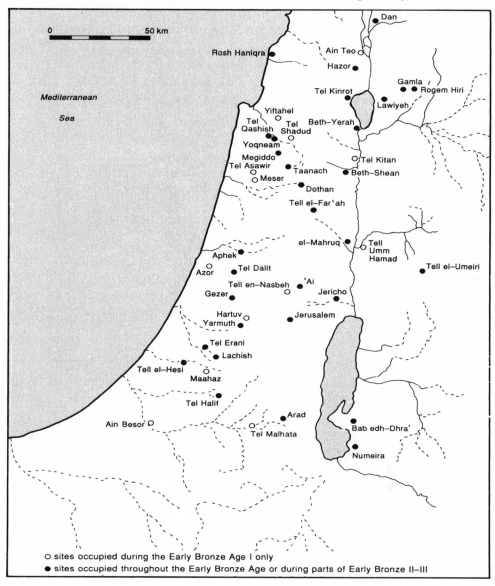

4.1   Map of Excavated Early Bronze Age Sites

centers—some of them the most important of the period, such as Megiddo, Beth-Shean, Beth-Yerah (near the southwestern corner of the Lake of Galilee), Tell el-Far'ah (north; biblical Tirzah, northeast of Shechem), 'Ai, Yarmuth, Tel Halif, Arad, and Bab edh-Dhra' (on the eastern side of the Dead Sea). There were, however, many EB I sites which were abandoned at the end of EB I, perhaps due to the concentration of population in the emerging cities.

Agriculture and sheep and goat herding formed the traditional base of the economy throughout the ancient history of Palestine, yet the significance of each factor varied from period to period. The distribution of sites in EB I points to agriculture as the main occupation of the settled population, rather than herding. During the Early Bronze Age new crops were introduced, particularly horticulture in the mountain areas; grapes and figs—two of the most typical Mediterranean crops—may have been cultivated during this period for the first time.[4]

The semiarid regions of Palestine and Sinai were inhabited by pastoralists in EB I. The vast cemetery at Bab edh-Dhra', east of the Dead Sea, and hundreds of circular graves known as *nawamis* and found in southern Sinai evidence the existence of such societies.

An outstanding phenomenon is the site of Jawa, a 25-acre fortified town from the end of the fourth millennium B.C.E. in the remote basalt desert separating Jordan from Iraq.[5] Amazing water supply projects found here, including dams and artificial reservoirs, would have demanded a comprehensive knowledge of the environment. The origin of the population at Jawa, and the relationship between this unique site and the cultural development in Palestine, are still open questions, and the short-lived Jawa culture remains an enigmatic phenomenon.

SITE PLAN AND ARCHITECTURE

Only a few EB I sites have been excavated to a sufficient extent to permit a comprehensive study of their plan and architecture. The best known among these include the eastern slope of Megiddo (Stages VII–IV and Stratum XIX of the mound proper); the large site of Yiftahel in the Lower Galilee; 'En Shadud in the Jezreel Valley; the sparse structures revealed at 'En Teo in the Huleh Valley; Beth-Yerah; Meser and Aphek in the Sharon Plain; Tel Kitan in the Beth-Shean Valley; Hartuv near Beth-Shemesh; and, in the Negev, Tel ʿErani, Tel Halif, Tel Malhata, and Arad. In Transjordan, Jawa in the eastern desert, Bab edh-Dhraʿ east of the Dead Sea, and Tell Umm Hamad in the Jordan Valley are the most important sites.[6] Most of these sites were unfortified small villages, although some covered a large area of more than a dozen acres (Beth-Yerah, Aphek, Tel ʿErani).

In the northern part of the country, there was a tendency to build curvilinear, elliptical, apsidal, or round structures. Groups of houses at ʿEn Teo, Yiftahel, and ʿEn Shadud, as well as at Jebel Mutawwaq in Transjordan, are elliptical in plan, recalling similar contemporary buildings known from Lebanon (Dakerman south of Sidon and Byblos).[7] At Megiddo, Meser, and Aphek, as well as at Byblos, there were apsidal buildings, while some of the dwellings at Yiftahel and all the structures at Jawa were round. This curvilinear architecture

4.2 Early Bronze I oval houses at Yiftahel.

was almost unknown in the Chalcolithic period, and it may represent a foreign tradition introduced by immigrants. Indeed, at most of the aforementioned sites, this architecture is associated with Gray Burnished pottery, which also evidenced a foreign tradition (see p. 103).

As in the Chalcolithic period, the only known EB I public buildings are temples. This fact perhaps hints at the role of the priests and the religious institutions as the leading power in the social and governmental hierarchy during this period. At Megiddo (Stratum XIX) there was a double temple composed of two broad rooms, each with a raised pedestal for the statue of the deity located opposite the entrance. A fenced courtyard in front of the temple proper was paved with flat stones, on which depictions of various animals as well as a man playing a lyre were incised. These engravings are almost the only artwork known from EB I, and one of the few artistic remains from the Early Bronze Age as a whole. The plan of this temple resembles that of the Chalcolithic temple at En Gedi, and thus provides the connecting link between the religious architecture of the two periods and that of the following EB II–III. At Hartuv (near Beth-Shemesh) a unique public architectural complex was discovered. The main feature here is a large broad-hall (5.10 × ca. 15 m), with a row of pillar bases along its longitudinal axis. A row of standing stones is incorporated in the southern wall of this hall; these appear to be sacred stones (*massebot*) which perhaps symbolized different deities or were related to an ancestor cult. Similar standing stones are known from fifth and fourth millennia B.C.E. open-air sacred sites in the southern Negev and eastern Sinai, where such stones were perhaps erected by groups of pastoralists and hunters. At Hartuv, it appears that the standing stones stood first in an open-air sacred area, and only later were they incorporated into the large temple building. This development may reflect processes of sedentation and settlement which passed over the EB I communities during the last centuries of the fourth millennium B.C.E.[8]

BURIAL CUSTOMS

Burials are one of the main sources of our knowledge concerning this period. The most common practice was multiple burial—several generations of one family being buried in the same artificial or natural cave together with a variety of offerings: pottery vessels, jewelry, and metal objects. Yet in most cases the skeletons were found disarticulated, the skulls separated from the bodies. At Tell Asawir bones were packed in pottery jars; at Azor there is some evidence of cremation; and at Jericho the skulls were separated and arranged in rows.[9]

In the vast cemetery at Bab edh-Dhraʿ, two phases of EB I burials were distinguished.[10] The first (termed "EB IA") included shaft tombs—caves approached through a vertical shaft. Their number was enormous, estimated at several thousand. As no settlement was established in this phase, the cemetery may have belonged to pastoral seminomads. This supposition is supported by the method of burial: not more than six or seven skeletons were found in each cave; they were disarticulated—the long bones arranged in one pile and the skulls laid out in a row. The flesh was probably extracted

4.3   Bad edh-Dhraʿ; plan and section of an Early Bronze I shaft tomb.

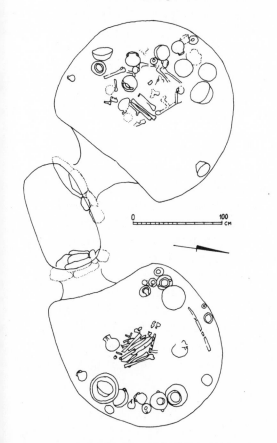

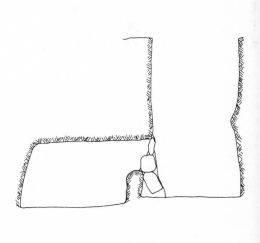

from the bones by boiling, a curious practice which would have suited the lifestyle of wanderers who may have kept the bones of the deceased in temporary graves or shelters until they could bring them to final burial in their central, possibly sacred cemetery.

In the following phase (termed "EB IB"), circular burial structures made of mud bricks were used for primary articulated multiple burials, perhaps for members of the same family or clan. These new tombs were constructed by the people who founded the first permanent settlement at Bab edh-Dhra᷑, which in the following EB II period was to develop into a fortified town. It thus appears that the transition to permanent settlement at this site was accompanied by the abandonment of the practice of secondary burial, which was common in the Chalcolithic period and in the early part of EB I.

Rounded burial structures from the end of the fourth millennium B.C.E. are also known from southern Sinai. These are *nawamis*—stone-built, rounded structures with corbeled roofs, probably constructed by groups of pastoral nomads.[11] Although the meager finds in these graves (particularly a type of flint arrowhead) point to relations with Egypt, the rounded built-up tomb recalls both the rounded burial structures of the Chalcolithic period in the Beer-sheba region and the built-up late EB I tombs at Bab edh-Dhra᷑.

POTTERY

The large number of complete ceramic vessels found in EB I tombs, as well as the less-known domestic pottery from settlement sites, are primary sources for the study of the culture's origins, regional variety, foreign influences, and international connections. The division of the EB I pottery assemblages into subgroups is not always easy, as there are features common to the entire country in addition to the characteristics peculiar to certain regions or subphases. The lack of sufficient stratified deposits makes it sometimes difficult to decide which features represent chronological development and which are regional variations. Nevertheless, there is a distinction between the northern and southern parts of the country, and between the earlier and later stages of EB I in each.[12]

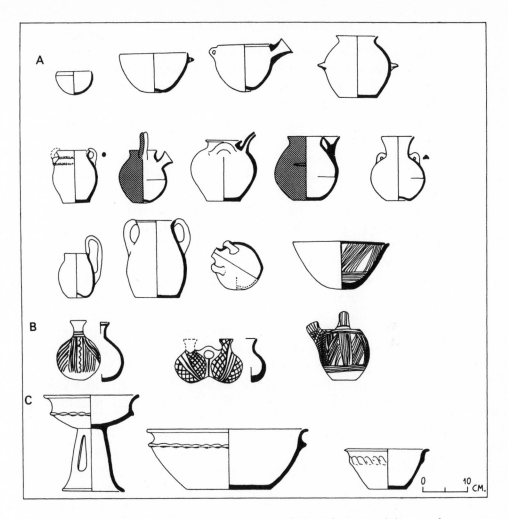

4.4   Selected pottery of Early Bronze I: (A) red slipped pottery; (B) painted pottery of central hill country sites; (C) Gray Burnished Ware.

Some of the domestic pottery displays traditions continued from the Chalcolithic period—such as the "hole mouth" jar, which remained the main cooking vessel throughout the Early Bronze Age. Yet new vessel forms and details such as ledge handles became hallmarks of the Early Bronze Age pottery. Decoration techniques and special shapes enable us to distinguish between the pottery of northern Palestine and that of the south. In the north, large jars were covered with bands of reddish brown paint applied with wide rough brushes, a technique known as "grain wash" or "band slip." This practice appeared in the later half of EB I, together with a variety of small vessels covered with a highly burnished red slip. In the south, however, red slip and burnish were rare in domestic pottery. The ornamentation there was one of the following, all of which were found, for example, at Hartuv: painting small jars with vertical orange-red parallel lines on a white slip background; incisions of diagonal short lines on necks and handles of small jars; and the application of clay bands with thumb indentations which recall Chalcolithic decoration.

The large assemblages found in tombs consist mainly of small vessels, many of which were intentionally prepared as burial gifts. Most common are small rounded bowls (sometimes with omphalos-depressed bases); amphoriskoi (small jars with two handles); cups with a high loop handle; bottles with a narrow neck and two lug handles; small jars with a "basket" handle or with an elongated cylindrical spout, or alternatively a false spout, and "teapots" with a bent spout. Some of the shapes appear throughout the country, while others are peculiar to certain regions. In the north, many of the vessels are covered by thick, well-burnished red slip, while in the south, the red slip is less frequent and is hardly burnished.

Two main burial-pottery groups are found in the central part of Palestine. K. M. Kenyon defined them in the terms "Proto-Urban A" and "Proto-Urban B." The two groups are contemporary and closely related; many shapes are common to both of them. The A group (known mainly from Jericho, Azor, and Tell el-Far'ah north) contains many unpainted vessels covered with red burnished slip; the B group features geometric patterns painted in red thin lines by using a delicate brush; the patterns appear to imitate weaving. However, unpainted vessels similar to those in the A group also appear in the B group. The B group was found in the central hill country (Jerusalem, Tell en-Nasbeh, and 'Ai), in some of the Jericho tombs, at Bab edh-Dhra', and in one tomb in northern Transjordan ('Arqub edh-Dahr). Vessels of both the A and B types were found also at northern sites such as Tell el-Far'ah and Beth-Yerah together with other forms typical of EB I in the north of the country. At Bab edh-Dhra', the earliest phase of EB I contained a local group of unpainted pottery, while the painted pottery of the B tradition and related shapes appeared only in a later phase of EB I at this site, in which the first permanent settlement was founded there.[13]

An important northern pottery group is the Gray Burnished Ware (known in the past as "the Esdraelon culture" and denoted by Kenyon as "Proto-Urban C"). It comprises open vessels only, made of gray ware with a thick dark gray and very well-burnished slip. The forms include large bowls and bowls on a fenestrated high foot (the latter resembling Chalcolithic vessels). The bowls are usually carinated and decorated with various knobs or "rope" decoration. Imitations were made in the usual brown or buff clay. Gray Burnished Ware was limited to the northern valleys (at sites such as Beth-Yerah, Megiddo, Afula, Tel Qashish, Beth-Shean, Tell el-Far'ah, Yiftahel, 'En Shadud, and Tell Umm Hamad [in the Jordan Valley]), where it appears together with other pottery of the period. Though Gray Burnished Ware was locally made, both the shapes and the decoration were foreign to the Levant; their parallels have to be sought in northeastern Anatolia. This ware, therefore, can be taken as evidence of immigration of small population groups from eastern Anatolia to northern Palestine via Syria. The immigrants probably assimilated with the local population, but they continued to produce a limited number of shapes of their traditional pottery. A similar phenomenon, though on a larger scale, is manifest in EB III with the appearance of Khirbet Kerak Ware (see p. 133).[14]

The interrelated regional pottery groups probably reflect closely connected communities which shared a similar socio-economic status but maintained independent cultural identities.

OTHER FINDS

Copper was the exclusive metal used for weapons and tools throughout the Early Bronze Age. The two main copper objects known are axeheads, similar to those of the Chalcolithic period, and tanged daggers, which appear for the first time. The Chalcolithic flint repertoire disappeared, and a new type of flint blade—known as the "Canaanean blade"—was manufactured in specialized workshops. It was to remain almost the sole flint type throughout the Early Bronze Age.[15] To some degree, basalt vessels, seemingly produced in the northern part of the country, continued the tradition established during the Chalcolithic period, yet new forms and decorations differentiated the EB I industry from its predecessor.[16]

Cylinder seals, and impressions of such seals made on storage jars before firing, are found in Palestine and at Byblos on the Lebanese coast.[17] Cylinder seals were invented in Mesopotamia during the fourth millennium B.C.E., and they were soon widespread throughout the ancient Near East, including Egypt. The rolling of such seals on jars before their firing is, however, unknown in Mesopotamia and may have been invented in Syria-Palestine. The impressions were most probably done with wooden stamps and were used either as potters' marks or, more likely, as symbols of ownership. The designs either are merely geometric or show rows of schematic animals, sometimes arranged in a tête-bêche arrangement. Close parallels between impressions from northern Palestine and those from Byblos point to close relations between these two regions. The seals and seal impressions from Palestine and Byblos are local in character, though some of them imitate the contemporary Mesopotamian glyptic style of the Jemdet Nasr period, while others show some Egyptian and Elamite influence.

THE ORIGINS OF THE EARLY BRONZE I CULTURE

The significant differences between the Chalcolithic period and the Early Bronze Age are expressed in various ways: settlement patterns, population size and density, agricultural methods, trade relations, and the new assemblages of artifacts and artistic forms. Do these changes reflect only a local, indigenous development, or do they represent an immigration of people from outside Palestine? Scholars differ in their interpretations of the archaeological phenomena. In the past, it was widely accepted that the EB I culture represented a massive immigration from outside Palestine. Thus, J. B. Hennessy claimed that the Proto-Urban A tradition indicated immigration from northern Syria and Cilicia,[18] while K. M. Kenyon determined that the newcomers came from regions east of Palestine. The finds at Jawa do point to the existence of a contemporary settled agrarian population in the eastern desert of Jordan, but fail to support Kenyon's theory. There are also some indications of Mesopotamian influence in the local EB I culture, such as the bent cylindrical spouts of pottery "teapots" and the appearance of cylinder seals. These elements could have arrived in Palestine via Sumerian colonies which are now known to have existed along the Upper Euphrates in the late fourth millennium B.C.E. (such as at Habuba Kabira). But whether such isolated elements are evidence of massive immigration or are a result of complex and indirect trade relations is still uncertain. Another school of thought argues that many EB I cultural elements, and particularly the painted pottery, are indigenous to Palestine and developed from the previous period.[19] Chalcolithic characteristics can indeed be seen in some of the EB I pottery, metal objects, and temple architecture, but such elements seem to be minor when compared to the innovations. Analysis of human bones apparently indicates that there was no drastic change in the population during the transition from the Chalcolithic to the Early Bronze Age.[20]

Thus it appears that the material culture of EB I Palestine was an intermingling of new features—originating in Syria, Anatolia, and Mesopotamia—with elements rooted in the local culture of the preceding period. Probably, to some extent, ethnic and demographic changes occurred; it is possible that new peoples arrived in Palestine mainly from Syria and mixed with the remnants of the autochthonous population. Many of these conclusions, however, are a result of guesswork, as central and southern Syria are in fact terra incognita from an archaeological point of view.

RELATIONS WITH EGYPT AND CHRONOLOGY

Sumerian influence on Egyptian culture was considerable during the Late Gerzean and Archaic periods in Egypt. These international relations during one of the most creative periods in the history of the ancient Near East may indicate movements of people over long distances—both by land, from Mesopotamia westward through Syria to Palestine and Egypt, and by sea, connecting Elam and southern Mesopotamia with Egypt around Arabia. Within this general framework, close though short-term connections between Egypt and southern Palestine in EB I are of particular significance.

Relations between Canaan and Egypt existed already during the late Pre-Dynastic Period, as evidenced by Egyptian pottery and flint blades of the Gerzean culture found in early EB I contexts. But the dramatic cultural development in Egypt which brought about the rise of the First Dynasty and the pharaonic culture also led to increased Egyptian presence for a short period in southern Canaan.

The route from Egypt to Palestine passed along almost 200 km of desert in northern Sinai. A survey of this route carried out by E. D. Oren revealed fourteen clusters of EB I sites in the sand dunes, each containing concentrations of pottery which may be the remains of campsites and short-lived settlements. The pottery is mainly Egyptian and dates to the late Pre-Dynastic Period as well as to the First Dynasty. About 20 percent of the ceramic finds at these sites date to EB I and originated in Palestine. Consequently it can be deduced that Egyptians lived in northern Sinai during the time of the First Dynasty and were in contact with southern Palestine.[21]

Sites from EB I in the southern part of Palestine produced substantial evidence of an Egyptian presence. The key site is Tel Erani, on the southeastern coastal plain west of Lachish.[22] During EB I, Tel Erani was perhaps the largest settlement in Palestine reaching an area of almost twenty hectares. The existence of seven occupation levels of EB I date (Strata XII–V) indicate that this period extended over a long time. Substantial mud-brick buildings erected in these levels present an urban lifestyle. Egyptian pottery and stone vessels typical of the late Pre-Dynastic and First Dynasty periods predominate in these strata. They include a jar fragment incised with the

4.5 The *Serekh* (name of) Narmer, first Pharaoh of the First Dynasty in Egypt, incised on a fragment of an Egyptian jar found at Arad.

name of Narmer, the first Egyptian pharaoh. It appears, therefore, that Egyptians were important, if not the major, occupants of this large site.

Egyptian pottery and other artifacts were found also at various smaller sites in the northern Negev and the southern coastal plain, such as Arad, Tel Malhata, Tel Halif, Maahaz, Rafiah and Afridar (near Ashkelon); incised inscriptions with the name of Narmer were uncovered at several of these places.[23] At ʿEn-Besor, an important water source on the bank of the Besor Brook, a settlement from this period has produced Egyptian finds from the First Dynasty, including clay jar stoppers impressed with Egyptian seals dating to the beginning of that dynasty. This settlement must have been either an Egyptian military position or a trading post which maintained commercial relations between southern Canaan and Egypt.[24]

In contrast to the situation in the northern Negev, only sparse Egyptian finds were found north of Tel Erani. Some EB I pottery originating in Palestine has, however, been revealed at several sites in the eastern Delta of Egypt. These vessels probably reflect limited imports of oil, wines, and ointments during the late Pre-Dynastic and early First Dynasty.[25]

Some scholars interpret the Egyptian finds in southern Palestine as merely representing trade relations; others argue for active Egyptian colonization in southern Canaan; still others claim that the Egyptians invaded the region.[26] A relief on the stone palette of King Narmer, the most important art object from the time of the First Dynasty, shows the pharaoh smiting Asiatic enemies and (shown in the form of a bull) conquering a fortified city surrounded by a city wall and towers. The combined evidence of this artifact and the finds from Sinai and southern Palestine seem to suggest a short period of strong Egyptian interest in Palestine, perhaps accompanied by a military presence as well as settlement that was probably centered at Tel Erani. This activity must have been economically motivated and may have been related to the exploitation of raw materials such as copper ores (perhaps brought from mines in the Arabah, between the Dead Sea and the Red Sea) and materials from the Dead Sea such as bitumen. This Egyptian colonization lasted less than a hundred years: it is limited to the time of Narmer and Hor Aha, and it came to an end in EB II.

The aforementioned finds make possible a correlation of EB I in Palestine with Egyptian history and chronology. The early part of EB I can be associated with the late Pre-Dynastic Gerzean culture, while late EB I was contemporary with Dynasty 0 and the beginning of the First Dynasty. As we will see later, EB II pottery from Palestine and Syria was found in Egyptian tombs of the latter part of the First Dynasty (starting from the reign of Djer).

The dates for the accession of the First Dynasty range between 3200 and 2900 B.C.E.; the most accepted date for Narmer is 3100 B.C.E.[27] The end of EB I, therefore, can be placed at ca. 3050 B.C.E., while its beginning would have occurred some two hundred to three hundred years earlier. Such dates are also supported by carbon 14 analyses.[28]

EB I, therefore, was a creative period whose cultural features may have been introduced by new population groups. The culture of this period became the foundation of further developments culminating in the emergence of urbanization in the following phase of the Early Bronze Age.

THE EARLY BRONZE II–III
URBAN CULTURE
(ca. 3050–2300 B.C.E.)

INNER PHASING AND CHRONOLOGY

The major part of the Early Bronze Age, denoted "EB II–III," saw the beginnings of an intensive urbanization throughout the Levant. Massively fortified cities with public buildings such as temples, palaces, granaries, and water reservoirs illustrate this process.[29] The development of city life began at the onset of EB II, which can be correlated with the time of Djer, the third king of the First Dynasty of Egypt (ca. 3050 B.C.E.).[30] The transition between EB II and EB III should be dated to the end of the Second Dynasty in Egypt (ca. 2700 B.C.E.),[31] and the urban culture of EB III continued most probably until the early days of the Sixth Dynasty; it seems that the third pharaoh of that Dynasty, Pepi I, conducted military raids against cities in Palestine. This correlation with Egypt provides the basis for establishing the chronology of the period. According to the Egyptian chronology suggested by S. Smith and I. E. S. Edwards,[32] the urban culture of EB II–III extended for some seven hundred to eight hundred years, from ca. 3050 to ca. 2300 B.C.E. It was contemporary with the Sumerian Early Dynastic period and the beginning of the Akkadian period in Mesopotamia.[33]

There is a great deal of continuity between the material culture of EB II and that of EB III. Although some of the cities were destroyed and abandoned at the end of EB II (see below), others were rebuilt and continued to flourish in EB III. Typological changes in the pottery are the best criteria for

Table 3. Comparative Stratigraphy of Early Bronze Age Sites

SUBPERIODS / SITES	c. 3300 B.C.E.	EB I	c. 3050 B.C.E.	EB II	2700 B.C.	EB III	2300 B.C.
Egypt		Pre-Dynastic	Dynasty 1 (Narmer & Hor Aha)	Dynasties 1–2		Dynasties 3–6	
Hazor		—		—		XXI XX XIX	
Beth-Yerah		XVI–XIV		XIII XII		XI–VII	
Beth-Shean		XVII XVI XV		XIV XIII		XII XI	
Megiddo		XIX		XVIII		XVII–XV	
Tell el-Farʿah (North)		III		IVa–f		—	
ʿAi		I–II		III–IV–V		VI–VIII	
Jericho		Q–M		L–G		F–A	
Gezer		XXV		XXIV—XXIII		—	
Yarmuth Area B				V–IV		III–II	
Yarmuth Area A				1–3		4–7	
Tell el-Hesi		11		10———→4			
Tel Erani		XI–V		IV–II		I	
Tel Halif		XIV				XIII XII XI	
Arad		IV		III–II I		—	

distinguishing between EB II and EB III, yet even the pottery indicates cultural continuity rather than a break between these two subperiods.[34]

THE BACKGROUND TO URBANIZATION

Cultural development in Syria and Palestine was undoubtedly influenced by the flourishing civilizations at both ends of the Fertile Crescent. The Egyptian interests in southern Palestine during the time of the First and Second dynasties were stopped from the time of the Third Dynasty onward in favor of naval connections with Byblos, the important export emporium for Lebanese timber. Byblos thus became the gateway through which Egyptian influence infiltrated the Levant. The local culture at Byblos was to a large extent similar to that of Palestine; in fact, southern Syria and Lebanon became part of one large cultural entity in this period.

Northern Syria—the region of the Upper Euphrates and Aleppo—was under direct Sumerian influence. Excavations along the Upper Euphrates, particularly at the site of Habuba Kabira, have brought to light a sophisticated urbanization existing already at the end of the fourth millennium B.C.E. in this region. During the second half of the third millennium B.C.E., Ebla (Tell Mardikh, south of Aleppo) was a center of a thriving literate civilization. Though the writing system and other aspects of this civilization were based on Sumerian prototypes, the Eblaites had their own language, the oldest West Semitic one known.[35] Ebla served as a bridge between Mesopotamia and the Levant, but to what extent it influenced the regions to its south cannot yet be determined. It flourished until sometime between 2290 and 2250 B.C.E., when its palace was destroyed by Naram Sin of Akkad, its downfall somewhat later than the end of the urban culture of EB III Palestine.[36]

Since V. G. Childe's first attempt (in 1936) to define the socioeconomic factors involved in the development of cities in the ancient Near East, various other explanations for the rise of urbanization have been put forth, most of which concentrated on its development in Egypt and Mesopotamia.[37] But the explanations given for developments in the great river valleys of Egypt and Mesopotamia cannot be transferred to the Levant, where completely different environmental conditions prevailed. Experiments in interpreting the rise of urbanization in Syria and Palestine are only in their beginnings,[38] and no clear-cut answers have been ascertained. In the past this process was seen as a result of a population influx from the north, particularly from northern Syria and even Mesopotamia. The current approach, however, tries to define inner socioeconomic factors which may have forced the agrarian population of EB I Palestine to move to city life. Certain internal changes—such as an increase in population, and progress in agriculture and trade creating a surplus—as well as the impact of outside developments in Mesopotamia, Egypt, and northern Syria brought about the rise of cities in Palestine.

SETTLEMENT PATTERN AND POPULATION

The Urban Environment   A comparatively large number of EB II–III fortified cities are known throughout Palestine, both west and east of the Jordan. Some are located near important water sources and close to the major roads of the country, such as Dan, Hazor, Qedesh in Galilee, Beth-Yerah, Beth-Shean, Megiddo, Tell el-Farʿah (north), Tell es-Saʿidiyeh, el-Mahruq (at the opening of Wadi Farʿah into the Jordan Valley), Jericho, Lachish, and Tell el-Hesi. Other major cities are located in surprisingly remote regions, far from roads, water sources, and fertile land: such are ʿAi, on a faraway ridge east of the main route crossing the central mountain ridge north of Jerusalem; Yarmuth, which is situated in an out-of-the-way area in the inner Shephelah; Arad, in the semiarid region of the northern Negev; and Bab edh-Dhraʿ and Numeira, found in the dry and desolate region east of the Dead Sea. These locations are enigmatic, especially as the first three cities rank among the largest of the period, each exceeding 25 acres in area.

In addition to these excavated towns, a large number of Early Bronze settlements are known from surface surveys. R. Gophna and M. Broshi counted 260 sites of various sizes in western Palestine alone. The most densely settled regions were the coastal plain, the hills of Samaria, the Shephelah, and the Jordan Valley. About 20 sites exceeded 20 acres in size; together they comprised an estimated area of 750 acres, about half the total built-up land throughout the country. The most prominent cities in this group were Beth-Yerah (55

4.6 Yarmuth: view of the excavations. In the background the higher mound is seen.

acres), Yarmuth (40 acres), Tell el-Hesi (25 acres), ʿAi and Arad (each about 25 acres). After them, there were 36 towns which averaged over 12 acres each, and finally about 160 smaller settlements, most of which measured no more than 2.5 acres in area. In all, the urban area of the Early Bronze Age is estimated as having included 1,500 acres. Accordingly, the population can be calculated as having been 150,000, based on an assumed coefficient of 100 persons per built-up acre.[39] The concentration of half the population in the hill country (Galilee, Samaria, and Judah) was peculiar to this early part of the Bronze Age and was unparalleled in the later stages of that era.

In Transjordan, too, numerous Early Bronze sites were revealed in surveys, some of them in remote regions.[40] Bab edh-Dhraʿ was the largest among a group of five sites situated

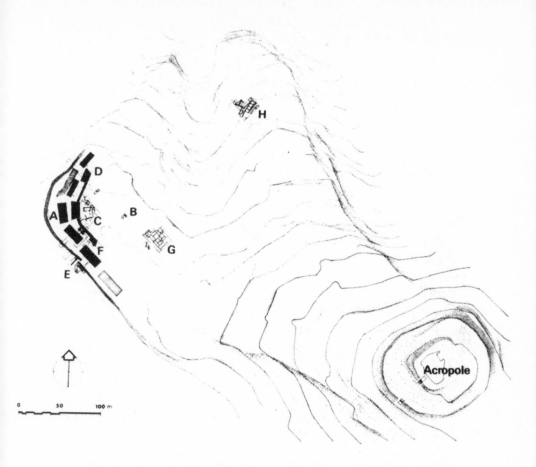

4.7 Yarmuth: site plan and main features discovered in the excavations.
A: rectangular structures at the western side of the city dating to the last
phase of Early Bronze III. B, C, G, H: dwelling areas; D: Early Bronze II
fortifications; E: Early Bronze III city gate.

in dry riverbeds leading to the Dead Sea.[41] Other large Early
Bronze Age settlements are known from surveys and some
excavations in the Jordan Valley and the plateaus of northern
and central Transjordan.

The Golan-Galilee Enclosures   Surveys in the Golan Heights
and in the eastern Lower Galilee have revealed enclosures
constructed close to the edge of ridges near the junction of
two deep ravines. The triangular area thus created was usually
surrounded by outer walls. A large enclosure such as that at
Lawiyeh on the Golan Heights is 1,000 m long and 250 m
wide and is subdivided by cross walls into smaller sections.
These enclosures are located on hilly grounds on both sides

of the shores of the Lake of Galilee and the northern Jordan Valley, in which large EB II–III cities flourished. The pottery and cylinder-seal impressions discovered in the enclosures are similar to those found in the cities of the valleys. Since the regions in which these enclosures are found are good pasture lands, the enclosures were thought to be paddocks for stock breeding, used seasonally by seminomadic people or by city dwellers of the upper Jordan Valley. However, recent excavations at one of the enclosures have shown that it was compactly built up during the EB III period, and thus it now appears that at least some of the enclosures were permanent settlements.[42]

The Negev and Southern Sinai Pastoralists Extensive research in the Negev and southern Sinai revealed a network of EB II settlements in these arid areas. In the region of St. Catherine Monastery in southern Sinai, I. Beit-Arieh discovered about fifty EB II sites and excavated six of them.[43] The settlements were clustered around the main routes, which ran along the wadis of the region, where water and pasture could be found. They comprised one or several units; each unit included a central courtyard surrounded by dwelling rooms and additional smaller structures. The dwellings recall the "broad room" houses of contemporary Arad, while the auxiliary structures appear to be circular huts similar to those found in the desert regions around Palestine since Neolithic times. Some of the pottery is similar to that found at Arad; petrographic examinations have shown that there were ties between Arad and these Sinai sites—as some cooking pots found at Arad contained granite which originated in Sinai as temper, while on the other hand, some large jars originated from Arad were found in Sinai.

The establishment of these villages must have been related to the exploitation of copper; this relation is evidenced by finds of copper-industry installations and equipment, as well as by the location of copper ores in the area. A continuous chain of sites connected southern Sinai with southern Palestine through the western Negev and Kadesh-Barnea region as well as via the Arabah. According to Beit-Arieh, the inhabitants of the Sinai settlements arrived from the urban regions of southern Palestine and adapted their way of life to

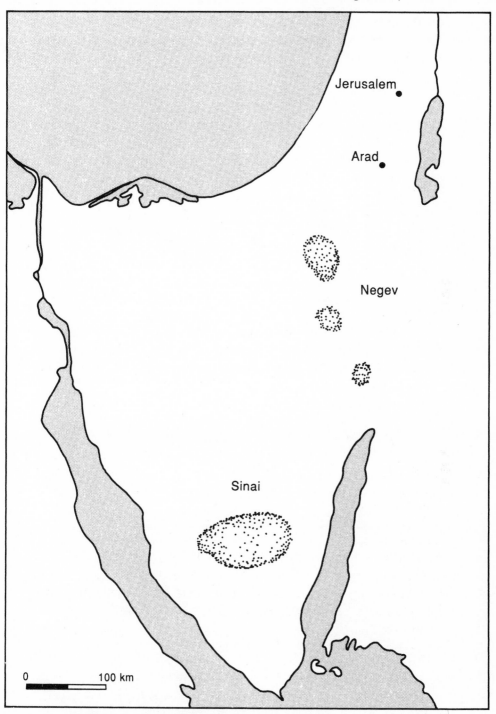

4.8 MAP OF SINAI AND THE NEGEV SHOWING DISTRIBUTION OF EARLY BRONZE AGE SITES. Dotted areas mark concentrations of Early Bronze settlements.

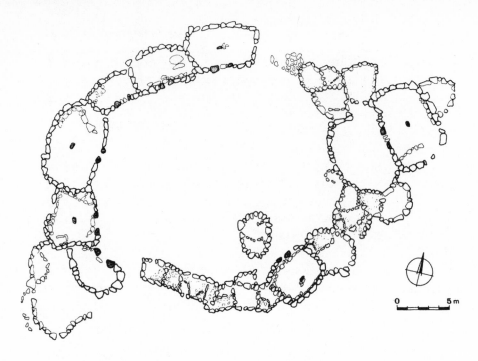

4.9 Plan of an Early Bronze II dwelling complex at Sheikh Muhsein, southern Sinai.

4.10 A dwelling at the Early Bronze Age II site of Sheikh Awad, southern Sinai. Note the benches along the walls and the pillar that supported the roof.

the local environment and conditions. The evidence, however, would imply a more complicated situation in which a symbiosis between local desert dwellers and northerners was formed.[44] This is seen in the extensive use of circular architecture and of tabular flint scrapers both of which were rooted in older local traditions.

This chain of sites in the Negev and southern Sinai, in addition to the city of Arad, were abandoned at the end of EB II—that is, toward the end of the Second Dynasty in Egypt. One possible explanation for this abandonment is political pressure by the Egyptians, who during this period began mining turquoise somewhat to the west, in Wadi Magharah in southern Sinai. Rock reliefs found there depict Egyptian pharaohs smiting Asiatics whom we can identify either as local nomads or as the Semitic people who came to Sinai from the Arad region to exploit copper, and who settled the sites in the region of St. Catherine. Thus an enterprise, probably initiated by people from southern Palestine, came to an end.

The evidence from Sinai and the Negev suggests that not only an urban population but also seminomads and pastoralists played a role in the environment of the Early Bronze Age. P. Lapp claimed that a seminomadic population lived next to the fortified settlement at Bab edh-Dhraᶜ. He further inferred that such an indigenous, nonurban population lived between the cities of western Palestine as well as in Transjordan throughout the third millennium B.C.E., and that they may have survived the collapse of the urban culture at the end of EB III. This survival may explain the continuation in cultural phenomena from EB I down to EB IV/MB I (see the following chapter).

It thus appears that during the seven hundred to eight hundred years of EB II–III, Palestine underwent one of the most intensive periods of settlement and urbanization in its ancient history. Though the process did not occur evenly— some important sites were abandoned at the end of EB II, and others were established only in EB III—there must have been a large population increase in comparison with the previous periods. The origins of this population may have been the descendants of the EB I agrarian communities, immigrants (perhaps from Syria), and/or seminomads who adopted city life.

AGRICULTURE

Studies of plant and animal remains and paleoenvironmental research enable us to reconstruct the agriculture and diet of the period. It appears that the traditional Mediterranean agriculture was already well developed. At Arad, various cereals (barley and wheat) and legumes (peas, lentils, chickpeas) were found. Flax was used for preparing oil and for weaving textiles. At other sites, remains of olives, figs, grapes, pomegranates, and dates are evidence of an evolved horticulture. Grape vines (the source of wine and raisins), and olive trees (the source of olive oil) appeared now for the first time as major crops in the hill country. It may be assumed that the establishment of large cities surrounded by many smaller settlements in the hilly regions of Samaria, in the land of Benjamin (for example, at ʿAi), and in the inner Shephelah (for example, at Yarmuth) was related to this emergence of horticulture as a major occupation.[45] Much of the oil and wine products of these regions was perhaps intended for trade with the cities of the plains, where cereals were the major crop, and with seminomadic pastoralists who supplied meat and skins. These products were also exported to Egypt. Thus, during the Early Bronze Age, agricultural specialization that was adapted to regional environmental conditions probably became an essential economic factor, allowing dense and varied settlement throughout the country. Another important innovation that probably arose during this time was the animal-drawn plow. This new method of plowing replaced the older hoeing stick and enabled faster and easier cultivation of the land.

Paleoenvironmental studies show that during the third millennium B.C.E. rainfall was heavier than today, and that the water table was consequently higher. Simple gravity-flow irrigation in low areas, such as the Shephelah and the coastal plain, was thus possible.[46] These natural conditions and agrotechnical innovations provided the basis for an economic surplus, which in turn resulted in the floruit of urbanization in Early Bronze Age Palestine.

ARCHITECTURE

Early Bronze Age remains are usually buried in the deepest strata of the major *tells* of Palestine, and thus they have been exposed only in a few of these *tells*—and even then mostly to a limited extent, insufficient for comprehensive study of urban layout. In only two of the multistrata *tells*—Megiddo and Tell el-Far'ah (north)—was a comparatively large area of the Early Bronze Age town uncovered. Extensive horizontal excavation of Early Bronze Age cities has been possible only at sites which were abandoned during most of the later periods, such as Arad, 'Ai, Yarmuth, Beth-Yerah, Tel Erani, Tell el-Hesi, and Bab edh-Dhra'. Of these, the excavations at Arad, 'Ai, and Yarmuth have been the most informative.[47]

Fortifications The formidable Early Bronze Age fortifications are the most expressive illustration of the intensity of urbanization in this period. During EB II, simple stone walls, 3–4 m wide, surrounded cities such as Arad, Megiddo (Stratum XVIII), Taanach, Tell el-Far'ah (north), 'Ai, Jericho, and Yarmuth. At Jericho and Megiddo, the walls were constructed in individual sections separated by vertical seams; such construction was possibly intended to prevent the total collapse of the wall in case of an earthquake or other disaster.

Horseshoe-shaped towers that are entered by way of narrow posterns are typical to the EB II phase; they are known at Arad, 'Ai, and Jericho. Such semicircular towers are a well known feature in Mesopotamia, Egypt and Greece in the third millennium B.C.E., but it is hard to say whether their appearance in Palestine was a result of outside influence. In fact, the EB II semicircular towers precede most of the other known examples.[48] Rectangular towers or small bastions were found at EB II levels at Megiddo, Taanach, Tell el-Far'ah (north), and Tel Yarmuth.

In the latter part of EB II and in EB III, the fortifications of cities were further strengthened and thickened, some reaching considerable dimensions. At Megiddo, Tell el-Far'ah (north), 'Ai, Yarmuth, Jericho, and Tel Halif, the walls were doubled in width by additions to the original wall. At Tell el-Far'ah, for example, the original 3-m-wide wall reached a width of 7 m in the late EB II phase. At Beth-Yerah the fortification system reached a total width of 8 m; at 'Ai the original EB II wall was replaced by a new wall which was later thickened, so that in their final form the defenses averaged 7–8 m in width.

At Yarmuth the simple EB II city wall was supported by a

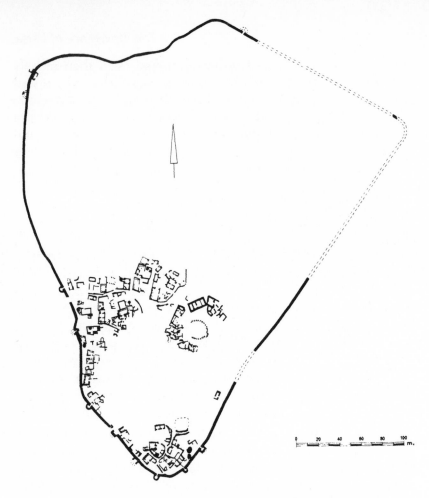

4.11 Arad: plan of the excavated remains of the Early Bronze II city.

4.12 Arad: view of the excavations. Left; the Early Bronze II city wall. Right: a dwelling unit.

huge stone retaining wall; in EB III a new city wall was built of cyclopean stones in front of the original wall, which continued to function. This outer wall, plastered on the outside, is still preserved to a height of almost 8 m. The entire system reached a width of approximately 40 m and surrounded an area of some 40 acres; it is the most formidable fortification system from this age.

4.13 Yarmuth: looking east at the western gate (Early Bronze III).

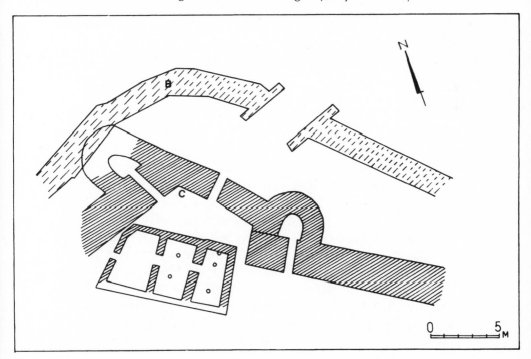

Elongated rectangular towers, 15–20 m in length and 6–8 m in width, defended the weakest points in the fortifications of cities, particularly during the EB III phase. Such towers were discovered at Tell el-Farʿah (north), Jericho, ʿAi (the "Citadel"), Yarmuth, and Tell el-Hesi.[49] At Tell el-Hesi a mud-brick tower of this type, 9.6 m wide and 27 m long, was part of a fortification surrounding an area of almost 25 acres.[50] At Yarmuth, several such towers, each about 30 m long and 10 m wide, were constructed along the western edge of the site in the last phase of EB III. A huge tower uncovered at Tel Halif in the southern inner Shephelah is the southernmost EB III fortification to be found in Palestine.[51]

The Early Bronze Age city walls were sometimes retained by earthworks glacis (artificial solid steep slopes) made of layers of earth or crushed lime; such earthworks have been found at Taanach, Tell el-Farʿah (north), el-Mahruq (in the Jordan Valley), Yarmuth, Tell el-Hesi, and Tel Halif. They were intended to strengthen the foundation of the wall against erosion and to prevent easy access to the city wall by the enemy with siege equipment. These are the forerunners of the formidable Middle Bronze II earth glacis (see p. 198).[52]

City gates of the Early Bronze Age known from Tell el-Farʿah (north), Beth-Yerah, ʿAi, and Arad were rather simple in comparison to those of the late fourth millennium B.C.E. settlement at Jawa, or to the gate of the Chalcolithic sacred enclosure at En Gedi.[53] The EB II gates were essentially simple openings in the city wall protected by flanking towers. At Tell el-Farʿah the opening in the city wall was flanked by two large square towers built of mud bricks. In a few cases there was an attempt to improve the city's defenses by creating a "bent axis" entrance. Thus an EB III gate at Yarmuth was approached by a winding ramp which created a well-defended "bent axis" approach.

These monumental fortifications could only be the work of a central authority in the cities—an authority who possessed the necessary organizational and economic power as well as commanding the engineering skill of the builders. Why were these formidable defenses necessary? One potential enemy was Egypt, though there is no evidence of Egyptian military activity in Palestine between the beginning of the First Dynasty and the documented raids during the Fifth and Sixth dynasties. Perhaps this latter danger was in the minds of the

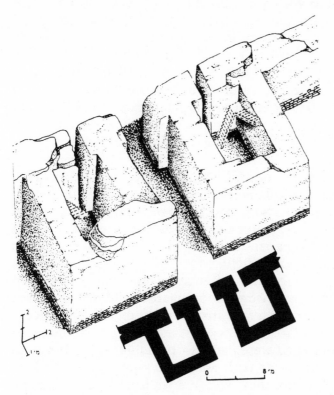

4.15 Tell el-Farʿah (north): reconstruction of Early Bronze II city gate.

Early Bronze city rulers. A more plausible reason seems to be internal struggles between the independent city-states, as was the case in the following Middle Bronze Age.

City Planning and Dwellings Exemplifying the development of a city quarter during the Early Bronze Age is Area BB at the eastern side of Megiddo.[54] The EB I village was abandoned, and during EB II (Stratum XVIII), a city wall with a square bastion was constructed. Inside this wall, there was a sacred area, separated from the rest of the city by a massive inner wall.

In EB III (Strata XVII–XVI) the steep slope west of the city wall was leveled by constructing a 4-m-deep fill on which a 800 sq m public building, possibly a palace, was built (Building 3177; see later). A massive terrace wall or inner fortification separated the latter from the sacred area farther to the west, where a large temple (4040) and a circular altar were constructed. Major changes were undertaken in the late EB III period (Stratum XV), when Building 3177 was replaced by a new structure, possibly a ceremonial gate, with a monumental staircase leading from the mound's eastern slope toward the sacred area in the west. In this latter area two new temples were erected next to the earlier one. Area BB at Megiddo and large areas exposed at Yarmuth are the best illustrations of the superb quality of EB III urban planning and monumental construction. Indications of similar large-scale and carefully planned operations have been detected at Beth-Yerah, Tell el-Far'ah (north), and 'Ai.

The best example of an EB II city plan is Arad. An EB I unfortified settlement developed there into a 25-acre city. The city wall, 2.4 m wide and 1,200 m long, was erected on ridges surrounding a crater-shaped area in the center of which was a well or a water reservoir. Narrow lanes ran parallel to the city wall or perpendicular to it, the perpendicular ones radiating from the central water reservoir. The dwellings on either side of the lanes were either isolated buildings, separated by open spaces, or clusters of structures arranged in no specific order.

Dwellings at Arad were usually "broad houses" consisting of a single main room with an entrance in one of the long walls; the flat roof of the house (known from a pottery model of a dwelling found at Arad) was supported by a wooden pillar with a stone base. The beaten earth floor was somewhat lower than the street level, and benches were built along the walls. Clay installations in the houses were constructed for storing food and so forth. Outside, there was usually a small courtyard including rounded or square foundations, probably for grain silos. A small room near the main chamber probably served as storage space. One cluster of such houses, isolated from the rest of the city by outer walls, was defined by R. Amiran as a palace, but it may have been the dwelling complex of an extended family or clan. Four other buildings at Arad similar to, but larger than, regular dwellings were defined as temples. These, however, may be interpreted as the homes of higher-class families.[55]

The Arad house type appears to have been common throughout the country in EB II, as exemplified at Jerusalem (the City of David) and Tell el-Far'ah (north). At the southern Sinai sites such single "broad room" chambers were combined into larger units around a central courtyard, and adjacent to them were rounded stone platforms which perhaps served as foundations for huts, storage spaces, and so forth. Each unit could serve an entire clan or extended family.

Few EB III dwellings are known. Those exposed at Yarmuth indicate the appearance of complex architectural units comprising several large rooms. These elaborate houses reflect an advanced phase of urban life, comprising social ranking, accumulation of wealth, and larger families.

Temples The Early Bronze Age temples were planned according to the concept of the "broad room" known from contemporary domestic architecture as well as from Chalcolithic and EB I temples. Most of the EB II–III temples were large, monumental edifices. The three EB III temples at Megiddo each measured approximately 17 × 18 m, and their walls were ca. 1.8 m thick. The temples comprised an open porch with two pillars; a wide entrance led from the porch into a broad hall (ca. 14 m wide and 9 m long). Two stone pillar bases in these halls present some of the earliest stone architectural decoration in the country: they were smoothed and ended in a sharply cut cavetto and a fillet. A raised dais

4.16 Megiddo: plan of Early Bronze Age III sacred area, including three temples and a rounded altar (Stratum XV).

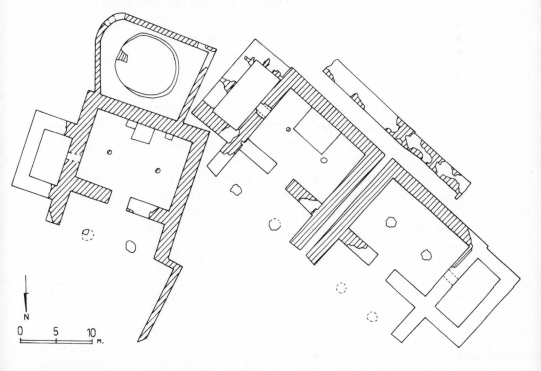

at the back of the hall probably was a pedestal for the statue of the god. The three temples seem to have been used for the worship of three different deities, perhaps an early example of a triad of gods known from later Semitic religions. A circular raised podium—about 8 m in diameter, built of stones and located at the back of the temples—was probably the sacrificial altar of the sacred enclosure.

The Megiddo temples are unique. They have been compared to the third millennium B.C.E. megaron temples of Troy as well as to other temples in the ancient Near East, but none of these comprises a broad hall and pillars, as at Megiddo. The closest parallel are three shrines in the center of the EB III Temple of Baalath at Byblos, each of which is similar in plan to the Megiddo temples, but much smaller in size and lacking pillars.

The main temple at ʿAi was located on the highest point of the town. It was a large broad building (the inner dimensions of the main hall were 17.2×5.8 m) built of massive stone walls. The main broad hall opened to the east; its roof was supported by a row of wooden pillars with curved rectangular stone bases. In the first phase of this structure (perhaps EB II), the main hall was surrounded by a narrow corridor with rounded corners. In the following EB III stage, this corridor was replaced by a series of rooms. In this period the building was constructed of flat small stones resembling bricks and was coated with a thick layer of white plaster.[56] A somewhat similar building was excavated at Yarmuth; its identification as a temple is supported by remains of a dais opposite the entrance.

Earlier we mentioned the architectural complex at Arad defined by R. Amiran as the sacred area of the city. The four buildings there appear to be elaborate dwellings of high-class families rather than temples, as neither focal points for the cult nor ritual objects were found.

The building known as the "Sanctuary" near the northern "Citadel" at ʿAi is a modification of a regular dwelling in the last phase of EB III. The cult objects found in it are of considerable significance, but its architecture represents a local improvisation.[57]

The large monumental temples at Megiddo, ʿAi, and Yarmuth are evidence of the importance of the religious center in the life of the Early Bronze Age city. As in contemporary

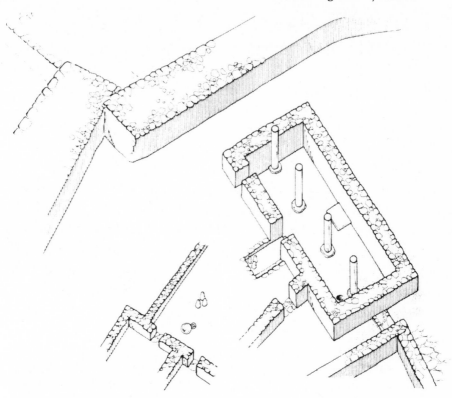

4.17 The "White Building" at Yarmuth, probably an Early Bronze III temple.

Sumerian cities, the temple was probably a center of economic wealth and power.

The Granary at Beth-Yerah   A unique EB III public building is the granary of Beth-Yerah. Surrounded by paved streets, the building was 30 × 40 m, and its outer walls were ca. 10 m wide. Foundations for nine circular silos were sunken in the outer wall, each ca. 8 m in diameter. Assuming that each silo was about 7 m high, it could hold 200–250 cu m of grain. Consequently, the total capacity of the granary was 1,800–2,250 cu m—almost 1,400–1,700 tons—of wheat.[58] The Beth-Yerah building has been compared to granaries found in eastern Anatolia (at Yanik Tepe); a stone model from the island of Melos in the Aegean dated to the third millennium B.C.E. features similar circular structures integrated in a temple (?) structure.[59]

4.18   The granary at Beth-Yerah during excavation.

This granary building may enlighten us not only on the civic architecture of the period but also on the demography and socioeconomic structure of Early Bronze Age cities. A granary of this magnitude must have been erected by a central authority who was responsible for harvesting and distributing grain. The average quantity of grain produced in traditional Arab agriculture is about 0.25 ton per acre (this number should perhaps be lowered when speaking of the third millennium B.C.E.); thus at least 5,600 to 6,800 acres of land would be required to fill this granary. The average Arab family could cultivate 20–50 acres, so up to about 350 families would be required for the work. Assuming a family size of 5 members, a population of up to 1,750 can be inferred. An average coefficient of 80–100 people per urban acre is used in demographic studies of ancient Near Eastern towns. As the area of ancient Beth-Yerah was about 50 acres, its population can be estimated at 4,000–5,000. Consequently, in order to fill the granary almost half of the population would be required. Furthermore, the traditional average grain consumption of the population in the Levant was ca. 0.14 ton per year. Even if only 70 percent of the grain could be consumed (the remainder being set aside for future sowing and/or being

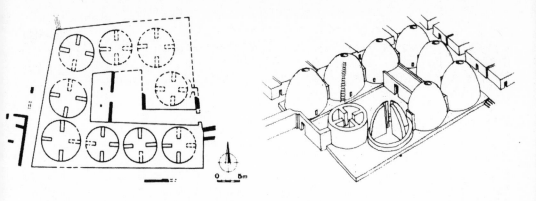

4.19   The granary at Beth-Yerah, plan and reconstruction.

damaged by insects and other pests), the granary could provide for 9,000–11,250 people. The surplus may have been used for trade or for long-term storage.

The central part of the Beth-Yerah granary includes a courtyard leading into a single large broad room whose roof was supported by two pillars. This hall resembles those in the temples at ʿAi and Yarmuth, and it tentatively may be regarded as a sanctuary, though a secular public administration center should not be ruled out.[60] The owner of this building— either religious or secular—perhaps possessed large portions of the city's land and ruled over much of the city's population as a feudal lord over serfs. Such a social structure recalls contemporary Sumerian city-states, where the temples owned large plots of land in the city and the priesthood supervised its economic life.

The ʿAi Water Reservoir   The desolate city of ʿAi was located far from any flowing water source. Its people solved the problem of water supply by building a large water reservoir— yet another illustration of the large-scale, probably centralized public works carried out in Early Bronze Age cities. Located at the lowest part of the city, the 25-m-long reservoir was constructed in EB III by building a dam over an earlier gate. It was sealed by layers of fine-grained clay and stones, and it could collect and store over 1,800 cu m (about 0.5 million gallons) of runoff water.

Thus the EB III material culture evidences the central authority, economic surplus, and a high level of technical and organizational knowledge characteristic of a mature urban society.

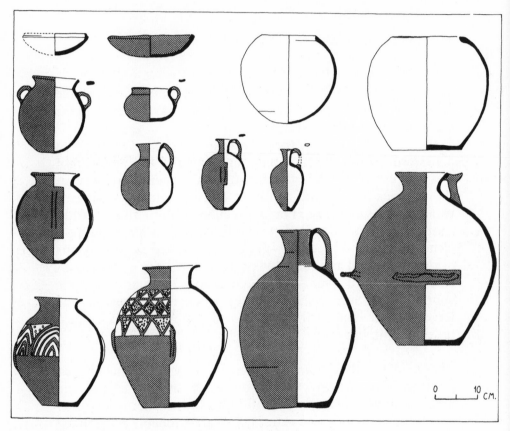

4.20   Selected pottery of Early Bronze II from Arad.

The pottery was still essentially handmade, though some parts of certain vessels were made on the potter's wheel. A potter's kiln at Tell el-Farʿah (north) is a two-story rounded structure similar to present-day traditional pottery kilns known in the Middle East. Many features were prevalent throughout the Early Bronze Age, such as flat bases, flaring rims of closed vessels, wavy ledge handles, and typical "hole mouth" cooking-pot jars. Distinctions can be made between the northern and southern parts of the country in regard to each of the two major subperiods: EB II and EB III.

Arad has provided the best EB II southern pottery assemblage.[61] It includes several types of storage jars, jugs, and amphoriskoi; cooking pots of the "hole mouth" type, with either a flat or a rounded base; and deep kraters, some with spouts below the rim, probably having a specific function such as preparing beer from barley. Little juglets were used for oils, and small, flat bowls served as oil lamps. Many of the vessels at Arad have a red slip, but burnish is not common. Shoulders of several jars at Arad are decorated with red painted friezes including dot-filled triangles and lozenges, a wavy

4.21 Early Bronze II painted jars from Arad.

continuous line, or concentric half circles. Vessels painted in this typical style are known also from the northern part of the country as well as in coastal Syria, and they are found as an import from the Levant in Egypt (see pp. 135–36). We have already mentioned the similarity between the pottery of Arad and that of the sites in southern Sinai, and the petrographic studies which have demonstrated the exchange of pottery between the two regions.[62]

EB II assemblages in the northern part of the country generally resemble those of the south, yet there are also significant regional distinctions. Jars and jugs of typical slender shape were very well fired to obtain a characteristic "metallic" touch, and the surface of jars was sometimes delicately combed. "Hole mouth" jars always have flat bases, and those with round bases common at Arad are not found in the north. Large flat platters with inverted sharpened rim and red burnished slip are the hallmark of the northern assemblages. Many of the vessels are covered with well-burnished red slip.

The transition from EB II to EB III was gradual, and the development in pottery is not easily defined. It appears that during EB III the homogeneity of the pottery throughout the country was greater than in EB II, perhaps indicating the growth of mass production resulting from the emerging urbanization. Large jars with flaring rim, flat base, and ledge or loop handles were now combed in a typical "pattern combing." Large platters and bowls with thickened flat rims were usually covered with well-burnished red slip; often the burnishing created net or "spiderweb" patterns, a technique known as "pattern burnishing." Jugs, juglets, and amphoriskoi had a tall "stump base" and were usually well burnished. Small juglets with narrow neck and pointed base appeared in the later part of the period and may be taken as forerunners of Middle Bronze Age II juglets which were to appear almost four hundred years later.

The northern EB II–III pottery has close parallels as far north as Byblos and Ras Shamra, demonstrating the homogeneity of the material culture of northern Palestine and the Lebanese and Syrian coast during this period. Inner northern Syria, on the other hand, had its own material culture.

An exceptional EB III pottery group is known as "Khirbet Kerak Ware," named after the site of Khirbet Kerak (Beth-Yerah), where it was first defined.[63] The vessels were handmade, with a thick body, and were fired at a comparatively low temperature. They were covered by a heavy slip and were highly burnished. The color of the slip was controlled by fire: on the outside it was either all black or black with red around the rim; on the inside it was red. Surface decoration includes ridges shaped in the form of triangles, spirals, or certain symbols. Khirbet Kerak vessels include small carinated bowls, large carinated kraters, deep small cups, little carinated jars, several types of jars, cylindrical and biconical stands, cooking-pot stands (or fenders?), and lids. This pottery is found mainly in the northern part of the country (at Beth-Yerah, Meggido, Beth-Shean, Hazor, and so forth), while only a few small vessels reached the south, probably through trade.

4.22 A Khirbet Kerak Ware krater.

Khirbet Kerak Ware was manufactured in Palestine and is found together with other local EB III pottery. But the manufacturing technique and the variety of shapes can be traced to northeastern Anatolia, where similar traditions are known from the third millennium B.C.E. Similar pottery was found in Syria, particularly in the Amuq region (yet it was not found at Tell Mardikh [Ebla], east of the Orontes Valley). This implies that the pottery of this kind was produced by immigrants who left eastern Anatolia, moved southward, and settled in certain selected locations, the most prominent of which were the Amuq Valley, the upper Jordan Valley, and the region of the Lake of Galilee. Limited in number, they probably settled among the local population, continuing to produce their traditional pottery. Most likely their arrival was peaceful, as there is no indication of a resulting cultural change in the country.

METALLURGY

Copper continued to be the main metal used throughout the third millennium B.C.E. in the Levant. Copper seems to have been either rare or very expensive, since tools and weapons are relatively sparse in Early Bronze Age contexts, perhaps due to repeated recycling of the metal. The establishment of EB II sites in southern Sinai (earlier, p. 114) is best explained as an effort by the city dwellers of southern Palestine (particularly Arad) to develop and control copper resources of their own, perhaps in cooperation with the local population of the region. Copper ores, crucibles, and even smelting furnaces with clay nozzles of bellows, as well as molds, chunks of copper, and complete copper tools evidence the southern Sinai copper industry. The products must have been sent to southern Palestine in exchange for goods.

The most complete assemblage of copper objects from the Early Bronze Age is a hoard of tools and weapons discovered in a field in the Sharon Plain, near Kefar Monash, dated to EB II or even to EB III.[64] The weapons in this hoard include tanged axes, daggers with a central rib, large spearheads with a central rib, and a crescentic axehead (found at some distance from the main hoard). As there are four specimens of most of the weapons, it is assumed that they belonged to four warriors. The tools are adzes, chisels, pegs, and a saw (the latter resembling contemporary Egyptian saws), all of which were of use in felling trees. Since an oak forest is known to have existed in the Sharon Plain in antiquity, it is possible that the hoard represents the equipment of soldiers and woodcutting laborers who were obliged to leave their equipment there. Most of the objects in this hoard are typical products of the local copper industry which had evolved since EB I. Some of the objects are forms known also from Syria, Anatolia, Cyprus,

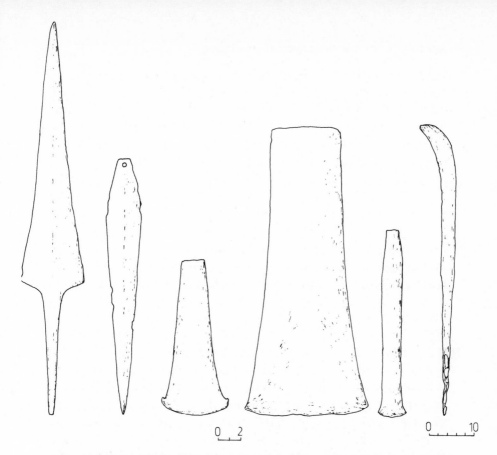

4.23 Kefar Monash hoard: selected copper objects (probably from Early Bronze II). From left to right: spearhead; dagger; axe; adze; chisel; large knife (perhaps for cutting trees).

and Mesopotamia. This wide geographic distribution of metal types is common in the ancient Near East, where wandering metalsmiths, trade connections, and wars spread fashions and techniques over vast regions.

INTERNATIONAL CONNECTIONS

Connections with Egypt EB II jars and jugs imported from Palestine and Syria were found in tombs of kings and nobles of the First Dynasty (starting with its third pharaoh, Djer) and the Second Dynasty at Abydos and Sakkarah.[65] The jars and jugs exported to Egypt are similar to types known in EB II contexts in Palestine, such as painted jars and jugs, and red slipped burnished pottery of the "metallic" type (sometimes designated "Abydos Ware"). This imported pottery in

Egypt is of prime importance for establishing chronological correlations between EB II in Syria-Palestine and the first two dynasties in Egypt. It also illuminates the economic relations between the two countries: Asiatic agricultural products, particularly olive oil and wines, found markets in Egypt. Copper, and perhaps bitumen and salt from the Dead Sea, were also exported to Egypt.

A few Egyptian objects from this period were found in Palestine, particularly pottery jars at Arad and perhaps a group of stone vessels found at 'Ai (see later). These may represent some return trade from Egypt, or they may have been brought by Egyptian officials who arrived in the southern part of the country. The Egyptian presence in southern Palestine, which was a dominant feature of the previous period, ceased during EB II, and the region was now settled by a local population. Nonetheless, it appears that travel by land, and perhaps by sea between Egypt and Palestine continued during EB II and was one source of the wealth of the emerging local city-states.

It seems that during EB III the connections with Egypt decreased, as almost no Egyptian finds from this phase are known.[66] On the other hand, the ties between Byblos and Egypt were now stronger, as evidenced by Egyptian objects found in the former and Syrian pottery found in the Old Kingdom cemetery at Giza. A relief on the mortuary temple of Pharaoh Sahure (Fifth Dynasty) shows a ship bringing people, bears, and pottery from Syria, perhaps from Byblos. Byblos now became the main port of call for ships transporting timber to Egypt, and Palestine was almost ignored, the land route along northern Sinai neglected.

Art Objects Indicating Relations with Syria, Anatolia, Mesopotamia, and the Aegean   The number and quality of art objects from Early Bronze Palestine is surprisingly low compared to their number and quality in the Chalcolithic period. The few known items, however, have special value, as most of them represent ties with various cultural centers.

Rough clay figurines of domesticated animals are found, but they are uncommon and of careless workmanship. An exceptional group includes five ivory or stone miniature bull heads which were probably the product of one workshop of EB III date. They recall bull-head figurines from Mesopotamia

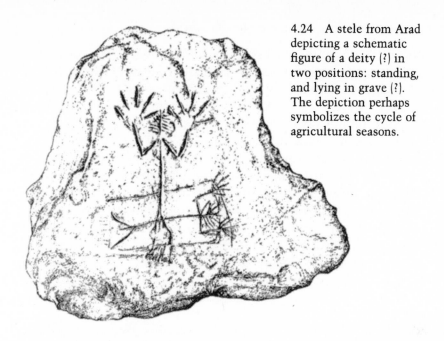

4.24 A stele from Arad depicting a schematic figure of a deity (?) in two positions: standing, and lying in grave (?). The depiction perhaps symbolizes the cycle of agricultural seasons.

and from Elam, but it is uncertain whether they indicate a direct Mesopotamian influence on local art in Palestine.[67]

A unique art object is a rather small, unsmooth, and roughly incised stele found at Arad showing a schematic figure in two postures: lying in a rectangular frame which most probably represents a grave, and standing with upright arms.[68] The figure is anthropomorphic, yet its head recalls an ear of corn and its feet roots. The scene was interpreted by R. Amiran as a depiction of the death and reincarnation of a fertility god. It might be related to a local myth connected to the agricultural seasons—recalling the Mesopotamian myth about Dumuzi, the god who dies in summertime and is reincarnated in fall.

Dozens of cylinder-seal impressions as well as a few actual cylinder seals and stamps provide significant information on local art as well as on foreign connections during the Early Bronze Age.[69] Several cylinder seals and stamp seals from Arad represent the local EB II style. The stamps, carved in a variety of geometric designs, are stylistically related to contemporary finds from Byblos, northern Syria, and northern Mesopotamia. The cylinder seals show a Mesopotamian glyptic influence of the Jemdet Nasr and Early Dynastic I periods.

The habit of using wooden cylinder seals for stamping jars before firing was common throughout the Early Bronze Age in Palestine and Syria, but is unknown from Mesopotamia proper. Seal impressions dated to EB II show various geometric motifs and processions of animals. Some sealings recall impressions from Byblos, and three impressions show a coiling snake, a motif known in Elamite glyptic art. EB III cylinder-seal impressions from northern Palestine schematically depict rows of human figures holding each other (perhaps dancing in a ritual dance), animals, and structures (perhaps temples). Some parallels to the schematic style and the themes were found in inner Syria—particularly at Hama, on the Orontes River. In northern Syria Mesopotamian seals from this period as well as imitations of such seals were found. The lack of such seals in Palestine indicates that the local culture was relatively isolated during the EB III period.

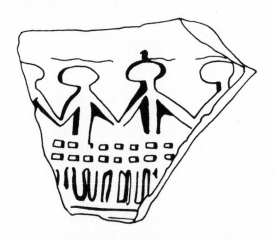

4.25 Drawing of a cylinder-seal impression on a jar, showing schematic human figures (dancers?) above an architectural facade (temple?); Early Bronze III.

Thus, the few classes of art objects from EB II–III Palestine reflect the existence of local workshops which were influenced to some degree by Mesopotamian art, perhaps through the mediation of northern Syria. Unfortunately, the third millennium B.C.E. culture of Syria prior to the civilization of Ebla is almost unknown. This latter civilization, which flourished in the twenty-fourth and twenty-third centuries B.C.E., appears to have been isolated from that of Palestine. Further discoveries in Syria will probably provide more evidence on the missing link between the Sumerian civilization of Mesopotamia and that of Palestine.

Two polished stone axes discovered at ʿAi are of types known from Asia Minor and inner Anatolia, and a decorated gold disc from a tomb near Beth-Yerah recalls finds from the royal tombs of Alaja Huyuk in central Anatolia. These objects may have arrived with the immigrants from Anatolia who introduced the Khirbet Kerak Ware tradition, or they may represent indirect trade with Anatolia via Syria.

The Early Helladic site of Lerna in the Peloponnese has produced two interesting links with the east that were mentioned earlier: horseshoe-shaped towers resembling those of EB II Palestine, and the sealing of jars with wooden stamp seals. Furthermore, three seal impressions from northern Palestine resemble impressions from Lerna in their decoration (particularly in the appearance of the spiral motif).[70] Incised bone tubes found at several EB III contexts in Palestine and Syria and a bone pin decorated with an animal head from Megiddo recall finds from the Cycladic Islands.[71] These sporadic finds hint at some remote connections between Syria-Palestine and the Aegean in the EB III period. Yet there is as yet an unresolved chronological discrepancy between the two regions.

BURIAL CUSTOMS

The common burial custom in EB II–III was multiple interment in caves, each of which usually contained many skeletons, dozens of pottery vessels, and other objects. Such a burial custom, in which several generations of one family could be buried in the same cave, would comply with the needs of an urban society.

A variation of this practice was found at the large cemetery at Bab edh-Dhraʿ, where EB II–III rectangular burial chambers (denoted "charnel houses") served for multiple interments.[72] The uniqueness of this vast burial site is emphasized by its peculiar pottery, which differed considerably from that of the rest of the country. It should be noted that at important Early Bronze Age cities such as Arad and Yarmuth no cemeteries have yet been found, in spite of extensive search. Can we assume that people from such cities were buried far from their homes in sacred cemeteries, as the cemetery at Bab edh-Dhraʿ may have been?

SOCIETY, POLITICS, AND ECONOMY

Reconstruction of the social and political structure of Early Bronze Palestine can be carried out only tentatively, as no written documents are available. The extensive archaeological data, however, does allow for some preliminary conclusions. The settlement pattern and comparisons with the situation in the second millennium B.C.E. present a country divided into about twenty city-states, each overseeing a distinct geographic region comprising smaller towns and villages. The homogeneity of the material culture throughout Palestine, Lebanon, and perhaps southern Syria demonstrates close cultural connections and interchange between these city-states, but it does not appear that there was one overriding authority or "state" controlling the entire country or a large part of it.[73] There was, most probably, an upper ruling class in each city-state that had the wealth and power to initiate the impressive public works, such as fortifications, temples, palaces, and the Beth-Yerah granary. Among these, the fortifications were necessitated by rivalry between the city-states. The importance of the theocracy in particular is indicated by the monumentality of the temples.

Specialized craftsmen, usually a common component of an urban society, were rare: they included metalsmiths, seal-cutters, professional potters, and some artisans of the minor crafts. The lack of evidence of any writing system is curious. It is hard to believe that such an urban system lacked bureaucracies employing some sort of written word. Could Palestine have remained illiterate, while in Mesopotamia, Egypt, and northern Syria writing was widespread? If so, then the hierarchical, urban society of Palestine was a backwater in comparison to the sophisticated civilizations of Mesopotamia, northern Syria, and Egypt in the third millennium B.C.E.

The rise of the urban culture of EB II–III in the time of the Archaic Period and Old Kingdom of Egypt is not a coincidence. The strong relations with Egypt at the beginning of the period and the trade between the two countries during EB II probably provided the impetus for the development of the city-state system in Palestine. This Egyptian connection seems to have been less prominent during EB III, when the cities of Palestine appear to have been more self-sufficient. The mighty fortifications of the EB III phase evidence rivalry between the cities, perhaps at a time when living conditions became harder, and the economic and social systems deteriorated.

THE COLLAPSE OF THE EARLY BRONZE AGE URBAN CULTURE

Some cities were deserted at the end of EB II. Arad was abandoned at that time; this was due perhaps to the shift in Egyptian economic policy in the Levant, a shift that put an end to the economic basis for Arad's survival. Tell el-Far'ah (north), el-Mahruq, and Tell es-Sa'idiyeh were destroyed, and they remained uninhabited throughout the EB III period. Yet these seem to be exceptional cases. Other cities did suffer from destructions during EB II–III, perhaps as a result of inner struggles, but in most cases they were rebuilt and continued to flourish until the end of EB III. The final annihilation or abandonment of these cities was one of the most fateful cultural crises in the history of Palestine: the entire Early Bronze Age urban culture in western Palestine collapsed within a short time, to be replaced by a totally different, nonurban pattern which lasted for about three hundred years. The exact date, nature, and causes of this crisis are among the major questions concerning the period.[74]

It appears that the downfall of the cities was abrupt. Excavations at Megiddo, Beth-Yerah, 'Ai, Yarmuth, and other EB III sites have shown that they were abandoned or destroyed when they were at the peak of their urban development. Various explanations have been offered for this phenomenon. Some scholars connect it with the Egyptian raids at the end of the Old Kingdom. A hymn found in the tomb of the Egyptian general Uni, who served ca. 2300 B.C.E. in the army of Pepi I (the third pharaoh of the Sixth Dynasty), describes a military invasion of the "land of the sand dwellers." The song mentions the destruction of fortresses, the felling of fig and wine orchards, the killing of thousands of enemies, and the capture of many others. A relief found at Dashasheh in Upper Egypt—dating to the end of the Fifth Dynasty—depicts the Egyptian siege of a fortified city in Asia. A siege ladder is depicted being used by the Egyptians, who are shown destroying the city wall with large bars or spears. The city wall has rounded towers, and its inhabitants wear typical Asiatic costume and headdress; local captives are depicted tied up by ropes.[75] These two sources can be taken as evidence of Egyptian military operations in Palestine and Syria during the time of the Fifth and Sixth dynasties.

If the Egyptians were responsible for the destruction of the Early Bronze Age culture of Palestine, what was their motive in doing so? Soon after the Sixth Dynasty, Egypt entered the First Intermediate Period, a time of inner turmoil and insecurity during which Asiatics penetrated Lower Egypt. Perhaps the Egyptians were aware of this danger already in the days of the Fifth Dynasty, and tried to prevent it by raids on Canaan. Another theory, which was popular in the sixties, connected the destruction with a hypothetical invasion by West Semitic "Amorite" tribes from Syria who were considered to have been responsible for the nomadic culture of the following period (see Chapter Five). A third approach looks for environmental conditions which might have caused the abandonment of cities and the collapse of urbanization.[76] Various studies point to a decline in the amount of precipitation, a drier climate, and a consequently lower water table. Such gradual changes, combined with more severe successive drought years, could bring about a crucial lack of drinking and irrigation water—and eventually starvation, plagues, and an upheaval in the delicate pattern of urban life. Coping with successive years of drought is a difficult task even in our own day; it must have been impossible in the Early Bronze Age, when cisterns were as yet unknown, and water supply depended on springs and collecting runoff water in open-air reservoirs. Overpopulation, resulting in land and water depletion as well as deforestation, has also been cited as a possible factor leading to the end of the Early Bronze Age civilization. The "environmental" explanation to the end of the EB urban civilization may be refuted in light of the discoveries in the Transjordanian plateau east of the Dead Sea, where a continuity of urban life in the following EBIV/MBI period was detected (see below, p. 158). This area of Transjordan appears to have been vulnerable to environmental difficulties even more than most of the Mediterranean regions of Western Palestine; if environmental problems caused the end of urban life in the rest of the country, why did they not affect this area? The discoveries in this part of Transjordan imply, in our mind, that the collapse of the urban system of Palestine at the end of EB III must have resulted to a large degree from human factors, such as internal warfare and perhaps Egyptian raids.

A multifactor model which includes most of the points just outlined should be taken into consideration (as suggested in principle by W. G. Dever). Deterioration of environmental conditions could have led to an economic and social crisis; in times of drought, desert nomads may have attacked settlements and their lands; and conflicts between the cities regarding water and land resources would have made the situation worse. And finally, the fatal blow to the vulnerable city-state system may have been delivered by Egyptian raids during the time of the Fifth and Sixth dynasties.

THE EARLY BRONZE AGE AND THE BIBLE

At first glance it appears that the Early Bronze Age was too early to be related to biblical history. Yet from time to time scholars attempt to relate this period to the biblical background, especially in connection with the traditions in the Book of Genesis. The discovery of the archive of Ebla in 1976 raised premature expectations in this regard. For a while it appeared that the patriarchal period had been identified.[77] It is now clear, however, that the Ebla archive can at best provide the general cultural background for the emergence of the West Semitic peoples in the third millennium B.C.E. Nonetheless, should we abandon any attempt to relate the Early Bronze Age to ancient biblical traditions?

The Book of Genesis, particularly its first part, may be seen as an attempt by Israelite authors to reconstruct the early history of their people by means of genealogical narrative. Some traditions assimilated into this book might be very early, having been orally transmitted by many generations of the local population of Palestine and finally adopted by the Israelites. Some of these stories could perhaps reflect events in the late third millennium B.C.E. Thus, the attempts to relate Genesis narratives to Early Bronze Age features cannot be completely excluded.

The most tempting supposition is to relate the narrative in Genesis 14 about the five "cities of the plain" (Sodom, Gomorrah, Admah, Zeboiim, Zoar) to the discovery of five Early Bronze Age sites close to the eastern shores of the Dead

Sea. At least two of these sites were fortified (Bab edh-Dhraꜥ and Numeira). Their destruction, which was followed by total abandonment for centuries, was presented by some as real archaeological evidence of the story in Genesis.[78] Perhaps a severe catastrophe bringing an end to these five cities was remembered and transmitted orally in legendary form over centuries down to the first millennium B.C.E., when it was adapted to its final form by the author of the Book of Genesis.

An alternative theory has an etiological basis. Some of the Early Bronze Age sites were prominent ruins visible to the inhabitants of the country in later periods. The remains of the ruined EB cities east of the Dead Sea, as well as of cities such as Arad, ꜥAi, and Yarmuth, were exposed for centuries. Even today, ancient fortifications at several of these sites protrude from the surface. Later inhabitants of the country—the Israelites among them—might have invented etiological legends related to these ruins, such as the legend about the cities of the plain, the story about the war against Arad (Numbers 21:1–3) and the conquest story of ꜥAi (Joshua 8). These people might also have used terms such as "Rephaim" and "giants" (Genesis 15:20; Deuteronomy 2:11, 20; Joshua 13:12; and so forth) to describe the ancient indigenous population of the country.

4.26 Egyptian troops lay siege to a fortified city in Asia. A relief from a tomb at Dashasheh (5th Dynasty, 24th century B.C.E.; see page 141).

NOTES

1. The dates here for Egypt and Mesopotamia follow those suggested by H. Kantor and E. Porada in: *COWA* 2, pp. 26–27, 176–79 respectively. Note that Porada dates the beginning of the Early Dynastic I in Mesopotamia at 2900 B.C.E., while Kantor, when correlating her Egyptian chronology to Mesopotamia, suggests 3100 B.C.E. for the same event. Differing views are found in other publications; compare, for example, W. W. Hallo and W. K. Simpson, *The Ancient Near East: A History*, New York 1971, p. 37, note 16.

2. G. E. Wright, *EI* 5 (1958), pp. 37*–45*; Wright (1961), pp. 81–85; R. de Vaux in: *CAH*, vol. 1, part 1, pp. 499–538; ibid., vol. 1, part 2, pp. 208–37; Hennessy (1967), pp. 26–48; P. de Miroschedji, *L'Epoque Pre-Urbaine en Palestine*, Paris 1971; Kenyon (1979), pp. 66–83; P. Lapp, *BASOR* 189 (1968), pp. 12–41; J. F. Ross in: K. Newmyer (ed.), *Historical Essays in Honor of Kenneth R. Rossman*, Crete 1980, pp. 147–70; R. T. Schaub in: Hadidi (1982), pp. 67–68; *BAT*, pp. 108–12, 145–51 (a symposium at which R. Amiran and P. de Miroschedji suggested continuity from the Chalcolithic to EB I, while A. Ben-Tor and R. Gophna emphasized the differences and break between the two periods; A. Kempinski, following J. Perrot and J. B. Hennessy, supported an overlap between EB I in the northern part of the country and the Ghassulian culture in the south). See also L. E. Stager in: *COWA* 3, and papers in *Emmaus Colloquium*.

3. See G. E. Wright, *The Pottery of Palestine from the Earliest Times to the End of the Early Bronze Age*, New Haven 1937. Wright 1958 and 1961 in previous note; D. L. Esse, *JNES* 43 (1984), pp. 317–30; Stager in: *COWA* 3.

4. L. E. Stager in: *Tufnell Festschrift*, pp. 172–88.

5. S. W. Helms, *Jawa: Lost City of the Black Desert*, London 1981.

6. E. Braun and S. Gibson, *BASOR* 253 (1984), pp. 29–39; E. Braun, '*En-Shadud*, Oxford 1985; M. Dothan, *IEJ* 7 (1957), pp. 217–18; ibid. 9 (1959), pp. 13–29; E. Eisenberg, *Excavations and Surveys in Israel*, vol. 2, Jerusalem 1983, pp. 111–13; J. Hanbury-Tenison, *Liber Annuus* 35 (1985), pp. 410–12; S. W. Helms, *Levant* 16 (1984), pp. 35–58; ibid. 18 (1986), pp. 25–50; E. Braun in: *Emmaus Colloquium*; E. Eisenberg in: ibid.

7. R. Saidah, *Berytus* 27 (1979), pp. 29–55.

8. For Megiddo see I. Dunayevsky and A. Kempinski, *ZDPV* 89 (1973), pp. 161–87. Some Chalcolithic pottery was found in the earliest occupation levels at Megiddo, and one cannot be sure whether the temple was not erected already in that period. The building at Hartuv was excavated in 1988 by P. de Miroschedji and the author. Another possible temple from this time is a small structure at Jericho Stratum VII (Garstang's excavations) which has an indirect entrance and benches along its walls. The only other public building from this period is a structure at Tel Erani (Stratum VI). It contains a hall roofed with nine pillars arranged in three rows.

9. A. Ben-Tor, *Two Burial Caves of the Proto Urban Period at Azor.* *Qedem* 1, Jerusalem 1975, pp. 1–54; K. M. Kenyon, *Excavations at Jericho,* vol. 2, London 1965, pp. 3–62.

10. Lapp (see note 2); R. T. Schaub, *AASOR* 45 (1979), pp. 45–68.

11. O. Bar-Yosef et al., *IEJ* 27 (1977), pp. 65–88; idem, *IEJ* 36 (1986), pp. 121–67.

12. See Amiran (1969) pp. 41–48, where a regional approach was suggested. For the development in the north, see Braun in: *Emmaus Colloquium.*

13. Lapp (see note 2).

14. Lapp's claim that the Gray Burnished pottery was invented locally as an imitation of basalt vessels of the Chalcolithic period is not convincing. There are indeed some resemblances in the forms (for example, the fenestrated high-footed bowls), yet other features of this pottery are missing in the Chalcolithic basalt industry, while, on the other hand, such features have parallels in eastern Anatolia. See Hennessy (1967), pp. 35–40.

15. S. A. Rosen, *IEJ* 33 (1983), pp. 15–29.

16. R. Amiran and N. Porath, *TA* 11 (1984), pp. 11–19; Braun in: *Emmaus Colloquium.*

17. A. Ben-Tor, *Cylinder Seals of Third Millennium Palestine, BASOR Supplement* 22 (1978); P. Beck, *Opuscula Atheniensia* 11 (1975), pp. 1–9; idem, *TA* 11 (1984), pp. 97–114.

18. Hennessy (1967), pp. 35–36.

19. R. T. Schaub in: Hadidi (1982), p. 71; de Miroschedji (see note 2); Stager in: *COWA* 3.

20. P. Smith in: *Emmaus Colloquium.*

21. E. D. Oren, *IEJ* 23 (1973), pp. 198–205; idem in: *Emmaus Colloquium.*

22. J. M. Weinstein, *BASOR* 256 (1984), pp. 61–69; B. Brandel in: *Emmaus Colloquium.* The excavations at Tel Erani were resumed by A. Kempinski in 1985.

23. Sh. Yeivin, *IEJ* 10 (1960), pp. 193–203; R. Amiran, *IEJ* 24 (1974), pp. 4–12; ibid. 26 (1976), pp. 45–46; R. Gophna and A. Schulman, *IEJ* 31 (1981), pp. 165–67; R. Amiran et al., *The Israel Museum Journal* 2 (1983), pp. 75–83.

24. R. Gophna, 'Atiqot 11 (1976), pp. 1–9; ibid. 14 (1980), pp. 9–16; idem, *TA* 3 (1976), pp. 31–37; idem, *Expedition* 20 (1978), pp. 5–7; R. Gophna and D. Gazit, *TA* 12 (1985), pp. 9–16.

25. K. Kroeper in: *Emmaus Colloquium.* This paper reports the discovery of EB I pottery at the cemetery of Minshat Abu Omar, approximately 50 km west of the Suez Canal on the Pelusiac branch of the Nile. Twenty vessels originating in Palestine were found here among the over two thousand local ones dating to the late Pre-Dynastic Period.

26. Y. Yadin, *IEJ* 5 (1955), pp. 1–16; Gophna and Schulman (see note 23). For other views, see the citations in notes 22–23.

27. Kantor in: *COWA* 2, pp. 1–46; W. Needler, *Predynastic and Archaic Egypt in the Brooklyn Museum,* New York 1984.

28. J. A. Callaway and J. M. Weinstein, *BASOR* 225 (1977), pp. 1–16; J. M. Weinstein, *Radiocarbon* 26 (1984), pp. 297–366; Stager in: *COWA* 3. Carbon 14 tests relating to EB I come from only four sites; some of the tests point to a high date in the first half of the fourth millennium. This may mean that the period was longer than previously believed, or that mistakes and distortions occurred in the C 14 tests.

29. Some general essays on this period: R. de Vaux in: *CAH*, vol. 1, part 1, pp. 208–37; Kenyon (1979), pp. 84–118; P. W. Lapp in: *Glueck Festschrift*, pp. 101–31; Amiran (1969), pp. 83–100; A. Kempinski, *The Rise of an Urban Culture*, Jerusalem 1978; idem, *IEJ* 33 (1983), pp. 235–41; J. A. Callaway in: *Kenyon Festschrift*, pp. 46–58; P. de Miroschedji in: *A propos des interpretations archeologiques de la poterie: Edition recherche sur les civilisations*, Paris 1986, pp. 11–46; S. Richard, *BA* 50 (1987), pp. 22–43. See also papers in *Emmaus Colloquium*. For earlier discussions see Anati (1963), pp. 317–62; Mellaart (1966), pp. 59–60. For a general bibliography on Early Bronze sites see J. F. Ross in: *Rose Festschrift*, pp. 315–53. For a general account of the development throughout the region, see C. L. Redman, *The Rise of Civilization: From the Early Farmers to Urban Society in the Ancient Near East*, San Francisco 1978.

30. The various terminologies used for the inner division of the EB I period led to some confusion concerning the exact date of the beginning of urbanization in Palestine (see Note 3 above). Thus R. de Vaux dated the beginning of urbanization at Tell el-Farʿah (north) to the phase which he called "EB IB." But in fact, de Vaux's EB IB phase can be regarded as part of the EB II phase. (Most of the assemblages which we include in EB I were attributed by de Vaux to "Late Chalcolithic.")

31. This date is based on the assumptions: (1) that the Third Dynasty corresponds to the beginning of EB III in Palestine; (2) that the high Egyptian chronology should be utilized. A lower chronology would place the end of EB II ca. 2600 B.C.E. It should be remembered, however, that both the inner division of the Early Bronze Age and Egyptian chronology can be interpreted in different ways, and thus there are considerable discrepancies between the dates given in various publications. Carbon 14 dates from EB II–III contexts are known only from Jericho, Bab edh-Dhraʿ, and Numeira. They appear to be problematic, as calibration based on dendrochronology provides a wide range of dates in the third millennium B.C.E., many of which appear to be too high when compared to those based on Egyptian correlations (see references in note 28).

32. W. C. Hayes in: *CAH*, vol. 1, part 1, pp. 173–80; ibid., vol. 1, part 2, pp. 994–95 (Narmer: 3100 B.C.E.; end of the Sixth Dynasty: 2181 B.C.E.).

33. The date 2300 B.C.E. for the end of EB III and the urban culture is suggested by W. G. Dever in *BASOR* 237 (1980), pp. 35–37.

34. There have been attempts to divide the period into further subperiods. See earlier (note 3) concerning the phase denoted by G. E. Wright "EB IC" and by K. M. Kenyon "EB I." The material ascribed to both these terms should be regarded as part of EB II. EB III is divided by several

scholars into two subphases: EB IIIA and EB IIIB. This division is based mainly on the supposed disappearance of Khirbet Kerak Ware in the second stage of EB III, but the division is still unclear (see later). The phase which Wright and Albright termed "EB IV" corresponds to the post-urban period and will be discussed in the following chapter.

35. P. Matthiae, *Ebla: An Empire Rediscovered*, London 1980, pp. 65–111, 150–225.

36. The Akkadian period is dated to 2370–2230 B.C.E. (Naram Sin: 2291–2255 B.C.E.) in: *CAH*, vol. 1, part 1, pp. 219–20 (followed by Porada in: *COWA* 2, pp. 178–79).

37. V. G. Childe, *Man Makes Himself*, London 1936, pp. 197–201; idem, *What Happened in History*, London 1939, pp. 70–72. For later attempts, see especially R. M. Adams, *The Evolution of the Urban Society: Early Mesopotamia and Prehistoric Mexico*, Chicago 1966; Redman (see note 29).

38. See Kempinski, *The Rise of an Urban Culture* (note 29); the criticism of Kempinski's theory in L. Marfoe, *JNES* 39 (1980), pp. 315–22; another such criticism in W. G. Dever, *IEJ* 31 (1981), pp. 254–57; and Kempinski's answer in *IEJ* (see note 29). See also R. Amiran in: *Glueck Festschrift*, pp. 83–100, and recently D. L. Esse in: *Emmaus Colloquium*.

39. M. Broshi and R. Gophna, *BASOR* 253 (1984), pp. 41–53. A coefficient of 100 persons per acre is based on various independent demographic research methods related to a number of periods and regions in the history of the Middle East. An estimation of the population in EB II Arad arrived at a similar result; see Marfoe (note 38), p. 320.

40. For a survey of the ʿAjlun region and its numerous Early Bronze sites, see S. Mittmann, *Beiträge zur Siedlungs und Territorialgeschichte des nördlichen Ostjordanlandes*, Wiesbaden 1970. See also J. A. Sauer, *BASOR* 263 (1986), pp. 3–4. A 15-acre fortified EB III city is reported at Tell el-Umeiri, close to Amman: see L. T. Geraty et al., *BASOR Supplement* 24 (1986), p. 139.

41. W. E. Rast and R. T. Schaub, *ADAJ* 19 (1974), pp. 5–54, 175–85; idem, *AASOR* 43 (1978), pp. 1–32; idem, *BASOR* 240 (1980), pp. 21–60; idem, *ASSOR* 46 (1981) (entire volume dedicated to Bab edh-Dhraʿ); idem, *BASOR* 254 (1984), pp. 35–60. See also T. L. Thompson, *ADAJ* 19 (1974), pp. 63–70.

42. C. Epstein, *IEJ* 22 (1972), pp. 209–17; Ben-Tor (note 17), p. 107. The excavations in the Lawiyeh enclosure (Mitham Leviʾah) were carried out by M. Kochavi and P. Beck (oral information).

43. I. Beit-Arieh, *TA* 1 (1974), pp. 144–56; ibid. 8 (1981), pp. 95–127; ibid. 9 (1982), pp. 146–56; idem, *BASOR* 243 (1981), pp. 31–55; idem, *Levant* 15 (1983), pp. 39–48; idem, *BASOR* 263 (1986), pp. 27–54.

44. Stager in: *COWA* 3.

45. Stager in: *Tufnell Festschrift*, pp. 172–88.

46. A. M. Rosen in: *Emmaus Colloquium*.

47. On Arad, see R. Amiran, *Early Arad*, Jerusalem 1978; on the later seasons, see R. Amiran et al., *Qadmoniot* 49–50 (1980), pp. 2–19

(Hebrew); idem, *IEJ* 36 (1986), pp. 74–76. Regarding 'Ai, see J. A. Callaway, *BASOR* 178 (1965), pp. 13–40; ibid. 196 (1969), pp. 2–16; ibid. 198 (1970), pp. 7–31; ibid. 207 (1972), pp. 41–53; idem, *The Early Bronze Age Sanctuary at Ai (et-Tell)*, London 1972; idem, *The Early Bronze Age Citadel and Lower City at Ai*, Cambridge, Mass., 1980. On Yarmuth, see A. Ben-Tor, *Qedem* 1 (1975), pp. 55ff.; P. de Miroschedji, *Yarmouth I*, Paris 1988. For a general account of Early Bronze architecture, see Wright (1985), passim; *Architecture*, pp. 47–78 (Hebrew).

48. Amiran (see note 47 [1978]), p. 13.

49. S. W. Helms, *Levant* 9 (1977), pp. 101–14.

50. L. E. Toombs, *PEQ* 115 (1983), pp. 35–44; R. W. Dorneman and V. M. Fargo, *PEQ* 117 (1985), pp. 12–22.

51. J. D. Seger, *BASOR* 252 (1983), pp. 1–3.

52. P. Parr, *ZDPV* 84 (1968), pp. 18–45.

53. S. W. Helms, *PEQ* 107 (1975), pp. 133–50; Z. Herzog, *Das Stadttor in Israel und in den Nachbarländern*, Mainz 1986.

54. Dunayevsky and Kempinski (see note 8). The views expressed by K. M. Kenyon in *EI* 5 (1958), pp. 51*–60* should be corrected in the light of the findings of Dunayevsky and Kempinski.

55. Regarding dimensions of Arad houses, see Marfoe (note 39), pp. 317–20.

56. Callaway in: *Kenyon Festschrift*, pp. 49–51. The building was defined as a palace by its first excavator, J. Marquet-Krause. Callaway first explained it as a fortress-palace, but later he, as well as other scholars, accepted its identification as the main temple of the city. He believes that it was attached to a palace, but he only hints that the latter was actually discovered. The Egyptian parallels drawn by Callaway are vague and unconvincing.

57. Callaway, *The Early Bronze Sanctuary at 'Ai (et-Tell)* (see note 47).

58. The numbers in this section are based on data assembled by B. Rosen in: I. Finkelstein, *Izbet Sartah*, Oxford 1986, pp. 171–85.

59. R. Amiran, *Anatolian Studies* 15 (1965), pp. 165–67. On Yanik Tepe, see C. A. Burney, *IRAQ* 23 (1961), pp. 138–53. Regarding Melos, see H. G. Buchholz and V. Karageorghis, *Prehistoric Greece and Cyprus*, London 1973, item no. 1122.

60. Anati (1963), p. 337 advocates the identification of the building as a sanctuary.

61. Amiran, *Early Arad* (see note 47), pp. 51–52; idem, *Levant* 6 (1974), pp. 65–68.

62. R. Amiran, I. Beit-Arieh, and J. Glass, *IEJ* 23 (1973), pp. 193–97.

63. Hennessy (1967), pp. 74–79.

64. R. Hestrin and M. Tadmor, *IEJ* 13 (1963), pp. 265–88; R. Gophna, *IEJ* 18 (1968), pp. 211–15; A. Ben-Tor, *IEJ* 21 (1971), pp. 201–6; T. F. Watkins, *PEQ* 107 (1975), pp. 53–63.

65. Hennessy (1967), pp. 49–61, pls. 39–45; Kantor in: *COWA* 2, pp. 1–

46; R. Amiran, *BASOR* 179 (1965), pp. 30–33; ibid. 195 (1969), pp. 116–21; idem, *AJA* 72 (1968), pp. 316–18; A. Ben-Tor, *AJA* 85 (1981), 449–51; idem, *Journal of Jewish Studies* 33: 1–2 (1982), pp. 3–18; Stager in: *COWA* 3.

66. The one possible exception is a collection of Egyptian alabaster vessels found at ʿAi in Sanctuary A near the "Citadel"; dated to the last phase of EB III. The collection was presumed to be evidence of Egyptian connections during this period, yet a study of the vessels suggests that they are earlier than EB III and probably were produced during the time of the first or second dynasties. They were probably brought to ʿAi during EB II and were preserved as precious heirlooms until the final destruction of the city. J. A. Callaway in: *Kenyon Festschrift*, pp. 299–306; Hennessy (1967), pp. 69–70; R. Amiran, *IEJ* 20 (1970), pp. 170–79.

67. A. Ben-Tor, *BASOR* 208 (1972), pp. 24–29.

68. R. Amiran, *IEJ* 22 (1972), pp. 86–88.

69. Ben-Tor (see note 17); Beck (see note 17, both references); Epstein (see note 42).

70. Ben-Tor (see note 17), pp. 96–99.

71. Hennessy (1967), pp. 82–83.

72. R. T. Schaub, *AASOR* 46 (1981), pp. 45–68.

73. Lapp (see note 29) has suggested that all the fortified cities of the Early Bronze Age were part of one kingdom established by "town dwellers" who immigrated to Palestine and established themselves over the local indigenous population of village dwellers and seminomads. This radical view is not accepted by scholars currently dealing with the subject.

74. For current approaches, see Kempinski *IEJ* (note 29); S. Richard, *BASOR* 237 (1980), pp. 5–34; Dever (see note 33), pp. 35–59; idem in: *Emmaus Colloquium*.

75. *ANET*, pp. 227–28; *ANEP*, p. 311.

76. On the last approach, see the papers of D. L. Esse, A. M. Rosen, and W. G. Dever in: *Emmaus Colloquium*.

77. D. N. Freedman, *BA* 43 (1980), pp. 202–3; M. Dahood, *BAR* 6:5 (1980), pp. 54–60; but see A. Archi, *BAR* 7:6 (1981), pp. 54ff.; ibid. 7:2 (1981), p. 62; idem, *Biblica* 60 (1979), pp. 556–66; idem, *BA* 44 (1981), pp. 145–54; L. Vigano and D. Pardee, *BA* 47 (1984), pp. 6–16. On Ebla in this period, see note 35.

78. W. C. van Hatten, *BA* 44 (1981), pp. 87–92; W. E. Rast, *Rose Festschrift*, pp. 186–201.

CHAPTER FIVE

AN INTERLUDE
The EB IV/MB I Period
(2300/2250–2000 B.C.E.)

INTRODUCTION

For about three hundred years following the collapse of the EB III urban culture, Palestine was sparsely populated, mainly by pastoralists and village dwellers. This period of decline parallels the First Intermediate Period in Egypt (Dynasties VII–XI), during which there was a decentralization of power and a break in the traditional connections between Egypt and Asia, particularly those with Byblos. The end of Palestine's period of decline also has a parallel in Egyptian history: the revival of urbanization in Palestine at the beginning of the Middle BronzeAge II corresponds with the rise of the Middle Kingdom in Egypt, ca. 2000 B.C.E. Mesopotamia also suffered from invasions and instability, though only for a relatively short duration (ca. 2230–2130 B.C.E.).

In Syria, it seems, the cultural development differed from one region to another. Ebla was destroyed by Naram Sin of Akkad ca. 2250 B.C.E., but urban life soon recovered. At the coastal cities of Ras Shamra and Byblos, a severe destruction occurred at the end of the Early Bronze Age; at Ras Shamra the destruction was followed by a transitional phase resembling that of Palestine, while at Byblos it appears that cultural continuity prevailed more than anywhere else.

The data concerning this period is limited; most of it has come from cemeteries, as only few settlement sites have been excavated. Nevertheless, the available evidence allows reconstruction of the major cultural developments and features.[1]

TERMINOLOGY

The varied views concerning this period are expressed by the terms used to denote it. W. F. Albright and G. E. Wright divided the phenomena under discussion in this chapter between two periods: Early Bronze IV (denoted by Wright in 1961 "Early Bronze IIIB") and Middle Bronze I (MB I). The first term was vaguely determined at that time; only a few tomb groups in western Palestine, and deposits from Trans-jordanian sites known from N. Glueck's surveys, were attributed to it. The term "Middle Bronze I" was widely accepted as designating most of the features to be described in this chapter.

The uniqueness of the period, and its outstanding divergence from those preceding and succeeding it, led other scholars to endow it with special terms. Olga Tufnell called it "the Caliciform culture," after the shape of one of its common pottery vessels; K. M. Kenyon, following her excavations at Jericho, called it "Intermediate Early Bronze–Middle Bronze Period"; and in the midsixties, P. Lapp and M. Kochavi denoted the period "Intermediate Bronze Age."[2] In 1968, however, P. Lapp reverted to the term "Early Bronze IV" as a result of his work at Bab edh-Dhraʿ, where he found a great deal of continuity between EB III traditions and those of the period under discussion. The term "Early Bronze IV" was later accepted by E. D. Oren, and a few years later by W. G. Dever and other writers.[3] In short, terminological chaos now reigns, resulting from the simultaneous use of all these terms. Furthermore, those who avoid using the term "Middle Bronze I" in relation to the period under discussion in this chapter, used this term to describe the following period in Albright's terminology, the one denoted by him as "Middle Bronze IIA." This caused further confusion (see below, p. 175). To avoid utter disorientation, we will use in this book the composite term "EB IV/MB I" (suggested already in 1966 by W. G. Dever) for the entire period under discussion in this chapter.

SETTLEMENT PATTERN AND ARCHITECTURE

Only at a few major *tells* did a scanty occupation level follow the end of EB III (Hazor, Megiddo, Beth-Shean, Jericho).

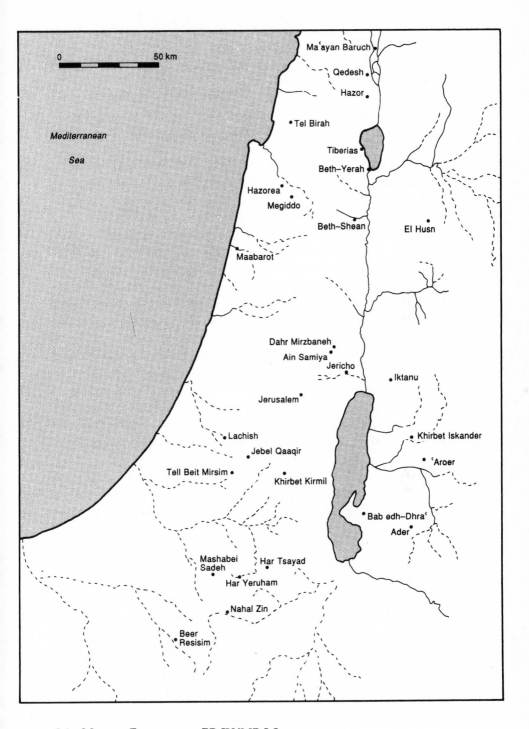

5.1 MAP OF EXCAVATED EB IV/MB I SITES.

Thus Megiddo Stratum XIV was an unfortified village with poor structures and large open spaces. Evidence was found of a continued use of the city's sacred enclosure: the ruined Temple 4040 became a small chapel, and gifts were found on a floor just above the circular altar of the Early Bronze Age. Other villages were now erected at new locations; these villages have been discovered, other than by chance, thanks to systematic archaeological surveys in such areas as the Jordan Valley south of the Lake of Galilee, the inner Shephelah, and the central hill country (for example, in Shaar Hagolan, Wadi Far'ah, 'Ain Samiya, and Nahal Rephaim, west of Jerusalem). Sometimes settlements were located on the outskirts of major *tells* (such as at the foot of Tel Birah [Bir el-Gharbi] in the valley of Acre, and on a hill opposite Lachish). Most of the above were occupied only during this one period.

One of the few excavated sites is Jebel Qaaqir, in the inner Shephelah west of Hebron. The dwellings there were in caves and poor huts, but a large cemetery was found nearby. At Dahr Mirzbaneh near 'Ain Samiya—an important spring at the eastern fringes of the hills of Ephraim—vast cemeteries from this period surrounded a large settlement which may have been a campsite or a seasonal village.[4] In the valley of Rephaim, stone houses from this period were constructed along natural terraces close to the riverbed. Although these one-period sites are difficult to discern due to their sparseness and remote location, their dispersion throughout the country is inferred from the distribution of cemeteries from this period. It is evident, therefore, that the settlement pattern in western Palestine during EB IV/MB I was considerably different from that of the Early Bronze Age.

A most peculiar feature of EB IV/MB I is the habitation of arid regions, particularly the central Negev and Sinai. The natural conditions in the central Negev highlands (between the modern Dimona–Beer-sheba road on the north, Machtesh Ramon on the south, and Nahal Zin on the east) would have been appropriate for pastoral nomadism. This area may have been inhabited by nomads throughout historical periods as it is today, but significant archaeological remains have been found here from only a few periods, one of the predominant of which is EB IV/MB I. Surveys and excavations conducted by N. Glueck, Y. Aharoni, M. Kochavi, and W. G. Dever, and the detailed research conducted by R. Cohen and a team of the Israel Survey, revealed a few large villages (2–5 acres in area), hundreds of smaller settlements, and vast cemeteries from this period scattered throughout this geographic zone and extending west into the northern half of the Sinai Peninsula.

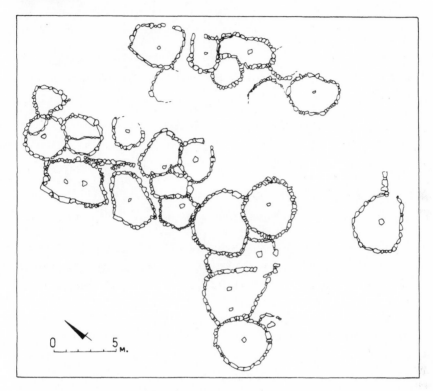

5.2   Beer Resisim: plan of a dwelling complex.

Many of the Negev sites consisted only of a few huts and pens, while the larger ones comprised several dozens of dwellings. The largest sites in this region are Beer Resisim, ʿEn Ziq (in Nahal Zin), a site near Kibbutz Mashabei Sadeh, and Har Tsayad on a narrow ridge south of Mamshit. At Beer Resisim the population of the site is estimated to have included about seventy-five individuals.[5] Several types of dwellings were found in the Negev sites. Most typical is a rounded structure with a single chamber, about 2–4 m in diameter (with an average floor space of 10 sq m). A stone pillar at the center of the structure supported a roof made of large slabs of stone. Such simple houses are clustered in groups

5.3   Dwellings at the EB IV/MB I site at Har Tsayad.

or in the form of small chains; each chain probably represents
dwellings of families of several adults and children. Several
of the houses comprise between two and five rooms, yet no
public buildings were detected. The small site excavated at
the top of the high ridge of Har Yeruham consisted of a few
houses with square rooms, such houses may have been roofed
with wool cloth laid on stone pillars. Animal pens here were
surrounded by stone walls, and a "high place" was located
near the settlement. Many burials in the form of stone tumuli
(see p. 161) can be found near and even inside the Negev
settlements.

As we have seen, the Negev and southern Sinai were to
some extent settled during EB II. In spite of superficial
similarities between the sites of the two periods, there seems
to be a fundamental difference between them: the EB II
settlements are found in small numbers throughout the Negev,

5.4   EB IV/MB I round dwellings at ʿEn Ziq (central Negev).

including in the Arabah, and they thus created a communication line between southern Palestine and southern Sinai,
while the EB IV/MB I sites are limited to the central Negev
and northern Sinai. The economy of the EB II sites may have
been based on the trade of copper which was mined in southern
Sinai and sold to the urban centers of southern Palestine,
while the EB IV/MB I sites do not appear to have been related
to any outside economic system. Differences in the plans of
the sites and of the individual houses are also significant:
while the EB II house units were of the "broad room" and
rounded types—both arranged in groups around an inner
courtyard—most of the EB IV/MB I dwellings were single-
room, rounded structures and did not enclose a courtyard.
Their planning resembles much earlier, Neolithic sites. They
probably reflect a social structure differing from that of EB II.

The EB IV/MB I Negev society appears to have been

egalitarian and tribal; the people were pastoralists and perhaps practiced transhumance. The Negev highlands would have served their winter needs, while in summer the herdsmen may have been obliged to wander north, perhaps to the Hebron Hills and to the Shephelah. In fact, the artifacts (pottery and metal objects) found in the Negev, in the Hebron Hills, and in the Shephelah are identical.[6]

The settlement of the central Negev in the EB IV/MB I period is enigmatic. This area was almost uninhabited at times when an urban culture flourished in the rest of the country (such as in EB III, in the Middle and Late Bronze periods); but the region was heavily settled in EB IV/MB I— when in the fertile areas of Palestine there probably was no lack of land and pasture, and population was relatively sparse. This paradox is sharpened by paleoclimatic studies showing that after the end of EB III drier conditions prevailed. Current research indicates that the number of settlements and their size had been larger than we previously believed, but no satisfactory explanation of the phenomenon has been suggested.

An even more extraordinary development took place in Transjordan in the area east and northeast of the Dead Sea, along the main north-south route there. A number of sites from this period—Iktanu, Khirbet Iskander, ʿAroer, and Ader— appear to have been agrarian sedentary settlements, and to have retained EB III cultural traditions more than other sites in the country.[7] This is the culture which Albright and Wright defined as "EB IV" (or "EB IIIB"). Both at Iktanu and at Khirbet Iskander, several occupation phases from this period were revealed. The 8-acre site of Khirbet Iskander was fortified by a massive wall, resembling Early Bronze fortifications, and dwellings of the "broad building" type definitely continued the urban architecture of the Early Bronze Age. The pottery in this region was a distinct Transjordanian variation of the EB IV/MB I repertoire, but in its early phases it was closer to EB III traditions than any of the EB IV/MB I assemblages in western Palestine: red slipped burnished pottery still appeared here, while elsewhere it was almost entirely nonexistent. It appears that this part of Transjordan became a refuge for population groups escaping from extermination which occurred at large parts of the country at the end of EB III.

BURIAL CUSTOMS

The vast EB IV/MB I cemeteries are a primary source in the study of this period. Three major types of burials are known, each typical of a different region: shaft tombs, known throughout western Palestine; megalithic dolmens covered by tumuli, known in the Golan Heights and Upper Galilee; and built-up tumuli, typical of the central Negev. All three are interments of one or a few individuals, in either primary or secondary burial, in strong contrast to the multiple family graves of EB I–III. This shift in custom reflects a change in the social structure and way of life: while the multiple burials would suit the needs of extended families living in an urban society, the individual and secondary burials conform with the nature of a seminomadic society in which the dead are brought to central cemeteries after primary burial elsewhere. Both secondary burials and shaft tombs were already known in EB I, but their use was abandoned during EB II–III.

Most of the cemeteries found in the country are composed of shaft tombs. These tombs are rock-cut vertical shafts leading to underground burial chambers. The details differ from site to site—and even within the same cemetery, as exemplified

5.5 Shaft-tomb cemetery at Jebel Qaaqir; note the shallow shafts, the openings to the burial chambers, and the large blocking stones.

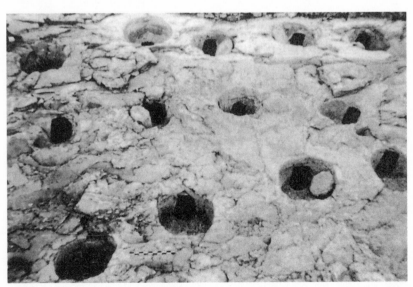

5.6   A shaft tomb
at Jericho: plan and
section.

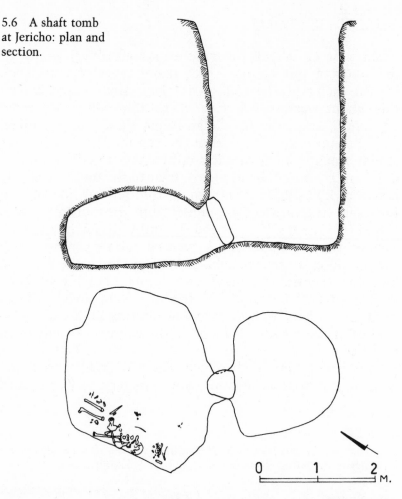

0   1   2
M.

at Jericho.[8] In some of the burial fields, such as those near
Ain Samiya, the shafts are circular; they were hewn with
great care, and they descend to depths of up to 6 m. The
shafts lead into one or two burial chambers, sealed by stone
slabs.[9] In other cases, the shaft is either square or irregular:
sometimes it is very shallow and the cave is small (such as
at Lachish); in other cases the shaft is elaborate and square,
and it leads into a cave with several rectangular rooms (as at
Megiddo). The burial caves generally contained a single or a
few articulated or disarticulated skeletons. The gifts usually
included only some pottery vessels and sometimes a number
of copper weapons (a dagger and/or a spear). Beads accompanied
female skeletons. Variations between cemeteries in close

proximity may indicate either a chronological sequence or the possibility that related tribal groups with somewhat different burial customs lived side by side.

In the Negev highlands, the dead were laid in stone structures known as "tumuli." These are circular cairns with an inner central cell where the body was placed with some gifts. Tumuli fields are found on summits of mountain ridges in the Negev and often are associated with settlement sites. High, overhanging locations were deliberately chosen for these tombs, so that many tumuli still protrude into the skyline in the central Negev. Tumuli are found also inside settlement sites, between houses. Many were found empty, as if they had been used for primary burial and the bones had later been removed for secondary interment elsewhere.

The megalithic dolmens found in the Golan and Galilee are tablelike structures composed of two or more vertical basalt blocks roofed by large rock slabs. A heap of stones usually covered the dolmens, creating a tumulus. Such structures are known in Transjordan from the Chalcolithic period, but in the Golan and Galilee they definitely date to EB IV/MB I. Dolmens generally served for the secondary interment of one person.[10] These dolmens recall similar megalithic burial structures known throughout Europe in the Bronze Age, but the significance of this resemblance is still unclear.

5.7   A large dolmen in the Golan Heights.

POTTERY

The Three Main Assemblages   The pottery assemblages found
in EB IV/MB I contexts, particularly the assemblages in the
vast cemeteries of the period, are a primary source for defining
the origin of the culture, its chronological framework, its
regional variations, and its foreign connections. Three main
regional pottery assemblages or families can be discerned: the
Transjordanian, the Northern, and the Southern.[11] Further
subdivision into regional subgroups was suggested (by Dever),
but such distinctions are less significant and may represent
only individual workshops possibly related to subtribal units.
There are shapes common to all three assemblages, such as
several types of goblets, amphoriskoi (small jars with two
handles) and "teapots." Lamps with four spouts; are one of
the hallmarks of the period. In all three families the pottery
is usually handmade; the potter's wheel was used only for
some small vessels and for producing jar necks in the Southern
group.

The Transjordanian group is known mainly from the sedentary sites east of the Dead Sea and from the cemetery at
Bab edh-Dhraᶜ. Both shapes and decoration in this group are
close to EB III traditions. Thus burnished red slip, a hallmark
of the Early Bronze Age pottery, is common in this family,
while it is almost nonexistent in the others.[12] Stratigraphic
excavations at Iktanu have shown the existence of two distinct
phases: the earlier one still retains the Early Bronze Age red
burnished slip, while in the later stage red slip is not evident.
This development may indicate that the earlier stage of the
EB IV/MB I period in Transjordan corresponds to a period of
occupational gaps in the southern part of western Palestine.

The Northern family can be divided into two subgroups:
the Upper Galilee (represented at the Qedesh cave and Maᶜayan
Baruch cemetery) and the Jezreel Valley group (represented at
cemeteries near Megiddo, Hazorea, and Beth-Shean).[13] Its
southern limit is Wadi Farᶜah, northeast of Shechem, where
an important concentration of sites from this period is known.
Although this group differs to a large extent from the Transjordanian, it too retains Early Bronze Age traditions. The Early
Bronze ledge handle developed here into a folded form known
as "envelope shaped." The jars tend to be globular. Distinct

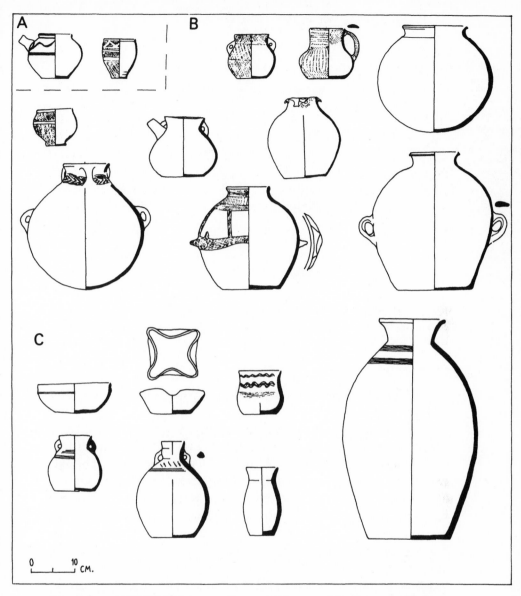

5.8 Selected EB IV/MB I pottery forms: (A) imported Syrian ware; (B) from tombs in the northern part of Palestine; (C) from tombs in southern Palestine.

northern vessels are squat globular jars with pinched mouth, and large mugs. Punctured decoration, made with a sharp tool, appears around necks of jars. Pale, unburnished red slip appears on some of the vessels and vaguely recalls Early Bronze red burnished slip. Poorly painted pale red stripes or circles decorate vessels, particularly in the Megiddo–Beth-

5.9 Finds from a cave at Qedesh, Upper Galilee. Left and center: imported Syrian wheel-made bottle and "teapot" (black ware and white painting); right: a local amphoriskos; foreground: beads.

Shean region. Imported Syrian Black Ware vessels are found in this assemblage (see below).

Under the designation "Southern family" we include pottery assemblages from the central hill country, the Jordan Valley, the Shephelah, the coastal plain, the Negev, and Sinai. Though there are minor distinctions among these regions, their assemblages still seem to have sufficient common features to categorize them under one major tradition. The main features of this group are light buff clay, lack of red slip or painted decoration, incised decorations, horizontal and wavy stripes created by a five-tooth narrow comb, and the appearance of various knobs and vestigial handles. The most common vessels are flat bowls, amphoriskoi, "teapots," several types of goblets, cups, four-spouted lamps and tall, handleless jars with flaring neck which was made on the wheel. This Southern group appears to be less related to Early Bronze traditions than the other two pottery families, though its "hole mouth" cooking pots are quite similar to those of the Early Bronze Age.[14]

Syrian Imported Pottery A number of imported "teapots" and goblets were found in the north, such as at a cave near

Qedesh in the Upper Galilee and in the Megiddo cemetery. The pots were made on the wheel and are of black or gray ware, painted with white horizontal or wavy lines. Both the shapes and the decoration are known from contemporary urban centers in northern Syria, such as Hama (Levels J1–4) and Tell Mardikh (= Ebla; Phase IIA–B, the palace and post-palace periods).[15] Yet there are some minor differences between the ware found in northern Syria and that found in northern Palestine, perhaps indicating that the import came from sites in southern Syria (the Damascus region and Lebanon) where no archaeological material from this period is available. This pottery group was considered in the past as evidence of an emigration from Syria to northern Palestine, but later research seems to indicate that it reached Palestine through trade rather than emigration. Pottery groups introduced by immigrants, such as the Gray Burnished and Khirbet Kerak wares of the Early Bronze Age, were produced locally, while this pottery was imported from Syria. The Syrian shapes were imitated by local potters both in the north and in the south of the country. Caravan routes apparently connected the urban culture of Syria with the poorer one of northern Palestine; but the nature of this trade has yet to be clarified.

METALLURGY

Weapons and Pins   The EB IV/MB I cemeteries contained a distinct group of weapons which were to accompany the dead to his afterlife. Most weapons in this period were still made of copper, but bronze alloy appears for the first time in one cemetery in the Upper Galilee, perhaps indicating Syrian influence in this region.[16] The selection of shapes is limited to certain daggers, spearheads, spear butts, and axeheads. The daggers developed from Early Bronze shapes; their tang is now more prominent, with several holes for connecting the handle. The spearheads are also based on the common Early Bronze tanged blade, but now they have a short blade and a long tang with a curled end intended to prevent the splitting of the wooden shaft when hitting a target. The spear butts are long, narrow, and sharpened, and they end in a curl. Axeheads from this period are known as "eye shaped"; they developed from the E-shaped crescentic axes of the previous period, but now they were equipped with a shaft for the wooden handle.

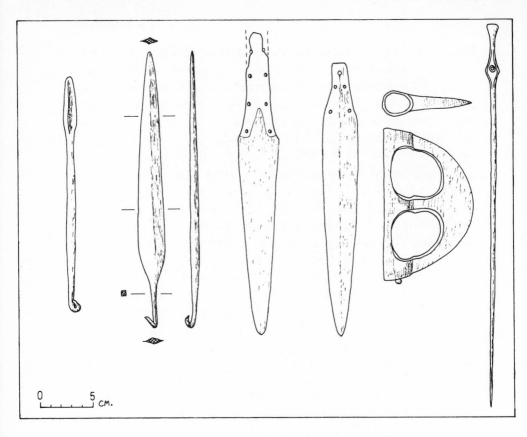

0 5 CM.

5.10   Selected weapons and a pin from EB IV/MB I tombs.

Similar axes were common along the Phoenician coast, particularly at Byblos and Ras Shamra.

Elongated copper toggle pins of types known in Syria are almost the only other type of metal object found (particularly in the northern part of the country) in this period.

Narrow elongated copper ingots found at several sites in the south served perhaps as a raw material for casting metal objects.[17] These ingots, as well as the numerous well-made metal weapons and pins, show that specialized, skilled metal-smiths operated in the country during this period. They were perhaps traveling metalsmiths, like those illustrated in a famous wall painting in a tomb at Beni Hasan in Egypt (1890 B.C.E.), where a family of West Semites is shown. Their main occupation appears to be metalworking, since the object carried by a donkey in this painting is probably a bellows (see p. 187).

The 'Ain Samiya Goblet An outstanding find from this period is a silver goblet decorated in repoussé technique and found in one of the shaft tombs near 'Ain Samiya.[18] Actually,

5.11   The silver goblet from 'Ain Samiya.

5.12   Drawing of the scene on the 'Ain Samiya goblet.

it is the only art object from this period. A mythological scene shown on the central frieze of the goblet has two parts: On the right, two men dressed in the Sumerian sheepskin kilt are shown holding a crescentic object which supports a twelve-petal disc with a human face. A snakelike dragon is shown below, between the figures. The left scene features a janiform mythological creature—with the bodies of two lions, a human torso, and a double face—feeding the same dragon-snake with plants; the left part of the scene is missing.

Y. Yadin suggested that the picture illustrated scenes from *enuma elish*, the Mesopotamian creation myth. He interpreted the creature on the left as the god Marduk, who in the epic has a double head. The story relates how Marduk neutralized with a special plant the poison of the snakelike dragons borne by Tiamat. The scene on the right perhaps shows how part of Tiamat's body, after she was slain by Marduk, became the sky; an alternative interpretation is that the right scene depicts Marduk's assistants catching Tiamat with a net. Though the known texts of the *enuma elish* are much later, its origin might have been in the third millennium B.C.E. (Perhaps the main god in the original version was not Marduk, who was probably incorporated into the myth by the Babylonians in the second millennium B.C.E.)

The ʿAin Samiya goblet, therefore, may be taken as evidence of both the early date of the myth and the wide scope of Mesopotamian cultural influence. It appears, however, that this important object was not manufactured in Mesopotamia, but rather in northern Syria—where a local north Syrian art, inspired by that of Mesopotamia, flourished during the second half of the third millennium B.C.E. Similarly shaped goblets (though undecorated) are indeed known from northern Syria.

CHRONOLOGY

The imported Syrian pottery found in northern Palestine is the only find from this period that allows correlation to another ancient Near Eastern culture. Similar pottery is found in north Syria both before and after the destruction of Palace G at Ebla ca. 2250 B.C.E. This "Caliciform" pottery was in use in northern Syria throughout the last three centuries of the third millennium B.C.E. A more precise chronological framework for our period is based on the dates of the end of EB III and the beginning of the following MB IIA. As we have seen, the end of the EB III urban culture can be dated to the beginning of the Sixth Dynasty in Egypt, ca. 2300–2250 B.C.E. The beginning of MB IIA should probably be determined at ca. 2000 B.C.E., corresponding to the beginning of the Middle Kingdom in Egypt (see pp. 190–91).[19]

INTERPRETATION

Who were the people of Palestine of the EB IV/MB I period? To what extent is this period a continuation of the preceding period? The most common view until the early seventies proposed a sharp break between this period and the preceding Early Bronze Age. The dominant opinion was that the country was invaded by West-Semitic seminomadic tribes from Syria, similar to those who emigrated during the same period from Syria toward Mesopotamia. These latter people are known in Mesopotamian documents as "Amurru" (Sumerian "MAR.TU"), namely "westerners," and are thus denoted "Amorites" by modern scholars.[20] Several scholars suggested that these "Amorite" newcomers were responsible for the destruction of the Early Bronze Age cities, while others propose that these pastoral nomads just entered the vacuum created in the aftermath. The wall painting at Beni Hasan in Egypt which was mentioned earlier was generally considered to be illustrating such pastoral nomads, as the leader of the group depicted has a typically West Semitic, "Amorite" name (*Ab-sha*).

W. F. Albright went one step further by identifying this period as the time of the Hebrew patriarchs. The supposed movement of "Amorite," West Semitic tribes along the Fertile Crescent, and the settlement activity in the Negev, appeared to him to be the best background for the traditions in the Book of Genesis.[21]

Another theory identified the peoples of Palestine during this period as intruders from far outside the Near East. During the thirties, C. F. A. Schaeffer uncovered, in Ras Shamra, graves which contained finds recalling those of EB IV/MB I in Palestine. These graves separated the Early Bronze and Middle Bronze urban phases at this important site in coastal northern Syria. The people were denoted by him "Porteurs de Torques," after the peculiar copper torques found in their graves. Based on parallels in Europe, he identified these people as Indo-Europeans. In the late sixties, P. Lapp and M. Kochavi, following M. Gimbutas, independently suggested that the people of Palestine in EB IV/MB I were an offshoot of one of the great waves of Indo-Europeans moving from central Asia toward Europe at the end of the third millennium B.C.E. The major similarities pointed out were the use of tumuli for burial and the frequent appearance of metal objects in the tombs. The extensive use of dolmens in this period may support this view, as they are one of the essential features of Indo-European cultures in Europe.[22]

The current approach of W. G. Dever, S. Richard, and others tends to negate any massive invasion of the country by a foreign population; they emphasize the indigenous nature of the culture, and its origins in the previous Early Bronze Age, as exemplified in pottery and metal forms. The Early Bronze settlements in the Negev and Sinai are considered predecessors of those of EB IV/MB I, and the finds in Transjordan are taken as evidence of a general continuation of sedentary, even urban life in this region. The EB IV/MB I culture is explained as a shift in the modes of life, social structure, and subsistence economy of the local population following the collapse of the Early Bronze Age urban system, not as a product of ethnic incursions.[23] According to this view, both the EB IV/MB I pastoral nomads as well as the sedentary villages of this period developed from the indigenous population. The use of the term "EB IV" as the sole denotation for this period reflects this outlook.

The general tendency to emphasize indigenous processes in explaining cultural changes is currently fashionable in scholarly circles. This approach forms the basis of current explanations of a series of other cultural changes and transitions in a number of regions.[24] The archaeological phenomena in the small region east of the Dead Sea have greatly influenced these current views. But, as mentioned earlier, this small and remote region may have been an exceptional case, a refuge, where the Early Bronze traditions and way of life were better preserved than elsewhere. In most of western Palestine, the change in the way of life between the two periods was extreme: a thriving, hierarchical urban culture with a city-state political system, surplus economy, and foreign trade relations was replaced by an egalitarian society based on pastoralism and agriculture, without any distinct political system. Although connections with Egypt were lacking, some trade relations with inner Syria were maintained. It is true that in terms of pottery and some of the metal objects, the EB IV/MB I period can be seen as the last echo of the Early Bronze tradition; many forms of the vessels and tools are based on Early Bronze prototypes. But the discontinuity from the previous period is expressed in the essential modes of life. The complete desertion of many Early Bronze sites, the poor villages constructed on some of the ruined cities, the establishment of new encampments on previously unsettled hills, the occupation of the arid Negev highland and northern and central Sinai, and the appearance of new burial customs are all demonstrative of a radical cultural break.

To claim that these changes were adopted by the remnants of the indigenous population of the previous urban Early Bronze Age does not seem feasible. An alternative to a foreign invasion would be to claim that autochthonous pastoral nomads, who lived in the country throughout the third millennium B.C.E. beside the urban system and were suppressed by it, thrived in the vacuum created by the collapse of the cities. Such pastoral tribes could perhaps have absorbed groups of survivors from the cities, who retained some of their own traditions and added to the number and economic power of these seminomads. It would appear, however, that such a revolution in lifestyle would also be accompanied by some ethnic change. Nonetheless, the extent of the crisis at the end of the Early Bronze Age—one of the greatest crises in the history of the land—and the subsequent cultural shift cannot be underestimated.[25]

5.13　A group of Semites (metalsmiths?) arriving in Egypt. A wall painting in a 12th Dynasty tomb at Beni Hasan in Middle Egypt (ca. 1900 B.C.E.).

NOTES

1. W. G. Dever in: *Glueck Festschrift*, pp. 132–63; idem, *Harvard Theological Review* 64 (1971), pp. 197–226; idem, *BASOR* 210 (1973), pp. 37–63; ibid. 237 (1980), pp. 35–64; idem in: *BAT*, pp. 113–35. See also S. Richard, *BASOR* 237 (1980), pp. 5–34; idem, *BA* 50 (1987), pp. 34–40. For a summary of previous views, see Wright (1961), pp. 86–88; Kenyon (1979), pp. 119–47.

2. P. Lapp, *The Dahr Mirzbaneh Tombs: Three Intermediate Bronze Age Cemeteries in Jordan*, New Haven 1966; M. Kochavi, "The Settlement of the Negev in the Middle Bronze I Age," unpublished Ph.D. dissertation, The Hebrew University of Jerusalem 1967 (Hebrew with English summary).

3. Dever, *BASOR* 210 (1973), pp. 38–41.

4. W. G. Dever, *IEJ* 22 (1972), pp. 95–112. The settlement was observed in a survey of the region carried out by the present author in 1979. Architectural remains of villages were found at three unpublished sites in addition to Megiddo: at Tel Birah in the Acre Valley (Black Syrian Ware was uncovered in an occupation level at the foot of the mound excavated by M. W. Prausnitz); at the fishing ponds of Kibbutz Shaar Hagolan in the upper Jordan Valley (surveyed by E. Eisenberg); and at the valley of Rephaim, southwest of Jerusalem (excavated by G. Edelstein and E. Eisenberg). I thank the excavators, all from the Israel Department of Antiquities, for permission to refer to these discoveries. Settlements from this period were also surveyed along Wadi Farʿah (by Y. Porath and R. Gophna, and later by A. Zertal).

5. R. Cohen and W. G. Dever, *BASOR* 232 (1978), pp. 29–45; ibid. 236 (1979), pp. 41–60; ibid. 243 (1981), pp. 57–77. For the village planning and the socioeconomic structure at Beer Resisim, see W. G. Dever, *EI* 18 (1985), pp. 18*–28*.

6. Dever in: *BAT*, pp. 116–21.

7. K. Prag, *Levant* 6 (1974), pp. 69–116; idem, *BASOR* 264 (1986), pp. 61–72; S. Richard, *ADAJ* 26 (1982), pp. 289–99; idem, *Expedition* 28 (1986), pp. 3–12.

8. K. M. Kenyon, *Excavations at Jericho*, vol. 1, London 1960, pp. 180–262; ibid., vol. 2, London, 1965, pp. 33–166; idem, *Digging Up Jericho*, London 1957, pp. 186–209.

9. Lapp (see note 2).

10. C. Epstein, ʿAtiqot 17 (1985), pp. 20–58. However, some dolmens in Transjordan are from the Chalcolithic period and others are now dated to the Early Bronze Age; see K. Yassine, *BASOR* 259 (1985), pp. 63–69.

11. In addition to the general studies mentioned in notes 1–2, see R. Amiran, *IEJ* 10 (1960), pp. 204–25; idem, ʿAtiqot, Hebrew series, 7 (1974), pp. 1–12.

12. R. T. Schaub, *BASOR* 210 (1973), pp. 2–19; Dever, *BASOR* 210 (1973), pp. 37–63.

13. E. D. Oren, *BASOR* 210 (1973), pp. 20–36; M. Tadmor, *IEJ* 28 (1978), pp. 1–30.

14. S. Gitin, *EI* 12 (1975), pp. 46*–62*; W. G. Dever, *EI* 15 (1981), pp. 22*–32*.

15. S. Mazzoni, *BASOR* 257 (1985), pp. 1–18. See also Tadmor (note 13).

16. E. Eisenberg, ʿ*Atiqot* 17 (1985), pp. 59–74; T. Stech-Wheeler, J. D. Muhly, and R. Maddin, ʿ*Atiqot* 17 (1985), pp. 75–82.

17. W. G. Dever and M. Tadmor, *IEJ* 26 (1976), pp. 163–69; R. Maddin and T. Stech-Wheeler, *IEJ* 26 (1976), pp. 170–73.

18. Z. Yeivin, *IEJ* 21 (1971), pp. 78–81; Y. Yadin, *IEJ* 21 (1971), pp. 82–85; R. Grafman, *IEJ* 22 (1972), pp. 47–51; M.-H. Gates, *Levant* 18 (1986), pp. 75–82.

19. B. Mazar, *IEJ* 18 (1968), pp. 65–97 (= Mazar [1986], pp. 1–34). Attempts to start MB IIA at ca. 1950 B.C.E. or even later were based on insufficient data and on the assumption that the wall painting at Beni Hasan in Egypt must have been related to MB I people. See Wright (1961), pp. 87–88 (where the end of EB IV/MB I is dated to 1900 B.C.E.); Kenyon (1979), p. 147 (where the end of the period is placed at 1900 B.C.E. with a margin of error of fifty years). The appearance of ceremonial gold axes of the "eye" type in Middle Kingdom contexts at Byblos appears to contradict the chronology used here, as the Eye Axe is supposed to be replaced by a new type (the "duckbill" axe) during MB IIA, which is claimed to be contemporary with the Middle Kingdom at Egypt. It is possible that ceremonial axes of the "eye" type continued to be produced at Byblos later than the appearance of regular axes of this type in Palestine.

20. K. M. Kenyon, *Amorites and Canaanites*, London 1966, pp. 1–52; Kenyon (1979), pp. 145–47.

21. W. F. Albright, *BASOR* 163 (1961), pp. 36–54.

22. See Lapp (note 2), pp. 86–116; Kochavi (note 2).

23. See the papers by D. L. Esse and W. G. Dever in: *Emmaus Colloquium.*

24. This antidiffusionist way of thinking, perhaps inspired by C. Renfrew's approach to developments in European archaeology, is reflected in the current interpretation of several transitional periods, such as that from the Neolithic to the Chalcolithic era; the transition from the Chalcolithic to EB I; and from the Late Bronze to Iron Age I. See pp. 87, 294, note 53 in this volume.

25. The crisis at the end of EB III, and the discontinuity between the EB III period and the following EB IV/MB I, were emphasized recently by R. Amiran and M. Kochavi in their Hebrew article in *EI* 18 (1985), pp. 361–65.

CHAPTER SIX

MIGHTY CANAANITE CITY-STATES:
The Middle Bronze II Period
(ca. 2000–1550 B.C.E.)

GENERAL OUTLINE

The Middle Bronze Age II (henceforth MB II), spanning some 450 years from ca. 2000 until 1550 B.C.E., began with the revival of urban life in the country—at first on a limited scale, and later more extensively. The result of this process was the establishment of the Canaanite culture, which flourished during most of the second millennium B.C.E. and then gradually disintegrated during the last three centuries of that millennium. The second half of MB II was one of the most prosperous periods in the history of this culture, perhaps even its zenith.

The evolvement of the Middle Bronze Age culture must be seen against the background of the general historical developments in the ancient Near East. The establishment of West Semitic, "Amorite" dynasties in Mesopotamia during the twentieth and nineteenth centuries B.C.E. (the Isin and Larsa period) brought about a constant interchange of ideas and knowledge, political connections, and even kinship relations between Syria and Mesopotamia, which in turn resulted in the extensive international relations of the eighteenth century B.C.E. (see p. 192).

Historical developments in Egypt during this period were also related to the cultural and historical processes in the Levant. MB II corresponded to two periods of entirely different character in the history of Egypt: the Middle Kingdom (Twelfth Dynasty, 1991–1786 B.C.E.) and the Second Intermediate Period (Thirteenth through Seventeenth dynasties, 1786–1567 B.C.E.). While the former was one of the greatest eras in Egyptian history, the latter was a period of gradual decline and inner instability, culminating in a foreign rule in Lower Egypt by the "Hyksos" Fifteenth Dynasty (mid-seventeenth to mid-sixteenth centuries B.C.E.).

Some Egyptian and Mesopotamian texts, as well as a few clay tablets found in Middle Bronze Age levels in Palestine, provide us for the first time with written documentation concerning the country and its population.[1]

THE MIDDLE BRONZE IIA PERIOD
(ca. 2000–1800/1750 B.C.E.)

INTRODUCTION

The first part of MB II was designated by W. F. Albright as "MB IIA" following his excavations at Tell Beit Mirsim, where he discovered two occupation levels (Strata G–F) preceding two other MB II levels (Strata E–D), the latter corresponding to the Hyksos rule in Egypt. This term is maintained by many and will be used in this book, though other scholars (such as K. M. Kenyon, W. G. Dever, E. D. Oren, and P. Gerstenblith) call the same period "Middle Bronze I" as a result of the renaming of the previous period.

In spite of the rich material from MB IIA found during the thirties in the excavations of Megiddo (Strata XIII–XII), Ras el-Ain (Aphek), and Tell el-Ajjul, the period remained relatively unknown and enigmatic. The situation has changed over the last twenty years as a result of a series of excavations and surveys carried out along the coastal plain of Israel, which uncovered an abundance of new material relating to the period.[2]

MB IIA is distinguished by an almost total revolution in all aspects of material culture: settlement pattern, urbanism, architecture, pottery, metallurgy, and burial customs. Basic questions relating to this period are: Who were the people responsible for the appearance of this new culture? How, where, and when did it originate? How long did it last?

SETTLEMENT PATTERN

Excavations and surveys along the coastal plain north of the Yarkon River have shown that large fortified cities were founded in this region during MB IIA. Some of the largest sites are located in the northernmost coastal plain, between the Lebanese border at Rosh Haniqrah and Mount Carmel. Among them are Kabri (located near important springs east of Nahariyah) and Acre, the latter of which was fortified by huge earth ramparts in this period.[3]

A chain of cities and forts was established in the Sharon Plain. Tel Burgah, south of the Carmel ridge, is a 50-acre site which was surrounded by earth ramparts in MB IIA. Somewhat to the west, defending the passage between the Carmel ridge and the seacoast, is the small settlement of Tel Mevorakh.[4] Farther south, at Tel Zeror (east of Hederah), an MB IIA town was defended by an artificial earth rampart, massive brick wall, and rectangular towers; even farther south, at Tell Ifshar ("Tel Hefer"), several occupation levels from MB IIA were detected, though no fortifications were preserved. At Tel Poleg, situated on the western *kurkar* (sandstone) ridge of the central Sharon Plain, MB IIA town fortifications included a brick wall, a glacis and a large rectangular tower. At nearby Khirbet Zureikiyeh, another fortified settlement has been uncovered. One of the most important sites of this period is Aphek—near the springs of Ras el-Ain, the source of the Yarkon River—where a large fortified city flourished during this period. Several occupation levels uncovered at Aphek provide the best stratified sequence for this period.[5]

Most of the aforementioned sites were founded on virgin soil, or in places which had not been occupied for many centuries (such as Aphek, which had been deserted since the end of EB II). The cities were usually situated near rich water sources, in an area which was to a large extent marshy and wooded. Surveys carried out along the coastal plain (particularly those by R. Gophna) have shown that, in addition to the chain of fortified cities and forts, there were also many small sedentary settlements and campsites scattered throughout the region.[6]

The MB IIA settlement in the coastal plain south of the Yarkon River appears to have been less extensive than in the

6.1 MAP OF MIDDLE BRONZE II AND LATE BRONZE AGE EXCAVATED SITES.

Place names in *italics* are ancient names; place names in roman letters are modern names.

north. At Yavneh-Yam, on the coast south of Jaffa, a large square area was surrounded by an earth rampart dated by J. Kaplan to MB IIA.[7] At Tell el-Ajjul—a large mound on the bank of the Gaza Brook south of Gaza—an MB IIA cemetery was found, but the existence of a city during this period has not been verified.[8]

The valleys of Jezreel and Beth-Shean are a natural continuation of the northern coastal plain, connecting the latter with the Jordan Valley. A chain of MB IIA settlements was found along the main East–West route connecting the coastal plain with the Jordan Valley. They include Tel Amar, Yoqneam, Megiddo, and Beth-Shean. Yoqneam and Megiddo were defended by solid city walls. Megiddo Strata XIII–XII designate the gradual growth of an urban center during MB IIA. At Beth-Shean, only a rich tomb from this period indicates occupation, since the mound itself has not been sufficiently excavated.[9] The small mound of Tell el-Hayyat southeast of Beth-Shean (east of the Jordan) was a sedentary village from the MB IIA period with a small temple.[10]

At other inland sites, MB IIA levels are either poor or completely lacking. At Tel Dan, rich finds were found in a tomb which predates the MB IIB earth rampart. The important city of Hazor was only beginning to develop at the end of MB IIA, and it appears that the huge earth ramparts there were constructed during the transition between MB IIA and MB IIB (see later). At Shechem (Tel Balatah), the city was founded in MB IIA; a large structure—perhaps a palace—has been discovered, yet no fortifications from this period have been identified.[11] Tell Beit Mirsim in the inner Shephelah is the only inland site in the south of the country where MB IIA occupation levels have been uncovered; they designate a beginning of urbanization. A city wall may have been constructed at the second phase of this MB IIA town (Stratum F).[12]

We thus have evidence of a wave of MB IIA settlement along the northern coastal plain and along the northern valleys of Israel. Large fortified cities, forts, and rural sedentary settlements were founded. This settlement pattern differs from that known from the Early Bronze Age, when the coastal plain was quite insignificant. The peculiar concentration of population along the northern coastal plain is of crucial

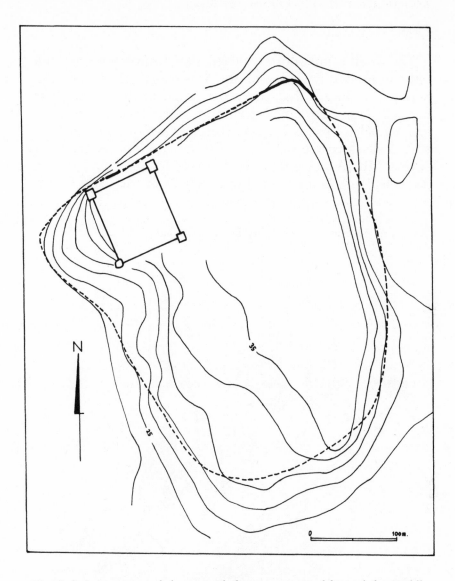

6.2 Aphek: contours of the mound showing assumed line of the Middle Bronze IIA city wall.

importance for understanding the origin of the MB IIA culture and population (see p. 188). The total lack of MB IIA settlements in the northern and central Negev as well as in inland Transjordan demonstrates the cultural break between this period and that of the preceding EB IV/MB I.

FORTIFICATIONS

The small number of excavated sites from MB IIA provide only limited knowledge of the urban architecture of this period. It appears that the cities founded in the northern coastal plain were large—sometimes 25–50 acres in area— and defended by massive fortifications. A new feature of this period was large freestanding earth ramparts which surrounded several MB IIA cities (Acre, Tel Burgah, Tel Zeror, and perhaps Yavneh-Yam). Unlike the modest glacis of the Early Bronze

6.3   Acre: Middle Bronze IIA city gate and rampart.

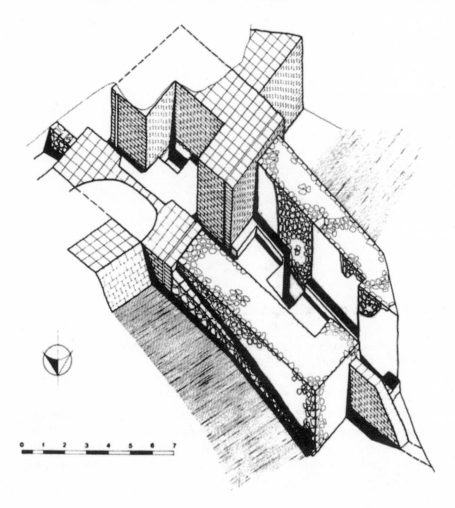

Age, which revetted the front of massive stone or brick city walls, these ramparts were tremendous artificial earthworks which changed the morphology of the site. A prerequisite of their construction would have been a strong central government, capable of organizing sufficient manpower. Similar artificial earth ramparts are known from contemporary northern Syria, particularly at Ebla (Tel Mardikh).[13] In Palestine, they were still rare during this period, but in the following MB IIB phase they became more common.

Other MB IIA cities were defended by solid brick walls, 3–4 m wide, with stone foundations (as at Yoqneam, Megiddo, Tel Poleg, Aphek, and Tell Beit Mirsim). At Tel Poleg, a freestanding brick wall was buttressed by a glacis recalling those of the Early Bronze Age. Rectangular towers were part of these fortification systems at Megiddo, Tel Poleg, and Tel Zeror.

City gates from MB IIA are known from Megiddo and Acre. Both have a long corridorlike approach; at Megiddo the corridor was stepped, and it ended in a gate chamber which necessitated an indirect entrance to the city. Although a "bent axis" was an advantage from the point of view of the defenders, it was inconvenient for chariots or other vehicles. At Acre, the entrance was direct through a long corridor and a gate chamber.[14]

Thus the art of fortification improved considerably during this period and laid the foundation for a further development in urban defenses in the following phase of the Middle Bronze Age.

URBAN ARCHITECTURE

At Aphek, three major phases from this period were distinguished. The first (Pre-Palace phase) marks the beginning of urban life in the city. A few fragmentary dwellings and graves were attributed to it. In the second phase, a large public building, perhaps a palace, was constructed on the northwestern spur of the mound. It included a large courtyard and halls surrounded by massive walls and paved with thick, well-made plaster floors. In the following Post-Palace phase, the palace went out of use, and many graves found in its area may indicate that the center of the town shifted slightly to the east, where later palaces were discovered. At Megiddo, a similar gradual growth of the city can be detected. A well-planned dwelling quarter was constructed in the eastern area of the mound (Area BB), and later, a large palace was erected in the western section of the same area. The sacred area of the Early Bronze Age became now an open cult place, where standing stones (*masebot* in the biblical terminology) stood.[15] A similar open cult area from the same period was found on the coast near Nahariyah.

At Shechem, a large MB IIA urban compound was found under the MB IIB temple. The complex was surrounded by massive thick walls and comprised inner courtyards and large rooms. It was defined by the excavator as a "Courtyard Temple," but in fact it was probably a large civil center, perhaps the residence of the local governor. This discovery can be related to an Egyptian Middle Kingdom inscription mentioning Shechem as the target of a military expedition.

Thus the architectural remains of fortifications, palaces, cult places, and dwellings indicate a consistent evolvement of urban life during MB IIA. The period lasted for a considerable time, as we learn from the several phases of occupation detected at some of the sites.

POTTERY

The cultural break between EB IV/MB I and MB IIA is reflected by the new pottery assemblage.[16] The innovation of the fast potter's wheel resulted in a large variety of new, elegant shapes. Globular jars and jugs, carinated thin bowls, flat large bowls, piriform juglets, and large dipper juglets are characteristic of this period. Most of the shapes are unrelated to those of the previous EB IV/MB I, but some surprisingly recall EB III pottery types which went out of fashion in the EB IV/MB I phase. This interesting phenomenon (pointed out by A. Kempinski) is of importance for tracing the origins of the MB IIA culture.

A hallmark of the pottery of this period is the well-burnished red slip which appears on many of the small vessels. Painted decoration usually includes horizontal bands in black or red.

In some cases more elaborate designs appear, such as triangles outlined in black and filled with red diagonal lines or a net pattern. A similar painting style was practiced in Byblos, as well as in inner Syria along the Orontes Valley. Comparisons have also been made with a painting tradition found in the region of the Habur River in northern Mesopotamia. Painted pottery was found there at the site of Chagar Bazar, in a level preceding that containing written documents from the time

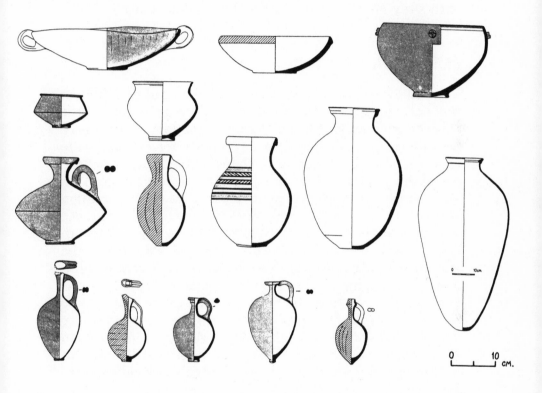

6.4   Selected Middle Bronze IIA pottery from Megiddo and Aphek.

of Shamshi-Adad I, king of Assyria of the late nineteenth century B.C.E. This could be a most important chronological and cultural synchronism; however, the relation between the painted pottery of the Habur region and that of Syria and Palestine is not entirely clear. It was suggested (by J. Tubb) that the similarity is superficial, and that the painting tradition found in Syria and Palestine is independent and unrelated to that of the Habur region.[17] Painted pottery of Levantine origin and other red burnished pottery typical of MB IIA was exported to Tell el-Dab'a (ancient Avaris) in the eastern Delta of Egypt and found there in contexts dated to the end of the Middle Kingdom and of the thirteenth dynasty. Relations with Anatolia are detected in certain pottery forms found in the northern part of the country—particularly red burnished jugs with a rim cut diagonally, and some painted vessels.

METALLURGY

In MB IIA, bronze replaced copper, which had been almost the only metal in use for tools and weapons since the Chalcolithic period. Bronze is an alloy of copper with 5–10 percent tin. It was found to be much stronger than pure copper, and it continued to be the essential metal until the end of the second millennium B.C.E. The nearest source of tin was thought to be Afghanistan. This led to the assumption that bronze manufacture was dependent upon a long-distance trading system. The Mari archive of the early eighteenth century B.C.E. recorded shipments of tin to other cities in the ancient Near East, among them Hazor in the Upper Galilee. Mari's geographic location on the Middle Euphrates was appropriate for an important station on an international trade route dealing in such raw materials. Recent surveys have discovered tin resources in the Taurus Mountains of southern Anatolia close to the border with Syria, but it is still unknown whether these resources were exploited in the Middle Bronze Age.

New types of metal weapons and tools appeared in MB IIA.[18] The typical axehead of the period was the elongated bronze "duckbill" type with two elliptical holes and a shaft for the handle. Evidently it developed from the earlier fenestrated copper axes. The duckbill axehead is found in northern Palestine, Lebanon, and Syria as far north as the Mari region (at the cemetery of Baghuz). Another type of battle-axe has a narrow, chisel-shaped blade, a shaft for the handle, and a notch which enabled one to tie the blade to the handle. This type is found only in Palestine and southern Syria. Shafted

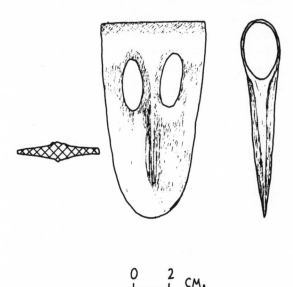

6.5 "Duckbill" axe: a typical Middle Bronze IIA bronze weapon.

0   2
└──┘ CM.

spearheads replaced the older tanged type, and a new dagger had a tang and ridges on the blade. A sickle-shaped sword with a long handle is another elaborate innovation of the period, though rarely found. Duckbill axes, notched axes and shafted spearheads appear also at Tell el-Dabʿa in Egypt, together with MB IIA pottery imported from the Levant, in datable contexts.

The offering deposits and princely tombs of Byblos, dated to the time of the Twelfth Dynasty in Egypt, contained superb examples of ceremonial weapons made of precious gold and silver, and decorated in local style. Some of these decorations are the earliest examples of the second millennium B.C.E. Canaanite art.

RELATIONS WITH EGYPT

The character of the relations between Egypt and Asia during the Middle Kingdom (corresponding to MB IIA) is open to different interpretations due to the nature of the evidence.[19] Egyptian documents relating to Asia are few: the Execration Texts, the Story of Sinuhe, and a few more short references.[20] The earliest text, dated to the first half of the twentieth century B.C.E., is the story of the Egyptian high official Sinuhe, who fled to Asia and found shelter somewhere in Syria, where he became an honorable guest in the court of a local tribal leader. His tale includes a lively description of the country, which appears to have been settled and to have produced rich crops such as barley, olives, wine, honey, and herbs, as well as having good flocks. Yet the population in the area where Sinuhe found refuge was settled in encampments, not in permanent cities or villages; his hosts were perhaps seminomadic pastoralists in a transitional phase to sedentary life. Such a way of life was perhaps common in the early part of MB IIA in the inland parts of the country.

The Execration Texts are three groups of short inscriptions on pottery bowls or figurines which include curses against peoples and places considered hostile to Egypt. These short inscriptions are of the utmost importance, since they contain the earliest known lists of cities, regions, and governors in Palestine and southern Syria. The difference between an earlier group of such texts (dated to around 1900 B.C.E.), and a later one (perhaps about one hundred years later) illustrates the expansion of urbanization in the country. In the earlier collection, only a few cities are mentioned (Jerusalem, Ashkelon, Rehob); most of the names are those of tribes, and in several cases there are two or three leaders or rulers of a tribe or town. The second group includes a longer list of cities, reflecting the emergence of city-states in the country around 1800 B.C.E. Among the names mentioned are Acre, Mishal, and Achshaf in the valley of Acre; Rehob (either the one in the same valley or the one south of Beth-Shean region); 'Iyon, Laish, Hazor, and Qedesh in the Upper Galilee; Shechem and Jerusalem in the central hills; and Ashtaroth, Qanah, and perhaps Maachah in Transjordan. The list does not, however, include major cities such as Gaza and Megiddo, either because they were not considered hostile to Egypt or because the inscriptions are not complete. The Execration Texts do not necessarily demonstrate direct control by Egypt over Palestine, yet they do reflect firsthand knowledge of the country and its peoples.

An additional historical document from the Middle Kingdom is the burial inscription of an Egyptian official named Hu-Sebech from the time of Senusert III (early nineteenth century B.C.E.), which mentions a military invasion of the land of Retenu (the name of Palestine in Egyptian sources) and, in particular, an attack on Shechem (*skmm*).

The wall painting at Beni Hasan (mentioned on p. 166) dating to the sixth year of Senusert II (1890 B.C.E.) depicts a group of Asiatics (*ʿamu*), perhaps metalsmiths, traveling to Egypt, led by a man with the typically West Semitic name of Ab-sha. This painting provides us with important information about the physical appearance of the peoples of Asia at that time: their bearded faces, hairstyle, as well as about their multicolored decorated dress, and weapons. They are shown mounting asses—a practice unknown in Egypt, yet illustrated on a decorated royal dagger from Byblos. The painting is important evidence for the presence of West Semites in Egypt during the Middle Kingdom, either as merchants or as wandering artisans.

Egyptian Middle Kingdom objects found at various sites in Palestine and Syria provide additional evidence of the contacts between these countries. The richest collection of such objects was found in Byblos—the main port from which Lebanese timber was shipped to Egypt, and consequently the gateway for Egyptian influence in the Levant. Egyptian merchants, officials, and ambassadors no doubt passed through this port on their way to inland Palestine and Syria, and they brought with them a stream of Egyptian goods and ideas, to be detected in the emerging Canaanite culture of that time. Egyptian artistic influence is indeed clearly expressed in the local art of Byblos. Other occasional Egyptian artifacts were found throughout the Levant: small statues (including those of officials) and votive sphinxes were uncovered at Tell el-Ajjul, Gezer, Megiddo, and other sites in Palestine, and at Ugarit and Qatna in Syria. An interesting example is that of the statue of Thuthotep found at Megiddo. In the tomb of this high official in Egypt he is shown bringing cattle from Asia (named Retenu). Thus we can conjecture that he was stationed at Megiddo as an Egyptian agent dealing with the shipment of cattle and other goods to Egypt. Egyptian scarab seals of the Twelfth Dynasty, including stamps with names of pharaohs, were also found in Palestine and Syria.

The excavations at Tell el-Dabʿa have revealed abundant evidence for connections with the Levant. MB IIA pottery and weapons typical to Palestine found there probably originated from southern Palestine, as shown by Neutron-Activation analysis. Many of the vessels were store jars which were used for transporting wine, olive oil and other agricultural products from Canaan to Egypt. The MB IIA finds were found in context of strata G and F, dated to the time of the late Twelfth Dynasty (nineteenth century B.C.E.) and Thirteenth Dynasty (first half of eighteenth century B.C.E.). M. Bietak explains these finds as evidence of the presence of Canaanite soldiers, metalsmiths and other artisans in Egypt at that time. Thus the finds at Tell el-Dab'a add an additional dimension to the relations between Egypt and Canaan at the end of the Middle Kingdom: there were strong trade relations as well as immigration of Canaanites to the Delta region. This phenomenon will eventually lead to the rise of the Hyksos rule in Egypt at the following period.

There must have been a great deal of Egyptian activity and interest in the Levant, but its extent in Palestine is disputable. Few scholars believe in a direct Egyptian rule in Palestine like that of the time of the New Kingdom. The majority maintains that the relations with the emerging Canaanite city-states were only commercial and diplomatic, and that at most the Egyptians may have maintained trading posts in Asia.[21]

THE ORIGIN OF THE MIDDLE BRONZE IIA CULTURE

The material culture of MB IIA appeared in the coastal plain of Palestine in a crystallized form. One cannot follow any gradual evolution from EB IV/MB I to MB IIA. The difference between the two periods is distinct, and the transition from one to the other is one of the most clear-cut in the history of Palestine. We thus must assume that the new culture appeared in the northern coastal plain of Israel as a result of an immigration from farther north. Later, the new culture spread to the south and east, and it eventually evolved into the MB IIB civilization of Palestine.

The origin of the MB IIA culture can be traced to the coastal plain of Lebanon and Syria, where there was almost no cultural break between the Early Bronze and Middle Bronze ages. This continuation between the third and second millennia B.C.E.

is particularly evident at Byblos. The Temple of the Obelisks there contained numerous MB IIA finds; it was built on top of an Early Bronze Age temple according to the same outer contours, thus demonstrating urban continuity between the two periods. The rich finds from this temple, as well as abundant offering deposits found in the so-called Field of Offerings, clearly demonstrate the wealth of culture at Byblos ca. 2000 B.C.E. Similarities between the Byblian civilization and that of MB IIA Palestine point to the former as being the most probable source of the new culture. We may assume that the narrow Lebanese coast was overpopulated during this period, and it would have been natural for the surplus population to move southward to the empty northern coast of Palestine.

Another possible origin may have been inner northern Syria (the Orontes Valley), where rich urban life flourished at cities such as Ebla and Hama in the early centuries of the second millennium B.C.E. Earth ramparts, gates, and temple plans in this region recall types characteristic of the later MB IIB period in Palestine. The MB IIA painted pottery also hints at traditions common to inner Syria, Byblos, and Palestine. We may conjecture that a stream of ideas and population from both the Lebanese coast and inner Syria flowed southward, but it appears that the coastal groups were the immediate responsibles for the establishment of the MB IIA culture in Palestine.[22]

Judging from the forms of personal names which appear in the Egyptian documents mentioned earlier, in the royal cemetery of Byblos, and in the Mari archive of the early eighteenth century B.C.E., we can infer that the population of Syria and Palestine was West Semitic, "Amorite." The term "Canaanite" appears for the first time in one of the documents of Mari, and it perhaps designates a certain part of the population of the Levant. In fact the "Amorite" personal names were very close to Canaanite ones of the later centuries. The MB IIA material culture may thus be seen as the beginning of the Canaanite civilization of the second millennium B.C.E.

CHRONOLOGY

Since W. F. Albright first determined a subdivision of and terminology for the MB II period, there has been much debate concerning the chronology of the MB IIA phase. Albright based his chronology on finds from Byblos, particularly from the royal tombs there. The earliest of these tombs could be dated by Egyptian finds to the second half of the Twelfth Dynasty in Egypt, that is, to the nineteenth century B.C.E. Accordingly, a date between 1900 and 1750 B.C.E. was suggested for MB IIA by Albright, who was followed by G. E. Wright. In later publications, Albright proposed a shorter duration of a mere fifty years for MB IIA, (1800–1750 B.C.E.), parallel to most of the Thirteenth Dynasty in Egypt thus extending the length of the preceding period to almost half a millennium. K. M. Kenyon adopted a similar short duration for MB IIA (her MB I), but she dated it from 1950 or 1900 B.C.E. until 1850 B.C.E.[23]

In 1968 B. Mazar has suggested that MB IIA must have covered the entire Middle Kingdom in Egypt, namely ca. 2000–1800 B.C.E. (for this later date, see p. 194). The several phases of MB IIA occupation levels detected at various sites necessitate a considerable time span; the Egyptian objects of the Middle Kingdom must have been brought to an urbanized country, and not to a seminomadic population such as that which existed during the previous period. Furthermore, EB IV/MB I could not have been as long as indicated by Albright's and Kenyon's low dating of MB IIA. The dates 2000–1800 B.C.E. seemed to settle most of the difficulties concerning the beginning and the end of the period.[24] However, the discoveries at Tell el-Dabʿa led M. Bietak to return to a low chronology for our period. MB IIA finds of Canaanite origin were detected at Tell el-Dabʿa in contexts dated to the latter part of the Twelfth Dynasty in Egypt—i.e. to the nineteenth century B.C.E. as well as to the Thirteenth Dynasty, which lasted 150 years between ca. 1786 and 1633 B.C.E. Furthermore, Canaanite pottery groups which were considered transitional between MB IIA and MB IIB were dated to the latter part of the Thirteenth Dynasty. Thus Bietak suggested to start the MB IIA ca. 1900 B.C.E. and to end it ca. 1710 B.C.E.[25] This low chronology raises many difficulties for archaeologists of Palestine. If accepted, it will create difficulties in correlation with Mesopotamian chronology and cause the abandonment of the Mesopotamian "Middle Chronology" which is considered the most acceptable by many scholars. The finds at Tell el-Dab'a appear to be crucial for dating the MB IIA in Palestine, but it appears that Bietak's view is too extreme. It seems to us that there is still insufficient data from Egypt concerning the beginning of MB IIA, and that the determination of the end of the period depends on exact definition of pottery groups which are denoted "transitional MB IIA/MB IIB." As the transition between MB IIA and MB IIB was a smooth and slow process of cultural development unaccompanied by a cultural crisis, the dating of this transition is hard to establish. A date between 1800 and 1750 seems to us feasible (see also p. 195).

THE MIDDLE BRONZE IIB–C
(ca. 1800/1750–1550 B.C.E.)

INTRODUCTION

The transition from MB IIA to MB IIB was a rather smooth and peaceful cultural development. Cities and rural settlements which were established in the new phase, in all parts of the country, witness a considerable population growth. The international political situation was conducive to a floruit in the Canaanite culture of Syria-Palestine. In Egypt, there was a decline following the Twelfth Dynasty. The pharaohs of the Thirteenth Dynasty still maintained some relations with the Levant, as evidenced by scarabs and inscriptions found at Byblos, at Ebla, and elsewhere. Yet the glory of the Middle Kingdom was over, and soon Egypt entered a period of weakness and instability known as the "Second Intermediate Period." The term "Hyksos" was used by Manetho, the Hellenistic Egyptian historian, to designate the foreign rulers of Lower Egypt (the Delta region) at that time. In fact, the name originated from the two Egyptian words *hekau khasut*, "foreign rulers." These foreigners were Canaanites who settled in the eastern Delta and founded a local dynasty, designated as the Fifteenth Dynasty in Egyptian history. Their capital was Avaris (biblical Zoan), identified with Tell el-Dab'a, where excavations have revealed a huge city with a material culture almost identical to that of MB IIB in Palestine and Syria.

The historical development in northern Syria is known to us mainly from the Mari archive as well as from the documents found at Alalakh (Tell Atchana in the Amuq Valley) Stratum VII (seventeenth century B.C.E.). These texts submit a general picture of the cultural and historical environment throughout the Fertile Crescent at their time. Expansion of "Amorite," West Semitic tribes from Syria into Mesopotamia continued from the beginning of the second millennium B.C.E., resulting in the establishment of West Semitic, "Amorite" kingdoms throughout Syria and Mesopotamia. Much of the Mesopotamian cultural heritage was adopted by these tribes, both in Mesopotamia and in northern Syria.

During the time of the Mari archive, a political status quo existed between the "Amorite" kingdoms of Babylon, Larsa, and Eshnunna in southern Mesopotamia, Assyria and Mari in northern Mesopotamia, Yamhad in northern Syria, Qatna in central Syria, and Hazor in the Upper Galilee. The whole northern part of the Fertile Crescent was thus integrated during this period by West Semitic hegemony. Yet soon competition between the main political centers eventuated in power struggles, finally resulting in the rise of Hammurapi, king of Babylon, who established an empire which lasted until the Hittite raid on Babylon (1595 B.C.E. according to the "Middle Chronology").[26]

During the latter part of the Middle Bronze Age new ethnic groups came to the fore. The Hurrians, who had been known in northern Mesopotamia since the third millennium B.C.E., increased in number and became an important factor there and in northern Syria. Some of them reached Palestine and assimilated into the Canaanite population, as evidenced by some Hurrian names on a cuneiform tablet found in Gezer. The Hittites, an Indo-European people, established themselves in eastern Anatolia, and during the seventeenth century B.C.E. they were strong enough to devastate the kingdom of Yamhad, including Alalakh, in 1630 B.C.E. and Babylon in 1595 B.C.E. Yet in Palestine, it appears that there was no real turmoil throughout the MB IIB period. Even the expulsion of the Hyksos from Egypt and the rise of the Eighteenth Dynasty did not bring in its wake a cultural break in Canaan, except for the destruction of cities in the southern part of the country.

SUBPHASING AND CHRONOLOGY

The continuous cultural development throughout the second millennium B.C.E. makes the definition of subphases, and the transitions between them, a difficult task. In the case of MB II, the difficulties exist in regard to both the beginning and the end of the period. The transition from MB IIA to MB IIB was gradual and cannot be easily pinpointed. A good number of pottery types and decoration techniques had a long duration and may be attributed both to the end of MB IIA and to early MB IIB.[27] As a result, special terms such as "Transitional MB IIA–MB IIB" were given to some eighteenth century B.C.E. tomb groups.[28]

W. F. Albright and G. E. Wright divided the period into two major subphases, denoting them "MB IIB" and "MB IIC," the latter comprising the last hundred years of the period. This subdivision is mainly based on refined ceramic typology and the relative sequence of phases, particularly at Shechem and at Gezer.[29] The definition of such subphases is valuable in the precise archaeological investigation of the period, but one should take into account the difficulties in making distinctions when dealing with a long period during which cultural changes were gradual and slow. In such a case, regional differences are sometimes easier to identify than chronological changes.

In a study of the rich MB IIB–C cemeteries at Jericho, K. M. Kenyon divided the tombs into five successive groups (I–V) representing gradual changes in the pottery assemblages at this site. A review of this subdivision shows that the changes are slow, and that there is much overlapping—though Groups I–II, of the early MB II period, are distinct from Groups IV–V, of the later part of that period. Thus, there is evidence for the existence of earlier and later assemblages in this period. In this chapter, however, we will discuss the entire MB IIB–C period as one unit.

The absolute chronology of the beginning and the end of MB IIB–C depends on correlations to Egyptian and Mesopotamian chronologies. A crucial chronological problem concerning the beginning of MB IIB is the correlation between the finds at Hazor and the mention of this city in the Mari archive. In several documents from this archive Hazor appears to be one of the most important cities in the ancient Near East. We must assume that the texts refer to the huge city of Hazor, including the Lower City. The definition of the archaeological phase in which the Lower City at Hazor was founded is thus essential, since its establishment should not postdate the time of the Mari Archive. Y. Yadin dated the foundation of this Lower City (Stratum XVII) to MB IIB. In fact, the pottery from the earliest phases as well as from a rich tomb from this period (mentioned in note 27) fits a date in the earliest stage of MB IIB, which could be defined also as "transitional MB IIA–MB IIB." This stage can thus be correlated to the time of the Mari Archive.

The date of the Mari archive in turn can be fixed by correlation to the reign of Hammurapi of Babylon, since the latter destroyed Mari in his thirty-sixth year. Alas, the date of this king's reign is controversial. Four different dates have been suggested for his accession to the throne: 1900, 1848, 1792 and 1728 B.C.E., based on different interpretations of astronomical observations of the star Venus known from the time of Ammisaduqa, one of Hammurapi's successors.[30] Of these chronologies, the third one is most commonly accepted by scholars and is known as the Middle Chronology. Accordingly, Mari was destroyed in the year 1756 B.C.E., and the Mari Archive must be dated to the first half of the eighteenth century B.C.E. We then conclude that the large city at Hazor was founded ca. 1800 B.C.E., and that the transition between MB IIA and MB IIB should be dated to around that time. Albright, however, followed by Yadin, used the lower Mesopotamian chronology; he thus suggested a date ca. 1750 B.C.E. for the beginning of MB IIB, conforming with his views concerning the correlation between the finds in the royal tombs at Byblos and Egyptian and Mesopotamian chronologies.[31]

Another important chronological pivot is the correlation between finds in Palestine and the history of the Hyksos in Egypt. Scarabs with names of pharaohs and high officials of the Fifteenth ("Hyksos") Dynasty were found at several sites in Palestine. The largest numbers of such scarabs was found at Tell el-Ajjul (perhaps Sharuhen), which must have been in close relations with the Hyksos rulers (it has even been suggested that Tell el-Ajjul was considered part of the Hyksos kingdom). Other Hyksos royal scarabs were found at Tell el-Far'ah (south), Jericho, Gezer, Lachish and a few other sites. These scarabs provide a chronological link between MB IIC contexts in Palestine and the time of the Fifteenth Dynasty in Egypt.[32]

Avaris, the Hyksos capital, was probably founded between 1720 and 1700 B.C.E., as can be deduced from the "four hundred years" stele, a memorial stele mentioning that Seti I, before he became Pharaoh, commemorated four hundredth anniversary to the god Seth, the main god of Avaris. The excavator of Avaris (Tell el-Dab'a), M. Bietak, suggested extremely low dates for MB IIB–C in Palestine.[33] His conclusions are based mainly on the finds of MB IIA material culture in contexts of the Thirteenth Dynasty at Tell el-Dab'a and the correlation of the MB IIC material culture of Palestine with the Hyksos Fifteenth Dynasty in Egypt. The dates used by Bietak (following several German Egyptologists) for this dynasty are 1650–1541 (the fall of Avaris was in the eleventh year of Ahmose, whose first year according to this method is 1552 B.C.E.). The date suggested by Bietak for the transition between MB IIA and MB IIB is 1720 and from MB IIB to MB IIC is 1570 B.C.E. This Low Chronology was severely attacked by W. G. Dever. It indeed contradicts the correlations between the Mesopotamian Middle Chronology and the archaeology of the Levant, particularly the correlation between the foundation of the Lower City at Hazor (early MB IIB) and the time of the archive of Mari (first half of the eighteenth century B.C.E.). But if one uses the Low Chronology for Mesopotamia, the chronology suggested by Bietak may be basically accepted, though even then his dates for the transitions between MB IIA to MB IIB and between MB IIB to MB IIC should be raised by twenty to thirty years.

It appears to me that a general division of the entire MB II period into three phases (A, B, C) is well documented on the basis of stratigraphy, pottery typology, and development of other artifacts. The first phase, MB IIA, can be correlated with the Twelfth and perhaps the first fifty years of the Thirteenth Dynasty (until 1800 or 1750 B.C.E.). The second phase—MB IIB—can be correlated with the rest of the Thirteenth Dynasty (until 1650 B.C.E.) and the third phase—MB IIC correlates with the Hyksos Fifteenth Dynasty (until 1540).

Table 4. Comparative Stratigraphy of Middle Bronze Age Sites

SITES	MB IIA ("MB I") ca. 2000 B.C.E. – 1800/1750 B.C.E.	MB IIB ("MB II") – 1650 B.C.E.	MB IIC "(MB III)"* – 1550 B.C.E.
Egypt	Dynasty 12	Dynasty 13	Second Intermediate Age "Hyksos"
Dan	tomb	walled city	
Hazor	——	XVII	XVI
Kabri	5 4	3	
Acre	rampart & gate ————————————————→		
Megiddo	XIVA XIII XII	XI	X
Beth-Shean	tomb	Xb	Xa
Shechem (Tel Balatah)	XXII XXI	XX→XVII	XVI XV
Tel Zeror	walled city	——	
Tel Poleg	walled city	——	
Aphek	walled city $X_{20}→X_{17}$	X_{16}	X_{15}
Shiloh	——	walled town	
Jerusalem (City of David)	——	18–17	
Jericho	——	groups I–II	group III groups IV–V
Gezer	XXII	XXI XX	XIX XVIII
Beth-Shemesh	——		V
Tel Batash	——	XII	XI X
Lachish	——		palace, rampart
Tell Beit-Mirsim	G F	$E_{1–2}$	D
Tel Nagila	——	fortified city	
Tel el-Ajjul	"courtyard cemetery"	city I	city II
Tell el-Farʿah (South)	——	fortified city	
Tel Masos	——	IV	
Tel Malhata	——	fortified city	

*Alternative term, following K. Kenyan, W. G. Dever, etc.

SETTLEMENT PATTERN

MB IIB–C was a period of increased settlement and urban growth throughout the country. Great fortification systems were the products of the social organization, centralized authority in the cities, and rivalry between the various city-states.

The foundation of the Lower City at Hazor around 1800 B.C.E. was one of the most important phenomena of this period;[34] Hazor is a superb example of grand-scale town planning. Its total area (Upper and Lower City), almost 200 acres, was unrivaled in the history of Palestine, and it was to remain the largest city in the country until the thirteenth century B.C.E. Hazor's special status is reflected in the biblical words concerning this city: "Beforetime the head of all these kingdoms" (Joshua 11:10).

Many other fortified cities throughout the country created the network of Canaanite cities which is known to us to a large extent from Egyptian documents of the Late Bronze Age. The main cities in the Upper Galilee were Hazor and Dan; in the northern valleys Kabri, Acre, Yoqneam, Megiddo, Taanach, and Beth-Shean—as well as yet unexcavated sites such as Tel Shimron and Rehob; along the coastal plain and in Philistia, Aphek, Tel Gerisa, Jaffa, Tel Poran, Tel Nagila, and Tell el-Ajjul. Ashdod and Tel Mor were founded toward the end of the period. Some of the earlier MB IIA cities in this region were, however, abandoned (Tel Burgah, Tel Zeror, "Tel Hefer"). In the Shephelah, the main cities were Gezer, Tel Batash (biblical Timnah), Beth-Shemesh, Lachish and Tell Beit Mirsim. In the central hills region Shechem, Tell el-Farʿah (north), Shiloh, Tell Sheikh Abu-Zarad (biblical Tappuah), Bethel, Gibeon, Jerusalem, Beth-Zur and Hebron (Tell er-Rumeideh). In the Jordan Valley an important city was at Jericho. The southernmost line of MB IIB–C cities was in the northern Negev, along the Beer-sheba and Gaza brooks: Tel Malhata, Tel Masos, Tell el-Farʿah (south). In Transjordan, our knowledge of the Middle Bronze Age is still limited, yet fortified cities are reported to have been found at Amman, Sahab (southeast of Amman), and Tell Safut (northwest of Amman).

In addition to the fortified cities, there were also many

small rural settlements. In surveys of the central hill country, hundreds of the latter were revealed to have existed in the Middle Bronze Age, only to be abandoned in the following Late Bronze period. A large site of this type was excavated along the valley of Rephaim, west of Jerusalem, where a previous EB IV/MB I settlement existed. This site comprised several dozen acres of built-up area on terraces extending around the slopes close to the brook bed, without any defenses.[35] Another village was excavated at Givat Sharet, on top of a hill southeast of Beth-Shemesh. These sites give us some idea of the substantial rural activity in this period.

Cemeteries and single burial caves are found in different parts of the country far from any settlement site, indicating that they belonged to a pastoral, seminomadic population. An example is the cemetery at Efrat, south of Bethlehem, where a number of MB IIB burial caves were found on a remote ridge; no contemporary settlement has been detected nearby, though the example of the valley of Rephaim shows that such settlements are sometimes hidden below later agricultural terraces.

FORTIFICATIONS

Ramparts and Glacis   During the eighteenth and seventeenth centuries B.C.E. the art of fortification reached a level of unparalleled sophistication. Tremendous efforts were invested by the Middle Bronze Age urban communities to defend their cities utilizing techniques which were by now widespread throughout the entire Levant. The idea was to surround the city with steep artificial slopes which will raise the level of the city wall high above the surrounding area and locate it as far as possible from the foot of the slope so that siege devices such as battering rams, ladders, and tunneling methods would not be effective.[36] Two major types of fortifications were adopted, both of which were intended to achieve the same effect: the earth rampart and the glacis.

Earth ramparts were constructed already in MB IIA at a few of the cities on the northern coastal plain (see p. 180). In MB IIB they became a common feature at new urban centers which were founded on shallow topography, such as Hazor (the Lower City), Dan, Kabri, Tel Mevorakh, Dor, Shechem, Tel Batash (Timnah), Ashkelon, and Tel Masos (in the northern

6.6 Hazor: vertical air view of the site; note the earth rampart along the edges.

Negev). The huge earth ramparts were erected by dumping large quantities of earth, sometimes on both sides of a central vertical core which served as a foundation for a freestanding city wall. At Hazor and Dan, the core wall was about 8–10 m wide and ca. 10 m high. In several cases there was a stone revetment wall at the foot of the rampart (as at Yavneh-Yam). The material used for the construction of the ramparts may have originated in a moat at its front, as at Hazor and perhaps at Tel Batash.

The ramparts tended to be built in geometric shapes. At Hazor, they have a generally rectangular appearance, and projections on the east were built at right angles to the main rectangle. At Yavneh-Yam, the preserved eastern part of the rampart is rectangular in shape, and at Tel Batash the rampart is an exact square (200 × 200 m at its base), oriented to the compass points.

6.7 Dan: air view. The Middle Bronze earth rampart shaped the steep slopes of the mound.

The creation of the rampart usually resulted in a huge crater, inside which the city developed. A variation of this phenomenon is found at Shechem (Tel Balatah), where the usual rampart with a stone retaining wall was replaced in the last phase of the period (MB IIC) by a huge retaining wall (still standing to a height of 8 m) behind which was a massive artificial fill.[37]

Similar earth ramparts are known in Syria: at Carchemish on the Upper Euphrates, at Ebla (Tell Mardikh), at Qatna in the middle Orontes Valley, and at Tell Sefinet Nuh north of Damascus. Some of these ramparts were huge: at Ebla the rampart surrounds an area of almost 150 acres; at Qatna it circumvents 250 acres. Only the site of Hazor with its 200 acres can rival these large Syrian cities.

It appears that the practice of constructing such ramparts was born in north Syria early in the second millennium B.C.E.

6.8   Tel Batash: air view. The Middle Bronze rampart creating the square form of the mound was constructed on a flat alluvial plain.

Those of Ebla were dated to the twentieth and nineteenth centuries B.C.E., contemporary with MB IIA in Palestine, from which time the earliest examples on Palestine's northern coastal plain date. Other ramparts, such as those at Hazor and Dan, were most probably erected in an early phase of MB IIB, ca. 1800 B.C.E. It thus appears that the ramparts were a characteristic feature of MB IIA and early MB IIB throughout the Levant; the main period of their construction was perhaps during the nineteenth and eighteenth centuries B.C.E.

Ramparts are also known at Tell el-Yehudiyeh and Heliopolis in the eastern Delta of Egypt, and they were considered to be a typical Hyksos fortification, originating in the culture of Syria-Palestine.[38]

The other type of MB IIB fortification is the glacis, or the artificial slope created by dumping compact earth (*terre pisée*) on an existing mound or hill. The glacis is in fact a rampart lacking the inner slope and core. These artificial solid steep slopes were slanted at an average of 30 degrees and they produced the same effect as the outer faces of the earth ramparts. Such glacis are known in particular from the Valley of Jezreel southwards, at such sites as Taanach (?); Megiddo (?); Shiloh; Tel Gerisa; Jaffa; Gezer; Jericho; Lachish; Tel Nagila; Tel Malhata (?); Tell el-Farʿah (south); and Tell el-Ajjul. They may have been very massive, and several methods were used to prevent erosion of the earth fills. At Gezer, for example, alternating bonded strata of earlier occupation debris and layers of chalk chips created the artificial slope. At Jericho, three layers of earth were interpreted by Kenyon as different phases of the glacis, but it appears that they merely represent a constructional method intended to strengthen the earthwork. At Tel Gerisa, layers of bricks were used to stabilize the slope. At Shiloh, retaining walls supported a huge earth and lime glacis. The outer slope was usually covered by a coat of lime, thus creating a smooth steep surface. At the foot of the slope there were sometimes stone retaining walls, such as at Jericho. Unlike the earth ramparts, the glacis appears to have been rare in Syria; one possible example is the earthwork found at Alalakh Stratum VII, dating to the seventeenth century B.C.E.

As we have seen, earth glacis were known already in the Early Bronze Age. The MB IIA glacis at Tel Poleg, the only one known from that period, recalls Early Bronze Age examples

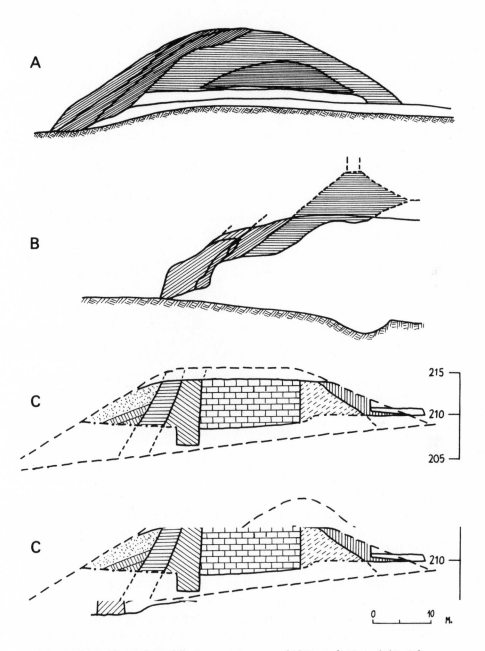

6.9   Sections through Middle Bronze ramparts: (A) Yavneh-Yam; (B) Jericho;
(C) Hazor; (D) Shechem
    (A: retaining wall of second Middle Bronze II rampart; B: fill of second Middle
Bronze II rampart; C: retaining wall of first Middle Bronze II rampart; D: inner
wall; E: wall of temple; F: reconstructed contour of first rampart).

6.10 Gezer: detail of the glacis, showing alternating layers of crushed limestone and occupation debris abutting a stone wall of a large tower.

in size and construction, but the MB IIB–C glacis are much larger than their prototypes and recall the freestanding earth ramparts, which do not have Early Bronze Age precedents. The possible connection between the Early Bronze and the Middle Bronze glacis is still an open question.[39] It thus appears that the peculiar defense systems of MB II comprised a combination of two traditions: The freestanding earth ramparts originated in north Syria in the early second millennium B.C.E. and reached the northern coastal area of Palestine in MB IIA, spreading to inland Palestine early in the eighteenth century B.C.E. This method was adapted during MB IIB–C to the existing mounds of Palestine where the technique of constructing earth glacis to support the city walls was known since the Early Bronze Age.

6.11 Shiloh: earth glacis and core wall of the Middle Bronze fortifications.

The effect of the earth ramparts and glacis on the shape of sites was tremendous and is visible to this day in the steep inclination and regular shape of many mounds in Palestine.

City Gates A new type of city gate was introduced during MB IIB–C. It was a rectangular, symmetrical, large gatehouse composed of two massive towers flanking an elongated passage; the passage was divided by three pairs of pilasters into two guard chambers. The towers usually had inner guardrooms and staircases leading to the second floor, which roofed the central passage. This type of gate demonstrates the architectural fashion common to both Syria and Palestine in this period. It appeared for the first time at Ebla, where it is dated to MB IIA; later Syrian examples are known from Alalakh Stratum VII, Qatna, and Carchemish. In Palestine, such gates were found at Hazor, Megiddo, Shechem, Gezer, Beth-Shemesh, Yavneh-Yam, and Tell el-Far'ah (south).[40] In Syria, large well-cut slabs of stone—known as "orthostats"—strengthened and decorated the lower part of the walls inside the gate passage. These orthostats became a common feature in Syrian architecture from then on, but in Palestine they were utilized on a limited scale (in both the gates of Gezer and Shechem, orthostats were only employed for constructing the pilasters

6.12 Selected plans of Middle Bronze IIB–C gates: (A) Gezer; (B) Hazor; (C) Yavneh-Yam; (D) Shechem.

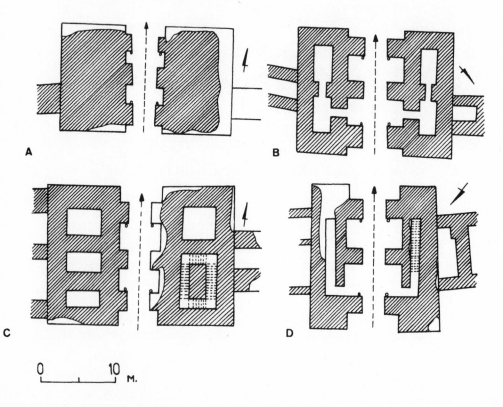

at the gate passage). When the gates were locked—by heavy wooden doors fixed between the two innermost and outermost pilasters—the structure could function as an independent defensible fort.

A smaller variation is the gate with only two pairs of pilasters, creating one guard chamber. Examples are the MB IIA gate at Acre, the eastern gate of Shechem (constructed probably at the end of the MB II period), and that of Dan.[41] The last was superbly preserved up to roof level, probably due to the fact that it went out of use shortly after its erection and was covered by the earth rampart. Brick arches supporting the roof of its passage are the only known examples of such a structure from the Bronze Age Levant.

The wide and straight gate passages and the wide ramps leading to them indicate that the MB II gates were intended to provide easy access to the cities for chariots and other wheeled carts. Battle chariots are thought to have been

6.13 A Middle Bronze IIB gate at Dan. Unique brick-built arches were preserved, perhaps because the gate structure went out of use and was buried under a later phase of the earth rampart.

introduced into Egypt by the Hyksos, and therefore chariots must have been well known in western Asia during the first half of the second millennium B.C.E.

The fortification systems of MB II reflect a period of great wealth and strong self-government in Syria and Palestine. As in the Early Bronze Age, it appears that these huge fortifications were intended to defend the city-states against each other. The capture of Mari by Shamshi-Aadad I, king of Assyria, and Hammurapi's many conquests are examples of the constant warfare among the "Amorite" states. This rivalry—as well as the introduction of new techniques of warfare, such as the battering ram and war chariots—led to the development of these new types of fortifications and city gates.

URBAN ARCHITECTURE

City Plan and Dwellings　The concepts of town planning in Middle Bronze cities are insufficiently known due to lack of wide-scale excavations in any one city. However, when combining the information from various sites, we get an impression of a high degree of urban planning prevailing in these cities. Public buildings were designed on a large scale and built in excellent technique, involving wide stone socles with plastered mud-brick superstructure. Paved streets built at right angles to one another and wide piazzas are evidence of planning by central authorities. At Shechem and Megiddo, areas of public buildings included a large palace and a monumental, freestanding temple located near the palace. Similar planning is known in northern Syria (at Alalakh and Ebla). At Shechem the public area was close to the city wall and the city gate; a large open piazza was located inside the gate, and rooms along the city wall were perhaps barracks. One of the structures near the gate was perhaps a second temple attached to the royal quarter. At Megiddo the huge palace was located near the sacred area, at the eastern part of the mound, away from the city gate. Evidence for planned urban pattern can also be seen at Kabri, Aphek, Gezer, and Tell el-Ajjul. There is thus sufficient evidence for a high degree of urban planning, with royal and sacred quarters, and dwelling quarters.

Dwelling quarters excavated at Megiddo, at Tel Nagila, at

Tell el-Ajjul, and even at a small village near Beth-Shemesh illustrate some principles of orthogonal town planning. At Megiddo, the dwelling quarter founded during MB IIA was changed several times during MB IIB–C (Strata XI–X), yet the basic layout of the area was retained: parallel streets enclosed square or rectangular blocks of dwellings. Tell el-Ajjul City II is a well-preserved example of a city from the end of the MB II period. Long streets divided the city into several quarters, each containing wealthy, multichambered houses. The houses in most of these sites included a small central courtyard surrounded by several rooms; this typical Mediterranean house appeared in Palestine for the first time during this period.

Palaces MB IIB–C palaces were discovered at Kabri, Megiddo, Aphek, Lachish, Tell el-Ajjul, and perhaps Hazor; however, none have been completely excavated. These were huge architectural complexes, some over 1,000 sq m in area, including large courtyards surrounded by halls, and various rooms. At Lachish and Tell el-Ajjul orthostats were found embedded in the lower part of massive plastered brick walls, exhibiting some Syrian influence.[42] At Aphek, a partly excavated MB IIB palace demonstrates the magnitude of these buildings. A wing of this palace, comprising some 1,000 sq m, included a large hall with a monumental entrance; the roof was supported by two pillars, the bases of which were

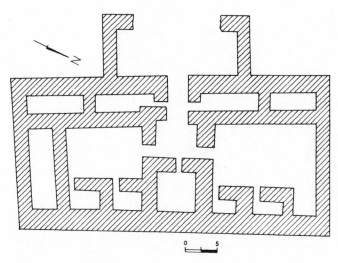

6.14 Middle Bronze IIB–C palace at Hazor (Stratum XVI); reconstructed plan.

1.8 m in diameter; the floor of the hall was covered with a layer of hard, compact plaster almost 0.25 m thick; and the foundations of the walls were 2 m deep. The palaces of Megiddo Stratum XI and Tell el-Ajjul City II contained spacious courtyards surrounded by rooms. At Kabri a large palace was elaborately decorated with painted floors in a technique recalling contemporary Minoan palace decorations known from Crete.[43] A huge architectural complex (23 × 46 m) at Hazor (Area F) was probably a large palace (though Yadin interpreted it as a double temple). It contained two attached square units, each with a central courtyard enclosed on all sides by large rooms. Tunnels below this building led to subterranean chambers which may have been royal tombs (p. 214).

The partially preserved palaces of MB II Palestine might have been similar to contemporary palaces in Syria, known

6.15 Aphek: a wing of a monumental Middle Bronze IIB palace (isometric view).

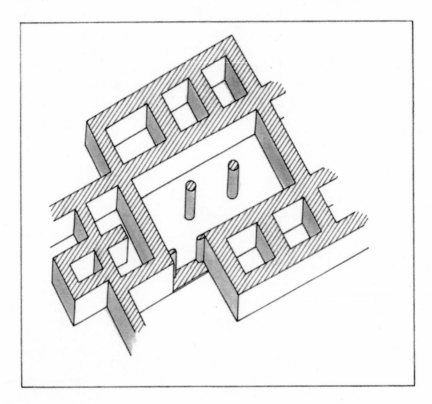

from Alalakh (Stratum VII), Ebla, and Tilmen Huyuk (the last located beyond the border of modern Turkey). Large courtyards and halls, porticoes, and the extensive use of orthostats along the walls are the characteristics of these Syrian palaces. The palace of Mari—the largest, most elaborate, and best-known residence of "Amorite" rulers from this period—was designed on a much larger scale recalling in its plan and design Mesopotamian principles of palace architecture. The palaces of Palestine and Syria are thus evidence of the prosperity and wealth of the local independent city rulers of the region during MB II.

Temples   The temple architecture of MB IIB–C is one of the best expressions of the architectural and perhaps religious uniformity which prevailed throughout the Levant at the time. Temples at Ebla, Alalakh, Ras Shamra (Ugarit), Hazor, Megiddo, Shechem, Tell el-Hayyat and Tel Kitan (in the Jordan Valley), as well as at Tell el-Dabʿa (Avaris) in the eastern Delta, show similarities in planning and design.[44] All of them were monumental rectangular or square buildings, with thick walls indicating considerable height. They com-

6.16   Plans of Middle Bronze Age temples: (A) Shechem; (B) Megiddo; (C) Hazor, Area H.

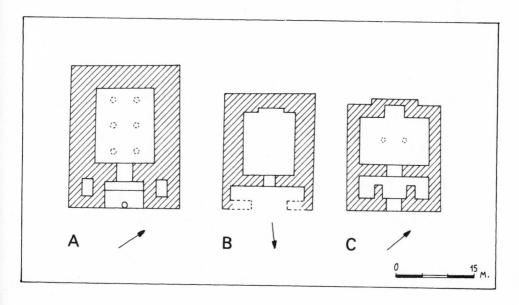

prise one major hall in which the Holy of Holies was located opposite the entrance.

The simplest temple (exemplified at Ebla and at Hazor Area A) includes just one rectangular hall—a long room—with a niche or a dais as a Holy of Holies. A more elaborate type has an entrance chamber in front of the main hall; examples include a second temple at Ebla and the temples at Alalakh, Hazor (Area H), Megiddo, Shechem, and Tell el-Dab'a. The design of the temple facade also varied: at Ebla there were two projections (*antae*) in front of a wide entrance hall; at Shechem and Hazor two massive square towers flanked the entrance; and at Alalakh and Tell el-Dab'a two broad rooms in the front created a tripartite division of the building.

The proportions of the main hall are of some significance. At Alalakh, Ras Shamra, Hazor (Area H), and Tell el-Dab'a (Temple III), the main hall is more broad than long, a proportion which recalls the EB III temples at Megiddo. In the other temples, the main hall is a "long room," possibly reflecting north Mesopotamian tradition known from several third millennium B.C.E. temples there. Such a development is demonstrated at Ebla, where the "long room" temples appear to have been founded during the twentieth and nineteenth centuries B.C.E. (though they probably continued in use in the eighteenth and seventeenth centuries also). At other sites the "long room" temples do not appear before MB IIB. These monumental, symmetrical temples may be regarded as the essential temple type of West Semitic civilization, where the main gods of the local pantheon—such as Hadad, Ishtar, Shamash, Dagan, and Reshef—were worshiped. It is no wonder that this type of temple continued to be in use also during the Late Bronze Age, and was eventually the major source of the design of the temple of Solomon in Jerusalem.

In small Middle Bronze towns and villages, such as Tel Kitan and Tell el-Hayyat (both in the Jordan Valley), we find small temples of the symmetrical plan recalling a megaron building: they comprise a major hall and an entrance chamber built with two *antae*. At Tel Kitan a line of ritual stones (*massebot*) stood in front of the temple. Though they are of small size, these country temples demonstrate the dominance of the symmetrical temple plan during this period.

Another type of Middle Bronze religious site is the open cult area. At Nahariyah, the open cult place founded in MB

IIA continued in use.[45] A large building constructed there near the open-air platform probably served as an auxiliary structure. An open cult center at Gezer contained ten large upright stones, a prominent demonstration of the use of the standing stone (biblical *massebah*) in Canaanite cult practices. The stones may have represented different deities or human figures such as ancestors and kings who were worshiped at this place.

The Middle Bronze Age architecture was to a large extent innovative and original. Together with the massive fortifications of this period, it evidences a thriving, prosperous urban culture. The magnitude of the palaces and temples manifests the wealth and power concentrated in the hands of the autocracy and theocracy of the period.

AGRICULTURAL INSTALLATIONS

Very little is known of Middle Bronze Age agrotechnology. An exception is a canalization system found in the fields outside the Lower City of Hazor. Stone-roofed canals were discovered there running for a length of hundreds of meters; they may have been connected to the nearby city gate (in Area P), through which they received drainage water from the city. This is the only evidence of irrigation systems from this period.

BURIAL CUSTOMS

The use of caves for multiple burials became popular again in MB IIB–C after a long gap. As in EB II–III, this method suited an urban society in which families wished to bury their dead in the same place over several generations. Dozens of rich burial caves from this period at Jericho are fine examples of the custom.[46] The corpse was laid on a wooden bed in the center of the cave. A similar practice, although possibly from a slightly earlier date, was evident in the cemetery of Baghuz near Mari. At Jericho, older burials were pushed to the sides to allow room for the new ones on the bed or near it. Dozens of skeletons were found in the same cave, together with a rich collection of burial gifts, including many pottery vessels (some containing food remains), wooden containers, weapons, tools of various kinds, jewelry, and seals. An extraordinary feature of the Jericho tombs is the preservation of organic material, and in particular of wooden furniture such as curved beds and stools.

Another burial practice of the Middle Bronze Age was the building of tombs beneath houses inside the city. This custom was common at Megiddo, where dozens of such tombs were uncovered.[47]

At Hazor, long rock-cut tunnels below the large building in Area F ended in spacious subterranean chambers which were found empty of finds. The feature resembles the underground burial caves below the MB II Palace Q at Ebla, where princely tombs were found together with opulent finds. As mentioned earlier, this building at Hazor was probably a palace below which members of the royalty were entombed. The practice is known in the Levant also from Late Bronze Age Ugarit and possibly in Megiddo.[48]

Another common form of burial in MB II was that of infants in pottery jars placed under the floors of rooms and courtyards. The upper part of the jar was deliberately broken, and the body of the infant was placed inside with gifts such as ointment juglets and jewelry. This practice was peculiar to MB II and did not continue in the Late Bronze Age. It may reflect a high rate of infant mortality.

POTTERY AND FOREIGN RELATIONS

The quality of MB IIB–C pottery is particularly good: the potters mastered the use of the wheel and produced a variety of distinct forms which usually had thin walls and were fired at high temperatures. Many of the vessel shapes evolved from those which were introduced in the preceding MB IIA period; this is a significant indication of the cultural continuity between the two periods. Only precise typological studies based on stratified deposits and on the sequence of tomb groups enable us to define the inner typological evolvement during this period.[49] In this section we will limit ourselves to a few prominent features.

The burnished red slip which was frequently applied to vessels during MB IIA gradually disappeared during the eighteenth century B.C.E. and was replaced by a white or creamy slip which appears on many of the small vessels. Painted decoration is rare, and when it does appear, it is usually unicolored

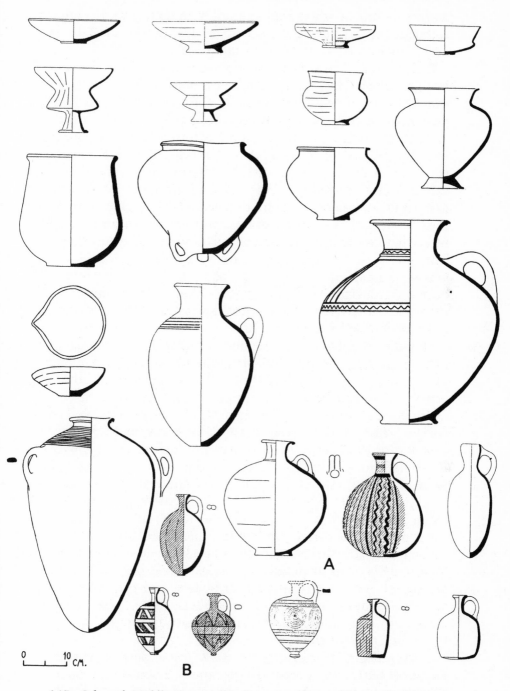

6.17 Selected Middle Bronze IIB–C pottery forms (from Megiddo and Jericho); among them (A) imported Cypriot jug; (B) Tell el-Yehudiyeh juglets.

(dark brown on a white background) with simple motifs such as horizontal stripes or concentric circles; in rare cases birds or antelopes are painted on ointment juglets.

Ointment juglets are one of the most popular types of vessel in this period. They have a distinct typological development from MB IIA down to the end of the Middle Bronze Age: piriform juglets are gradually replaced by those with a cylindrical body. While the juglets of the MB IIA phase are usually red slipped and burnished, those of MB IIB–C are mostly plain, or in some cases painted. A distinct group is the so-called Tell el-Yehudiyeh Ware, named after the site in the eastern Delta where it was first identified. The group consists mainly of juglets but also contains zoomorphic vessels (shaped like fish, birds, and even human heads) and fruitshaped vessels. This group is distinguished by its "puncturing" decoration, which was applied by means of a sharp tool and consisted of geometric designs such as stripes, circles, and triangles. In many cases the vessels have a black surface and the punctured holes were filled with white lime.

Outside Palestine, Tell el-Yehudiyeh Ware appears in Egypt (mostly in the eastern Delta), along the Phoenician coast, and in Cyprus. The group thus demonstrates the cultural homogeneity of Palestine, the Phoenician coast, and the eastern Delta during the time of the Hyksos rule in Egypt as well as trade relations with Cyprus. But a recent study (by M. Kaplan) established the existence of various production centers with local traditions. Thus at Afula, in the valley of Jezreel, a potter's workshop produced juglets of distinct shape, size, and local buff ware. Independent production centers in the eastern Delta manufactured slightly different forms of juglets, with the typical black surface and white lime-filled dots.[50]

Characteristic sharply carinated bowls made of fine, well-levigated clay appear mainly in the last phase of MB II. They are superb vessels with very thin bodies, and thus they are sometimes dubbed "Eggshell Ware." In fact, these bowls constitute one of the most delicate pottery groups known from ancient Palestine.

During the sixteenth century B.C.E. two fine and distinct groups of pottery appeared: the so-called Chocolate on White Ware and Bichrome Ware. The former includes beautifully shaped bowls, kraters, and jugs covered with thick white slip and painted in a dark brown decoration. The motifs are

6.18   Anthropoid vase from Jericho, manufactured in the technique of Tell el-Yehudiyeh Ware.

geometric, although there are a few antelopes and fish. This group is rather rare and its distribution is limited. It is found mainly in the northern part of the country, particularly along the Jordan Valley (the region of Beth-Shean and Pella), where it probably was manufactured. The Bichrome group is more important and much more widely distributed. Its appearance before the end of the MB IIC is proved by finds at Tell el-Ajjul (City II) and Megiddo (Stratum X), as well as at Tell el-Dab'a, where it was found in the last phase before the expulsion of the Hyksos rulers. But the Bichrome group continued during Late Bronze IA until the time of Tuthmosis III, and thus it will be discussed in further detail below (p. 259).

Trade relations with Cyprus during MB II resulted most probably from the need for copper ingots, which this island could supply. Exchange of pottery between Cyprus, Egypt, and the Levant is important evidence of this trade and enables us to link the archaeological sequence in Cyprus to that of the Levant. Imports of Cypriot pottery started at the end of MB IIA and increased during MB IIB, though even then they were limited in comparison to the massive amount in the following Late Bronze Age. The Cypriot pottery displays distinct manufacture and decoration techniques which enable scholars to classify it according to well-defined typological groups. It is mostly handmade; the gourd shape is common; and the painted decoration is applied to the whole body. "Pendant lines" and groups of strips are painted in brown-black paint on a white slip background (in the White Painted group), or red painting appears on black background (Red on Black group). During the early sixteenth century B.C.E., the first examples of the hemispherical bowls known as "Milk Bowls" (White Slip Ware) started to appear. Tell el-Yehudiyeh juglets found in Cyprus represent the other end of this trade connection. Meager connections with the Minoan culture of Crete are evidenced by a few sherds of Minoan pottery found in Palestine.

The close relations between the inhabitants of Canaan and the Hyksos settlements in the eastern Delta of Egypt finds expression in an influx and local imitation of Egyptian goods in Palestine. This phenomenon is exemplified by valuable objects such as alabaster and faience vessels, scarab seals, and Egyptian influence on local glyptic art.

WEAPONS

Bronze weapons developed in MB IIB–C from the types known in MB IIA. The duckbill axe disappeared, and a new type of narrow, small, chisel-shaped axe prevailed; daggers had a leaf-shaped multiple-ridged blade and a wooden handle with a stone pommel; the blades of spearheads were elongated and their handles had a long shaft. Two warrior tombs, one at Jericho and one at Tell el-Far'ah (north) contained the full equipment of a warrior: a dagger, an axe, and a wide bronze belt.

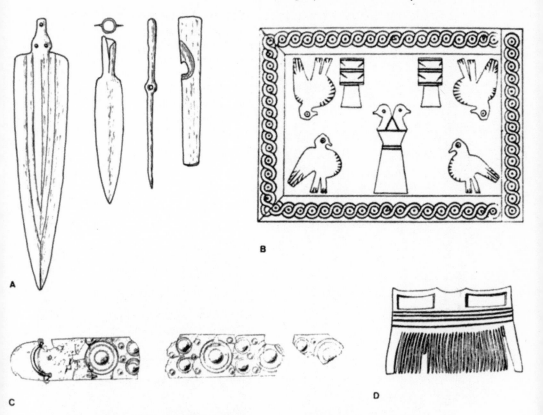

6.19 Weapons, ornaments and seals of the Middle Bronze IIB-C. (A) bronze dagger, spear head, toggle pin and an axe head; (B) bone inlays used for decorating wooden cosmetic boxes; (C) two bottom parts of Hyksos scarabs; (D) an impression of a cylinder seal; a local variant of the "Syrian" style.

A unique bronze axe, shaped like the palm of the hand, was discovered at Shiloh and has parallels in northern Mesopotamia and thus confirms relations with this region.[51]

ART

A developed MB IIB–C miniature art is represented by metal figurines, jewelry, cylinder seals, scarabs, and bone and ivory inlays. These miniature artifacts give witness to a Canaanite art form which was to develop in the following period.

Metal Figurines The manufacture of metal figurines of male and female deities became popular in the Levant during the Middle Bronze Age.[52] These figurines appear for the first time

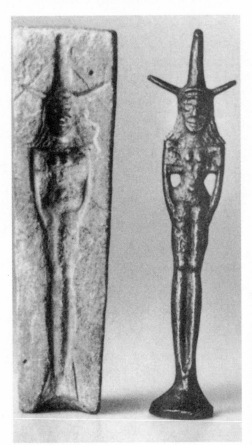

6.20 Left: a stone mold for casting bronze figurines, found at the temple at Nahariyah. Right: a modern cast made into this mold, showing a naked horned goddess.

6.21 Sheet-gold female figurines from Gezer, sixteenth century B.C.E. (the right figurine is 16 cm high).

in the early second millennium B.C.E. in Byblos, northern Syria, and Anatolia; later they spread to Palestine and to inland Syria. Over a thousand figurines found in the offering deposits at Byblos are dated to the time of the Middle Kingdom. Similar examples were found in Palestine, particularly at the temple of Nahariyah and at Megiddo. Some female figurines were made of gold, silver or bronze sheets cut to shape, while the details were produced by hammering. Elaborate gold examples of these latter figurines were found at both Gezer and Tell el-Ajjul in a late MB II context.[53] Other figurines were cast in open molds, or in closed ones in the "lost wax" technique. An open mold of a naked horned female goddess found at the temple at Nahariyah would imply that metal figurines were cast at Canaanite shrines. The female statuette made from this mold probably represented the Canaanite goddess Astarte; she is known also from cylinder seals of this period and from later Canaanite figurines.

Jewelry Long bronze or silver toggle pins were used in the Middle Bronze Age to fasten garments made of a rectangular piece of cloth which was wrapped around the body. Repre-

6.22   Three gold pendants and a band (diadem?) from Tell el-Ajjul—most probably from City II, which was destroyed in the mid–sixteenth century B.C.E. This jewelry is made by fine granulation, engraving, and repoussé techniques.

sentations of these garments and heavier mantles as the dress of high officials and kings are found on cylinder seals from this period, and the abundant use of silver and gold reflects the wealth of the ruling class. Three hoards of fine gold jewelry from Tell el-Ajjul "City II" probably predate the destruction of this prosperous city, which may have been related to the expulsion of the Hyksos from Egypt.[54] The jewelry includes some fine pins, rings and earrings, one made in the form of a bird in elaborate granulation technique. Gold sheet pendants found there were engraved with a symbolic presentation of the fertility goddess, showing only her head and female organs. Similar elaborate gold jewelry was found in the Hyksos cemetery at Tell el-Dabʿa, as well as in the royal tombs at Ebla.

A silver pendant found at Shiloh was decorated with the symbol of the weather god, well known from Anatolia. This pendant indicates relations with the Hittite culture of Anatolia during that time.

Glyptic Art   Two kinds of seals are found in MB II contexts: scarab and cylinder seals. They reflect the two main sources of influence on Canaanite civilization: Egypt and Mesopotamia.

During the Second Intermediate Period in Egypt a particular class of scarabs appeared, known as "Hyksos scarabs."[55] They retained the general shape of the Egyptian scarab seal, yet their decoration comprises either geometric designs or false, meaningless, Egyptian hieroglyphs. These artifacts illustrate the character of the Hyksos culture in Lower Egypt: Egyptian motifs were adopted by these foreign people, sometimes without understanding their meaning. Only a few of the Hyksos scarabs note the names of Hyksos kings and officials in hieroglyphs. Many such scarabs, some with royal names, were found in MB IIB–C contexts in Palestine, particularly in City II at Tell el-Ajjul. They are significant evidence of the close connections between the Hyksos rulers of the eastern Delta and their relatives, the Canaanites of southern Palestine.[56]

A fine, well-defined style of glyptic on cylinder seals emerged in Syria during the eighteenth century B.C.E. and is known as the "Syrian Style." One of its important production centers was at Aleppo, the capital of the kingdom of Yamhad, and seals and sealing from this center were found at Alalakh, another of Yamhad's major cities.[57] Other manufacturing centers were probably located farther south at important political centers such as Qatna and Hazor. This glyptic style combined Mesopotamian traditions, local stylistic and iconographic innovations, and Egyptian motifs which found their way to Syria. It demonstrates, better than any other art form from this period, the emergence of the Canaanite art and iconography. Thus, here we have the first representations of the Canaanite storm god Hadad (Baal) and of the Canaanite fertility goddess Astarte, as well as of the royal and official dress fashion. The decoration on the fringes of the scenes includes motifs such as the sphinx, the griffin, and the lion attacking animals. These motifs will continue to be popular in Canaanite art for centuries to come. Local workshops of seal-cutters in Palestine produced cylinder seals that merged Syrian and Egyptian traditions into a local, eclectic style.

Another local class of miniature art from this period is the carving of small, flat bone inlays used to decorate wooden objects such as jewelry boxes.[58] The designs included combinations of concentric circles made with a drill, Egyptian *Jed* symbols, silhouettes of birds, and other motifs. Exceptional bone works include silhouettes of humans and animals (the male figures wear Egyptian-like short kilts) and small plaques incised with one of the earliest illustrations of antelopes featured in a flying gallop, a motif which is known to have originated in the Aegean.

Ivory carving is rare in this period. An ivory plaque from Megiddo shows a lion attacking a mountain goat—a subject also known as a subsidiary motif on MB II Syrian cylinder seals, and which was to become common in Late Bronze Age Canaanite ivory carvings.

Monumental Art The only example of a large work of art in stone from Middle Bronze Age Palestine is the lower part of a small stele found at Tell Beit Mirsim. It depicts a human figure wearing a garment with thick fringes—the common dress of Canaanite kings and priests as featured on cylinder seals and metal figurines from this period.[59] Evidence of monumental sculpture in stone is found in northern Syria, where a good number of reliefs, statues, and stelae were recovered at Ebla, Ras Shamra, and Alalakh. These works of art exhibit a high degree of skill, and some—such as the head of a king found at Alalakh and a male head from the region of Jabbul—show high artistic skill and fine facial features. A famous stele from Ugarit showing the storm god Baal could belong to this period, though its date is not entirely certain.

WRITING

The few written documents found in MB IIB–C contexts are cuneiform Akkadian texts written on clay tablets. Akkadian became the lingua franca of the entire ancient Near East. Professional scribes in the large urban centers of Syria and Palestine (such as Hazor) mastered Akkadian and were acquainted with Mesopotamian literature. At Hazor, four Akkadian inscriptions were found: a clay tablet with a judicial document; an inscribed model liver used by priests as an omen; a fragment of a Mesopotamian study text (a list of weights and measures); and a local West Semitic name incised on a jar. A clay tablet from Gezer lists names, and another one from Hebron was a register of sacrifices.[60] These sparse finds demonstrate the use of Akkadian language by official scribes in the country during that period, while the imitation of Egyptian hieroglyphs on Hyksos scarabs demonstrates how unfamiliar this latter writing system was to the Semitic population of Palestine.

Sometime during the second millennium B.C.E. the Canaanites developed an alphabetic system of writing known as "Proto-Canaanite." The dating of this revolutionary invention is disputed; one view (of A. Gardiner, followed recently by B. Zass) place it in the MB II (see below, pp. 274–76).

THE PATRIARCHAL NARRATIVES AND THE MIDDLE BRONZE AGE

Various scholars have suggested that the cultural environment of MB II provides the most suitable background for the patriarchal sagas in the Book of Genesis.[61] The land of Canaan appears in these stories as having a prosperous urban culture with pastoral clans living in between the cities, just as was the situation in MB IIB–C. The biblical chronology, giving four hundred years for the sojourn in Egypt from Jacob until Moses, points to the seventeenth century B.C.E. as the time of Jacob. The high position of Joseph in Egypt could fit the Hyksos period, when Semitic princes ruled Lower Egypt.

Most of the cities mentioned in the patriarchal stories were occupied and fortified during MB IIB–C, particularly those along the central mountain ridge: Shechem, Bethel, Jerusalem, and Hebron. In general, the ancient Near Eastern setting during this period conforms to that of the patriarchal narratives: the wandering of Abraham from Ur to Haran and from there to Canaan can be explained as part of the general movement of clans and peoples in the Fertile Crescent. Furthermore, the Mari archive has supplied abundant information concerning the social structure and daily manners of the time, which are reminiscent of a number of phenomena described in the Book of Genesis. Other parallels have been found in the Nuzi archive dating to the fifteenth century B.C.E. Personal names appearing in the patriarchal stories are of West Semitic form known from the first half of the second millennium B.C.E.

Various phenomena in the Book of Genesis which apply to a later period (such as the extensive use of the camel and the appearance of Arameans and of Philistines) were considered by scholars as anachronisms, introduced by later editors and compilers of the old oral traditions. The essential stories were considered as reflecting traditions which go back to the Middle Bronze II Age. This approach, which was common during the sixties and early seventies, has been severely opposed by some current authors who believe that the stories themselves reflect a much later period, closer to the time of their compilation. Thus B. Mazar has suggested that the Book of Genesis was compiled in the court of David and Solomon, and that it is an expression of the reality of their time or of the slightly earlier period of the Judges. Others, such as T. L. Thompson and J. Van-Seters, have offered even more extreme ideas, suggesting much later dates for the patriarchal traditions.[62] I find the similarities between the MB II culture and that illustrated in the Genesis stories too close to be ignored. The patriarchal narratives known to us from the Book of Genesis must have been very old traditions which were orally passed on from generation to generation until they were written for the first time, perhaps during the time of the United Kingdom of David and Solomon. To substantiate this theory and identify the earliest nucleus of these traditions, we should note the many details which do not correspond to the period of the Israelite settlement and Monarchy. As is the nature of oral transmission, many features have been added, yet the origin of the traditions might go back as early as MB II.

THE END OF THE
MIDDLE BRONZE AGE

The formidable and homogeneous urban culture of Palestine, Syria, and the Delta of Egypt during the Middle Bronze Age signified a peak in the cultural history of this region. Two important events brought an end to this period: the Hittite raids on northern Syria and the expulsion of the Hyksos from Egypt. Northern Syria suffered from Hittite raids at the end of the seventeenth century B.C.E.; the raids caused the collapse of the great kingdom of Yamhad, centered at Aleppo. This collapse was followed by an interruption in the flourishing West Semitic civilization of northern Syria and by an influx of Hurrian population from northern Mesopotamia into Syria; a thinner stream of these people advanced farther to the south and appeared in Palestine. Thus some change in the ethnic composition of Canaan occurred and was to become an important factor in the following period.

The most significant event concerning Palestine was the expulsion of the Hyksos from Egypt in the mid–sixteenth century B.C.E. The Hyksos princes fled from the eastern Delta of Egypt to southern Palestine; the Egyptians followed them there and put them under siege in the city of Sharuhen. This event was probably followed by turmoil and military conflicts throughout the country, as a significant number of Middle Bronze cities were destroyed during the mid–sixteenth century B.C.E.[63] These destructions caused a collapse in entire urban clusters in the country. Thus, in the south, cities along Beersheba and Besor brooks were destroyed, and they hardly continued to exist in the following period. These include Tell el-Ajjul (Sharuhen?), Tell el-Far'ah South, Tel Malhata, and Tel Masos. In the coastal plain and the Shephelah, Tell Beit Mirsim, Gezer, Tel Batash and Aphek suffered from destructions and severe changes in their occupation history. In the northern coastal plain, the large city at Kabri was abandoned.

In the central hill region and the Jordan Valley, a chain of Middle Bronze cities and villages came to an end, and only few revived in the following period. Examples are Jericho, Hebron, Beth-Zur, Jerusalem, and Shiloh.

However, unlike the great collapse of the urban culture at the end of the EB III period, the turmoils in the mid–sixteenth century B.C.E. did not cause a total break of the Canaanite urban culture. Important cities in the northern part of the country, such as Hazor and Megiddo, suffered some disturbance at this period but soon were rebuilt on the same outline. Major temples at these cities were rehabilitated and continued to be in use in the Late Bronze period. The cultural continuity can be seen also in terms of pottery production, crafts, and art. Thus, the wide-scale destructions in the mid–sixteenth century B.C.E. which mark the end of the Middle Bronze Age, did not bring an end to the Canaanite civilization.

NOTES

1. For comprehensive synthesis of archaeological and historical data, see B. Mazar, *IEJ* 18 (1968), pp. 65–97 (= Mazar [1986], pp. 1–34; idem in: *WHJP*, vol. 2, pp. 169–87; K. M. Kenyon, *Amorites and Canaanites*, London 1966, pp. 53–77; idem in: *CAH*, vol. 2, part 1, pp. 77–116; J. Van-Seters, *The Hyksos: A New Investigation*, New Haven 1966; de Vaux (1978), pp. 55–81; Aharoni (1979), pp. 137–50; W. G. Dever, *BA* 50 (1987), pp. 148–77.

2. W. G. Dever in: *Wright Festschrift*, pp. 4–29; P. Gerstenblith, *The Levant at the Beginning of the Middle Bronze Age*, Philadelphia 1983; idem, *BASOR* 237 (1980), pp. 65–84.

3. M. Dothan, *BASOR* 224 (1976), pp. 1–48. A. Kempinski et al., *Excavations at Kabri, Preliminary Reports of 1986–1987 Seasons*, Tel Aviv, 1987–88 (Hebrew).

4. E. Stern, *Tel Mevorakh, Part Two. Qedem* 18, Jerusalem 1984, pp. 46–69.

5. For a synthesis of the finds at Aphek, Tel Poleg, Tel Zeror, and Tel Burgah, see M. Kochavi, P. Beck, and R. Gophna, *ZDPV* 95 (1979), pp. 121–65.

6. R. Gophna and E. Ayalon, *TA* 7 (1980), pp. 147–50; R. Gophna and P. Beck, *TA* 8 (1981), pp. 45–80; R. Gophna, *IEJ* 34 (1984), pp. 24–31.

7. J. Kaplan, *ZDPV* 91 (1975), pp. 1–17. The evidence is as yet unpublished, and consequently the date cannot be verified. A six-pier gate found at this site is built according to a typical MB IIB plan. Since there is almost no accumulation of debris inside the rampart, and it appears that the site was deserted shortly after its founding, the gate cannot be

a later addition to an earlier rampart. This evidence raises a question about the MB IIA date of the rampart. Perhaps, as at Hazor and Dan (see later), the rampart at Yavneh-Yam should be dated to the eighteenth century B.C.E.

8. O. Tufnell, *Bulletin of the Institute of Archaeology, University of London* 3 (1962), pp. 1–37.

9. E. D. Oren, *ZDPV* 87 (1971), pp. 585–86.

10. B. Magness-Gardiner and S. E. Falconer, *BASOR* 254 (1984), pp. 49–74. The discovery of a series of temples at this site was reported by Falconer at the annual meeting of The American Schools of Oriental Research, Atlanta, November 1986.

11. G. E. Wright, *Shechem: The Biography of a Biblical City*, New York 1961, pp. 103–22.

12. A. Eitan, *BASOR* 208 (1972), pp. 19–24. Y. Yadin attributed the city wall to Stratum E of the MB IIB period; see *BASOR* 212 (1978), pp. 22–25.

13. P. Matthiae, *Ebla: An Empire Rediscovered*, London 1980, pp. 112–49.

14. M. Dothan and A. Raban, *BA* 43 (1980), pp. 35–39.

15. I. Dunayevsky and A. Kempinski, *ZDPV* 89 (1973), pp. 161–87.

16. P. Beck, *TA* 2 (1975), pp. 45–85; ibid. 12 (1985), pp. 181–203; Gerstenblith, *The Levant* (see note 2), pp. 59–87.

17. Amiran (1969), pp. 112–14; Gerstenblith, *The Levant* (see note 2), pp. 59–64; J. Tubb, *Levant* 15 (1983), pp. 49–62. Amiran, Dever, and Gerstenblith support the relation to the Habur pottery, while Tubb opposes it.

18. Oren (see note 9); Gerstenblith, *The Levant* (see note 2), pp. 89–100.

19. G. Posener, *CAH*, vol. 1, part 2, pp. 532–83; W. A. Ward, *Orientalia* 36 (1967), pp. 39–54; A. F. Rainey, *Israel Oriental Studies* 2 (1972), pp. 369–408.

20. *ANET*, pp. 328–29; Aharoni (1979), pp. 144–47; Mazar (1986), pp. 9–10.

21. An extreme view claims that all these Middle Kingdom objects which were not found in a stratigraphic context arrived in Palestine as a result of tomb robbing in Egypt during the Second Intermediate and later periods; see J. M. Weinstein, *BASOR* 217 (1975), pp. 1–16.

22. K. M. Kenyon was the first to suggest that the MB IIA (her MB I) culture originated in Byblos, and this she did even before knowing of the importance of the northern coastal plain of Palestine during this period; see Kenyon (1979), pp. 148–49; idem, *Amorites and Canaanites* (see note 1), p. 76. W. G. Dever proposed northern inland Syria as a possible origin (see note 2). J. Tubb proposed a local development, but his view is unconvincing (see note 17).

23. W. F. Albright, *The Archaeology of Palestine*, Harmondsworth 1960, p. 84. For Albright's later views, see his series of papers in *BASOR*— 176 (1964), pp. 38–46; 184 (1966), pp. 26–35; 209 (1973), pp. 12–18; *COWA* 2, pp. 54–57; Kenyon (1979), p. 155.

24. Mazar, *IEJ* (see note 1). These dates were accepted by W. G. Dever and P. Gerstenblith; see the comprehensive discussion in Gerstenblith, *The Levant* (note 2), pp. 101–8.

25. M. Bietak, *AJA* 88 (1984), pp. 471–87.

26. J.-R. Kupper in: *CAH*, vol. 2, part 1, pp. 1–39.

27. An example is a tomb group found at Hazor which was considered by Y. Yadin as essential for establishing the foundation date of the Middle Bronze Age city there. Yadin defined this group as belonging to MB IIB, yet many of its forms are clearly MB IIA, only a few conforming to the MB IIB definition. As the duration of the tomb's use was short, it appears that it was in use for a short time during the transitional phase between MB IIA and MB IIB, ca. 1800–1750 B.C.E. See Y. Yadin, *Hazor: The Head of All These Kingdoms*, Jerusalem 1974, pp. 265–72.

28. C. Epstein, ʿ*Atiqot* 7 (1974), pp. 13–39 (Hebrew).

29. D. Cole, *Shechem I: The Middle Bronze IIB Pottery*, (*ASOR Excavations Reports*) Winnona Lake, 1984.

30. H. Tadmor in: *WHJP*, vol. 2, pp. 63–84. But see now P. J. Huber et al., *Astronomical Dating of Babylon I and Ur III*. Occasional Papers on the Near East 1:4, Malibu 1982; see also P. J. Huber in: P. Aström (ed.), *High, Middle or Low?* Acts of an International Colloquium on Absolute Chronology Held at the University of Gothenborg 20th–22nd August 1987, Gothenborg 1987, part 1, pp. 5–17. This new view claims that the high (or "long") chronology of Hammurapi (1848–1806 B.C.E.) is the only one acceptable. This high chronology, however, would make the correlation with Egypt more difficult in light of the suggestions of M. Bietak to lower the dates of the Middle Bronze in the Levant on the basis of finds from Egypt (see note 25).

31. W. F. Albright, *BASOR* 144 (1956), pp. 27–30; ibid. 176 (1964), pp. 38–46; ibid. 179 (1965), pp. 38–43. The significance of the finds from the royal tombs of Byblos is not entirely clear. The main tombs belong to the last pharaohs of the Twelfth Dynasty (from Senusert III onward). Only the last one dates to the Thirteenth Dynasty, and it may be linked with the transition between MB IIA and MB IIB.

32. J. M. Weinstein, *BASOR* 241 (1981), pp. 8–11.

33. Bietak (see note 25) and see the response of W. G. Dever in *Tufnell Festschrift*, pp. 69–87.

34. Yadin (1972), pp. 27–125.

35. Excavated by E. Eisenberg and G. Edelstein on behalf of the Israel Department of Antiquities (1984–87).

36. Y. Yadin, *BASOR* 137 (1955) pp. 23–32 suggested that the earthworks were mainly intended to defend the cities from the battering rams. Yet it appears that this was only one purpose of these artificial slopes. For a general discussion, see P. Parr, *ZDPV* 84 (1968), pp. 18–45; Kaplan (see note 7).

37. Wright (see note 11), pp. 57–79; J. D. Seger, *EI* 12 (1975), pp. 34*–45*; W. G. Dever, *BASOR* 216 (1974), pp. 30–52.

38. G. R. H. Wright, *ZDPV* 84 (1968), pp. 1–17; ibid. 85 (1969), pp. 24–34. Wright claims that the dates of these Egyptian ramparts is not certain and that they have nothing to do with our period.

39. Parr (see note 36) suggested that the glacis in Syria-Palestine were essentially intended to stabilize the slopes of the mounds against erosion, and that the Middle Bronze earthworks continue a tradition known since the Early Bronze Age. Though glacis are indeed known in the Early Bronze Age, there is no third millennium B.C.E. example of the artificial freestanding ramparts which appear to have been the main new invention of the Middle Bronze Age.

40. *Architecture*, pp. 107–19 (Hebrew); Z. Herzog, *Das Stadttor in Israel und in den Nachbarländern*, Mainz 1986; G. R. H. Wright, *ZDPV* 101 (1985), pp. 1–8; B. Gregori, *Levant* 18 (1986), pp. 83–102.

41. J. D. Seger, *Levant* 6 (1974), pp. 117–30; A. Biran, *IEJ* 34 (1984), pp. 1–19.

42. D. Ussishkin, *TA* 10 (1983), pp. 105–8.

43. J. R. Stewart, *Tell el-Ajjul: The Middle Bronze Remains*, Gothenborg 1974; for the finds at Kabri, see note 3.

44. P. Matthiae (see note 13), pp. 125–32, 200–3; L. Wooley, *Alalakh*, Oxford 1955, pp. 43–59; C. F. A. Schaeffer, *Syria* 12 (1931), p. 9; ibid. 14 (1933), p. 122; ibid. 16 (1935), pp. 154–56; Yadin (1972), pp. 67–105; Wright (see note 11), pp. 103–22; M. Bietak, *Proceedings of the British Academy* 65 (1979), pp. 247–52, 284–85. For general studies, see G. R. H. Wright, *PEQ* 103 (1971), pp. 17–31; P. Matthiae, *Rencontre Assyriologique Internationale*, Leiden 1975, pp. 43–72; *Architecture*, pp. 136–60 (Hebrew); Wright (1985), pp. 229–47.

45. M. Dothan in: A. Biran (ed.), *Temples and High Places in Biblical Times*, Jerusalem 1981, pp. 74–81.

46. K. M. Kenyon, *Digging Up Jericho*, London 1957, pp. 233–55; idem, *Excavations at Jericho*, vol. 1, London 1960, pp. 263–518; idem, *Excavations at Jericho*, vol. 2, London 1965, pp. 167–478.

47. K. M. Kenyon, *Levant* 1 (1969), pp. 25–60.

48. P. Matthiae, *Archaeology* 33 (1980), pp. 68–77; idem, *Ugarit Forschungen* 11 (1979), pp. 563–69, where Matthiae suggests the existence of an ancestor cult in these cases and at other sites in this period.

49. Kenyon (see note 46, Jericho I–II); Cole (see note 29). For a general survey, see Amiran (1969), pp. 93–124.

50. M. Kaplan, *The Origin and Distribution of Tell el-Yahudiyeh Ware*, Gothenborg 1980.

51. I. Finkelstein and B. Brandel, *The Israel Museum Journal* 4 (1985), pp. 17–26.

52. O. Negbi, *Canaanite Gods in Metal*, Tel Aviv 1976.

53. J. D. Seger, *BASOR* 221 (1976), pp. 133–39. The figurines from Tell el-Ajjul were dated by Negbi to the LB IA phase, i.e. to the second half of the sixteenth century B.C.E. See: O. Negbi, *The Hoards of Goldwork from Tell el-Ajjul*, Gothenborg 1970; A. Kempinski, *IEJ* 24 (1974),

pp. 145–52. It appears to me that the hoards belong to City II, which was destroyed after the expulsion of the Hyksos. The contents of this stratum should be defined as belonging to late MB II.

54. Negbi, op. cit. and see previous note.

55. O. Tufnell, *Studies on Scarab Seals*, Warminster 1984.

56. A. Kempinski, *Syrien und Palästina (Kanaan) in der Letzten Phase der Mittelbronze IIB Zeit*, Wiesbaden 1983; J. M. Weinstein, *BASOR* 241 (1981), pp. 8–10; R. Giveon, *JNES* 51 (1965), pp. 202–4.

57. D. Collon, *The Seal Impressions from Tell Atchana/Alalakh*, Neukirchen-Vluyn 1975; idem, *Ugarit Forschungen* 13 (1981), pp. 33–43.

58. H. A. Liebowitz, *IEJ* 27 (1977), pp. 89–97.

59. R. Merhav, *The Israel Museum Journal* 4 (1985), pp. 27–42. The title "Serpent Stele" given to this stele by Albright should be abandoned.

60. M. Anbar and N. Na'aman, *TA* 13–14 (1986–87), pp. 3–12 (includes previous bibliography).

61. de Vaux (1978), pp. 161–266; E. A. Speiser and Sh. Yeivin in: *WHJP*, vol. 2, pp. 160–68, 201–18; W. G. Dever in: J. H. Hayes and J. M. Miller (eds.), *Israelite and Judaean History*, London 1977, pp. 70–119.

62. B. Mazar, *JNES* 28 (1969), pp. 73–83; T. L. Thompson, *The Historicity of the Patriarchal Narratives: The Quest for the Historical Abraham*, Berlin 1974; J. Van-Seters, *Abraham in History and Tradition*, New Haven 1975, pp. 5–122.

63. Weinstein (see note 56), pp. 1–10.

CHAPTER SEVEN

IN THE SHADOW OF
EGYPTIAN DOMINATION:
The Late Bronze Age
(ca. 1550–1200 B.C.E.)

HISTORICAL BACKGROUND

For four hundred years from the mid–sixteenth century B.C.E., the history of the land of Canaan was, to a large extent, interrelated with and dictated by Egyptian activity in Asia and the reactions of Egypt's northern enemies. The Canaanite city-states as well as other population groups in the country were under the yoke of Egyptian domination and exploitation for most of this period; this resulted in the deterioration of Canaanite culture. Nevertheless, the Canaanites played an important role in the international cultural sphere during the Late Bronze Age.[1]

The expulsion of the Hyksos and the reunification of Egypt by Pharaoh Ahmose (1550–1525 B.C.E.),[2] the founder of the Eighteenth Dynasty, culminated in a strong Egypt both militarily and economically, and in renewed Egyptian interest in Canaan. Ahmose himself crossed the Sinai Desert and laid siege to the Hyksos troops who found refuge at Sharuhen.[3] Yet, it appears that during this early phase of the Eighteenth Dynasty, lasting about eighty years, there were only sporadic Egyptian incursions into Canaan. It was Tuthmosis III (1479–1425 B.C.E.) who consolidated Egyptian rule over that country. In the battle of Megiddo, Tuthmosis faced a united force, including troops from many Canaanite city-states in Syria and Palestine. In this battle and in a series of campaigns in the following years, he defeated the league of Canaanite rulers and established direct Egyptian rule over Palestine and southern Syria as far as Kadesh on the Orontes. Meticulous records of these events have been preserved—including a list of 119 Canaanite cities defeated at Megiddo, depicted on a wall relief in the great temple of Amun at Thebes (Karnak); this is the most detailed list of Canaanite cities at our disposal, even though it does not include places in southern Canaan conquered by Tuthmosis' predecessors.[4]

The Egyptians continued to make war in northern Syria, particularly against the kingdom of Mitanni, a Hurrian state which during the fifteenth century B.C.E. ruled northern Syria and northern Mesopotamia. During these campaigns, conducted by Tuthmosis III and his successor Amenophis II, the Egyptian troops crossed the so-called Via Maris (The Way of the Sea)—the international road connecting Egypt and Syria by way of the coastal plains and the northern valleys of Palestine. Amenophis II led two campaigns into Palestine itself; cities in the Sharon Plain, in the valley of Jezreel, and in the Upper Galilee are mentioned in inscriptions from his time. A group of cuneiform tablets from Taanach records the demand for troops and tribute to be sent from that city to Amenophis' headquarters, thus demonstrating the exploitation of Canaan by the Egyptians particularly at the time of their military campaigns. A fragment of an Egyptian stele found at Tel Kinrot (Tell el-ʿOreme) on the western bank of the Lake of Galilee, mentioning a war against people from the kingdom of Mitanni, is the only Egyptian monument from this time as yet found in Palestine.

The situation in Canaan in the mid–fourteenth century B.C.E. is known to us in detail thanks to the documents found in the palace of Amenophis IV (= Akhenaten, 1352–1336 B.C.E.) at Tell el-Amarna, in Middle Egypt. The archive, which contains over 360 documents written in Akkadian on clay tablets, is part of the diplomatic correspondence of Akhenaten and his father, Amenophis III. Most of the letters are from or to rulers of Canaanite cities, though there are also letters from important powers outside the Egyptian empire, such as Babylon, the Hittite empire, and Alashya (most probably Cyprus). From these documents, we have extensive information about and insight into the entire political, social, and cultural world of the fourteenth century B.C.E.

Weakness and internal turmoil in Egypt during the second half of the fourteenth century B.C.E. led to the establishment of the Nineteenth Dynasty, which had a strong interest in maintaining its control over Canaan. The second pharaoh of this dynasty, Seti I (1294–1279 B.C.E.), resumed military operations in Asia. A stele found at Beth-Shean commemorates his suppression of the Canaanite rebellion in the Jordan Valley—a rebellion led by the cities of Hamath (Tell el-Hama south of Beth-Shean) and Pella (Tabaqat Fahil, on the eastern side of the Jordan River opposite Beth-Shean). Seti also fought in Syria to reestablish Egyptian domination over Kadesh on the Orontes and over the kingdom of Amurru, a mountainous country in Lebanon which tried to maintain its autonomy.

During the fourteenth century B.C.E. the Hittites established an empire which included all of Anatolia and northern Syria. Their capital was Hattusha—modern Boghazkoy—in central Anatolia, and Carchemish on the Upper Euphrates was their central base in Syria. This Hittite kingdom replaced that of Mitanni as Egypt's main rival in northern Syria, and eventually a great battle between the two took place at Kadesh in the fourth regnal year of Ramesses II (1279–1213 B.C.E.). Notwithstanding the five huge wall reliefs erected in Egyptian temples to commemorate Ramesses' victory over the Hittites, the battle probably ended in a status quo—the Hittites remaining rulers of northern Syria and even of the kingdom of Amurru. A few years later Ramesses II and Hattushili III, king of the Hittites, signed a peace treaty. The border between the Egyptian province of Canaan and the area controlled by the Hittites passed in the center of the Lebanon Baq'ah Valley. The peace between the two empires lasted until the collapse of the Hittite empire at the end of the thirteenth century B.C.E.

Ramesses II's successor, Merneptah (1213–1203 B.C.E.) conducted a campaign in Canaan of which we know from a memorial stele known as "the Israel Stele." Poetic lines on this monument mention the conquest of the cities Ashkelon, Gezer, and Yenoam, as well as of Israel, which appears here (as a name of a tribe) for the first and only time in Egyptian sources. Merneptah was also the first to fight the Sea Peoples (see pp. 303–4), who in his time were allied with the Libyans.

The recurrence of inner political unrest in Egypt resulted

7.1 The capture of Ashkelon by Egyptian troops. Drawing of a relief from the temple of Amun at Karnak, thirteenth century B.C.E. (the time of Ramesses II or Merneptah).

in the rise of the Twentieth Dynasty. This was a period of turmoil throughout the ancient Near East. The Mycenaean civilization of the Aegean world, the Hittite empire in Anatolia, and important cultural centers in the Levant such as Ugarit collapsed and vanished around 1200 B.C.E. The incursions of the so-called Sea Peoples and widespread drought were significant factors in the general changes that occurred. In Canaan, the most important event of the time was the clash between Ramesses III and the Sea Peoples in his eighth regnal year (see pp. 303–7). In contrast to their predecessors, the pharaohs of the Nineteenth and Twentieth dynasties left in Canaan a wealth of monuments, buildings, and artifacts which are evidence of their overwhelming presence in the country.

The Egyptians maintained their control over Canaan from several administrative centers. The most important were Gaza (where the chief governor of Canaan resided), Jaffa, and Beth-Shean. In Syria, the cities of Kumidi (Khamid el-Loz in the Lebanese Baq'ah), Sumur, and Ulasa (both located on the coast) served the same purpose. In these cities the Egyptians installed administrative staff as well as small garrisons to maintain their control of the country. Larger forces arrived from Egypt either in times of military conflict with a northern enemy or, as in the time of Seti I, in order to suppress a local revolt.

The Egyptian conquests in the Levant were carried out in order to guard the main routes to Lebanon and Syria, and for the gains from the economic exploitation of the occupied country.[5] Wood, oil, wine, wheat, cattle, copper, slaves, and concubines were brought from Canaan to Egypt. The Egyptians retained the structure of the Canaanite independent city-states established during the previous period; however, these city-states now became their vassals. The most important independent cities known to us from the Amarna archive were Yurza (in the southern coastal plain, perhaps Tell Jemmeh), Lachish, Gath (perhaps Tell es-Safi in the Shephelah), Ashkelon, Ashdod (not mentioned in the Egyptian documents, but known from the Ugaritic documents), Jerusalem, Gezer, Shechem, Gath-Padalla (Jatt, in the Sharon Plain), Taanach, Megiddo, Rehob (south of Beth-Shean), Pehel (Pella), Shimon (Tel Shimron in the western part of the valley of Jezreel), Anaharath (perhaps Tel Rekhesh in Wadi Bireh, east of Mount Tabor), Acre, Achshaf (one of the mounds in the valley of Acre), Hazor, and three cities in Transjordan: Ashtaroth, Kenath, and Bezer. To the north, a series of cities in Lebanon and Syria had similar status. Among the most important of these were Byblos (Gebal), Tyre, Sidon, Beirut, Arwad, Damascus, Kadesh, and Qatna. In each of these Canaanite city-states a local dynasty of rulers and nobles (*maryannu*) governed the domain, which included a number of minor towns. Yet all these city-states were dependent on Egyptian overlordship. The princes of these petty kingdoms were educated in Egypt and thus were acquainted with Egypt's culture and trained to be loyal to its pharaoh. The rulers of the city-states had to pay heavy tribute and taxes to the Egyptian authorities; they were required to supply food and goods to Egyptian troops when these passed through their territory on military expeditions. The Egyptians seem to have cleverly exploited the principle of "divide and rule," as rivalry between these city-states was the common phenomenon.

The Amarna documents often mention danger from the Habiru, a class of people without permanent citizenship who from time to time attack the territory of the city-states, though they may also serve the cities as military mercenaries, workmen and so forth. Shechem appears as the capital of a very large territory where many of the Habiru resided. Labaya, this territory's ruler during the Amarna Period, tried to gain control of an even larger area, the plains north and southwest of his territory, until he was stopped by a united force of several Canaanite cities.

There was also a widespread nomadic or seminomadic pastoral population in the country, particularly in the mountains and on the desert fringes. The Egyptians used the general title "Shasu," to denote this population. In times of drought and crisis these pastoralists could become raiders and endanger the settled, cultivated regions.

The economic exploitation of the country by the Egyptians for over three hundred years, the inner rivalry between the cities, and the invasions of the Habiru and seminomadic raiders brought about a gradual deterioration in the Canaanite culture.

In general, the population of Palestine was basically Canaanite—that is to say, West Semitic in origin. During the Late Bronze Age, however, it was mixed to a large extent with a non-Semitic population—particularly Hurrians, who had been emigrating from northern Syria since the sixteenth century B.C.E. This can be deduced from Hurrian names and theophoric components which appear in this period aside from the traditional West Semitic names.

The importance of Palestine as a bridge between Egypt and northern Syria is well documented in the historical texts of the Late Bronze Age. Most of these documents were found in Egypt, but some were discovered in Canaan itself. Thus a cuneiform tablet from the thirteenth century B.C.E. found at Aphek was a letter sent by a high official at Ugarit to the Egyptian governor of Canaan asking for a shipment of wheat;

a fragment of a Hittite royal seal impression from Aphek provides evidence of direct correspondence between the Egyptian and Hittite administrations in northern Syria.[6]

The city of Ugarit (Ras Shamra) in northern Syria has provided the most significant and authentic documentation for the study of Canaanite culture. Although this important coastal city-state was outside the borders of the Egyptian province of Canaan, and its own inhabitants did not consider themselves Canaanites, the Ugaritic language was a Canaanite dialect, and Ugarit's local culture may be viewed within the broader context of Canaanite civilization. The rich archives of Ugarit's palace and the libraries of the city's temples contained documents written in Akkadian as well as those inscribed in a locally developed alphabetic cuneiform script in the Ugaritic language. Both kinds of documents are invaluable sources for studying the political, economic, and social structure of the city and its periphery, the international relations, and the local religious literature—the latter became invaluable sources for the study of the origins of biblical language and literature.

In addition to north-south cultural, political, and trade relations, Canaan was also connected during this period to the Mediterranean world. Transactions with Cyprus and the Mycenaeans of Greece were fundamental to Canaanite culture during the Late Bronze Age.

INNER DIVISION AND TERMINOLOGY

The Late Bronze Age, termed by some Israeli scholars the "Late Canaanite period," has been subdivided in several ways. The following division, which we utilize, is based on W. F. Albright's suggestion, with slightly modified subdivisions and dates:

LB IA	1550–1470 B.C.E.
LB IB	1470–1400 B.C.E.
LB IIA	1400–1300 B.C.E.
LB IIB	1300–1200 B.C.E.

An alternative approach, adopted by several scholars (C. F. A. Schaeffer, O. Tufnell, and R. Amiran), divides the Late Bronze Age into three main phases:

LB I	1600/1550–1450 B.C.E.
LB II	1450–1350 B.C.E.
LB III	1350–1200 B.C.E.[7]

These subdivisions reflect the major historical developments related to the Egyptian history: LB IA is parallel to the period of the Eighteenth Dynasty, between the expulsion of the Hyksos and the conquest of Canaan by Tuthmosis III; LB IB is the time between this event and the eve of the Amarna period; LB IIA is parallel to the latter part of the Eighteenth Dynasty, including the Amarna period and the following period of weakness and turmoil; LB IIB is parallel to the Nineteenth Dynasty. According to the terminology used here, the time of the Twentieth Dynasty is included in the following period (Iron Age IA). It should be noted, however, that there was a great deal of continuity in the local Canaanite culture throughout the period as well as in the transitional periods between MB II and LB I and between LB II and Iron Age I. Thus the distinctions between the subphases is sometimes obscure and can be done mainly on the basis of certain distinct groups of pottery or other artifacts, mainly imported ones.

SETTLEMENT PATTERN

In the Late Bronze Age, the population and density of settlement declined in comparison with the preceding period. The fringe areas were deserted, and some of the sites which had been important urban centers in MB II were either fully or partially abandoned. This process of deterioration can be seen in the Beer-sheba Valley, where fortified towns existed in MB IIB–C; in the central hills; and in the Jordan Valley. Thus, at sites such as Shiloh, Beth-Zur, Jericho, and Hebron, the Late Bronze Age occupation was very poor or completely nonexistent. Important Middle Bronze Age towns such as Tell el-Ajjul and Tel Nagila either were unsettled or became the locations of small fortresses. Even in the central and northern fertile regions of the country, some flourishing MB II cities became impoverished; examples are Kabri, Aphek, Tel Gerisa, Shechem, and Dan. It appears that some of these sites in fact ceased to be cities and functioned only as strongholds of the Egyptian government (as perhaps at Tell el-Ajjul and Aphek). There was also a decline in the rural settlement, particularly in the hill country. The archaeological surveys in Samaria and Ephraim have shown that the many small Middle Bronze Age agricultural settlements in these regions disappeared in the Late Bronze Age. This phenomenon is symptomatic of a demographic decline which was perhaps followed by an increase in a seminomadic pastoral population.

A survey of the Late Bronze Age settlement has led R. Gonen to argue for a general decline in urbanization during this period.[8] Her research has also given support to the argument (previously expressed by Kenyon) that the deterioration was particularly notable during LB I following the expulsion of the Hyksos, and that during LB II there was a partial revival in urbanization. However, this argument might be questioned, as an insufficient number of LB I sites were excavated.

Indeed, it appears that southern Palestine suffered from a wave of devastation in the sixteenth century B.C.E.; such devastation was probably brought about by the Egyptians in their struggle against the Hyksos, who retreated to this area after their expulsion from Egypt. Yet population decline does not seem to have been universally experienced throughout the country. Some of the most important Middle Bronze urban centers continued to flourish throughout the Late Bronze Age. Such was the situation at Lachish, Ashdod (which was founded toward the end of MB IIB–C), Gezer, Megiddo, Beth-Shean, and particularly Hazor. Hazor maintained its status as the largest city in Canaan, and its entire area, about 200 acres, remained settled in the Late Bronze Age.[9] Extensive Late Bronze occupation took place at a series of mounds and smaller sites, particularly along the coastal plains, in the Shephelah, and in the Jezreel and Beth-Shean valleys.

The international marine trade, one of the most important economic factors of the period, led to the foundation of several port towns along the Mediterranean coast. These include Tell Abu Hawam, Shiqmona, Tell Nami (near 'Atlit), Tel Michal, and Tel Mor (the last was founded at the end of the preceding period).

In contrast to conclusions of N. Glueck, it now appears that there were a number of Late Bronze Age cities in most of the fertile areas of Transjordan: in the central Jordan Valley and at several mounds along the "King's Highway," the main road transecting Transjordan from north to south.[10] This settlement, however, has a distinct southern demarcation; no Late Bronze sites were found south of Madeba (which is approximately opposite the northern end of the Dead Sea).

This coincides with the evidence from the west of the Jordan, as Late Bronze settlements have not been discovered south of the Hebron Hills.

THE OCCUPATION HISTORY OF LATE BRONZE SITES

At a number of important sites, three major occupational phases from the Late Bronze Age have been defined. This tripartite division was determined at Hazor, Megiddo, Beth-Shean, Gezer, Lachish (the Fosse Temple on the slopes of the mound), Shechem, Tel Mevorakh, Jaffa, Tel Sera^c (Tell esh-Shari^{c}a), and Tel Halif. At some sites, more than three successive Late Bronze Age occupation levels were found. Thus at Tel Batash (Timnah), five levels have been detected—the first four of which, all destroyed by conflagration, extended from the mid–sixteenth to the fourteenth century B.C.E. The port towns established during the Late Bronze Age also underwent decisive changes: Tell Abu Hawam Stratum V can be divided into several subphases; at Shiqmona six occupation levels were detected and at Tel Mor five. On the other hand, at several other sites only one or two occupation phases from this period were discerned, as at Tell Beit Mirsim (Stratum C) and Beth-Shemesh (Stratum IV, which may be divided into two subphases).

Because much of the disruption in this period was a result of local conflicts between cities, and of raids by Habiru or seminomadic tribes, settlements underwent destructions at different times and it is difficult to correlate destructions and rebuildings throughout the country. However, it appears that many towns were destroyed during the fourteenth century B.C.E. and that there was a general decline in settlement in the thirteenth century. Thus at the last Canaanite level at Hazor (Stratum XIII), a deterioration of the city was evident.

Scholars have suggested occupation gaps of various lengths at various sites during the LB age. Thus it was suggested that a gap occurred in the first phase of the Late Bronze (LB I) at such sites as Tell Beit Mirsim, Jericho, and Shechem.[11] Such suggestions should be taken with caution, as gaps are usually determined on the basis of the lack of certain ceramic groups, and this "evidence from silence" is not always conclusive.

Table 5. Comparative Stratigraphy of Late Bronze Age Sites

SITES / SUBPERIODS	LB IA (ca. 1550 B.C.E.)	LB IB (1470 B.C.E.)	LB IIA (1400 B.C.E.)	LB IIB (1300 B.C.E. – 1200 B.C.E.)
Egypt	Dynasty 18			Dynasty 19
Hazor	XV		XIV	XIII
Tel Yin'am				VIB
Beth-Shean		IXB	IXA	(VIII) VII
Megiddo	IX		VIII	VIIB
Tell Abu-Hawam	V_1 ——————→ V_5			
Shechem (Tell Balatah)		XIV	XIII	XII
Aphek	X_{14}		X_{13}	X_{12} X_{11}
Gezer	XVIII	XVII	XVI	XV XIV
Beth-Shemesh	IV			
Tel Batash	X IX	VIII	VII	VI
Ekron (Tel Miqne)	——	IX	VIIIB	VIIIA
Ashdod				XIV
Lachish*		IX	VIII	VII
Tell Beit-Mirsim			C_1	C_2
Tel Halif	X	IXB	IXA	VIII
Tel Sera'	XII		XI	X
Tel el-Ajjul		IIIA	IIIB	
Deir el-Balah			settlement	fortress, cemetery
Tell el-Far'ah (South)				citadel→

* Tel Aviv University excavations.

ASPECTS OF CANAANITE TOWN PLANNING AND ARCHITECTURE

Fortifications   One of the most amazing features of the Late Bronze Age is the almost total lack of fortifications. At most sites excavated, none have been found, although at some sites the mighty Middle Bronze defenses may have continued in use during the Late Bronze period. Thus at Hazor, the city gates and a segment of a double casemate wall of the Middle Bronze Age were rebuilt in LB I after a destruction; in fact, they were continually restored and reconstructed throughout the Late Bronze Age. Yet Hazor is an exceptional case, as it was the most powerful city-state in the country. At Megiddo there was a six-pier gatehouse leading to the palace area. The purpose of this gate appears to have been more ceremonial than defensive; its corners were constructed of ashlars, yet it lacked the side towers which appear in all Middle Bronze Age triple gates. No city wall abuts the Megiddo gate, and apparently the external northern wall of the nearby palace served as the city wall. At Lachish and Tel Batash, large buildings of the Late Bronze Age were built at the edge of the mound, and there were definitely no city walls at these places during the entire Late Bronze Age. At Tel Batash, open alleys between the buildings on the edge of the mound were blocked by sections of walls in which drainage holes were constructed. At Gezer, a massive stone, defined by Macalister as the "Outer Wall," is the subject of debate. W. G. Dever argues that it was founded in the Late Bronze Age, yet it appears to be part of the Iron Age defense system.[12] Only at a few other sites— Ashdod, Tell Abu Hawam, and Tell Beit Mirsim—is there evidence of fortification walls constructed during the fourteenth and thirteenth centuries B.C.E.

How can we explain the lack of fortifications at cities which in the preceding period were heavily defended? The most plausible assumption is that Egyptian policy in Canaan outlawed the building of fortifications by Canaanite rulers.

Town Planning   The town planning of Late Bronze Canaanite cities is relatively unknown, as only limited areas have been exposed.[13]

At Hazor and Megiddo, two of the most important cities in

the northern part of Palestine, major components of the Middle Bronze town plan and public buildings (gates, palaces, temples) appear to have been retained in the Late Bronze Age, though various changes and modifications were made to individual buildings. In the southern part of the country, however, the fate of the Middle Bronze Age cities was quite different: their devastation was followed by either an occupation gap or distinct changes in the city plan.

Orthogonal planning was retained in places where it existed in the preceding period, such as Megiddo. At other sites, however, an irregular network of narrow streets with various branches and dead-end alleys is found (such as at Area C at Hazor). Large cities such as Hazor and Ugarit probably comprised several quarters, and at Hazor, the existence of a cult center in each of the quarters has been confirmed.

The separation of the palace from the city's main temple was a characteristic of Late Bronze Age urban planning in both Palestine and Syria. Thus at both Alalakh and Megiddo, while the Middle Bronze palace was close to the temple, in the Late Bronze Age the palace was moved to a new location near the city gate. A similar change may have been made at Lachish, where an MB–LB I palace at the center of the city was abolished in LB II, part of a major temple being superimposed on its ruins. At Hazor, the temple on the acropolis near the palace of the city ruler (Area A) went out of use in the last years of LB I, while the public temple in Area H continued to function until the end of the Late Bronze Age.

Palaces The palace of Megiddo exemplifies a gradual local development of a Canaanite palace from the sixteenth century (Stratum X) until the early twelfth century B.C.E. (Stratum VIIA). In the first two phases it was a square building, comprising a large courtyard surrounded by rooms on all four sides. In the fourteenth century B.C.E. (Stratum VIII) it was enlarged and made rectangular in shape with an area of at least 33×50 m, or 1,650 sq m. (As its excavation may not be complete, it could in fact have been larger.) In the center of the building there was a large rectangular courtyard. West of the latter was a reception unit, comprising two large halls connected by a wide entrance within which stood two columns. A bathroom south of the courtyard was joined to the reception unit, and large dwelling rooms lay to the east and

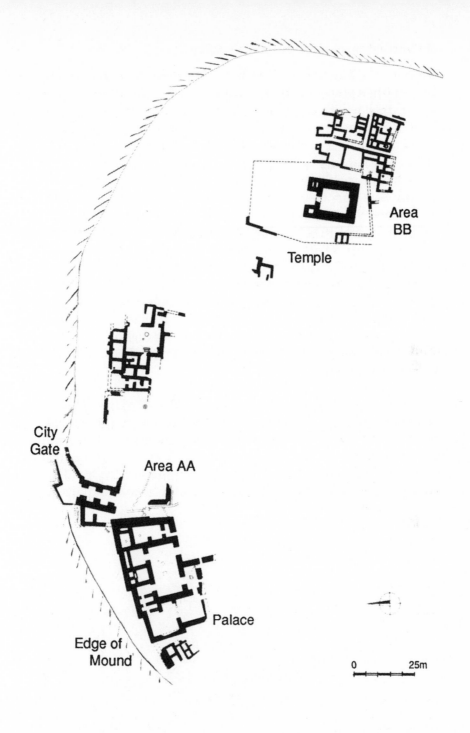

Area
BB

Temple

City
Gate

Area AA

Palace

Edge of
Mound

0   25m

7.2 Megiddo: plan of Stratum VIII (fourteenth century B.C.E.). Left: the
city gate and palace (Area AA). Upper right: the sacred area and dwelling
quarter (Area BB).

north of the bathroom. Possibly a staircase led to a second floor. In the succeeding level (Stratum VIIB, thirteenth century B.C.E.), this palace underwent extensive renovation particularly in its western wing, where a smaller reception hall was added. The palace was destroyed during the latter part of the thirteenth century B.C.E.; it was reconstructed in the early twelfth century (Stratum VIIA) with a tripartite annex possibly serving as a chapel or a treasury. Here, the famous Megiddo ivories were discovered (see pp. 269–71).

The palace of Megiddo has some interesting similarities to that of Ugarit. The latter, which served one of the most important and influential rulers of the period, was a huge architectural complex covering an area of ca. 5,000 sq m. It comprised a cluster of individual units, each of which recalls the palace at Megiddo. It seems, therefore, that similar principles of palace planning were adopted throughout Canaan, the size of the edifice varying according to the status and wealth of its owner.

Domestic Architecture   Several large and well-planned buildings from this period may be defined as local patrician houses. At Megiddo such a building was discovered east of the royal palace and beyond a piazza. It comprised a large central courtyard surrounded by good-sized rooms and halls. This building may have been the residence of a noble—perhaps

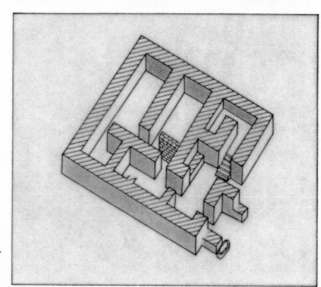

7.3   Aphek: isometric view of a residency (perhaps an Egyptian stronghold; thirteenth century B.C.E.).

one of the *maryannu*, whose status ranked only after that of the king during this period. Other examples of patrician, official residences in Canaan are the West Building at Taanach and the Residency at Aphek. The first was a 18×21 m structure comprising a square corner courtyard, a corridor (perhaps a staircase to the second floor), and a series of nine square chambers. The somewhat similar building at Aphek, from the thirteenth century B.C.E., was 14×16 m; it had a series of halls and rooms on the ground floor, and a staircase leading to a second floor.[14] The written documents found in this building indicate that it was the seat of Egyptian administrative officials.

Buildings at Tel Batash (Strata IX, VIII and VII) are examples of large patrician houses, perhaps of landlords. They are rectangular, and include pillared halls, storage rooms and staircases leading to a second floor, where the main dwelling area probably was. In a building of Stratum VII there were two rows of wooden pillars with stone bases, which supported the upper floor. Such rows of pillars were to become common in Iron Age architecture, and the Tel Batash building may be considered a Canaanite prototype of this later architectural form.[15]

7.4 A patrician house at Tel Batash: isometric view of ground floor (fourteenth century B.C.E.).

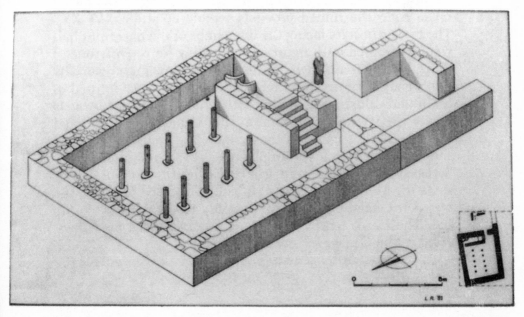

Most of the other Canaanite dwellings are courtyard houses—namely, they are composed of a central courtyard surrounded on several sides by rooms of no defined proportion or design. Such houses began to appear in the Middle Bronze Age, and they continued to be the major type of Canaanite dwelling.

Temples A variety of Late Bronze Age temples provides rich data concerning the physical aspects of Canaanite religion and art. Such temples are known at Hazor, Megiddo, Beth-Shean, Tel Mevorakh, Lachish, and Amman in Palestine, at Khamid el-Loz in the Lebanese Baq'ah, and at Alalakh and Ugarit in north Syria.[16]

Some of the major temples of the period had been erected during the preceding Middle Bronze Age. Such are the temples at Hazor (Area H) and Megiddo. Both these monumental structures were constructed during MB IIB–C and continued to function in the Late Bronze Age, when they were rebuilt and renovated.

At Hazor, the Middle Bronze temple of Stratum XVI in Area H served also in LB I (Stratum XV) with only slight changes to the interior layout. In its front courtyard, an altar and a ceremonial gate were constructed. In the fourteenth century B.C.E. (Stratum XIV), the temple was entirely rebuilt after being destroyed. The outline of the previous building was retained, but a new entrance hall was added, elongating the structure. Large, well-cut basalt orthostats were placed along the inner sides of the walls in this phase (they may have been taken from the ruined previous temple of Strata XVI–XV). The two orthostats facing the doorjambs of the new front hall were sculptured with figures of crouching lions. Only one of these, found intentionally buried in a pit, was preserved. The lion's body is shown in relief, while its head is sculptured in the round. Illustrating superb artistic skill, this orthostat is one of the few relics of monumental Canaanite art. A relief on a basalt altar found in the main hall of the Hazor temple shows a spoked circle—a simplification of an Anatolian–north Syrian symbol for the storm god Hadad (Baal), a symbol known since the Middle Bronze Age. A badly preserved basalt statue of a deity standing on a bull possibly represented the same god. The Hazor temple, therefore, seems to have been dedicated to the Canaanite storm god Baal.

The cultural homogeneity in Syria and Palestine during the

7.5   Hazor: the temple at Area H, general view, looking southeast.

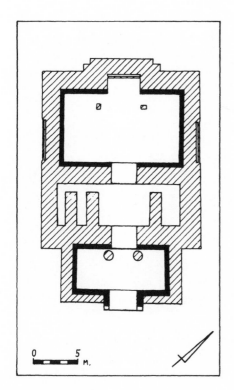

7.6   Hazor: plan of the temple at Area H, Stratum XIII (thirteenth century B.C.E.).

7.7 Hazor: cult objects as found on the floor of the temple in Area H. Note the basalt altar with relief showing the symbol of the storm god, and two stone offering tables.

7.8 Hazor: a doorjamb orthostat from the Area H temple (length 1.82 m; height 0.91 m). The body of the lion is shown in relief, while the head is sculptured in the round, intended to protrude from the front of the building.

Late Bronze Age is demonstrated by the similarities between the temple at Hazor and the temples at Alalakh. Although the Alalakh edifices underwent severe changes during this period, those of the fifteenth century (Stratum IV) and the thirteenth century B.C.E. (Stratum I) resemble the Area H temple at Hazor in plan, furniture, and decoration. At Alalakh as at Hazor, lion orthostats guarded the temple entrance, and a similar basalt altar was used. The temples of Hazor, Alalakh, and Ugarit have a broad main hall of similar proportions.

The elongated Tower Temple at Megiddo, founded in the MB IIB–C period, was important and strong enough to survive for more than five hundred years through the twelfth or even the eleventh century B.C.E. Two towers built of ashlars were added to its front sometime during the Late Bronze period, and the shape of the Holy of Holies was changed. The temple was now enclosed in a sacred compound, comprising a large forecourt surrounded by auxiliary rooms and storage spaces.

The temple at Shechem had a more complicated history. Stratigraphic examination of the remains left by the original excavators of the building during the twenties led G. E. Wright to conclude that the temple went out of use at the end of the Middle Bronze Age. During the Late Bronze Age, a new temple was constructed on its ruins; the new structure (Temple 2) was 16 m wide and 12.5 m long, its proportions now being those of a "broad building" as at Hazor, Alalakh, and Ugarit. In front of the temple, in the courtyard, stood a sacrificial altar and a huge standing stone (*massebah*); the latter was undoubtedly of considerable importance in the local cult. (Wright suggested that this stone was the "great stone at Shechem" of Joshua 24:26–27.) This new temple was maintained until Iron Age I, and thus it can be identified, according to Wright, with the temple of El-Berith ("the god of the covenant")—a temple also called "the tower of Shechem" and mentioned in the Abimelech narrative (Judges 9:46–49).[17]

It thus appears that the major type of Canaanite temple building during the Late Bronze Age was a monumental, symmetrical building, entered from a porch in front of the main hall; the Holy of Holies was inside the main hall, opposite the entrance. In most cases, the main hall of the building was an almost square broad room—a long room plan being incorporated only in cases where a Middle Bronze Age temple was retained, such as at Megiddo. This broad room tradition is deeply rooted in the religious architecture of Palestine, as exemplified at Megiddo in the Early Bronze Age.

A variant of Canaanite temples, combining Canaanite and Egyptian traditions, was found in thirteenth century B.C.E. levels at Beth-Shean and Lachish. At Beth-Shean, the temple of Stratum VII was erected on the site of an earlier sacred enclosure. The approach to the temple was indirect through an entrance chamber. The building was essentially square in plan (14.8 × 14.2 m), comprising a hall with benches along the walls, two columns which supported the roof, and an offering altar. A flight of seven steps led to a raised Holy of Holies, close to which was a chamber which may have served as a treasury. The temple was destroyed at the end of the thirteenth century B.C.E. and rebuilt in the following level, dating from the time of Ramesses III (Stratum VI, see p. 297).

7.9 Plans of thirteenth and twelfth century B.C.E. temples. Right: Beth-Shean Stratum VII (late thirteenth century B.C.E.). Left: Lachish Stratum VI (early twelfth century B.C.E.).

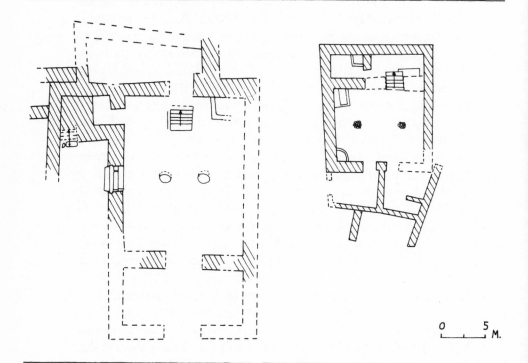

In this later temple, Egyptian-styled architectural fragments were found, including stone friezes and papyrus-shaped capitals (the latter perhaps originating in the earlier Stratum VII temple). A. Rowe compared the Beth-Shean temples to fourteenth-century chapels known at Tell el-Amarna in Egypt; he thus believed that the former temples were half roofed. His supposition, however, is unacceptable, as the Beth-Shean temples appear to have been fully roofed buildings; they should be defined as variants of the local Canaanite temple.

The temple at Lachish (Area P), located at the center of the mound,[18] recalls the temples of Beth-Shean in its general dimensions, plan, and architectural details. At Lachish, however, entrance to the building seems to have been direct by way of a porch on the west. A well-cut stone flight of steps with a unique stone parapet led to the Holy of Holies. In addition to the two main columns with papyrus-shaped stone capitals in Egyptian style, there were decorative columns, some featuring Egyptian fluted shafts. Fragments of wall plaster painted in black, white, red, yellow, and blue are rare remains of interior wall painting in Canaan and are another reflection of the influence of Egypt. Cedar beams, which must have been brought from Lebanon, were used in the building, recalling the use of this wood in the Solomonic temple in Jerusalem.

The combination of Canaanite concepts and Egyptian architectural decoration in these temples at Beth-Shean and Lachish typifies the thirteenth–early twelfth centuries B.C.E., when the Egyptian presence in the country was at its peak. Such temples were built both at Canaanite city-states such as Lachish and at Egyptian government centers such as Beth-Shean. This architecture may reflect religious syncretism, also suggested by some cultic art objects combining Egyptian and Canaanite motifs.

A number of Canaanite shrines and temples of various plans may be denoted "irregular". These buildings lack consistency in plan, most of them having individual characteristics. At Hazor, a small shrine in Area C of the Lower City probably served families residing nearby. It comprised a single broad room and was built on the inner slope of the Middle Bronze Age rampart. A row of eleven stelae was erected in this room—the central one of which was carved in relief, depicting two hands in prayer posture below a moon-and-

7.10 Hazor: finds from the shrine in Area C, including basalt stelae, statue of a seated male, relief of a crouching lion, and offering table.

crescent symbol. The shrine included also a miniature relief of a crouching lion, a statue of a sitting male figure (possibly depicting a god or a priest) and an offering table made of one stone slab. A pottery mask and a silver scepter were some of the cult objects used in this temple. The use of standing stones, the biblical *masseboth*, in the Late Bronze Age Canaanite cult is best exemplified in this Hazor temple. Consequently, this temple forms the link between the Middle Bronze open cult places and the similar practice in the period of the Monarchy (see p. 377).

The best manifestations of Canaanite irregular temples are the Fosse Temples at Lachish—three superimposed edifices constructed during the fifteenth through thirteenth centuries B.C.E. outside the mound of Lachish in the old Middle Bronze Age moat. All three temples had an indirect approach leading into a main hall, the roof of which was supported by wooden columns. The Holy of Holies was a raised platform located at the end of the main hall. Benches in the main hall probably functioned as places to put offerings. One or two other rooms served for auxiliary purposes or perhaps as treasuries. The third temple was destroyed by violent attack toward the end of the thirteenth century B.C.E., and a variety of offering vessels and cult objects was found smashed on its floor. *Favissae* (pits used for burying obsolete offerings and cult objects) were found outside these temples and contained an abundance of finds. Among these finds were ivory fragments of a statue, including a palm of a hand and an eye. Presumably,

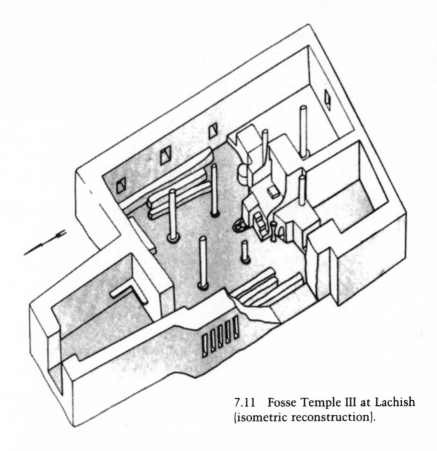

7.11 Fosse Temple III at Lachish
(isometric reconstruction).

these fragments belonged to a composite statue of a deity
made of ivory, wood and cloth.

A Late Bronze Age temple found at the small site of Tel
Mevorakh recalls the Fosse Temples at Lachish in its architectural features.[19] It may have been an isolated road sanctuary,
unrelated to any town. Since both the Lachish and Tel
Mevorakh structures differ from the regular, symmetrical and
monumental temples of the Canaanite cities, and since both
are located in unusual places (one extramural and the other
in a small site unrelated to any city), one may surmise that
they reflect a side stream in the Late Bronze Age temple
architectural tradition.

An enigmatic building was discovered in the area of the
Amman airport.[20] It was an isolated building, located several kilometers away from the Canaanite city at Amman.
The building was a well-planned, massive square structure
(15 × 15 m) with rooms surrounding a central space, perhaps
a roofed hall or an open courtyard. A round stone at the center
of this space has been alternatively interpreted as an altar, a

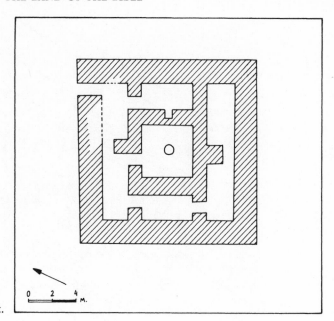

7.12 Plan of the square building at the Amman airport.

base for a sacred pillar, or merely a pillar used to support the roof. A rich variety of finds—including a large quantity of imported Mycenaean and Minoan pottery, Egyptian stone vessels and scarabs, cylinder seals, and gold jewelry—demonstrate the importance of this building. In addition, quantities of burnt human bones, both of children and of adults, were found. Widely differing opinions regarding the function of this building have been suggested: J. B. Hennessy explained the building as a temple, seeing in the bones evidence of child sacrifice; G. E. Wright and E. F. Campbell have suggested that it was a religious center for a tribal league in Transjordan; G. R. H. Wright suggested that it was a "fire temple" of Iranian type; V. Fritz denied the ritual function of the building and explained it as a residency; L. G. Herr has shown that the human bones are mainly those of adults, and he explains the building as a mortuary used for cremation. The practice of cremation was unknown among the Canaanites, yet it was practiced by Indo-Europeans—among them Hittites, some of whom may have settled in Transjordan during the thirteenth century B.C.E.[21]

The building at Amman has been compared to two other structures: one at Tananir on the slopes of Mount Gerizim overlooking Shechem,[22] and the other at Hazor (Area F, Stratum XV). The three were thought to comprise a group of Late Bronze "square temples"; however, they differ from one another in function and date. The Mount Gerizim structure has been dated to the end of the Middle Bronze Age; although it was similar to the Amman edifice in general plan, its central courtyard was much larger. Perhaps it should be interpreted as a residency outside the city. The building at Hazor is an LB I renovation of the large Middle Bronze Age edifice which stood in the same area (see p. 210). There are no indications of its use as a temple, and it probably was a large residence or palace like its predecessor. The chronological gap between the Mount Gerizim and Hazor structures (MB IIC and LB I, respectively) and the Amman building (apparently LB II) also separate them, and therefore the three cannot be conclusively grouped together as one class of temples.

Open cult places were used in the Late Bronze Age as in previous periods. At Area F at Hazor, such a cult place from the fourteenth and thirteenth centuries B.C.E. comprised an open courtyard with a drainage canal and a large, monolithic sacrificial altar.

Thus, the variety of religious architecture in Late Bronze Age Canaan may reflect not only the complexity of religious practices during that time but also demographic heterogeneity.

POTTERY AND INTERNATIONAL TRADE

A rich variety of local and imported pottery is an important indication of the evolvement of Canaanite culture and of international trade during this period. The extent and development of this trade, which was then one of the most dominant features of the civilization in the eastern Mediterranean, can be analyzed in the light of well-defined stylistic groups of Cypriot and Mycenaean pottery, as well as Syrian and Egyptian wares.

Local Pottery   The local pottery of Canaan in the Late Bronze Age features a gradual and direct evolvement from that of the preceding Middle Bronze Age, as there was no distinct cultural break between the two periods. In fact, the distinction between the end of the Middle Bronze and the beginning of the Late Bronze Age in pottery is not always clear and can be defined

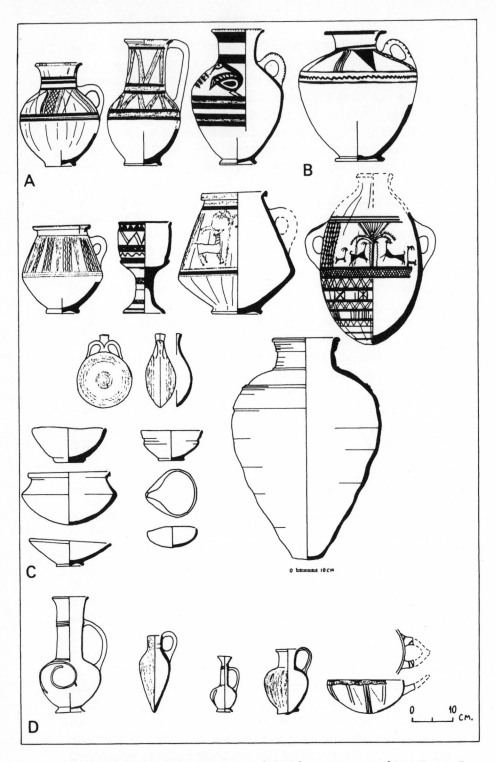

7.13 Selected Late Bronze pottery: (A) Bichrome pottery of Late Bronze I;
(B) Chocolate on White pottery of sixteenth century B.C.E.; (C) local pottery
of Late Bronze I–II; (D) imported Cypriot pottery.

only after minute typological study. The appearance and disappearance of certain forms and styles are important criteria for this distinction: Tell el-Yehudiyeh Ware becomes obsolete, and a rather rare type of gray ware juglet appears at the beginning of the Late Bronze Age. Gradually, the local Canaanite pottery changed in form, manufacture, and decoration. It became coarser and rougher, and there is evidence of a mass production of rough, cheap, local ware.

Aside from the simple, undecorated vessels, painted decoration now became common. It was usually red or red and black, applied directly on the plain buff surface of the vessels or on light buff slip. The motifs are mainly geometric: concentric circles decorate the inside of bowls, and horizontal bands appear on the outer shoulders of jars and jugs. Kraters, biconical jugs, and some jars were decorated with friezes divided by vertical geometric patterns (triglyphs) into a series of rectangular panels (metopes). The metopes were filled either with geometric designs or with the popular motif of a sacred tree flanked by two antelopes. The latter theme perhaps originated in the glyptic art of the kingdom of Mitanni in the fifteenth century B.C.E., where it was common on local cylinder seals. Such seals also had a wide distribution in Canaan, perhaps due to Hurrian immigration, and they may have inspired the pottery artists. In a few cases more complicated scenes appear on Canaanite pottery: on a jar from Tel Batash a procession of human figures and animals is depicted, and on a jug from Megiddo various animals are shown on both sides of a sacred tree.

The Bichrome Group   The pottery group known as Bichrome Ware due to its distinct red and black decoration started to appear around 1600 B.C.E. in late MB IIC contexts (see p. 216) and continued to be distributed during the entire sixteenth century and early fifteenth century, perhaps until the conquests of Tuthmosis III.[23] It is a homogeneous group, defined by its manufacturing technique and variety of forms. Most of its forms, such as the kraters, jars, and jugs, are rooted in the local Syro-Palestinian Middle Bronze Age tradition, but some, such as certain bowls and jugs, have Cypriot traits. This duality can be seen also in the decoration: the Canaanite frieze of metopes and triglyphs is prevalent, yet some vessels are painted with crosslines over the whole body, a typical

7.14 A krater of the Bichrome group from Tel Nagila (sixteenth or early fifteenth century B.C.E.).

Cypriot decorative approach. Fish, water birds (sometimes shown on fish backs), antelopes, and bulls painted in a specific style characterize this ware.

The Bichrome pottery was distributed throughout Palestine (particularly in the coastal plain, the Shephelah, and the northern valleys), along the coast of Syria (at Ras Shamra [Ugarit]), and in Cyprus. Neutron activation analysis has shown that many of the vessels in this group were produced in one region of eastern Cyprus. Only a few vessels from Megiddo were shown to be locally made.[24] If indeed most of this ware was created in Cyprus, one has to explain the overriding Canaanite features in the vessels' shapes and decoration. One possibility is to assume that the ware was created by Cypriot potters for the Canaanite market, and that these potters adapted their technique and style to their customers' taste. Another possibility—more plausible to my mind—is that Bichrome pottery was manufactured by immigrants from Syria or Palestine who settled in eastern Cyprus in the sixteenth century B.C.E. and created an eclectic style in which their own traditions were prominent. It may be suggested that these immigrants were Hurrians, as there are some similarities (as shown by C. Epstein) to Hurrian pottery decoration of the sixteenth and fifteenth centuries B.C.E. The Bichrome pottery was exported from Cyprus to the Levant, but it was also produced locally at places such as Megiddo.

Aside the Bichrome group, the Chocolate on White group (see p. 216) most probably also continued to appear throughout the sixteenth century. The continuation of these two groups as well as of the bulk of local pottery throughout the sixteenth century is an indication of the cultural continuity between the MB and LB periods.

Cypriot Imported Pottery   The import of pottery vessels from Cyprus to the Levant began in limited quantities in the Middle Bronze Age, becoming more extensive in the Late Bronze Age until it reached its zenith in the late fifteenth and fourteenth centuries B.C.E.[25] The phenomenon has to be seen against the wider background of eastern Mediterranean trade. Cyprus played a central role in this commerce as an exporter of copper and as middleman between the Aegean world and the Levant.

The Cypriot pottery was usually handmade and is defined by its wares, method of manufacture, color, and decoration. Swedish scholars divided this pottery into several major stylistic groups, which were further subdivided according to refined typological analysis of the forms and decoration. Some of the most prominent Cypriot wares were exported to Syria, Palestine, and Egypt. Among the most common of these were what is known as Base Ring Ware (mostly small juglets, jugs, flasks, bowls, and bull-shaped libation vessels); White Slip (mainly hemispheric bowls known as "milk bowls"; the decoration is brown on a white slip); Monochrome (small reddish bowls); White Shaved (the majority are juglets; the ware is white, and the body is treated in a technique known as "knife shaving"); White Painted (small jugs and juglets painted in brown-black on a white background); and Bucchero Ware (jugs with a ribbed body).

Each of the aforementioned groups has its own history. White Painted Ware was found in Palestine already in MB II (together with several other Cypriot wares); it continued in LB I and then disappeared. Monochrome, White Slip, and Base Ring, the most widespread forms, appeared in LB I (though White Slip "milk bowls" started to appear in small numbers already during MB IIC). The import of these groups to Palestine gradually increased, reaching a zenith in the fourteenth century B.C.E.[26]

As the imported Cypriot pottery included many bowls which could not be used as containers, the market demand was evidently for the pottery itself, which was considered as fine "table ware." Closed vessels—particularly the small Base Ring juglets which were very common among the Cypriot imports—were sold perhaps as containers for a particular Cypriot product such as a perfume or oil. R. S. Merrillees has suggested that the latter juglets were used to export opium; he points to similarities between the shape of these vessels and that of a poppy.[27]

Mycenaean Imports Mycenaean pottery originated in the Mycenaean civilization of Greece and the Aegean Islands and was distributed throughout the Mediterranean from southern Italy to the coasts of Turkey, and to Egypt. This pottery demonstrates the vitality of the Mycenaean mercantile emporium established during the Late Bronze Age.

The Mycenaean vessels were made on a fast wheel from fine, well-levigated clay. A light cream lustered slip covered the surface; on this slip, the decoration was applied in one color, usually in dark brown. The shapes and decorative motifs were well defined and repetitious. Most of the vessels imported to the east were small and closed, such as flasks, cylindrical boxes (known as "pyxides"), "stirrup jars," and piriform amphoriskoi; a few, such as flat bowls and large kraters, were open. The decoration consisted usually of horizontal bands, concentric circles, spirals, and various particular stylized motifs; some large deep kraters were decorated with a painted frieze showing a procession of chariots.

E. Furumark divided Mycenaean pottery into three major successive stylistic groups, termed "Mycenaean I–III"; these in turn were subdivided. The earliest found in the Levant is Mycenaean II (parallel to LB IB, fifteenth century B.C.E.), yet in this phase imports were rare. In Palestine, Mycenaean II is represented by only a cup decorated with ivy leaves found in Lachish Fosse Temple I, and a few sherds found in the Amman square structure. The Mycenaean imports greatly increased throughout the Levant, Cyprus, and Egypt in the fourteenth and thirteenth centuries (Mycenaean IIIA and IIIB).[28] In Pal-

7.15 Mycenaean krater from Dan painted with chariot scene.

estine they are found in various contexts in occupation levels as well as in tomb deposits—and in all parts of the country, including Transjordan. They are particularly abundant at Tell Abu Hawam near Haifa, where the largest collection of Mycenaean pottery in Palestine has been found. This phenomenon led some scholars to suggest that Tell Abu Hawam was founded as a Mycenaean trading colony; however, it is doubtful whether Mycenaeans settled in the east during the Late Bronze Age. The abundance of Mycenaean pottery in Tell Abu Hawam is perhaps due to the site's having been a major trading port of the period. A variety of Mycenaean pottery found in the Amman square building demonstrates that such vessels were circulated from the port towns along the Mediterranean coast to the inner parts of Transjordan.

The Mycenaean vessels, like most of the Cypriot ones, were most probably traded as objects of art and precious tableware within the broader framework of marine commerce between Greece, Cyprus, Egypt, and the Levant in the Late Bronze

Age. The nature of this commerce is not entirely clear. Some scholars believe that Mycenaeans established trade colonies in Cyprus, and perhaps even at Ugarit and Tell Abu Hawam, and it has been suggested that Mycenaean pottery was produced in some of these colonies (particularly in Cyprus) and from there distributed farther east. Others believe that all the Mycenaean products found in the Levant, including clay figurines and ivory works, originated in Greece and were brought to the Levant either directly or via Cyprus by Cypriot or Canaanite merchants.

Two shipwrecks discovered in underwater excavations off the southern coast of Turkey (at Cape Gelidonya and at Kash, near Budrum) throw light on this trade.[29] Both ships were on their way to Greece, carrying a cargo of copper ingots which probably originated in Cyprus. Yet the equipment of the crew was Canaanite, indicating in the opinion of G. Bass that Canaanite seafarers were active in the marine commerce between the Levant, Cyprus, and Greece. The ships perhaps sailed from a Canaanite port, loaded the copper in Cyprus, and continued along the coasts of Syria and southern Turkey toward Greece. These shipwrecks, however, probably represent only one side of the naval trade. It is more than likely that Mycenaean ships also sailed to the east via Rhodes and Cyprus. Thus the Late Bronze Age was a time of peculiar bilateral relations between the Greek Bronze Age culture and that of the eastern Mediterranean.[30]

The imported Cypriot and Mycenaean pottery was valued and appreciated in the markets of Canaan—so much so that local Canaanite potters imitated these vessels with their own techniques.

METALLURGY

Cyprus was the main source of copper throughout the eastern Mediterranean during the Late Bronze Age. Oxhide-shaped copper ingots originating in Cyprus were exported to all parts of the Mediterranean: they were found near Ugarit, in Cyprus, in Greece, and in southern Italy, and hundreds were sunk in the two shipwrecks just mentioned. Copper was one of the major items of the international trade in which the Canaanites probably played a central role. Tin ingots were also traded, as evidenced by their discovery in the sea near

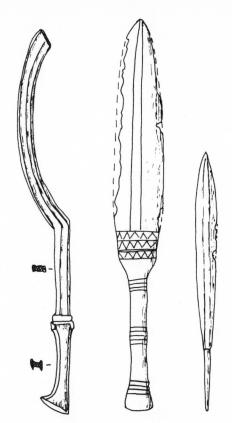

7.16 Selected Late Bronze weapons: a scimitar, a dagger, and an arrowhead.

Haifa. Copper ores in the Arabah were exploited in the Late Bronze Age only from the beginning of the thirteenth century B.C.E., when the Egyptians established mines at Timnaᶜ.

Workshops where copper ingots were alloyed to bronze and cast into tools and weapons were discovered in several Late Bronze and Iron Age I sites. A metalworking area at Tel Zeror in the Sharon Plain is a good example; it was an open area with several smelting kilns; the kilns were equipped with clay crucibles and bellows. Thick layers of ash indicate a long period of production. Abundant Cypriot pottery found in this area suggests connections with Cyprus, where the copper ingots originated.

The types of bronze objects in this period developed from those known in the preceding era. Sickle-shaped scimitars are known both from actual finds and from Egyptian artistic depictions; daggers were now cast as one unit with their hilt; tanged and shafted spearheads and narrow, elongated arrowheads were common. Other bronze artifacts were chisels, cymbals, and figurines.

Gold and silver were employed for jewelry, and occasionally

for casting small silver figurines or sheeting bronze statuettes. These precious metals were apparently less common after the sixteenth century B.C.E., perhaps due to the continuous exploitation of Canaan under Egyptian rule.

ART

The variety of Canaanite art objects includes only a few examples of large stone reliefs or sculpture; in the main, Canaan featured miniature art represented by cylinder seals, carved ivories, metal and clay figurines, and jewelry. These artifacts are invaluable in the research of the iconography, physiognomy, costumes, and other aspects of daily life in Canaan. They shed light on the extent and identification of foreign elements in Canaanite culture as well as on the nature of local artistic styles. Some imported art objects provide additional information on international relations during the period.

Sculpture in Stone Several stone statues and reliefs are indications of a Canaanite tradition in stone sculpture, apparently rooted in north Syrian Middle Bronze art known from Ebla and Alalakh. The crouching lion carved on the doorjamb orthostat of the temple at Hazor (see p. 250) and a lioness's head from that site are superb examples of this monumental Canaanite art. The motif of guarding lions is well known in the Levant: a row of lions' heads decorated one of the sculptured stone troughs in one of the Middle Bronze Age temples of Ebla, and such sculptured orthostats guarded the Late Bronze temples. Canaanite architectural sculpture is also exemplified by a relief on a basalt slab from Beth-Shean depicting a lion fighting a dog or a lioness. Each of the two stages of the combat is presented in a separate register. This work of art demonstrates narration in Canaanite art, as do several of the Megiddo ivories.

Small stone statues from Hazor and Tel Sippor (in the southern coastal plain) show a seated male holding a symbolic object in his hand—either a cup or a lotus flower. Prototypes of such figures are a Middle Bronze Age statue from Ebla and the statue of Idrimi, king of Alalakh during LB I. It is probable that the smaller Late Bronze seated figures from Canaan also represent kings.

7.17 A basalt architectural relief from Beth-Shean showing two phases in a struggle between a lion and a dog or a lioness (height 89 cm).

Sculptured stelae are another form of Canaanite monumental art. Several stelae from Ugarit depict gods such as Baal, shown as a young warrior god, or El, shown as an aged seated god. It is possible that a fragmentary stele from Tell Shihab in Transjordan, showing a young warrior god wearing a typical headdress and holding a spear, also depicts Baal; it should perhaps be dated to the Middle or Late Bronze Age. Another stele from Transjordan, found at Baluaʿ, shows a leader of what appears to be a nomadic tribe (Shasu?) in front of an Egyptian god.

Glyptic Cylinder seals are a most important source for studying the art, iconography, and international relations of the Late Bronze Age. The almost four hundred seals found in Palestine and the many more uncovered in Syria represent varied styles and a rich iconography. Seals in the Syrian Style of the Middle Bronze Age are still found in Late Bronze Age contexts, mostly as a result of their continued use as heirlooms. But seals were also produced during the Late Bronze Age and based on the Syrian Middle Bronze style, though these later seals were now of an inferior quality. The young warrior god Baal and the naked or dressed goddess (Astarte?) were popular motifs in this latter group.

During the fifteenth century B.C.E. a particular glyptic style emerged in the kingdom of Mitanni. About half of the seals found in Late Bronze Age contexts in Palestine represent this so-called Mitannian popular style. These seals were made of soft frit and engraved with friezes of birds, antelopes, or fish; priests and antelopes are often shown beside a stylized sacred tree. Most of the seals of this kind found in Palestine are later than the original Mitannian seals of the fifteenth century B.C.E. and are simpler in composition. It appears, therefore, that they were produced in local workshops in Canaan, perhaps by Hurrian artists who immigrated to the south during the fourteenth century B.C.E. after the conquest of Mitanni by the Hittites.[31]

7.18 A cylinder seal from Late Bronze II tomb near Acre, and its impression. The seal is made of haematite and has gold caps. The motifs and style are typical of the elaborate Mitannian style. Upper register: two lions attacking a bull; a winged goddess and a priest sacrificing a horned animal. Lower register: a sacred tree flanked by two horned animals and two griffins.

There were also local Canaanite seal-engraving workshops. Their simply made products depict a variety of themes, mainly animals and deities. Other seals were imported from Cyprus; some originated in Assyria, providing the only evidence we have of connections with Assyria during the Late Bronze Age. The foreign seals either arrived as imported objects of art or signify the presence in Canaan of foreigners from these countries, perhaps messengers and merchants.

Egyptian scarab seals are found in large numbers in Canaan. Scarabs with royal names are naturally of particular importance for dating archaeological contexts. In this regard, however, they must be used with caution. Scarabs could have been kept as sacred objects for several generations, and others, incised with the name of a pharaoh, were used as talismans and often postdated the time of the ruler mentioned. Thus scarabs with the name of Tuthmosis III were produced for several hundreds of years after his time.

Ivories Carved ivories are perhaps the best representation of the artistic world of the Late Bronze Age.[32] The richest collection, including almost three hundred pieces, was discovered in a subterranean wing of the palace of Megiddo Stratum VIIA; the latest work in this collection dates to the first half of the twelfth century B.C.E., as evidenced by the name of Ramesses III found on one of the objects.[33] As will be seen later (p. 298), Stratum VIIA at Megiddo belongs in our view to the first phase of the Iron Age (Iron Age IA), but from the point of view of cultural history it is the last phase in the succession of Canaanite cities at Megiddo. The palace of this level is a rebuilding of the older palace. Thus it is possible that the ivories found in Stratum VIIA were collected by the kings of Megiddo for several generations, and many of them perhaps decorated the palace furniture already in Stratum VIIB. Additional ivories were found at other sites, such as Lachish and Tell el-Farʿah (south). An ivory box from the latter site depicts hunting scenes and banquet scenes in Egyptian style. A common Canaanite ivory object is a cosmetic box designed in the shape of a duck; the latter object is also influenced by Egyptian prototypes. Elaborate Canaanite ivory artworks are known from Ugarit, where mythological and palace scenes appear on a series of plaques decorating a bed.

H. Kantor has divided the ivories found in the Levant into

several stylistic categories: pure Canaanite; Canaanite with Egyptian influence; a hybrid group combining Mycenaean and Canaanite traditions; and finally, imported ivories, mostly from the Mycenaean world and one imported from the land of the Hittites.[34] The first group includes decorated panels, plaques, boxes, and even fully sculptured figures. The motifs comprise a variety of stylized plants, animals, and mythological creatures; many of these motifs—such as female sphinxes, griffins, lions, or antelopes—were already known from the earlier "Syrian" glyptic style. Female figures, dressed or naked, are common. Scenes from palace life are shown on the bed panels from Ugarit and on several works from Megiddo, such as a plaque depicting an enthroned king approached by his queen, a musician behind her, and servants serving the king food from elaborate vessels. The other half of the same plaque shows the king returning from battle in his chariot, to which two captives are tied. Narration is represented in four panels from Megiddo which probably depict various stages of one event: a chariot battle between Canaanites; a victory procession after the battle; a sacrificial ceremony in which soldiers and nobles or priests participate; and finally a royal banquet.[35]

7.19 An ivory plaque from Megiddo (perhaps used for decorating a chair armrest). Two scenes from Canaanite palace life are depicted by incision. Left: the king on his throne, approached by the queen and a lyre player; servants carrying elaborate vessels are shown behind the throne. Right: the king is shown returning from battle on a chariot to which two captives are tied.

These scenes are a firsthand source for studying the physical appearance, the furniture, dress, weapons, and chariots of Canaanite rulers, nobles, and soldiers.

The Egyptian-influenced ivories include objects and themes which are almost purely Egyptian, including plaques showing deities, bottles in the shape of swimming girls, bird-shaped cosmetic boxes, and typical stylized plant motifs such as the papyrus. But most of these works were locally made by artists who copied the Egyptian motifs, frequently in an inaccurate and innovative way. Thus Egyptian motifs became part of the hybrid Canaanite art. The ivories which were made in a hybrid Mycenaean-Canaanite style include combs, a gaming board, and plaques showing animal combats, pinnate foliage and drooping palm branches; the style and many of the motifs in this group are taken from the Mycenaean repertoire. This ivory group may have been produced in Cyprus, where superb examples were discovered. Some imported Mycenaean ivories were also found at Megiddo and Ugarit. An exceptional Hittite ivory plaque from Megiddo illustrates superimposed rows of deities, kings, animals, and winged sun discs.

In summary, the Late Bronze ivory collections from Canaan demonstrate a vivid local art as well as international connections and influences. Toward the end of the Late Bronze Age and in the first half of the twelfth century B.C.E. the Canaanite rulers possessed a variety of art objects reflecting the cosmopolitan nature of the period.

7.20 An ivory cosmetic box from Megiddo, depicting lions and sphinxes in high relief.

Metal Art Objects Figurines and decorated pendants of bronze, silver, and gold were popular in the Late Bronze Age, as they were in the preceding period.[36] The most popular subjects were the young warrior god, most probably Baal (Hadad), striding and holding weapons; an enthroned male god identified as El, the head of the Canaanite pantheon, dressed in a long mantle; and a naked female goddess—probably Astarte, the love and fertility goddess—usually depicted on triangular gold-sheet pendants. Sometimes the full body of this goddess is shown, while in other cases only the head and fertility organs are featured. Another goddess, pos-

7.21 A bronze figurine from Megiddo depicting the "smiting god," most probably Hadad (Baal).

7.22 A bronze plaque from Hazor depicting, in shallow relief, a Canaanite noble or king dressed in official costume; his hand is raised in a blessing gesture.

sibly the consort of the enthroned El, is shown seated and dressed in a long robe.

There are several Egyptian and Canaanite representations of a naked goddess standing on a lion. In Egypt she is identified as Qudshu, "the holy one." A variation of this figure appears on a large gold sheet found in the temple at Lachish (Area P): she is shown in profile wearing an Egyptian crown, standing on a horse, and holding two lotus flowers.[37]

Few metal figurines represent mortals. A superb example is a bronze plaque from Hazor on which a beardless king or priest is dressed in a long Canaanite mantle, his hand raised in a characteristic blessing gesture.

Clay Figurines Clay figurines made by pressing clay into molds were common Canaanite art objects. In general, they represent the naked fertility goddess, and like the biblical *teraphim* (Genesis 31:19–35; I Samuel 19:13–16) they were

7.23 Pottery plaque figurine showing a fertility goddess, possibly Astarte (unknown provenance).

probably used by women.[38] The naked goddess usually is standing and holds snakes or lotus flowers; in most cases her hair is styled with the typically Egyptian "Hathor locks," a style adorning comparable female heads made of ivory. Another class of Canaanite figurine seems to depict a mortal woman lying on a bed, a subject known from Egypt during this period.[39]

Thus the various Canaanite art objects provide a comprehensive insight into the artistic world, the iconography, and the daily life of the Canaanites during the Late Bronze Age. Though this art absorbed much from foreign sources, particularly Egyptian, it had its own expressive stylistic features which define it as a unique and vivid decorative art.

WRITING

A variety of writing systems found in Late Bronze Age Canaan is a further indication of the cosmopolitan character of this period, as well as of the creativity and ingenuity of the Canaanites themselves.

Throughout the period, Akkadian continued to be the lingua franca of the entire ancient Near East. Thus the Amarna documents, most of the correspondence and secular documents at Ugarit, and texts found in Canaanite cities were written in this language. Each independent ruler must have had in his service professional scribes who had mastered Akkadian. Akkadian was studied in local scribal schools, as demonstrated by bilingual and trilingual dictionaries (a fragment of such a dictionary tablet was found at Aphek). A number of hieroglyphic Egyptian inscriptions was also discovered in Canaan, showing that the Egyptian system of writing must have been known to some Canaanite scribes. Yet for the Canaanites, both Akkadian and Egyptian were foreign languages and strange writing systems. Unattached to sacred traditions, as in Mesopotamia and Egypt, which necessitated the use of traditional scripts, the Canaanites had the creative freedom that enabled them to develop an alphabetic writing system. This is perhaps their most important contribution to Western civilization, as the later Phoenician and Greek scripts were a direct evolvement from the Canaanite alphabet.

There were two separate forms of the Canaanite alphabet.

At Ugarit, where Akkadian was in extensive use, the local scribes invented a script based on cuneiform signs—twenty-seven in number—which enabled them to inscribe on clay tablets. Indeed, most of the mythological texts found in the temple library at Ugarit were written in this revolutionary alphabet. This form, however, was limited to Ugarit itself; only a few short inscriptions of this kind were found in Palestine, and they were perhaps brought to the country from Syria.

The Canaanites who lived in the Egyptian province of Canaan developed a separate group of signs based on acronyms.[40] This script had two variations: the Proto-Sinaitic and the Proto-Canaanite. Several dozen Proto-Sinaitic inscriptions

7.24 A Proto-Canaanite inscription found on the shoulder of a jar from the Fosse Temple at Lachish. The inscription consists of a blessing to a goddess. The letters were written above and between a painting of gazelles flanking sacred trees.

were carved on the rocks at the turquoise mines of Serabit el-Khadem in Sinai, perhaps by Canaanites of high rank attached to the Egyptian mining expeditions. The Proto-Canaanite script is found in Canaan proper.

Unfortunately, the Proto-Canaanite and Proto-Sinaitic writing systems are known only from a few short and mostly incomplete inscriptions written on rocks, pottery vessels, and stone and metal objects. Most of these texts cannot be deciphered with certainty, and the origin and development of both script forms are still obscure. Even the dating of their introduction is vague. Two very short inscriptions from Lachish and Tel Nagila, and perhaps a longer one from Shechem found on a small, sculptured stone plaque, are said to belong to the end of the Middle Bronze Age. If this dating is correct, the alphabetic script might have appeared in Canaan in the sixteenth century B.C.E. Yet most of the other known inscriptions belong to the thirteenth century B.C.E. The dating of the Proto-Sinaitic writing is controversial; while most scholars follow W. F. Albright and date it to the New Kingdom—perhaps to the fifteenth century B.C.E.—others, following the original suggestion of Sir A. Gardiner, believe in a Middle Kingdom date.

The few deciphered inscriptions appear to be dedications related to cult practices. The longest in Proto-Canaanite script was written on the shoulder of a painted jar found in the Lachish Fosse Temple; it is a dedication to a goddess who perhaps was worshiped in the temple. The only Proto-Sinaitic word securely deciphered and which is repeated in the inscriptions is also a dedication to a goddess: *lbʿlt*, "for (or 'belonging to') the lady." This word is perhaps an epithet of Astarte, who may have been identified with Hathor, the protector of the mines.

In spite of the meager finds, it is clear that the invention of the alphabet was a revolution in the history of mankind. In the words of F. M. Cross: "The invention of the Proto-Canaanite alphabet was an act of stunning innovation, a simplification of writing which must be called one of the great intellectual achievements of the ancient world . . . With the creation of the alphabet came the first opportunity for the democratization of culture . . . literacy spread like wildfire and a new epoch of cultural history may be said to begin . . ."[41]

BURIAL CUSTOMS

A number of burial customs was simultaneously prevalent in Canaan.[42] Natural or artificial caves were used for multiple burials, perhaps of members of the same family over several generations. Some of the largest of these caves were used to bury hundreds of people. The burials were accompanied by numerous pottery vessels, weapons, jewelry, seals, and other precious objects. Cemeteries containing simple dug-out tombs for individual burials were common in the coastal and northern plains of Canaan. At Acre, tombs of this type were accompanied by rich Mycenaean and Cypriot objects, suggesting that these were burials of rich merchants or highly ranked people who traded with the Aegean or could afford its products. Sometimes the individual tombs were more elaborate and built up: tombs at Tell es-Saʿidiyeh in the eastern Jordan Valley were built as boxes made of bricks, and they contained a rich collection of objects from the end of the Late Bronze Age and the beginning of the twelfth century B.C.E. LB II tombs at Tell el-Ajjul were built of stones with a corridor (dromos) leading to them.

Several other burial practices from this period possibly reflect particular population groups. The use of anthropoid coffins in the thirteenth century B.C.E. can be related to Egyptian officials or troops (see p. 285). Another burial form is a central shaft with side niches in which individual corpses were laid. Square rock-cut chambers at Tell el-Farʿah (south) with burial benches along their walls are probably from the early twelfth century B.C.E.; they thus will be discussed in the following chapter.

Burials inside towns, a practice known from the Middle Bronze Age, became rare, perhaps reflecting some change in religious beliefs. An exception was stone-built tombs—roofed in a corbeling technique—that were found at Megiddo, Dan, and Aphek in LB II contexts. They resemble the much more elaborate, royal tombs, constructed of ashlar masonry, found in the palace at Ugarit. The resemblance of the corbeled roof to that of the Mycenaean Tholos tombs, and the abundance of Mycenaean pottery in the tombs at Dan and Aphek implied a possible Mycenaean inspiration; but in fact, the simple corbeling technique is found in the Levant in structures and

7.25 A built tomb at Megiddo, roofed in the corbeling technique. This large tomb, found close to the Canaanite palace, may have been a royal burial place. Schumacher, the excavator of Megiddo between 1903 and 1905, is seen in this old picture.

tombs from the Middle Bronze Age onward, and therefore the built tombs of the LB II probably continue a local Canaanite tradition.

Two pottery bathtub-shaped containers for bones, found in tombs at Gezer and Acre, resemble the Greek larnax, known in the Mycenaean culture. The evidence for cremation in the Amman square building (see p. 256) if correctly interpreted, is a unique evidence for the practice of cremation in the LB period in Palestine. It may indicate the presence of some Indo-Europeans (Hittites?) in this part of the country.

The multiplicity of burial customs in such a small country probably reflects the existence of a number of population groups. In her study of the subject, R. Gonen has defined at least one clear regional distinction: burials of individuals in simple pits or built-up cist tombs occurred mainly in the coastal plain, while multiple burials in rock-cut caves appear mainly in the Shephelah and the hill country. The Bible denotes the population of the plains as "Canaanite," while the indigenous population of the hill country is called "Amorite." Was there a true distinction between two major population groups in this period—a distinction reflected in their burial customs? Ascertaining a definite answer to this question appears to be beyond our ability at this stage of research.

As in the preceding period, we encounter in the Late Bronze Age the phenomenon of cemeteries without any significant related settlement in the vicinity. At Tell el-Ajjul, for example, a large cemetery of the fourteenth and thirteenth centuries B.C.E. was discovered, yet no settlement is known to have existed at the mound at that time. Such cemeteries may have belonged to a seminomadic population which increased during this period but left no trace of its presence except its burials.[43]

THE EGYPTIAN PRESENCE IN CANAAN

The Egyptian presence in Canaan was intensified during the period of the Nineteenth and Twentieth dynasties—a period starting ca. 1300 B.C.E. and ending in the middle of the twelfth century B.C.E. As this period, according to the schema used in this book, covers the end of the Late Bronze Age and the beginning of the Iron Age, Egyptian finds related to the thirteenth century B.C.E. will be reviewed here, while those dated to the twelfth century B.C.E. will be discussed in the following chapter (see pp. 297–300).

Egyptian Forts and Residencies   A wall relief carved on the outer wall of the temple of Amun at Karnak during the time of Seti I (ca. 1300 B.C.E.) is one of the earliest attempts at cartography known; it is a map of the road leading from the easternmost branch of the Nile Delta (the Pelusiac branch, which is dry today) to Gaza, the main stronghold of the Egyptians in Canaan. This road was named "Horus Road" in Egyptian, and it is mentioned in the Bible as "the road of the land of the Philistines," detoured by the Israelites in the Exodus tradition (Exodus 13:17). The Karnak relief shows over twenty stations along this northern Sinai desert route, each having a small fort and a water reservoir. Archaeological surveys (carried out by E. D. Oren) indeed revealed about

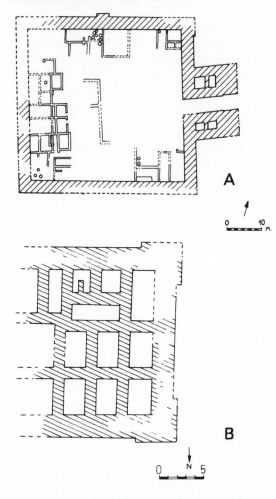

A

0   10 M.

B

0   N   5

7.26   Plans of Egyptian fortresses along the "Horus Road" connecting Gaza and the eastern Delta of Egypt: (A) fortress at Haruvit, near el-Arish; (B) fortress at Deir el-Balah, south of Gaza.

sixty New Kingdom sites along this route.[44] Excavations at two sites—Haruvit and Deir el-Balah—illustrate the Egyptian activity in this region.

At Haruvit (el-Harubah, east of el-Arish), a New Kingdom administration center was revealed. In the sand dunes close to the seashore, elongated storage rooms and a pottery workshop of the fourteenth century B.C.E. (Amarna Period) were uncovered. During the thirteenth century B.C.E. (Nineteenth Dynasty) a large fortress was constructed nearby. It was a 50 × 50 m mud-brick structure with 4-m-thick outer walls and an elongated gate. A large inner courtyard in this desert fortress was surrounded by dwelling rooms and cooking facilities. Rich Egyptian, Canaanite, and Aegean finds indicate extensive movement of people and goods along this route.

Deir el-Balah, south of Gaza, was a major Egyptian base near the end of the "Horus Road."[45] The site comprises a large settlement and a cemetery which was covered in time by sand dunes up to 13 m high. Remains of large Egyptian-style residencies from the Amarna Period confirm the Egyptian presence here during the fourteenth century B.C.E. An artificial water reservoir, a common feature in fourteenth-century Egyptian residencies of this type, was discovered nearby. In the thirteenth century, a square fortress (20 × 20 m) was constructed over the previous, ruined residencies and close to the artificial pond—this combination of a square fort and a water reservoir recalls the depictions of the Egyptian forts along the Horus Road in the relief of Seti I from Karnak. The mud-brick fort had wide walls and was divided into about fifteen small chambers; it was at least two stories high. During the second half of the thirteenth century B.C.E. the pond was filled with rubble and dirt, and its area was used for artisan workshops where potters prepared and fired large coffins for the nearby cemetery.

Additional square forts and residencies have been discovered at a number of sites in the northern Negev. These structures

7.27 Excavations at Deir el-Balah. The Egyptian settlement and fortress were discovered below deep sand dunes.

were erected during the Nineteenth Dynasty, and some of them continued into the Twentieth Dynasty.[46] The residency at Tell el-Farʿah (south), is a square structure of 25×25 m with a small central courtyard surrounded by various rooms and corridors; a residency at Tel Seraʿ (Stratum IX), of the early twelfth century B.C.E., was a square structure, 22×22 m, and resembled that at Tell el-Farʿah. An earlier structure (Stratum X), from the thirteenth century B.C.E., is believed to have had a similar layout. Buildings at Tell Jemmeh and at Tell el-Hesi may have been residencies of similar date and plan.

Egyptian forts were located in at least two additional sites along the coast: Tel Mor and Jaffa. At Tel Mor, situated at the mouth of the Lachish Brook (Wadi Suchreir) northwest of Ashdod, a square fortress (23×23 m) dating to the thirteenth century B.C.E. was uncovered. It had outer buttresses and was divided on the inside into several elongated halls and square chambers. The plan recalls the fort at Deir el-Balah, as do the finds, which included Egyptian, Canaanite, and Aegean pottery. The Tel Mor fortress was most probably an Egyptian stronghold on the coast, guarding the nearby port at the mouth of the Lachish Brook.

At Jaffa, the names of Ramesses II were found inscribed on the door jambs of an Egyptian fortress. Bronze hinges for the large wooden doors of the gate were found nearby. This Egyptian fortress at Jaffa fits a description in one of the most detailed Egyptian literary sources concerning the Land of Canaan—Papyrus Anastasi I (an ironic letter from an Egyptian scribe to his colleague)—in which Jaffa is mentioned as an Egyptian stronghold. The Akkadian letter from Ugarit found at Aphek also mentions Jaffa as the seat of an Egyptian official.

We have mentioned earlier (p. 246) the thirteenth-century governor's residency at Aphek, which might have been the strategic observation post of an Egyptian garrison at the point where the "Via Maris" ran along the narrow passage between the sources of the Yarkon and the hills to the east.

At Beth-Shean—the most important Egyptian stronghold in the northern part of the country—the largest concentration of Egyptian monuments outside of Egypt was uncovered. During the thirteenth century (Stratum VII), a tower-like fort was constructed at Beth-Shean not far from the temple. Inscribed monumental stelae of Seti I and of Ramesses II (found in secondary use in later levels) are evidence of the importance of Beth-Shean during the time of the Nineteenth Dynasty. Additional Egyptian buildings and finds were prominent in Stratum VI, dated to the time of the Twentieth Dynasty (early twelfth century B.C.E.; see below, pp. 297–98). Both levels contained numerous small objects imported from Egypt and locally made pottery in Egyptian shapes.

These finds demonstrate the existence of a network of military and administrative strongholds along northern Sinai, the northern Negev, the coastal plain, and the Beth-Shean Valley—a network constructed by the Egyptian pharaohs of the Nineteenth and Twentieth dynasties to enforce their presence and control in Canaan.

Anthropoid Coffins Burial in clay anthropoid coffins can be related to the Egyptian presence in the country in the thirteenth and early twelfth centuries B.C.E.[47] The lids of these coffins were shaped in the form of a human head and upper torso, with hands usually crossed on the chest. This burial custom was undoubtedly inspired by Egyptian prototypes, as suggested by the wig and Osiris beard formed on many of these coffins; but the execution is original and far removed from the Egyptian coffins. The best examples of these anthropoid coffins come from Deir el-Balah and Beth-Shean. At the cemetery of Deir el-Balah, dozens of them are rendered

7.28 Burial in anthropoid coffin at Deir el-Balah.

7.29　A group of pottery anthropoid coffins from Deir el-Balah.

7.30　A lid of an anthropoid coffin from Deir el-Balah (grotesque style).

in a grotesque style in which the facial features are exaggerated and unnatural. The burials were accompanied by a wealth of finds, including local, Egyptian, and Aegean pottery; a variety of gold, carnelian, and other jewelry; alabaster vessels; bronze vessels; Egyptian seals; ushabti figurines (symbolic representations of the servants of the deceased); and funeral stelae.

At Beth-Shean, the human face on the coffins is usually presented in a more naturalistic style, but some of the later coffins were made in the grotesque style, like those of Deir el-Balah (see p. 298). An anthropoid coffin found at Lachish in an early twelfth century B.C.E. burial was inscribed with an Egyptian hieratic inscription.

These burials were most probably of Egyptian officials and army officers, but the coffins were possibly prepared by local artisans. Perhaps some of the deceased were mercenaries of foreign origin who adapted Egyptian practices to their own taste and style. Aside from the coffin burials, the cemetery at Deir el-Balah contained simple poor graves, dug into the ground. These may have belonged to ordinary soldiers or to Canaanites who also served at this important Egyptian base.

Egyptian Mines Another aspect of the Egyptian activity in Asia was the exploitation of natural resources in remote regions. The turquoise mines of Serabit el-Khadem in southern Sinai continued in use throughout the New Kingdom, and Canaanites participated in the mining expeditions (see pp. 275–76).

In the Timnaʿ Valley, located in the remote southern Arabah north of Elath, the pharaohs of the Nineteenth and Twentieth dynasties operated a copper mine.[48] The Egyptians reached the place via difficult desert routes through the Sinai Peninsula. A high level of mining technology was acquired: the copper ore was quarried from horizontal underground galleries, which were either cut straight into the cliffs or approached through deep vertical and narrow shafts, some of the latter exceeding a depth of 30 m. The copper was then extracted in working camps set up in the valley and was smelted in furnaces located in these camps. The copper ingots could then be transported to Egypt or Canaan and used for casting metal objects.

As at Serabit el-Khadem, the Egyptians erected at Timnaʿ a temple dedicated to Hathor, the patroness of the mine. The

7.31 Timnaᶜ: view of the Egyptian temple near the copper mines.

Timnaᶜ temple was a modest structure which magnificently exploited the natural vertical cliffs of red sandstone known today as "the Pillars of Solomon." The temple included a rectangular chamber (which may have been unroofed) with a naos decorated in Egyptian style at its corner. Stone stelae were placed in the temple, some of them having a relief decoration showing the head of Hathor. The varied finds in the temple included small offerings brought from Egypt, such as seals, jewelry, and objects of art.

The mine was probably operated by a rather small number of Egyptian officials, experts, and soldiers; in addition to the Egyptians, there were workmen who most probably came from the northwestern part of the Arabian Peninsula, as is indicated by a particular kind of handmade pottery known also in Arabia. This pottery, known as "Midianite" (though the ethnic identification of the potters cannot be proved), was decorated in elaborate black and red designs.[49] A few such vessels reached southern Canaan, where they were found in contexts of the thirteenth through eleventh centuries B.C.E.

THE END OF THE LATE BRONZE AGE

Toward the end of the thirteenth century B.C.E. the political, social, and economic structure throughout the ancient Near East underwent a crisis. Within a short time we witness dramatic changes in the most important cultural centers of the eastern Mediterranean. The Hittite empire collapsed ca. 1200 B.C.E.; simultaneously, a wave of destruction swept through the Mycenaean world, resulting in the abandonment of some important cities. These events eventually led to the so-called Dark Age in Greece. Both from Greece and from Anatolia, there was a population movement to the east. The new peoples who arrived in Cyprus and the Levant are known as the "Sea Peoples" (see pp. 300–8).

These momentous events terminated the east-west international trade—one of the dominant characteristics of the Late Bronze Age. A manifestation of this termination was the disappearance in the Levant of imported Mycenaean and

7.32 A letter from Takuhlinu, governor of Ugarit, to Haya, the Egyptian high official in Canaan, written in Akkadian on a clay tablet. Found in the "governor's building" at Aphek and dated to the mid–thirteenth century B.C.E.

Cypriot pottery ca. 1200 B.C.E. At the same time in Syria, some of the most important urban centers were destroyed, including Ugarit and Alalakh. In Cyprus, however, cities destroyed at the end of the thirteenth century were resettled by new Aegean peoples, and there was a subsequent period of prosperity in some of the coastal cities of the island.

In Egypt, a short crisis at the end of the thirteenth century (which brought the Nineteenth Dynasty to a close) was followed by a renaissance which lasted for almost all of the first half of the twelfth century B.C.E. under the first rulers of the Twentieth Dynasty (Ramesses III–Ramesses VI). During this period, Egyptian domination in Canaan was still strong, in spite of the Egyptian confrontation with the Sea Peoples. Eventually Egypt suffered the fate of the other great powers. Following the reign of Ramesses VI, it entered a long period of decline.

Various theories have been proposed to explain this widespread phenomenon of destruction and migrations of peoples.[50] The collapse of the Mycenaean culture was credited in the past to a Doric invasion from the north, but currently, other factors—such as economic difficulties and, in particular, successive years of drought—have been suggested as the main causes. The Hittite kingdom also suffered from a lengthy drought and subsequent famine, but its abrupt end may have resulted from an invasion by northern peoples. The decline of the Egyptian empire still eludes decisive explanation. Although the wars against the Sea Peoples during the days of Ramesses III, early in the twelfth century B.C.E., were concluded with no immediate effect on Egyptian power, this invasion might have had deeper implications and, together with internal factors, possibly brought about the end of the Egyptian New Kingdom.

The determination of the end of the Late Bronze Age in Canaan proper is not an easy task. The land underwent a complicated cultural process at the end of the thirteenth and beginning of the twelfth centuries B.C.E., with diverse consequent developments at various sites. Some important Canaanite cities were totally destroyed around the second half of the thirteenth century B.C.E., the largest and most influential of which was Hazor.[51]

At Tell Deir Alla in the Jordan Valley, a faience bottle with the name of the last ruler of the Nineteenth Dynasty, Queen

7.33 A stele from Beth-Shean, showing an Egyptian official practicing ritual in front of the Canaanite god Mekal.

Tausert, was found in a clear Late Bronze context which included imported Mycenaean and Cypriot pottery. This discovery is of prime importance, as it provides a terminus postquem for this assemblage—around 1200 B.C.E (1185 B.C.E, according to current low Egyptian chronology—see p. 297). Many other cities were destroyed at the end of the thirteenth century B.C.E.: Megiddo (Stratum VIIB), Beth-Shean (Stratum VII), Tell Abu Hawam (Stratum V), Tel Zeror, Aphek, Gezer (Stratum XV), Timnah (Tel Batash; Stratum VI), Lachish (Stratum VII and Fosse Temple III), Tell Beit Mirsim (Stratum C), Tel Sera' (Stratum X), and Ashdod (Stratum XIV). But the fate of these cities differed: in some (such as Hazor and Aphek) the destruction was followed by a gap in occupation or a completely new cultural pattern, while others were rebuilt during the first half of the twelfth century B.C.E. along the same lines (Megiddo, Beth-Shean, Lachish, Tel Sera', Ashdod, and Tell el-Far'ah [south]; see details on pp. 297–301). The revival of these latter cities lasted for about fifty years, corresponding with the last phase of Egyptian control in Canaan during the Twentieth Dynasty. This short period ended in another wave of destructions, corresponding with the termination of Egyptian presence in Canaan in the mid–twelfth century B.C.E.

The traditional division of periods, suggested by W. F. Albright and G. E. Wright, terminates the Late Bronze Age toward the end of the thirteenth century (ca. 1200 B.C.E.). The period ca. 1200–1150 B.C.E., corresponding to the last phase of Egyptian domination and to the revival of certain Canaanite cities, should be termed "Iron Age IA." An alternative method, suggested by D. Ussishkin, terminates the Late Bronze Age ca. 1150 B.C.E.[52] I prefer to retain the older schema for two main reasons. First, such retention avoids adding to the existing terminological confusion regarding earlier transitional periods. Second, some of the essential characteristics of the Late Bronze Age do not continue after the end of the thirteenth century B.C.E.: the international trade connections cease, major Canaanite metropolises such as Hazor are destroyed, and various other Canaanite cities undergo crises (for example, the abandonment of the Lachish Fosse Temple). Furthermore, some of the new Iron Age features are already present in the first half of the twelfth century B.C.E., such as the initial settlement of Sea Peoples and probably that of the Israelites in the hill country (see Chapter Eight).[53] The inclusion of the period between ca. 1200 and 1150 B.C.E. in the Late Bronze Age would require the coining of a special term for this phase, such as "LB IIC." Thus, in spite of the true continuation of Canaanite culture in this phase, I prefer to draw the dividing line between the periods at ca. 1200 B.C.E. The detailed discussion of the first half of the twelfth century is presented, therefore, in the following chapter.

NOTES

1. M. S. Drower in: *CAH*, vol. 2, part 1, pp. 467–83, ibid., vol. 2, part 2, pp. 102–16; de Vaux (1978), pp. 82–152; B. Mazar in: *WHJP*, vol. 3, pp. 3–22; Aharoni (1979), pp. 150–90. On the history of Egyptian domination, see in particular J. M. Weinstein, *BASOR* 241 (1981), pp. 1–28, (with extensive bibliography) and I. Singer, *BASOR* 269 (1988), pp. 1–10.

2. We cite the chronology proposed by K. A. Kitchen, who follows the most recent studies on Egyptian chronology; see K. A. Kitchen in: P. Aström (ed.), *High, Middle or Low? Acts of an International Colloquium on Absolute Chronology Held at the University of Gothenburg 20th–22nd August 1987*, Gothenborg 1987, part 1, pp. 37–55. An even lower chronology for the Eighteenth Dynasty is proposed by W. Helck in: ibid., part 1, pp. 18–26 (Tuthmosis III: 1467–1413 B.C.E.). Compare the higher chronology used by W. C. Hayes in *CAH*, vol. 1, part 1, pp. 173–92 (Tuthmosis III: 1490–1436 B.C.E.). For the chronology of the Ramesside period, see E. F. Wente and C. C. Van Siclen in: *Studies in Honor of George R. Hughes*. Studies in Ancient Oriental Civilization 39, Chicago 1976, pp. 217–61 (followed by Kitchen [see in this note] see p. 297).

3. A. Kempinski, *IEJ* 24 (1974), pp. 145–52.

4. Sh. Ahituv, *Canaanite Toponyms in Ancient Egyptian Documents*, Jerusalem 1984.

5. N. Na'aman, *IEJ* 31 (1981), pp. 172–85. For a different view, see Sh. Ahituv, *IEJ* 28 (1978), pp. 93–105.

6. D. Owen, *TA* 8 (1981), pp. 1–17; I. Singer, *TA* 4 (1977), pp. 178–90; ibid. 10 (1983), pp. 3–25.

7. I would date the phases in this method as follows:
   LB I: 1550–1470 B.C.E.
   (From the expulsion of the Hyksos to the conquests of Tuthmosis III)
   LB II: 1470–1300 B.C.E.
   (The period of the Eighteenth Dynasty's rule over Canaan, including the Amarna Period)
   LB III: 1300–1200 B.C.E.
   (The Nineteenth Dynasty)

8. R. Gonen, *BASOR* 253 (1984), pp. 61–73. On Megiddo in the Late Bronze Age, see idem, *Levant* 19 (1987), pp. 83–100.

9. Y. Yadin (1972), pp. 27–109; 125–28; P. Bienkowski, *PEQ* 119 (1987), pp. 50–61.

10. J. A. Sauer, *BASOR* 263 (1986), pp. 4–9 (with extensive bibliography).

11. K. M. Kenyon in: *CAH*, vol. 2, part 2, pp. 526–56.

12. I. Finkelstein, *TA* 8 (1981), pp. 136–45; S. Bonimovitz, *TA* 10 (1983), pp. 61–70. It was suggested (by Bonimovitz) that the Middle Bronze glacis at Gezer was enlarged and strengthened in the beginning of the Late Bronze Age, and that the Middle Bronze fortifications continued in use. Yet it is not clear at what exact date this enlarged glacis was constructed and to what extent the city was fortified in LB II. Remains of dwellings from the latter period found on top of the Middle Bronze massive wall and "Inner Wall" indicate that this fortification was obsolete by the fifteenth century B.C.E. at least. W. G. Dever strongly claims a Late Bronze Age date for the foundation of the "Outer Wall" at Gezer following his excavations there in 1984 (*BASOR* 262 (1986), pp. 9–34); but there does not appear to be any actual proof of this date, and the evidence is circumstantial at best. See also J. D. Seger in: *Rose Festschrift*, pp. 119–22, for further support for a Late Bronze date for the "Outer Wall." (For further discussion, see Chapter Nine, note 17.)

13. Y. Baumgarten in: *Architecture*, pp. 120–27 (Hebrew).

14. M. Kochavi, *BA* 44 (1981), pp. 75–86.

15. G. L. Kelm and A. Mazar, *BASOR Supplement* 23 (1985), pp. 94–100.

16. M. Ottosson, *Temples and Cult Places in Palestine*, Uppsala 1980; A. Mazar, *Excavations at Tell Qasile, Part One. Qedem* 12, Jerusalem 1980, pp. 62–66; idem in: *Architecture*, pp. 136–60 (Hebrew); Wright (1985), pp. 229–47.

17. Wright (1965), pp. 80–102. It should be remembered, however, that only poor remains of Temple 2 were preserved, so Wright's conclusions must be considered with caution. It is possible, in my mind, that Shechem's monumental temple of the Middle Bronze Age continued in use throughout the Late Bronze Age, as did the temple at Megiddo. The remains of Temple 2 can be understood as foundations of the Iron Age "granary building," which has the same outer contours. See Y. Yadin, *BASOR* 150 (1958), p. 34.

18. D. Ussishkin, *TA* 5 (1978), pp. 10–25. The temples of Lachish VI and Beth-Shean VI, as well as the Megiddo ivories found in Stratum VIIA are discussed in this chapter, though they were found in contexts which have been determined by us to be "Iron Age IA." These levels are an integral part of the Canaanite culture of the Late Bronze Age. Their inclusion in the archaeological phase denoted "Iron Age IA" is explained in the next chapter.

19. E. Stern, *Tel Mevorakh Part Two. Qedem* 18, Jerusalem 1984, pp. 28–39.

20. J. B. Hennessy, *PEQ* 108 (1966), pp. 155–62; G. R. H. Wright, *ZAW* 78 (1966), pp. 351–57; E. F. Campbell and G. E. Wright, *BA* 32 (1969), pp. 104–16; G. R. H. Wright, *ZDPV* 78 (1966), pp. 351–57.

21. L. G. Herr, *BA* 46 (1983), pp. 223–29; idem, *AASOR, The Amman Airport Excavations, 1976*, Winona Lake, 1983. Herr's historical postulations should be taken with caution, as a direct Hittite political stronghold in Transjordan during the thirteenth century B.C.E. has no credence.

22. R. Boling, *BASOR Supplement* 21 (1975), pp. 25–85.

23. C. Epstein, *Palestinian Bichrome Ware*, London 1966.

24. M. Artzy, F. Asaro, and I. Perlman, *Journal of the American Oriental Society* 93 (1973), pp. 446–61; idem, *Levant* 10 (1978), pp. 99–111; B. Wood, *Levant* 14 (1982), pp. 73–79.

25. E. Sjöquist, *Problems of the Late Cypriote Bronze Age*, Stockholm 1940; P. Aström, *The Late Cypriote Bronze Age: Swedish Cyprus Expedition*, vol. IV Paris 1c–1d, Lund 1972; E. D. Oren, *Opuscula Atheniensia* 9 (1969), pp. 127–50; B. M. Gittlen, *BASOR* 241 (1981), pp. 49–59 (an updated survey of the subject).

26. B. M. Gittlen has suggested that during the thirteenth century B.C.E. Cypriot imports to Palestine stopped. This seems to be an extreme view; perhaps there was some decline, but the continuation of Cypriot imports is evidenced in many contexts.

27. R. S. Merrillees, *Antiquity* 36 (1962), pp. 287–92; idem, *Levant* 11 (1979), pp. 161–71. The suggestion was recently rejected by Gittlen (see note 25), p. 55.

28. F. H. Stubbings, *Mycenaean Pottery from the Levant*, Cambridge 1951; V. Hankey, *Annual of the British School at Athens* 62 (1967), pp. 107–47. On the finds in the Amman building, see idem, *Levant* 6 (1974), pp. 131–78.

29. G. Bass, *Cape Gelidonya: A Bronze Age Shipwreck*, Philadelphia 1967; idem, *AJA* 90 (1986), pp. 269–96.

30. See *The Mycenaeans in the Eastern Mediterranean: Acts of the International Archaeological Symposium*, Nicosia 1972.

31. H. Kantor in: C. W. McEwan (ed.), *Soundings at Tell Fakhariyah*, Chicago 1958, p. 83.

32. R. D. Barnett, *Ancient Ivories in the Middle East. Qedem* 14, Jerusalem 1982.

33. G. Loud, *The Megiddo Ivories*, Chicago 1939.

34. H. Kantor, *JNES* 15 (1956), pp. 153–74. For a general updated discussion, see H. Liebowitz, *BASOR* 265 (1986), pp. 3–24.

35. H. Liebowitz, *IEJ* 30 (1980), pp. 162–69.

36. O. Negbi, *Canaanite Gods in Metal*, Tel Aviv 1976.

37. Ch. Clamer, *TA* 7 (1980), pp. 152–62.

38. J. B. Pritchard, *Palestinian Figurines in Relation to Certain Goddesses Known Through Literature*, London 1943.

39. M. Tadmor in: T. Ishida (ed.), *Studies in the Period of David and Solomon and Other Essays*, Winona Lake 1982, pp. 139–73.

40. W. F. Albright, the Proto Sinaitic Inscriptions and their Decipherment, Cambridge, Mass., 1966; F. M. Cross, *EI* 8 (1967), pp. 8*–24*; idem in: *Symposia*, pp. 97–124; J. Naveh, *The Early History of the Alphabet*, Jerusalem 1982, pp. 13–42; M. Dijkstra, *Ugarit Forschungen* 15 (1983), pp. 33–38.

41. Cross in: *Symposia*, pp. 101, 111.

42. The subject was extensively discussed by R. Gonen, "Burial in Canaan

of the Late Bronze Age as a Basis for the Study of Population and Settlements," unpublished Ph.D. dissertation, The Hebrew University of Jerusalem 1979 (Hebrew), idem, *Burial Patterns and Cultural Diversity in Late Bronze Canaan* (ASOR Dissertation Series), in press.

43. R. Gonen, *EI* 15 (1981), pp. 69–78 (Hebrew).

44. E. D. Oren in: A. F. Rainey (editor), *Egypt, Israel, Sinai*, Tel Aviv 1987, pp. 69–119.

45. T. Dothan, *National Geographic Research*, vol. 1 (1985), pp. 32–43.

46. E. D. Oren, *Journal of the Society for the Study of Egyptian Antiquities* 14:2 (1985), pp. 38–56. For a current treatment of the Nineteenth Dynasty activity in southern Canaan see: I. Zinger, *BASOR* 269 (1988), pp. 1–10.

47. T. Dothan, *IEJ* 22 (1972), pp. 65–72; ibid. 23 (1973), pp. 129–46; ibid. 31 (1981), pp. 126–31; idem, *Excavations at the Cemetery of Deir el-Balah*. *Qedem* 10, Jerusalem 1979; E. D. Oren, *The Northern Cemetery of Beth Shean*, Leiden 1973, pp. 101–50.

48. B. Rothenberg, *Timna: Valley of Biblical Copper Mines*, London 1972; idem, *The Egyptian Mining Temple at Timna*, London 1988. The mine was discovered by N. Glueck, who incorrectly dated it to the time of Solomon. B. Rothenberg's surveys and excavations in the valley have shown that the mine was founded by the Egyptians in the beginning of the thirteenth century B.C.E. and was in operation until the end of the Egyptian presence in Asia in the middle of the twelfth century B.C.E.

49. B. Rothenberg and J. Glass in: J. F. A. Sawyer and D. J. A. Clines (eds.), *Midian, Moab and Edom*, Sheffield 1983, pp. 65–125.

50. F. H. Stubbings in: *CAH*, vol. 2, part 2, p. 338–58; V. R. d'A. Desborough in: ibid, pp. 658–71; H. E. Wright, *Antiquity* 42 (1968), pp. 123–27; A. Bryson et al., *Antiquity* 48 (1974), pp. 46–50; P. P. Betancourt, *Antiquity* 50 (1976), pp. 40–47; Aström (see note 25), pp. 775–81.

51. There is no decisive evidence for the dating of Hazor's destruction; some place it in the first half of the thirteenth century B.C.E., though in my opinion there is no reason to exclude a date during the second half of that century (P. Beck and M. Kochavi, *TA* 12 [1985], p. 38).

52. D. Ussishkin in: *Tufnell Festschrift*, pp. 213–30.

53. The complicated situation concerning the transition between the periods caused A. Kempinski to define the period between the mid–thirteenth and mid–twelfth centuries B.C.E. as one of cultural overlapping, the older Canaanite culture surviving side by side with the new features attributed to Sea Peoples and Israelite settlers. See A. Kempinski, *EI* 18 (1985), pp. 399–407 (Hebrew). He does not suggest any terminology to describe this phenomenon.

CHAPTER EIGHT

THE DAYS OF THE JUDGES:
Iron Age I
(ca. 1200–1000 B.C.E.)

During the Iron Age the ethnic makeup and the material culture of Palestine underwent significant changes. The Bronze Age Canaanite city-state system was replaced by an ethno-political structure in which the various regions of the country were inhabited by different peoples. Thus, in western Palestine there were Israelites; Philistines and other related Sea Peoples; and the remnants of the indigenous Canaanite population. In Transjordan, there were Israelites, Edomites, Moabites, Ammonites, and Arameans. Our discussion here will revolve around the regional ethnic cultures crystallized by each of these population groups.

TERMINOLOGY AND INNER DIVISION

By the term "Iron Age" we refer to the period between the end of the Late Bronze Age around 1200 B.C.E. and the destruction of the first temple in Jerusalem in 586 B.C.E.[1]

Subdivisions of the period have been proposed in various ways. The approach of W. F. Albright is reflected in the following division, suggested by G. E. Wright in 1961:

Iron Age IA	1200–1150 B.C.E.
Iron Age IB	1150–1000 B.C.E.
Iron Age IC	1000–918/900 B.C.E.
Iron Age IIA	900–700 B.C.E.
Iron Age IIB	700–587 B.C.E.

In this division, still maintained by several scholars, both the period of the Judges (twelfth and eleventh centuries B.C.E.) and that of the United Monarchy are included in Iron Age I. The division of the Iron Age employed in this book is based on the division proposed by Y. Aharoni and R. Amiran in 1958 following the Hazor excavations.[2] Our schema differs from Aharoni and Amiran's only in regard to the transitions between the subperiods of Iron Age II, for which we prefer dates related to two major historical events: the division of the Monarchy, and the Assyrian conquest of the northern kingdom of Israel.

Iron Age IA	1200–1150 B.C.E.
Iron Age IB	1150–1000 B.C.E.
Iron Age IIA	1000–925 B.C.E.
Iron Age IIB	925–720 B.C.E.
Iron Age IIC	720–586 B.C.E.

Thus the present chapter on Iron Age I relates to some two hundred years corresponding to the period of the Judges in Israelite history.

IRON AGE IA: THE LAST PHASE OF EGYPTIAN CONTROL IN CANAAN

We use the term "Iron Age IA" to describe the first half of the twelfth century B.C.E., contemporary with the Twentieth Dynasty in Egypt. During this time, the Egyptians still dominated the country, and Canaanite culture continued to thrive in many centers. This transitional phase could be included in the Late Bronze Age (as suggested by D. Ussishkin; see pp. 290–91). Nonetheless, as previously explained, the disappearance of some important Late Bronze Age features (such as the international trade connections) and the introduction of significant new factors (such as the initial settlement of the Sea Peoples) argue for maintaining the traditional term "Iron Age IA" for this phase.[3] There is not, however, a sharp dividing line between the periods, and the local material culture in many regions in Iron Age IA was almost identical to that of LB II.

The time span for Iron Age IA has been determined (by dated Egyptian objects) as covering the fifty years between the early days of Ramesses III and the time of Ramesses VI.

The table below presents several key dates according to the two current major chronological methods (see Chapter Seven, note 2).

	M. B. Rowton Method (CAH)	Wente–Van Siclen Method
Tausert	1200 B.C.E.	1185 B.C.E.
Ramesses III	1198–1166 B.C.E.	1182–1151 B.C.E.
Ramesses VI	1156–1148 B.C.E.	1141–1133 B.C.E.

The continuation of Canaanite culture and the strong Egyptian presence in the country during this time are evident at several key sites, the most important of which are Beth-Shean, Megiddo, Lachish, Tel Mor, Tel Seraᶜ, and Tell el-Farᶜah (south).

Beth-Shean, a major Egyptian center in Late Bronze Age Canaan, was destroyed toward the end of the thirteenth century B.C.E. (Stratum VII), but it was rebuilt (Stratum VI) shortly after.[4] The new temple was a modified form of its predecessor (see p. 252) and was decorated with stone capitals and lintels made in Egyptian style.

Building 1500, a large square building north of the temple, was apparently the residency of a high Egyptian official; its plan and architectural elements, such as T-shaped stone

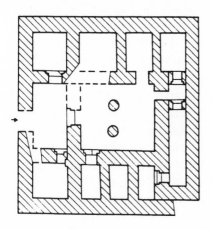

0   10

M

8.1 Plan of the
Twentieth Dynasty
Egyptian residency at
Beth-Shean, Stratum VI.

8.2 Anthropoid coffin lids from Beth-Shean. The headgear resembles that of Sea Peoples on the Medinet Habu relief.

thresholds, are typically Egyptian. A lintel from a nearby area bears a dedicatory inscription dated to the time of Ramesses III, and a statue of that king, found in secondary use in a later level, apparently originated in this stratum. Most of the anthropoid coffins in the cemetery to the north of the mound (see p. 283) date to Iron Age IA (though such coffins probably were introduced in the time of the previous Stratum VII), and they were apparently manufactured for Egyptian officials and soldiers, some of whom may have been foreign mercenaries. Thus, Beth-Shean continued to be a thriving Egyptian stronghold until at least the time of Ramesses III and possibly somewhat later.

Like Beth-Shean, Megiddo was destroyed at the end of the thirteenth century B.C.E. (Stratum VIIB) and rebuilt soon after according to the same ground plan (Stratum VIIA). The cause of the destruction of these two cities at the end of the thirteenth century B.C.E. is unknown, but their rapid reconstruction demonstrates the continuation of Late Bronze Age Canaanite culture in the first half of the twelfth century B.C.E. in the Jezreel and Beth-Shean valleys.

At Megiddo Stratum VIIA major buildings of the Canaanite city, such as the royal palace and the temple, were reconstructed.[5] A subterranean wing attached to the palace on the west included three chambers arranged in a row, which may have served as the treasury or a chapel. Here the famous Megiddo ivories (see pp. 269–71) were found. Many of these precious objects had apparently been manufactured during LB II and collected by the kings of Megiddo over a period of several generations. The latest of the ivories, however, were made in the first half of the twelfth century B.C.E., for one of them bears the name of Ramesses III. The base of an Egyptian bronze statue bearing the name of Ramesses VI and found in an unclear context probably also belongs to Stratum VIIA.

At Lachish, after the thirteenth century B.C.E. destruction of the Stratum VII city and Fosse Temple III, at least part of the Canaanite city was rebuilt during the first half of the twelfth century (Stratum VI). The temple in Area P (described on p. 253) belonged to this town. Like its similar Beth-Shean counterpart, this temple was decorated with Egyptian architectural elements such as papyrus-shaped stone capitals. Various finds in Stratum VI evidence Egyptian presence at Lachish during the Twentieth Dynasty: a bronze plaque inscribed with the name of Ramesses III; pottery bowls bearing Egyptian hieratic script; and a tomb with an anthropoid clay coffin bearing such an inscription.[6] The pottery recalls that of the previous period, except that imported Mycenaean and Cypriot ware of the preceding period are missing. Thus Lachish retained its Canaanite character at least until the time of Ramesses III.

The fate of Tel Seraᶜ on the banks of the Gerar Brook resembles that of Beth-Shean, Megiddo, and Lachish. The thirteenth century B.C.E. residency (Stratum X) was destroyed at the end of that century and rebuilt in the early twelfth century (Stratum IX) on the same ground plan. It stood until the cessation of Egyptian rule in Palestine in the mid–twelfth century B.C.E. This building was probably an Egyptian stronghold, as evidenced by Egyptian pottery—including a number of bowls inscribed with Egyptian hieratic dedicatory inscriptions. One text included the date "year 20," probably referring to a regnal year of Ramesses III.[7]

A similar though smaller fort, perhaps Egyptian, was located at the port site of Tel Mor, near modern Ashdod. Here, too, a thirteenth century B.C.E. square fortress was destroyed and rebuilt in Iron Age IA (Strata VI–V).

At Tell el-Farᶜah (south), on the Besor Brook, the Iron Age I phase can be distinguished in Cemetery 900. Aside simple graves intended for a single interment, there were in this cemetery several hewn chamber tombs, each including a stepped corridor (*dromos*) and a burial chamber with wide benches. These chamber-tombs recall Cypriot and Aegean burial caves; thus they may have belonged to mercenaries, perhaps of Aegean or Cypriot origin, serving in the local Egyptian fortress.[8] The pottery in these tombs is Late Bronze in general character but lacks Cypriot and Mycenaean imported vessels. Scarabs of Ramesses III, Ramesses IV, and perhaps Ramesses VIII date the tombs to the Twentieth Dynasty.

Egyptian activity in Canaan during this period is also evident at the Timnaᶜ copper mine (see pp. 285–86), which was in operation at least until the time of Ramesses V. The carved name of Ramesses III was found on the rocks of "the Pillars of Solomon" and near Beerot-Oded in the southern Negev, through which the route from Egypt to Timnaᶜ ran.

As mentioned earlier, in spite of the continued Egyptian presence side by side with Bronze Age Canaanite culture, various phenomena typical of the Iron Age were already in evidence in the first half of the twelfth century B.C.E. This half century, denoted in this book "Iron Age IA," can be regarded as a transitional phase between the Late Bronze and the Iron Age IB.

The sites discussed earlier met destruction again around the mid–twelfth century B.C.E. The destructions perhaps were an effect of the strength gained by both the Sea Peoples and the Israelites. To some extent, the destructions of these last Egyptian and Canaanite strongholds may have been related to the collapse of Egyptian control in Canaan, which coincided with this devastation. In any case, the two waves of assault— that in the second half of the thirteenth century B.C.E. (perhaps during the reign of Merneptah and in following years), and that in the mid–twelfth century B.C.E.—were severe blows to the Canaanite culture.

THE SETTLEMENT OF THE PHILISTINES AND OTHER SEA PEOPLES

The arrival and settlement of those ethnic elements collectively denoted by scholars as "Sea Peoples" is one of the most

Table 6. Comparative Stratigraphy of Iron Age I Sites*

SITES	ca. 1200 B.C.E. — IRON IA	IRON IB			ca. 1000 B.C.E.
Egypt	Dynasty 20	Dynasty 21			
Dan	VI	V			
Hazor	——	XII			XI
Beth-Shean	VI	"Upper VI"			Lower V
Megiddo	VIIA	VIB			VIA
Yoqneam	——	XVIII			XVII
Tel Qiri	——	IX			VIII
Taanach	IA	IB			——
Tell Keisan	12	11	10		9c→9a
Tell Abu-Hawam	Vb				IV
Tel Mevorakh	——				VIII
Shechem (Tel Balatah)	XI	——			
Tell es-Saʿidiyeh	cemetery				
Tell Deir Alla	A————→D	E————————————→L			
Shiloh		town			
Gibeah (Tell el-Ful)	Period I			Period II	
Tel Aphek	X$_{11}$	X$_{10}$			X$_{9}$
Izbet Sartah	III			II	I
Tell Qasile		XII		XI	X
Gezer	XIV	XIII	XII	XI	X
Beth-Shemesh				III	
Timnah (Tel Batash)				Vc–a	
Ekron (Tel Miqne)	VII	VI		V	IV
Ashdod	XIII	XII		XI	X
Lachish	VI	——			
Tell Beit-Mirsim	B$_{3}$		B$_{2}$		
Tel Halif				VII———→	
Tel Seraʿ	IX		VIII		
Tel Beer-sheba				IX	VIII | VII
Tel Masos	III?			II	I

* Many small sites, particularly in the hill country, are not mentioned in this chart.

fascinating episodes of Iron Age I in the Levant. This event was the outcome of the profound cultural crisis in the Aegean and Anatolian region toward the end of the thirteenth century B.C.E. The most well known among these people are the Philistines, but they were only one of several new peoples involved in a broad process of migrations and settlements throughout the eastern Mediterranean basin. Given this background of insufficient historical sources, the archaeological data is of prime importance. The historical and archaeological research of the Philistines and other Sea Peoples started already at the turn of the century, but gained great momentum during the last decades, due to excavations in some of the major Philistine centers and thanks to synthetic work, particularly that of T. Dothan.[9]

HISTORICAL SOURCES

Since the fourteenth century B.C.E., the Egyptians had encountered some of these peoples either as mercenaries serving in the Egyptian Army or as their foes in battle. In the Amarna letters the Sherden are mentioned as mercenaries serving in the Egyptian Army, and Lukka are noted as pirates. During the reign of Ramesses II, Sherden served in the Egyptian Army, notably in the battle of Kadesh against the Hittites. Under Merneptah, five different peoples are noted as being in league with the Libyans against Egypt, including Sherden, Shekelesh, Lukka, Tursha, and Akawasha, all denoted by the Egyptians as "foreigners from the Sea." The most significant source concerning the arrival of these peoples are the monumental reliefs and inscriptions on the walls of the mortuary temple of Ramesses III at Medinet Habu (Thebes), where the battles against these peoples during his eighth regnal year are documented.

The main inscription at Medinet Habu describes in poetic, literary form the formidable invasion by these peoples of the land of the Hittites, Cilicia (Kode), western Anatolia (Arzawa), and Cyprus (Alashya). The land of Amurru (in Lebanon) is mentioned as the place of their camp. Ramesses describes how he prepared for the onslaught of these foreigners and how he beat them both in a land battle and in the river mouths (probably at the Delta), where a naval attack was

8.3 Egyptian unit attacks Sea Peoples warriors, who are accompanied by ox-driven cart with women and children. Detail from Ramesses III's reliefs at Medinet Habu showing the land battle between the Egyptian Army and Sea Peoples.

expected. Finally the inscription lauds the great Egyptian victory over the invaders.

The Medinet Habu inscriptions name seven peoples. The main inscription mentions five names: The Plst (Philistines), well known from the Bible, are listed here, as are the Shekelesh and Weshesh. The Tjekel (or Shkl) are referred to as sea raiders in a letter from Ugarit and the inhabitants of Dor in the tale of the Egyptian priest Wen-Amon of the early eleventh century B.C.E. (it is from their name that the name "Sicily" is derived); finally the inscription mentions the Dnn (Denyen), who are also known as the Dnnym, living in Cylicia (southern Turkey), as evidenced by the eighth century B.C.E. inscription of Azi-tawada found at Karatepe; they were known as Danaoi in

Hellenistic times. The Sherden and Teresh (the latter perhaps related to the later Etruscans) are mentioned in other inscriptions related to this invasion.

A land and a naval battle are depicted in the Medinet Habu reliefs. In the naval battle, ships of the Sea Peoples appear with bow and stern ornamented with bird's heads; their square sails are furled as if the ships were stationary during the battle.[10] On three of the vessels the warriors are wearing a headgear often denoted as a "feather helmet." This helmet has a horizontal band bearing various geometric ornaments; above the band there are vertical lines possibly depicting leather strips. In another scene, captives with such a headdress are identified as Philistines, Denyen, and Tjekel. The warriors in the other two ships wear horned helmets which, as known from earlier reliefs, belonged to Sherden. The weapons employed by the Sea Peoples include a long, straight sword; spears; and round shields.

In the depiction of the land battle we see "feather-helmeted" Sea Peoples in battle chariots with six-spoked wheels. Each chariot is hitched to a pair of horses and holds three warriors, two of them holding spears or lances. Foot soldiers, armed

8.4 Detail from the Medinet Habu reliefs showing the naval battle between Egyptians and Sea Peoples. The upper part of this section shows a ship of Sea Peoples who wear "feather helmets"; in the lower part, other Sea Peoples are depicted wearing horned helmets.

with lances, long swords, and round shields, are portrayed in groups of four. The families (women and children) and belongings of the warriors are drawn in heavy ox-driven carts with solid wooden wheels. Thus the Sea Peoples appear as migrants and not merely as military invaders.

Although the majority of the Sea Peoples are clean-shaven, there are a few bearded Philistines and Tjekel among the captives. These bearded figures recall two contemporary artistic depictions found at Enkomi, the most important city during this period in Cyprus. One, on the lid of an ivory box, features the local ruler in his chariot with a bearded, "feather-helmeted" warrior behind him holding a battle-axe and another weapon. The other depiction, on a seal, shows a similar warrior, also bearded, holding a round shield. These two finds are of considerable significance for relating the Sea Peoples to Cyprus.

The outcome of these battles is related in Papyrus Harris I, according to which the Sea Peoples were repulsed by the Egyptians. However, many remained as mercenaries in Egyptian fortresses:

> "I slew the Denyen in their islands, while the Tjekel and the Philistines were made ashes. The Sherden and the Weshesh of the Sea were made nonexistent, captured all together and brought in captivity to Egypt like the sands of the shore. I settled them in strongholds, bound in my name. Their military classes were as numerous as hundred-thousands. I assigned portions for them all with clothing and provisions from the treasuries and granaries every year."[11]

In spite of Ramesses' boasting, it appears that the arrival and settlement of the Sea Peoples within the Egyptian kingdom was one of the factors which eventually led to the decline of that empire and to the end of its rule in Canaan. Two Egyptian sources from the following period relate to the status of the Sea Peoples at the time of Egypt's downfall. The Onomasticon of Amenope, an encyclopedic list from the end of the twelfth century B.C.E., mentions the Sherden, Tjekel, and Philistines. Three major Philistine cities are also listed: Ashkelon, Ashdod, and Gaza. It would seem then that the peoples mentioned in the Onomasticon were already settled in Canaan. The second source is the Tale of Wen-Amon, a literary text relating to the trials of an Egyptian official who passed through Canaan around 1100 B.C.E. on his way to purchase cedarwood at Byblos. Wen-Amon stayed for a while at Dor with its Tjekel inhabitants. They seem to have been the major body of Sea Peoples who settled north of the Philistines in the Sharon Plain, while the Sherden may have inhabited the northern plains and valleys of Palestine.

The role of settled Sea Peoples as navigators along the eastern Mediterranean is indicated by Wen-Amon's description of eleven Tjekel ships which pursued him to Byblos. He also designates the rulers along the coast who may have governed the Philistine cities. Their names are foreign to Canaanite private names. It seems, therefore, that the Philistines and the Tjekel controlled the coastal trade and shipping along the eastern Mediterranean littoral—alongside, and occasionally in league with, the rising Phoenician city-states of Byblos, Tyre, and Sidon on the coast of Lebanon.

The Bible is, of course, our only written source of further details on the Philistines. Their pentapolis included the cities Gaza, Ashkelon, Ashdod, Gath (apparently Tel Safit [Tell es-Safi]), and Ekron (Tel Miqne); it seems to have comprised a coalition of city-states similar to that found in Bronze Age Greece. At the head of each city stood a *seren*; the term is probably related to the Greek *tyranos*, "tyrant." The complex relations between the Philistines and the Israelites can be learned from the stories in the books of Judges and Samuel. Their conflict mainly concerned the control of the inner Shephelah and the Philistine attempt to penetrate the hill country and stop the development of an Israelite kingdom under Saul and David.

Various suggestions have been raised by scholars concerning the origins of the Philistines and other Sea Peoples. The Bible identified the homeland of the Philistines as "Kaphtor," probably referring to Crete (Amos 9:7; Jeremiah 47:4. Compare also Zephaniah 2:5 and Ezekiel 25:16. The expression "Cherethites and Pelethites"—found, for example, in 2 Samuel 15:18—would seem to refer to Cretans and Philistines.)

Most of the evidence points to the Anatolian coast (Ionia) and/or the Aegean world as the homeland of the various Sea Peoples. Some Philistine personal names and terms recorded in the Bible are related to Luvian languages of western

Anatolia, but the evidence is far from concrete. The archaeological data discussed in the following sections is a prime source and would indicate a Mycenaean origin for the Philistines at least. Cyprus featured prominently in the eastward journey of these peoples, but probably was not their homeland.

THE INITIAL SETTLEMENT OF THE SEA PEOPLES

After the wave of destruction which swept through Greece at the end of the thirteenth century B.C.E., new forms of Mycenaean pottery appeared. In the main, the new types were based on the previous tradition, but there were stylistic innovations and regional differences between various production centers. This new phase is denoted "Mycenaean IIIC," and it is further subdivided according to chronological and regional developments. One subgroup, denoted "Mycenaean IIIC1b," was especially common in Cyprus, where scholars associate it with a settlement of refugees from destroyed centers in Greece. The vessels in this group are typically Mycenaean in form: monochrome brownish black paint was applied on a light, sometimes greenish background to depict typical Mycenaean motifs such as spirals, various geometric patterns, birds, and fish. At the Philistine cities Ashdod and Ekron, pottery identical with that found in Cyprus was uncovered in the earliest settlement levels of the Sea Peoples (Ashdod Stratum XIII and Ekron Stratum VII).[12] At both sites it was found in a level succeeding the last Late Bronze level. Neutron activation analysis has shown that the Mycenaean IIIC1b pottery found at Ashdod and Ekron was produced locally.[13] Similar Mycenaean IIIC pottery, though in smaller quantity, was found at Acre and Beth-Shean, as well as along the coast of Lebanon and Syria.

The great similarity between Mycenaean IIIC1b in Philistia and that in Cyprus, and its appearance in both areas in large quantities, imply settlements of migrants with common origins. In Cyprus, scholars denote these peoples "Achaeans," referring to Mycenaean refugees; in Philistia, the producers of Mycenaean IIIC pottery must be identified as Philistines.[14] The logical conclusion, therefore, is that the Philistines were a group of Mycenaean Greeks who immigrated to the east, clashed with the Egyptians in the eighth regnal year of

Ramesses III, and later inhabited Philistia. In the initial phase of their settlement they retained their native monochrome pottery and produced it locally. Within several decades, however, due to their acquaintance with the local Canaanite and Egyptian artistic traditions, stylistic development occurred and a new bichrome style, known as "Philistine," appeared in Philistia (see pp. 313–17).

Thus, the initial phase of the Philistine settlement should be dated between the eighth regnal year of Ramesses III and the end of the Egyptian rule in Canaan ca. 1150 B.C.E. During this period—Iron Age IA—the Philistines retained their Mycenaean traditions while establishing the urban centers in Philistia described in the Bible as the five cities of the *seranim*.

SETTLEMENT PATTERN AND STRATIGRAPHY

Of the five main Philistine cities, Gaza, Ashkelon, and Ashdod are located in the coastal plain: the first two on the coast, and the third some 3 km inland beyond the line of the dunes. Gath and Ekron are situated in the lower Shephelah. Of these five, only at Ashdod, Ekron (Tel Miqne), and to some extent Ashkelon have excavations reached Philistine levels.

At Ashdod the first Philistines settlement (Stratum XIII), although unfortified, was a well-planned and densely built city, some twenty acres in area. Mycenaean IIIC1b Ware was manufactured locally in this city along with other pottery made in Canaanite traditions. The next two levels at Ashdod (Strata XII–XI) denote successive rebuildings of the Philistine city in the twelfth and eleventh centuries B.C.E. In Stratum XII the ruined fortifications of the last LB II city (Stratum XIV) served as foundations of a solid city wall. At the end of the eleventh century B.C.E. (Stratum X), Ashdod expanded to a size of about 100 acres, thus becoming one of the largest cities in the country. In this time Ashdod was surrounded by a solid wall with a four-chamber gate. This enlarged city endured for a long time in Iron Age II.[15]

The identification of Ekron as Tel Miqne is based on the description of the northern border of the tribe of Judah (Joshua 15:10–11); according to this description, it was located west of Beth-Shemesh and Timnah, south of the Sorek Brook. Tel Miqne, almost 50 acres in size, is one of the largest Iron Age sites in Palestine. The widespread distribution of My-

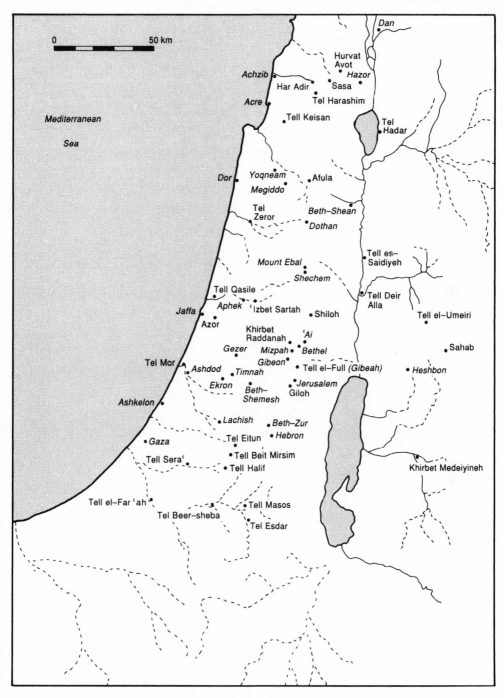

8.5   MAP OF IRON AGE I SITES. Ancient names are in italics; modern names are in roman.

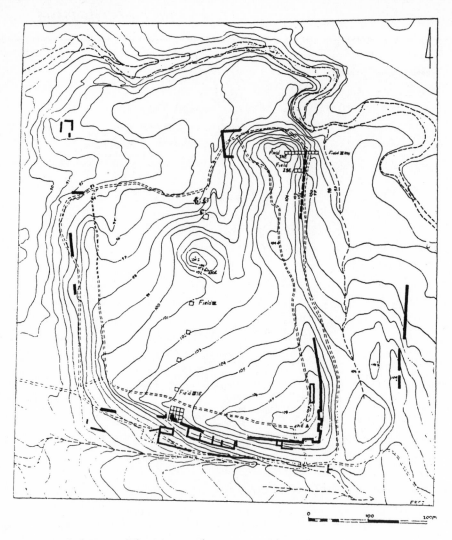

8.6   Tel Miqne (Ekron): site plan.

cenaean IIIC1b pottery on the mound indicates that the entire
50 acres of site were inhabited by the Philistines already in
the initial phase of their settlement (Stratum VII). Already in
this phase (first half of the twelfth century B.C.E.) Ekron
appears to have been an important urban center. It continued
to flourish in the following three strata (VI–IV; mid–twelfth
through early tenth centuries B.C.E.). During this period the
city was fortified, and it included large public edifices and
industrial quarters. Elaborate finds of this period indicate
relations with Cyprus and the Aegean. In Strata VI–V the

typical Philistine bichrome pottery was abundant, while in Stratum IV it gave way to new traditions in pottery making, characterized by drab red slip.[16] At Ashkelon, the third excavated major city of the Philistines, only few remains of the Philistine levels have so far come to light.

The extent of Philistine settlement in the heart of Philistia is still obscure. Except for the excavations just noted, few sites have been studied, and survey results have not yet been analyzed. At Tel Mor, following the destruction of the Egyptian fortress, the unfortified village (Strata IV–III) perhaps served as the port for Ashdod. Tel Ṣippor, in the southern coastal plain east of Ashkelon, is the single example from this period of a small, rural settlement continuing from a Late Bronze village.

A series of sites were settled by the Philistines along the Yarkon River; of these, Tell Qasile was the most important and extensively settled and is a unique example of an urban settlement founded by the Philistines on virgin soil.[17] The town is located on the northern bank of the Yarkon, on a *kurkar* (sandstone) ridge some 2 km from the sea. The choice of the site must have been associated with Philistine maritime activity along the Mediterranean coast, as the Yarkon River provided a convenient anchorage. Three occupation levels (Strata XII–X) denote building phases starting in the second half of the twelfth century B.C.E. The town was finally destroyed in a mighty conflagration apparently early in the tenth century B.C.E., during the Israelite conquest of this area by David. Other sites settled by the Philistines in the Yarkon region are Aphek and Tel Gerisa, but they appear to have been only partially settled and of little significance. Jaffa, the most natural port in the area south of the Yarkon, was surprisingly unimportant during this time, but at nearby Azor, a cemetery was exposed which indicated the existence here of a substantial Philistine settlement.

Three mounds in the northern Shephelah—Gezer, Tel Batash, and Beth-Shemesh—demonstrate the Philistine penetration of this region. At Gezer, four strata are ascribed to Iron Age I—one of which (Stratum XIV) is poor and dates to Iron Age IA, prior to the appearance of bichrome Philistine pottery. The other three (Strata XIII–XI) signify urban development in the twelfth and eleventh centuries B.C.E., though no fortifications have been detected. Philistine pottery appears in small quantities; it seems, therefore, that Gezer basically continued as a Canaanite town, with some Philistine population or overlordship.[18]

Tel Batash—on the bank of the Sorek Brook, 9 km south of Gezer and 7 km east of Ekron—is identified with Timnah, the Philistine city associated with Samson (Judges 14–15). This identification is based on the description of the northern border of Judah (Joshua 15:10); according to this description, Timnah was situated between Beth-Shemesh and Ekron. Only one Philistine occupation level has been distinguished (Stratum V). It was a densely built town and thrived for a lengthy period. There is some evidence of a fortification system, and Philistine painted pottery is abundant.[19]

At Beth-Shemesh, some 7 km farther east, a single Iron Age I level (Stratum III) contained abundant Philistine pottery. Beth-Shemesh appears in the Bible as an Israelite town during the period of the Judges (see particularly 1 Samuel 6:9–15), but the material culture at the site is indistinguishable from that of its Philistine neighbor, Timnah. This phenomenon exemplifies the difficulty of defining ethnicity on the basis of material culture.

The evidence concerning Philistine settlement in the southern Shephelah is rather confusing. At Lachish, the main Canaanite city in this region, there was a gap in occupation from the destruction of Stratum VI of the mid–twelfth century B.C.E. until the time of the United Monarchy in the tenth century B.C.E. Philistine finds are evident, however, at sites in the inner Shephelah. In richly furnished burial caves near Tel Eitun, southeast of Lachish, some of the most splendid Philistine pottery, figurines, and other finds have come to light. Though petrographic analysis of the Philistine pottery has located its origin in the coastal plain, these exceptional tombs are evidence of Philistine occupation at Tel Eitun. Philistine pottery was found also at Tell Beit Mirsim (Stratum B₂) and Tel Halif (Stratum VII), where unfortified and only partially built-up settlements existed during Iron Age I.[20] It is difficult to estimate the extent of Philistine habitation in this region.

In the northwestern Negev and the southern coastal plain, Philistine occupation appears to have been substantial. Tel Seraʿ Stratum VII was an unfortified town containing Philistine pottery dated mainly to the eleventh century B.C.E. At

Tell Jemmeh, several occupational strata were exposed; they include the only pottery kiln from a clear Philistine context to have been found to date. At Tell el-Farʿah (south), the Philistines seem to have utilized the Egyptian fortress from the end of the Late Bronze Age, and a cemetery adjacent to the mound is of considerable importance (see p. 327). At Deir el-Balah, remains of a poor Philistine settlement were revealed above the ruined Late Bronze Egyptian fortress.

The Philistines were thus responsible for a vivid and dynamic settlement process, during which large planned cities as well as smaller rural settlements were founded and intensively developed in Philistia. In contrast to this situation, major Canaanite cities such as Hazor and Lachish were abandoned during the same time. Thus the Philistines, as well as perhaps other Sea Peoples (such as the Tjekel at Dor), were responsible for the continuation of urban life in Palestine during the twelfth and eleventh centuries B.C.E. This aspect of their culture is of significance in the search for their origin, as an urban way of life must have been part of their cultural heritage.

Mycenaean IIIC1b pottery, denoting in our view the initial phase of Philistine settlement, was found in Philistia only at Ashdod and Ekron, both cities of the Philistine pentapolis. At all the other sites just mentioned, Philistine habitation began only after the evolvement of the Philistine bichrome pottery, which occurred in our view after the end of the Egyptian occupation in the mid–twelfth century B.C.E. Thus we evidence a process of expansion of the Philistine settlement from its nucleus in the major cities to peripheral areas of Philistia. The process probably did not involve the obliteration of the local Canaanite population, but rather the replacement of Egyptian overlordship with that of the Philistines throughout these regions.

PHILISTINE BICHROME POTTERY

The typical bichrome Philistine pottery developed from the locally produced Mycenaen IIIC1b Ware, which characterized the first phase of Philistine settlement. The new style appeared in the mid–twelfth century B.C.E. and survived with some slight changes until the end of the eleventh century B.C.E.[21] Though the main influence on it was Mycenaean, Philistine pottery borrowed from Canaanite traditions as well, mainly in the use of red and black paint (unknown on Mycenaean pottery) and in some shapes and designs Egyptian influence can also be detected in this eclectic pottery style.

The majority of the shapes are Mycenaean in tradition. The most common ones are bell-shaped bowls with two horizontal handles; kraters resembling the bowls, but larger and with profiled rims; "stirrup jars" (small closed vessels with two handles and a false spout adjoining the rim); strainer jugs; and cylindrical boxlike pyxides. Two types of bottles are similar to contemporary Cypriot vessels: a narrow, tall bottle and a horn-shaped one. Only the few vessels whose shape was derived from the local Canaanite repertoire (such as certain jugs and flasks) were painted with Philistine decoration.

The transition from monochrome, locally produced Mycenaean IIIC Ware to the new style (featuring black and red designs painted on light, whitish slip) was stratigraphically and stylistically detected at Tel Miqne (Stratum VI), where the earliest bichrome Philistine pottery appears together with local Mycenaean IIIC monochrome ware. A few vessels (particularly a jug from Tel Eitun and a bell-shaped bowl from Ashkelon) clearly demonstrate this transition, as their bichrome decoration is very similar in its details to the unicolored (monochrome) Mycenaean IIIC designs (Fig. 8.8).

8.7   Selection of Philistine pottery.

The ornamentation on Philistine Ware was generally applied in friezes bordered by groups of horizontal lines and often vertically divided into triglyphs and metopes. Most of the stylized motifs painted in the friezes are essentially Mycenaean in origin, particularly the bird representations. The latter were apparently considered sacred, as they also decorate the Philistine ships in the Medinet Habu reliefs and appear on Philistine cultic vessels. Fish, which appeared frequently on Mycenaean IIIC1b pottery, are rare on the bichrome Philistine Ware. Among the geometric motifs, mostly taken from Mycenaean IIIC traditions, the most common are spirals, presented both singly and in antithetical pairs. The Egyptian lotus pattern appears once in naturalistic form, but as a rule it is rendered schematically as a row of elongated triangles. Only a few motifs are Canaanite in inspiration.

8.8 A Philistine jug from Tel Eitun. The decoration of this jug is very similar to that of the Mycenaean IIIC style, though the jug is painted in two colors.

8.9 A Philistine "stirrup jar" from Tell Qasile. The shape retains Mycenaean tradition.

8.10 A Philistine horn-shaped vessel from Tell Qasile. The shape resembles contemporary vessels in Cyprus.

During the second half of the eleventh century B.C.E. there was a slight deterioration in the quality of Philistine pottery, and certain motifs, such as the bird, disappeared. Nonetheless, the style seems to have survived until the end of the century.[22]

Philistine Ware is always found together with another typical Iron Age I assemblage based on the Canaanite pottery tradition. At Tell Qasile, for instance, the decorated Philistine vessels comprise 20 percent of the entire corpus; both the

Philistine pottery and the other pottery uncovered there were locally made (perhaps in the same workshops), as shown by neutron activation analysis.[23] Presumably, at least some of the potters producing Philistine pottery were of local Canaanite origin; they adopted the Aegean traits brought by their new overlords, and thus they produced wares in the new Philistine style as well as in their local tradition.

Philistine pottery is found mainly in the regions of Philistine settlement. Small amounts found in the central hill country, the Sharon Plain, the Jezreel and Beth-Shean valleys, and even the Upper Galilee (Dan) most probably originated in Philistia and reached these areas through trade or military invasions.

ARCHITECTURE

Fortifications, Town Planning, and Dwellings The major cities of the Philistines were strongly defended. At Ashdod, the city wall in Stratum XII was constructed following an initial, unfortified stage of Philistine occupation in Stratum XIII. This was a solid wall, based on the ruined casemate wall of the Late Bronze Stratum XIV. At Ekron a massive brick wall defended the Philistine city, and the border town of Timnah appears to have been fortified by a modest city wall.

Philistine town planning is known mainly from Tell Qasile and to some extent from Ashdod. At the 4-acre site of Tell Qasile, the gradual development of the town was followed in three successive strata. In the earliest level (Stratum XII), the central part of the town was densely built, while the periphery was more sparsely settled. The town's sacred precinct was set apart by a wall running 25 m from east to west. Farther south, there was a public building. In the following level (Stratum XI), the town was more densely built up, many new buildings being erected. Substantial changes in the layout were found in the third level (Stratum X, mid–eleventh century B.C.E.), where a regular orthogonal street network was introduced, dividing the town into well-defined blocks.

Philistine secular public buildings are known only at Tell Qasile and Tel Miqne (Ekron). The building at Tell Qasile was found in the earliest occupation level on this site (Stratum XII); it comprised a large hall (inner length 6.70 m) built of plastered mud-brick walls with mud-brick benches along their inner face. In the center of the hall there was a freestanding

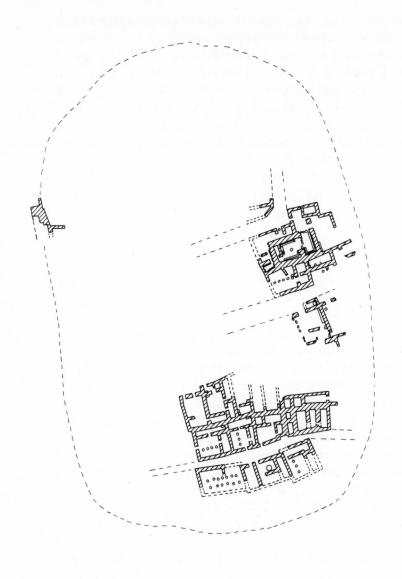

15 m.

8.11 Plan of Tell Qasile, showing architectural remains of Stratum X (eleventh century B.C.E.).

hearth, built of plastered mud bricks. The building at Tel Miqne (Strata V–IV, late eleventh and early tenth centuries B.C.E.) was probably a palace or a patrician house. It comprises a large hall (or courtyard) with two pillar bases and a free-standing hearth; three square rooms on the east open to this main space. The appearance of freestanding hearths in both these buildings is of significance: such hearths are unknown in Canaanite architecture but are a well-known feature in the Aegean and Anatolian world, and they appear in Cyprus during the same period. This foreign architectural feature was thus probably brought by the Philistines from their homeland.

The dwellings in Stratum X at Tell Qasile mostly had a uniform plan known also in other parts of the country in this period: They were square or rectangular buildings with an average dimension of 10×10 m, and they included a courtyard in which there was a row of wooden pillars resting on unworked stone bases. One part of the courtyard was left open, while the other was roofed and intended for household animals. At the back of the courtyard, and occasionally parallel to it, were dwelling rooms. The pillars in the courtyards were a prominent feature in these typical Iron Age houses, which accordingly are termed "pillared buildings"; some of them were planned in the "four-room" layout which was to become common from the eleventh century onward (see pp. 485–87). In the courtyards there were ovens, looms (of which only clay loom weights are preserved) and installations for grinding and crushing agricultural produce (cereals, olives, and grapes).

In Ashdod the only complete dwelling uncovered had a completely different plan (perhaps preserving foreign traditions): it comprised a large hall, the roof of which was supported by two pillars, and side chambers.

The Tell Qasile Temples   The excavations at Tell Qasile have revealed the only Philistine cultic center to be found to date. Three successive temples were discovered (Strata XII–X).[24] The earliest (Stratum XII) was a small brick structure (outer dimensions 6.4×6.6 m) comprising a single hall entered from the east. Opposite the doorway there was a raised platform on which the statue of the deity probably stood, and benches for offerings lined the walls. East of the temple, a broad courtyard was situated, in which accumulated layers of ash,

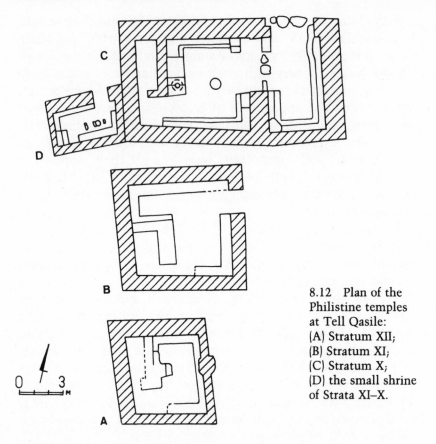

8.12 Plan of the Philistine temples at Tell Qasile: (A) Stratum XII; (B) Stratum XI; (C) Stratum X; (D) the small shrine of Strata XI–X.

organic material, and animal bones evidence the sacrificial activity there.

In the following phase (Stratum XI), the brick structure was superseded by a stone building, slightly larger than its predecessor (external dimensions 5.75 × 8.50 m). The doorway was now located at the northeastern corner. Along the interior walls were benches; in the western part a small room, which served as the temple treasury, revealed a rich group of cultic objects and offerings. West of the main temple, a secondary shrine was constructed; this was a rather small room with a "bent axis" entrance, benches along its walls, and a raised platform at its corner. Perhaps it was the temple of some secondary deity, possibly the main god's "spouse." This practice of constructing a minor shrine near the main temple was unknown in Canaanite religious architecture but had parallels in the Aegean and in Cyprus during the thirteenth and twelfth centuries B.C.E. In the final phase of Stratum XI, a *favissa* was dug in the courtyard; it contained ritual objects, abundant pottery vessels, and many animal bones.

In the third phase (Stratum X), the temple was rebuilt utilizing three older exterior walls. The floor level was raised and an entrance chamber was appended to create a "bent axis" approach. Plastered benches were constructed along the walls; a raised platform was located in the western part of the building, and behind it there was a treasury room. The ceiling of the main hall rested upon two cedarwood pillars which had well-worked cylindrical limestone bases. The temple courtyard was enclosed by stone walls, setting it off from the rest of the city. Within the courtyard a square sacrificial altar stood. The small shrine to the west, built in the previous stratum, continued in use, now having its own courtyard.

The three temples at Tell Qasile are different in plan even though they belong to the same culture and were built within

8.13   Tell Qasile: looking west at the temple of Stratum X.

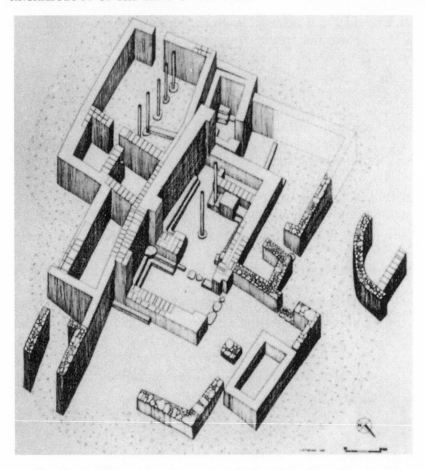

8.14   Tell Qasile: isometric view of Area C in Stratum X. Right: the cultic complex. Left: dwelling area.

a relatively short time span of some 150 years. Such variations in temple architecture are unprecedented within the Canaanite sphere, in which temples retained their basic form for lengthy periods. It seems, therefore, that the Philistine population—as was the case with the Mycenaeans—did not have a crystallized tradition of religious architecture. The Tell Qasile temple plans, in the main, do not conform to the bulk of Canaanite temples, although they do reflect traditions prevalent in some Late Bronze Age temples in Palestine, such as the Lachish Fosse Temples and the sanctuary at Tel Mevorakh (see p. 254). On the other hand, there are similarities to temples in the Aegean (at Mycenae, and at Phylakopi on the island of Melos) and in Cyprus (Kition). All these temples in the Aegean and Cyprus date to the thirteenth and twelfth centuries B.C.E., and do not have earlier roots in the Aegean architectural tradition. Temples of this kind appeared earlier in the LB period in Canaan, but as suggested above (p. 255) they appear to be unusual in Canaan itself and perhaps are not typical Canaanite temples. It remains unclear whether there were any influences in temple architecture between the Levant, Cyprus and the Aegean, and what was the direction of such influences. It appears, however, that there were some common features of temple architecture throughout the Eastern Mediterranean during the end of the Mycenaean period and the time of the expansion of the Sea Peoples.

CULT OBJECTS

Two types of Philistine clay figurines are a continuation of a decidedly Mycenaean tradition.[25] One figurine type (denoted "Ashdoda" due to the discovery of the only complete example at Ashdod) is a schematic depiction of a goddess seated on a chair. The particular style in which these statuettes were fashioned provides a direct connection with Mycenaean clay figurines of goddesses occasionally seated on chairs. A second type shows mourning woman with hands on her head; such figurines were attached to the rims of pottery kraters used as funerary offerings. Both figurine forms are demonstrative of the Mycenaean religious heritage preserved by the Philistines, though these forms underwent major stylistic changes.

Abundant pottery ritual vessels were uncovered in the Tell Qasile temples. Some of them continue Canaanite artistic traditions, others are original works of art, while still others indicate connections with Cyprus in this period. Ornamented cylindrical stands, one of which depicts dancers and another two lionesses, supported bowls probably used to serve sacred meals in the temples. The heads and wings of birds ornamenting several of the bowls recall the birds' heads which decorate the Sea Peoples' ships in the Medinet Habu reliefs. A cup in the form of a lion's head is the best-preserved in a group of similar vessels found at other Iron Age I sites related to the Sea Peoples in Palestine. Late Bronze prototypes of such cups are known from Ugarit, where they may have been based on Aegean examples.[26] A unique libation vessel is

8.15 "Ashdoda"—
a pottery figurine
(height 17 cm) de-
picting a seated fe-
male, probably a
goddess. Stylisti-
cally this figure re-
tains Mycenaean
traditions.

8.16 Figurine (height 10.8 cm)
showing a mourning woman; it
was probably attached to the rim
of a krater, in a fashion similar to
Mycenaean prototypes. Found in
a tomb at Tel Eitun.

fashioned in the form of a female figure. Her head serves as
the vessel's neck and her breasts form the libation spouts.
The vessel was probably employed in some kind of a fertility
cult. Other libation vessels were kernoi (tubular rings with
attached spouts in the shape of animals, pomegranates, and
jars) and kernos bowls (bowls with tubular rims and animal-

8.17 Tell Qasile: woman-shaped libation vessel (height 32.5 cm) with breasts used as spouts: probably the vessel functioned in a fertility cult. Found in a pit (*favissa*) of Stratum XI.

8.18 A bird-shaped offering bowl from Tell Qasile (diameter 24 cm). Birds also decorate the Sea Peoples' ships shown at Medinet Habu, and they are a common motif on Philistine pottery.

shaped spouts). Both these vessels are common finds from this period in Philistia and Cyprus.

Other cultic vessels include a jar with five openings in which sacred plants may have been grown. A pottery plaque is shaped in the form of a temple facade with two gods or goddesses shown in relief. The two figures appear to have been deliberately erased, perhaps by the conquerors of the town, before the last temple—in which the plaques were found—was burnt down. Pottery masks in the form of human and animal faces may have been worn by priests during rites, and a triton shell served as the horn blown during rituals, a practice carried out throughout the Mediterranean Basin. Among the offerings in the temples were precious objects such as beads, metal artifacts, ivory objects, alabaster vessels, and many pottery vessels. They illustrate the wealth and artistic vitality of the population at Tell Qasile during Iron Age I.

GLYPTIC ART AND WRITING

Among the objects found at Philistine sites is a number of stone seals, mostly of conical or pyramidal shape, with schematic and linear depictions of animal and human figures. On two seals (from Ashdod and Tel Batash), seated human figures are shown playing a stringed instrument (a sort of harp). These seals apparently represent Philistine and related schools of glyptic art.

Short inscriptions appear on two of the seals from Ashdod. The letters are linear, recalling the still undeciphered Late Bronze Cypro-Minoan script known from Cyprus. Although only a few letter signs are known, they demonstrate the existence of a Philistine writing system, probably of Aegean inspiration.

BURIAL CUSTOMS

Philistine cemeteries have been uncovered at Azor, Tell el-Farʿah (south), and Tel Eitun, and necropolises at Tel Zeror and Beth-Shean are attributed to other Sea Peoples. A variety of burial customs have been observed. At Azor, single graves were dug into the ground, others were built as rectangular cists, and there were also "coffins" created by breaking the necks of and joining two large storage jars. These three types have also been found at a cemetery adjacent to Tel Zeror; this latter cemetery can be related to the Tjekel, whose center was at nearby Dor. Some evidence for cremation was found at Azor, but the importance of this practice among the Sea Peoples is still obscure.

Cemetery 600 near Tell el-Farʿah (south) in the northern Negev contained dozens of simple graves, and five burial caves hewn in the bedrock there apparently belonged to Philistine aristocratic families. The latter were chamber tombs, similar in shape to those found in the earlier Cemetery 900 of the Iron Age IA phase (see p. 300). Thus the tradition of using chamber tombs was retained by the Philistines during the twelfth and eleventh centuries B.C.E.[27]

Pottery anthropoid coffins were considered in the past as examples of Philistine burial practice. This hypothesis was based on two such coffins discovered in chamber tombs with Philistine pottery at Tell el-Farʿah (south), and on the forehead decoration on some of the Beth-Shean coffins—decoration recalling the headdress of the Sea Peoples at Medinet Habu (see Fig. 8.2, p. 298). More recent studies, however, particularly those made at Deir el-Balah, have shown that this practice was common in Palestine toward the end of the Late Bronze Age at Egyptian government centers. The grotesque-style coffins may be attributed to Sea Peoples mercenaries serving with the Egyptian Army who were inspired from the Egyptian burial customs (see pp. 283–85). The custom was passed on to the Philistines and possibly to other Sea Peoples after the end of the Egyptian rule, though on a very limited scale.[28]

THE END OF THE PHILISTINE CULTURE

The archaeological study of the Philistines is a "laboratory case" in the research of the emergence, development, and disappearance of the material culture of an immigrant people. We have to assume that the Philistine immigrations in the mid–twelfth century B.C.E. was one episode and was not followed by successive waves of immigrants. We also have to conclude that the newcomers did not replace the local population, but rather became a numerically limited military and civil aristocracy which dominated it. The bilateral relations between the two populations produced an eclectic culture archaeologically expressed by phenomena such as the Philistine bichrome pottery. Isolated from the source of their culture, the Philistines were inspired by the indigenous population and were assimilated into it. This was a long and gradual process. Toward the end of the eleventh century B.C.E., the Philistine bichrome ware gave way to a new pottery style—characterized by burnished red slip—which was to become popular in the succeeding centuries. At Tell Qasile, this innovation appeared for the first time in Strata XI–X of the eleventh century B.C.E. together with Philistine bichrome pottery; in Stratum X, the link between the two techniques is demonstrated by the appearance of black spirals painted on red slipped kraters. But by the time of Stratum IX in the tenth century B.C.E., the painted pottery disappeared and was fully replaced by the red slipped and burnished pottery.

The Philistines' cultural assimilation, however, did not bring an end to their identity. The independence of their city-states was retained throughout Iron Age II, as demonstrated by both their political history and their distinct material culture (see pp. 531–36).

THE MATERIAL CULTURE OF THE ISRAELITE TRIBES IN THE PERIOD OF THE JUDGES

INTRODUCTION

The origins of the Israelites and the crystallization of their national entity are among the most controversial topics of biblical history. Various opinions have been put forth, ranging from the fundamentalist approach—which strictly adheres to the biblical text regarding the patriarchal traditions, the enslavement in Egypt, the Exodus, and the conquest of Canaan—to the contradictory position, which entirely negates any historicity in the biblical tradition, regarding it as fiction and proposing various alternative reconstructions of Israelite origins.[29]

In the present discussion we shall confine ourselves to the contribution of archaeological research to this debate. Serious methodological problems are involved, as on its own the dry archaeological data lends itself to various interpretations. The destruction layer of a Canaanite town mentioned in the biblical conquest traditions can be considered as confirming the historicity of the biblical account, or can be interpreted differently. Some settlements which are regarded by certain archaeologists as evidence of Israelite habitation during the period of the Judges are explained by others as settlements of non-Israelite ethnic groups. The relative sparsity of archaeological finds relating to this problem hinders unequivocal conclusions. Despite these objective difficulties, recent research—using the modern tools of intensive surface survey, ecological studies, and ethnographic comparisons—has brought forth much new data, enabling a better understanding of the settlement process of the Israelite tribes.

THE ISRAELITE CONQUEST OF CANAAN IN THE LIGHT OF ARCHAEOLOGICAL EVIDENCE

In examining the archaeological aspect of the conquest of Canaan, we shall concentrate on the factual situation at the various sites which are related to the conquest by biblical tradition.[30] This approach may seem anachronistic in the light of some current views concerning the reality behind the Exodus and conquest narratives. Nonetheless, since archaeology is probably the only tool available for verifying the factual data in these stories, a survey of the subject in some detail is called for.

Archaeological material is sometimes utilized indiscriminately in historical studies. We must take into account that excavation data can lead to different interpretations; such interpretations are often subjective and slanted toward a particular historical view. An overall examination of the conquest tradition in the archaeological context illustrates the complexity of the subject and the various possibilities for interpretation of the finds.

Included in the narrative of the wanderings of the Israelites in the Book of Numbers is a battle against "the Canaanite king of Arad who lived in the Negev" (Numbers 21:1). Concerning the Israelite victory, the text continues (Numbers 21:3 and compare 33:40): "they completely destroyed them and their towns, so the place was named Hormah." According to this tradition, the Israelites journeyed to the region of Arad from Kadesh-Barnea via Hor Hahar. A thorough archaeological research at the oasis of Kadesh-Barnea did not reveal even one sherd from the Late Bronze Age or Iron Age I. The place was only populated during the third millennium B.C.E. and in the time of the Israelite Monarchy, when a royal fortress was established.

Extensive research in the Arad Valley, too, has revealed no evidence of any Canaanite settlement of the Late Bronze Age. At Arad proper there was an occupational gap after the destruction of the EB II city until the time of the United Monarchy, when a small Israelite settlement was founded there. Facing this problem, Y. Aharoni sought Canaanite Arad at other sites in the region, but all were uninhabited during the Late Bronze Age, although two mounds were settled in MB II (Tel Malhata and Tel Masos).[31] This archaeological determination is important for assessing the biblical tradition's historical reliability in regard to the region. Does the biblical narrative reflect an earlier period (in this case, perhaps MB II) during which Canaanites settled the region? Or does the phrase "king of Arad" refer to the leader of a nomadic or seminomadic population of which no material remains have survived (as suggested by B. Mazar followed by Aharoni)? Both possibilities seem unlikely. It is more feasible that the biblical stories were formulated as a literary tradition of no historical value when the Israelites began settling this region at the end of the period of the Judges and at the time of the Monarchy.

The tradition concerning the wars in Transjordan is even more problematic due to insufficient archaeological data. Numbers 21:21–32 tell of the wars of the Israelites against Sihon, king of the "Amorites," and of the conquest of Heshbon. Heshbon (Tell Hesban) was settled for the first time in Iron Age I, but very sparsely according to the remains. There is no archaeological testimony of an "Amorite" state in this region which could have been conquered by the Israelites. Nor is there evidence of a Moabite kingdom in Iron Age I, in spite of the discovery in the region of several sites from this period. The tradition about Balaam the seer, hero of Numbers 22–24, is now well attested archaeologically by the plaster inscriptions found at Tell Deir Alla near the mouth of the Jabbok, but these inscriptions date to Iron Age II (eighth and seventh centuries B.C.E.) and do not confirm the historicity of the tradition in the decisive period in question.

There are varying evaluations of the literary narrative

concerning the Israelite conquest in Joshua 1–11. While some scholars regard the narrative as demonstrating an actual military campaign under the leadership of Joshua (Y. Kaufmann, Y. Yadin, and others), others regard it as a literary creation from a much later time. Nonetheless, even this latter view does not exclude the possibility that the stories echo individual historical events which may have occurred during the process of the Israelite settlement. In fact, the stories in Joshua (excluding the onomastic list in Chapter 12) refer to a small number of cities: Jericho, 'Ai, the league of cities under the leadership of Jerusalem, and Hazor. Let us examine the archaeological data at these sites.

At Jericho, no remains of Late Bronze fortifications were found; this was taken as evidence against the historical value of the narrative in the Book of Joshua. The finds at Jericho, however, show that there was a settlement there during the Late Bronze Age, though most of its remains were eroded or removed by human activity. Perhaps, as at other sites, the massive Middle Bronze fortifications were reutilized in the Late Bronze Age. The Late Bronze settlement at Jericho was followed by an occupation gap in Iron Age I. Thus, in the case of Jericho, the archaeological data cannot serve as decisive evidence to deny a historical nucleus in the Book of Joshua concerning the conquest of this city.

The description of the conquest of 'Ai details its location: "Ai, which is near Beth Aven to the east of Bethel" (Joshua 7:2). The identification of Bethel with the village of Beitin is almost universally accepted because of the geographic and archaeological compatibility of the latter. Between Beitin and the desert to its east, there is only one site which could have been referred to as "'Ai"—the large mound of et-Tell near Deir Dibwan. The mound's name is actually an Arabic translation of the Hebrew biblical name "'Ai," meaning "ruins." A long gap in occupation followed the large Early Bronze Age city at 'Ai until a small village was established there during the Israelite settlement in the twelfth and eleventh centuries B.C.E. This lack of any Late Bronze Canaanite city at the site or in the vicinity contradicts the narrative in Joshua 8 and shows that it was not based on historical reality despite its topographical and tactical plausibility. The 'Ai story can only be explained as being of etiological nature, created at a time when there was an Israelite settlement on the site—which was the case in the period of the Judges (during the Monarchy, the site was deserted). The 'Ai settlers were surely acquainted with the substantial remains of the Early Bronze Age city, and it was these which inspired the name of the site and the formation of the story regarding the conquest of a Canaanite city there. The topographical details which were integrated into the narrative were based on firsthand observation.[32]

The Joshua 10 narrative relates to the wars against the league of kings in the hill country and in the Shephelah under the leadership of Jerusalem; the league included Jerusalem, Hebron, Yarmuth, Lachish, and Eglon. The story notes the military conquest of Makkedah, Libnah, Lachish, Eglon, Hebron, and Debir, and in its summary there is an allusion to the acquisition of extensive territories: "the hill country, the Negev, the western foothills (Shephelah) and the mountain slopes ... from Kadesh Barnea to Gaza and from the whole region of Goshen to Gibeon" (Josh. 10:40–41).

Remains of Canaanite cities have been discovered at Jerusalem, Lachish, and Debir (Khirbet Rabud). At Lachish the cartouche of Ramesses III determines the terminus post quem for the destruction of the last Canaanite city there (see p. 299).[33] Hebron was an important stronghold during MB II, but it was probably uninhabited during the whole of the Late Bronze Age until the settlement revival in Iron Age I.[34] Additional Canaanite towns in the northern and southern Shephelah, such as Beth-Shemesh, Timnah, Tell Beit Mirsim, and Tel Halif, were destroyed toward the end of the Late Bronze Age. Thus the evidence at most of the sites in this region, except Hebron, does not explicitly contradict the biblical tradition.

Hazor is described in the Book of Joshua as the greatest of the Canaanite cities: "Hazor had been the head of all these kingdoms" (Joshua 11:10). After the battle fought at the waters of Merom, Hazor was razed: "Yet Israel did not burn any of the cities built on their mounds—except Hazor, which Joshua burned" (Joshua 11:13). We have seen that Hazor was indeed the largest Canaanite city throughout the Middle and Late Bronze ages. The latest Canaanite city there (Stratum XIII), which was rather poor in comparison to its predecessors, was destroyed sometime during the thirteenth century B.C.E., probably about half a century before the annihilation of

Lachish. The excavators assumed that the end of Canaanite Hazor should be ascribed to the Israelites.[35]

The Book of Judges preserves several additional conquest traditions, especially in its first chapter. Mention is made of the military subjugation of Jerusalem by the tribe of Judah (Judges 1:8); this contradicts a later verse (1:21) in the same chapter, as well as 2 Samuel 5:6–9, where Jerusalem is described as a Jebusite city until its capture by David. The excavations in the City of David have revealed a series of massive stone terraces erected on the steep eastern slope above the Gihon Spring as foundations for buildings of the Jebusite-Canaanite city. No significant data concerning a specific Jebusite material culture or regarding the city's subjugation was found. It would seem that the tradition in Judges 1:8 either is fictional or relates to an earlier conquest not associated with a subsequent Israelite occupation.

Other sources in Judges 1 concern the conquest of Debir, Hormah, Hebron, and Bethel. Several of these cities have already been discussed. At Bethel, a fortified Late Bronze Canaanite city was destroyed toward the end of the period and was rebuilt in Iron Age I as an Israelite town. This is one of the few cases where archaeology might confirm a conquest tradition.

In Judges 1:27–35 as well as in Joshua 13:2–6, the unconquered territories in Canaan are listed. These include Beth-Shean, Taanach, Dor, Jibleam, Megiddo, Gezer, and Acre, as well as cities in the valley of Ajalon and others. At several of these sites, such as at Beth-Shean, Megiddo, and Gezer, Canaanite culture with additional Sea Peoples elements existed during Iron Age I, thus supporting the biblical tradition concerning these cities. At others, however, the picture is much more complex. Thus, at Taanach the Canaanite city seems to have been destroyed at the end of the Late Bronze Age and replaced by an Israelite village.

Shechem, one of the major Canaanite centers in Palestine, was located in the heart of the tribal allotment of Manasseh and Ephraim. Its central role in Israelite history is expressed in the tradition that at Shechem the covenant between the tribes of Israel and their God was made (Joshua 24). The story of Abimelech (Judges 9) depicts the continued existence of a local Canaanite population at Shechem until a late stage in the period of the Judges; indeed, in the opinion of the excavators, the Canaanite city at Shechem continued to thrive until the eleventh century B.C.E.[36]

This rather superficial review shows that in some cases (southern Transjordan, Arad, 'Ai, Yarmuth, and Hebron) there is an outright conflict between the archaeological findings and the conquest narratives, while in others (Lachish, Hazor, Bethel) archaeology does not contradict these stories. Since the dates of the various destructions differ considerably (for example, Hazor was ruined several decades earlier than Lachish), we may conclude that even if the Israelites were the invaders of certain cities, the devastation was not carried out in one sweep during the same military campaign; rather, such destruction was a result of a drawn-out process of regional wars, in which a tribe or a group of tribes succeeded in destroying certain Canaanite cities. Such successive local clashes between Israelites and Canaanites were digested in the Book of Joshua to yield a tradition of a single conquest. Thus, the conquest tradition must be understood as a telescoped reflection of a complex historical process in which some of the Canaanite city-states, weak and poor after three hundred years of Egyptian domination, were replaced during Iron Age I by a new national entity, Israel.

THE ISRAELITE SETTLEMENT

Intensive archaeological surface surveys revealed an entirely new settlement pattern in Iron Age I. Hundreds of new small sites were inhabited in the mountainous areas of the Upper and Lower Galilee, in the hills of Samaria and Ephraim, in Benjamin, in the northern Negev, and in parts of central and northern Transjordan. Much of this activity can be related to Israelite tribes, though the ethnic attribution in some of these regions is still questionable.[37]

In the Upper Galilee, within the allotment of the tribe of Naphtali, some twenty-five such settlements have been discovered; these were centered around Mount Meron. Additional sites were discovered on the hills of the western Galilee, in the tribal territory of Asher. The Galilee sites are small agricultural villages approximately 1 acre in area. An exception is the well-planned fortress uncovered at Har Adir (see p. 344).[38]

At both Hazor and Dan, the most important mounds in the Huleh Valley, occupational strata attributable to the Israelites have come to light. At Hazor, there was a small village (Strata XII–XI) on the upper mound. At Dan, on the other hand, the settlement of the tribe of Dan was identified over the entire area of the mound (some 25 acres). Its principal components were silo pits, flimsy structures and bronze industry installations; these components were found in two successive levels (Strata VI–V).[39] The migration of the Danites from central Palestine is evidenced by the appearance of the large storage jars denoted Collared-Rim jars, which were common in central Palestine but foreign to the Galilee (see p. 347).

In the Lower Galilee, the surveys have turned up fifteen sites, most of them in the hilly regions of Shefarᶜam and Nazareth within the tribal territory of Zebulun. In contrast, on the basalt heights of Issachar, the settlement process began only in the tenth century B.C.E., possibly in the wake of the tribe of Issachar's migration here during the period of the Monarchy from its initial allocation in the Samarian Hills.[40]

The greatest number of Iron Age I sites is located within the tribal territories of Manasseh and Ephraim in the central hill country of Palestine. Here the settlement process was intensive. In the territory of Manasseh, between Shechem and the Jezreel Valley, about one hundred sites have been recorded to date. The largest were 10–20 acres in area, while others ranged between 2 and 5 acres or less.[41] This region is exceptional for its broad, fertile, inner valleys, in which Canaanite cities such as Shechem, Tell el-Farᶜah (north), Dothan, and Jibleam flourished during the Late Bronze Age. Many of the Iron Age I sites were situated close to the valleys, and some were even found in the eastern Sharon Plain, west of the hill country.

Surveys in the land of Ephraim have revealed some one hundred sites from Iron Age I; seven additional sites were located on the foothills east of Aphek.[42] Most of the settlements in this remote, hilly area are very small, extending from a few houses to 1–1.5 acres of built-up area. Some of the important sites excavated are Shiloh, the main Israelite cultic center in this period; ᶜAi; Bethel; Khirbet Raddanah near Ramallah; and ᶜIzbet Sartah on the foothills east of Aphek.

In the land of Benjamin, some twelve Iron Age I sites have been located, most of them along the mountains' watershed and slightly to the east. Excavations have been carried out at

Tell en-Nasbeh (near Ramallah), identified with biblical Mizpah, and at Tell el-Ful, presumed by W. F. Albright to be Gibeah of Benjamin, Saul's capital city. The biblical description of the war against Benjamin in Judges 20–21 refers to a walled city of great importance. The level that corresponds with the period of the Judges at Tell el-Ful is "Period I"—the lowest occupation level at this site; however, the finds at this level are scanty and include only thin occupation debris which point to the existence of a poor village at the site during this period. Thus either the identification of Tell el-Ful with Gibeah is mistaken or the biblical tradition exaggerated and distorted the proportions of the event. The latter possibility is more plausible, as the location of Gibeah is well attested in the Bible, and there is no other site which could be identified with it in this region.

The phenomenon of many small, one-period sites attributable to the Israelite settlement is almost completely non-existent in the Hebron Hills south of Bethlehem and in the Shephelah of Judah. Here, perhaps the Israelites contented with a smaller number of sites, which later, in the period of the Monarchy, developed into towns. At such sites, Iron Age I remains can be found only by systematic excavation, as indeed occurred at Hebron, Beth-Zur, and Tell Beit Mirsim. The only excavated one-period Iron Age I site in this region is Giloh, south of Jerusalem.[43]

In the semiarid Arad and Beer-sheba valleys, in which no Late Bronze settlement had existed at all, only a few sites were established in Iron Age I. The most prominent is Tel Masos, one of the largest settlements from this period in the entire country (20 acres). Smaller sites are Tel Esdar and Tel Beer-sheba, both of which have been excavated. Tel Masos features a concentration of population in one central site, perhaps due to a combination of ecological factors (particularly water sources), security considerations, and possibly the special role of this site in relation to the trade routes connecting the Arabah and Transjordan with the coastal plain. The material culture at Tel Masos is close to that of coastal Palestine, and the finds point to connections with Philistia, Phoenicia, and the Arabah. Canaanites and perhaps Philistines probably settled there alongside the local tribal population, which may have comprised part of the Israelite league.[44] At Tel Beer-sheba (Tell es-Saba), gradual development was observed from the eleventh century B.C.E. onward. During the earliest occupation (Stratum IX), the settlers perhaps lived in tents and poor hamlets, for only storage pits and cisterns were found. In the following phase (Stratum VIII, late eleventh century B.C.E.), a small village developed; it was possibly that in which Samuel's sons resided (1 Samuel 8:2).

Intensive settlement occurred farther south, in the Negev highlands. Some scholars tend to date it to the eleventh century B.C.E., namely contemporary with the occupation at Tel Masos; but we agree with the view that it should be dated to the tenth century B.C.E., and thus we will discuss this subject in the following chapter (see p. 390).

In Transjordan, dozens of small Iron Age I sites in Gilead (north of the Jabbok River) may be related to the half tribe of Manasseh. They mirror the settlement process of that tribe in the Samarian Hills. Fewer sites are known farther south in Transjordan (see p. 357).[45]

In addition to illuminating the change in settlement pattern, the surveys and regional studies throw light on the population size, subsistence economy, and environmental adaptation of the new settlers. The population in the settlement regions of western Palestine was estimated by I. Finkelstein at about 60,000; he arrived at this figure by multiplying the known built-up area by a factor of 100 persons per acre.

We have only vague knowledge of the sequence of settlement emergence and its development in the various regions. It appears that the process began in the early twelfth century B.C.E. in the central hill country and to some extent in Transjordan and the northern Negev, while most of the sites in the Galilee appear to belong to the eleventh century B.C.E. Apparently, in Iron Age I there was a simultaneous, independent settlement of various regions by loosely related population groups. We can determine the background of these peoples in only a general way. They perhaps emerged from a pastoralist and unsettled population which partly was indigenous and partly originated from the periphery of the country.

At both Tel Masos and 'Izbet Sartah, a poorly built settlement was founded in the twelfth century B.C.E., gradually becoming more established in the eleventh century. At Giloh, the settlement had only one phase and was abandoned probably sometime in the twelfth century B.C.E. Most of the other excavated sites in the central hill country, such as Shiloh and

'Ai, appear to have been founded during the twelfth century B.C.E. and to have flourished in the eleventh century. Two occupation phases were observed at Hazor and Dan, but their differentiation could not be determined.

Many settlements were deserted at the end of the eleventh century and beginning of the tenth century B.C.E. Some of them (such as Shiloh, 'Ai, Khirbet Raddanah, Tel Masos, and sites in the Upper Galilee) were not resettled, while others (such as Tell en-Nasbeh, Tell Beit Mirsim, Beth-Zur, Hebron, Dan, and Hazor) were reinhabited as towns and cities in the period of the Monarchy. This change in settlement pattern must have been related to the concentration of population in the emerging Israelite towns in the period of the Monarchy, from the tenth century B.C.E. onward.

SETTLEMENT PLANNING AND ARCHITECTURE

Only a few of the Iron Age I sites have been extensively excavated to permit the study of planning and architecture. Most of the excavated sites were open villages—the houses arranged along their circumference, leaving large open spaces inside the settlement (for example, Hurvat Avot in the Galilee, 'Ai, 'Izbet Sartah, Giloh, Tel Masos, and Tel Esdar). At Shiloh, the outer walls of the external row of houses formed a continuous line which served as a sort of defense, as at some Late Bronze towns. At 'Izbet Sartah the early settlement phase (Stratum III, twelfth century B.C.E.) comprised an area of 0.5 acre. Its plan (largely postulated) included about twenty-two rooms arranged in an oval plan around an open space. According to Finkelstein, this layout recalls seminomadic Bedouin camps, and thus he explains it as echoing the previous pastoral life of the 'Izbet Sartah settlers. At Tel Esdar, an eleventh-century 1-acre site in the northern Negev, houses separated by open spaces were arranged on the periphery of a circle, the inner part of which was left open. At Tel Beersheba Stratum VII there was (though according to a postulated plan, based on fragmentary evidence) a 0.75-acre village which included about twenty houses compactly arranged in an oval around a central open space (this level should probably be dated to the time of David, see p. 374). In contrast, at the exceptionally large site of Tel Masos, the entrances to the houses faced outward, as if there were no defense considerations.

Giloh is the only site of this group which was partly defended by a wall; this wall surrounded an area of 1.5 acres. The wall comprised separately built segments, each of which can possibly be attributed to a different family or group living in the adjacent area. A massive square foundation for a tower, found at the northern end of the site outside of the fortified area, is a rare example of defense architecture in this type of site (but see p. 350).

The large open spaces in these villages probably served as livestock paddocks and for storing grain in round dug or built-

8.19   Giloh: schematic plan of the settlement, twelfth century B.C.E.

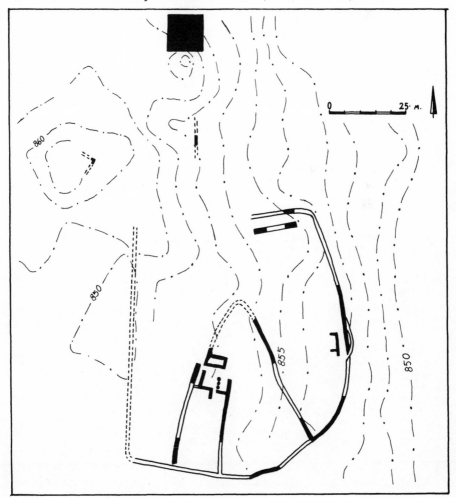

up silos (see p. 345). The site of Giloh, located on a remote rocky ridge, was divided by stone walls into large areas—apparently animal pens—with attached dwellings. Herding, therefore, probably played an important role in the local subsistence economy.

The typical Iron Age I dwelling was the "pillared house" type, based on a courtyard divided by a row of pillars. We have seen a precedent to such a pillared house in the LB II patrician house at Tel Batash (above, p. 247), but in that period the use of pillars in private dwellings was still rare, whereas in Iron Age I it became common in all parts of the country. A dwelling at Giloh, dated to the early twelfth century B.C.E., is one of the earliest examples of such houses in the hill country; the pillars in this house were little more than crudely worked blocks of stone.

During the eleventh century B.C.E. the specific form of pillared house known as the "four-room house" (see discussion on pp. 485–88) was widespread at such sites as Tel Masos

8.20 'Izbet Sartah: a "four-room house" (after reconstruction) and stone-lined silos, Stratum II (late eleventh century B.C.E.).

and 'Izbet Sartah, as well as in Philistia. Such houses are usually rectangular or square in shape, and have a central rectangular courtyard surrounded by rooms or pillared porticoi on all three sides. The entrance leads in most cases directly into the central courtyard. A common variation of this architectural form is the "three-room house," consisting of a courtyard, an area parallel to it whose roof was supported by

8.21   Tel Masos: general plan of the site.

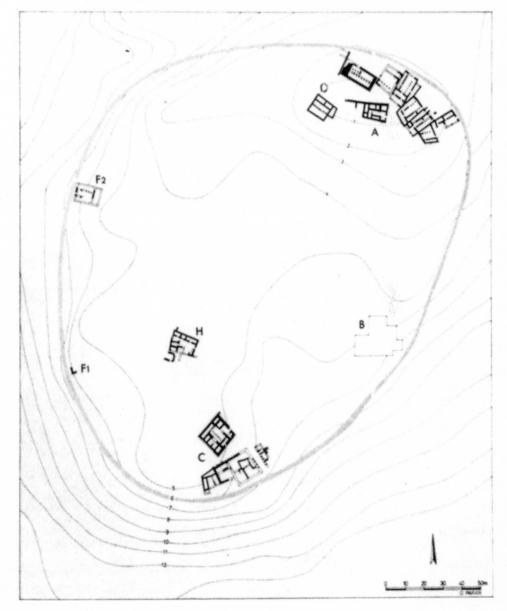

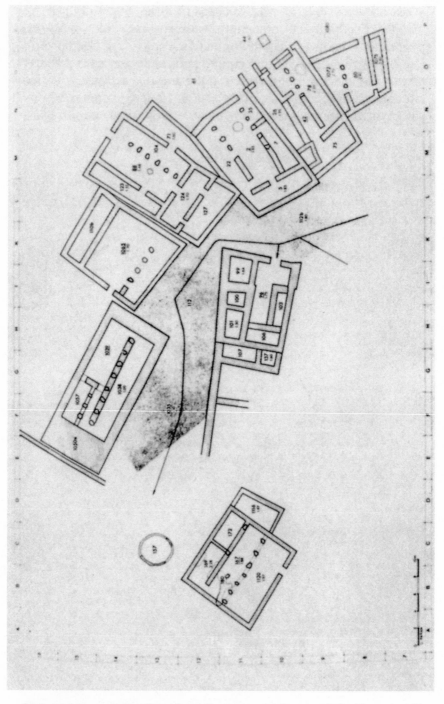

8.22   Tel Masos: plan of residential quarter with houses of the "four-room" type (Stratum II, eleventh century B.C.E.).

pillars, and a chamber at the back. Stone and wooden pillars were deployed in various ways, such as in the elongated storage rooms at Shiloh.

The pillared-house type is regarded by some as having developed among Israelite tribes who settled in the central hill country and in the northern Negev. Some scholars have even suggested that this type evolved from the pastoralist's tent. It is not, however, limited to the Israelite settlement sites. In fact, pillared houses are found in Iron Age I strata in various regions of the country and at different types of sites, such as those of the Canaanite-Phoenicians in the northern plains (Megiddo Stratum VIB; Tell Keisan in the plain of Acre), those in Philistia, and those in various parts of Transjordan. Thus, pillared houses were the building fashion of the period—possibly rooted in the domestic architecture of southern Canaan in the Late Bronze Age, but eventually adopted by all the peoples living in Palestine during Iron Age I. Among the Israelites inhabiting the central hill country and the northern Negev, this type of house became the most popular

8.23 Tel Masos: air view of Iron Age I dwellings.

form; later, in the period of the Monarchy, it became a hallmark of Israelite domestic architecture.

At Tel Masos, dwelling quarters comprising "four-room houses" were located at the northern part of the site, while in its southern part different kinds of buildings were erected. One of the latter had a square plan and was 15 × 15 m in size; it consisted of an inner courtyard divided by a row of pillars and surrounded by rooms. The layout recalls the Egyptian "governor's residencies" in southern Palestine from the end of the Late Bronze and from Iron Age IA. Another large building had a central courtyard surrounded by rooms, resembling Canaanite dwellings. The finds in this latter structure are indicative of the wealth of its inhabitants and of their ties with the coastal region and Phoenicia. This quarter may have belonged to an elite group of Canaanite-Phoenician origin, perhaps merchants with commercial connections in the coastal region, Transjordan, and the southern Negev.

Monumental structures, fortifications, and public buildings are almost unknown at the Israelite settlement sites. One exception is Har Adir in the Upper Galilee, where an eleventh century B.C.E. square fortress was surrounded by a casemate wall (a double wall with rooms in between). The fortress was located in the midst of a group of small villages considered to have been typical Israelite settlement sites. The fortress may have been constructed by the mountain settlers as a military outpost against the rising power of the Phoenician cities, or, alternatively, by the Tyrians or Sidonians as a stronghold in their mountainous hinterland, located in the heart of the Israelite settlement around Har Adir.

Another exception is a solid square (11.2 × 11.2 m) foundation built of large, unworked stones, discovered at Giloh. It probably was a foundation for a tall tower with inner rooms. Towers are mentioned in the Book of Judges as a common feature of towns in this period (for example, at Shechem, where the tower is identified with the city temple [Judges 9:46–49]; at Penuel [Judges 8:17]; and at Tebez [Judges 9:50–52]). But it is surprising to find such a massive example at the small and remote site of Giloh, and its discovery adds a new dimension to the character of the Israelite settlement sites in the hill country. Such a tower must have been intended to be the settlers' stronghold in case of attack. In the case of

Giloh, which overlooked the Valley of Rephaim and Jerusalem, the potential threat was Jebusite Jerusalem, which according to the biblical sources remained unconquered until the time of David.

Cisterns, silos, and agricultural terraces demonstrate the means by which the settlers adapted to their new environmental conditions. W. F. Albright, followed by Y. Aharoni, stressed the importance of plastered cisterns, invented by the Israelites, to allow settlement at places in the hill country lacking a perennial water source. But this view should be abandoned in light of later research. Cisterns already existed in the Middle Bronze Age (at Hazor), and they are in fact found only at a few sites related to the Israelite settlement ('Ai and Khirbet Raddanah). Water supply at many of the settlements came from minor springs often located at a considerable distance from the settlement proper (as at Giloh). The widely used large pottery pithoi at these sites may have served for water storage.

At most of the Israelite settlement sites located in areas suitable for cereal crops, storage pits and silos dug into the ground and plastered or lined with stones are found in large numbers (as at Dan, Tell Deir Alla, Tel Zeror, 'Izbet Sartah and Tell Beit Mirsim). The capacity of the 'Izbet Sartah silos was calculated and found to be greater than the quantity of grain required by the settlement's inhabitants; it was concluded, therefore, that the economy of this and similar sites was based on barter with the inhabitants of the hill country who specialized in horticulture and herding.

Agriculture in the steeply sloping and forested hill country necessitated the clearing of the land, surely one of the more difficult tasks of the settlers. Such land clearing is reflected in the words of Joshua to Ephraim: "Go up into the forest and clear land for yourself there" (17:15). Deforestation was followed by the construction of terraces on the steep slopes. The process of building terraces continued for many centuries and culminated in the stepped landscape of the hill country of Palestine visible today.[46]

POTTERY

A characteristic of the material culture in the hill country settlements is the poor pottery repertoire limited to types essential for basic subsistence. Large storage jars (pithoi), probably used as water containers, are a hallmark of this culture, and their number overwhelms that of other ceramic forms. There are also smaller storage jars (used for carrying and storing liquids such as oil and wine), cooking pots, and a limited selection of other shapes. Painted decoration is totally lacking, but in certain regions incisions and simple impressed decorations appear. The assemblage as a whole differs widely from that of the Canaanite-Philistine culture of the coastal plain and the valley of Jezreel.

The pithoi constitute an important criterion for distinguishing regional differences. The "Collared-Rim" pithos is most common in the central part of Palestine on both sides of the Jordan, from the Jezreel Valley in the north to the region of Hebron in the south. This is a large vessel (ca. 1.2 m in height)

8.24 Group of pottery vessels from Shiloh (eleventh century B.C.E.). The large jars (pithoi) are of the "collared-rim" type.

and ovoid in shape; its rim is thick and folded, and its neck has a ridge or "collar." The earliest example of such a pithos is known from Aphek in a context dating to the thirteenth century B.C.E.; the widespread use of these pithoi in Iron Age I settlement sites led scholars to identify them as distinctive of the material culture of the Israelites. The ethnic attribution, however, should be used with caution; similar pithoi were found also at Megiddo and Tell Keisan, where Canaanite culture survived until the eleventh century B.C.E., and at Sahab in Transjordan, probably an Ammonite site.[47] On the other hand, they did not reach the northern Negev, where there were also Israelite settlement sites.

The discovery of "Collared-Rim" pithoi at Dan, when they have not been found elsewhere in the Galilee, is possible evidence of the northward migration of the Danites from

8.25 Pottery from an Iron Age I silo at Dan. The pithoi are characteristic to the Galilee; they retain Canaanite northern traditions (compare Figure 7.13).

central Palestine. At other sites in Galilee, the prevalent pithoi are of the Galilean type, which developed from a northern Canaanite form known in the Late Bronze Age at Hazor.

It appears that the Israelite settlers in the hill country lacked their own pottery-making tradition, and that initially they obtained the most necessary pottery vessels from their Canaanite neighbors. When they did begin producing pottery, they manufactured a limited repertoire of forms based on Canaanite prototypes, without adopting the Canaanite decoration.

In settlements adjacent to Canaanite or Philistine regions, such as 'Izbet Sartah, the pottery assemblage is more variegated and much closer to that of the coastal plain. A strong coastal influence is also evident in the pottery at Tel Masos.

RELIGIOUS PRACTICE

The archaeological evidence for Israelite religious practices during the period of the Judges is meager. At Shiloh, the central part of the site where the tabernacle probably stood has been thoroughly destroyed by erosion and by Byzantine building activities.[48] Evidence of the existence of a cult place at this site already in the Late Bronze Age is of considerable significance. It probably served seminomadic pastoralist tribes who lived in the vicinity, as no actual settlement from this period was found on the mound. Shiloh, therefore, seems to have been a sacred place long before the Iron Age, and perhaps this tradition led to its choice as the religious center of the Israelites during the period of the Judges.

An ambiguous and controversial discovery was made on Mount Ebal, north of Shechem. Early Israelite tradition regards this mount as the place where Joshua built an altar (Joshua 8:30–32; see also Deuteronomy 11:29; 27:4–8). The painstaking survey of the entire mount revealed only one Iron Age site. The material culture found in the excavation of this site is similar to that of other Iron Age I settlements in the central hill country.[49] Yet peculiarities in the architecture and finds led the excavator, A. Zertal, to suggest that this was the early Israelite shrine on Mount Ebal. The 1-acre site was surrounded by a stone wall; in an early phase of the site's history, a circular, 2-m-wide installation was constructed on

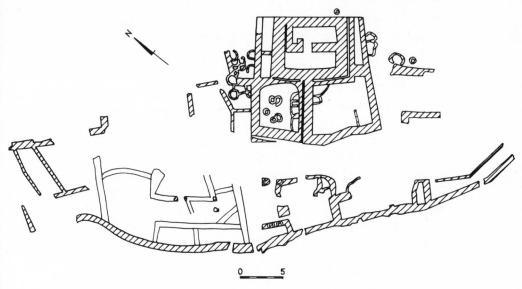

8.26   Plan of the nucleus of the site at Mount Ebal.

8.27   The central structure of the Mount Ebal site (interpreted by A. Zertal as an Israelite altar).

its highest point. The site's ritual purpose is suggested by the animal bones—probably originating in this phase—found in the fill of the superseding structure. The bones include those of ritually clean young male animals which may have been sacrificed here. Two scarabs, one dating to Ramesses II, are attributed to this phase.

Later, above the installation, a rectangular structure (8 × 9 m) with massive outer walls was constructed. Its interior was divided by a partition wall into two chambers, but in spite of the good state of preservation, no opening was found. The inside space of the structure was filled with stones, earth, ash, and animal bones. On its southern side and attached to it were two large rooms or courtyards separated from each other by a wide wall. Zertal interpreted this rectangular structure as a large altar and identified some of the components as its parapet and ramp. He alluded to the Jerusalem altar described in the Mishnah, and he proposed that the Mount Ebal structure was the very altar noted in the Books of Joshua and Deuteronomy. This interpretation caused a scholarly controversy, as there are no archaeological parallels for such a large monumental altar anywhere else, and Zertal's view was thought by some as a naive correlation between archaeological features and biblical tradition, which perhaps is of much later date. The critiques (especially that of A. Kempinski) claimed that the central structure at Mount Ebal was of a secular nature, a watchtower in the center of an Israelite farmstead of the settlement period, like the square tower found at Giloh.[50] The case of Mount Ebal illustrates the difficulties in interpreting an archaeological discovery, particularly in relation to biblical sources. Zertal may be wrong in the details of his interpretation, but it is tempting to accept his view concerning the basic cultic nature of the site and its possible relationship to the biblical tradition. This tradition came to us indeed in the framework of Deuteronomistic literature of a much later date, but it is very possible that this literature preserved old traditions which go back to the period of the settlement. The biblical references to the sanctity of Mount Ebal could be one of these old traditions.

On a high ridge in the northern Samarian Hills, in the heart of the Israelite settlement region, an open cult place has been found which is perhaps one of the few examples known of the biblical "high places" built "on every high hill and under every spreading tree" (1 Kings 14:23).[51] On the ridge's summit a circle of large stones was laid, some 20 m in diameter; the empty center of the circle was perhaps reserved for a sacred tree. On the circle's eastern side, a large stone was found standing on its narrow long side. Due to this stone's position in front of a paved area on which several offerings were found, it seems to have served as a *massebah*, a "standing stone." A unique find here was a 0.18-m-long bronze statuette of a bull, which apparently was a major object of worship at this site; it is reminiscent of the golden calf described in the Bible in connection with the Exodus tradition and with the temples erected by Jeroboam I at Bethel and at Dan. In the Canaanite religion, the bull was the accompanying animal and symbol of Baal, the storm god; in several Canaanite and later Syrian artistic depictions the storm god is seen standing on the back of a bull. It is thus possible that in the religion of the northern tribes of Israel the bull was considered either as the symbol of the god of Israel or its pedestal (recalling the function of the Cherubim in the temple of Jerusalem). Bronze statuettes

8.28 Bronze bull figurine, found at a cult site in the northern Samarian Hills (length 18 cm).

8.29   Canaanite-type bronze
figurine showing a seated deity
found in the Stratum XI "high
place" at Hazor.

of bulls are to be found in the Canaanite culture (at Hazor
and Ugarit), and thus our example may have been made in a
Canaanite workshop, in cities such as Beth-Shean or Megiddo,
where extensive metalworking industries flourished during
Iron Age I. However, though of possible Canaanite origin, the
figurine was probably used by Israelite settlers in this region
of the northern Samarian hills.

Similar evidence for the use of Canaanite-type bronze
statuettes by the settling Israelites is the figure of a seated
deity found in a ritual place in the eleventh century B.C.E.
village at Hazor (Stratum XI).

THE PROBLEM OF ETHNIC IDENTITY
AND ORIGINS OF THE ISRAELITE CULTURE

How can we judge the ethnic identity of the settlers in an Iron Age I site or a cluster of sites? This problem is complicated by the differing theories regarding the origin of the Israelites and the processes which led to the amalgamation of the new nation. The definition by archaeologists of certain features or sites as "Israelite" has to be regarded with caution. Various population groups who settled in the country during this time may have identified themselves as "Israelites" and amalgamated with this emerging national body in a slow process which lasted from the late thirteenth century B.C.E. until the early Monarchy. Consequently, defining a distinctively "Israelite" material culture is a difficult venture. Our departure point in this issue should be sites which according to biblical tradition were Israelite during the period of the Judges, such as Shiloh, Mizpah, Dan, and Beer-sheba; settlements with similar material culture in the same region can then be defined as Israelite.

The question of ethnic identification becomes more complicated when dealing with certain regions or sites. Thus, in the hill country, Jerusalem and the four Gibeonite cities to its northwest are considered in the biblical tradition as non-Israelite Jebusite and Gibeonite enclaves in the period of the Judges. Excavations at Jerusalem (the City of David) and at Gibeon have yielded only scanty remains relating to the period. These remains do not differ from the ones at those sites farther north which are considered Israelite; nothing in these remains points to the existence of a distinct "Jebusite" or "Gibeonite" material culture which differs from that in other sites of the central hills country. The unique cultural features of Tel Masos led to the suggestion that it was either an Amalekite, Canaanite, or Philistine settlement (see p. 344).[52] Giloh was thought to be a Jebusite outpost rather than an Israelite habitation, and the "Bull Site" in the Samarian Hills was considered a Canaanite place of worship.[53] The identification of the people of the sites in the Upper Galilee and Transjordan is also questionable.

Our survey has pointed out the regional differences among the material cultures of the Galilee, the central mountains, the foothills, and the northern Negev. As these regions constitute the heartland of Israel, and since the various population groups there eventually joined and became part of the new nation of Israel, our term "Israelite" as it relates to the Iron Age I period can only be a general designation for cultural phenomena in an area specified in later biblical tradition as Israelite.

Assuming the ethnic identification used in this chapter is correct, we can draw some conclusions concerning the socio-economic structure of Israelite society. In fact, these conclusions correspond to the social structure described in the biblical sources concerning this period. This was a nonurban, sedentary population of small communities, each numbering several dozens of people who subsisted on farming and herding. It appears to have been an egalitarian society, striving for a livelihood in the difficult environmental conditions of the forested mountains and semiarid regions of Palestine.

Having no traditions of their own, the settlers at first utilized the pottery, arts, crafts and some architectural features of the Canaanite culture—a culture which continued to flourish in various areas of the country. Only later did these settlers begin producing their own artifacts along lines adapted from Canaanite prototypes. Nonetheless, the nature of the settlers' culture as a whole differed to a large extent from that of the Canaanites.

Can archaeology throw light on the question of the origin of Israel? The answer is not affirmative, as the interpretation of the archaeological evidence is not clear-cut. However, the role of archaeology should not be underestimated, as it is the only extrabiblical source on this subject other than the "Israel Stele" of Merneptah (see p. 234). Nothing in the archaeological findings from this period points to foreign traditions or objects brought by the Israelites from outside the country. The discoveries appear to depict a settlement by tribal groups who once followed a seminomadic, pastoral way of life. No actual evidence of this previous lifestyle can be located, but its impact is felt in the distribution of the settlement sites and their planning.

I. Finkelstein pointed to the resemblance between the settlement process in the central hill country in Iron Age I and a similar phenomenon in this region during MB II. He proposed that the MB II sedentary population, after having been forced to adopt a pastoralist and seminomadic existence in the Late Bronze Age, exploited the opportunity of changing conditions in Iron Age I to return to sedentary life.[54] This interpretation can be linked with the theory that the Israelites emerged from local unsettled Late Bronze groups, such as the Habiru and Shasu known from the Egyptian sources.[55] Such a theory perhaps explains the origin of most of the components of the Israelite confederation, but it still does not elucidate the identity of that confederation's nuclear group, which initiated Yahwism and was responsible for the traditions concerning slavery in Egypt, the Exodus, Mount Sinai, and the role of Moses. At present archaeology can contribute nothing to answering this question.

THE CANAANITES
AND THE EMERGENCE
OF THE PHOENICIAN CULTURE

Throughout Iron Age I the Canaanite culture continued to survive in the coastal plain and in the northern valleys of the country. In Philistia, Canaanites probably lived under Philistine control, and the Philistines absorbed many of the Canaanite cultural traits.

Two areas in northern Israel demonstrate the cultural phenomena related to the Canaanites in the eleventh century B.C.E.: the valley of Jezreel (and its eastern extension at Beth-Shean); and the valley of Acre from the Carmel ridge northward. The phenomena in the first region are best illustrated at Megiddo and Beth-Shean. Beth-Shean Stratum VI and Megiddo Stratum VIIA, destroyed in the mid–twelfth century B.C.E. at the end of the Egyptian rule, were succeeded by a short transitional phase consisting of poor dwellings and storage pits (Megiddo Stratum VIB; Beth-Shean, the phase denoted "Upper VI"). Both sites were rebuilt on a grand scale in the eleventh century B.C.E. by the bearers of a distinct local culture based on Canaanite traditions and some Sea Peoples inspiration.

At Beth-Shean, the level denoted "Lower Stratum V" was a well-planned, densely built town whose cultic center included two adjacent temples, the Northern Temple and the Southern Temple. Though these temples have been badly disturbed, the basic outline of their plans can be traced. The Northern Temple was a massive structure (with walls 1.5 m thick), its roof resting on four pillars; the entrance was in a corner. The Southern Temple comprised an elongated hall divided by two rows of three columns into a narrow nave and two aisles. In both temples, the Holy of Holies was not preserved. The existence of two adjacent temples in the same sacred enclosure, the unconventional plan of these temples, and their corner or indirect entrance are comparable to the contemporary temples at Tell Qasile. A large, open courtyard in front of the Beth-Shean edifices contained some earlier statues and stelae dating to the time of the Egyptian control during the thirteenth and early twelfth centuries B.C.E. For some reason, these had been reerected in the eleventh century B.C.E. A rich collection of cult vessels found in these temples include square and round pottery stands; these stands are ornamented with reliefs of human figures and snakes, or painted in black and red geometric patterns.

Megiddo in the eleventh century B.C.E. (Stratum VIA) was also a densely built, flourishing city. The city had a palace and a city gate, but appears to have lacked a city wall. The city was destroyed in a conflagration at the beginning of the tenth century B.C.E., possibly by David. Numerous finds in this destruction layer attest to the wealth of the town; they include metal objects, jewelry, small artifacts, and abundant painted pottery inspired by Canaanite traditions. Certain pottery vessels and bronze objects can be related to the Sea Peoples; outstanding among these items is the so-called Orpheus Jug, whose painted decoration is closely related to the Philistine style. A painted frieze on this jug displays a procession of various animals and a lyre player in front of a sacred plant. Cypriot pottery found at Beth-Shean and Megiddo proclaim the renewal of trade connections with Cyprus.

Thus, in the plains of Jezreel and Beth-Shean, in spite of the crisis in the second half of the twelfth century B.C.E., there was a revival of local Canaanite culture in the eleventh century possibly connected with a limited settlement of Sea Peoples.

During the eleventh century B.C.E., a new aspect of the Canaanite culture developed on the Phoenician coast. This is known as the "Phoenician culture," a term based on the Greek word for the descendants of the Canaanites who

8.30 A pottery plaque figurine from the cemetery at Tel Zeror in the Sharon Plain.

developed their own civilization in the cities of Tyre and Sidon and later in colonies established by them in the western Mediterranean. The Phoenician culture is outside the scope of our survey, but we should mention the discoveries in the valley of Acre, north of the Carmel ridge, where some of the earliest finds relating to this culture have been uncovered at the sites of Achzib, Tell Keisan, and Tell Abu Hawam.[56] A well-planned dwelling quarter at Tell Keisan has pillared buildings resembling contemporary dwellings at Tell Qasile Stratum X. A specific pottery group, which may be denoted "Phoenician Bichrome Ware," is typical of this earliest phase of the Phoenician culture; it comprises globular flasks and jugs decorated with concentric circles in red and black and sometimes white on burnished buff red background. By means of trade such pottery arrived in Philistia, the northern Negev, Egypt, and Cyprus, evidence of the beginning of Phoenician commerce.

TRANSJORDAN IN IRON AGE I

According to the biblical narrative, the tribes of Reuben and Gad and half of Manasseh settled in Transjordan alongside the Edomites, Moabites, Ammonites, and Amorites. To what extent is this ethnic multiplicity reflected in the archaeological finds?

The material culture of Transjordan in Iron Age I is only vaguely known.[57] The main finds are from the central Jordan Valley, a continuation of the Beth-Shean Valley, where the material culture was always related to that of western Palestine. Excavations at two of the mounds in this region, Tell es-Sa'idiyeh (either Zarethan or Zafon) and Tell Deir Alla (probably biblical Succoth), had considerably different results. The early twelfth century B.C.E. cemetery at Tell es-Sa'idiyeh is rich in finds of Canaanite character—finds reminiscent of those at contemporaneous Beth-Shean. Several metal objects point to connections with Cyprus and Europe and may indicate the presence of some Sea Peoples.[58] At Tell Deir Alla, however, a Late Bronze sacred place was destroyed in a conflagration around 1200 B.C.E.; above it were the settlement remains of a seminomadic populace—remains consisting mainly of silo pits which were renewed and redug over a long time span.[59] These remains resemble those at sites in western Palestine related to the Israelite settlement in the twelfth and eleventh centuries B.C.E. It thus appears that Tell Deir Alla was one of the Israelite settlement sites of this period.

We have mentioned earlier the results of the surveys in Gilead, north of the Jabbok River, where many small sites established in Iron Age I probably reflect Israelite settlement in this region. Surveys in inner Transjordan south of the Jabbok revealed additional, although less numerous, sites. The land of the Ammonites is known mainly from the site of Sahab (southeast of Amman)—one of the largest Iron Age I sites in the country, covering some 60 acres.[60] The material culture evident there is similar to that found in western Palestine: it includes pillared houses, Collared-Rim pithoi, and "jar coffins." The evidence at Sahab indicates that Ammon was the most developed kingdom in Transjordan during Iron Age I.

In the land of Moab, excavations of major biblical towns, such as Dibon and Heshbon, have yielded only meager remains from Iron Age I. The two sites named Khirbet Medeiyineh, located on a high ridge overlooking the crossing of the Arnon River, are examples of the few settlements dating to this period in the region.[61] A few similar settlements were located in the survey of Wadi Hesa (Zered Brook) in the northern part of Edom, but almost no Iron Age I remains are known from the heart of this kingdom farther south.

The archaeological picture in Transjordan is thus complex and heterogeneous. Essentially, it does not confirm the biblical traditions concerning Edom, Moab, and the "Amorite" kingdom of Sihon during the time of the Exodus and period of the Judges. It does, however, correspond to the biblical sources about Ammon and the Israelite settlements in Gilead and the valley of Succoth.

METALLURGY, ART, AND WRITING IN IRON AGE I

METALLURGY

The replacement of bronze by iron as the main metal for daily use was gradual, culminating only in the tenth century B.C.E. In Iron Age I, bronze was still the major metal for casting weapons, tools, metal vessels, and art objects. Bronze workshops similar to those of the Late Bronze Age are prominent at Iron Age I sites throughout the country: Dan and Tel Harashim in the Upper Galilee; Tell Deir Alla; Tell Qasile; Beth-Shemesh; Tel Mor; and Tel Masos. The raw material probably came from the Arabah (Timna° and Punon), from Cyprus, and from the recycling of older objects. Most of

8.31 A bronze ax-adze from Tell Qasile. The shape is unknown in local Canaanite tradition and probably signifies Aegean-Cypriot metallurgical traditions retained by Sea Peoples.

the bronze objects were shaped according to Late Bronze prototypes; even figurines such as the seated deity from Hazor and the bull from the Samarian Hills were made in the Canaanite tradition.[62] Other bronze utensils reflect Aegean and Cypriot influence, apparently related to the immigration of Sea Peoples. These utensils include weapons found at Megiddo, Tell Qasile, Tel Zeror, Achzib, and Tell es-Saʿidiyeh; among these weapons are double axes, axe-adzes, elongated shafted spearheads and a European-type bronze sword with a contemporary Cypriot parallel. Bronze stands and a cauldron from Beth-Shean and Tell Saʿidiyeh are also typical products of this bronze industry, which flourished mainly during the twelfth century B.C.E. It has been suggested that the transition to iron was to some extent dictated by the difficulty in obtaining copper and tin—difficulty resulting from the termination of Late Bronze Age international trade relations.

Iron, particularly from meteorites, had long been known in the ancient Near East as a precious metal. During the twelfth and eleventh centuries B.C.E., iron objects which were produced from ores appeared in various parts of the ancient world, but the birthplace of this technology eludes us. It was once thought that the Hittites held a monopoly over iron technology in the Late Bronze Age, and that after the collapse of their empire the knowledge spread throughout the ancient world, being transmitted especially by the Sea Peoples. But this theory is no longer regarded as valid. As the earliest iron implements in Palestine were found in Philistine contexts (a sword at Tell el-Farʿah [south], knives at Tell Qasile and Ekron, and jewelry), it was assumed that the Philistines introduced ironworking during the twelfth century B.C.E.[63] A passage in 1 Samuel 13:19–22 mentioning Philistine monopoly over metal production was cited as support of this hy-

8.32 An iron pick from the citadel at Har Adir, Upper Galilee (eleventh century B.C.E.). This is one of the earliest known examples of steel tools.

pothesis, but in fact this passage does not specify the metal in question. The finds show that in Iron Age I, iron was still rare and expensive; it was chosen for jewelry (bracelets and earrings) and a limited number of weapons and knives. Iron tools began appearing only in the eleventh century B.C.E., and even then in meager quantity.

A pick found in the eleventh century B.C.E. fortress at Har Adir in the Upper Galilee is the earliest known iron implement made of real steel produced by carbonizing, quenching, and tempering. This technological revolution opened the way for the widespread use of iron.[64]

ART

The twelfth and eleventh centuries B.C.E. have been considered a "dark age" in the history of the ancient world. The decline of Egypt, and the collapse of the Hittite kingdom and the Mycenaean emporium, are also reflected in the deterioration in art and architecture in these areas. In Palestine and Phoenicia, the Canaanite miniature art of the Late Bronze Age apparently continued to thrive during the twelfth and eleventh centuries B.C.E. The last of the Megiddo ivories were made during the time of Ramesses III in the mid–twelfth century B.C.E. A carved ivory box from Stratum VIA at Megiddo, dated to the eleventh century B.C.E., as well as additional ivory works from Tell Qasile, Tel Miqne, and other sites illustrate the continuation of the art of ivory carving in Canaan throughout Iron Age I.

Both in Philistia and in the northern valleys and plains, creative and imaginative artists were producing objects which blended Canaanite traditions with motifs and concepts probably brought by the Sea Peoples. Their products are exemplified by the variety of cult artifacts from Beth-Shean, Megiddo, Ashdod, and Tell Qasile. This art is a link between that of the Late Bronze Age and that which developed in Palestine and Phoenicia during Iron Age II.

WRITING

A meager number of inscriptions represents the development of alphabetic writing during Iron Age I.[65] An incised ostracon from 'Izbet Sartah was apparently a pupil's exercise.

One of its lines lists the letters of the alphabet with several omissions and changes from the canonical order, while other lines are unintelligible sign combinations. An inscription incised on a pottery bowl from Qubur el-Walaydah in southern Philistia included two Canaanite names; the inscription was apparently a dedication (possibly an offering to a deity). These two texts can be ascribed to the twelfth century B.C.E. A seal carved in the common Philistine style and found in Philistia (in the vicinity of Ekron) bears the words "Belonging to Aba," written in the alphabetic script of this period. This seal and the inscription from Qubur el-Walaydah show that the Canaanite alphabetic writing system was utilized in Philistia (perhaps by Canaanites living under the Philistine rule) alongside the undeciphered linear Philistine writing system known from the Ashdod seals.

Five inscribed arrowheads found near el-Khadr, south of Bethlehem, feature the most important inscriptions from the eleventh century B.C.E. Four of the arrowheads state, "Arrow of ʿAbd lbʾt"; the fifth is inscribed with "ʿAbd lbʾt" on one side, while the obverse reads, "Ben ʿAnat." This last name is a well-known Canaanite name at Ugarit and Egypt as well as in the Bible, where Shamgar Ben ʿAnat is known as one of the Israelite "minor" judges who fought the Philistines (Judges 3:31). The title lbʾt probably means "lionesses"; it recalls the presence of mercenary archers called lebaʾim (= "lions") among David's warriors prior to his ascension to the throne: "I am in the midst of lions, I lie among ravenous beasts—men whose teeth are spears and arrows, whose tongues are sharp swords" (Psalms 57:4). The date of these arrowheads and the fact that they were found near Bethlehem, David's birthplace, suggest that they could have been connected with his activities in

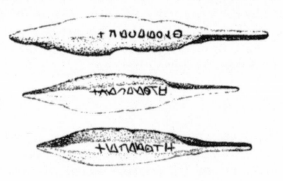

8.33 Bronze arrowheads from el-Khadr, near Bethlehem, with incised alphabetic inscription: "arrow of ʿAbd Ibʾt."

the vicinity. The arrowheads—as well as short texts on jar handles, and possibly the 'Izbet Sartah inscription—exemplify the knowledge of alphabetic writing among the Israelites in this period.

The direction of writing had not yet crystallized in this period: sometimes it was from left to right, while in other cases it was from right to left or from top to bottom. The letters were far more advanced than those of the Proto-Canaanite inscriptions of the Late Bronze Age. They represent an important stage in the evolvement toward the mature forms of the Hebrew-Phoenician alphabet in Iron Age II.

NOTES

1. The term "Israelite period," used for the Iron Age by some Israeli archaeologists, is not employed in this book, because the term "Iron Age" in addition to conforming with the sequential terminology starting from "Stone Age," does not exclude the non-Israelite factors and material cultures of the period.

2. Y. Aharoni and R. Amiran, *IEJ* 8 (1958), pp. 171–84. The wide variety of suggestions concerning the inner division of the Iron Age is exemplified in a recent table of the archaeological periods of Palestine, published in: P. J. King, *American Archaeology in the Mideast*, Philadelphia 1983, and cited in *Callaway Festschrift*, p. 469. In this table the tenth century B.C.E. is included in the Iron Age I, and the Babylonian period—from 605 until 539—is termed Iron Age IIC. The date 586 B.C.E. is not cited at all. The division suggested is as follows:

Iron Age I	1200–930 B.C.E.
Iron Age IIA	930–721
Iron Age IIB	721–605
Iron Age IIC	605–539

3. A. Mazar, *IEJ* 35 (1985), pp. 95–107.

4. F. James, *The Iron Age at Beth Shan*, Philadelphia 1966; Y. Yadin and Sh. Geva, *Investigations at Beth-Shean, The Early Iron Age Strata. Qedem* 23, Jerusalem 1986.

5. Dothan (1982), pp. 70–74; Mazar (see note 3).

6. D. Ussishkin in: *Tufnell Festschrift*, pp. 213–30.

7. E. D. Oren, *EAEHL* pp. 1059–67; for the inscriptions, see O. Goldwasser, *TA* 11 (1984), pp. 77–93.

8. Dothan (1982), pp. 29–30, 260–68; J. Waldbaum, *AJA* 70 (1966), pp. 331–40, contra W. H. Stiebing, *AJA* 74 (1970), pp. 139–43.

9. For general discussion, see R. D. Barnett in: *CAH*, vol. 2, pp. 359–78; Dothan (1982), particularly pp. 1–24, 289–96; idem, in: *BAT*, pp. 165–76; idem in: S. Deger-Jalkotzy (editor), *Griechenland, die Ägäis, und*

die Levante während der "Dark Ages," Vienna 1983, pp. 99–120. N. K. Sanders, *The Sea Peoples,* London 1968; B. Mazar in: *WHJP,* vol. 3, pp. 164–82; J. F. Brug, *A Literary and Archaeological Study of the Philistines.* B.A.R. International Series 265, Oxford 1985; A. Mazar (see note 3).

10. S. Wachsman, *The International Journal of Nautical Archaeology* 10 (1981), pp. 187–219; 11.4 (1982), pp. 297–304.

11. *ANET,* pp. 261–62.

12. Dothan (1982), pp. 37–41; J. Balensi, *Revue Biblique* 88 (1981), pp. 399–401. See also note 16.

13. M. Dothan, F. Asaro, and I. Perlman, *Archaeometry* 13 (1971), pp. 169–75; T. Dothan et al., *BASOR* 264 (1986), pp. 3–16.

14. M. and T. Dothan suggested that the Mycenaean IIIC1b pottery in Philistia denotes an earlier phase of Sea Peoples, who arrived there before the time of Ramesses III's eighth year. The Philistines, according to this theory, can be defined only with the appearance of the characteristic black and red painted Philistine pottery, which in the opinion of Dothan appeared already during the time of Ramesses III. I claim that the Philistine Bichrome Ware developed about one generation later, and that the local production of Myc. IIICI signifies the initial settlement of the Philistines in Philisitia during the time of Ramesses III and his successors. See my discussion (note 3) and I. Singer, *TA* 12 (1985), pp. 109–22.

15. M. Dothan and Y. Porath, *Ashdod IV. 'Atiqot* 15, Jerusalem 1982.

16. T. Dothan and S. Gitin, *BA* 50 (1987), pp. 197–222.

17. B. Mazar, *IEJ* 1 (1951), pp. 61–76, 77–140; A. Mazar, *Excavations at Tell Qasile, Part One. Qedem* 12, Jerusalem 1980; idem, *Excavations at Tell Qasile, Part Two. Qedem* 20, Jerusalem 1985.

18. W. G. Dever (ed.), *Gezer,* vol. 4, Jerusalem 1986, pp. 60–116.

19. G. L. Kelm and A. Mazar, *BASOR* 237 (1982), pp. 15–19; idem, *BASOR Supplement* 23 (1985), pp. 100–1.

20. On Tell Beit Mirsim, see R. Grinberg, *BASOR* 265 (1986), pp. 55–80; on Tel Halif, see J. D. Seger, *BASOR* 252 (1983), pp. 9–10.

21. Dothan (1982), pp. 94–218.

22. Dothan (1982), pp. 94–218 suggested three phases in the development of Philistine pottery, the third of which was defined as debased when the black and red decoration was replaced by black decoration on a red slip with simple motifs of detached spirals and horizontal bands. The decorated vessels in this third group are mainly kraters and jugs, both traditional local shapes. This division was based primarily on the excavations at Tell Qasile from 1950 to 1951, where Stratum X was considered the hallmark of the third phase of the Philistine culture. But the excavations at that site since 1972 under the direction of the present author have shown that Stratum X contains abundant decorated red and black Philistine pottery. The debased Philistine decoration appears there together with elaborately decorated vessels. This poor decoration with black spirals on kraters is characteristic only of Tell Qasile and of certain other sites along the Yarkon River (Tel Gerisa

and Tell Abu-Zeitun). It is thus a regional feature not found at other sites in Philistia. See Mazar, *Part Two* (note 17), p. 104.

23. J. Gunneweg and J. Yellin in: Mazar, *Part Two* (see note 17), pp. 111–17.

24. Mazar (see note 17).

25. Dothan (1982), pp. 234–49.

26. C. F. A. Schaeffer, *Ugaritica*, vol. 7, Paris 1978, pp. 149–54; U. Zevulun in: *Israel—People and Land, Haaretz Museum Yearbook*, vol. 1 (19), 1984, pp. 41–54 (Hebrew).

27. See note 8.

28. Oren (see note 7), contra Dothan (1982), pp. 268–76, 288; see also Chapter 7, note 47.

29. Bright (1981), pp. 120–76; A. Malamat in: *WHJP*, vol. 3, pp. 129–63; de Vaux (1978), pp. 488–824; J. H. Hayes and J. M. Miller (eds.), *Israelite and Judaean History*, London 1977, pp. 213–332; N. K. Gottwald, *The Tribes of Yahweh*, New York 1979; G. W. Ahlström, *Who Were the Israelites?*, Winona Lake 1986; B. Halpern, *The Emergence of Israel in Canaan*, Chico-California, 1983; J. M. Miller and J. H. Hayes, *A History of Ancient Israel and Judah*, Philadelphia 1986, pp. 54–79.

30. In addition to the works cited in the previous note, see W. F. Albright, *BASOR* 74 (1939), pp. 11–23; P. W. Lapp, *Concordia Theological Monthly* 38 (1967), pp. 283–300; B. Mazar in: *WHJP*, vol. 3, pp. 69–93; G. E. Mendenhall, *BA* 25 (1962), pp. 66–87; Y. Yadin in: *Symposia*, pp. 57–68; Sh. Yeivin, *The Israelite Conquest of Canaan*, Istanbul 1971.

31. Y. Aharoni, *BA* 39 (1976), pp. 55–76. See also N. Na'aman, *ZDPV* 96 (1980), pp. 136–52.

32. For a slightly different approach, see Z. Zevit, *BAR* 11:2 (1985), pp. 58–69. For an earlier, unacceptable view, see J. A. Callaway, *JBL* 87 (1968), pp. 316–19. Lately Callaway himself has rejected his previous ideas and has come up with a much more sceptical view; see his paper in: *Rose Festschrift*, pp. 87–99.

33. Ussishkin in: *Tufnell Festschrift*, pp. 215–26.

34. The excavations at Hebron (Jebel Rumeideh) were carried out by A. Ofer and M. Kochavi following earlier excavations by P. Hammond.

35. Yadin (1972), p. 199; idem in: *Symposia*, pp. 57–68; idem in: *BAT*, pp. 22–26. See also Chapter 7, note 51.

36. L. E. Toombs in: *Symposia*, pp. 69–84.

37. For some recent discussions on the subject, see M. Weippert, *The Settlement of the Israelite Tribes in Palestine*, London 1971; Y. Aharoni in: *WHJP*, vol. 3, pp. 94–128; Y. Aharoni, *The Archaeology of the Land of Israel*, Philadelphia (1978), pp. 153–80; B. Mazar, *BASOR* 241 (1981), pp. 75–85; M. Kochavi, A. Mazar, and responses in *BAT*, pp. 31–94; L. E. Stager, *BASOR* 260 (1985), pp. 1–35; Ahlström (see note 29), pp. 25–36; J. A. Callaway, *Tufnell Festschrift*, pp. 31–49; I. Finkelstein, *Izbet Sartah*, Oxford 1986, pp. 211–17; idem, *The Archaeology of the Israelite Settlement*, Jerusalem 1988. The latter is the most comprehensive and updated treatment of the subject.

38. Y. Aharoni, *The Settlement of the Israelite Tribes in Upper Galilee,* Jerusalem 1957 (Hebrew). The excavations of the Israel Department of Antiquities at Har Adir, Sasa, and Hurvat Avot are as yet unpublished.

39. A. Biran, *BA* 43 (1980), pp. 168–82.

40. Z. Gal, *TA* 9 (1982), pp. 79–86.

41. A. Zertal, *Arubboth, Hepher and the Third Solomonic District,* Tel Aviv 1984 (Hebrew); idem, *The Israelite Settlement in the Hill Country of Manasseh* (Ph.D. thesis), Haifa 1988 (Hebrew).

42. See the publications of Finkelstein cited in note 37.

43. A. Mazar, *IEJ* 31 (1981), pp. 1–36.

44. W. Fritz and A. Kempinski, *Ergebnisse der Ausgrabungen auf der Hirbet el Masas (Tel Masos) 1972–1975,* Wiesbaden 1983; F. Fritz, *BASOR* 241 (1981), pp. 61–73; Z. Herzog, *Beer Sheba II: The Early Iron Age Settlements,* Tel Aviv 1984; M. Kochavi, *'Atiqot* 5 (1969), pp. 14–48 (Hebrew).

45. M. Weippert in: *Symposia,* pp. 15–34; idem in Hadidi (1982), pp. 153–62.

46. Stager (see note 37).

47. See discussions by M. M. Ibrahim in: *Kenyon Festschrift,* pp. 116–26; A. Mazar (see note 43), pp. 27–31.

48. I. Finkelstein, *TA* 12 (1985), pp. 123–77; idem, *BAR* 12:1 (1986), pp. 22–41.

49. A. Zertal, *BAR* 11:1 (1985), pp. 26–43; ibid 12:1 (1986) pp. 42–53; idem, *TA,* 13–14 (1986–87); pp. 105–65.

50. A. Kempinski, *BAR* 12:1 (1986), pp. 44–49. N. Na'aman suggested that this is the "tower of Shechem" mentioned in Judges 9:49 as located on "Mount Zalmon" and burnt by Abimelech, but it appears that the tower of Shechem was located in Shechem itself; see N. Na'aman, *Zion* 51 (1986), pp. 259–80 (Hebrew).

51. A. Mazar, *BASOR* 247 (1982), pp. 27–41.

52. G. W. Ahlström, *ZDPV* 100 (1984), pp. 35–52 suggests that Tel Masos was populated by Canaanites; Z. Herzog and A. F. Rainey accepted M. Kochavi's suggestion that Tel Masos was inhabited by Amalekites. See Herzog (note 44), pp. 72, 101; and the discussion in Finkelstein (note 37), pp. 41–46 (objection of identifying Tel Masos as Israelite site, but no alternative solution suggested).

53. G. W. Ahlström, *IEJ* 34 (1984), pp. 170–72; M. D. Coogan, *PEQ* 119 (1987), pp. 1–8.

54. Finkelstein, *Archaeology of the Period of Settlement* (see note 37), pp. 307–14.

55. There are several points which led some scholars to identify the early Israelites as part of this body of Shasu: Some Shasu emigrated to Egypt, just as Jacob did. In one Egyptian document the land of Shasu is called "Yahu," possibly a distortion of the name of the God of Israel. See Weippert in: *Symposia,* pp. 25–34; B. Mazar in: A. Biran (ed.), *Temples and High Places in Biblical Times,* Jerusalem 1981, pp. 5–9. The ideas of Mendenhall and Gottwald (see notes 29–30) concerning the emerg-

ence of Israel in the peasant communities of Late Bronze Age Canaan have become popular in recent years. The archaeological evidence cannot prove or disprove these ideas, as we don't have any direct archaeological evidence to the proto-history of the Israelites. The archaeological evidence for the Israelite settlement which is presented in this chapter relates to a time when the Israelites were already settled in the hill country. The Canaanite traditions which can be seen in their material culture are general to the entire country in Iron Age I, and they do not necessarily point to the origin of the Israelites in Canaanite society.

56. J. Briend and J. B. Humbert, *Tell Keisan (1971–1976)*, Paris 1980, pp. 197–234.

57. For summary and detailed literature, see J. A. Sauer, *BASOR* 263 (1986), pp. 10–14.

58. J. B. Pritchard in: W. V. Ward, *The Role of the Phoenicians in the Interaction of Mediterranean Civilizations*, Beirut 1968, pp. 99–112; J. B. Pritchard, *The Cemetery at Tell es-Saʿidiyeh, Jordan*, Philadelphia 1980; J. N. Tubb, *Levant* 20 (1988), pp. 23–88.

59. H. J. Franken, *Excavations at Tell Deir Alla*, Leiden 1969.

60. M. M. Ibrahim, *ADAJ* 17 (1972), pp. 23–36; ibid. 19 (1974), pp. 55–61; ibid. 20 (1975), pp. 69–82. Tell el-Umeiri appears now to be another important Iron Age I site in this region.

61. E. Olavarri, *ADAJ* 22 (1977–78), pp. 136–49.

62. O. Negbi, *TA* 1 (1974), pp. 159–72.

63. J. Waldbaum, *From Bronze to Iron*, Göteborg 1978; idem in: T. A. Wertime and J. D. Muhly, *The Coming of the Age of Iron*, New Haven 1980, pp. 69–98; T. Stech-Wheeler et al., *AJA* 85 (1981), pp. 245–68.

64. D. Davis et al., *JNES* 44 (1985), pp. 41–52.

65. For discussion and previous literature, see F. M. Cross in: *Symposia*, pp. 97–123; idem, *BASOR* 238 (1980), pp. 1–20. For the ostracon from ʿIzbet Sartah, see M. Kochavi, *TA* 4 (1977), pp. 1–13; A. Demsky in: Finkelstein, ʿIzbet Sartah (see note 37), pp. 186–97.

CHAPTER NINE

THE UNITED MONARCHY:
Iron Age IIA
(ca. 1000–925 B.C.E.)

INTRODUCTION

The period of the Monarchy (ca. 1000 B.C.E. until 586 B.C.E.) is illuminated by vast written sources. Biblical and extrabiblical documents provide insight into the history of the country, the relations of the Israelites with their neighbors, the historical geography of Palestine, and the social structure, spiritual life, moral values, and religious beliefs of the population. In a period so well known from written sources, archaeology has a somewhat different role than it has for earlier periods. In addition to its major goal—the reconstruction of material culture and cultural changes—it is instrumental in the verification, illumination, and supplementation of the written sources. Thus, while biblical narratives refer in the main to the Israelites, archaeology adds information on Israel's neighbors and can evaluate the Israelite material culture against the broader background of the time. A large number of Iron Age inscriptions, mostly from the eighth and seventh centuries B.C.E., are a major addition to the corpus of written documents from this period.

The vast material regarding the Israelite Monarchy is discussed in the next four chapters according to the following main subjects: the Israelite culture during the United Monarchy (in the present chapter); outline of the main discoveries relating to the separated kingdoms of Israel and Judah, in-

368

cluding the settlement pattern and development of the settlements (in Chapter Ten); discussion of common aspects of the Israelite material culture (in Chapter Eleven); and Israel's neighbors and the evidence for the Assyrian and Babylonian domination (in Chapter Twelve).

HISTORICAL OUTLINE

The Bible is the only written source concerning the United Monarchy, and it is therefore the basis of any historical presentation of the period. Although the historical evaluations of the biblical sources relating to the United Monarchy vary, historians treat it in general with credibility, believing it to be rooted in the Jerusalem royal "court history."[1]

The tribal structure and leadership of the Israelites during the period of the Judges did not withstand the test of time. The greater the pressure from neighboring states, the greater was the need for a centralized form of government. In the last quarter of the eleventh century B.C.E., Saul of the tribe of Benjamin became the first Israelite king. During his reign, which is thought to have lasted for ten to twenty years, the Israelite tribes of the north, of Gilead, and of Judah were molded into a single political entity, but it was a precarious unification. Large parts of Palestine remained outside Israelite control at the end of Saul's reign; Philistia on the coast, the Canaanite enclaves in the northern valleys and plains, and much of Transjordan. His rule was characterized by continuous warfare and struggle against these peoples and the Amalekites of the Negev.

Following Saul's death, David became king in Hebron and was recognized by both Judah and the other tribes of Israel. He ruled for a long time, ca. 1000–965 B.C.E. Decisive in the formation of his kingdom was the conquest of Jebusite Jerusalem, a foreign enclave separating Judah from the northern tribes. Thenceforward, Jerusalem became known as the "City of David" and was the seat of the Davidic dynasty—one of the longest-surviving royal houses in world history, lasting for over four hundred years. Jerusalem, under David and his son Solomon, also became the religious center of the nation.

David's warfare and policy of expansion led to the consolidation of a mighty empire stretching (according to the biblical tradition) from the Negev to the Euphrates in the north, and

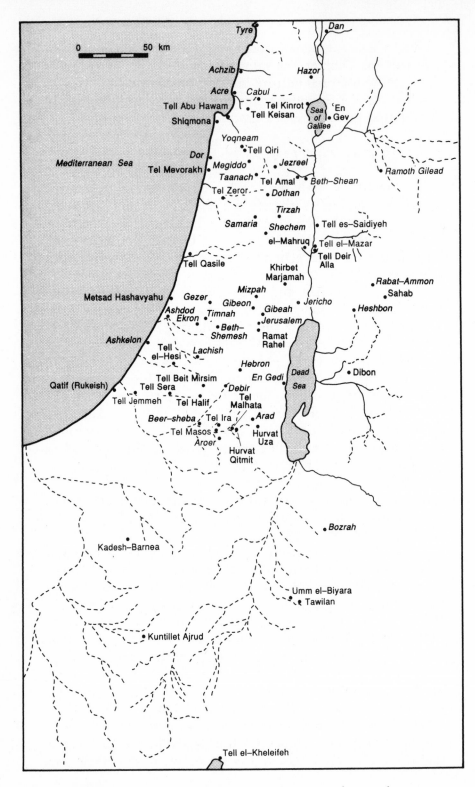

9.1 MAP OF IRON AGE II SITES. Ancient names are in italics, modern names in roman.

comprising most of Palestine and Transjordan (except the Philistine coastal plain), parts of Syria, and some of the Phoenician coast. This kingdom was governed by means of an innovative apparatus based on older, traditional bureaucracies.

The biblical tradition recalls David as a warrior and the creator of a great state, but not as the initiator of elaborate building projects. This task was left to his son Solomon, who also maintained most of David's political and territorial achievements. Solomon's reign was a time of economic wealth and administrative reorganization. According to the biblical sources, Solomon's widespread commercial network included Cylicia and Egypt. A breakthrough in trade was achieved with southern Arabia (the kingdom of Sheba) by way of the newly developed port of Ezion-Geber on the Gulf of Elath. Close relations between Solomon and Tyre, the most important Phoenician city, greatly facilitated the former's trade activity and extensive building projects. Solomon's reign, however, involved the imposition of a taxation system (including a corvée) under which the northern tribes were treated unfairly. After the death of Solomon, a division between the northern and southern parts of the kingdom was inevitable.

ARCHAEOLOGY OF THE TIME OF SAUL AND DAVID

Several basic questions face the archaeologist studying the United Monarchy: Can archaeology throw light on the transition from tribal life in the period of the Judges to the centralized rule of a monarchy? Do the discoveries reflect the existence of a mighty kingdom as that described in the biblical sources? To what extent are the elaborate international commercial and political relations evidenced in the remains? Do the material finds reflect the internal development of the kingdom from Saul until the time of Solomon? Unfortunately, the archaeological evidence for the period of the United Monarchy is sparse, often controversial, and it does not provide unequivocal answers to these questions.

The time of Saul hardly finds any expression in the archaeological record. Saul's capital is said to have been Gibeah of Saul, also known as "Gibeah of Benjamin." W. F. Albright identified this place with Tell el-Ful, a strategically located

Table 7. Comparative Stratigraphy of Iron Age II Sites

SITE \ SUBPERIOD	IRON IIA (ca. 1000 B.C.E. — ca. 925 B.C.E.)	IRON IIB (ca. 925 — 732/722/701 B.C.E.)	IRON IIC (732/722/701 — 600/586 B.C.E.)	Babylonian Period (600/586 — 530 B.C.E.)
Dan	IV	III II		
Hazor	X IX	VIII VII VI VB VA		
Tel Kinrot	IV	III II	I	
Beth-Shean	Upper V	IV		
Megiddo	VB IVB–VA	IVA	III	II
Taanach	IIA IIB	III IV	V	
Yoqneam	XVI XV XIV	XIII XII	XI	
Tel Qiri	VIIA	VIIB–C	VI V	
Tell Keisan	8c→a	7 6	5 4b 4a	3b
Tell Abu-Hawam	III	——	——	
Tirzah (Tell el Far'ah [North])	VIIb	VIIc VIId VIIe	$VIIe_1$	
Shechem (Tell Balatah)	X	IX VIII VII	VI V	
Tell es-Sa'idiyeh	XII(?) XI	X————→VI		
Tel Mevorakh	VIII VII	——	——	
Samaria	Pottery I–II	Pottery III–IV–VI	Pottery VII	
Tell el-Ful	II→?	——	III	
Jerusalem (City of David)	14	13 12	11 10	10A
Ramat-Rahel	——	VB	VA	
Aphek	X_8	X_7 X_6	——	
Tell Qasile	IX VIII	——	"VII"	
Gezer	IX VIII	VII VI	V	
Beth-Shemesh	IIa	IIb	IIc	
Timnah (Tel Batash)	IV	III	II	

SITE \ SUBPERIOD	ca. 1000 B.C.E.	IRON IIA	ca. 925 B.C.E.	IRON IIB	732/722/701 B.C.E.	IRON IIC	600/586 B.C.E.	Babylonian Period 530 B.C.E.
Ekron (Tel Miqne)		IV	(III)		(II)	Ic	Ib	Ia
Ashdod	X	IX			VIII	VII	VI	
Lachish		V	IV		III	II		
Tell Beit-Mirsim		B₃		A₂		A₁		
Tel el-Hesi				VIId→VIIc		VIId	VI	
Tel Halif		VII		VIB		VIA		
Tel Seraᶜ		VII		—		VI		
Tel Jemmeh		"EF"		"CD"		"AB" (Assyrian buildings)		
Tel Beer-sheba	VII VI	V	IV		III	II —		
Arad		XII	XI X IX	VIII		VII–VI		
Tel Ira		—		—		city		
ᶜAroer		—		—		II	I	
En Gedi (Tel Goren)		—		—		V		
Qadesh Barnea		early fort		middle fort		late fort		
Tell el-Kheleifeh		Period I(?)			II	III IV		

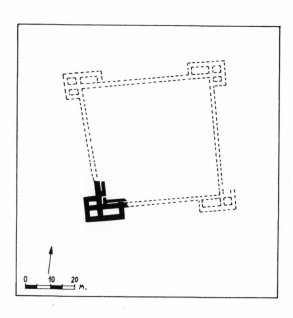

9.2 Tell el-Ful: P. Lapp's suggested reconstruction of the Period II fortress, perhaps the stronghold of Saul.

0 10 20 M.

hill about 7 km north of Jerusalem, along the main route leading from the latter. A corner of an extensive fortress which was discovered there may have been part of Saul's headquarters.[2] The fortress was a large public structure (ca. 57 × 62 m), but its full plan is unknown.

The archaeological evidence concerning David's reign is also poor and ambiguous. Jebusite Jerusalem, which he conquered, was located on a narrow spur demarcated on the east by the deep brook of Kidron, and on the west by the Tyropoeon Valley. Excavations on the steep eastern slope of this hill, above the spring of Gihon, have revealed an imposing edifice, known as the "stepped structure," which may tentatively be attributed to the tenth century B.C.E.; it is a huge retaining wall, preserved to a height of 16.5 m, which apparently supported a monumental building of which no remains were found. The identification of this construction with David's "fortress of Zion" (metsudat Zion) (1 Chr 11:5) is tempting. The wall's location, on the summit of the hill above the Gihon Spring, would be more appropriate for David than for Solomon, whose acropolis was constructed farther north. Later during the period of the Monarchy, when the city expanded to the eastern slopes of the hill, this enormous structure became obsolete (see map on p. 418).[3]

Violent destructions by fire of flourishing Canaanite and Philistine towns such as Megiddo Stratum VIA and Tell Qasile Stratum X can perhaps be attributed to David. At both these sites, the succeeding modest habitation can be dated to his reign. At Megiddo (Stratum VB), houses were constructed along the perimeter of the mound, their outer walls creating a defensive line. No fortifications or public buildings should be attributed to this phase.[4] At Tell Qasile (Stratum IX), the ruined town was reconstructed to some degree, but within a more limited area.

Several small village sites may be attributed to the time of David's reign—such as Khirbet Dawara near biblical Michmash in the land of Benjamin, where a circular-shaped settlement was defended by a casemate wall; or Tel Beer-sheba Stratum VII, where dwellings were built around a central open area. New types of pottery appear in these levels, characterized by distinct shapes and hand-burnished red slip.

It would appear that the first half of the tenth century B.C.E. was a transitional period in which the Israelites began to

9.3 Jerusalem, City of David. View of the "stepped structure," possibly a retaining wall of the "Fortress of Zion" (on the left: Hasmonean wall).

develop an urban culture. The modest archaeological data from the time of David, although not conforming with the image of an empire founder, is consistent with the biblical accounts, which do not attribute to him any building operations.

THE TIME OF SOLOMON

The intensive building activity of Solomon and his encouragement of the arts, both intricately portrayed in the Bible, find expression in discoveries in the outlying cities, but in Jerusalem are illuminated only by indirect sources.

Solomonic Buildings in Jerusalem   In spite of the lack of any remains, the detailed biblical descriptions enable us to reconstruct in outline the plan and ornamentation of Solomon's temple and palace complex located on the Temple Mount, the peak of the ridge of the City of David. Several basic points, however, do remain debatable.

Detailed descriptions of the Solomonic temple appear in 1 Kings 5:16–6:38 and 2 Chronicles 4. To those may be added the firsthand evidence of Ezekiel (Chapters 40–44).[5] The measurements of the building are given in cubits. Two standard cubits were employed during the biblical period: the long, or royal, one of 52.5 cm, and the short cubit of 44.5 cm. The former was most probably utilized in the construction of the temple. The temple was a rectangular structure, measuring 50 × 100 cubits, or approximately 25 × 50 m—larger than any Canaanite or Phoenician temple known to us. Its height was also exceptional, 30 cubits (ca. 15 m). The walls are said to have been 12 cubits thick—a width recalling that of the Middle Bronze Age temple at Shechem. The interior is described as having had a tripartite division into a porch (ulam), a sanctuary (hechal), and the Holy of Holies (debir); the entrance to each lay on the central axis. No wall dividing the sanctuary from the Holy of Holies is described; perhaps the separation was achieved by means of a curtain or a wooden partition. On either side of the temple, there were three stories

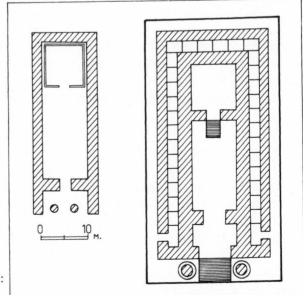

9.4 Two suggestions for the reconstruction of the temple of Solomon in Jerusalem. Left: after F. Fritz. Right: after K. Watzinger.

of auxiliary chambers which probably served as the kingdom's treasury.

The plan of the temple is rooted in the religious architecture of the second millennium B.C.E. in Canaan and northern Syria: the Middle Bronze Age temples at Ebla, Megiddo, and Shechem are clear prototypes. A later example is the eighth century B.C.E. edifice at Tell Tainat in northern Syria. The extensive use of cedarwood in the temple of Solomon recalls its use in Canaanite and Philistine temples (Lachish and Tell Qasile). The cedars are said to have been brought to Jerusalem by way of the "Sea of Jaffa," perhaps via the Yarkon River near Tell Qasile. Cult appurtenances described in connection with Solomon's temple, such as the sacrificial altar and the "molten sea" (a huge bronze basin supported by twelve bull figures), can be reconstructed on the basis of actual finds and artistic depictions from Phoenicia, Cyprus, and Palestine. The two ornamental columns Jachin and Boaz stood at the temple's facade, probably without having any constructional role. They recall two column bases in the Late Bronze Age temple at Hazor (Area H), which also lacked constructional function. Similar columns appear on the facade of a pottery model-shrine from Tell el-Farʿah (north).

The ark of the covenant stood in the Holy of Holies beneath

9.5 Temples resembling the temple of Solomon: (A) a Middle Bronze Age temple at Ebla, north Syria; (B) a Late Bronze temple at Tel Mumbakat, north Syria; (C) plan of the *Bit Hilani* palace (I) and attached tripartite temple (II) at Tell Tainat (north Syria, eighth century B.C.E.).

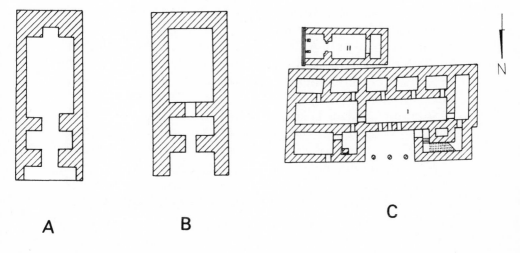

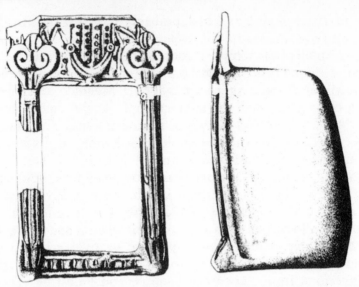

9.6 A pottery model shrine from Tell el-Farᶜah (north), with two pillars at the front recalling Jachin and Boaz.

the outstretched wings of the olive-wood cherubim. The latter were probably sphinxlike, with the body of a lion or bull, the wings of an eagle, and the head of a man—a well-known motif in Canaanite, Phoenician, and Syrian art of the Bronze and Iron ages. The various ornaments in the temple—the networks, palmettes, fringes, and chains—are also paralleled in Phoenician depictions, especially on carved ivories of the ninth and eighth centuries B.C.E. The tenth century B.C.E. was considered by some art historians as a "dark age" in the history of art in the ancient Near East.[6] The only example of monumental art from this century is the Phoenician sculptured sarcophagus of Ahiram, king of Byblos.[7] The descriptions of Solomon's temple are thus important evidence for the existence of monumental, elaborate art during the tenth century B.C.E..

Solomon's palace is described in 1 Kings 7:1–11. It included the following units: the "house of the Forest of Lebanon"; the "hall of pillars"; the "hall of the throne where he [Solomon] was to pronounce judgment"; "his own house where he was to dwell"; and the "other court." Contemporary or slightly later palaces have been discovered at Megiddo and at several cities in Syria; they are known as *bit-hilani*, an Akkadian term apparently based on the Hittite reference to palaces having a colonnaded entrance porch (see pp. 377, 382–83). D. Ussishkin has proposed that the different elements of Solomon's mansion in Jerusalem followed the plan of such a *bit-hilani*: the "hall of pillars" was the entrance porch with its ornamented columns.[8] In palaces of this type, the porch gave access to the throne room; the latter was a broad hall in which the throne stood at one of the narrow ends. Behind the throne room there were dwelling rooms, sometimes arranged around an inner courtyard like the "other court" of Solomon's palace.

The palace which Solomon built for Pharaoh's daughter, his most prestigious wife, may have been a separate *bit-hilani*. Such clusters of palaces are known at other royal cities of the Iron Age, such as Sinjirli, capital of the kingdom of Sama'l. The "house of the forest of Lebanon" is described as a separate building with four rows of cedarwood columns. This feature is paralleled in the pillared halls of the kingdom of Urartu in eastern Anatolia, as well as in a ninth century B.C.E. Phoenician temple at Kition on Cyprus, where there were four rows of pillars.[9]

The Bible describes the palace as having been built of stones "sawed with saws, back and front," "stones of eight and ten cubits." The courtyard is said to have been constructed of "three courses of hewn stone round about, and a course of cedar beams." These details conform to the character of monumental Israelite ashlar masonry known from Solomonic times at Megiddo (see p. 472).

The archaeological parallels to the biblical descriptions of Solomon's buildings in Jerusalem validate the accuracy of these descriptions and further illuminate the Israelite royal architecture of the time. Solomon was aided by Phoenician architects and craftsmen sent from Tyre who probably brought with them the traditions of Canaanite art and architecture. But as no contemporary buildings are known from Phoenicia proper, the description of the Jerusalem buildings is almost the only link presently known between the public architecture of the Late Bronze Age and that of the Iron Age throughout the Levant.

In addition to the temple and the palace, the Bible relates that Solomon built the wall of Jerusalem and the "Millo" (1 Kings 9:15). The latter term must have been connected with some artificial fill required to overcome a topographic

9.7 An elaborate cult stand from Taanach (height 53.7 cm). The stand is decorated with a rich variety of motifs taken from the Canaanite-Phoenician repertoire. From bottom to top: naked goddess flanked by two lions; two sphinxes; two lions and two gazelles flanking a sacred tree; and an animal (calf?) supporting a winged sun disc, with sphinxes on the sides. Tenth century B.C.E.

obstacle, perhaps a depression in the saddle between the City of David and the Temple Mount.

Solomonic Buildings Outside Jerusalem In 1 Kings 9:17–19 Solomon is credited with the building of Hazor, Megiddo, Gezer, Lower Beth-Horon, Baalath, and Tadmor (Palmyra, in the Syrian Desert). It is also noted that he built "store cities," "chariot cities," and "cavalry cities." The excavations at Hazor, Megiddo, and Gezer have substantially uncovered Solomonic urban architecture.

Megiddo was an administration center; it served as the seat of Ba'ana son of Ahilud, who was the governor of the Jezreel and Beth-Shean valleys—the "grain barns" of the kingdom. The excavations at Megiddo by the Oriental Institute of the

University of Chicago rank among the largest archaeological projects at an Iron Age site in Israel, yet the interpretation of the finds is the subject of a continuous debate.

Remains of four Iron Age II levels, Strata V–II, were identified by the excavators. The earliest, Stratum V, was noted as having subphases in certain areas of the site, termed "Stratum VA" and "Stratum VB." W. F. Albright, followed by G. E. Wright, suggested that the excavators missed an entire occupation level to which several buildings of Phase VA and some of Stratum IV should be attributed. He called the new level "Stratum IVB–VA." Y. Yadin's probes at Megiddo during the sixties successed in defining this stratum more precisely and resulted in a comprehensive view of Megiddo's architectural history during the period.[10] Yadin concluded that after the massive conflagration which destroyed the Stratum VIA city ca. 1000 B.C.E., Megiddo was rebuilt as an unwalled town with dwellings along the perimeter of the mound (Stratum VB). He dated this phase to the first half of

9.8 Plan of Megiddo Stratum IVB–VA (according to Y. Yadin) (1) City gate; (2) Palace 6000; (3) Palace 1723; (4) Dwellings.

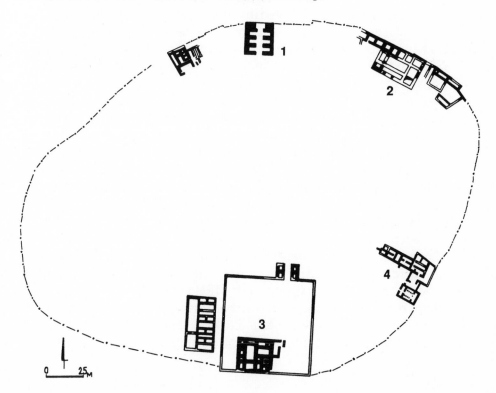

the tenth century B.C.E., the time of David. The following Stratum IVB–VA, identified as the Solomonic city, included two palaces (6000 and 1723) and other buildings of a public nature. In Yadin's view, this city was surrounded by a casemate wall which he suggested to be identified in his excavations along the northern edge of the mound. He conjectured that this casemate wall abutted a monumental, ashlar-built six-chamber gate, 17.8×20.0 m in size, which was attributed by the original excavators to Stratum IV. This interpretation was based on the fact that at Hazor and Gezer casemate walls were found in relation to similar six chamber gates at Solomonic levels; but it should be taken into consideration that the excavators of Megiddo did not discover any such casemate wall near the gate structure. In the following Stratum IVA, attributed by Yadin to the ninth century B.C.E. (the time of Ahab), a solid "offsets and insets" city wall and a large complex of "stable buildings" were constructed; the six-chamber gate was retained for a while, but eventually it was replaced by a four-chamber type. This new city survived until the conquest of Megiddo by the Assyrians in 732 B.C.E.

Yadin's conclusions were criticized by Aharoni and Herzog, essentially on two grounds: the identification of the casemate wall and the stratigraphic attribution of the six-chamber gate.[11] They accepted the view of the first excavators that the "offsets and insets" wall was the first and only wall related to the six-chamber gate and that both this wall and the gate were constructed as one unit in "Stratum IV," which they dated to the time of Solomon. Since palaces 6000 and 1723 were admitted to be earlier than this stratum, they were allocated by Aharoni to Stratum V, which he dated to the time of David. According to this theory, the Solomonic city included the six-chamber gate, the "offsets and insets" wall, and the "stable buildings" (identified by Aharoni and Herzog as storehouses). In our discussion we retain Yadin's suggestion in spite of ambiguities concerning the gate area (see p. 399, note 15).

The two palaces of Stratum IVB–VA clearly demonstrate the emergence of Israelite royal, monumental architecture characterized by ashlar masonry, stone molding and specific plans.[12] The northern palace (Palace 6000) is similar in plan to the *bit hilani* of northern Syria, and particularly to those at Sinjirli in southern Turkey. The southern palace (Palace 1723) has a more complicated plan, though it too may

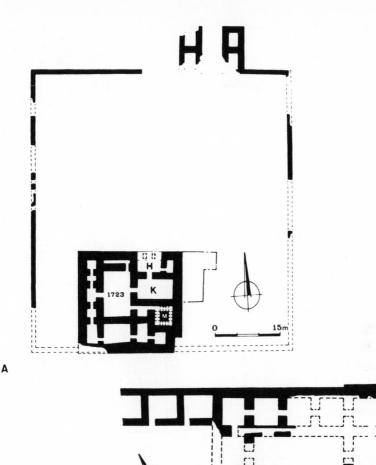

A

B

9.9 Reconstructed plans of the tenth century B.C.E. palaces at Megiddo: (A) Palace 1723; (B) Palace 6000.

be interpreted as a variation of the *bit hilani*.[13] The latter palace stood at the back of a large square courtyard which was surrounded by a wall constructed of ashlar piers separating segments built of fieldstones. This building technique is well known in later Israelite and Phoenician architecture. A four-chamber gate leading to the courtyard was decorated with stone capitals carved in the Proto-Aeolic style, which was to characterize Israelite royal architecture throughout the Iron Age. It is feasible to assume that similar elaborate architectural

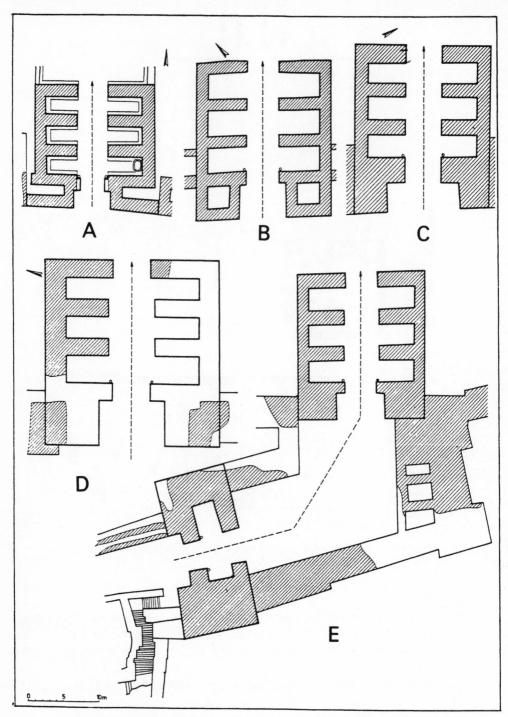

9.10 Plans of six-chamber gates: (A) Gezer; (B) Hazor; (C) Ashdod; (D) Lachish; (E) Megiddo (shown with the outer gate and the offsets-insets city wall).

384

components were also employed in the Solomonic royal buildings in Jerusalem.

The city gates of Megiddo, Hazor, and Gezer were noted by Y. Yadin as the bold illustration of a centralized, royal building operation attributable to Solomon on archaeological grounds as well as on the basis of the biblical reference in 2 Kings 9:15–17. These three monumental gates, as well as two additional examples found at Lachish and Ashdod, were rectangular structures comprising six guard chambers and four gateways. The facades of the gates at Megiddo, Hazor, and Gezer included projecting towers, and their central passage was 4.20 m in width, almost equal to 8 royal Egyptian cubits of 52.3 cm each. Other measurements, details of layout, and building technique in these gates varied.[14] The six-chamber inner gate of Megiddo was built of high-quality ashlar masonry. It is the only one of these gates which was completely built of ashlar stones, like the Megiddo palaces. We have mentioned earlier the complex stratigraphic difficulties relating this gate

9.11   Gezer: view of the six-chamber gate, from inside the city.

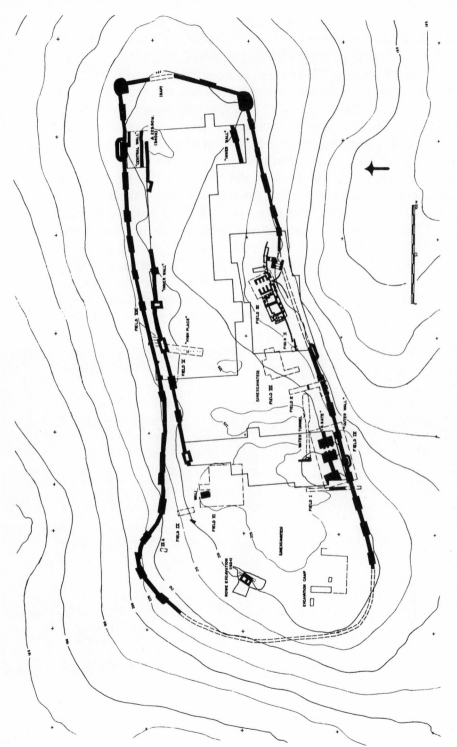

9.12 Gezer: general site plan. The Solomonic gate is seen on the right lower side; the Middle Bronze gate and tower are seen on the left lower side. The "Outer Wall" with its ashlar towers surrounds the entire site.

structure.[15] An outer gate constructed on the slope of the mound can most probably be attributed to a second phase in the history of this gate, probably in the ninth century B.C.E.

Solomonic Hazor (Stratum X) only occupied the western half of the upper mound, an area of 8 acres. The city was surrounded by a casemate wall, and entrance to it was gained through a six-chamber gate similar to that of Megiddo, though built of uncut fieldstones. Almost no details concerning other parts of the city are known.

At Gezer, the six-chamber gate was constructed of large fieldstones, ashlars being used only for parts of its facade.[16] A casemate wall, similar to the one at Hazor, flanked the gate but probably did not surround the entire city. The city was approached through an outer gate constructed of fine ashlar masonry and related to the solid "Outer Wall" with its ashlar towers (on this wall see earlier, p. 243). This latter wall was thought by Dever to be founded in the Late Bronze Age and rebuilt by Solomon. But in our opinion it is possible that this wall was added to the Solomonic fortifications of Gezer during the time of the Divided Monarchy.[17] This formidable fortification system was in use until the Assyrian conquest of Israel. A large public building, perhaps an administrative center, stood during the Solomonic era west of the gate, abutting the casemate wall.

SETTLEMENT AND ARCHITECTURE

The rise of the Monarchy brought about changes in the socioeconomic structure of Israelite society, and in consequence a new pattern of settlement was formed. Many of the small sedentary villages typical of the period of the Judges were abandoned, and others developed into towns, but our knowledge of this process is still limited.

In addition to the royal cities of Megiddo, Hazor, and Gezer, Israelite occupation levels from the tenth century B.C.E. were identified at Dan (Stratum IV), Tel Kinrot (Tell el-ʿOreme, Stratum IV), Taanach (Period II), Yoqneam (Stratum 11), Tel Amal, Tell Abu Hawam (Stratum III), Shiqmona, Tel Mevorakh (Stratum VII), Tell el-Farʿah (north; Tirzah, Stratum VIIb), Tel Hamath (Tell el-Hama in the Jordan Valley south of Beth-Shean), Tell el-Mazar (in the valley of Succoth, near the junction of the Jabbok and the Jordan), Tell Qasile (Strata IX–

VIII), Beth-Shemesh (Stratum IIa), Timnah (Tel Batash, Stratum IV), Tell Beit Mirsim (Stratum B3), Lachish (Stratum V), Arad (Stratum XII and perhaps Stratum XI), and Tel Beer-sheba (Strata VII–VI).[18] The evidence from most of these sites indicates the initial renewal of urbanization, though it seems that towns were still not densely populated or built up. This was the beginning of the gradual process of urbanization which reached its zenith in the succeeding centuries.

Fortifications The sparse fortifications found at these sites are mostly casemate walls. In addition to those at Hazor, Gezer, and possibly Megiddo, casemate walls fortified the tenth-century city of Yoqneam, and perhaps also Tell Beit Mirsim, Tell en-Nasbeh, and Beth-Shemesh. This type of defense was also common at the Negev "fortresses" of this period (see pp. 390–97). The versatility of its structure made it advantageous: the space between the outer and inner faces of the walls could serve as storage space or as the inner rooms of adjacent houses. Casemate walls occasionally appeared in the Middle and Late Bronze ages (at Hazor and Ashdod), but it is doubtful whether these early examples inspired those of the Iron Age. The latter may have developed from Iron Age I Israelite settlements in which the rear rooms of pillared houses created the outer defense ring of the settlement.[19]

It has been suggested that some solid walls—at Tel Kinrot, Tel Beer-sheba Stratum V, and Gezer (the last according to Dever)—belonged to the tenth century B.C.E., but the dating of the last two is debatable. At other sites there was no city wall at all during this period, and the outer walls of houses built along the perimeter of the town seem to have been the only defense. This was definitely the case during the time of David (at Megiddo Stratum VB, Tell Qasile Stratum IX, Beer-sheba Stratum VII), and at some sites dated to Solomon (Tell Qasile Stratum VIII, Tel Batash Stratum IV, Lachish Stratum V, and perhaps Megiddo Stratum IVB–VA).

Town Planning Our data concerning the inner planning of the tenth-century towns and cities is meager. It appears that in this initial phase of Israelite urbanization, large areas of the cities remained unsettled. Lachish is a good example, since it was to become one of the major cities of Judah in the following centuries. After a gap in occupation which began in the mid–twelfth century B.C.E., Lachish was reinhabited in the tenth century B.C.E. on a limited scale: no fortifications were erected, and extensive parts of the mound remained uninhabited. The excavators attributed to this stratum the first phase of a large palace-fort. In this phase, denoted Palace A, the building stood on a square stone platform, 32×32 m in size. However, in my view the attribution of this palace to Stratum V is not sufficiently proved, and it may be suggested that it was founded in the following Stratum IV, of the Divided Monarchy.[20]

The emergence of Israelite urbanization is demonstrated also at Tell Beit Mirsim and at Timnah (Tel Batash). At the latter, the ruined Philistine town was replaced in the tenth century B.C.E. by a town with houses built around the circumference of the mound. Entrance to the city was perhaps gained through a gate composed of two square towers.

Tirzah (Tell el-Farʿah [north]) is an exceptional example of a developed town—well planned and densely occupied—in this period. It is characterized by orthogonal planning (almost nonexistent in later Israelite towns) and the repeated appearance of typical "four-room houses" (both elements recall Tell Qasile Stratum X of the late eleventh century B.C.E. see p. 466).

Other Settlement Features Related to the United Monarchy
The expansion of settlement along the Palestine littoral may have been the outcome of the special ties between the kingdom of David and Solomon and the Phoenician cities of Tyre and Sidon. At Tell Qasile, the ruined eleventh century B.C.E. Philistine town was rehabilitated in a diminished area, large open spaces being left in the town. A partial reconstruction of the ruined Stratum X temple (in Strata IX and VIII which should probably be dated to the times of David and Solomon respectively) suggests that some of the local population may have remained as navigators for the Israelites, who lacked the seagoing knowledge necessary for the development of the maritime ties with Phoenicia. The contemporary settlements along the Mediterranean coast at Tel Michal, Tel Mevorakh, Shiqmona, and Tell Abu Hawam tell a similar story.

A large public building of the tenth century, discovered near Tell el-Mazar in the Jordan Valley (near the junction of the Jabbok and the Jordan rivers), was in use during the time of Solomon until it was destroyed by a heavy conflagration.

The floor plan can be recovered only in part, but it included casemate rooms along one side of a large courtyard, recalling the plan of the compound around Palace 6000 at Megiddo. There is no reason to accept the identification of this building as a temple, as suggested by its excavator. It may have been a royal Solomonic building related to the official metal-processing activity in the Jordan Valley between Succoth (probably Tell Deir Alla) and Zarethan (1 Kings 7:46).[21]

SETTLEMENTS IN THE NEGEV

The Central Negev Highlands The region defined as the "Negev highlands" is demarcated on the east by the cliffs of Nahal Zin, on the south by the precipices of Machtesh Ramon, and on the west by the oasis of Kadesh-Barnea and the eastern Sinai Desert. This mountainous arid region, where the annual rainfall does not surpass 100–200 mm, was always more suited for pastoral nomadism than for permanent settlement. In order to foster agriculture in the riverbeds, settlers had to devise sophisticated techniques to divert runoff water and to store water for both man and animal.

Thorough surveys and excavations in this region have shown that following the wave of settlement in the third millennium B.C.E. (see pp. 114–17), the area was unoccupied throughout the second millennium. Surprisingly, however, rapid and wide-scale settlement occurred in this area, most probably during the time of the United Monarchy.[22] About fifty fortified enclosures (commonly referred to as "fortresses"), and many additional small settlements and isolated farmsteads, were part of this phenomenon. They are found close to water sources (such as the Kadesh-Barnea oasis) or wadi beds, where some agriculture could be practiced and water could be collected in open, large reservoirs. Most of the "fortresses" are located on hills within sight of each other between the present-day towns of Yeruham and Mitspe Ramon, and as far as Kadesh-Barnea in the west. However, they were not constructed along any particular route; on the contrary, their widespread distribution seems to have been planned to achieve settlement all over the region.

Most of the "fortresses" were 25–70 m in diameter; they were circular, oval, rectangular, or amorphic in shape and followed the contours of the hill on which they were estab-

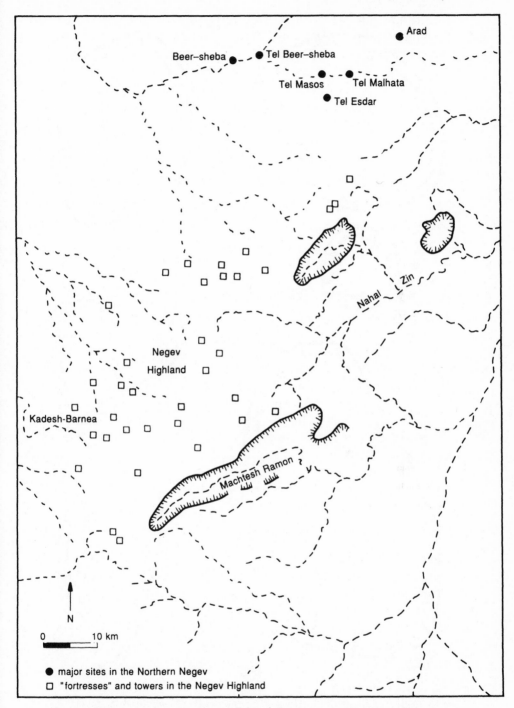

9.13 Distribution map of tenth-century "fortresses" in the central Negev highlands.

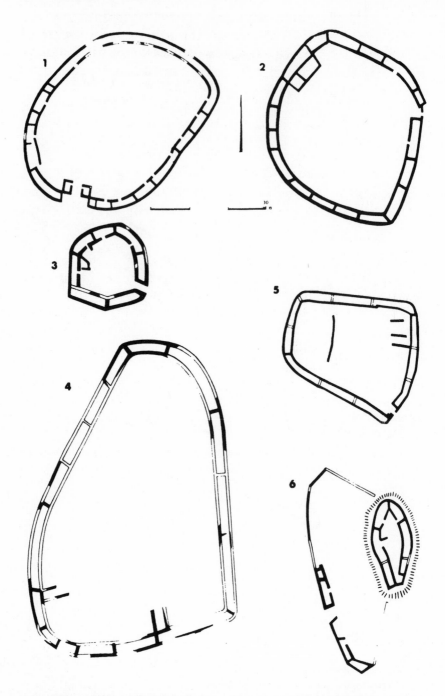

9.14 Selected plans of "fortresses" in the central Negev highlands: (1) ʿEn Kadesh; (2) Atar Haroʿa; (3) Hurvat Haluqim; (4) Hurvat Rahba; (5) Hurvat Ketef Shivta; (6) Ramat Matred.

lished. Usually they included a row of casemate rooms surrounding a large central courtyard; the latter was entered through a narrow entrance. In some cases actual buildings adjoined the casemates, while in others the "fortresses" were rather smaller structures or towers. Groups of dwellings are located either adjacent to the "fortresses" or independent of them; these dwelling groups can be found scattered at a considerable distance in the plains and along riverbeds, particularly in the region just north of Machtesh Ramon. These unfortified settlements lacked any central planning, and often the houses were isolated, at a considerable distance from one another. Some of the buildings were simple in plan, comprising between one and three rooms arranged in a row, sometimes with a fenced courtyard at their front. There were also structures, particularly in the northern part of the region, which were similar in plan to the pillared houses found since Iron Age I in other parts of the country. Several were fully developed "four-room houses" and others were variants of this form, both utilizing the principle of a courtyard divided by pillars.

The sites were inhabited for a short period of time. There are two groups of pottery vessels found in them. One of these groups includes wheelmade shapes, identical in form and decoration to the pottery found throughout the southern part of the country in the tenth century B.C.E. The second group is denoted "Negebite Ware"; it comprises rough handmade

9.15 View of the site at Metsudat 'Akrab, central Negev highlands. The settlement is seen at the front; the "fortress" is located on the hill in the background.

vessels similar to those found in the Timnaʿ mines from the end of the thirteenth and beginning of the twelfth centuries B.C.E. This latter group can safely be attributed to local Negev nomads.

The significance and precise date of these central Negev settlements and forts are debated issues. One group of scholars (B. Rothenberg, D. Eitam, I. Finkelstein) ascribe them to the desert nomads, the Amalekites, or even to Israelites of the tribe of Simeon. Finkelstein points out a resemblance between the casemate "fortresses" and tent enclosures of pastoral Bedouins. He dates these settlements to the second half of the eleventh century B.C.E., and he believes that they were terminated with the wars of Saul against the Amalekites.[23] This theory, however, does not explain what motivated the local pastoralists to move to permanent settlements, why they suddenly adopted northern pottery and architectural forms, and finally what brought about the end of this settlement wave. Furthermore, Finkelstein's dating of this process seems to be too early.

9.16 Casemate rooms in the "fortress" of Metsudat ʿAkrab.

Other scholars view these settlements as evidence of Israelite penetration, but there are various opinions regarding their date and development. Y. Aharoni suggested a gradual Israelite penetration to the Negev highlands by a surplus Israelite population in the northern Negev. He dated these settlements to the eleventh century B.C.E., contemporary with Tel Masos and Tel Esdar. N. Glueck, Z. Meshel, and R. Cohen (and initially Y. Aharoni) view these sites as a result of royal initiatives.[24] Accordingly, settlers arriving from Judah established a network of agricultural settlements in the Negev highlands. The "fortresses" were the headquarters of officials and landowners. Major aspects of the material culture of the Negev sites (such as house plans and wheel-made pottery) are correlated to Judah in the time of the United Monarchy.

Z. Meshel dates this process to the time of Saul, explaining it as a strategy against the desert nomads, particularly the Amalekites. R. Cohen, who carried out the most intensive study of the subject, accepts the earlier views of Aharoni and Glueck dating the settlements to the time of David and Solomon. In Cohen's view, which we tend to accept, these sites reflect an overall Israelite policy to control the Negev and its inhabitants in order to secure the routes crossing the Negev through Kadesh Barnea toward the Red Sea, where commercial ties with Arabia had been established.

The Negev highland region served as a link between the heartland of Judah and the arid regions of the southern Negev. The southern limit of these settlements corresponds to the description of the southern border of Judah: ". . . south of Scorpion pass (*maale 'Akrabim*), continued on to Zin, and went over to the south of Kadesh Barnea. Then it ran past Hezron . . ." (Joshua 15:2–3). This demarcation, therefore, may have originated in the period of the United Monarchy. The new settlements would of course have been a source of livelihood for the local desert nomads who subsequently concentrated around them. This demographic symbiosis is reflected in the handmade Negebite pottery and the poor scattered dwellings; it recalls similar earlier and later phenomena, such as those in the EB II Negev and southern Sinai.

These Negev highland settlements were probably destroyed and deserted as a result of Pharaoh Shishak's military campaign in the region five years after the death of Solomon (see p. 397 and note 29). Shishak's topographical list, preserved on the walls of the temple of Amun at Karnak, includes almost seventy place-names in the Negev. Some of them can be identified in the area of Arad and Beer-sheba, but others were perhaps located farther south, in the Negev highlands. The prefix *hgr* appears and is possibly an Egyptian transcription of the Hebrew term *hagar*, "belt" or "enclosure," which could have denoted the casemate "fortresses" of the Negev. Shishak's goal may have been to disrupt the Israelite and Phoenician trade with southern Arabia and restore Egyptian hegemony over this trade as it had been during the New Kingdom. This supposed Egyptian invasion of the Negev can be taken as indirect evidence of the significance of the Negev settlements in the Solomonic kingdom.

The Northern Negev   Toward the end of the eleventh century B.C.E., a crisis occurred in the northern Negev (the Arad–Beer-sheba region), witnessed in the destruction and abandonment of the large settlement at Tel Masos. This crisis may have been related to the wars against the Amalekites during the time of Saul and in the early days of David, and to the disruption of the specific economic arrangements and ties with the coastal plain which ensured the prosperity of Tel Masos during the eleventh century B.C.E. Later in the period of the United Monarchy, new sites were founded in the region, though on a smaller scale.[25]

At Tel Beer-sheba, the village of Stratum VII (see p. 374) should probably be dated to the time of David. The destruction of this village was followed by a short, impoverished intermediate phase (Stratum VI), which in turn was succeeded—in Stratum V, apparently during the time of Solomon—by a well-planned 3-acre town defended by a solid wall buttressed by a solid earth rampart.[26]

At Arad, a village developed during the period of the United Monarchy (Stratum XII), perhaps around a sacred shrine which served Kenite families who joined Judah (Judges 1:16). A square fortress surrounded by casemate walls (Stratum XI) replaced this village. It was dated by Aharoni to the time of Solomon, and it was identified by him as *p-Hgr Arad Rbt*, "the fortress of great Arad," noted in Shishak's list of conquered sites in the Negev. Yet it may be proposed that this fortress was founded later—in the ninth century B.C.E.—and that the Arad mentioned in Shishak's list was a settlement surrounded by a belt of casemates or buildings.[27]

Ezion-Geber The Bible relates that Solomon carried out an active trade with Sheba and Ophir, apparently to be identified with southern Arabia and Somali respectively (1 Kings 9:26–28; 10:1–13). Ezion-Geber, the port of call for this trade, was identified by N. Glueck in 1937 with Tell el-Kheleifeh, at the head of the Red Sea (between Elath and Aqaba). He described a large building at this site as a smelting center for copper ores brought from the Timna‘ mines. Glueck's proposals, however, became questionable when it was clarified that what he identified as copper crucibles are handmade "Negebite" vessels and that the copper mines at Timna‘ are earlier than Solomon by some three hundred years.[28] The architectural complex of the earliest level at Tell el-Kheleifeh (Period IV) includes a square compound surrounded by casemate wall and a central building of the "Four-Room" plan. New study of the finds from the excavation (by G. Pratico) did not reveal any clear evidence for the date of this level. The combination of casemate wall, Four-Room building, and handmade Negebite pottery recall the central Negev sites of the tenth century B.C.E., though the compound at Tell el-Kheleifeh is much better planned than any of these sites. The identification of Tell el-Kheleifeh with Ezion Geber was questioned in light of the criticism on Glueck's interpretation. But since the pottery from this level was not preserved and never published, I don't see in the present state of our knowledge any clear negative evidence for a tenth-century B.C.E. date for this compound. Thus the identification of the site with Ezion-Geber should at least be regarded as a legitimate possibility. Ezion-Geber could thus be in fact no more than a royal fortress with a central administration building, from which the Red Sea trade could have been managed (see also p. 450).

THE OUTCOME OF SHISHAK'S CAMPAIGN

The Egyptian campaign to Israel led by Pharaoh Shishak ca. 923 B.C.E. resulted in the destruction of numerous settlements and even entire regions. The campaign is known from the Bible (1 Kings 14:25–29) as well as from the Karnak inscription mentioned earlier.[29] We have already noted the southern thrust of the campaign into the Negev; the northern and central operations took place in the hill country, the heart of Israelite territory. Shishak crossed the Shephelah via the Ajalon Valley and ascended to Kiriath-Jearim and Gibeon, thus threatening Jerusalem from the northwest. Rehoboam, king of Judah, forestalled an Egyptian siege of the capital by paying a heavy indemnity: ". . . he carried off the treasures of the temple of the Lord and the treasures of the royal palace; he took everything, including all the gold shields Solomon had made" (1 Kings 14:26). The newly born northern kingdom of Israel suffered considerably; Shishak's incursion spread in an arc from Gibeon and Bethel through the Jordan Valley as far as the valley of Jezreel. He then swept along the historical coastal route ("The Way of the Sea") from Megiddo to Gaza. Some of the numerous destructions of this period can be ascribed to Shishak's campaign: Timnah (Tel Batash, Stratum IV), Gezer (Stratum VIII), Tell el-Mazar, Tell el-Hama, Tell el Sa'idiyeh (these last three sites in the Jordan Valley), Megiddo (Stratum IVB–VA), Tell Abu Hawam (Stratum III), Tel Mevorakh (Stratum VII), Tel Michal, and Tell Qasile (Stratum VIII). Megiddo was apparently only partially destroyed—as the six-chamber gate seems to have continued in use in the following period, and Shishak erected a victory stele there, a fragment of which was found in the excavations.

NOTES

1. Bright (1981), pp. 195–228; B. Mazar and D. N. Freedman in: *WHJP*, vol. 4, pp. 76–125; J. M. Miller and J. H. Hayes, *A History of Ancient Israel and Judah*, Philadelphia 1986, pp. 149–217.

2. N. Lapp (ed.), *The Third Campaign at Tell el-Ful: The Excavations of 1964. AASOR* 45 (1981), pp. 1–38.

3. Y. Shiloh, *Excavations at the City of David I. Qedem* 19, Jerusalem 1984, pp. 16–17, 27.

4. Y. Aharoni ascribed to the time of David a series of public buildings and occupation levels, including Palaces 6000 and 1723 at Megiddo, the city gate at Dan, and Stratum V at Beer-sheba with its four-chamber gate and massive wall (Aharoni [1982], pp. 192–211). This view was based on assumptions rather than on actual facts. The finds from Beer-sheba Stratum V were not yet published. For the publication of the preceding Levels VII–VI see: Z. Herzog, *Beer Sheba II: The Early Iron Age Settlements*, Tel Aviv 1984. The pottery from levels VII–VI appears

to me to have been contemporary with Tell Qasile IX–VIII of the tenth century B.C.E. I suggest the late eleventh century B.C.E. for the Beersheba Stratum VIII pottery; the first half of the tenth century B.C.E. for Stratum VII; and the second half of the latter century for Stratum VI. Stratum V can thus be related to the time of Solomon or even later (see note 26). The gate at Dan was ascribed by its excavator, A. Biran, to the time of the Divided Monarchy, and there is no reason to dispute this dating. The pottery found on the floors of Palace 6000 in Yadin's excavations at Megiddo (unpublished) appears to fit the time of Solomon (for further discussion see p. 382 and note 15).

5. Th. A. Busink, *Der Tempel von Jerusalem*, vol. 1, Leiden 1970; Wright (1985), pp. 254–67; F. Fritz, *BAR* 13:4 (1987), pp. 40–49.

6. H. Frankfort, *The Art and Architecture of the Ancient Near East*, Harmondsworth 1954, pp. 163–67, contra W. F. Albright, *EI* 5 (1956), pp. 1*–9*.

7. E. Porada, *Journal of the Ancient Near East Society of the University of Columbia* 5 (1973), pp. 355–72.

8. D. Ussishkin, *BA* 36 (1973), pp. 78–105.

9. V. Karageorghis, *Kition*, London 1976, pp. 107–17.

10. Yadin (1972), pp. 147–64; idem, *BA* 33 (1970), pp. 66–96.

11. Aharoni (1982), pp. 192–239, followed by Herzog (see note 4). See also idem in: *Architecture*, pp. 195–231 (Hebrew).

12. Y. Shiloh, *The Proto–Aeolic Capital and Israelite Ashlar Masonry. Qedem* 11, Jerusalem 1979; W. G. Dever in: T. Ishida (ed.), *Studies in the Period of David and Solomon and Other Essays*, Winona Lake 1982, pp. 269–306.

13. D. Ussishkin, *IEJ* 16 (1966), pp. 174–86; ibid. 20 (1970), pp. 213–15.

14. In addition to the literature in notes 10 and 13, see D. Milson, *ZDPV* 102 (1986), pp. 87–92. Milson claims that the builders of all three gates utilized the Egyptian cubit of 52.3 cm, but that the plans of each of the three were designed separately, according to different geometric patterns.

15. Yadin (1972), pp. 147–64 suggested that the lower part of the gate, considered by the excavators to be a foundation, was in fact the original superstructure of the Solomonic gate. The floor level in this phase was, according to his view, a white lime floor found at the gate's foundation level and attributed by the excavators to the earlier Stratum V. The advantage of Yadin's view is that it explains the fine ashlar masonry in the lower courses of the gate's structure, as it is hard to believe that such beautiful stonework would have been intentionally buried in foundation courses where it could not be seen. The problem with Yadin's proposal, however, is that it leaves the massive gate without any subterranean foundation. In support of Yadin's view, see Y. Shiloh, *Levant* 12 (1980), pp. 69–76. For Y. Aharoni and Z. Herzog views see p. 382 and note 11. D. Ussishkin accepts Aharoni and Herzog's view concerning the separation of the gate from palaces 1723 and 6000, yet he also accepts Yadin's dating of the palaces to the time of Solomon and thus proposes dating the six-chamber gate to the following level

(IVA) of the ninth century B.C.E. See D. Ussishkin, *BASOR* 239 (1980), pp. 1–18, and Yadin's answer there, pp. 19–23.

A weak point in Yadin's argumentation concerns the casemate wall. The fact that such a wall was not observed by the first excavators raises strong doubts regarding its existence; the rooms found by Yadin east of Palace 6000 can hardly be taken as evidence of such a casemate wall, and those west of this palace appear to have been part of an enclosure surrounding it. Even if a casemate wall never existed at Megiddo, the six-chamber gate still could have had a phase antedating the erection of the "offsets and insets" wall. The gate could have formed the entrance to a city which lacked a city wall and in which the outer walls of the outer belt of buildings created a defense line. Similar town planning in the time of the United Monarchy can be observed at Tell Qasile, Tel Batash, and perhaps also at Gezer, where only a small segment of a casemate wall was discovered. In a later period (Stratum IVA), when Palaces 6000 and 1723 went out of use, the massive city wall was constructed at Megiddo and attached to the existing six-chamber gate. See also p. 526, note 4.

16. The Solomonic gate at Gezer was first identified by Yadin from a plan in R. A. S. Macalister's report on his excavations there. Later, the gate was excavated by the Hebrew Union College expedition; the outer gate, discovered by Macalister, was explored by Dever in 1983. See Y. Yadin, *IEJ* 8 (1958), pp. 80–86; W. G. Dever, *BA* 34 (1971), pp. 94–132; idem, *Journal of Jewish Studies* 33:1–2 (1982), pp. 19–34; idem, *BASOR* 262 (1986), pp. 9–33.

17. Dever's dating of the Gezer outer gate and "Outer Wall," published in his preliminary report in *BASOR* (see note 16) on the 1983 excavations, should be taken with caution. The evidence for the original Late Bronze Age dating of the "Outer Wall" is too meager (see Chapter Seven, note 12), and the association of the "rebuild" phase of this wall with the tenth century B.C.E. is based on sherds from fills, mainly from outside the wall itself. Evidence of this type can give at best a terminus post quem for the erection of the wall. In addition, our ability to distinguish sherds of the late tenth century from those of the ninth century B.C.E. can be questioned. More general considerations, therefore, should be taken into account. I doubt the existence of two major walls at Solomonic Gezer (a casemate wall on top of the mound and a solid one on the slope); the latter would have become necessary only when the Assyrian threat developed. I, therefore, tend to date the erection of the "Outer Wall" and perhaps the adjoining outer gate at Gezer to the time of the Divided Monarchy, perhaps in the ninth century B.C.E.

18. On Taanach, see W. E. Rast, *Taanach I: Studies in the Iron Age Pottery. American Schools of Oriental Research Excavation Reports* (1978); on Tel Amal, see S. Levy and G. Edelstein, *Revue Biblique* 79 (1972), pp. 325–67; on Tel Kinrot, see F. Fritz, *ZDPV* 102 (1986), pp. 1–39; on Yoqneam, see A. Ben-Tor et al., *IEJ* 33 (1983), pp. 30–54; on Tell Abu Hawam, see J. Balensi, *BASOR* 257 (1985), pp. 65–74; on Tel Mevorakh, see E. Stern, *Excavations at Tel Mevorakh. Qedem* 9, Jerusalem 1978, pp. 46–65, 77; on Tell el-Farʿah (north) see A. Chambon, *Tell el-Farʿah,*

l'Age du Fer, Paris 1984; on Tell el-Mazar, see K. Yassine, *ZDPV* 100 (1984), pp. 108–18; on Tel Batash, see G. L. Kelm and A. Mazar, *BASOR Supplement* 23 (1985), pp. 101–3. On Beer-sheba see Herzog in note 4 above and note 26 below.

19. Y. Aharoni, *BASOR* 154 (1959), pp. 35–39; N. Lapp, *BASOR* 223 (1976), pp. 25–42; A. Kempinski, *Expedition* 20 (1978), pp. 35–36; Y. Shiloh, *IEJ* 28 (1978), pp. 44–46. "Enclosed settlements" arranged around a central courtyard (such as the one at 'Izbet Sartah) were proposed by I. Finkelstein as a possible origin of the casemate walls in Israel. But 'Izbet Sartah Stratum III is the only example of such a site, and the reconstruction of its plan is largely speculative. The Negev sites cited by Finkelstein are probably from the tenth century B.C.E. and thus should not be seen as a prototype of the casemate walls; see I. Finkelstein, *The Archaeology of the Israelite Settlement*, Jerusalem 1988, p. 263.

20. D. Ussishkin, *TA* 5 (1978), pp. 28–31; ibid. 10 (1983), pp. 171–73. Ussishkin follows Starkey and Tufnell in attributing Palace A—the earliest phase of the citadel-palace—to Stratum V, which he dates to the time of Rehoboam. Y. Yadin has suggested associating Stratum V with the time of the United Monarchy and Stratum IV with Rehoboam (*BASOR* 239 [1980], pp. 19–23). W. G. Dever believes that both the erection of Palace A and the six-chamber gate belong to Stratum V, which he dates to the time of Rehoboam or even Solomon (*BASOR* 262 [1986], pp. 26–28). I accept Dever's view that both Palace A and the six-chamber gate belong to the same building phase, but I believe that they should be attributed to Stratum IV. According to this interpretation, Stratum V would remain an unfortified town from the time of the United Monarchy, lacking a palace or a fortress. The foundation of Stratum IV should be dated to the time between the reigns of Rehoboam and Jehoshaphat, a more precise dating being impossible.

21. On Tell el-Mazar see Yassine (note 18); the new excavations at Tell el-Sa'idiyeh revealed a sequence of Iron Age strata. See J. Tubb, *Levant* 20 (1988), pp. 1–88. Stratum XII was dated by Tubb to the twelfth century B.C.E., but the pottery published appear to me to belong to the tenth century B.C.E., and thus this densely built level may perhaps be identified with Solomonic Zarethan. The level was destroyed by heavy fire, perhaps during the conquest of the region by Shishak.

22. R. Cohen, *BASOR* 236 (1980), pp. 61–79; idem, *BAR* 11:3 (1985), pp. 56–70; ibid. 12:4 (1986), pp. 40–45. On specific sites, see Y. Aharoni, *IEJ* 10 (1960), pp. 97–111; ibid. 17 (1967), pp. 1–17; Z. Meshel, *TA* 4 (1977), pp. 110–35; R. Cohen, *'Atiqot* 11 (1976), pp. 34–50; Z. Meshel and R. Cohen, *TA* 7 (1980), pp. 70–81. The most extensive work on this subject is R. Cohen, "The Settlement of the Central Negev," unpublished Ph.D. dissertation, The Hebrew University of Jerusalem 1986.

23. Z. Herzog, *BASOR* 250 (1983), pp. 41–49; I. Finkelstein (see note 19), pp. 242 and passim; idem *TA* 11 (1984), pp. 82–84; idem, *BAR* 12:4

(1986), pp. 46–53; similar opinions were expressed previously in Hebrew publications by B. Rothenberg and D. Eitam.

24. See the views of Meshel and Cohen (papers cited in note 22). For Aharoni's first opinion see *IEJ* 17 (1967), pp. 1–17. See also Mazar (1986), pp. 148–50.

25. See p. 353 for the different opinions concerning the identity of the settlers at Tel Masos. For a discussion of the history of the entire region, see Herzog (note 4), pp. 70–85, 88–104.

26. The dates suggested in the preceding section for Strata VII–VI at Beersheba are lower by several decades than those recorded by the excavators (see also note 4). The acceptance of the former set of dates naturally involves changes in Herzog's and Rainey's historical interpretations. See Herzog (earlier, note 4), pp. 70–84; Rainey, ibid., pp. 96–104. The dating of Stratum V to Solomon (rather than to the time of David as suggested by the excavators) is tentative, since the pottery from Strata V–III has not yet been published. We suspect that the city of Stratum V could have been founded even after the division of the Monarchy.

27. On the first village at Arad (Stratum XII), see M. Aharoni, *EI* 15 (1981), pp. 181–204 (Hebrew). On Strata XI–VI see Z. Herzog et al., *BASOR* 254 (1984), pp. 1–34. I suggested lowering the date of the fortress of Stratum XI to the ninth century B.C.E.; see A. Mazar and E. Netzer, *BASOR* 263 (1986), pp. 87–91; B. Mazar, *JNES* 24 (1964), pp. 297–303; N. Naʾaman, *TA* 12 (1985), pp. 91–92.

28. For a comprehensive discussion and previous bibliography, see G. D. Pratico, *BASOR* 259 (1985), pp. 1–31.

29. B. Mazar, *Vetus Testamentum Supplementum* 4 (1957), pp. 57–66 (= Mazar [1986], pp. 139–50); Aharoni (1979), pp. 323–30; K. A. Kitchen, *The Third Intermediate Period in Egypt*, Warminster 1973, pp. 293–300, 432–47.

CHAPTER TEN

THE DIVIDED MONARCHY:
Iron Age IIB–C
(925–586 B.C.E.)

HISTORICAL OUTLINE[1]

The United Monarchy created by Saul and David was not to endure for long. The conflicting interests of the southern and northern Israelite tribes were stronger than the political drive of the Davidic dynasty to maintain a unified nation. After the death of Solomon, his son Rehoboam was unable to preserve the unification, and Jeroboam son of Nebat split the Monarchy, establishing the northern kingdom of Israel. To accomplish the separation from the united capital in Jerusalem and the temple erected there just several decades earlier, Jeroboam founded cultic centers at both ends of his realm— at Dan in the north and at Bethel in the south.

During the reigns of Asa in Judah and Baasha in Israel, the two kingdoms fought over the demarcation of their common frontier. The Arameans of Damascus, however, became a danger for Israel, and in the time of Omri and Ahab (882–851 B.C.E.) Israel was preoccupied with struggles against this new enemy, balanced by friendship with Judah under Jehoshaphat and Jehoram, as well as with the Phoenicians to the north. Together with Jehoshaphat, Ahab campaigned in Transjordan, where he gained control of significant parts of Moab. The ties with the Phoenicians found political expression in his marriage to Jezebel, daughter of the king of Sidon, which in turn led to the infiltration into Israel of Phoenician religious and artistic concepts. Israel's capital during its early years was moved from Shechem to Penuel (in Transjordan), from there to Tirzah (Tell el-Far'ah [north]), and finally to Samaria by Omri.

The Assyrian threat to Israel and its neighbors was first felt during the rule of Ahab. The Assyrians had amassed a formidable military machine and, as of the early ninth century B.C.E., had begun the systematic conquest of much of the ancient Near East. They carved out an empire which eventually—some two centuries later—was to encompass even Egypt. The danger of Assyrian conquest was so acute already in the mid–ninth century B.C.E. that the kings of southern Syria and Palestine, including Ahab, were motivated to overlook their own conflicts and form an anti-Assyrian league. In the battle of Qarqar (853 B.C.E.) they succeeded in stemming Shalmaneser III, king of Assyria, at least for some time. Shortly after, however, conflicts again erupted among the allies, and in a battle with the Arameans, Ahab was killed.

The succeeding Israelite dynasty founded by Jehu persisted for almost a century. During this period, there was a withdrawal from Phoenician influence, a turning inward of the northern kingdom, and even submission to Assyria in time of peril. Shalmaneser III's Black Obelisk depicts, graphically and literally, the submission of "Jehu son of Omri." At Judah, during the same time, Athaliah, Ahab's daughter, married Jehoram son of Jehoshaphat. After the murder of her son, Ahaziah, Athaliah seized power in Jerusalem, seeking to eliminate the Davidic line. During her rule (842–836 B.C.E.) the cult of the Tyrian Baal was introduced into the capital of Judah. Eventually, however, the Yahwist priests in the temple, as well as other elements in Judah, instigated a counter-revolution and enthroned Joash, the young crown prince, thus securing the continuity of the Davidic dynasty.

After a military struggle between Amaziah of Judah and Joash of Israel (early eighth century B.C.E.), the two kingdoms entered a period of stability and prosperity under Uzziah, king of Judah, and Jeroboam II, king of Israel (785–745[?] B.C.E.). The Assyrian military campaigns during the second half of the eighth century B.C.E. brought an end to this period. The subsequent numerous changes of kings and dynasties in the kingdom of Israel are indicative of its weakness. In 732 B.C.E., Tiglath-Pileser III of Assyria conquered the Galilee and exiled its inhabitants. Samaria proper remained independent for only another decade, then it too was conquered and its population exiled (720 B.C.E.). The kingdom was annexed to the Assyrian empire and divided into several provinces. Foreign peoples were brought from afar and resettled in the Israelites' stead. Eventually, these foreign people came to be known as "Samaritans," centered at Shechem and Samaria.

In Judah, this was the time of Hezekiah (727–698 B.C.E.) and of the prophet Isaiah. The Assyrian threat, and the lesson of Samaria's destruction, led Hezekiah to organize a rebellion against Assyria with Egyptian support. He forced Ekron, his independent western neighbor, to enter into an alliance with him. After prolonged preparations which included the fortification of Jerusalem and the reorganization of the kingdom, the revolt broke out, and the Assyrian retaliation was prompt and forceful. King Sennacherib's campaign, in 701 B.C.E., began with the conquest of the Phoenician coastal cities, victory over an Egyptian expedition (at Eltekeh in Philistia), and the conquest of Timnah and Ekron. The Assyrian Army then turned toward Judah, probably conquering Gath and Azekah. The main battle was at Lachish, second in importance only to Jerusalem. Numerous other towns in Judah were subsequently razed, but the Assyrian siege of Jerusalem was terminated abruptly (probably due to internal problems in Assyria), an event which was seen by the Judeans as a miraculous deliverance.

The seventh century B.C.E. was marked by the long reigns of two kings in Jerusalem: Manasseh (698–642 B.C.E.) and his grandson Josiah (639–609 B.C.E.). Judah was still in a state of devastation following Sennacherib's campaign when Manasseh came to the throne. He submitted to Assyrian hegemony, but Judah remained autonomous and Manasseh set about rebuilding his kingdom. Josiah took advantage of Assyria's weakness and the subsequent disintegration of this empire to expand his realm northward into the territories formerly belonging to Israel, and westward toward the coastal plain. He also initiated a significant religious reform involving the elimination of all foreign practices and the centralization of the cult in Jerusalem. The rising might of Babylon, however, indirectly led to Josiah's fall. In 609 B.C.E. he was killed while attempting to block an Egyptian military campaign to north Syria directed against Babylon.

Between 609 and 586 B.C.E., Judah had a roller-coaster existence consisting of complex relations with Egypt on the one hand and the ever advancing threat from Babylon on the other. The rebellion of Jehoiakim, the son and second successor of Josiah, against Babylon led to the latter's punitive campaign, which culminated in the death of the king and the exile of his son Jehoiachin and much of the aristocracy (in 597 B.C.E.). The final destruction of Judah came a decade later, in 586 B.C.E., following the failure of the last king of Judah— Zedekiah, the youngest son of Josiah—to stave off the Babylonian onslaught.

THE NORTHERN KINGDOM OF ISRAEL

SAMARIA

The new capital of the northern kingdom was named *Shomron* by its founder, Omri, after the name *Shemer*, the family who originally owned the hill (1 Kings 16:23–24). Ahab, Omri's son, completed the construction of the city, which thrived as the capital for about 150 years till the Assyrian conquest in 720 B.C.E. Its location was perhaps related to Omride foreign policy: it was situated northwest of Shechem, near an important road running toward the Sharon Plain on the coast, and on another leading northward through the Jezreel Valley to Phoenicia, where the Omrides had close ties. The city was strategically positioned on a steep hill offering a good view of the surrounding countryside. The excavations at Samaria concentrated on the royal acropolis, and very little is known of the city itself, which probably covered an area of several dozen acres.[2]

The extent of the planning and building operations on the acropolis of Samaria was unprecedented in the architectural history of the country, except perhaps in Solomon's buildings in Jerusalem. Samaria demonstrates the power and great wealth of the Israelite royalty at the time of Ahab, probably the result of successful economic enterprises carried out in cooperation with the Phoenicians of Tyre. The royal acropolis was a huge leveled rectangular enclosure, measuring 89 × 178 m—covering an area of 4 acres, the average size of a town in the countryside. The plan perhaps derived from

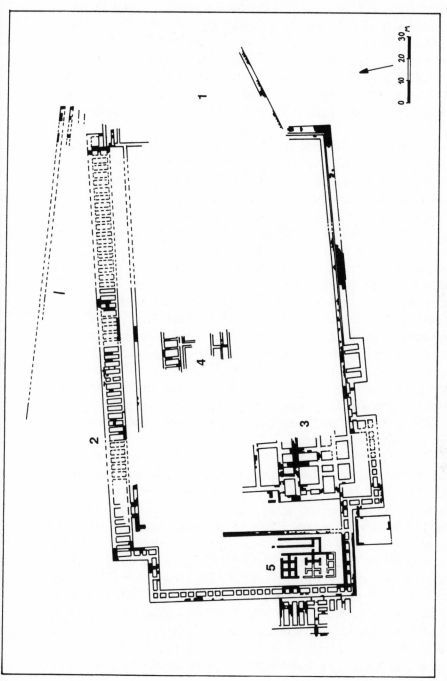

10.1 Samaria: plan of the royal acropolis. (1) Approach; (2) Casemates; (3) Royal palace; (4) The Ivories building; (5) The Ostraca building.

some foreign (Phoenician?) model, as it was suited more to flat terrain than to the hilly topography of Samaria. In order to build on this rounded hilltop, the architects had to erect an artificial rectangular platform supported by massive retaining walls. We may assume that the construction of the retaining walls and platform was inspired by similar solutions employed on the hilly site of Jerusalem during the time of Solomon.

The palace complex displays two main phases of planning and construction. In the first—represented by Building Period I, probably from the reign of Omri—the main part of the acropolis was paved with a thick lime floor and was surrounded by a fine ashlar masonry wall, 1.6 m thick, built in the "headers and stretchers" technique. As we have seen, such stonework is known from Israel since the time of Solomon, but the smooth cutting and precision of the dry masonry are finer than the Solomonic prototypes. Nothing is known of the buildings inside the enclosure in this initial phase. In the second stage—"Building Period II," which apparently should be ascribed to Ahab—the outer wall on the northern and western sides was replaced by a casemate wall. In the north, the long axis of fifty-four elongated casemates was perpendicular to the line of the wall, and fifty-two smaller rooms were on the south and west. The casemate rooms comprised an extensive storage space for the royal treasures, arsenal, and food stocks.

The area surrounded by the casemate wall was an open, paved surface, on which the palace was erected. The main building was badly preserved and its complete plan is unknown. At its center was a large, rectangular courtyard, flanked by several wings. Of these, only the southern one was preserved to any extent; it comprised rectangular rooms surrounding a square inner courtyard. This plan, with its large central courtyard, is reminiscent of Late Bronze Age Canaanite palaces such as those of Ugarit and Megiddo; but it differs from the *bit-hilani*, which was the main palace type during the Solomonic era at Megiddo, and perhaps also at Jerusalem. While the *bit-hilani* is related to the Syrian interior, Ahab's royal residence may have been inspired by Canaanite-Phoenician architectural traditions.

A smaller structure on the acropolis contained a hoard of carved ivories—the most important collection of such artwork

10.2 Ashlar wall, probably a foundation of a gate structure leading to the royal acropolis at Samaria.

from Iron Age Israel. This find might shed light on the biblical term "houses of ivory," applied by the prophet Amos to describe the houses of the rich (Amos 3:15; and see p. 503). Furthermore, only in this structure at Samaria was it possible to discern various building phases and to determine the internal development of pottery.

The eastern facade of the Samaria acropolis has not been preserved, but six Proto-Aeolic capitals found in its vicinity apparently topped pilasters at an elaborate gate structure. Long ashlar walls found farther to the east (near the Roman basilica) seem to have belonged to an entryway with a "bent axis" leading into the acropolis from the city proper. This entrance was protected by a huge tower.

The Samaria Ostraca In the western part of the acropolis of Samaria, between the early inner wall and the later casemate wall, there was an administrative complex comprising on its eastern side elongated storerooms, and on its west three units each with square chambers flanking a passage. Identical contemporaneous units are known from Hazor, adjacent to the governor's citadel there, and it would seem that this was a standard design for royal administrative headquarters in Israel.

A group of sixty-three ostraca (brief inscriptions written in ink on pottery sherds) was found in this building. They are records of oil and wine deliveries received at Samaria from the outer townships probably as taxes. The listings note the year (apparently the regnal year of one of the kings of Israel), the place of origin, the name of a person (possibly the royal official) who received the merchandise, and the type of goods (such as "old wine," or "bathing oil").[3]

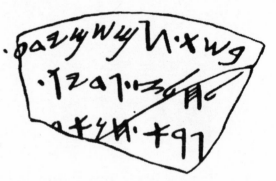

10.3 A drawing of Ostracon 30 from Samaria. Translation: "In the fifteenth year. From Shemida' to Hellez [son of] Gaddiyau. Gera [son of] Hanniab."

These ostraca are the only large group of inscriptions known from the kingdom of Israel, and they reveal some of the administrative and fiscal procedures current at the time, as well as being instructive on linguistic and onomastic matters pertaining to the northern kingdom. The common suffix of personal names was *-yw*, or *-baal*, in contrast to *-yahu* dominant in Judah. Many of the toponyms mentioned can be identified with sites surveyed in the Samarian Hills. As to the date of the ostraca, there have been various suggestions ranging from the reign of Ahab till the days of Menahem.

A subsidiary capital was erected by Ahab at Jezreel, overlooking the valley of the same name. Chance discoveries at this site revealed a huge quarried moat which separated the hill from its surroundings; evidence of ashlar masonry and thus of large-scale building activities was also uncovered.

MAJOR CITIES IN THE KINGDOM OF ISRAEL

Excavations at four of the major cities in the kingdom of Israel—Dan, Hazor, Megiddo, and Tirzah—have provided information regarding their planning, fortification, public and domestic architecture, and occupation history.[4] This section will survey several aspects of the archaeology of these cities, but a general survey of Israelite architecture can be found in conjunction with the finds from Judah in the following chapter.

In all of the aforementioned cities, extensive changes were made during the ninth century B.C.E. Massive fortifications which were erected at that time, most probably intended to withstand the Assyrian threat, continued to serve in much the same form until the Assyrian conquests. Inside the cities, on the other hand, several alterations and occupation phases can be detected.

10.4 Dan: topographic map of the site showing main remains of the Iron Age city.

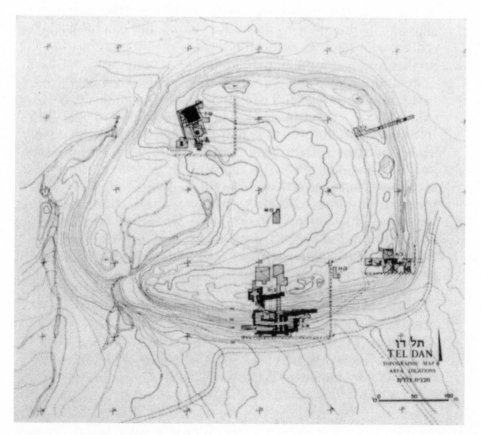

At Dan, two main occupation levels from the time of the Divided Monarchy (Strata III and II) were defined. Dan appears to have been a densely built, well-planned city with massive fortifications and public buildings, and streets paved with cobblestones. The main structures uncovered were the city gates and the cultic center, both of which will be discussed in Chapter 11.

At Hazor, five occupation phases belong to the period between the division of the kingdom and the Assyrian conquest (Strata IX–V). During this span of two hundred years, far-reaching changes were made as a result of destructions. Stratum IX succeeded the Solomonic city almost without any deviation. It was perhaps destroyed during the wars with the Arameans. During the time of Ahab (Stratum VIII), the city was doubled in area and was surrounded by a solid wall. A governmental citadel was located on the narrow western spur of the mound, separated from the rest of the city and entered by way of an elaborate gate decorated with ashlar pilasters carrying Proto-Aeolic capitals. The citadel was rectangular and divided into elongated spaces; it recalls the "four-room houses" in the principles of its planning. Two buildings adjacent to the citadel, inside its compound, were probably offices or residences of royal officials, as they were identical in plan to the administrative buildings at Samaria.

A public storage complex and a large granary erected on an eastern lower terrace of the mound establish the role of Hazor as a regional center for royal food administration. A magnificent underground water system supplied water to the city. The residential houses were densely built along the streets and alleys, sometimes with forecourt areas believed to have served as shops. Several of the residences are large and well-planned "four-room houses"; others are less elaborate and vary in plan. Evidence of extensive alteration in the city during the eighth century B.C.E. was found in Area A, where the public storehouse went out of use and its area was utilized for private dwellings.

The continuous changes in Hazor can be associated with various historical events. Stratum VI was destroyed in an earthquake, probably that mentioned by Amos (1:1) and Zechariah (14:5). Many of the buildings collapsed but were later rebuilt on the same lines. On the eve of the Assyrian invasion of the Galilee by Tiglath-Pileser III (732 B.C.E.), the for-

10.5 Hazor: model of the citadel in Area B (ninth and eighth centuries B.C.E.).

10.6 Hazor: store building (Stratum VIII, ninth century B.C.E.).

tification wall around the citadel was broadened (Stratum VA), eliminating the area of the administrative buildings. But even these stronger defenses could not withstand the Assyrian siege when Hazor was conquered by Tiglath-Pileser. Following this devastation, only poor squatters (Stratum IV) occupied Hazor.

The numerous defined building phases at Hazor provide the best background for the study of changes in architecture and artifacts in the northern part of the kingdom of Israel. In contrast, at Megiddo only a single level (Stratum IVA), most probably built as an important royal center during the time of Ahab, is attributable to the period of the Divided Monarchy. This city was surrounded by a massive 3-m-wide "offsets and insets" wall and entered via an outer and inner gate. A large area inside the walls was devoted to the pillared public buildings identified as royal stables (see pp. 476–78). Elaborate palaces (such as Building 338 at the eastern part of the city) probably served as the residencies of high officials. Water supply was provided by means of an underground shaft and tunnel.

At Tirzah, following the destruction of the planned city of

10.7   Megiddo: plan of Stratum IVA. (1) City gate; (2) Stable complexes; (3) Building 338; (4) Water shaft.

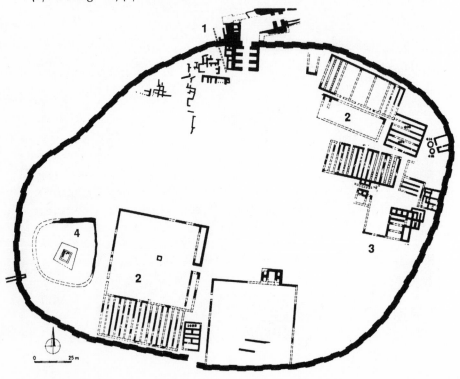

the United Monarchy (Stratum VIIb), the city was rebuilt (Stratum VIIc) but not completed, perhaps due to the shift of the capital to Samaria during the time of Omri. In the following phase (Stratum VIId, the ninth and eighth centuries B.C.E.), the city was rebuilt, developed, and fortified. Adjacent to a gatehouse with a "bent axis" approach there was a public piazza containing a cult place. A residential quarter south of this piazza continued the basic planning of the previous levels in that the houses were arranged in blocks along parallel streets. The dwellings, however, which in the tenth century were of almost identical plan and size, were now diverse: the larger and more elaborate houses were located close to the city gate, the poorer ones being more to the south. This feature implies rigid social ranking during this time. The city's annihilation was part of the general destruction of the kingdom in 720 B.C.E.; it was later rebuilt during the Assyrian rule (Stratum VIIe).

OTHER TOWNS AND FORTS IN THE NORTHERN KINGDOM

Our knowledge of the settlement history of the kingdom of Israel is still deficient; surveys in different parts of that realm have been carried out, but their results are still to be published and processed. It appears that fortified towns and villages were abundant. In addition to the major excavations mentioned earlier, smaller excavations have helped to illuminate various aspects of the material culture of this period. Fortified cities were discovered at strategic locations. Thus Tel Kinrot, overlooking the route running along the western side of the Lake of Galilee, was a fortified town with a solid wall, square towers, and a single-chambered gate. Yoqneam, the strategically located mound northwest of Megiddo, was defended by a unique double wall encircling the 10-acre Iron Age city. In both cases, the new fortifications replaced tenth century B.C.E. city walls. At Khirbet Marjamah, near the fountain of Ain Samiya northeast of Ramallah, a 10-acre town on a steep slope above the fountain was fortified by a solid wall and by the natural defenses of the surrounding cliffs. The town was densely built up with stone houses erected along winding narrow streets. At the southwestern border of the kingdom, Gezer was an important stronghold, protected by the massive "Outer Wall" with its square ashlar towers.[5]

Smaller towns and villages from this period were revealed at Tel Zeror in the Sharon Plain, Tel Qedesh and Tell Qiri near the valley of Jezreel, Shiqmona (a port town near modern Haifa), Dothan, and Shechem. The remains in these sites are fragmentary or insufficiently published, but it appears that all were densely built up and successively rebuilt until the Assyrian conquests.

Forts and isolated defensive towers protected important strategic points and roads in the kingdom. About a dozen fortresses, discovered in a survey of the vicinity of Samaria, created a defensive belt around the capital and protected all its access roads. A round and a square tower defended the promontory el-Mahruq, overlooking the important road connecting the Jordan crossing at Damiah with Wadi Farʿah.

THE SOUTHERN KINGDOM OF JUDAH

The kingdom of Judah enjoyed a much longer period of independence than did its northern counterpart. Many cities of Judah developed from an Iron Age I settlement site to a fortified town or city. This was a gradual, peaceful process, lasting from the tenth century until the eighth century B.C.E., usually without the abrupt destructions evident in the northern kingdom. The Assyrian invasion of Judah in 701 B.C.E. resulted in the destruction of many of these sites. The seventh century B.C.E. was a period of great revival. The Babylonian invasions in the early sixth century B.C.E. were fatal to large parts of Judah. Due to intensive archaeological research, Iron Age Judah is one of the best-known segments of the archaeology of Palestine. The bulk of the data, however, relates to the latter part of the period (the late eighth and seventh centuries B.C.E.), while the ninth and early eighth centuries are less known, perhaps due to the continuity and lack of destruction levels from that time.

SETTLEMENT PATTERN

A predominant demographic factor in Judah was the concentration of its population in the capital. As we shall see later, Jerusalem greatly expanded until it became a huge city in the eighth and seventh centuries B.C.E., spreading over some 150 acres. Jerusalem's domain now equaled the size of dozens of towns in the countryside combined. Lachish, the second largest city of Judah, had an area of only 20 acres, while other Judean towns averaged only 5–8 acres. The population of Jerusalem, estimated at between ten thousand and twenty thousand, must have constituted a large portion of the entire population of the kingdom.

In the rural periphery of Judah there were dozens of small fortified towns, unfortified villages, and isolated farms and hamlets. Towns were concentrated along the backbone of the hill country, in the Shephelah, and in the southern Hebron Hills. They sometimes are found only 3–4 km apart. It appears that Judah was settled to the maximum of its carrying capacity. Furthermore, during the last two centuries of Judah's existence, the northern Negev and the Judean Desert were also densely inhabited.

Joshua 15:20–63 lists the Judean cities and their satellites according to four major geographic regions: the mountains (*Har*), the Shephelah, the Negev, and "the desert" (*midbar*, namely the Judean Desert). These four units comprise twelve administrative districts. The list would appear to reflect the zenith of settlement in Judah, in the seventh century B.C.E., as several of the places mentioned were not founded until that time, such as En Gedi and ʿAroer in the Negev.[6]

JERUSALEM

Jerusalem, the capital of Judah during the latter's 350 years of existence, underwent extensive growth during this period. For many years, scholars argued over the size and limits of the city during the Divided Monarchy; however, extensive archaeological investigation since 1967 has now enlightened us on this subject.[7]

The excavations at the City of David have demonstrated that during the eighth and seventh centuries B.C.E. a solid, thick city wall was built well down the eastern slope of the hill, thus expanding the built-up area of the city. Above the wall, terraces were densely covered with dwellings, the roofs of one row of houses being level with the floors of those above. The "stepped structure" of the early period of the

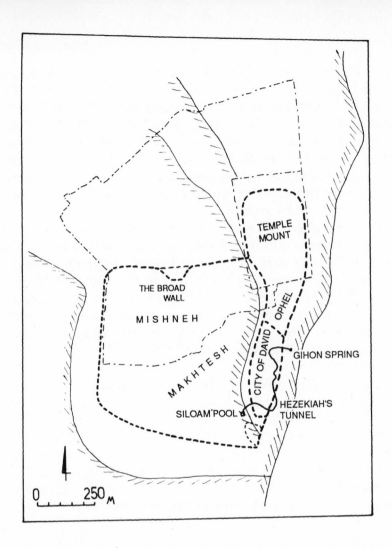

10.8 Jerusalem: topographic map of the city, showing the fortification lines in the Jewish Quarter and the assumed contours of the city wall during the late eighth and seventh centuries B.C.E.

Monarchy went out of use, and several houses were built over it. The lack of space caused the settlement of the eastern slope of the City of David to spill over beyond the city walls, as evidenced by building remains and by the utilization of natural caves there. This residential quarter was burnt down during the destruction of the city by the Babylonians. Among the finds on the burnt floors was a group of fifty-one inscribed bullae (seal impressions; see pp. 518–20). Two water projects related to the Gihon Spring can be dated to this period: the "Warren Shaft" and Hezekiah's Tunnel (see pp. 480–85).

In the area denoted "the Ophel," between the spur of the City of David and the Temple Mount, most of the Iron Age remains disappeared due to later building operations. Part of a large public building, however, was preserved in the lower part of this area, close to the edge of the capital's acropolis. The building is located beside a huge tower—discovered by Ch. Warren in the nineteenth century—which overlooks the Kidron Brook. The building was erected on steep bedrock and leveled with fills of stone and earth, and its thick walls were solidly constructed. Features of the building's plan indicate that it was of administrative and official nature. Parts of it may have served as a city gate with four chambers, defended on the outside by Warren's tower. Other parts were employed for storage—as evidenced by large pottery pithoi, one inscribed with the title of an official.[8] (See plan on p. 423.)

The spur of the City of David and the Temple Mount were probably entirely built early during the Divided Monarchy. On the east, this area was demarcated by the steep slope descending to the Kidron Brook; on the north, the Temple Mount was set off from an extended plain farther to the north by a shallow saddle, where particularly strong fortifications would have been required. The area of the Temple Mount, however, remains unexplored.

The eastern ridge of Jerusalem, comprising the Temple Mount and the City of David, was bordered on the west by the Central Valley (later called the Tyropoeon Valley), which descends from the area of the present-day Damascus Gate and joins the Kidron Brook at the southern tip of the City of David. The ridge to the west of this valley, known as the "Western Hill," is a large, broad spur comprising today's Jewish and Armenian quarters in the Old City, as well as "Mount Zion," now outside the Turkish city walls. This hill is bordered on the west and south by the Hinnom Valley and on the north by a minor valley called the "Cross Valley." The role of the Western Hill in the history of the Iron Age city has been a debated question. Several scholars (such as K. M. Kenyon) held that the city never spread westward beyond the Central Valley during this period. However, research at various spots since 1967 has clearly demonstrated that Jerusalem of the late Monarchy encompassed the entire Western Hill.

On the eastern slopes of the Western Hill, close to the bed

of the Central Valley, what seem to have been Iron Age burial caves may have belonged to the city's ninth century B.C.E. aristocratic families. The plan of the caves points to Phoenician influence, which during this period was especially strong in Jerusalem. The caves were cleared of burials in a later phase of the Iron Age, very possibly due to the city's expansion westward.

In the Jewish Quarter of the Old City, at the top of the Western Hill, remains of massive Iron Age fortifications are the most important evidence of the expansion of the city. A segment of a 7-m-thick stone city wall, the thickest Iron Age wall known, was interpreted by N. Avigad as being the wall built by Hezekiah as a part of his preparations for war with Sennacherib. The thickness and the solidity of the wall were designed to withstand the Assyrian battering rams. In the process of constructing the wall, older houses were demolished, recalling Isaiah's description of Hezekiah's acts: "You counted the buildings in Jerusalem, and tore down houses to strengthen the wall" (Isaiah 22:10).

The wall ran south and made a sharp turn apparently dictated by the existence of a gully descending toward the "Cross Valley"; it then continued westward, probably until just south of the present-day Jaffa Gate. From here its direction was probably southward along the edge of the slope above the Hinnom Valley, until it swung to the east to meet up with the southern tip of the City of David at the confluence of the Hinnom, Central, and Kidron valleys. At this latter point, the wall probably crossed the Central Valley on top of a dam which demarcated a reservoir behind it. Such a reservoir can be identified with the biblical "Lower Pool" (Isaiah 22:9), or with the "reservoir between the two walls for the water of the Old Pool" mentioned two verses later. The "two walls" here may have been the old wall of the City of David and the new one encompassing the Western Hill. This course of the fortification line explains the logic in hewing Hezekiah's Tunnel, as the latter diverted the waters of the Gihon Spring from the Kidron Brook (east of the City of David) to the Central Valley, which was now within the new city walls (see pp. 483–85). The area encircled by this wall is almost 150 acres.

Another fortification system, discovered north of the massive wall in the Jewish Quarter, consists of a large tower and

10.9 Jerusalem: looking northeast at the 7-m-wide city wall uncovered in the Jewish Quarter. The wall was probably built by Hezekiah just before 701 B.C.E.

10.10   Jerusalem: tower uncovered in the Jewish Quarter (the walls at the front of the picture are remains of the Hasmonean First Wall of Jerusalem, which utilized the Iron Age tower in secondary use). This tower was part of the fortifications of Jerusalem destroyed by Nebuchadnezzar in 586 B.C.E.

a section of a city wall, both preserved to a height of 8 m. The tower's walls were 4 m thick, built of large, crudely hewn stones and ashlar corners. This fortification was apparently intended to enclose the area of the gully descending to the "Cross Valley." The tower was interpreted by Avigad as part of a huge city gate, perhaps the Middle Gate of Jerusalem (Jer. 39:3). The construction of this fortification would probably have made the section of the massive wall found to the south of it obsolete, indicating that major changes were made to the fortifications in this area during the period between Hezekiah and the destruction of the city in 586 B.C.E. Dramatic evidence of the conquest of Jerusalem by Nebuchadnezzar was discovered next to the tower in the form of an ash layer containing arrowheads of Babylonian type.

The expansion of Jerusalem to the west is indicated also by finds of Iron Age remains on Mount Zion and in the

Armenian Quarter. Impressive quantities of earth containing numerous amounts of broken pottery of the eighth and seventh centuries B.C.E. were found at several locations on the Western Hill, and even farther north in the Muristan area (close to the Holy Sepulchre).[9] This is apparent evidence of large-scale shifting of fills in later periods involving the destruction of Iron Age houses which seem to have been spread over the entire Western Hill. An additional illustration of the growth of the city is numerous burial caves from the late Monarchy located in a broad arc around the city—in the north (near the Damascus Gate), and in the west and south (along the Hinnom Valley). Some are exceptionally large and fine and undoubtedly belonged to the nobler families of the city (see pp. 520–25).

The newer quarters of Jerusalem are mentioned several times in the Bible, particularly in the Book of Zephaniah

10.11 Jerusalem: plan of a large architectural complex uncovered at the Ophel, between the City of David and the Temple Mount. This complex was probably an administrative building and possibly included a gate to the acropolis of the capital.

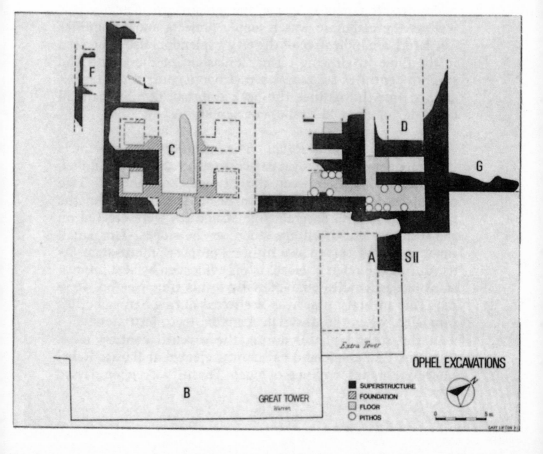

OPHEL EXCAVATIONS

■ SUPERSTRUCTURE
▨ FOUNDATION
□ FLOOR
○ PITHOS

B

GREAT TOWER
Warren

(1:10–11): "'On that day,' declares the Lord, 'a cry will go up from the Fish Gate, wailing from the *Mishneh*, and a loud crash from the hills. Wail, you who live in the *Machtesh!*'" In the *Mishneh* ("New Quarter," or "Secondary Quarter"), the prophetess Huldah is known to have lived (2 Kings 22:14). The term most probably refers to the Western Hill, the newer residential area of the city, where the upper class lived. The *Machtesh*, literally "Mortar", would appear to refer to the lower reaches of the Central Valley. In Avigad's opinion, the expression in Psalms 122:2–3—"Our feet are standing in your gates, O Jerusalem. Jerusalem is built like a city that is closely compacted together."—may refer to the city of the later Monarchy when its two major parts, the Eastern Hill and the Western Hill, were surrounded by the same single city wall. Numerous places within the city are mentioned in the biblical sources, but we are still unable to identify most of them with any certainty. Such is the case with the various city gates, towers, and pools, often specifically denoted, as well as certain other locations such as the "Millo."[10]

Although the data concerning the planning of Jerusalem under the Monarchy is sparse, the remains just described, as well as the elaborate water supply projects and cemeteries (see later), are indicative of the city's splendor, also expressed in the Bible in glowing terms. Jerusalem of the eighth and seventh centuries B.C.E. was a metropolis, one of the largest at this time. It signifies the peak of urban development in Israel during the Old Testament period.

The Palace at Ramat Rahel The splendor of Jerusalem is illustrated by a Judean royal palace discovered at Ramat Rahel, a prominent ridge between the city and Bethlehem.[11] Two main periods of use were distinguished at this site. In the first (Stratum VB), several large structures were erected on the summit, and dwellings stood on the slopes. This small town may have served as a military outpost of Jerusalem. Its use during the reign of Hezekiah is evidenced by seal impressions on jar handles characteristic of his time (see pp. 455–58). This military base was destroyed during Sennacherib's campaign, when the Assyrian Army besieged Jerusalem.

In the second phase, during the seventh century B.C.E. (Stratum VA), a splendid palace was erected at Ramat Rahel under one of the later kings of Judah. The hill was encompassed

10.12 Plan of the Judean palace at Ramat Rahel, south of Jerusalem.

by a solid wall enclosing an area of some 4 acres, and the space within was leveled off with fills. Both this artificial fill and the plan of the palace recall, though on a smaller scale, the royal enclosure at Samaria. The palace was rectangular in shape, measuring 50 × 75 m. It was surrounded by an ashlar casemate wall of an overall thickness of 5.2 m. The masonry, particularly the finely dressed ashlars in the walls facing the central courtyard, resembles that of Samaria. The casemates served as storerooms. A broad gateway gave access from the east to a spacious lime-paved courtyard. Although little remained of the residential buildings, one of them can be reconstructed as having an inner courtyard surrounded by rooms.

As at Samaria, here too the palace was decorated with Proto-Aeolic capitals. A special architectural detail was a stone window balustrade carved in the form of four colonnettes with petals and voluted capitals. Identical balustrades appear on Phoenician ivory plaques featuring a "woman in the window."

The palace at Ramat Rahel, therefore, incorporated the finest architectural forms current in Phoenicia and Palestine in Iron Age II, and it must give us some idea of the style and plan of the palaces in the capital itself, such as the palace

10.13   Proto-Aeolic capital from Ramat Rahel.

10.14   Stone window balustrade from Ramat Rahel.

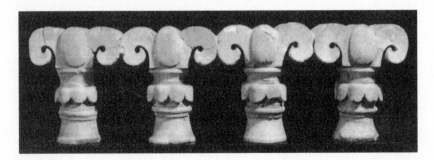

constructed by Jehoiakim (Jeremiah 22:14).[12] Indeed, one Proto-Aeolic capital, similar to though larger than the ones from Ramat Rahel, was found in Jerusalem. It seems, therefore, that both the plan of the royal enclosure known from Samaria and the ashlar masonry, including Proto-Aeolic capitals, remained in fashion from the tenth and ninth centuries B.C.E. until the end of the Iron Age.

LACHISH

Lachish Before 701 B.C.E. Lachish, the second most important city in Judah, is identified with Tell el-Duweir, a mound 20 acres in area located in the lower Shephelah near the main road leading from the southern coastal plain. During the United Monarchy (Stratum V) Lachish was only partly built up and remained unfortified. The following levels at Lachish (Strata IV–III) are of particular interest due to their association with the unique combination of archaeological, biblical, and Assyrian textual and pictorial data relating to the conquest of Lachish by Sennacherib in 701 B.C.E.[13]

The fortifications of Lachish in these two levels consisted of an outer wall at the middle of the mound's slope and an

10.15 Lachish: air view, looking east. The city gate is seen on the front of the mound, and the Assyrian siege-ramp on the lower right corner.

427

inner wall at the summit. The latter, 6 m thick in several sections, was built of mud bricks laid on a stone foundation. The city gate complex included an access ramp along the slope of the mound and an outer and inner gate (related to the outer and inner walls respectively), recalling similar arrangements at cities such as Dan, Megiddo, and Timnah (see p. 468). The outer gate was protected by a huge bastion erected on the slope of the mound. A piazza inside the outer

10.16 Lachish: plan of the site showing main structures of Stratum III (eighth century B.C.E.): (1) bastion; (2) six-chamber inner gate; (3) outer wall; (4) inner wall; (5) palace-fort; (6) inner defense wall of administration center; (7) shaft (quarry?); (8) well; (9) Assyrian siege-ramp.

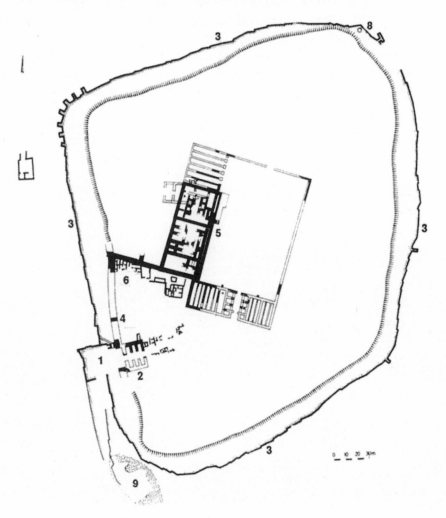

gate led to a six-chamber inner gate recalling in plan those of Megiddo, Hazor, and Gezer, though somewhat larger. Large drainage canals drained the city's streets.

It is tempting to attribute this tremendous defense system to Rehoboam, since Lachish is mentioned as one of the cities fortified by him (2 Chronicles 11:9). Yet the date of the list of Rehoboam's fortresses is a debated issue, and several scholars claim that it reflects a later period. On this basis, D. Ussishkin tends to believe that the fortifications were erected by either Asa or Jehoshaphat. They were in use for almost two hundred years, until the Assyrian conquest of 701 B.C.E.

From inside the gate, a street flanked by shops and houses led to a residential quarter. The northern part of the city was allocated to a royal governmental area and was separated from the rest of the city by a thick wall. Its main structure was the great palace-fort erected on a high podium. Palace A, the first phase of this building, was a square structure of 32×32 m standing on a high stone podium. Its date is unclear; it was built either in Stratum V of the United Monarchy or in the following Stratum IV of the early Divided Monarchy (see p. 401, note 20). In the next phase of this building (Palace B), it was enlarged to the south by 44 m while in the third phase (Palace C) it was enlarged to the east, resulting in final dimensions of 36×76 m—the largest Iron Age building ex-

10.17 Lachish: reconstruction of the city during the late eighth century B.C.E.

10.18   The siege on Lachish: detail from the Lachish reliefs found at the palace of Sennacherib at Nineveh. This section shows the city of Lachish with its inner and outer walls and projecting gate tower; Assyrian battering rams are approaching the city on built-up ramps and are attacked by torches thrown from the city walls. Exiles are shown leaving the gate, and on the lower right side, captives are being executed.

posed as yet in Israel. The podium elevated the palace's ground floor some 6 m above the surroundings so that the building looked over the entire city. Nothing remained of the super-structure of this palace, but its plan can be guessed on the basis of constructional walls inside the podium.

East of the palace there was a spacious, paved, square courtyard surrounded by a defense wall and entered through a six-chamber gate structure. Elongated rectangular buildings on the sides of the courtyard were storerooms, and perhaps stables, similar to those of Megiddo. This large royal enclosure was, most probably, the administrative and military head-quarters of the Judean government in the southern Shephelah.

The Conquest of Lachish by Sennacherib The siege of Lachish and its conquest by Sennacherib in 701 B.C.E. are perhaps the best documented events from the period of the Monarchy. The large wall relief from Sennacherib's palace at Nineveh details the city of Lachish, the siege, and the results of the conquest: surrender, execution, and deportation. The relief was most probably made in Assyria from sketches prepared during the actual war by an artist viewing the onslaught from Sennacherib's camp; the camp was perhaps located (according to D. Ussishkin) southwest of the city. The relief probably depicts the two defense walls of the city and the protruding gate on the western slope. The towers along the wall are shown with balconies which provided a conve-nient position for the defenders. The Assyrian siege operations are also illustrated in detail: battering rams were hauled to the city walls on built-up siege ramps. The wooden and leather rams were intensively attacked by the Judeans with torches, while the Assyrians defended them by pouring water on them and by returning fire with slingstones and arrows.

The siege ramp built by Sennacherib's troops at Lachish was discovered and is the only known example of such an Assyrian ramp. It was constructed at the southwestern corner of the city, which was connected by a shallow saddle to a hill on which the Assyrian camp was probably located. The ramp was constructed of huge quantities of stones piled perpendic-ular to the city walls until it reached the bottom of the wall. Evidence of the actual battle was found at the point of junction between the ramp and the city wall, in the form of hundreds of iron arrowheads, sling stones, heavy weight stones which

10.19 Detail from the Lachish reliefs showing the gate area of Lachish.

were thrown from the city onto the enemy, and charred wood. A fragmentary chain found in this place could have been part of the battering ram machine, or used by the defenders to catch and stop the ram's horns (suggestion of Y. Yadin). The most surprising discovery in this area was a massive counter-ramp built by the defenders inside the city opposite the Assyrian siege ramp. It was intended to protect the wall against the ram, and to provide the city an alternative defense if the wall was ruptured by the Assyrians.

These tremendous efforts to protect the city failed; the biblical and Assyrian documentation of its conquest have been completed by archaeological discoveries, the most dramatic of which was the mass burial of thousands of massacred people discovered in a cave outside the city. The buildings of the Stratum III city were found burnt. Among the finds were many storage jars of the *lamelech* type, which can be placed within the framework of Hezekiah's revolt against the Assyrians (see p. 458).

The date of the destruction of Stratum III at Lachish was a debated issue. Tufnell placed it in 701 B.C.E., but W. F. Albright and G. E. Wright (following the original view of the first excavator, J. L. Starkey) suggested that the stratum was destroyed in the first invasion of Judah by Nebuchadnezzar in 597 B.C.E. This view had considerable impact on Iron Age comparative chronology. However, the recent excavations at Lachish by D. Ussishkin verified Tufnell's chronology, and the dating of the destruction of Stratum III at Lachish to 701 B.C.E. can now be taken as axiomatic.

10.20   View of the Assyrian siege ramp discovered at Lachish.

Lachish in the Seventh Century B.C.E.   Lachish was rebuilt sometime during the seventh century B.C.E. (Stratum II). This last Iron Age city survived until the ultimate destruction of Judah by the Babylonians in 586 B.C.E. Its fortifications were less solid and the gate complex was weaker: the bastion and outer gate were partly reconstructed, and the inner gate was a simple opening in a new, thinner city wall. Eighteen ostraca known as the "Lachish letters," one of the two largest groups of written documents from the period of the Monarchy (see p. 458), were found in the destruction level of a guardroom in the piazza between the outer and inner gates. Inside the city, storage rooms and dwellings were exposed. The excavators claim that the palace-fortress was not in use during this period, but it is hard to believe that such a huge structure stood in ruins throughout the seventh century B.C.E., particularly when the same podium served as the foundation for a large palace during the Persian period.

JUDEAN COUNTRY TOWNS

Many of the towns in the lists of cities of Judah and Benjamin (Joshua 15:20–63, 18:21–28) can be identified with mounds in the Judean Hills, in the Shephelah, and in the northern Negev. Excavations carried out at a comparatively large number of these sites have enlightened us on various aspects of the Judean material culture. The most important excavations in the hill country are Tell en-Nasbeh (Mizpah), Tell el-Full (Gibeah), Gibeon, Hebron, and Debir (Khirbet Rabud); in the Shephelah: Beth-Shemesh, Timnah (Tel Batash), Azekah, Tell Beit Mirsim, and Tel Halif (Rimon or Hormah?); in the northern Negev: Beer-sheba, Tel 'Ira, 'Aroer; in the Judean Desert: En Gedi. In the following passages we will deal only with main features of town planning and the occupational history of these towns.

A look at the general outline of those sites excavated on a large scale, such as Tell en-Nasbeh, Beth-Shemesh, Tell Beit Mirsim, and Beer-sheba, pinpoint several features common to all of their town plans.[14] In general they were rounded or oval in accordance with the natural contours of the hills. At Timnah the square plan was dictated by the shape of the mound formed in the Middle Bronze Age. The average area of these towns was 5–8 acres, and thus the population can be estimated to have included approximately five hundred to one thousand persons per settlement.

The towns were strongly fortified and had a single gate; the latter was constructed according to the principles common throughout the region (see p. 467). A piazza behind the gate facilitated public activities such as commerce. At several of these towns, a street followed the circular line of the city

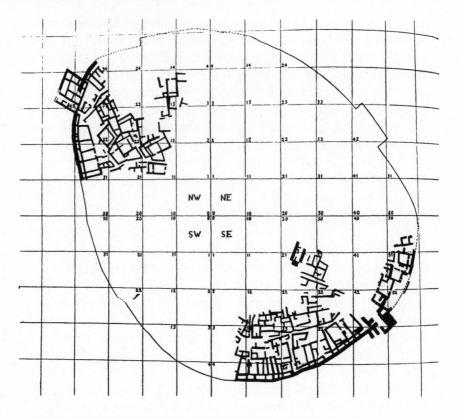

10.21   Tell Beit Mirsim: plan of the city.

wall and was separated from the wall by a row of dwellings. At Tell Beit Mirsim and Beer-sheba, the inner rooms of these dwellings were in fact casemates of the city wall. From this street, other routes radiated toward the center of the town, creating a network of alleys and lanes which were sometimes blocked by buildings. At Timnah a street running along the city wall separated the latter from a row of dwellings to its south and facilitated access to it—a feature which in the other towns in Judah was lacking.

In hilly terrain, the buildings were constructed on terraces—as on the eastern slope of the City of David in Jerusalem, at En Gedi (Tel Goren), and at Khirbet Marjamah in the territory of the northern kingdom of Israel.

Public buildings are rare in these towns. Exceptions are the large storage structures found near the gate at Beer-sheba; these structures indicate the town's function as an administrative center in the northern Negev. Most of the dwellings were average in size (see pp. 485–88), yet sometimes exceptionally large and elaborate houses are found. These latter houses probably belonged to the higher social classes—landlords and royal officials; examples are three "four-room houses" at Tell en-Nasbeh, and an elaborate building at Beer-sheba. The towns usually had a drainage system in which the sewage passed in open or roofed canals through the streets and the city gate.

It appears that most of the country-town population was composed of farmers who cultivated the surrounding land. Industrial installations found in the houses, such as oil presses and wineries, are always related to the working of agricultural products. An Israelite countryside town was thus a combination of an agricultural village and a fortified town with governmental, military, commercial, and industrial functions; there was no clear differentiation between "town" and "village," and agriculture dictated the character of life in the towns. In the vicinity of the towns, there were isolated farms and groups of buildings known in the Bible as the "daughters" of the towns or *Hatzerim* (farmsteads). These also served as homes for farmers but their number was limited, and it appears that the majority of the farmers were town dwellers.

Occupation History of Judean Towns   It appears that many towns in Judah (such as Tell en-Nasbeh and Tell Beit Mirsim) underwent a process of gradual development from the tenth century until the eighth and seventh centuries B.C.E. The details of the towns' growth can be ascertained only in a few cases, either because some of the sites were excavated a long time ago utilizing old methods, or due to objective difficulties involved in observing stratigraphy in places where stone buildings were in use for a long period, sometimes for hundreds of years. At several Judean towns, no more than one or two building phases could be defined between the tenth and the eighth centuries B.C.E. It appears that the density of construction gradually increased during this period. An exception is Tell en-Nasbeh (Mizpah), where a small tenth-century (or perhaps even earlier) town was surrounded by a casemate wall. This town was enlarged and enclosed by a massive wall perhaps during the time of Asa, who is said to have built Mizpah (1 Kings 15:22).

The wide-scale annihilation of Judean towns by Sennacherib in 701 B.C.E. can be observed at several sites. At Lachish, Timnah, Ramat Rahel, and perhaps also Gezer (which was for a while under Judean domination) destruction levels can be related to this event. All of these towns were rebuilt later, during the seventh century B.C.E. According to the view of Y. Aharoni, both Beer-sheba (Stratum II) and Tell Beit Mirsim (Stratum A) were also destroyed at that time and remained practically uninhabited throughout the seventh century B.C.E.[15]

The seventh century was a period of great prosperity in Judah. Jerusalem reached the peak of its development, many other towns flourished, and sites in the Judean Desert and in the northern Negev were established. This floruit came to an end with the Babylonian conquest of 586 B.C.E., when most Judean cities were destroyed and abandoned.

THE NORTHERN NEGEV

The painstaking study conducted by Y. Aharoni and his colleagues in the area of Arad–Beer-sheba has made the latter one of the best-known regions in Iron Age Judah. This is probably the region to which the Bible refers as "the Negev," more so than the arid deserts bordering it on the south and east. Here the Judean kingdom defended itself not only from the desert nomads, but also from the rising power of the kingdom of Edom in southern Transjordan. It was also through this area that commercial transactions were made with the southern Negev and the Red Sea region. In Chapter Nine, we mentioned the development of settlement in the northern Negev during the tenth century B.C.E. (p. 396). The importance of this region during the period of the Divided Kingdom is demonstrated by a wealth of discoveries in royal fortresses and fortified towns.

Arad At Arad, the small village of the tenth century B.C.E. (Stratum XII) was replaced by a royal fortress which must have served as an important administrative and military stronghold of the kingdom of Judah in this region, guarding the road from the Judean Hills to the Arabah and to Moab and Edom.[16] The fortress was a square structure, approximately 50×50 m in size, located on a high hill dominating the whole region. The initial fortress (Stratum XI) was surrounded by a casemate wall; this phase was dated by the excavators to the Solomonic era, though a later date, in the ninth century B.C.E., should not be excluded. In the following stage (Stratum X, probably early eighth century B.C.E.; perhaps the time of Uzziah), a new fortress with a solid stone wall was constructed. It included an entrance gate protected by two towers, a central courtyard, storage and dwelling rooms, and a temple located in its northwestern corner (the temple will be discussed later, p. 496). The water supply came from a deep, stone-lined well in the valley at the foot of the hill, from where it was brought by donkeys to a canal which passed through the outside wall of the fortress and led to rock-cut cisterns inside.

According to Aharoni and his team, the fortress with the solid walls underwent further stages of development (Strata IX–VII), until finally, at the end of the seventh century B.C.E., it was replaced by a new fortress with a casemate wall (Stratum VI). Following Y. Yadin and I. Dunayevsky, we argue that the fortress with the solid walls continued in use until the end of the Iron Age and that the casemate fortress belongs to a much later period (perhaps the Hellenistic age). A severe

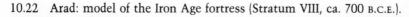

10.22   Arad: model of the Iron Age fortress (Stratum VIII, ca. 700 B.C.E.).

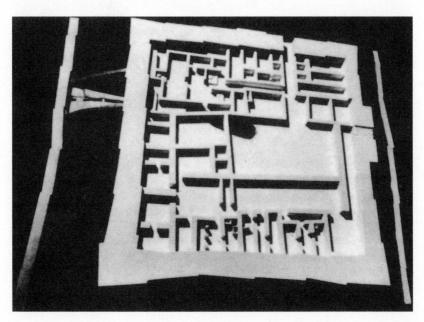

destruction of the fortress at the end of Stratum VIII was perhaps perpetrated by Edomites following Sennacherib's conquest of Judah. The rebuilding of the fortress, almost according to the same layout, in Strata VII–VI occurred during the seventh century B.C.E.

The ostraca uncovered in various levels at Arad constitute the largest and most varied group of Iron Age inscriptions found in Israel.[17] One letter, dating most probably to the time of Hezekiah (Stratum VIII), was sent to a commander of the fortress named Malkiyahu, and mentions conflicts with Edom. Most of the ostraca belong to the archive of Elyashib son of Ashiyahu, the commander of the fortress in its last phase (Strata VII–VI). They demonstrate Arad's importance as a military stronghold in the Negev during the last days of Judah. Some consist of orders to Elyashib from a higher commander; several were sent from Jerusalem—including a most fragmentary letter from one of the last kings of Judah (whom Aharoni believes to have been Jehoahaz), who announces his enthronement and discusses matters of international policy, mentioning the king of Egypt. One ostracon orders the dispatching of

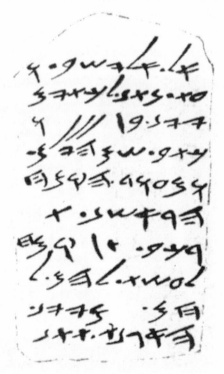

10.23 Ostracon 1 from Arad. Translation: "To Elyashib: And now, give the Kittim three *baths* of wine, and write the name of the day. And from the rest of the first flour, send one *homer* of flour in order to make bread for them. Give them the wine from the *aganoth* vessels."

troops from a place called Qinah to Ramot Negev (perhaps the fortress at Hurvat Uza) as an emergency measure to withstand the Edomite danger.

Several other Arad letters include instructions to send supplies to the Kittim, probably mercenaries in the Judean Army whose name may derive from the city of Kition in Cyprus. Their presence in the northern Negev is also suggested by the discovery of Cypriot and Eastern Greek pottery at several sites in the region. Arad appears in the ostraca as a receiver and distributor of food supplies: flour, oil, and wine are sent here from towns in the southern Hebron Hills (perhaps as royal taxes) and in turn are allocated by Arad to other Negebite forts and troops. Several ostraca are letters of introduction to the commander of Arad from officials elsewhere in Judah requesting that food supplies be assigned to a certain messenger. There are also lists of names, perhaps related to the military administration. In general, the Arad inscriptions comprise a wealth of varied data that reveals much about the historical geography of the region, the role of the fortress, the Judean military hierarchy, linguistic usages, the structure of private names in Judah, quantities of food consumed by troops, and aspects of daily life such as the system of numbers, measures, and distances.

Other Sites in the Northern Negev   Another Judean fortress from the eighth and seventh centuries B.C.E. was discovered at Hurvat Uza, south of Arad. It guarded the road descending toward the Dead Sea and Transjordan. The fortress was surrounded by casemates and was entered through an elaborate gate; near it a small village existed. Almost twenty ostraca were found here, including an Edomite letter of considerable historical importance.[18]

During the ninth and eighth centuries B.C.E., the small town at Tel Beer-sheba was the main Judean site in the entire region.[19] It was well planned, and it underwent several stages of development. Initially, perhaps at the end of the tenth or early in the ninth century B.C.E. it was a fortified town surrounded by a solid wall and a massive earth rampart and entered through a four-chamber gate. Later (Strata III–II), the solid wall was replaced by a casemate wall, and the gate was reconstructed. A circular street was separated from the casemate wall by a line of houses integrated into the wall itself,

10.24 Hurvat Uza: general view. The Iron Age fortress is seen on the plateau above the wadi; a small settlement is built on the slope overlooking the wadi.

a feature present at several other Judean towns. A large altar found dismantled, its stones used for construction in Stratum II, confirms the existence of a cult place or a temple in an earlier phase of Beer-sheba (see p. 495). Adjacent to the gate were three storage buildings—probably intended, like those at Hazor, for the storage and distribution of food supplies. These storage buildings establish the function of the town as the main administrative center in the northern Negev. Tel Beer-sheba was destroyed toward the end of the eighth century or in the early seventh century B.C.E. (during or after Hezekiah's time).

During the seventh century B.C.E. the northern Negev prospered: new towns were established and flourished, such as Tel ʿIra, ʿAroer, Tel Masos, Tel Malhata, and a large site in the modern city of Beer-sheba which can be identified as the biblical city of Beer-sheba at this time.[20] Tel 'Ira and 'Aroer are located on top of steep ridges, while Tel Malhata, Tel Masos, and the site in modern Beer-sheba are situated on lowland along the Beer-sheba Brook. It appears that occupation at most of these sites started in the eighth century B.C.E., and they prospered in the seventh century B.C.E. Tel 'Ira and 'Aroer were defended by solid walls, and at Tel 'Ira a large gate (probably with six chambers) led into the city.

Various finds throw light on the role of the northern Negev in international economic activity during the seventh century B.C.E. The prosperity of the region can be related in part to Assyrian economic and political interests which developed trade connections between Edom, Judah, and the coast through the Negev. This commercial activity, however, appears to have continued even after the Assyrians left. The finds include imported pottery originating from Edom and Philistia as well as valuable Assyrian artifacts. Some Cypriot and Eastern Greek pottery may be related to the Cypriot mercenaries, the

10.25 'Aroer: vertical air view of the site.

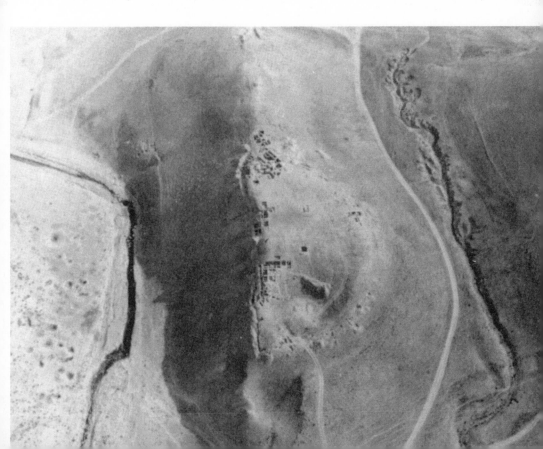

Kittim of the Arad inscriptions mentioned earlier. The Edomites appear to have played an important role in the northern
Negev toward the end of the seventh century B.C.E. This is
shown by the Edomite letter found at Hurvat Uza, the mention
of Edom as a threat in one of the Arad letters, and the Edomite
pottery found in the region. An exceptional discovery in this
connection is the cult place at Hurvat Qitmit which probably
dates to the very last days, or right after the destruction, of
Judah by the Babylonians (see p. 498). In the following Persian
period, the Edomite occupation reached such proportions that
southern Judah became known as "Idumea."

THE CENTRAL AND SOUTHERN NEGEV

Kadesh-Barnea Following the destruction of the tenth century B.C.E. settlements (see pp. 390–97), the central Negev
region remained unsettled for the rest of the Iron Age. Only
three Iron Age II sites are known south of Beer-sheba: Kadesh-
Barnea, Kuntillet ʿAjrud, and Tell el-Kheleifeh.

Ain el-Qudeirat, the site of biblical Kadesh-Barnea, is the
most important oasis on the border between Sinai and the
Negev. During the tenth century B.C.E., an elliptical casemate
enclosure was constructed at Tell el-Qudeirat, the mound at
this oasis. It was the westernmost in the cluster of some fifty
"fortresses" of the tenth century in the central Negev highlands.[21] Like the others in this group, the "fortress" at Kadesh-
Barnea was destroyed toward the end of the tenth century,
probably during Shishak's campaign. Kadesh-Barnea, however,
as opposed to the other sites of the Negev highlands which
were abandoned after this destruction, continued to be an
important Judean stronghold in the following centuries, though
perhaps after a gap of some one hundred years. The new
fortress erected there became the main Judean base along the
"Gaza Road," which led from Gaza to the Red Sea and was
essential to the trade relations with Arabia. This stronghold
was also critical in controlling the nomadic population of the
Negev and eastern Sinai.

The fortress at Kadesh-Barnea was a rectangular structure
of 40 × 60 m, enclosed by a 4-m-wide solid wall with eight
rectangular towers. The wall was surrounded by an earth
rampart supported by a retaining wall. In spite of the good
preservation of the walls, a gate was not found; perhaps entry

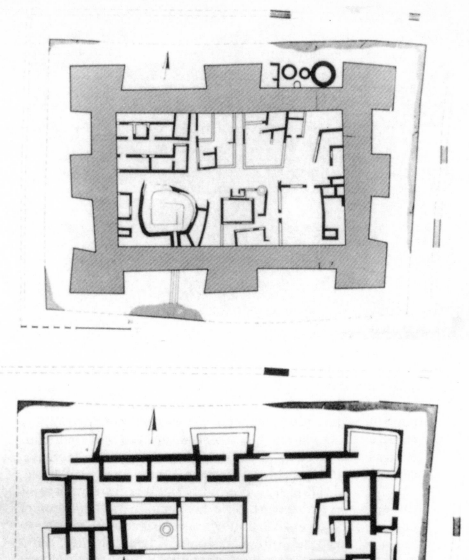

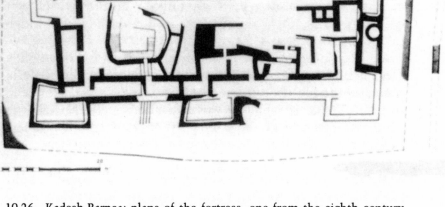

10.26 Kadesh-Barnea: plans of the fortress, one from the eighth century
B.C.E. (above) and one from the seventh century B.C.E. (below).

10.27 Kadesh-Barnea: model of the fortress.

was gained by way of a ramp on top of the earth rampart. A built-up water reservoir inside the citadel was filled from a canal bringing water from the spring Ain el-Qudeirat. This fortress was probably erected sometime in the early eighth century B.C.E. (perhaps by Uzziah? compare 2 Chronicles 26:10); like Tel Beer-sheba Stratum II, it was destroyed during the early seventh century B.C.E.—possibly by Edomites or nomads during the years following Sennacherib's invasion of Judah or during the time of Manasseh. Later in the seventh century B.C.E. the fortress was rebuilt, this time with outer casemate walls. It was finally destroyed with the rest of Judah in 586 B.C.E.

As was the case for the tenth century B.C.E., handmade Negebite pottery found in the various levels at Kadesh-Barnea indicates the presence of a seminomadic local population who lived alongside the Judean garrison and benefited from the royal resources. The handmade pottery often imitates typical Judean forms brought from Judah to this place.

Kuntillet ʿAjrud A unique site along the "Gaza Road," about 50 km south of Kadesh-Barnea, is Kuntillet ʿAjrud ("the solitary hill of the water wells").[22] An isolated building was constructed in this desolate place on top of a steep hill, near a crossroad leading into the Sinai Desert and close to water wells. The building was rectangular in shape (15 × 25 m) and consisted of a large central courtyard surrounded on three sides by long casemate rooms with projecting corner towers. The entrance was through a gate chamber which created a "bent axis" approach into a broad room. In both rooms benches were constructed along the walls, and white plaster covered the walls, floors, and benches. Among the varied finds in this site were unique objects made of organic materials, such as basketry, ropes, and textiles, whose preservation is due to the dry desert conditions.

Fascinating finds at Kuntillet ʿAjrud were inscriptions and drawings found on wall plaster, on two large jars, and on a stone vat. Some of the inscriptions were written on the plaster of doorjambs (compare Deuteronomy 6:9). The texts are

10.28 Kuntillet ʿAjrud: paintings and inscription on a pithos. The inscription mentions "Yahweh of Samaria and his Asherah."

blessings and dedications, such as that on the rim of a large stone trough which reads, "'Obadyau, son of 'Adnah, may he be blessed by God." The title *Sar 'ir*, "the governor of the city," which appears in several of the inscriptions, perhaps designates the official in charge of the place. The ink script on large jars is accompanied by drawings. The jar inscriptions are blessing formulae which include the astounding combination *lyhwh šmrn wl'šrth*, "Yahweh of Samaria and his Asherah." These important texts throw light on aspects of Israelite theology in the Old Testament period, of which there are few traces in the Bible.

Some of the paintings on the jars are imitations of artistic motifs well known from Phoenician ivory carvings, such as a cow nursing its calf, and two animals on both sides of a stylized tree. Other subjects are a sitting woman playing the lyre; two figures shown with interlocked hands (one of them is most probably the Egyptian god Bes), and a procession of five male figures with arms raised in prayer. The drawings

10.29 Kuntillet 'Ajrud: painting on a pithos showing suppliants in a procession.

were done in a simple, unprofessional style, perhaps by an amateur artist who copied some of his themes from more elaborate artworks.

The building appears to have been established and used for a short time by people who came from outside the region. The lack of Negebite handmade pottery of the type found at Kadesh-Barnea shows that here there was no cooperation with the local nomads. The pottery assemblage indicates a date between the mid–ninth and mid–eighth centuries B.C.E. It consists of forms known from both Judah and Israel. Connections with the northern kingdom are also seen in the theophoric suffix -*yw* of personal names appearing in the inscriptions (as opposed to the Judean -*yahu*), and in the mention of Yahweh of Samaria. The imitation of Phoenician motifs in the drawings on the jars also reflects ties with the kingdom of Israel, where Phoenician influence was strong. The large jars themselves, however, are typically Judean, and neutron activation studies have proven that they were produced in the Jerusalem region.

Kuntillet ʿAjrud thus shows a unique combination of Judean and Israelite traditions and connections. Its excavator, Z. Meshel, has suggested that the site served as a religious center located near the road to the Red Sea in a time when there was Israelite trade activity related to the Red Sea and Ezion-Geber—such as the Judean-Phoenician attempt to re-establish this trade during the time of Jehoshaphat (1 Kings 22:49). The combination of Israelite and Judean elements may reflect a time when the northern kingdom's sphere of influence extended to Judah, such as during the reign of Athaliah.

The religious activity at the site may have been related to some peculiar sect in Israel such as the Rechabites, mentioned in connection with Kenites and scribes in 1 Chronicles 2:55. The location of the site may be related to traditions concerning Mount Sinai, as almost during the same period Elijah is said to have gone to "Horeb, the mountain of God" a synonym for Mount Sinai (1 Kings 19:8).

The discoveries at Kuntillet ʿAjrud open a window onto the world of contemporary Israelite religion in a period prior to the Deuteronomic theology of Jerusalem which inspired our Masoretic Old Testament. They also illustrate the special role of the desert, and perhaps of Mount Sinai, in Israelite religion and spiritual life, as known also from biblical literature.

Tell el-Kheleifeh We have mentioned earlier (p. 397) the difficulties involved in N. Glueck's identification of Tell el-Kheleifeh with biblical Ezion-Geber. Glueck's excavation at this southernmost Iron Age site in Palestine revealed two successive square fortified enclosures. The first (Period I) was an open courtyard measuring 45 × 45 m, surrounded by a casemate wall. Inside the courtyard stood a single building planned as a "four-room house" with exceptionally thick walls strengthened by sloping revetments. In the next phase (Period II), the enclosure was enlarged to ca. 60 × 60 m, entered through a four-chamber gate and defended by a solid "offsets and insets" wall, a sloping glacis, and an outer defense wall. The layout of the enclosure resembles the fortress of Arad, though the latter is somewhat smaller. In the following Period III, various structures were built inside the fortified enclosure, which was still used.

The well-planned, fortified enclosures at Tell el-Kheleifeh appear to be of a military or administrative nature, constructed by a central authority. Glueck attributed the first phase to the time of Solomon (tenth century B.C.E.), the rebuilding in Period II to the activity of Jehoshaphat, and Period III to the reign of Uzziah (mid–eighth century B.C.E.). A seal with the name "Jotham" was thought to be related to King Jotham, the son of Uzziah. Glueck related the history of the site to the naval and mercantile activity of the Israelites in the Red Sea. In Period IV many small structures were constructed inside the area of the older enclosures; Glueck identified this phase as an Edomite town which survived from the end of the eighth century B.C.E. until the beginning of the sixth century B.C.E. His interpretation was based on the Edomite pottery as well as on a seal impression of an Edomite official: "Qaws'anal, servant of the king." Assyrian pottery pointed to some Assyrian presence in this level, perhaps related to that known from Transjordan (see p. 544).

A renewed analysis of the material from Tell el-Kheleifeh (by G. D. Pratico) suggests a revision of Glueck's chronology and historical interpretation.[23] While no new evidence on the date of period IV came to light, the pottery from Periods II–IV appears to belong to the eighth and seventh centuries B.C.E.

One possibility is that Tell el-Kheleifeh was initially a Judean stronghold, located at the end of the routes leading to the Red Sea, and that during the seventh century B.C.E. it passed into Edomite hands. An alternative supposition could be that the site was founded as an Edomite fortress and was never related to Judah. This last interpretation is less plausible, due to the finds of Judean pottery at the site. Handmade Negebite pottery demonstrates cooperation between the outsiders who founded the fortress and the local nomadic population, such as at contemporary Kadesh-Barnea.

The early phases of Tell el-Kheleifeh and the fortress at Kadesh-Barnea probably represent a major Judean effort to control the approach to the Red Sea along the "Gaza Road" during the eighth and seventh centuries B.C.E. It appears that trade relations with Arabia through the Red Sea continued during this period, perhaps as part of the international cooperation between Edom, Judah, and the Phoenicians under Assyrian guidance. Later in the seventh century B.C.E., Edom took possession of the approach to the Gulf of Elath and the Red Sea.

THE JUDEAN DESERT

The Judean Desert, separating the Judean Hills from the Jordan Valley and the Dead Sea, was almost totally unsettled since the Chalcolithic period. Only toward the end of the Iron Age, mainly in the seventh century B.C.E., was settlement activity reinitiated here. The most prominent site was the small town at the oasis of En Gedi (Tel Goren).[24] This town was constructed on hilly terrain and built on terraces. Industrial installations found in the houses were interpreted by B. Mazar as workshops for preparing an exclusive product—perhaps balsam perfume, which is known to have been the most important product of this region during the period of the second temple.

Smaller villages were found at other oases north of En Gedi along the Dead Sea. Farther inland in the desert, in the Buqeʿah Valley west of Qumran, three small Iron Age sites may have been centers of royal or private estates founded during the seventh century B.C.E.; in two of them a large rectangular fortified building was the major and perhaps the only structure. In the fields related to these sites, L. E. Stager identified sophisticated irrigation systems based on diversion of winter floodwaters to the fields by dams and canals.[25]

At Jericho, the most important oasis in the Jordan Valley, Iron Age II settlements existed both at Tell es-Sultan—the ancient mound of Jericho—and near Wadi Qelt. Farther south, at the site of Vered Jericho, an exceptional seventh century B.C.E. isolated structure was discovered at a place remote from the water sources and fertile lands of the Jericho oasis.[26] The building was rectangular in shape, its entrance defended by two flanking towers. Inside, a rectangular courtyard led to two attached "four-room house" units. The regular planning of the structure and its defensive character indicate that its function was official; it may be interpreted as a unique type of Judean fortress or administration center guarding the road from Jericho to the Dead Sea.

An isolated Iron Age building at Hurvat Shilhah—west of Jericho, on the road connecting the latter with the land of Benjamin—is an example of another type of desert settlement. The building was a 30×30 m square, comprising a large courtyard with rooms on two of its sides and a pillared structure at its corner. It could have served either as a caravanserai or as a farmstead based on livestock and some farming.[27]

10.30   Vered Jericho: plan of seventh century B.C.E. fortified building.

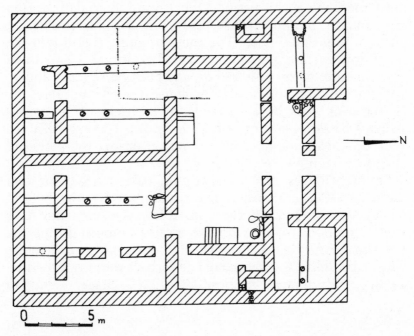

0 _____ 5 m

The dynamic settlement activity in the Judean Desert during the seventh century B.C.E. seems to be reflected in the list of desert cities in Joshua 15:61–62, supporting the view that this list was compiled sometime in that century, perhaps during the reign of Josiah.

OTHER FORTS AND TOWERS IN JUDAH

Several fortresses and towers discovered in the Judean Hills and the Shephelah show that such military and administrative structures were not limited to the Negev and the Judean Desert. The fortresses were square or rectangular in shape and had a large central courtyard surrounded by casemate rooms. The only building of this type excavated is that at Khirbet Abu et-Twein on the western slopes of the Hebron Hills (west of Kefar Ezion).[28] It was located on a high hill, with an excellent view of the Shephelah and the Valley of Elah. The building was 30 × 30 m in size; it had a gate chamber

10.31   Khirbet Abu et-Twein: plan of the fortress.

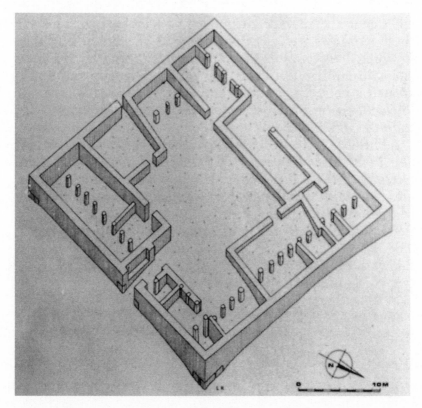

10.32 Khirbet Abu et-Twein: room in the fortress; notice the use of monolithic pillars.

and a central courtyard surrounded by a double row of rooms; these two rows were separated by rows of monolithic pillars to which division walls were attached. Khirbet Abu et-Twein, and two similar fortresses located on ridges to the north, created a network of strongholds in this hilly (and probably forested) region which separated the Hebron mountain ridge from the inner Shephelah.

Additional fortresses are known from Judah—such as that at Hurvat Eres, located on a high ridge west of Jerusalem offering a view of the coastal plain as well as of the Jerusalem area. The location of the Judean strongholds suggests that one of their main functions was to facilitate communication by fire signals between different parts of the kingdom of Judah. The use of such a communication and warning system is known both from biblical references (Jeremiah 6:1) and from one of the Lachish letters (see p. 459).

In addition to the fortresses with a central courtyard, there were freestanding, isolated, solid towers, usually built on a podium elevating their ground level above the surrounding countryside. Two are known from the Jerusalem area: one on a high ridge north of the city (in the suburb called the French Hill), and the other on a ridge south of the city (in the quarter of Giloh). Since Jerusalem is surrounded by mountains which cut off the view from the city, it was essential to establish such towers on the surrounding ridges in order to guard the roads leading to the capital from north and south, and to permit communication by fire signals.

Thus, settlement in Judah was at its peak in the eighth and seventh centuries B.C.E. New areas such as the Judean Desert were now inhabited, and the number of towns and forts in the Judean Hills and the Shephelah was unprecedented.

THE LAMELECH AND ROSETTE SEAL IMPRESSIONS

One of the most significant finds in Judah is seal impressions found on jar handles—impressions known as *lamelech* due to the word *lmlk* on the upper part of the sealing, meaning "belonging to the king."[29] Almost a thousand such sealings are known; they were impressed on the handles of jars of a very typical ware and form, made of the same clay, possibly even in the same workshop (as indicated by neutron activation analysis). The jars had a narrow neck, wide shoulders, a narrow base, and four handles; their capacity varied from 12 to 14 gallons (45 to 53 liters). Almost thirty such jars in one storage space were found at both Lachish (Stratum III) and Tel Batash (Stratum III), but only some of the jars had seal impressions on their handles. *Lamelech* sealings can appear on all four or on fewer than four handles. The sealings were often carelessly made, as if in haste. Studies have shown that the number of actual seals used was in fact small, approximately twenty.

There are two types of *lamelech* sealings: one featuring a four-winged beetle (a motif originating in Egypt), and the other decorated with a two-winged elongated object resembling the winged sun disc. These were perhaps royal Judean insignia. For many years it was believed that one replaced the other, but at both Lachish and Tel Batash the two forms appear together in the same storage room, and there is no satisfactory explanation for their simultaneous use. The word

10.33 *Lamelech* jar with stamped handles and two scoops from Tel Batash (Timnah).

10.34 Stamped *lamelech* jar handles

lmlk is placed above the symbol; below the latter, one of the four place-names Hebron, Ziph, Sochoh, and *mmšt* is inscribed. The first two cities are well known and located in the Hebron Hills. Sochoh is probably that in the Shephelah, and not the town of identical name south of Hebron. *Mmšt* is unknown from any other source. It may have been a title of Jerusalem (shortening of *mmšlt*, "government," as suggested by H. L. Ginsberg), but it may have been the name of an otherwise unknown city or administrative center in Judah.

In addition to the *lamelech* sealings, sealings with personal names appear on the same jars, but they are much less common; thirty-four different names have been noted. Their owners could have been officials who were involved in the manufacture of the jars, the preparation of their contents, or their distribution. Identical "private" sealings of this type have been found at different sites, indicating that the jars were produced and stamped in the same workshop, under the supervision of one official who was responsible for their distribution to various cities.

The date and function of the *lamelech* jars have been the subject of a volatile debate. Lachish and Tel Batash provided the firm stratigraphic grounds for determining their date, as at both of these sites they were found in a destruction level which can be safely associated with the conquest by Sennacherib in 701 B.C.E. The jars, therefore, were most probably produced in the years preceding the revolt of Hezekiah against Sennacherib. As to their function, some scholars have suggested that they were intended to contain the products of royal estates, particularly wine.[30] According to this view, the place-names denote centers of royal estates. A more probable explanation is that the jars were associated with some kind of administrative and military organization. Aharoni suggested that the four names reflect the fourfold administrative division of Judah mentioned in Joshua 15: the "mountain," the Negev, the "desert" (probably the Judean Desert), and the Shephelah. "Hebron" signified the mountains, "Ziph" the Judean Desert, "Sochoh" the Shephelah, and *"mmšt"* the Negev. Yadin emphasized a military association.[31] We suggest that the jars were related to a short-term military system of food provision organized according to the administrative divisions of the kingdom.

The *lamelech* jars and sealings are mainly found in the

regions invaded by Sennacherib: Jerusalem and its environment (at sites such as Tell en-Nasbeh, Gibeon, Ramat Rahel)
and the Shephelah of Judah (Gezer, Tel Batash, and Lachish).[32]
More than four hundred sealings were uncovered at Lachish,
the main fortress of Judah in the war of 701 B.C.E., while only
few were found in other parts of Judah. It is thus probable
that the jars contained the food supply of Hezekiah's army.
The jars were probably produced during the time of Hezekiah,
in the few years during which the revolt against Assyria was
prepared. They appear to have been distributed to garrisons
in cities where an Assyrian attack was considered inevitable,
and there they were found in the destruction layers associated
with this war.

Since Jerusalem was not captured by Sennacherib, we may
surmise that many jars of this kind, stored in the royal store
buildings of the capital, were available during the following
seventh century B.C.E. Such jars can stand in storage for
decades, and they may have been employed for a long time
after their production. This would explain the fact that
stamped *lamelech* jars are found occasionally in late seventh
century B.C.E. contexts. During the seventh century B.C.E.,
however, a new type of jar appeared with different details of
shape and ware, although in general form it recalls the
lamelech jars. The handles of the new jar were stamped with
a petaled rosette, which may have been a royal insignia during
the days of the last kings of Judah.

JUDAH'S DOWNFALL

The archaeological record of the destruction of Judah by
the Babylonians is extensive. Jerusalem was heavily destroyed
and burnt, as shown by the finds near the tower in the Jewish
Quarter, and by the burnt houses on the eastern slope of the
City of David. Outside Jerusalem, the palace at Ramat Rahel
fell into ruins.

Lachish (Stratum II) was destroyed in a heavy fire. The
Lachish letters, found in the burnt debris at the city gate,
were written by a certain Hoshayahu to his commander Yaush
probably during the last days of Judah. They contain important information on this period, but their contents are fragmentary and the interpretation is not easy. Hoshayahu was

considered by N. H. Tur-Sinai and other scholars to have been the commander of a small fortress outside Lachish, and Yaush was explained by them as the commander of Lachish. Y. Yadin, on the other hand, believed that the ostraca were drafts of one and the same letter sent from Lachish to Jerusalem, Hoshayahu being the commander of Lachish and Yaush a high official in the capital.[33] One of these letters ends with the sentence "And may my lord know that we are watching for the beacons of Lachish, according to all the signs which my lord has given, for we cannot see [the signals] of Azekah." These words must refer to the importance of fire signals in the last war against the Babylonians.

Most of the Judean towns and fortresses excavated in the Shephelah, the Negev, and the Judean Desert were destroyed during the Babylonian invasion. In the Shephelah, evidence of a fatal destruction by fire was uncovered at the large independent city of Ekron and its "daughter" Timnah. Their annihilation may have been perpetrated when Nebuchadnezzar fought along the coastal plain between 605 and 600 B.C.E.,

10.35   Lachish: Ostracon No. 4 (See translation of last lines on this page.)

somewhat before the destruction of Judah. Farther east and north, Gezer and Beth-Shemesh were overthrown, and their refugees probably fled to caves in the Shephelah (compare Ezekiel 33:27). Prayers found incised on the walls of a burial cave east of Lachish may have been written by such refugees. (See p. 515.)

All the fortresses and towns of the northern Negev, and the fortress at Kadesh-Barnea, were devastated, perhaps by Edomites who invaded the region following the Babylonian conquests in the heart of Judah. The Edomite threat in this region is reflected in the Arad letters. A similar fate befell the sites in the Judean Desert.

Only in the land of Benjamin, north of Jerusalem (at Tell el-Ful, Mizpah, Gibeon) was the Babylonian conquest not obliterative. In this region, it appears, there was no severe destruction, and life continued under Babylonian rule (see p. 548).[34]

NOTES

1. In addition to the relevant chapters in the books cited in Chapter Nine, note 1, see also W. W. Hallo in: E. F. Campbell and D. N. Freedman (eds.), *The Biblical Archaeologist Reader*, vol. 2, New York 1964, pp. 152–88; I. Eph'al in: *WHJP*, vol. 4, pp. 276–89.

2. J. W. Crowfoot, K. M. Kenyon, and E. L. Sukenik, *Samaria Sebaste I: The Buildings at Samaria*, London 1942; J. W. and G. M. Crowfoot and K. M. Kenyon, *Samaria Sebaste III: The Objects from Samaria*, London 1957; G. E. Wright, *BA* 22 (1959), pp. 67–78; O. Tufnell, *PEQ* 91 (1959), pp. 90–105; K. M. Kenyon, *Royal Cities of the Old Testament*, London 1971, pp. 71–91, 124–25; *EAEHL*, pp. 1032–50.

3. *ANET*, p. 321; Gibson (1971), pp. 5–13 (with earlier bibliography); Aharoni (1979), pp. 356–68; Y. Yadin, *Scripta Hierosolymitana* 8 (1961), pp. 9–25; idem, *IEJ* 12 (1962), pp. 64–66; A. F. Rainey, *PEQ* 99 (1967), pp. 32–41; ibid. 102 (1970), pp. 45–51; Mazar (1986), pp. 173–88, with previous bibliography.

4. On Hazor and Megiddo see Yadin (1972), pp. 147–200; on Dan see Chapter 11, note 25; on Tirzah see A. Chambon, *Tell el Far'ah I: L'Age du fer*, Paris 1984.

5. On Tel Kinrot and Yoqneam see Chapter 9, note 18; on Khirbet Marjameh see A. Mazar, *BA* (1982), pp. 171–74; on Gezer see Chapter 9, note 16 and J. D. Seger, *Rose Festschrift*, pp. 113–27.

6. Aharoni (1979), pp. 347–51; Z. Kallai, *Historical Geography of the Bible*, Jerusalem 1986, pp. 372–97.

7. K. M. Kenyon, *Digging Up Jerusalem*, London 1974, pp. 129–71; N. Avigad, *Discovering Jerusalem*, Nashville 1983, pp. 23–60; Y. Shiloh, *Excavations at the City of David I. Qedem* 19, Jerusalem 1984; see also the papers of P. J. King, A. D. Tushingham, Y. Shiloh, B. Mazar, N. Avigad, and respondents in *BAT*, pp. 435–78; B. Mazar, *The Mountain of the Lord*, New York 1965.

8. E. Mazar, *IEJ* 37 (1987), pp. 60–63; E. Mazar and B. Mazar, *Excavations in the South of the Temple Mount, the Ophel of Biblical Jerusalem* (Qedem 29), Jerusalem 1989 (in press).

9. A. D. Tushingham, *Excavations in Jerusalem, 1961–1967*, Toronto 1985, pp. 1–24.

10. In addition to the literature in note 7, see in particular J. Simons, *Jerusalem in the Old Testament*, Leiden 1952.

11. Y. Aharoni, *Excavations at Ramat Rahel*, vol. 1, Rome 1962; ibid., vol. 2, Rome 1964. Further excavations were carried out at the site in 1984 by G. Barkai.

12. Y. Yadin in: *Kenyon Festschrift*, pp. 127–35 suggested identifying the building at Ramat Rahel with the "temple of Baal" which Athaliah erected in Jerusalem (2 Kings 11:18). His argumentation is based on the similarity of Ramat Rahel to the palace at Samaria. However, the pottery and seal impressions of *lamelech* type found in the fill below the floor of the courtyard date the Ramat Rahel construction to the seventh century B.C.E. Aharoni associated the palace at Ramat Rahel with the one erected by Jehoiakim in Jerusalem, but the latter was probably located in the city itself.

13. D. Ussishkin, *TA* 5 (1978), pp. 1–97; ibid. 10 (1983), pp. 97–181; idem, *The Conquest of Lachish by Sennacherib*, Tel Aviv 1982; idem, *BAR* 5:6 (1979), pp. 16–40; ibid. 10:2 (1984), pp. 66–73.

14. Y. Shiloh, *IEJ* 28 (1978), pp. 36–51; Th. L. McClellan, *ZDPV* 100 (1984), pp. 53–69; Z. Herzog, *Expedition* 20:4 (1978), pp. 38–43.

15. Y. and M. Aharoni, *BASOR* 224 (1976), pp. 73–90. The rich pottery assemblage found in the destruction level of Beer-sheba Stratum II was dated by Aharoni to c. 700 B.C.E., while others date it somewhat later. See K. M. Kenyon, *PEQ* 108 (1976), pp. 63–64 and Y. Yadin, *BASOR* 222 (1976), pp. 5–17 (the latter dated it to the time of Josiah). The assemblage appears indeed to contain forms which are later than Lachish III (701 B.C.E.) and earlier than Lachish II (586 B.C.E.), but it is difficult to give a more precise date at this stage of research.

16. Z. Herzog et al., *BASOR* 254 (1984), pp. 1–34; idem, *BAR* 13:2 (1987), pp. 16–39; M. Aharoni, *BASOR* 258 (1985), p. 73; A. Mazar and E. Netzer, *BASOR* 263 (1986), pp. 87–91.

17. Y. Aharoni, *Arad Inscriptions*, Jerusalem 1981.

18. I. Beit-Arieh and B. Cresson, *TA* 12 (1985), pp. 96–101.

19. Y. Aharoni (ed.), *Beer-Sheba*, vol. 1, Tel Aviv 1973, pp. 106–15; Z. Herzog, *Beer-Sheba II: The Early Iron Age Settlements*, Tel Aviv 1984; Rainey, ibid., pp. 88–104.

20. On ʿAroer, see A. Biran and R. Cohen, *EI* 15 (1971), pp. 250–73 (Hebrew);

on Tel 'Ira, see I. Beit-Arieh and A. Biran, *Qadmoniot* 69–70 (1985), pp. 17–28 (Hebrew); on Tel Masos see: W. Fritz and A. Kempinski, *Ergebnisse der Ausgrabungen auf der Hirbet el Masas (Tel Masos) 1972–1975*, Wiesbaden 1983, pp. 123–38.

21. R. Cohen, *BA* 44 (1981), pp. 93–107; idem, *BAR* 7:3 (1981), pp. 20–33.

22. Z. Meshel, *Kuntillet 'Ajrud: A Religious Centre from the Time of the Judaean Monarchy on the Border of Sinai.* Israel Museum Catalogue 175, Jerusalem 1978; idem, *Expedition* 20 (1978), pp. 50–54; idem, *BAR* 5:2 (1979), pp. 24–35; P. Beck, *TA* 9 (1982), pp. 3–68.

23. G. D. Pratico, *BASOR* 259 (1985), pp. 1–32 (a reappraisal with detailed earlier bibliography).

24. B. Mazar, *En Gedi: The First and Second Seasons of Excavations, 1961–1962. 'Atiqot* 5, Jerusalem 1966; B. Mazar and I. Dunayevsky, *IEJ* 17 (1967), pp. 133–43.

25. L. E. Stager, *BASOR* 221 (1976), pp. 145–58.

26. A. Eitan, *Excavations and Surveys in Israel*, 2 (1983), pp. 106–7; idem, *BAR* 12:4 (1986), pp. 30–35.

27. A. Mazar, Z. Ilan, and D. Amit, *EI* 17 (1984), pp. 236–50 (Hebrew).

28. A. Mazar, *PEQ* 114 (1982), pp. 87–109.

29. D. Ussishkin, *BASOR* 273 (1976), pp. 1–13; idem, *TA* 4 (1977), pp. 54–57, with previous bibliography.

30. See A. F. Rainey, *EI* 16 (1982), pp. 177–81 (Hebrew).

31. Aharoni (1979), pp. 394–400; Y. Yadin, *BASOR* 163 (1961), pp. 6–12.

32. N. Na'aman, *Vetus Testamentum* 29 (1979), pp. 61–81; idem, *BASOR* 261 (1986), pp. 5–21.

33. Y. Yadin in: H. Shanks and B. Mazar (eds.), *Recent Archaeology in the Land of Israel*, Washington and Jerusalem 1981, pp. 179–86.

34. For a general survey of the seventh century B.C.E. and the end of Judah see: E. Stern, *BA* 38 (1975), pp. 26–53.

CHAPTER ELEVEN

GENERAL ASPECTS OF THE
ISRAELITE MATERIAL CULTURE

ASPECTS OF ISRAELITE TOWN PLANNING AND ARCHITECTURE

The main components of the Iron Age Israelite towns are the fortification system, the city gate, a piazza near the gate, the street network, public structures of various types (palaces, store buildings, cult places, royal stables), drainage and water supply systems, dwellings, and various industrial installations. In the following sections, we will briefly discuss the appearance of these components in the Israelite cities; we will also include a brief discussion of the appearance of some of these features in non-Israelite regions of the country, if they are known in such regions.

Classification of Cities Israelite cities can be divided into several categories: capitals of the kingdoms, district administration centers, and country towns.[1] The capitals of Judah and Israel (Jerusalem and Samaria respectively) as well as those of neighboring city-states in Philistia (Ekron, Ashdod) were very large, comprising several dozen or even hundreds of acres in area, and their population must have surpassed ten thousand. They included massive fortifications, a royal acropolis, public buildings, markets, and residential quarters. Unfortunately, however, only small portions of these cities are known archaeologically.

The second category includes cities which served as regional administrative and military centers. Such were Hazor, Megiddo, Lachish, and perhaps Tel Beer-sheba. Most of these averaged 20 acres (except Beer-sheba, which was much smaller) and their population numbered approximately two thousand to three thousand. Significant areas of these cities were set apart for public edifices such as palaces, administration buildings, storehouses, and stables. These were usually separated from the rest of the town by walls and gates (such as at Hazor, Megiddo Palace 1723, and Lachish). Other cities also had specific public buildings, such as the large religious center at Dan.

The third category consists of country towns, which were usually not more than 5–7 acres in area; their population can be estimated as having been about five hundred to a thousand. They were fortified, and they contained mainly dwelling quarters.

Town Planning Orthogonal town planning is known only at Tell el-Far'ah (north) and perhaps also at Timnah; in the former, houses were constructed in well-defined insulae. In

11.1 Beer-sheba: town plan (Stratum II).

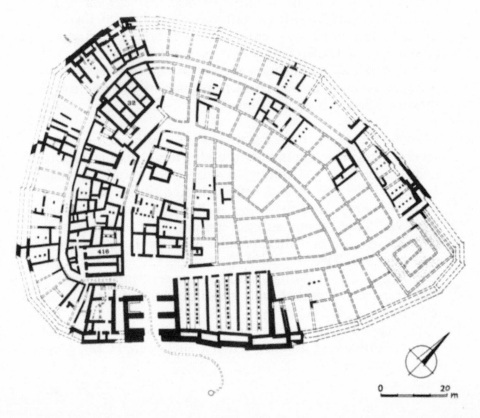

Judah, "peripheral" planning has been traced at several towns such as at Tel Beer-sheba, Tell Beit Mirsim, Tell en-Nasbeh, and Beth-Shemesh. In this town plan, a belt of houses is built along the circumference of the town, along a city wall. A circular street separated this outer belt from the inner core of the city, which included dwellings and other buildings arranged along radial streets and lanes. The core is often agglutinative, without a preconceived layout.[2]

Fortifications   As we have seen in Chapter Nine, the only defense of several Israelite cities during the tenth century B.C.E. was the outer belt of houses. In the latter half of that century, certain cities were surrounded by city walls, the shape of which varied according to fashion and local needs, with casemate walls prevailing (see p. 388).

Casemate walls became very rare after the tenth century B.C.E. They were used in royal enclosures (such as at Samaria and Ramat Rahel) and in fortresses (such as Kadesh-Barnea and Tell el-Kheleifeh), but only at Tel Beer-sheba and at Tell el-Ful were they built as the town's fortification. In the case of Tell Beit Mirsim, the tenth-century casemate wall was employed until the town's final destruction. At several Judean cities the casemates served also as the inner broad rooms of houses attached to the wall (as at Tell Beit Mirsim, Beer-sheba Strata III–II, and perhaps also Beth-Shemesh and the earlier stage at Tell en-Nasbeh).

Solid walls appear in rare cases already during the tenth century (at Ashdod, Tel Kinrot, and Tel Beer-sheba Stratum V; the last may date to the ninth century B.C.E.). They became the prevalent type of city wall only from the ninth century B.C.E. onward, as exemplified in almost all the cities excavated in the northern kingdom (Dan, Hazor, Tel Kinrot, Megiddo, Yoqneam, Tell el-Farʿah [north], Gezer, Khirbet Marjamah), in many Judean cities (Jerusalem [where the widest wall of this type was discovered], Lachish, Tell en-Nasbeh, Ramat Rahel, Timnah, Khirbet Rabud [Debir], Beer-sheba [Strata V–VI], Tel ʿIra, ʿAroer) and fortresses (Arad, Kadesh-Barnea earlier phase, Tell el-Kheleifeh later phase). Such solid city walls are also found at those independent city-states of Philistia which were excavated (Ekron and Ashdod).

The walls had a solid stone or brick superstructure on a stone foundation; their width averaged between 2 and 7 m.

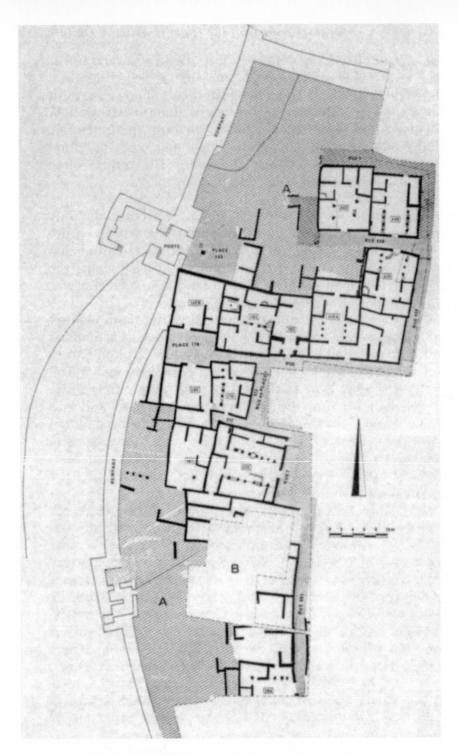

11.2 Tirzah (Tell el-Farᶜah [north]): plan of dwelling area near the city gate, tenth century B.C.E..

466

The details of construction and planning varied: the walls were sometimes strengthened with outside "saw teeth" offsets or were constructed with "offsets and insets" (as at Megiddo). A unique double wall was found at Yoqneam. Solid rectangular or slightly rounded towers defended weak points in the cities' defense system. The upper part of the walls can be reconstructed from Assyrian reliefs which show protruding balconies that enabled enfilade and vertical fire on the attackers. The city wall was usually constructed on the upper slope of the mound. In several cases (Lachish, Timnah, and perhaps Tel Halif) an outer retaining wall was constructed farther down the slope, creating a double defense line and serving as an additional obstacle for siege equipment and troops.

The steep inclination of mounds susceptible to erosion endangered the foundations of the walls. This problem was overcome at several Judean sites by the construction of earth glacis resembling those of the Middle Bronze Age. Such earthworks are known from Tel Beer-sheba, Tel Malhata, and Tel Halif in the southern part of the country, from Ashdod-Yam (on the coastline west of Ashdod), and possibly also from Timnah.

Y. Yadin suggested that the shift from casemate to solid walls was the answer to the Assyrian battering ram and other siege techniques, which appeared in the region from the mid–ninth century B.C.E.[3] Indeed, the more solid and wide the wall was, the greater its resistance to destruction by rams. Thus, the 7-m-wide solid stone wall of Jerusalem was perhaps the main obstacle in the path of Sennacherib's rams. However, even the solid walls failed to fend off the Assyrian siege machines. The 6-m-wide city wall at Lachish is just one example of a wall breached by the Assyrians.

There are few exceptions to the typological development of city walls suggested by Yadin. Among these exceptions are the few appearances of solid walls during the tenth century B.C.E. (p. 388) and the replacement of a solid wall with a casemate wall at Beer-sheba in the ninth and eighth centuries B.C.E. As a rule, however, this schema is supported by the majority of the sites excavated.

The gate complex is one of the most imposing features of Israelite cities. It was usually planned as a combined system creating an indirect approach to the city between an outer gate located on the slope of the mound and an inner gate

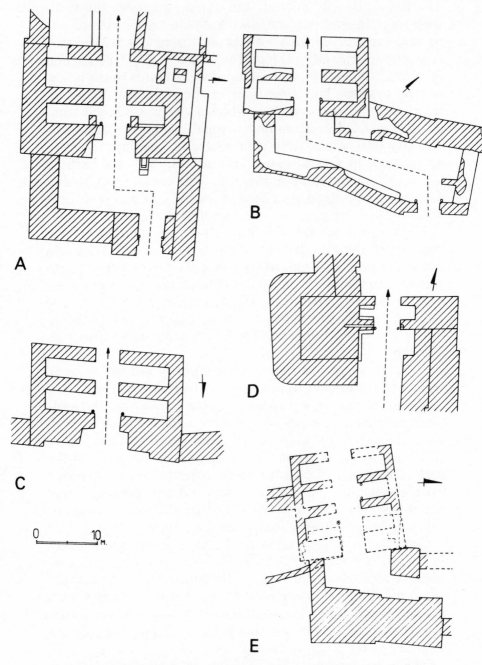

11.3 Selected plans of Iron Age II city gates: (A) Dan; (B) Beer-sheba; (C) Megiddo Stratum III; (D) Tell en-Nasbeh; (E) Tel Batash Stratum III (Timnah; see reconstruction of this gate on p. 534).

situated on the summit of the mound. A ramp supported by retaining walls led to the outer gate. Such gate complexes are known at Dan, Megiddo, Tirzah, Gezer, Timnah, Lachish, Beer-sheba, and perhaps the Ophel site in Jerusalem. The details of their planning vary according to topographic conditions. Thus, an outer gate was omitted wherever it was found unnecessary.

As we have seen (p. 385), six-chamber inner gates (with or without an outer gate) were a common feature in the Solomonic era and shortly after (at Gezer, Hazor, Megiddo, Lachish, and Ashdod). Exceptional later examples of such gates were found at Tel Batash (Timnah) Stratum III of the eighth century B.C.E. and at Tel ʿIra in the seventh century B.C.E. Four-chamber gates started to appear in the early tenth century outside Israel (at Ashdod), and at the end of that century or at the beginning of the ninth century B.C.E. at Tel Beer-sheba. They then became the most common gate type, appearing at Megiddo Stratum IVA,[4] Dan (where two gates of this type were discovered), Dor, Timnah Stratum II, Gezer (?), Beer-sheba, and Tell el-Kheleifeh. Such four-chamber gates were also the most common form in northern Syria during these centuries. Simpler gate forms had only one guard chamber (Megiddo Stratum III, Tel Kinrot, Tell en-Nasbeh), or none at all (Tell el-Farʿah [north] and Lachish Stratum II). It appears that the simpler versions were more common in the later part of the Iron Age. Several of the gates were defended by enormous solid towers (Lachish, Tell en-Nasbeh, Timnah, and perhaps the Ophel at Jerusalem, where the "Warren Tower" could have served in such a role; see p. 423).

In addition to their defensive function, the gates also played an important role in the daily life of the city: as a market (2 Kings 7:1), a place of judgment by the elders (Deuteronomy 21:19, 22:15; Amos 5:12; Ruth 4:1–11), and a general assembly area where rulers made appearances and prophets spoke (1 Kings 22:10; Isaiah 29:21; Amos 5:10; Jeremiah 38:7; 2 Chronicles 32:6). Cult practices were also carried out at the city gates. At Dan, an ashlar installation had a canopy supported on four stone column bases; the bases were ornamented in a style reminiscent of Neo-Hittite architecture in north Syria.[5] This installation could have been a focal point for cult practices (compare 2 Kings 23:8), though

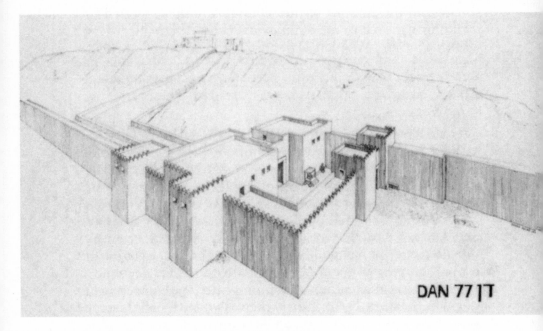

DAN 77 דן

11.4   Dan: reconstructed view of the city gate.

it can also be explained as a podium for the throne of an official: governor, judge, or ruler.

The civil activities could take place in a piazza adjacent to the city gate inside the city, or in a small piazza between the outer and inner gates. Other activities, such as trade, may have been conducted inside the guard chambers of the inner gate, as evidenced by benches and water troughs found there.

Streets   The layout of the streets—the skeleton of any city— is known only in a few cases, and it appears to have varied according to local conditions. In the hilly country of Judah, towns were circular in shape, and we have seen the arrangement there of circular and radial streets; at other sites, the plan is more orthogonal (Tell el-Farʿah [north] and perhaps Timnah). The streets averaged 2.5–3 m in width. They were usually paved with beaten earth, or with cobblestones; at Dan, a cobblestone main street leading from the gate at the bottom of the mound winds up the slope. Accumulation of garbage necessitated repavement from time to time, resulting in an eventual elevation of the street level, in some cases to the extent that the street was higher than the floors of the adjacent houses. Stone-lined drainage canals were constructed along streets and connected to a main drain leading outside the town via the city gate or next to it. Some streets opened onto piazzas, usually located inside the city gate, while others were alleys with dead ends. Front rooms of houses along main streets may have served as shops and workshops.

Royal Architecture and Ashlar Masonry   The royal buildings of Jerusalem, Ramat Rahel, Samaria, Megiddo, Hazor, and Lachish were described in the previous two chapters. Here we will discuss some major issues of a more general nature concerning this architecture.[6]

The royal enclosures in the capitals were very large and well planned. The acropolis of Samaria, about 6.5 acres in area, and the royal enclosure at Jerusalem (which perhaps was even larger) equaled the size of an average town in the kingdoms of Israel and Judah. The provincial government centers, such as Megiddo and Lachish, also occupied substantial parts of the town. At Lachish it was 3.5 acres in area, and an additional sector of the city was enclosed for the royal headquarters. The royal enclosures were well fortified, and they incorporated extensive building operations. Leveling was carried out by erecting artificial fills supported by high retaining walls. The great podium at Lachish demonstrates that even at provincial palaces care was taken to raise the building

11.5   Lachish: looking north at the podium of the Judean palace-fort.

above the surrounding countryside, and thus to emphasize the strength of the ruler. Spacious, lime-paved courtyards are a common feature in these Israelite royal compounds, providing space for military maneuvers, chariot and cavalry movement, public appearances of the rulers, and other convocations. Storage space was provided in casemates or elongated storage rooms located at the periphery of these complexes.

The individual structures inside the royal enclosures seem to comprise several contemporary traditions. We have seen the appearance of the *bit hilani* as the dominant type of Solomonic palace in Jerusalem and Megiddo, pointing to relations with northern Syria. In contrast, at Samaria, the palace plan followed the form of the "courtyard palace" of Canaanite tradition. The "four-room" principle, characteristic of many private dwellings of this time, formed the nucleus of the inner planning of royal citadels at Hazor and Shechem (the latter being the so-called "Granary" building above the ruined Middle Bronze–Late Bronze temple) and the central building at Tell el-Kheleifeh.

The formal architectural style employing ashlar masonry, Proto-Aeolic capitals, carved windows, and stone-cut crenellation on the upper part of the walls typifies Israelite royal buildings from the tenth century B.C.E. until the collapse of the kingdom of Judah. Three different types of ashlar walls have been identified: (1) those comprising ashlars laid in "headers and stretchers," the stones smoothly dressed; this technique was utilized in the facades of buildings, in palace walls which were seen from public courtyards and so forth; (2) the same, with stones marginally dressed and an unworked boss left at the center; this technique was utilized in foundation courses and retaining walls; (3) walls consisting of ashlar piers separated by a fill of field stones; this technique was utilized in walls of lesser importance such as fences of courtyards and walls of certain dwellings. Ashlar masonry was used extensively in the main palaces (Samaria, Jerusalem, Ramat Rahel), in some provincial royal residencies (at tenth century B.C.E. Megiddo), at royal ritual centers (such as that at Dan), and to some extent in other official buildings, such as at the gate to the citadel at Hazor (where we also find Proto-Aeolic capitals). In contrast, however, there were not any ashlars in the important palace of Lachish, perhaps due to economic considerations or lack of knowledge.

11.6 Samaria: ashlar masonry at the outer retaining wall of the acropolis. Note the drafted masonry and the gap between two of the courses, perhaps intended for insertion of wooden beams.

11.7 Dan: ashlar masonry at the "high place."

Ashlar masonry is also found outside Israel. At Ekron, Ashdod, and Tel Sera' in Philistia it was used for strengthening certain parts of mud-brick structures; in Moab, a royal citadel or a palace at the site of Medeibiyeh had a gate built of ashlars and decorated with Proto-Aeolic capitals identical to those of Jerusalem and Ramat Rahel. In Phoenicia ashlar masonry was employed in a few structures and tombs at Sarepta, Tyre, and Achzib. The fact that this type of masonry is particularly well known in Israel may be due to the extensive excavation and good preservation of Israelite sites.

What is the origin of this superb architectural style? Its roots can be traced to the Late Bronze Age: ashlar masonry was used in the palace of Ugarit and at some points at Megiddo; it is also known from the thirteenth and twelfth centuries at Cyprus. But both at Ugarit and in Cyprus the ashlars were used only for the outer facings of walls—not as the sole building material, as in Israel. Though the Iron Age ashlar building technique was probably rooted in this Canaanite tradition, the ethnic identity of the innovators of this style is still an open question. The fact that its earliest examples are preserved in the Israelite Solomonic and Omride architecture tempts us to assume that Phoenician artisans and architects were responsible for its introduction to Israel, as these Israelite kings are known to have had close connections with Tyre. However, the fact that all the examples of ashlar masonry outside Israel are later to the time of Solomon and Ahab, led Y. Shiloh to suggest that it, and the related Proto-Aeolic capitals, were original Israelite innovations. Unfortunately, no Phoenician royal architecture is known for comparison. Ashlar masonry was a common Phoenician architectural feature in the late Iron Age; it was also common in the succeeding period in Cyprus, Phoenicia, and in the Phoenician Mediterranean colonies.[7] The fact that its earliest known examples are Israelite may be due to the fact that Israelite sites have been more extensively excavated than those in Phoenicia.

The Proto-Aeolic capitals found at Megiddo (thirteen examples, including fragmentary ones), Samaria (seven), Hazor (two), Jerusalem (one), Ramat Rahel (ten), and Medeibiyeh in Moab (several) were comprehensively discussed by Y. Shiloh. He differentiated between those found in the kingdom of Israel from the tenth and ninth centuries B.C.E. and the group

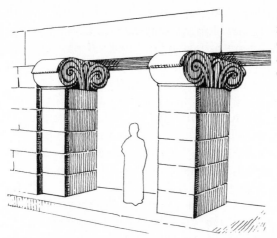

11.8 Hazor: reconstruction of the citadel's gate, built with ashlars and Proto-Aeolic capitals.

of later capitals (eighth and seventh centuries B.C.E.) of almost identical shape found at Jerusalem, Ramat Rahel, and Medeibiyeh. The volutes decorating these capitals are a stylized form of the palmette, one of the best-known motifs in Canaanite and Phoenician art. Representations of similar patterns appear on several Iron Age miniature works of art (ivory, stone, and metal).

Proto-Aeolic capitals have not been discovered in Phoenicia proper, but closely related capitals decorate later Phoenician rock-cut tombs in Cyprus. Y. Shiloh suggested that the stone examples in Israel were a local innovation based on Phoenician wooden prototypes which did not survive. As in the case of ashlar masonry, the lack of evidence from Phoenicia cannot be taken as proof that such stone capitals were not in use there as early as the tenth century B.C.E.

The stone balustrade from Ramat Rahel is practically identical to depictions of window balustrades on Phoenician ivories, indicating a clear connection between ashlar masonry (of which the window from Ramat Rahel is a detail) and Phoenician formal architecture. It can only be conjectured that the palaces of Tyre, Sidon, and Byblos from the tenth century B.C.E. onward were constructed of similar ashlar masonry and had similar windows.

The wide-scale use of ashlar masonry and Proto-Aeolic capitals in Israel and Judah expresses the integration of their regnal dynasties in the general cultural environment of their time. It also illustrates their wealth and efforts to exploit the best available artistic achievements of the time.

Stables and Store Buildings A common Israelite public building was a rectangular, elongated structure divided internally by two rows of stone pillars into a central passage and two flanking aisles. Such units began to appear on the coastal plain during the eleventh century B.C.E. (at Tell Qasile and Tell Abu Hawam), and they became common at Israelite sites from the ninth century B.C.E. onward. At Hazor, one such building was constructed in the ninth century B.C.E. At Megiddo there were seventeen examples grouped in two clusters; at Lachish two buildings stood at the southern side of the royal enclosure; and at both Tell el-Hesi and Tel Beer-sheba three adjoining public edifices of this type were discovered (at Beer-sheba next to the city gate). The dimensions of the structures varied from 16 to 18 m in length and 10 to 12.5 m in width. In each row there were ten to fourteen pillars, usually consisting of solid monoliths with a square section. In most cases, the aisles were paved with cobblestones and the central passage with beaten earth. The buildings are thought to have had a higher roof in their central part with clerestory windows providing light and air for the interior.

The largest group of such public buildings was discovered at Megiddo Stratum IVA (dated to the time of Solomon by the excavators and by Y. Aharoni and Z. Herzog, and to the time of Ahab by J. W. Crowfoot, by Y. Yadin, and in this

11.9 Plans and reconstruction of pillared buildings. From right to left: plans of buildings at Hazor and Megiddo; reconstruction of a pillared building at Beer-sheba.

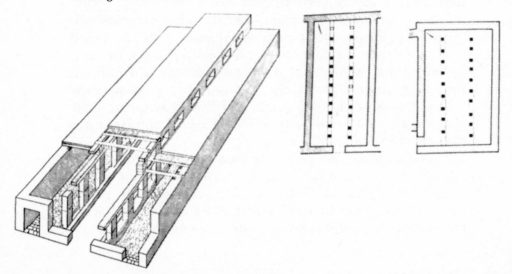

book). Five were located on the southern side of the mound, at the back of a large square courtyard surrounded by a wall. The other twelve were in the northern part of the mound arranged in three groups around a rectangular courtyard. The plan of these buildings—and details such as the stone troughs found between the pillars, holes in the pillars for tying, and the dimensions of the aisles—led to their identification as royal stables. The large fenced courtyard in front of the southern complex was explained as a training area, and large mangers at the courtyard's side could have been the parking place of battle chariots. If this interpretation is correct, the Megiddo stables could have accommodated about 450 horses.

The allocation of precious area inside the fortified city of Megiddo for stables, and the expense involved, are not surprising in light of the great importance of horses at that time. Solomon is said to have erected "cavalry cities" and "chariot cities," and to have fourteen hundred chariots and twelve thousand cavalry men (1 Kings 9:19 and 10:26–29). Ahab is mentioned in the Assyrian description of the battle of Qarqar as having had twelve hundred battle chariots, the largest number among the allied forces in this battle. The valuable battle horses and chariots had to be well maintained in appropriate structures, such as those at Megiddo.

Other pillared buildings of a public nature were explained by their excavators as public storehouses—the biblical *miskenot*—intended for storing grain, oil, and wine (2 Chronicles 32:28). Their existence in such regional administrative centers as Beer-sheba and Hazor is expected, as these cities may have been responsible for the collection and redistribution of agricultural products, and for storing the supplies for army units in the region.

The function of these rectangular pillared buildings, however, has been a matter of controversy. J. B. Pritchard, followed by Y. Aharoni and Z. Herzog, suggested that the Megiddo buildings were royal store buildings. This view was strongly opposed by Y. Yadin and J. S. Holladay; Holladay even suggested that all pillared buildings of this type should be identified as stables.[8] In our view, there is no reason to deny the identification of the Megiddo structures as stables, and at the same time we can accept the association of similar buildings elsewhere with storehouses. The same architectural

11.10   Beer-sheba: looking east at store buildings of Stratum II.

form could have had different functions, dictated by local needs.

In addition to the pillared buildings, public storage space was also allocated in casemates of citadels and royal enclosures, or in specially designed elongated storage rooms such as those discovered at Hazor, Samaria, Jerusalem (the Ophel site), and Lachish. The biblical terms *otsarot* and *miskenot*, which appear aside *urvot* (stables) in the description of Hezekiah's wealth (2 Chronicles 32:27–28), may refer to such royal storage spaces.

Water Supply Projects   The water supply projects in Israelite cities are one of the most impressive achievements of the period. They are evidence of great skill in engineering and practical hydro-geology as well as of astute ability in organizing large labor gangs for public works. Such projects have been found throughout the country: at Hazor, Megiddo, Yoqneam, Yibleʿam, Tell es-Saʿidiyeh, Gezer, Gibeon, Jerusalem, Beer-sheba, Arad, and Kadesh-Barnea.[9] In two cases we find more than one system in the same city: at Gibeon two projects were constructed, one replacing the other, while at

478

Jerusalem three waterworks were found, all related to the Gihon Spring.

The water projects may be divided into several types according to the principles of their planning. The first type consists of underground shafts and tunnels leading to a known spring located outside the town. Such were the projects at Megiddo, Yible'am, Gibeon (the stepped tunnel), and the "Warren Shaft" in Jerusalem. The details of planning vary in each of these sites according to the local conditions.

At Megiddo, during the time of the United Monarchy (Stratum IVB–VA), a passage constructed of ashlars allowed access to the slope of the mound, where a path led down to the outside spring. Later, most probably during the time of Ahab (Stratum IVA), a large underground passage leading to the spring from inside the city was hewn.[10] The upper part of the system cut through earlier occupation debris and was

11.11   Megiddo: Plan and section through the water supply system, Stratum IVA: (1) city wall; (2) and (3) retaining walls; (4) vertical shaft; (5) rock-cut diagonal staircase, canceled in later phase; (6) horizontal tunnel; (7) deepening of vertical shaft in later stage; (8) original steps leading to the spring prior to the construction of the water supply system; (9) the spring.

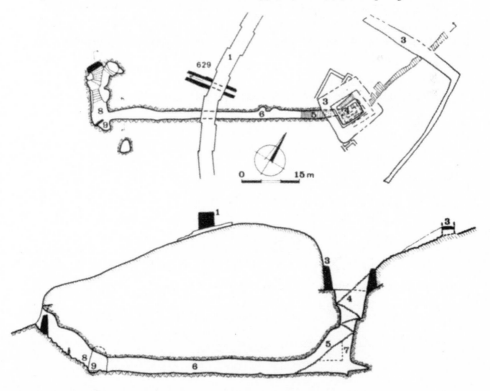

supported by retaining walls. When bedrock was reached, a vertical shaft was cut; inside the shaft, spiral stairs led to a steep diagonal flight of steps, ending in a horizontally hewn tunnel which provided access to the spring. Initially, one had to descend the steps to reach the fountain; in a later phase, the diagonal flight of steps was cut away, and the rock-hewn shaft was extended to become a 16-m-deep vertical shaft reaching the level of the horizontal tunnel. The latter, 50 m long, was elongated and deepened to enable the water to flow to its inner end, at the bottom of the shaft. Thus the shaft became a kind of well, from which water could be brought into the city by aid of pulley, ropes, and leather containers. Such a pulley is pictured in an Assyrian relief of an unknown city in Syria or Palestine.[11]

The "Warren Shaft" in Jerusalem (named after Ch. Warren, the great nineteenth-century explorer of Jerusalem, who discovered it in 1867) was similar to the Megiddo system, but here the engineers made use of a karstic vertical fissure in the bedrock. They reached the top of this natural shaft by hewing—into the steep slope of the hill—a bending, steep underground passage starting from inside the city wall. A lower horizontal tunnel led the water of the Gihon fountain to the bottom of the shaft. Water could then be raised by rope and containers, as at Megiddo. The "Warren Shaft" should probably be dated to the period of the Divided Monarchy—

11.12 Jerusalem; section through the "Warren Shaft." (1) Gihon spring; (2) horizontal tunnel of "Warren Shaft"; (3) beginning of Hezekiah's tunnel; (4) vertical shaft (natural); (5) diagonal tunnel; (6) city wall; (7) natural cavity.

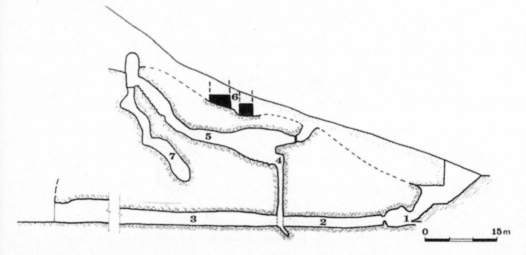

sometime before the time of Hezekiah, who made use of the lower horizontal gallery to begin his own tunnel (see p. 483).[12]

Simpler approaches to springs outside the city were constructed at Gibeon and Yibleʿam, where stepped underground tunnels led from inside the city along the slope of the hill directly to the spring. A similar method was employed at Tell es-Saʿidiyeh, but here the passage was a built-up roofed stairway of about 140 steps, constructed on the slope of the mound. The Gibeon system included an additional, unique feature: a feeder tunnel was cut from the spring into the subterranean water-bearing stratum (the aquifer) to increase the water flow. This is the only known Iron Age example of such a feeder tunnel, which is well known in the Judean Hills in later periods.[13]

Such high-level knowledge of practical geology and hydrology is also apparent in the second type of Iron Age water projects, known from Hazor, Gibeon (the so-called "pool"), and perhaps also Gezer. This type consisted of a deep shaft and tunnel hewn inside the city to the depth of the water level. The most imposing example is the water-system at Hazor. The total depth of this system is 40 m. It consists of three parts: an entrance structure with descending ramps; a vertical square shaft, some 13 × 16 m in size and about 19 m deep, with a wide, sloping stepped tunnel, 25 m long and 11 m deep, ending in an underground water room. The spiral steps hewn into the sides of the shaft were wide and shallow to enable descent by pack animals. The Hazor system, dated to the ninth century B.C.E., was probably the work of King Ahab, who carried out the extensive rebuilding of this city.[14]

The second water system at Gibeon starts with a great circular shaft, 11.3 m in diameter, cut into the bedrock with spiral steps. At a depth of 10.8 m, it ends in a spiral-stepped tunnel descending a further 13.6 m to the subterranean water level. This system was probably constructed later than the nearby stepped tunnel, which led directly to the spring.[15]

The Gezer water project probably followed a principle similar to that at Hazor and Gibeon. The sloping tunnel here was some 41 m long and was approached from a 7-m-deep shaft. The system terminated in an enormous, 38-m-long underground cavity, but the bottom of the latter was not reached by the excavators. We presume that it was an underground vertical shaft leading to water level. The water project

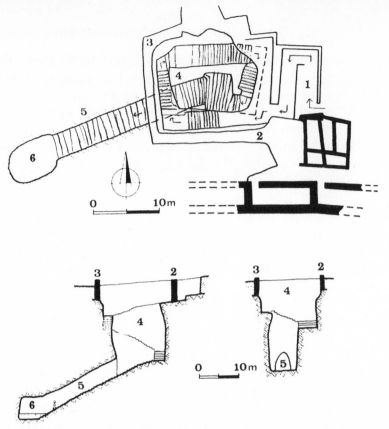

11.13 Hazor: plan and section of the water supply system (1) descending ramp; (2) and (3) retaining walls; (4) vertical shaft; (5) sloping tunnel; (6) underground water room.

11.14 Hazor: view of the vertical shaft in the water supply system.

at Tel Beer-sheba was probably also planned according to the same idea. A large, square shaft with wide spiral steps was hewn at the corner of the town in order to reach the water level 25 m below, near Beer-sheba Brook.

The ability to solve water supply problems is demonstrated also at the Israelite fortresses of Arad and Kadesh-Barnea. At Arad, a large circular stone-lined well was constructed at the bottom of the hill on which the citadel stood. Water was transported by pack animals and poured into cisterns inside the citadel by way of a feeder canal.[16] At Kadesh-Barnea, a similar arrangement was found, but here the water originated at the spring of Ain el-Qudeirat and was conducted by an open aqueduct through an opening in the citadel's wall to a large built-up cistern. This aqueduct is among the earliest examples known.

In addition to the one at Arad, deep stone-lined wells are known also from Lachish and Tel Beer-sheba. The well at the latter is located on the eastern slope of the mound, where remains of Iron Age I houses were revealed. Influenced by B. Mazar's theory concerning the possible Iron Age I background of the patriarchal stories, Y. Aharoni suggested identifying this well with that mentioned in the patriarchal narratives (Genesis 21:22–33). However, the date of the well cannot be clearly determined.[17]

Two other water projects in Jerusalem related to the Gihon Spring are the Siloam canal and Hezekiah's Tunnel (known erroneously as the "Siloam Tunnel"). The first is an aqueduct-canal along the outside slope of the City of David, conducting Gihon's water into a large reservoir at the lowest part of the Tyropoeon Valley; openings in the canal allowed irrigation of fields along the Kidron. The canal may be identified with the "Shiloah" mentioned by Isaiah during the reign of King Ahaz (Isaiah 8:6).

Hezekiah's Tunnel is the most fascinating and daring of all the Israelite water supply projects. It led all the water of the Gihon Spring through an underground tunnel to the Tyropoeon, on the other side of the hill of the City of David. At this time the Tyropoeon was already included inside the fortified city. The tunnel is referred to in the biblical narrative as one of Hezekiah's major achievements; it is said to have brought water "into the city," namely into the newly fortified area, west of the City of David (2 Kings 20:20; 2 Chronicles

32:3–4). The tunnel was discovered by E. Robinson in 1838 and later explored by Ch. Warren and Père H. Vincent.[18] It runs under the ridge of the City of David in extraordinary S-shaped curves. The hewing was carried out by two groups of laborers working from opposite ends until they met at a point which is easily discerned. Inaccuracy in direction close to the meeting point was possibly a result of the confusing sound of voices. Unlike most later water tunnels (in the Hellenistic and Roman periods), the almost 600 m long Hezekiah's Tunnel was cut without vertical shafts, making the work exceedingly difficult due to air and light deficiency and the distance from the outlet through which the hewn rock chips were removed. The dramatic moment in which the two groups met was perpetuated in the Siloam inscription, incised on the tunnel's wall close to its end. Written in a poetic style, it is one of the longest and most important monumental Hebrew texts from the period of the Monarchy. It reads as follows:

> ... and this was the matter of the tunnel: While [the hewers wielded] the axe(s), each man towards his fellow, and while there were still three cubits to be he[wn, there was hear]d a man's voice calling to his fellow; for there was a fissure (?) in the rock on the right and [on the left]. And on the day it was tunneled through, the hewers struck [the rock], each man towards his fellow, axe against axe. And the water flowed from the spring towards the pool for one thousand and two hundred cubits. And a hundred cubits was the height of the rock above the head(s) of the hewers.[19]

The factor which brought about the successful underground meeting of the two groups of workers was described in the inscription as *zdh*, a word unknown from other texts. We assume that it denotes a fissure in the rock followed by the cutters.

Hezekiah's Tunnel most probably filled a water reservoir in the Tyropoeon Valley, perhaps the one "between the two walls" mentioned by Isaiah (22:11). The overflow ran through a continuation of the tunnel and a canal (partly utilizing in reverse direction the older Siloam canal) back to the Kidron Valley south of the City of David. The total length of the project, including the overflow part, was 643 m, or almost

1,200 cubits; the latter measurement was noted as the tunnel's length in the Siloam inscription (calculated according to the long cubit of 52.5 cm, see map on p. 418).

The Iron Age water projects were, so far as we know, original Israelite innovations, unparalleled in contemporary neighboring countries. Simpler water shafts and tunnels are known in Mycenaean Greece and in Iron Age Anatolia (at Urartu and Phrygia), yet these do not seem to have any direct connection with or influence on the Israelite projects. The latter, therefore, are an extraordinary achievement of local engineers who were well acquainted with hydrological conditions, and who were capable of carrying out outstanding technical projects requiring skill, sagacity, and organization of manpower.

Dwellings The prevailing type of dwelling used by the Israelites during the period of the Monarchy was the pillared house, which was common already in Iron Age I (see p. 340).[20] This general term describes structures of various sizes and plans divided by one or two rows of pillars into several rectangular units. The pillars were usually monolithic stones with a square section and were 1–1.5 m in height. Where suitable rock was unavailable (as in the northern Negev), the pillars were made of several stones. Stone lintels preserved in several cases show that the passageways between the pillars were low, suitable for domestic animals such as sheep and goats. The area behind the pillars was usually paved with cobblestones. Rooms at the side of the central unit or at its rear were usually elongated, rectangular spaces. The existence of a second story can be deduced from stone steps preserved in several cases as well as from the massiveness of the stone pillars on the ground floor. Where stone steps did not exist, access to the second floor could be gained by a wooden ladder. In the Bible, a second story of a dwelling is denoted *aliyah* (2 Kings 4:10).

The central unit of these houses is usually interpreted as an open courtyard, and the pillars are thought to have supported a roofed area alongside the courtyard serving the household animals. An alternative interpretation (by E. Netzer) is that the entire house was roofed on the ground floor; this floor was used only for storage, domestic workshops, and livestock, the living quarters being on the second story, where

11.15   A "four-room house" at Hazor. Monolithic pillars divide the court-yard.

there was a central unroofed space. Such a reconstruction, however, would leave the ground floor without sufficient light and air.

The area of such houses varied between 50 and 110 sq m; their size, plan, and quality of construction were determined by the social status of the owner and the space available for construction. The most advanced form was the so-called four-room house (see pp. 341, 344). This was a rectangular building with average dimensions of 10×12 m. The entrance usually led directly into a rectangular courtyard flanked by various spaces on three of its sides. One of the spaces along the courtyard was usually a pillared roofed area. There were many variations to this plan: pillars were sometimes found on both sides of the courtyard; in other cases, no pillars at all were used. "Four-room houses" were built for the first time in the eleventh century B.C.E. at sites such as Tel Masos, ʿIzbet Sartah, and Tell Qasile (see p. 319). During the tenth century B.C.E. they were common at Tell el-Farʿah (north), Tell Qasile,

11.16   A dwelling at Hazor, showing stone steps leading to second floor.

and the central Negev sites. During the time of the Divided
Monarchy they were known mainly in the northern kingdom
of Israel (Hazor, Tell el-Far'ah, Shechem), while in Judah they
appear on rare occasions (such as three houses at Tell en-
Nasbeh). At Hazor, Shechem, and Tell en-Nasbeh, the houses
of this type appear to have belonged to high officials, rich
families, or landlords, as they are the largest and most elaborate
buildings in the town. Several "four-room houses" uncovered
at small country sites (near Jerusalem, in the Samarian Hills,
and inside the isolated enclosure south of Jericho) were perhaps
homes of landlords constructed close to their land plots.

Tell el-Far'ah (Tirzah) is the only Israelite town where the
"four-room" plan determined the standard for all the houses
in several occupation levels. In the tenth century B.C.E.
(Stratum VIIb, see p. 466), the structures there were of almost
identical size and plan, while in the ninth and eighth centuries
they varied in area, perhaps reflecting increasing social differentiation.

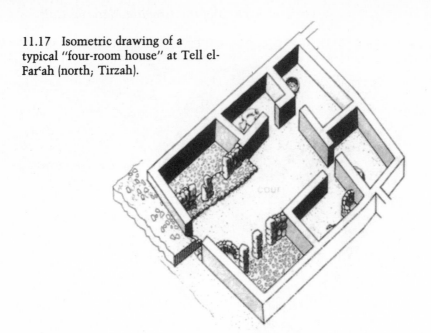

11.17 Isometric drawing of a typical "four-room house" at Tell el-Farʿah (north; Tirzah).

Most of the less elaborate houses in the Israelite cities appear to be smaller or diminished versions of this ideal plan. They include a courtyard unit divided by pillars with one or two rooms at its rear. In several cases, such as at Beer-sheba and Tell Beit Mirsim, the back room was part of a casemate wall surrounding the town. The rectangular form of the houses was retained whenever possible, but in a number of towns agglutinative development necessitated an irregularity. A front room, which in several cases separated the courtyard from a street, may have served as a shop or workshop.

The house courtyard was utilized for conducting various household duties. Baking ovens made of clay were often located here (or they were outside the house, in an open area or special small chamber). Cereals were ground in the courtyard on grinding stones usually made of basalt or other hard stone. Stone or plastered vats with attached working surfaces may have functioned as simple wine presses; clay weights were used in wooden looms; olive presses of specific forms are also often found (see later); and other built-in installations represent specific activities.

Rock-cut cisterns have been found only at places where the rock was suitable for cutting and easily accessible, such as Tell en-Nasbeh. In general, however, the daily water supply was based on nearby springs, wells, or public water projects. Two of the houses excavated in Jerusalem contained sanitation devices, probably lavatories. These devices, however, are unparalleled elsewhere. Small clay models depict furniture such as chairs, beds, and tables (compare 2 Kings 4:10).

The number of people who lived in each unit is mere estimate. It can be assumed that the average dwelling housed a "nuclear family" of five to seven persons. Larger houses perhaps served extended families of up to three generations, numbering approximately ten or eleven people in all. The amount of pottery vessels found in a house provides some indication of the number of its occupants. Houses at Timnah (Tel Batash) contained an astonishingly large quantity of pottery vessels. In one rather small dwelling, comprising a courtyard and two square rooms, there were thirty bowls, eight kraters, eleven cooking pots, fourteen storage jars, twelve jugs, eight dipper juglets, and several other vessels, so the number of tenants in this unit must have been relatively high.

Industrial Installations Several types of industrial installations are known in the Israelite culture. All of them were small, household workshops for processing agricultural products: oil and wine presses, looms and spindles, and installations of an unknown nature.

The olive oil industry is perhaps the best known. Special installations were devised to extract the oil by crushing the olives and then pressing them. The details differed from region to region. In the north the common oil press consisted of a circular flat stone with a groove along its perimeter. After the olives were crushed in special basins or on rocks, they were put in baskets on top of the round stone; weights then pressed the contents of the baskets, and the oil would seep through the groove into special containers.

A more sophisticated type of olive press was found in the Judean and Philistine Shephelah and at small farms on the western slopes of the mountains of Ephraim.[21] Here the olives were crushed inside stone basins, and beam presses with heavy stone weights then pressed straw baskets containing the crushed olives which were piled on specially designed cylindrical stone press-vats. The olive oil poured into these vats. Similar installations at Tel Beit Mirsim were thought

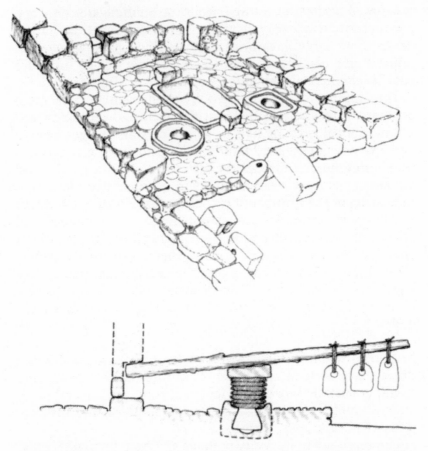

11.18   Oil press at Tel Batash (Timnah). The installation includes a crushing vat and two pressing vats. The section shows reconstruction of the beam press at work.

by W. F. Albright to be dyeing vats, yet they can now be interpreted as oil presses typical of the entire region. At the independent city-state of Ekron, and at nearby Timnah, this industry was exceptionally advanced in the seventh century B.C.E. At Ekron over one hundred such oil presses, each containing two sets of beams and pressing vats, were discovered in surface surveys, and at Timnah similar oil presses were found in two of the five houses excavated. At all of these sites, the oil presses are found inside ordinary houses, indicating that the manufacture of olive oil was a cottage industry practiced by families at their homes. The number of presses, however, surpassed the number required for local consumption, and thus it appears that the seventh century B.C.E. oil industry in this region was a major economic enterprise, most probably involved in export.

Wine production is known in particular from the winery excavated at Gibeon.[22] According to Pritchard, it contained surfaces for treading on the grapes, settling basins, and fermentation tanks, all cut in the rock. Sixty-three rock-hewn bell-shaped cisterns are explained as cellars in which the wine was stored in jars. Pritchard calculated the capacity of these cellars at twenty-five thousand gallons. Their interpretation as wine cellars rather than water cisterns is essentially based on their concentration in a small place, and on the discovery of handles of a particular jar type inscribed with the name of the city Gibeon followed by the title *gdr* and one of six personal names, probably well-known wine manufacturers of the time.

This large-scale wine and oil production exemplifies the sophistication of specialized agricultural industry in Judah and in the city-state of Ekron. The products were most probably supplied to the large population in Jerusalem and other parts of Judah; parts of it were perhaps exported to markets outside of the region.

Other specific home industry installations have been found, but their function is difficult to explain. We have mentioned the possible perfume industry found at En Gedi. A specific type of installation found at Ekron and Timnah is composed of two stone vats: a deep one and a flat one, the latter located at the entrance to the house with drainage into the street. These may have been related to flax or leather manufacture, but their exact operation remains uncertain.

Textile weaving from sheep wool and from flax was a common home industry. Stone and bone spindle whorls and clay loom weights are frequently discovered in Iron Age houses. They were used with warp-weighted looms, common throughout the ancient Near East and Greece.[23] Textiles found at Kuntillet ʿAjrud give some idea of the technical aspects of weaving. Some of them were found painted in red and blue, and several pieces from this site combine wool and linen, which was in conflict with the Torah law of *shaatnez*.

The important industries of metallurgy and pottery making will be discussed later.

ISRAELITE CULT:
TEMPLES, ALTARS, AND ARTIFACTS

Israelite religious practices are detailed in various biblical narratives such as the Book of Leviticus, the biblical descriptions of the Jerusalem temple, and the various prophecies against foreign cults. Further knowledge of the realia of the Israelite cult has been provided by a variety of archaeological finds, some of which were discussed in previous chapters (the Iron Age I cultic sites in Chapter Eight; the reconstruction of the Solomonic temple in Chaper Nine; and Kuntillet 'Ajrud in Chapter Ten). In the present section, discoveries relating to the Israelite cult during the time of the Divided Monarchy are discussed. These discoveries include the royal cult center at Dan, the temple in the fortress of Arad, the sacrificial altar at Beer-sheba, and various other altars, religious installations, and artifacts.[24]

Dan After the division of the kingdom, Jeroboam I erected two religious centers on the borders of his kingdom, at Bethel and at Dan (1 Kings 12:26–33). His purpose was to undermine the monopoly of the ritual center at Jerusalem founded by David and Solomon just half a century before. He also introduced the golden calf into his temples as a cult symbol; it probably was a statue of a young bull (compare the one found at the "Bull Site," p. 351). The bull was possibly considered to be the pedestal for the unseen God of Israel, like the cherubim in the Jerusalem temple.

The ritual center at Dan, uncovered at the northern edge of the mound near the spring, is the only structure mentioned in the Bible that has been positively identified in archaeological excavations.[25] It lay above earlier cultic remains from the eleventh and tenth centuries B.C.E.—remains which may be identified as the shrine erected by the Danites after their migration here (Judges 18). The sanctuary erected by Jeroboam and maintained by his successors is a unique example of an Iron Age temenos: a sacred enclosure intended for formal royal cult practices. It comprised three parts: a podium for a temple structure, a square open area where the main sacrificial altar was located, and side chambers used for ritual, minor sacrifice, and administration.

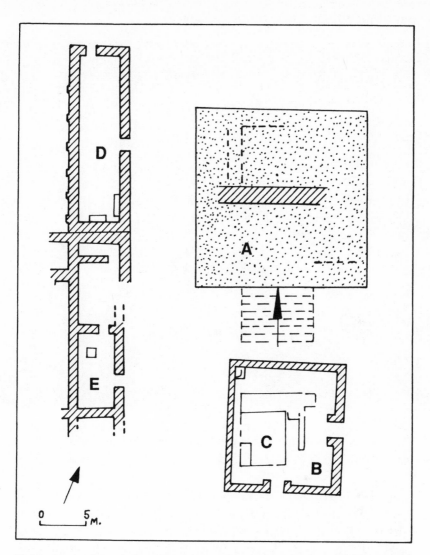

11.19 Dan: plan of the sacred area: (A) podium for a temple or "high place"; (B) square enclosure; (C) sacrificial altar; (D) hall; (E) altar room.

The first phase of this sacred enclosure is only partly known. The podium was an imposing structure, with a 19-m-long facade of large ashlars. A. Biran first explained the podium as an open-air platform, a *bamah* ("high place"), but later he changed his mind and concluded that the podium, recalling in function the palace's podium at Lachish, served as a foundation for a temple. A rectangular sacrificial altar 5 × 6 m in size, built of ashlars, stood to the south of the podium in

11.20   Dan: general view of the podium in the sacred enclosure.

an open courtyard. Two large pottery pithoi found nearby, on which a snakelike decoration was applied, probably contained libation liquids. Farther south, there was a small plastered pool whose water, derived from the nearby spring of Dan, must have been used in the ritual. Another installation was explained by the excavator as related to water libation ceremonies, while others interpret it as an oil press from which first-quality olive oil was produced for the religious ceremonies.[26] This first sacred enclosure was severely burnt in a violent conquest—perhaps during the invasion of Ben-Hadad I, king of Aramean Damascus, in 883 B.C.E.

Later during the ninth century B.C.E., perhaps in the reign of Ahab, the sacred enclosure at Dan was rebuilt on a larger scale. The temple's podium, built of ashlars, was repaired and enlarged, measuring 19 × 19 m; ashlar steps led to it from the south. The altar to the south of the podium was now approached by a flight of steps and surrounded by a square enclosure (12.5 × 14 m) which was fenced by an ashlar wall. Of the altar itself, only a fragment of a corner horn was preserved, but this permits the reconstruction of a large ashlar altar with four horns, similar in shape to but larger than the altar discovered at Beer-sheba (see p. 496). A smaller horned altar, made of a single stone, stood at the corner of the enclosure. A well-paved courtyard surrounded the podium and the altar. On the west side of the temenos, several elongated rooms arranged in a row had various functions related to the cult practices. One was probably an assembly room; it was a long rectangular hall and had a pedestal at one of its narrow walls. Another room contained the square foundation of an altar, and three iron shovels.

The ritual complex at Dan is the only actual example of an Israelite royal ritual center. Its architectural components are similar to those employed in the royal palaces of the kingdom—such as the ashlar masonry, the locating of monumental structures in large, paved open courtyards, and the raising of important buildings above their surroundings by erecting podiums.

Dan was destroyed in the Assyrian conquest of the Galilee in 732 B.C.E., but the sanctity of the site was remembered for centuries. During the Hellenistic period the enclosure was rebuilt and used again. A bilingual Greek-Aramaic inscription found there is a dedication "to the God who is in Dan."

Beer-sheba The prophet Amos refers to the sanctuaries at Dan and Beer-sheba in the same context (Amos 8:14); he further mentions Beer-sheba together with Gilgal and Bethel as places of worship (Amos 5:5), and a "high place" at Beer-sheba is said to have been destroyed by Josiah (2 Kings 23:8).

A large ashlar altar with horn-shaped cornerstones was discovered at Tel Beer-sheba.[27] It was found dismantled, its stones used as building materials for the storehouses of Stratum II. This latter level was destroyed in a heavy conflagration in the late eighth or early seventh centuries B.C.E. Consequently, the altar must have been in use earlier, during the ninth and eighth centuries B.C.E., and could well have been known to Amos. Perhaps its demolishment can be associated with Hezekiah's religious reform (2 Kings 18:3–4, 22). Its original location in the town of Beer-sheba is unknown,

11.21   Beer-sheba: sacrificial altar built of ashlars, with corner horns.

in spite of several suggestions.[28] Perhaps it stood in an open-air sanctuary, or in the courtyard of a temple which was not preserved. The construction of the Israelite altars at Dan and Beer-sheba from ashlar should be noted, as it is contrary to the biblical law which demands that their construction be of uncut stones (Exodus 20:25–26; Deuteronomy 27:5–6).

Arad   The fortress of Arad contained a small temple, the only known provincial shrine in Judah.[29] It was erected on the site of an earlier open cult place belonging to a tenth century B.C.E. village (Stratum XII); this village may have been related to the settlement of Kenite families at Arad (Judges 1:16). Thus the sanctity of the place was retained for hundreds of years. A temple in a royal fortress probably did not contradict the official policy of the Judean authorities, in spite of the rejection of such sanctuaries by the Jerusalem prophets. Y. Aharoni suggested that the Arad temple was one in a series of Judean "border temples," erected along the border of the kingdom, like the temples at Dan and Bethel in the kingdom of Israel. The temple probably served the garrison of the fortress and perhaps also the population of the region around Arad.

The temple comprised a large courtyard, a broad room, and a Holy of Holies in the form of a raised niche at the western end of the structure. A sacrificial altar in the courtyard was built of fieldstones and measured 2.5 × 2.5 m (about 5 × 5

496

11.22   Arad: model of the temple.

cubits), complying, in both building technique and dimension, to the biblical law (Exodus 20:24–25). Placed inside the niche, against its rear wall, were two standing stones (*massebot*); one, painted red, was larger than the other. At the entrance to the Holy of Holies, there were two monolithic stone altars of different dimensions, each standing opposite the *massebah* of comparable size. We have seen that the ninth century B.C.E. inscriptions from Kuntillet ʿAjrud mention Yahweh and his consort, Asherah (see p. 448). Such a theology, completely deleted from our Masoretic Bible, is now also reported in an inscription from Khirbet el-Kom in the Shephelah.[30] May we assume that the finds at Arad reflect a similar theology? If so, the larger standing stone would symbolize the God of Israel and the smaller one his consort, Asherah. The two altars would have been used to sacrifice animal fat, birds, or incense. Names such as "Pashhur" and "Meremoth" written in ink on potsherds found near the temple are of special interest, since these are names of priestly families known in Jerusalem during the time of Jeremiah and Ezra (Jeremiah 20:1; Ezra 8:33).

According to Aharoni, the temple at Arad was founded in

the tenth century B.C.E. (Stratum XI) and continued in use, undergoing various renovations, until the time of Josiah. The sacrificial altar in the courtyard became obsolete in Stratum VIII, perhaps as a result of the religious reform of Hezekiah, a reform evidenced also at Beer-sheba. In the last Iron Age level (Stratum VI), the use of the temple was deliberately terminated, as evidenced by the fact that the small altars in the Holy of Holies were found lying on their sides covered by plaster. The cancellation of the temple before the final destruction of the fortress may be attributed to the religious reform of Josiah (2 Kings 23).[31]

Hurvat Qitmit   Another cult place, probably non-Israelite, was discovered at Hurvat Qitmit, a remote hill a few kilometers southeast of Arad.[32] It was erected during the late seventh or early sixth century B.C.E. as an isolated structure, unrelated to any settlement. Its cultic focus was a three-celled building opening onto a courtyard at the south, where ritual installations such as water basins and a simple altar were located. The three chambers were most probably a triple Holy of Holies used for the worship of three deities. Triads of deities as well as triple shrines are known from later religious practices in our region, such as at some Nabatean temples. The temple at Qitmit provides one of the earliest examples of this practice.

A variety of artifacts of cultic nature found in the courtyard of the Hurvat Qitmit structure included unique ceramic art objects, completely foreign to the artistic tradition of Judah. They include stands with human faces, fragments of complex pottery sculptures, and ritual objects decorated with motifs such as human faces, animals, sphinxes, pomegranates, and a model clay sword. A horned god (or goddess?) head sculptured in the round is an outstanding piece of art.

The pottery uncovered at this site is a combination of local Judean and Edomite forms. Short inscriptions found incised on pottery sherds mention Qaus, the chief Edomite god. These finds led the excavator, I. Beit-Arieh, to identify Hurvat Qitmit as an Edomite sanctuary. Why and how an Edomite temple was established inside the territory of Judah is a matter of conjecture. One possibility is that it was erected by Edomites just after the destruction of Judah (in 586 B.C.E.) in relation to the beginning of Edomite penetration into the southern part

11.23 Hurvat Qitmit: sculptured pottery head, representing a horned god or goddess (late seventh or early sixth century B.C.E.).

of Judah—penetration which culminated in the establishment of the province Idumea during the period of Jerusalem's second temple. Alternatively, this Edomite temple may be associated with Edomite mercantile activity in the territory of Judah in the seventh century B.C.E. Edomites leading trade caravans to the Mediterranean coast may have been permitted to establish a cult place on their route in a region which was under Judean control. The latter possibility may be supported by the Edomite finds, including a letter and seals, discovered at pre-586 B.C.E. contexts at Hurvat Uza and 'Aroer (see p. 444).[33]

Other Cult Installations   Rooms used for cultic practices are found in several Israelite sites. At Megiddo, a cult place was found in a large residential building in the Solomonic level (Stratum IVB–VA) close to the city gate; at Lachish (Stratum V) a separate room with benches along its walls may have served as a small shrine;[34] at Taanach and Tel Amal, cultic installations were found in what appear to have been domestic buildings. All these examples are dated to the time of the

United Monarchy. The finds at Lachish and Megiddo consist of similar assemblages, which include monolithic horned altars, pottery cylindrical stands bearing offering bowls, chalices used to serve offerings, and additional pottery vessels used in religious ceremonies. Similar monolithic stone altars, mostly with four corner horns, are common throughout Iron Age II in Israelite dwellings as well as in sanctuaries (Dan, Arad, Megiddo, Lachish, Tel Qedesh). Such altars were also prevalent in the city-state of Ekron, where they were discovered adjacent to oil presses and may have served a local cult related to the oil industry during the seventh century B.C.E. At Timnah, a cult corner was found in the piazza of a dwelling quarter of the seventh century B.C.E. It consisted of a raised brick platform; chalices and fragmentary ritual vessels indicate its function.

Evidence of religious practices near the city gates was found at Tirzah, where a *massebah* and a large stone trough were located in the piazza inside the gate. The decorated canopy base found at the gate of Dan (see p. 469) can be explained either as a cult corner or as the base of a throne of a dignitary.

Israelite open cult places outside towns are often mentioned in the Bible but are rarely detected archaeologically. We have seen evidence of them in the period of the Judges (see p. 350). One possible example of such a place from the period of the Monarchy was found outside Samaria. It includes a rock-cut

11.24 Horned altar used in tenth-century cult corner at Megiddo.

trapezoidal ditch, approximately 3.5 m deep and 4–6 m wide, surrounding an inner flat area 26 × 30 m in size which was approached from "bridges" in the ditch. The unusual shape and location of this installation and the finds in it call for its identification as a "high place."

A group of about thirty huge stone piles known by their Arabic name, *rujum*, is located on hilltops west of Jerusalem. Small-scale excavations at two of the *rujums* revealed remains of rounded structures of the late Iron Age. It was suggested (by R. Amiran) that these structures were cultic "high places" used for ritual on the hills west of Jerusalem; this is a tempting suggestion, though no definite proof for this function was found. The high stone piles artificially heaped on the round structures may be the signs of desecration during the rule of Josiah.

Clay Figurines Pottery clay figurines were prominent in daily Israelite religious practice. They depict a goddess of fertility, Ashtoret, worshiped probably by women. Stylistically, the statuettes from Israel differ from those of Judah. The female figure from Israel is portrayed naturalistically,

11.25 Pottery "pillar figurines" from Judah, most probably depicting fertility goddesses. The figurine in the center was found in the Jewish Quarter of Jerusalem.

possibly due to Phoenician artistic influence. She appears naked; her hands hold her breasts or a circular object (a tambourine?) or are stretched out alongside the body. In Judah, a particular type known as the "pillar figurine" was common. Its lower part looks like a solid pillar, while the upper torso and head are of a naked female usually supporting her breasts with her hands. The face, made in a mold, is generally detailed with care, but it is sometimes rendered schematically, resembling a bird's head. Such figurines are found in large numbers in Judean sites—particularly in Jerusalem, from where the finest examples come—dating mostly to the eighth and seventh centuries B.C.E.[35]

Cult Stands Several pottery stands from the tenth century B.C.E. found at Megiddo and Taanach are an important source for the iconography of the period. They are designed in the shape of tall buildings and are richly decorated with a variety of applied figures, including female sphinxes, lions, "the tree of life," the winged sun disc, and a calf(?). The rich iconography of a stand from Taanach (p. 380) may be related (according to R. Hestrin) to the cult of Asherah.[36] The motifs are all known from Late Bronze Age Canaanite art, and they appear in modified fashion on later Phoenician ivories. Their existence in this context demonstrates the strength of the Canaanite heritage—particularly in the region of the valley of Jezreel during the United Monarchy.

ART IN ISRAEL AND JUDAH

There are very few classes of art objects which can be considered genuine Israelite works. Whereas in northern Syria monumental sculpture and wall reliefs were common in Iron Age public buildings, the almost only evidence of such art discovered in Israel are the Proto-Aeolic capitals and carved window balustrades which are part of the ashlar masonry tradition (discussed on pp. 471–75). Few works of sculpture are a limestone statue of a crouching lion from Tell Beit Mirsim and two reliefs of lions' heads found in a burial cave at Tel Eitun (both in the Shephelah of Judah). These works are poorly executed and may be considered provincial art, a faint echo of the elaborate stone sculpture known in Syria during the Iron Age.

The only other original Israelite artworks were all minia-tures: seal engravings, pottery figurines, cult stands decorated in relief, and some paintings on pottery (from Kuntillet ʿAjrud; see p. 447). Other artifacts were imported from Phoenician and Aramean production centers; they included carved ivories, stone cosmetic bowls, metal bowls, and engraved tridacna shells. Here we will confine our discussion to ivories and seal engravings.

The Samaria Ivories   The main group of ivories from Israel, including over two hundred pieces, was discovered in the royal acropolis at Samaria.[37] The majority were uncovered in a building which may be identified with the "ivory building" erected by Ahab (1 Kings 22:39). The Samaria pieces belong to the Phoenician ivory-carving school, known from such sites as Salamis in Cyprus, Arslan Tash in Syria, and Nimrud

11.26   The Samaria ivories: a plaque depicting a sphinx and lotus flowers.

11.27 The Samaria ivories: a lion attacking a bull.

11.28 The Samaria ivories: palmettes decorating an ivory plaque.

504

in Assyria, where elaborate works of this school were brought as booty.[38]

Most of the ivories were small plaques intended to decorate furniture, such as the "ivory beds" mentioned by Amos (6:4). Practically all the techniques of Phoenician ivory carving are represented. Plaques carved in low relief were ornamented with inlays of polychrome glass, paste, gold foil, and lapis lazuli (a precious blue stone imported from Afghanistan). In several cases, these different materials were separated from one another by narrow partitions, a technique known as "cloisonné." The majority of the motifs in this group are Egyptian, including gods and mythological scenes. There are also plaques made in high relief, others made in openwork (ajour), and still others sculptured in the round. The themes featured in the last two types include stylized plants (such as the palmette, the voluted "tree of life," and rosettes), a sphinx (perhaps the biblical cherub), a lion attacking a bull, a cow nursing a calf, two antithetical lions, and the "woman in the window" (a woman's head in a window, with a balustrade similar to that found in the palace of Ramat Rahel).

The Samaria ivories must have been produced during the ninth and eighth centuries B.C.E.; a more exact date cannot be determined, although various suggestions have been made. It is tempting to think that they were brought to Samaria from Phoenicia during the time of Ahab and his wife, the Tyrian princess Jezebel, who introduced Phoenician cult practices to the Israelite capital. If this was the case, most of the ivories should be dated to the first half of the ninth century B.C.E. Indeed, excellent examples of Phoenician ivories from this time are known from the palace of Shalmaneser III at Nimrud, and an ivory from Arslan Tash was inscribed with the name of Hazael, king of Aram in the late ninth century B.C.E.

No ivories have been discovered in Judah, but their existence may be assumed due to Sennacherib's reference to ivory tribute presented to him by Hezekiah.

The influence of Phoenicia on local Israelite art can also be discerned in the painted motifs on pottery jars from Kuntillet 'Ajrud—motifs imitating those on Phoenician ivories.

Seal Engravings   The art of seal engraving was well developed throughout the Levant in the Iron Age. Phoenician, Hebrew,

11.29   Iron Age seals (from the collection of the Israel Museum).

Ammonite, and Aramean seals were produced with high skill from hard, sometimes semiprecious stones.[39] Many of the seals were decorated, though many others bore only the names of the owner and his father and sometimes the owner's title. Local workshops of seal-cutters probably operated in Samaria and Jerusalem. The engraved Hebrew seals, dated from the

11.30 A seal ring decorated with the Egyptian scarab motif; the ring is inscribed, "Belonging to Shafat."

eighth and seventh centuries B.C.E., are the most important source of our knowledge of art and iconography in Israel and Judah. The themes were inspired mainly by Phoenician art, and thus indirectly from Egyptian traditions, but these foreign symbols were probably employed only as decoration without any religious significance. Original local motifs are also featured.

Among the motifs are various animals (roaring lion, cock, horse, bull, gazelle, cow nursing a calf, monkey, and locust), mythological creatures (griffin, sphinx), and adaptations of Egyptian themes, such as the winged sun disc, the Uraeus snake, and the scarab. Plant patterns include the lotus flower, papyrus, pomegranate, and palmette. Sometimes specific objects are shown, as the lyre. The more complicated scenes depict humans in various attitudes—such as priests in praying posture, and a figure presenting the symbols of government to the owner of the seal (see further pp. 518–20).

ISRAELITE POTTERY

The vast subject of pottery production in Israel and Judah can be dealt with in this book only in outline. The period of the United Monarchy is characterized by the appearance of a variety of new shapes. A most typical feature of this period is the abundance of red slip and rough, irregular burnish applied by hand on various vessels.[40]

After the division of the Monarchy, separate traditions of pottery making developed in Israel and Judah. In the northern kingdom, a characteristic inventory of forms and decoration appeared in the ninth and eighth centuries B.C.E. The development of this pottery, characterized by burnished red slip applied to bowls and jugs, could be traced at Hazor, Samaria, and Tell el-Far'ah (north).[41]

The term "Samaria Ware" was applied in archaeological literature to two different groups. The first included bowls with thick walls and a high foot, red slipped and burnished or in some cases black slipped. These were limited to Samaria and its vicinity. The second group consisted of thin flat bowls made of fine, well-levigated clay and decorated in concentric stripes of red and yellowish burnished color. In the case of the latter thin bowls, the use of the term "Samaria Ware" should be abandoned, as they most probably originated in Phoenicia and were imported to Samaria and other sites in Israel.

In Judah, there was a slow and gradual development in pottery forms, reflecting the rate of the changes in the material culture of this kingdom over the four hundred years of its existence. The length of this period makes research problematic, as many pottery forms in Judah endured for a long time. Thanks to stratigraphic evidence from several sites, we can define the homogeneous pottery assemblages related to the two major destructions experienced by Judah: the Assyrian conquest of 701 B.C.E., when Lachish (Stratum III) and many other cities were destroyed (perhaps followed by somewhat later devastations in the Negev), and the final destruction of the kingdom in 586 B.C.E. Though there is considerable continuity between these two assemblages, a distinction between them can be made. Finer, inner changes in the pottery of Judah, however, particularly between the tenth and the end of the eighth centuries B.C.E., are difficult to pin down.[42]

The Judean pottery of the eighth and seventh centuries B.C.E. includes a repetitive repertoire of shapes appearing throughout the kingdom in almost identical form and production technique. An orange-red slip, burnished while the vessels were turned on the potter's wheel (a process therefore known as "wheel burnish"), is characteristic. The quality of the pottery

11.31   Typical Judean pottery assemblage, found in the store buildings of Beer-sheba and dated to ca. 700 B.C.E.

is particularly good in Jerusalem and its surroundings. It appears that this assemblage was mass-produced in specialized workshops which distributed their products to vast areas of the kingdom. Neutron activation analysis of the typical *lamelech* jars (see pp. 455–58) confirmed that all samples were made of the same clay, possibly in the same workshop. This would imply a centralized production of these particular jars.

METALLURGY

Iron made its initial appearance in Iron Age I (see p. 360), but it was to become the dominant metal only from the tenth century B.C.E. onward. Sporadic attempts at quenching and carbonization to turn iron into steel were already made in Iron Age I, but these techniques were developed and became more widespread in Iron Age II.[43] Iron objects included tools such as knives, plows, shovels, and picks, and such weapons as arrows and spearheads. In the Bible, *barzel*, the Hebrew word for iron, became a synonym for strength (see, for example, Psalms 2:9 and Proverbs 27:17).

In contrast to the significant number of bronze workshops found in Late Bronze and Iron Age I levels, no remains of iron manufacturing workshops have been discovered. Iron ores are present in several places in Transjordan, but the extent of their exploitation in the Iron Age is unknown.

Bronze continued to play a role in the Iron Age, particularly for producing art objects. Such were the Solomonic temple copper vessels, which were smelted in the Jordan Valley (1 Kings 7:45–46). Bronze bowls are known from Israelite sites, as well as from the Phoenician culture, where they were elaborately decorated.

Silver was employed as the chief form of payment in Israel as well as for making jewelry and quality vessels. It is mentioned in many biblical references in connection with these two uses, as well as in metaphors. The origin of silver is placed by the Bible in Tarshish and Ophir. The former should be identified with southern Anatolia or with Spain, from where Phoenician traders could have brought it to the east. Jewelry and amorphic lumps of silver were found at Israelite sites, such as the tenth century B.C.E. hoard from Eshtemoa.

Gold is well known from the biblical descriptions of Solomon's treasures in Jerusalem. "Gold of Ophir" is mentioned on a Hebrew ostracon found at Tell Qasile as shipped by, or belonging to, Beth-Horon (either the city or a temple of Horon). Ophir is said to have been the source of gold during Solomon's time (1 Kings 9:28). Gold, however, is seldom found in Israel and Judah, except in small jewelry pieces such as earrings. The treasures of gold and silver goods mentioned in the Bible were probably kept in royal treasuries; such treasures were given as taxes and gifts to the Assyrian and Babylonian rulers, or looted when Samaria and Jerusalem were conquered.

TRADE AND FOREIGN CONNECTIONS

Internal Trade   Biblical references concerning internal trade are meager and insufficient. It appears that there were no merchants who dealt with domestic commerce per se.[44] Such commerce was carried out in casual street encounters, in special market-streets referred to in the Bible as *hutsot* (1 Kings 20:34), at the city gate (2 Kings 7:1, 18), or at the large adjacent piazza.

Payment was in silver ingots of amorphic form. A large treasure of silver objects—mainly composed of broken jewelry—demonstrates the use of silver in that period. It was found in Eshtemoa (es-Sammo'a) in the southern Hebron Hills and was dated to the tenth century B.C.E., the time of the United Monarchy. Eshtemoa is noted as one of the towns to which David distributed the booty taken from the Amalekites of the Negev (1 Samuel 30:26–28). The treasure consisted of five pottery jugs, each containing a little more than 5 kg of silver, almost equal to five units of 100 biblical shekels. Indeed, three of the jugs were marked with the Hebrew word *hmsh*, namely "five."[45] A treasure of several rough silver ingots was

11.32 Scale used for weighing silver ingots, with the ingots on the left and shekel stone weights on the right.

11.33 Silver ingots found in a pottery cooking pot below a floor of a house at En Gedi (end of the Iron Age).

found at En Gedi in a pottery cooking pot hidden below the floor of a house late in the seventh century B.C.E.

During the seventh century B.C.E. a system of marked dome-shaped stone weights came into use in the kingdom of Judah, most probably for weighing silver in trade transactions. The use of the weights is well attested in biblical references (Deuteronomy 25:13–15; Genesis 23:16), and bronze scales have been found in Iron Age sites. The basic unit of weight was the shekel, averaging 11.4 gm, and there were stone weights of 1, 2, 4, and 8 shekels. During the century, each piece was incised with the special sign for "shekel" and its amount. In addition, there were special weights designated *beqaʿ*, *pym*, and *nsf*. According to one suggestion, each of these represented one of the six subunits of the shekel. The *beqaʿ* stood for ½ shekel (compare Exodus 38:26) and had an average weight of 5.7 gm. The *pym* probably designated ⅔ shekel; its average weight was 7.6 gm. The *nsf* seems to have equaled ⅚ shekel, 9.5 gm, though here the relationship is not so obvious.[46]

Judean weights were employed throughout Judah as well as

Philistia (they were found in the latter at Ashdod, Ekron, and Timnah). Ostraca from Israel and Judah refer to the shekel system. In the "gold of Ophir" ostracon from Tell Qasile, the value of the gold is noted by the letter *sh* followed by three horizontal lines, probably denoting 30 shekels.

The numbers used in economic and administrative documents in Judah were taken from the Egyptian hieratic script, as seen on ostraca from Arad and Kadesh-Barnea.

The goods and their quality, or the name of the manufacturer, was sometimes noted on pottery containers. Such are the Gibeon inscriptions mentioned earlier (p. 491), or inscriptions denoting types of wine—such as the words "Belonging to Peqah, Semadar" found on a jar from Hazor, where "Semadar" probably denotes a type of wine.

International Trade[47]   Biblical references to international trade mainly concern King Solomon's activities. The story of the visit of the Queen of Sheba (1 Kings 10) reflects commercial connections with south Arabia. The goods brought by her are known from other sources as typically Arabian: gold, precious stones, rare timber and particularly perfumes which in later times were the main merchandise of the south Arabian international trade.

The transactions with south Arabia were part of a wider commercial network established by Solomon, particularly with the Tyrians (1 Kings 9:26–28; 10:22). According to the Bible the Israelites and the Tyrians established a mercantile enterprise from the port at Ezion-Geber (see p. 397) through the Red Sea with Ophir, from which materials such as gold, precious stones, ivories, monkeys, and precious wood were brought. The identity of Ophir remains enigmatic; some place it in the Somali region in East Africa, from which the Egyptians brought similar goods during the New Kingdom; others believe it to have been in south Arabia. The large quantities of gold in the possession of Solomon probably derived from this southern trade. We may assume that Shishak's invasion of the Negev five years after Solomon's death was intended to disrupt this connection. Later kings of Judah (Jehoshaphat, Ahaziah, Uzziah) tried to reestablish this trade, as implied in the Bible and perhaps in the establishment of the royal forts at Kadesh-Barnea and Tell el-Kheleifeh. No archaeological finds can throw direct light on the Solomonic Arabian trade.

Excavations at the City of David have produced some indications for connections between South Arabia and Judah in the form of South Arabian letters incised on local pottery vessels, but these date to the eighth and seventh centuries B.C.E.[48]

The trade relations with Tyre during the time of Solomon were based on direct interchange. Solomon is said to have supplied agricultural products to the Tyrians in return for wood and the professional manpower required for his building operations in Jerusalem. Another of this king's enterprises involved horses brought probably from Asia Minor and sold to Egypt and other markets in exchange for Egyptian chariots (1 Kings 10:28–29). Evidence of transactions with Phoenicia is seen in the form of Phoenician pottery found throughout the kingdom since the late eleventh century B.C.E., and in small objects of art, such as ivories, glass and decorated tridacna shells. Most of these art objects, however, are later than the Solomonic era.

Trade with Cyprus and the Aegean is indicated by a small amount of Cypriot and Eastern Greek pottery found in Israelite sites from the late tenth century onward. Such imported pottery found in seventh-century sites in the Arad–Beer-sheba region is associated either with trade or with the presence of Aegean and Cypriot mercenaries in Judah at that time.

LITERACY AND INSCRIPTIONS

In the course of the last two chapters, we surveyed some of the most important written documents found in Israel and Judah. In the following paragraphs, we will discuss them as illustrations of the degree of literacy in ancient Israel.[49]

The Hebrew inscriptions known from the period of the Monarchy include monumental, official texts; ostraca; short notations on pottery vessels; dedications; prayers; and even literary texts. The inscriptions are written on walls, jars, stone vats, metal talismans, and pottery sherds, and in addition there are many seals and seal impressions. It should be remembered that, in spite of their variety and richness, these inscriptions represent only a small portion of the written texts in Israel, which were mostly taken down on papyrus (brought from Egypt) or on parchment, both of which are perishable. The literary works, including the first biblical texts, were written on scrolls (Jeremiah 36) perhaps made of papyrus, and official documents were undoubtedly inscribed on papyrus and sealed with strings and stamped clay sealings. If anything of these official documents has been preserved, it is the stamped pieces of clay (bullae) alone; only one papyrus from the time of the Monarchy has been found—that in the remote cave of Muraba'at in the Judean Desert. The ostraca and simple inscriptions on potsherds and pottery jars as well as the abundance of seals are evidence that, at least during the last two centuries of the Monarchy, the knowledge of writing was widespread.[50]

Monumental inscriptions incised on stone in lapidary Paleo-Hebrew script were known in Israel and Judah, particularly in their capital cities. The only complete text of this kind is the Siloam inscription (see p. 484). The rest are fragmentary: two found in Jerusalem and one at Samaria (the latter includes only one word). These fragments may have been from royal stelae erected in the capitals, like that of King Mesha of Moab (see p. 542). Such royal inscriptions were inscribed in a formal script most probably by royal scribes.[51] A specific type of official notation is curses against tomb robbers, found on the facades of monumental tombs in Jerusalem (see p. 525).

On three occasions, dedications and prayers were found incised on cave walls in the Shephelah and in the Judean Desert.[52] One of these, in a cave at Khirbet Beit-Lei in the Shephelah, includes a prayer to Yahweh and notes of concern for the fate of Jerusalem. The Khirbet Beit-Lei graffiti were perhaps written by refugees who fled from Jerusalem after its fall in 586 B.C.E.[53] The texts from Kuntillet 'Ajrud from around 800 B.C.E. provide the best collection of Israelite prayers, blessings, and dedications (see p. 447).

Ostraca are the richest group of Hebrew inscriptions. The most important among these are the Samaria ostraca (see p. 410), the Lachish letters (see p. 458), the Arad letters (see p. 440), ostraca from Hurvat Uza, and some from Jerusalem, Tell Qasile, and Metsad Hashavyahu. Most of these ostraca are dated to the seventh and early sixth centuries B.C.E.—except those from Samaria, which must antedate the conquest of Samaria in 720 B.C.E., and a few from Arad which belong to the ninth and eighth centuries B.C.E. The ostraca were written in black ink (except for a few incised ones) on potsherds, a cheap and readily available writing material. Their contents relate to various daily activities: lists of names or goods, receipts or delivery notes (such as the Samaria letters), letters or copies of official documents (most of the Arad ostraca and the Metsad Hashavyahu letter), and rough drafts of texts which were to be copied onto papyrus or parchment (as suggested by Y. Yadin concerning the Lachish letters). The longest and one of the most interesting ostracons from this period was found at the coastal fort Metsad Has-havyahu. It is a complaint of a worker, probably written for him by a professional scribe and addressed to a high official.[54]

Graffiti and short notes on pottery vessels are additional evidence of the widespread knowledge of writing in Israel. In Jerusalem, a special chiseling technique was employed for writing on pottery vessels. Names of owners, the contents of vessels, or their capacity were incised or written in ink. Examples of this practice are the incised handles of the wine jars at Gibeon (see p. 491), and a jug from Judah inscribed with the name of its owner and the type of wine (or the name of the winery): "Belonging to Yahzeyahu, wine of Khl."

Inscriptions engraved in miniature letters on two silver talismans found by G. Barkai in a repository of a burial cave at Ketef Hinnom (Jerusalem) are of the utmost importance

11.34 A Judean wine jug inscribed with the words "Belonging to Yahzeyahu, wine of Khl" followed by a sign denoting quantity. The word "Khl" probably denotes a kind of wine or the name of the winery.

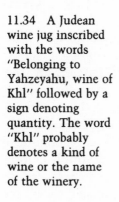

for the study of the antiquity of the biblical text (see p. 524).[55] They include the earliest verses of biblical texts known so far. In fact, the earliest biblical texts known until this discovery are those of the Dead Sea Scrolls, of the second and first centuries B.C.E. One of the texts in the silver talismans is almost identical to Numbers 6:24–25, which comprises a blessing that became known in later times as one of the most sacred Jewish blessings known as the Priestly Benediction. The other text is a shorter version of the same blessing. This biblical text was attributed by modern scholars of biblical criticism to the Priestly Code, which is considered to be the latest of the four hypothetical sources of the pentateuch. The discovery shows that at least this particular blessing was well known and widely used by Jews in Jerusalem already before the destruction of the first temple.

11.35   A group of stamped clay bullae found in Stratum II at Lachish.

Another outstanding inscription which was purchased in the antiquities market is incised in miniature letters on a small ivory pomegranate-shaped object which perhaps was used as a ceremonial scepter. A. Lemaire deciphered and reconstructed the inscription as following: *lby[t Yhw]h qds khnm*, namely: "belonging to the tem[ple of the Lor]d [Yahweh], holy to the priests." He dated the inscription on the basis of paleography to the end of the eighth century B.C.E. If the reconstruction is correct, the object may have been used by priests in the temple of Jerusalem, and thus may be the only object and inscription which can be related directly to the temple of Jerusalem during the Biblical time.[56]

Israelite Seals and Seal Impressions   Seals made of different types of hard, semiprecious stones, and their impressions on jar handles and on clay bullae, are an important source for the study of personal names, official titles, the administrative system, and the iconography of the period (on the last, see p. 505). Most of the seals from controlled excavations are found in eighth- and seventh-century levels at Judean sites, but some have also been uncovered in the northern kingdom of Israel. Seals of Israel's neighbors (Phoenicia, Ammon, Edom) were made with similar iconography and manufacturing technique and are differentiated mainly by their personal names. The seals belonged to dignitaries, members of the royal family, and other prestigious personalities.[57]

A superb example of an official's seal from the kingdom of Israel features an artistically carved figure of a roaring lion and bears the name "Shemaʿ servant of Jeroboam"; Shemaʿ may have been a minister of Jeroboam II. This seal, as well as others from the northern kingdom, were probably inspired by Phoenician and Aramean artistic traditions.

Among the seal impressions from the last decades of the kingdom of Judah, three groups of clay bullae are of special importance: (1) a group found at Lachish Stratum II; (2) a collection uncovered in a house in the City of David; and (3) a group from an unknown context.[58] The first two were found in destruction levels from the last days of Judah (586 B.C.E.). The majority of Judean seals and seal impressions were undecorated and included only the name and title of their owner; others featured certain artistic motifs (see p. 507).

The *lmlk*-type seal impressions and the accompanying

11.36 Two stamped bullae from Judah. Left: impression mentioning *sar ha'ir* ("the governor of the city," possibly Jerusalem). Right: the seal impression of Gemaryahu son of Shaphan, found at the City of David (compare Jeremiah 36:10–12).

"personal" stamps (see p. 455) are a distinct group related to the royal military administration during the time of Hezekiah. Other seals belonged to specific dignitaries, such as princes (titled "son of the king"); a seal of a princess carries the words "Maa'danah, daughter of the king" and is decorated with a lyre. Other titles noted include "who is over the house" (perhaps denoting the prime minister—the highest rank in the Judean administration, as known from the Bible), "servant of the king" (in several cases accompanied by the king's name, as in "Abiyau servant of Uzziah"), and that of the functionary named "over the tax." Another courtier was the *na'ar*, "steward," exemplified by "Benayahu steward of Haggai"; these stewards probably served important personages. Two stamps belonged to *sar 'ir*, "city governor" (perhaps governor of Jerusalem?). This title was also inscribed on jars at Kuntillet 'Ajrud.

Only a few of the names on the seals and seal impressions are actually known from the Bible: these include the names of "Berachyahu son of Neriyahu the scribe," who may be identified with Baruch, Jeremiah's scribe during the time of Jehoiakim (Jeremiah 36); "Jerahmeel the king's son," whom we presume was Jehoiakim's son sent to arrest Jeremiah (Jeremiah 36:26);[59] "Gemaryahu son of Shaphan," an important official in Jerusalem during the time of Jeremiah (Jeremiah 36:10–12), whose seal impression was discovered among the fifty-one bullae uncovered in the City of David and "Gedalyahu Over the House," whose seal impression was found at Lachish; the latter may be identified with Gedaliah Son of Ahikam, the appointed governor of Judah after the destruction of Jerusalem (Jer. 39:14).

Table 8

The Development of the Hebrew Alphabet during the Iron Age. (1). 11th century B.C.E. (mainly Isbet Sartah ostracon); (2). 10th century B.C.E. (Gezer tablet); (3). 9th century B.C.E. (Mesha stele); (4). 8th century B.C.E. (Siloam inscription); (5). 7th century B.C.E. (Lachish letters).

		1	2	3	4	5				1	2	3	4	5
א	A							ל	L					
ב	B							מ	M					
ג	C							נ	N					
ד	D							ס	S					
ה	H							ע	C					
ו	W							פ	P					
ז	Z							צ	S					
ח	H							ק	Q					
ט	T							ר	R					
י	Y							ש	Sh					
כ	K							ת	T					

BURIAL CUSTOMS

The custom of burying in family burial caves was inherited by the Israelites from the Canaanites. However, while the Canaanite Bronze Age caves were mostly amorphic, we find a deliberate shaping of rock-hewn tombs in Israel and particularly in Judah.[60] The most common type included a square room entered through a small square opening which could be closed by a large stone. Rock-cut benches on three sides of the chamber provided space for three bodies. More elaborate examples had an additional rear chamber. In several cases (at Jerusalem, Gibeon, and Khirbet el-Kom), "headrests" were shaped on the benches in the form of a horseshoe or a curled "Hathor headdress." The bones and gifts were collected from the benches to a special repository—a sunken pit or a small side chamber—to clear space for more recent burials.

The origin of these burial caves can be traced to the benched chamber tombs known at Tell el-Farᶜah (south) and elsewhere from the beginning of the Iron Age, including those with Philistine offerings. However, in spite of the similarity between these chamber tombs and the caves of Judah, their relationship is unclear, as the earliest Judean examples seem to have appeared only in the ninth century B.C.E. From then on, this form predominated. The plan of a simple Judean burial cave recalls that of the "four-room house," and it is not improbable that the latter inspired the design of the cave. Such house-like burial caves demonstrate the belief in an afterlife.

The cemeteries of Jerusalem are of special interest. They were found scattered around the city, and each has its own characteristics. The most elaborate tombs were identified in the area of the St. Etienne monastery, north of the Damascus Gate.[61] Two exceptionally large and elaborate caves there included a large central hall surrounded by several rectangular benched rooms. Architectural details in these caves, such as the cornices along the upper edges of the walls in the central hall, recall royal burial caves in the kingdom of Urartu in Anatolia; such resemblance indicates remote cultural connections, perhaps with Phoenician mediation. The burial rooms in the caves consisted usually of three benches, each with special headrests cut from the rock and repositories for collecting the bones. The headrests are typical of the Jerusalem cemeteries and are found in most of them, while outside Jerusalem they are rarely found. In one of the St. Etienne caves there was an inner room with rock-cut tub-shaped burial places, perhaps intended for important heads of the families to which the caves belong, people whose bones were never

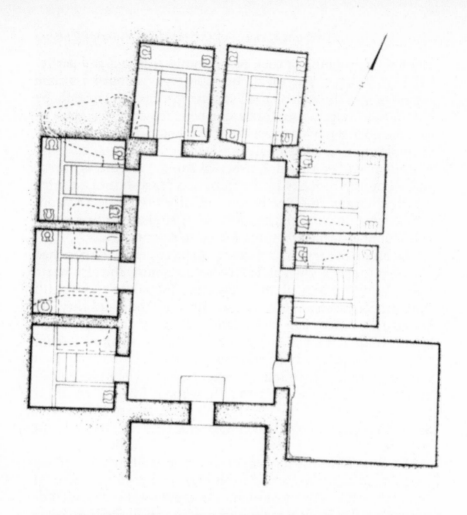

11.37 Plan of the largest Iron Age burial complex in Jerusalem, found in the grounds of the St. Etienne Monastery (north of the Damascus Gate).

collected for secondary burial. These two caves must have served as the burial place of important families in Jerusalem, perhaps even the last kings of Judah.

Many additional burial caves were discovered on the slopes of the Hinnom Valley. These are closer in form to the common Iron Age burial caves in Judah but some of them, particularly those discovered by G. Barkai on the site known as "Ketef Hinnom" (near St. Andrew's church), are large and elaborate. The location of these two cemeteries reflects the expansion of the city to the Western Hill in the eighth and seventh centuries B.C.E.[62]

An exceptional Iron Age cemetery was found in the Siloam

11.38   Interior of the burial cave at St. Etienne.

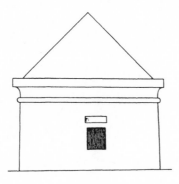

11.39   Reconstructed facade of a monolithic tomb at Siloam.

village, opposite the City of David. It consisted of elaborate tombs hewn from the cliffs in architectural shapes.[63] Some of the tombs are freestanding monolithic chambers decorated with Egyptian cornices which probably carried a pyramidal built-up or hewn roof. These monolithic tombs probably belonged to important personalities in Jerusalem, such as Shebna who was "over the house," whose burial monument in Jerusalem enraged Isaiah (Isaiah 22:15–16). On one of the facades of the tombs, the following Hebrew inscription was incised: "This is [the sepulchre of] . . . yahu who is over the house. There is no silver and no gold here, but [his bones] and the bones of his maid servant with him. Cursed be the

11.40 Incised inscription on a silver talisman from the Ketef Hinnom cemetery, Jerusalem. The miniature letters are incised into the silver sheet. The central part of the text is an abbreviated version of Numbers 6:24–25, the Priestly Benediction. This is the earliest biblical text so far known.

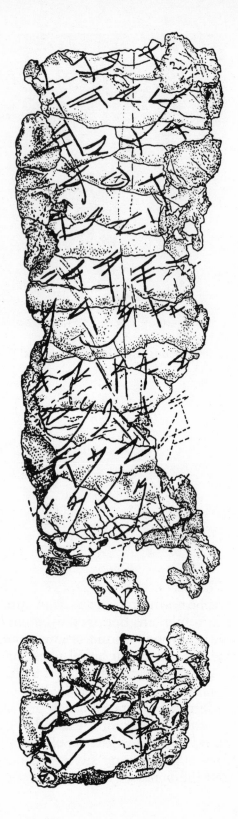

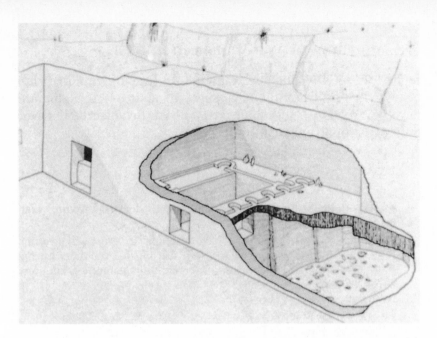

11.41 A burial cave in the valley of Hinnom, Jerusalem. Burial benches with carved "headrests" are seen. The silver talisman in fig. 11.40 was found in the repository of this cave (seen on the right).

man who will open this."[64] Other tombs in Siloam are smaller; they include a small cave chamber with a gabled roof and a side room with a sunken area intended for the burial of one or two bodies. The form of these tombs is foreign to Judah and was probably inspired by Phoenician prototypes.

Additional caves which appear to have been rock-cut tombs were those discovered on the west slope of the Tyropoeon Valley near the southwest corner of the Temple Mount (see p. 420). They must date to the ninth and eighth centuries B.C.E., prior to the expansion of the city to the Western Hill. Their form expresses Phoenician influence in Jerusalem.

Thus, while in the rest of Judah there was one dominant type of burial chamber, in Jerusalem we find a variety of forms, perhaps due to the heterogeneous population, social hierarchy, and impact of foreign influence in this city during the four hundred years it presided as the capital of Judah.

Varied offerings are found in Israelite burials. They include numerous pottery vessels, many of which probably contained food and drink for the dead, and abundant oil lamps to light his way to the afterlife. The seal of the deceased was sometimes placed in his tomb together with various weapons, jewelry, and other objects. The finds from the Ketef Hinnom caves exemplify the profusion of the offerings in this period. One repository, containing the remains of almost a hundred deceased, had 263 complete vessels, in addition to elaborate jewelry, weapons, and such artifacts as the inscribed silver talismans mentioned earlier (p. 516).

NOTES

1. Z. Herzog, *Expedition* 20 (1978), pp. 38–43; idem in: *Architecture*, pp. 209–31 (Hebrew).
2. Y. Shiloh, *IEJ* 28 (1978), pp. 36–51. The examples of peripheral planning in Israelite cities are sparse and are limited to Judah. Even there, among those towns extensively excavated, irregularity in planning is far more prevalent than the well-thought-out examples.
3. For his most recent view, see Y. Yadin in: *WHJP*, vol. 5, pp. 187–235. This opinion was severely attacked in Y. Aharoni, *Beer-Sheba*, vol. 1, Tel-Aviv 1973, pp. 108–10.
4. See Chapter Nine, note 15 for the problems regarding this gate. Yadin at first suggested that the six-chamber gate was replaced by one with four chambers in Stratum IVA. Later he accepted the fact that the six-chamber gate coexisted—at least in its later phase—with the "offsets and insets" city wall, and since he attributed the latter to Stratum IVA, the six-chamber gate necessarily continued in use in the early stages of this stratum with a higher floor level. Yadin adjusted his view by asserting that the six-chamber gate was replaced in a later phase of Stratum IV by a four-chamber gate. The different opinions of Aharoni, Herzog, and Ussishkin are also referred to in Chapter Nine, note 15. For a general discussion of city gates, see Herzog (Chapter 6, note 40).
5. A. Biran, *BA* 13 (1980), pp. 172–82.
6. Y. Shiloh, *The Proto Aeolic Capital and Israelite Ashlar Masonry. Qedem* 11, Jerusalem 1979; W. G. Dever, in: T. Ishida (ed.), *Studies in the Period of David and Solomon and Other Essays*, Winona Lake 1982, pp. 269–306.
7. G. and O. Van Beek, *EI* 15 (1981), pp. 70*–77*.
8. The Megiddo stables were published in R. S. Lamon and G. M. Shipton, *Megiddo*, vol. 1, Chicago 1939, pp. 32–47. On the rejection of their identification as stables, see J. B. Pritchard in: *Glueck Festschrift*, pp. 268–76; Z. Herzog, in: Y. Aharoni (ed.), *Beer-Sheba*, vol. 1, Tel Aviv 1973, pp. 23–30; idem in: *Architecture*, pp. 189–94 (Hebrew). For views supporting the identification of these structures as stables, see Y. Yadin, *EI* 12 (1975), pp. 57–62 (Hebrew); J. S. Holladay in: L. T. Geraty and L. G. Herr (eds.), *The Archaeology of Jordan and Other Studies* (Siegfried Horn Festschrift), Berrien Springs 1986, pp. 103–65. This last work is a most convincing and comprehensive study of the subject.
9. For a general survey, see D. Cole, *BAR* 6:2 (1980), pp. 8–29; Y. Shiloh in: *Rose Festschrift*, pp. 203–44.
10. R. S. Lamon, *The Megiddo Water System*, Chicago 1935; Yadin (1972),

pp. 161–64. The excavators dated the Megiddo system to the twelfth century B.C.E. I follow Yadin's dating to the ninth century B.C.E. based on the fact that the preceding ashlar "gallery" belongs to the tenth-century city, and also because of the Hazor analogy (see later).

11. P. Albenda, *BASOR* 206 (1972), pp. 42–48. Albenda suggested to identify the city with Hazor. But at Hazor the Assyrian troops could not have reached the end of the shaft while besieging the city from the outside. Megiddo would be a better alternative.

12. Shiloh (see note 6), pp. 21–22. In the past, the "Warren Shaft" was identified with the "Sinnor" mentioned in connection with the conquest of Jerusalem by David (2 Samuel 5:6–9). But this identification is unacceptable on both linguistic and archaeological grounds; no parallel to such an early water project is known in Palestine.

13. J. B. Pritchard, *The Water System at Gibeon*, Philadelphia 1961. On the water system at Tell es-Saʿidiyeh, see recently: J. Tubb, *Levant* 20 (1988), p. 46; S. Millard, op. cit., pp. 84–87. Tubb accepts Pritchard's dating of the system to the twelfth century B.C.E., but the date is based on pottery which he claims to be similar to that of Stratum XII. The latter, however, appears to be of the tenth century B.C.E. (see Chapter 9, note 21).

14. Yadin (1972), pp. 172–78.

15. The relationship between the two water projects at Gibeon and their dating are not clear. Pritchard had two arguments on which he based his claim that the circular shaft was earlier than the sloping tunnel: (1) the fact that the sloping tunnel starts with a "bent axis" corridor to avoid the already existing circular shaft; (2) the identification of the circular shaft as the "pool of Gibeon" where men of Abner and Joab fought after the death of Saul (2 Samuel 2:13). Neither argument is convincing. The turn of the entrance to the stepped tunnel may have been intended to avoid a building at that spot. The second point is dubious: the shaft is not a pool, and a date in the late eleventh century B.C.E. is too early and without precedent for such a water shaft. D. Cole's proposal that the shaft was first a pool and only later was converted into a shaft (see note 9) is also unconvincing; the steps and the parapet lead down to the bottom of the shaft and continue directly into the lower tunnel, indicating that the circular shaft and the tunnel were designed and planned as one unit.

16. R. Amiran et al., *Qadmoniot* 69–70 (1985), pp. 15–17 (Hebrew).

17. For the excavators' view, see Z. Herzog, *Beer-sheba II: The Early Iron Age Settlements*, Tel Aviv 1984, pp. 4–6. In my opinion, there is no clear indication of an Iron Age I date for this well. It could have been cut during the Hellenistic period, as its stone masonry and finds suggest. The hypothetical connection between the drainage system inside the city (explained as a water-collecting system) and the well is not clear. The presence of the large water project inside the town of Beer-sheba would exclude the need for another water source in this small town during the Iron Age.

18. H. Vincent, *Underground Jerusalem*, London 1911; J. Simons, *Jerusalem*

in the Old Testament, Leiden 1952, pp. 157–94; D. Ussishkin, *Levant* 8 (1976), pp. 82–95.

19. *ANET*, p. 321; Gibson (1971), p. 21.

20. Y. Shiloh, *IEJ* 20 (1970), pp. 180–90; H. Keith-Beebe, *BA* 31 (1968), pp. 49–58; G. E. Wright, *Tufnell Festschrift*, pp. 149–54; F. Braemer, *L'Architecture domestique du Levant a L'Age du Fer*, Paris 1982; E. Netzer in: *Architecture*, pp. 165–72 (Hebrew); E. Stern in: *WHJP*, vol. 5, pp. 265–70.

21. D. Eitam, *Tel-Aviv* 6 (1979), pp. 146–55; G. L. Kelm and A. Mazar, *BASOR Supplement* 23 (1985), pp. 104–19; S. Gitin and T. Dothan, *BA*, 50 (1987), pp. 206–22.

22. J. B. Pritchard, *Winery, Defenses and Soundings at Gibeon*, Philadelphia 1964, pp. 1–27.

23. A. Sheffer, *TA* 8 (1981), pp. 81–83.

24. For general surveys, see Y. Shiloh in: *Symposia*, pp. 147–58; R. de Vaux, *Ancient Israel*, New York 1961, pp. 271–339, 406–14; G. W. Ahlström, *An Archaeological Picture of Iron Age Religions in Ancient Palestine.* Studia Orientalia 55:3, Helsinki 1984; W. G. Dever in: C. L. Meyers and M. O'Connor (eds.), *The Word of the Lord Shall Go Forth: Essays in Honor of D. N. Freedman*, Winona Lake 1983, pp. 571–87.

25. A. Biran, *EI* 16 (1982), pp. 15–43 (Hebrew); idem, *BA* 37 (1974), pp. 168–82; ibid. 43 (1980), pp. 168–82; idem, *IEJ* 30 (1980), pp. 89–98; ibid. 36 (1986), pp. 179–87; idem, *BAR* 13:4 (1987), pp. 12–37; 15:1 (1989), pp. 29–31.

26. L. E. Stager and S. R. Wolf, *BASOR* 243 (1981), pp. 95–102.

27. Y. Aharoni, *BA* 37 (1974), pp. 2–6.

28. Aharoni thought that the altar had stood in the courtyard of a temple (similar to the temple found at Arad) which he believed was located at the western part of Tel Beer-sheba—at a location where, in a later phase of the Iron Age (Stratum II), a building with a large cellar was constructed. Y. Yadin suggested that the altar was situated in a structure south of the city gate—a structure which he identified as the *bamah* destroyed by Josiah. See Y. Aharoni, *TA* 2 (1975), pp. 156–65; Y. Yadin, *BASOR* 222 (1976), pp. 5–17; Z. Herzog, A. F. Rainey, and Sh. Moshkovitz, *BASOR* 225 (1977), pp. 49–58. Both these ideas are unconvincing. Yadin's proposal would necessitate the dating of the storehouses (in which the altar stones were found in secondary use) to the end of the seventh century B.C.E. But the pottery assemblage in the destruction level of these buildings belongs to the first half of that century. In fact, there is no evidence at Tel Beer-sheba for any occupation during the time of Josiah. The "high place" destroyed by this king may have stood within the area of seventh-century Beer-sheba, which lies under the modern city. The dating of the destruction of the altar to the reign of Hezekiah would place the erection or restoration of the storehouses in the later years of Hezekiah's reign, or possibly even in the time of Manasseh. N. Naʾaman suggested that the identification of Tel Beer-sheba with the biblical city of Beer-sheba should be abandoned and that the latter was always located at the large site in the area of the modern city of Beer-sheba. See: *ZDPV* 96 (1980), pp. 149–51.

29. Y. Aharoni, *BA* 31 (1968), pp. 2–32; B. Mazar, *JNES* 24 (1965), pp. 297–303. Z. Herzog et al., *BASOR* 254 (1984), pp. 1–34; *BAR* 13:2 (1987), pp. 16–39.

30. W. G. Dever, *BASOR* 255 (1985), pp. 21–37; Z. Zevit, *BASOR* 255 (1984), pp. 39–47.

31. Even if we do not accept the attribution of the Arad casemate wall to Stratum VI of the Iron Age (see p. 439), there is still evidence that the temple became obsolete before the final destruction of the citadel. See Z. Herzog et al. *BASOR* 254 (1984), p. 22, fig. 23. See also A. Mazar and E. Netzer, *BASOR* 263 (1986), pp. 87–91; D. Ussishkin, *IEJ* 38 (1988), pp. 42–57.

32. I. Beit-Arieh, *Qadmoniot* 19 (1986), pp. 72–81 (Hebrew); I. Beit-Arieh and P. Beck, *An Edomite Shrine: Discoveries from Qitmit in the Negev.* Israel Museum Catalogue 277, Jerusalem 1987.

33. It could be surmised that this foreign cult place belonged to the Kittim, as implied in the Arad letters; in one of these letters, oil and wine are said to have been sent from Arad to the Kittim. Such goods may have been delivered to the temple of these foreigners, which was not far from, but intentionally located outside, any permanent Judean settlement. The possible relationship between the Kittim and the temple at Hurvat Qitmit, as well as the possible origin of the Kittim in Kition on Cyprus, requires further verification. It should be emphasized, however, that Cypriot pottery was found at other sites in the region but not at Hurvat Qitmit.

34. Y. Aharoni, *Investigations at Lachish (Lachish Vol. 5)*, Tel Aviv 1975, pp. 26–32. This room resembles in many respects the small shrine attached to the main temple of Tell Qasile in the eleventh century B.C.E.

35. T. Holland, *Levant* 9 (1977), pp. 121–55.

36. R. Hestrin in: E. Lipinski (editor), *Studia Phoenicia* V (Orientalia Lovaniensia Analecta 22), Leuven 1987, pp. 61–77.

37. J. W. and G. M. Crowfoot, *Samaria Sebaste II: Early Ivories from Samaria*, London 1938.

38. R. D. Barnett, *The Nimrud Ivories*, London 1957; idem, *Ancient Ivories in the Middle East. Qedem* 14, Jerusalem 1982, pp. 43–55; I. J. Winter, *IRAQ* 38 (1976), pp. 1–22.

39. R. Hestrin and M. Dayagi, *Ancient Seals: First Temple Period. From the Collection of the Israel Museum*, Jerusalem 1979.

40. Examples of tenth-century stratified pottery can be seen in the publications of Period II at Taanach and Stratum VII–VI at Beer-sheba: W. E. Rast, *Taanach I: Studies in the Iron Age Pottery.* American Schools of Oriental Research Excavation Reports, 1978; F. R. Brandfon in: Herzog (see Chapter Nine, note 4).

41. Amiran (1969), pp. 208–320.

42. Y. and M. Aharoni, *BASOR* 224 (1976), pp. 73–90.

43. J. Waldbaum, *From Bronze to Iron*, Göteborg 1978; T. Stetch-Wheeler et al., *AJA* 85 (1981), pp. 245–68.

44. M. Eilat in: *WHJP*, vol. 5, pp. 173–78.

45. Z. Yeivin, *Qadmoniot* 5 (1972), pp. 45–46 (Hebrew).

46. Y. Meshorer, *Qadmoniot* 9 (1976), pp. 54–55 (Hebrew); R. B. Y. Scott, *BASOR* 153 (1959), pp. 32–35.

47. M. Eilat in: *WHJP*, vol. 5, pp. 178–86.

48. Y. Shiloh, *PEQ* 119 (1987), pp. 9–18.

49. N. Avigad in: *WHJP*, vol. 4, pp. 20–39, 315–17; J. Naveh, *The Early History of the Alphabet*, Jerusalem 1982, pp. 65–78. On the various inscriptions, see A. Lemaire, *Inscriptions hebraïques I: Les Ostraca*, Paris 1977; Gibson (1971).

50. A. Millard, *BA* 35 (1972), pp. 98–111; idem, *The Biblical Archaeologist Reader* 4 (1983), pp. 181–95; idem in: *BAT*, pp. 301–12; A. Demsky in: *BAT*, pp. 349–53.

51. J. Naveh, *IEJ* 32 (1982), pp. 195–98.

52. On the inscriptions from Khirbet el-Kom, see W. G. Dever, *Hebrew Union College Annual* 40–41 (1970), pp. 139–204; D. Barag, *IEJ* 20 (1970), pp. 216–18; A. Lemaire, *Revue Biblique* 84 (1977), pp. 597–608; Zevit (see note 30), pp. 39–46. The other two inscriptions are from Khirbet Beit Lei (see following note) and from a remote cave near En-Gedi. On the latter see: P. Bar-Adon, *EI* 12 (1975), pp. 77–80.

53. J. Naveh, *IEJ* 13 (1963), pp. 74–92; F. M. Cross in: *Glueck Festschrift*, pp. 299–306.

54. J. Naveh, *IEJ* 10 (1960), pp. 129–39; 14 (1964), pp. 158–59; F. M. Cross, *BASOR* 165 (1962), pp. 34–46; S. Talmon, *BASOR* 176 (1964), pp. 29–38.

55. G. Barkai, *Ketef Hinnom: A Treasure Facing Jerusalem's Walls*. Israel Museum Catalogue 274, Jerusalem 1986, pp. 34–35.

56. A. Lemaire, *Revue Biblique* 88 (1981), pp. 236–39; idem, *BAR* 10:1 (1984), pp. 24–29.

57. N. Avigad in: *WHJP*, vol. 5, pp. 35–39, with previous bibliography; Hestrin and Dayagi (see note 38); Gibson (1971), pp. 59–64.

58. N. Avigad, *Hebrew Bullae from the Time of Jeremiah*, Jerusalem 1986; Y. Aharoni (see note 34), pp. 19–22; Y. Shiloh, *EI* 18 (1985), pp. 73–87 (Hebrew).

59. N. Avigad, *IEJ* 28 (1978), pp. 52–56. On other seals, see ibid. 4 (1954), pp. 236–38; ibid. 13 (1963), pp. 133–36, 322–24; ibid. 14 (1964), pp. 190–94, 274–76; ibid. 16 (1966), pp. 50–53; ibid. 18 (1968), pp. 52–53; ibid. 26 (1976), pp. 178–82; ibid. 28 (1978), pp. 146–51; ibid. 30 (1980), pp. 170–73; idem, *BASOR* 246 (1982), pp. 59–61.

60. Stern *WHJP* IV:2, pp. 270–78; P. S. Loffreda, *Liber Annuus* 18 (1968), pp. 244–78.

61. A. Mazar, *IEJ* 26 (1976), pp. 1–8; G. Barkai and A. Kloner, *BAR* 12:2 (1986), pp. 22–39; G. Barkai, *BAR* 12:2 (1986), pp. 40–57; A. Kloner, *Levant* 18 (1986), p. 121; idem, *BAR* 13:4 (1987), pp. 54–56.

62. G. Barkai (see note 55).

63. D. Ussishkin, *The Village of Silwan*, Jerusalem 1986 (Hebrew).

64. N. Avigad, *IEJ* 3 (1953), pp. 137–52; ibid. 5 (1955), pp. 164–66.

CHAPTER TWELVE

ISRAEL'S NEIGHBORS
AND THE ASSYRIAN
AND BABYLONIAN DOMINATIONS

In addition to Israel and Judah, which were the dominant powers in Palestine during Iron Age II, there were other independent nations and city-states in various parts of the country. These included the Philistine independent cities, the Phoenician city-states along the northern coast, the kingdoms of Aram, Ammon, Moab, and Edom in Transjordan. The archaeological exploration of all these entities, however, is only beginning, in contrast with the situation in Israel and Judah. Recent excavations and surveys have provided a basis for studying the cultural sequence in some of these areas. These studies further emphasize the sharp differences between the coexisting regional cultures of Iron Age II Palestine.

PHILISTIA

The major Philistine city-states retained their independence throughout the period of the Monarchy. Even David and Solomon, who conquered all other parts of the country, annexed only the northern part of Philistia including the Sorek Valley and the Yarkon region. Thus the Bible refers to Gath during the time of Solomon as an independent city-state; it remained so until its destruction by Uzziah (2 Chronicles 26:6). The other Philistine principalities—Gaza, Ashkelon, Ashdod, and Ekron—maintained power throughout the period.[1] They dominated the fertile lands of the coastal plain and the lower Shephelah, and they controlled the passage from Syria to

Egypt. They also played an important role in the international trade among Arabia, Egypt, and Phoenicia, and thus gained great economic strength. Ashkelon's sphere of influence extended to the region of Jaffa during the eighth century B.C.E. Continuous struggles with Judah resulted in border changes. During the eighth century B.C.E., King Uzziah conquered parts of Philistia (2 Chronicles 26:6); but soon afterward, during the reign of Ahaz, the Philistines took advantage of Judah's weakness and annexed towns in the Shephelah (2 Chronicles 28:18).

The Assyrian expansion policy aiming at Egypt brought the Assyrian armies to Philistia during the second half of the eighth century B.C.E. In the year 734 B.C.E. Tiglath-Pileser III reached Gaza, and the Philistine principalities succumbed to his rule. Although they were allowed autonomous government, the following years saw a series of rebellions supported by Egypt and Judah against the foreign conquerors. These resulted in several Assyrian military invasions during the time of Sargon II and Sennacherib—invasions which brought about the surrender, but not destruction, of Gaza (720 B.C.E.), Ashdod (712 B.C.E.), and Ekron (701 B.C.E.). Local vassal rulers were enthroned and the Assyrians established strongholds in the region, making it a logistic base from which incursions into Egypt were initiated in the seventh century B.C.E. under the kings Esarhaddon and Assurbanipal.

After the fall of Assyria, the Philistines found themselves in the midst of a struggle between Egypt and Babylon which terminated in the latter's gaining supremacy throughout the region. Eventually, in approximately 600 B.C.E., the Philistine cities were destroyed during Nebuchadnezzar's military campaigns.

Excavations at the great Philistine cities (Ashdod and Ekron) and in minor towns of Philistia (such as Tel Sera῾ and Timnah) have revealed distinct local material cultures. We can even draw distinctions between the cultures of Ashdod and Ekron.

The urban development of the Philistine city-states was remarkable. During the tenth century B.C.E. Ashdod grew from 20 to about 100 acres. Three destruction levels at Ashdod were attributed respectively to David (or alternatively to the Egyptian Pharaoh Siamun), to Uzziah, and to the Assyrian conquest by Sargon II in 712 B.C.E. Ekron (Tel Miqne), which comprised 50 acres from the twelfth to the early tenth centuries B.C.E., diminished to a smaller size (about 10 acres) for most of Iron Age II; but it flourished in the seventh century, when it again extended to its original size of about 50 acres. Formidable fortifications surrounded these cities. At Ashdod two superimposed gates were exposed. The development of the gates is exceptional: unlike at other cities of the Iron Age, the earlier gate (constructed ca. 1000 B.C.E.) had four chambers and two towers at its front, while the later gate (constructed most probably at the end of the tenth century B.C.E. and surviving until the eighth century B.C.E.) was of the six-chamber type. The latter gate resembles the Solomonic gates at Megiddo, Hazor, Gezer, and Lachish.[2] The corners of the six-chamber gate at Ashdod were constructed of ashlar masonry, the rest of the structure being made of mud brick; a similar combination of ashlars and brick construction was also found in the solid city wall of Ekron in the Iron Age II and in a tenth century B.C.E. residency at Tel Sera'. It thus appears that the new architectural fashions evident in Israel during the United Monarchy, such as ashlar masonry and the six-chamber gate, were also adopted in Philistia. The distinction between the regional cultures is clearer in the pottery and art objects.

A floruit in settlement in southern Philistia, along the Besor Brook and farther north, is manifested by the numerous, short-lived sites dating mainly from the tenth century B.C.E. This phenomenon is comparable to the contemporary flourishing of settlement in the central Negev discussed in Chapter Nine.[3]

The painted Philistine pottery of the twelfth and eleventh centuries B.C.E. disappeared ca. 1000 B.C.E. A new pottery style then emerged, characterized by elaborate and delicate shapes and a highly burnished red slip sometimes decorated with black stripes. This style is best known from Ashdod, where its development from the early tenth century B.C.E. (Stratum X) until the late seventh century B.C.E. (Stratum VI) was followed. At Ekron and its "daughter," Timnah, a distinctive pottery assemblage of the seventh century B.C.E. illustrates a regional variety.[4] Clay figurines from Philistia are vivid and individually rendered, and they display great skill. They are completely different from contemporary examples at Judah.

The economic wealth and vitality of the material culture in Philistia are demonstrated in the industrial and residential quarters at Ashdod, Ekron, and Timnah. At Ekron and Timnah,

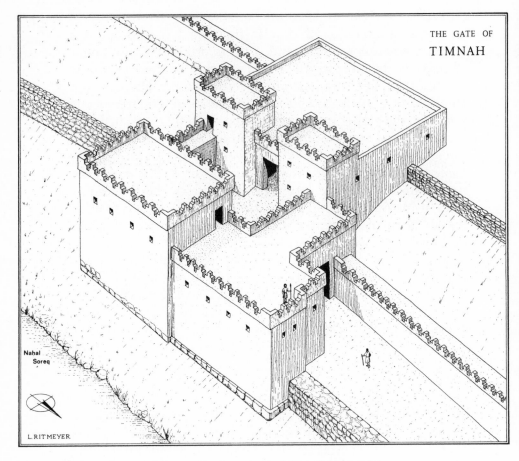

THE GATE OF
TIMNAH

Nahal
Soreq

L.RITMEYER

12.1   Reconstruction of city gate at Tel Batash (Timnah.)

a specialized olive oil industry developed during the seventh century B.C.E. (see p. 490). Relations with Greece are evidenced by the appearance of Greek and Eastern Greek pottery of the late seventh century B.C.E. in the well-planned fortress of Metsad Hashavyahu on the coast north of Ashdod, as well as at Ekron and at Timnah.

Because the modern city of Gaza was built on the ancient *tell*, excavation of ancient Gaza is impossible. To the south, however, on the coast, a tremendous urban center was erected during Iron Age II at the site of Qatif (Rukeish). Rectangular in area, comprising approximately 25 acres, it was surrounded by a massive brick wall with rectangular towers. The area inside was hardly excavated, but a nearby cemetery revealed

534

12.2   Male figurine heads from Ashdod.

rich finds with distinct Phoenician and Assyrian features. Perhaps this site was an important trade center where Phoenicians, Assyrians, Philistines, and possibly Egyptians and Arabs conducted international trade, as implied in a document from the time of Sargon II.[5]

Timnah's location on the border between Judah and Philistia and its passing from one hand to the other in Iron Age II make its history particularly interesting. In the tenth century B.C.E. (Stratum IV), it was under Israelite control; toward the end of that century it was destroyed, probably during Shishak's invasion, and it remained unoccupied until the eighth century B.C.E., when perhaps Uzziah rebuilt it as a typical Judean town. Later in the same century, during the reign of Ahaz, the Philistines took it from Judah; but soon after, Hezekiah seized it as part of his preparations for the revolt against Sennacherib. Evidence of Judean occupation under Hezekiah exists in the form of dozens of jars stamped with the Judean royal sealing (see p. 456). The town was destroyed by Sennacherib, but it was rebuilt and was prosperous, well planned,

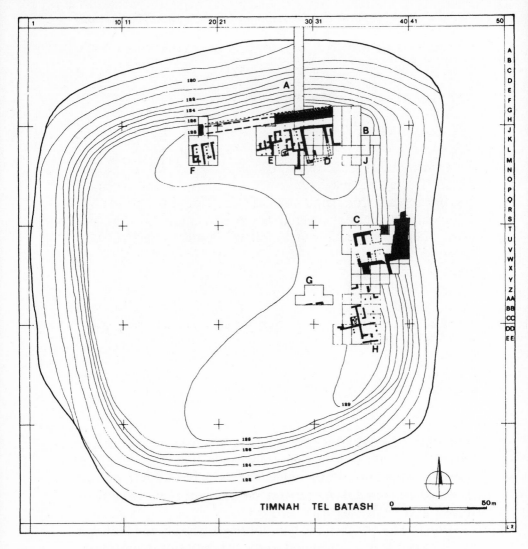

12.3 Plan of Tel Batash (Timnah) Stratum II, late seventh century B.C.E.

and densely built throughout the seventh century B.C.E. until it fell to the Babylonians about 600 B.C.E. (Stratum II). The local material culture, in this period was distinct from that of Judah; rather, it resembled that of Ekron.

PHOENICIA

The term "Phoenician culture" denotes the culture which developed during the Iron Age in Phoenicia itself (extending from the Carmel ridge in the south to the Syrian coast in the north) as well as in the colonies established by the Phoenicians along the Mediterranean from Cyprus to Spain. Rooted in Late Bronze Age Canaan, the Phoenician culture developed in the heartland of Phoenicia—the cities of Tyre, Sidon, Byblos, and Arwad. The archaeology of Phoenicia is beyond the scope of this book;[6] we shall limit ourselves to a brief survey of Phoenician finds from inside the geographic borders of Palestine. These have particular importance in view of the small amount of data from the Phoenician metropolises proper.

Phoenician sites excavated between Mount Carmel and Rosh Haniqra (Israel's northwestern border point) include Achzib, Tell Keisan, Acre, and Tell Abu Hawam. Additional sites along the narrow Carmel coastal plain are Shiqmona, Tel Mevorakh, and Dor, the last having been one of the largest cities on the Mediterranean in Palestine. The excavations at these sites were limited in scope; at none were public buildings or a substantial part of the Phoenician town excavated, and thus our knowledge of their material culture is rather meager. The available data relates mainly to the pottery sequence and to such aspects as burial practices, jewelry, and pottery figurines.

Three main Phoenician pottery groups are known. Their development can be followed in stratified sequences in Phoenicia itself (at Sarepta, Tyre, and Tell Keisan), in Phoenician cemeteries (at Achzib), and at sites outside Phoenicia, to which this ware was imported. The earliest group, which appeared during the mid–eleventh century B.C.E., is the Phoenician Bichrome Ware. (see earlier, p. 357).[7] Its presence in limited numbers in Philistia, the northern Negev, Egypt, and Cyprus signify the beginning of Phoenician trade activity there. This pottery continued to be produced during the tenth and ninth centuries B.C.E. with slight modifications.

A second distinct group, known as Black on Red (sometimes defined as Cypro-Phoenician), made its appearance in the early tenth century B.C.E. The ware is reddish with a reddish brown burnished slip and horizontal lines or concentric circles painted in black. Juglets and some bowls in this delicate fine ware were found throughout Palestine. Both this and the Phoenician Bichrome Ware were brought to Cyprus by Phoenician settlers there and eventually were locally produced with the addition of new shapes.

12.4   Phoenician Red Slip Ware from Achzib.

The third and dominant group is the Red Slip Ware, which was introduced in Phoenicia proper, spreading from there with Phoenician colonization to Cyprus, North Africa, Sicily, Sardinia, and Spain. It comprises mainly jugs with a trefoil mouth or "mushroom" rim; the vessels are covered with a superbly applied red burnished slip. Thin, delicate bowls with a red slip and concentric burnished red and yellowish stripes, known as "Samaria Ware," in fact belong to this group. The Red Slip Ware was probably introduced during the ninth century B.C.E., when it replaced the Phoenician Bichrome group. Other Phoenician forms which appear together with the red-slipped vessels are jars used in mercantile commerce and amphorae serving as cremation urns. Altogether, this Phoenician assemblage is well known in contexts of the eighth and seventh centuries B.C.E., both in Phoenicia and in the Phoenician colonies along the Mediterranean.

The dating of these three pottery groups is crucial in the debate regarding the chronology of the Phoenician colonization in the western Mediterranean.[8] It seems that the Phoenician colonies in Cyprus were established already in the late eleventh century B.C.E., while further expansion to the west probably started in the ninth century B.C.E.

During the latter part of Solomon's reign, the Bible tells us, he was forced to transfer to Tyre a group of towns in the Acre Valley denoted "the land of Cabul" (1 Kings 9:12–13). This ancient name is preserved in the name of the Arab village Cabul which overlooks the Acre Valley in the western Galilee. In its vicinity, at Hurvat Rosh Zayit, a large Phoenician fortress containing considerable quantities of pottery was discovered and partly excavated. This was perhaps a border citadel erected by the Tyrians after the Land of Cabul had been returned to Tyre.[9]

The cemetery at Achzib demonstrates Phoenician burial customs. Two kinds of Iron Age II burials have been identified there. The first is rock-cut or ashlar-built burial chambers approached through shafts. In some cases the rooms had an opening in the roof, perhaps intended to connect the chamber with a memorial structure on the surface. Second, there are cremation burials in amphora urns. This practice appears in Palestine in the late eleventh century B.C.E. cemetery at Azor,

12.5 Phoenician male mask from Achzib (height 13.2 cm).

east of Jaffa, and is also known from the early Iron Age necropolis at Hama in northern Syria. Since it was unknown to the Canaanites, it may have been introduced by foreign immigrants from Anatolia via northern Syria in the eleventh century B.C.E. The custom was adopted by the Phoenicians, as evidenced at Achzib, and later was common among the Phoenician settlers in the western Mediterranean.

The finds in the cemeteries, such as elaborate jewelry, seals, metal objects, and miniature art objects, illustrate the richness of the Phoenician material culture. Typical Phoenician clay figurines depict fertility deities and scenes of daily life. Strong Egyptian influence can be seen in many of these objects.

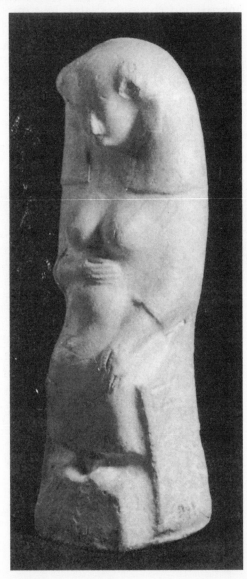

12.6 Phoenician pottery statuette showing a seated pregnant woman (height 23.5 cm). This statuette is perhaps from the Persian period.

The masterpieces of Phoenician art are the tenth century B.C.E. sarcophagus of King Ahiram found at Byblos; the Phoenician ivory works (see pp. 503–7); and decorated metal bowls. These magnificent works, mostly found outside Phoenicia proper, illustrate the superb combination of Egyptian and Canaanite traditions developed by the talented Phoenician artists into a new and lively art. It is no wonder that the great Israelite builders, Solomon and Ahab, turned to Phoenician artists and architects for assistance when erecting their royal centers in Jerusalem and Samaria.

TRANSJORDAN

During the reigns of David and Solomon, large parts of Transjordan, including Gilead and northern Moab, were under direct Israelite control, and Ammon, Moab (the portion south of the Arnon River), and Edom were Israelite vassal states. These last three regions regained their independence with the division of the kingdom, and Mesha, king of Moab, freed northern Moab from Israelite control after the death of Ahab. Gilead (the plateau north of the Jabbok River), however, remained Israelite until the Assyrian invasion in the eighth century B.C.E.[10]

After Tiglath-Pileser III's conquests in 732 B.C.E., northern Transjordan was annexed to the Assyrian empire, and Ammon, Moab, and Edom again became vassal states. Under Assyrian and Babylonian control, these kingdoms experienced prosperity and economic growth because they protected the main road through Transjordan to Arabia—and thus their masters' economic and political interests in Arabia and the Red Sea.

Although various surveys and excavations have been carried out in Transjordan, the study of this region is only in its initial stages.[11] The remains prior to the Assyrian conquests in 732 B.C.E. are sparse. At the site of biblical Ramoth Gilead (Tell er-Rumeith) in the Israelite territory of Gilead, a casemate wall was destroyed by the Assyrians in 732 B.C.E. At Tell es-Sa'idiyeh in the Jordan Valley a well-planned residential quarter was destroyed, probably at the same time.[12] The most fascinating discovery in this region is the ink inscriptions on a plastered wall of a large building at Tell Deir Alla. This structure was destroyed by fire, perhaps also during the Assyrian conquest, though a later date cannot be ruled out.[13]

The most interesting texts here tell a story about Balaam the seer, well known from the biblical account of the Exodus (Numbers 22–24). The practice of writing on walls is known also at Kuntillet ʿAjrud. At Tell Deir Alla the inscription is written in a local West Semitic language; it may have been a draft notation from a professional scribe's school located at this place.

The Moabite Stone, found in 1868 at Dhiban (biblical Dibon, the capital of Moab), carries the longest and most important Iron Age inscription found on either side of the Jordan River.[14] It commemorates the liberation of Moab from Israelite rule by King Meshaʿ, and it contains invaluable information regarding historical events, building operations, and the geography of this kingdom. Furthermore, the stele is invaluable in the study of Moabite script and dialect, both of which were related to Hebrew. The Moabite Stone, however, remains a unique discovery; excavations at Dibon and Heshbon revealed only scanty remains from the time of Mesha and his descendants.[15]

Most of the Iron Age remains in Transjordan relate to the prosperous period of Assyrian and Babylonian domination from the late eighth until the early sixth centuries B.C.E. This is particularly true concerning the land of Ammon.[16] The rich finds in this area include decorated inscribed seals, several short inscriptions, burial caves, and an important group of stone sculptures. Two of the seals belonged to servants of Amminadab, an Ammonite king mentioned in Assyrian records inscribed during the time of Esarhaddon. A building inscription on a stone discovered in Amman mentions the Ammonite god Milkom. A series of round towers found in the Amman region may have been a defense line surrounding the capital of the Ammonites during Iron Age II. Unfortunately, almost no Iron Age remains were found at the mound of Amman, the site of biblical Rabat-Ammon.

A group of Ammonite stone statuettes and statues are of particular interest, as they are the only freestanding stone sculptures from Iron Age Palestine. Depicted are standing, bearded males, and life-size human heads, both recalling contemporary Cypriot sculpture and Phoenician art.[17] Ammonite tombs of the seventh and sixth centuries B.C.E. contained rich groups of pottery with Phoenician and Assyrian features.

12.7   Ammonite limestone sculpture showing a male head.

Like Ammon, Edom also flourished during the latter part of the Iron Age. At Buseirah (biblical Bozrah, Edom's capital), the acropolis in the Assyrian period was uncovered, but no remains of earlier Edomite structures such as those mentioned by Amos (1:12) were identified.[18] A large palace from the period of Assyrian domination is inspired in its planning by Assyrian palace architecture. Farther south, Umm el-Biyara, Ghara and Tawilan also produced evidence of Edomite material culture.[19] Among the finds from Umm el-Biyara was a seal impression with the name of Qaus-Gabar, who was the king of Edom during the time of Esarhaddon and Assurbanipal. The theophoric component *qaus* is typical of Edomite names and appears on a number of seals and ostraca.

As we have seen (p. 450), the excavations at Tell el-Kheleifeh need now to be reinterpreted. It seems that at least during the time of Periods III and IV the place became an Edomite stronghold connected with the trade route to Arabia, a route which the Assyrians were anxious to control. A sealing of an Edomite official, perhaps the governor of the citadel, found on jars from Period III reads, "Qaus ʿanal, servant of the king."

A distinct group of Edomite pottery is decorated with red and black painted geometric designs.[20] This ware appears at Edom in eighth- and seventh-century levels, and it was also found in seventh century B.C.E. strata in the northern Negev, reflecting relations between Edom and Judah. These ties are also exemplified by an Edomite ostracon found at Hurvat Uza, and particularly by the possibly Edomite temple at Hurvat Qitmit (see p. 498). On the other hand, two ostraca from Arad mention Edom as an enemy toward the end of the Iron Age. Indeed, the slow Edomite penetration into southern Judah toward the end of the Iron Age culminated in massive Edomite settlement in the region after the Babylonian conquest of Judah; this settlement, in turn, resulted in the eventual establishment of the province Idumea there in the following periods.

THE ASSYRIAN CONQUESTS AND DOMINATION

As a result of the Assyrian conquests during the second part of the eighth century B.C.E., most of Palestine was under direct Assyrian rule, and only Judah retained its independence. This situation lasted through much of the seventh century B.C.E. during the reigns of the last two great Assyrian kings, Esarhaddon (680–669 B.C.E.) and Assurbanipal (668–627 B.C.E.). Toward the end of the latter's rule (perhaps already from 650 B.C.E.), Assyria's strength declined until it eventually collapsed and was replaced by Babylon after 609 B.C.E.

The Assyrians documented their conquests of Palestine in texts, monumental wall reliefs, and commemorative stelae. Fragments of these stelae from the time of Sargon II were discovered at Samaria and Ashdod. Assyrian reliefs schematically depict the conquest of Ashtaroth, Ekron, Gibbethon, Gezer, and Raphiah. The largest and most detailed of these relates to the suppression of Lachish at the hands of Sennacherib (see p. 432).[21]

The Assyrian conquests caused a tremendous change in the political and demographic structure of the country. The kingdom of Israel was divided among several Assyrian administrative districts, two of the capitals of which were established at Megiddo and Samaria. Other provinces were created in northern Transjordan and possibly at Dor in the northern coastal plain. Large masses of people were deported, and in their place a new population was brought in. In other parts of the country, independent entities such as the kingdoms of Transjordan and the city-states of Phoenicia and Philistia became Assyrian vassals.

Vast archaeological material illuminates the Assyrian domination of the country. This material includes Assyrian palaces and residencies, inscriptions, seals, pottery, and metal objects.[22]

Megiddo Stratum III exemplifies an Assyrian district capital. This city comprised an orthogonal town plan, in which blocks of houses were separated by parallel streets. The "offsets and insets" city wall of the previous period was maintained, but a new gate with only two guard chambers was constructed. The residency and administrative headquarters of the Assyrian governor were located in the vicinity of the gate. These official buildings feature an interesting combination of Assyrian and Syrian planning traditions. Their general layout is inspired by Assyrian architecture: they have a large central open courtyard surrounded by rooms on four sides. The reception unit of the palace, however, recalls the north Syrian–Palestinian *bit-*

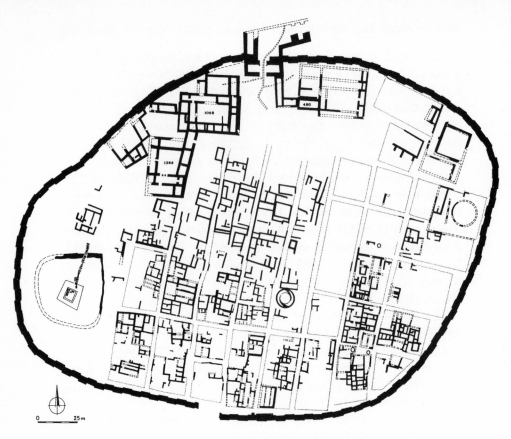

12.8 Plan of Megiddo Stratum III (seventh century B.C.E.).

hilani: leading to the broad reception chamber was a broad anteroom entered through a portico. Such a combination of the Syrian *bit-hilani* unit and the Assyrian type of "open court" building is evident also in the Upper Palace at Sinjirli, the capital of the kingdom of Sama'l in southern Turkey.

Two Assyrian buildings were found at Hazor. A large public structure, resembling in plan the Assyrian headquarters at Megiddo, was erected on top of the ruined Israelite citadel in Area B. Probably it was an isolated Assyrian administrative stronghold erected on an unsettled mound. At the foot of this mound (in the area of Kibbutz Ayelet Hashahar), the remains of a building were identified by R. Reich as the reception hall of a large palace built in typical Assyrian style.[23] The palace's presence at this particular location is enigmatic; perhaps it served an Assyrian district governor. The palace at Buseirah

546

in Edom (see p. 544) was also planned according to the Assyrian "open court" principle, and a shrine there recalls Assyrian shrines. Thus Buseirah reflects Assyrian influence or direct intervention in Edom.

The southern part of Palestine was particularly important for the Assyrians during the seventh century B.C.E., since it guarded the road to Egypt, the target of the Assyrian strategy. The archaeological evidence reflects massive Assyrian presence in this region. At Gezer, two administrative documents from the mid–seventh century B.C.E., a group of objects, and some architectural remains indicate that this city was an Assyrian stronghold.[24] Assyrian finds are abundant farther south along the southern coastal plain and in northeastern Sinai, where the land route to Egypt passed. At Tel Seraʿ, part of a large seventh century B.C.E. citadel contained Assyrian metal objects, including a scepter of a type used to decorate Assyrian chariots.[25] Tell Jemmeh, farther to the west along the Gerar Brook, was identified by B. Mazar with Arsah (Yurza), a city conquered by the Assyrians in 679 B.C.E. Mudbrick buildings found here—featuring unique Assyrian-type vaulted ceilings and floors, and containing Assyrian "Palace Ware"—are the remains of an important Assyrian military and administrative base.[26]

Sargon II mentions the "sealed *karu* [harbor or trading station] of Egypt" as being built by him to facilitate the Assyrian-Egyptian trade. This was after Sargon's conquests in Philistia, but long before the invasion of Egypt. There are two possible sites which could be identified with this trading station. One is the large fortified site at Qatif on the coast south of Gaza (see p. 534), and the other is Tell Abu Salima, east of El-Arish on the main road leading to Egypt. At Tell Abu Salima, Sir. F. Petrie excavated a structure recently interpreted by R. Reich as an Assyrian citadel incorporating a temple.[27]

Among the Assyrian objects found in Palestine are cylinder seals, sometimes inscribed with names of officials; imported Assyrian "palace style" pottery reached even the table of the kings of Judah, as indicated by finds at the palace of Ramat Rahel. Local imitations of this pottery were common in the coastal plain, the northern Negev, and Transjordan. Other Assyrian quality goods, such as elaborate metal bowls and glass objects, were also imported into the country.

THE BABYLONIAN PERIOD

After sacking Nineveh (612 B.C.E.), the Babylonians and the Medes inherited the territory and structure of the Assyrian empire. The struggle between Babylon and Egypt in 609 B.C.E. necessarily resulted in Babylonian incursions into Palestine. Between 605 and 601 B.C.E. Philistia was sacked, and Judah was attacked by Nebuchadnezzar first in 597 B.C.E. and again in 586 B.C.E., when Jerusalem was destroyed.

Unlike the Assyrians, who deported the entire population of Israel after the conquest of Samaria, the Babylonians only exiled the upper classes, the poorer people being left to till the land (2 Kings 25:12; Jeremiah 39:9–10, 52:15–16); furthermore, the Babylonians did not introduce a new populace into the region. For Judah, therefore, this conquest was not as traumatic as the Assyrian suppression was for the northern kingdom. The Babylonian occupation of the country continued until 539 B.C.E., when Cyrus brought about the collapse of Babylon and founded the Persian empire. There are almost no historical sources for the period of Babylonian occupation of the country, except for a short time after the fall of Jerusalem, when Gedaliahu son of Ahikam, a pro-Babylonian minister of Zedekiah, tried to establish an autonomous government at Mizpah (Tell en-Nasbeh) before he was killed.[28]

The destruction levels caused by the Babylonian invasions were detected at many sites in Philistia (Ashdod, Ekron, Timnah) and in Judah (see p. 458). However, there is some evidence of a continuation of life at several Judean sites, particularly north of Jerusalem.[29] The most prominent of these is Mizpah (Tell en-Nasbeh), where occupation was uninterrupted throughout the sixth century B.C.E., corresponding to the biblical account which describes this city as the center of continued Judean autonomy. Similar continuous settlement during the sixth century B.C.E. was also evident at other sites in the region, such as Tell el-Ful (Gibeah), Gibeon, and Bethel, and at the fortress of Khirbet Abu et-Twein in the Hebron Hills. Perhaps most surprising of all is the evidence from Jerusalem itself—in the burial caves in the Hinnom Valley, where G. Barkai uncovered rich burial goods from both the end of the Iron Age and the Babylonian period.

Outside Judah, the Babylonian period is hardly known. At Megiddo Stratum II, a huge citadel (68 × 48 m) was erected at the eastern end of the mound, on top of the ruined "offsets and insets" city wall of the previous period. The dating of this fortress, and the identification of its builders, are disputed: some believe that it was erected by Josiah; others think it was Babylonian; A. Malamat suggested associating it with the Egyptian stronghold at Megiddo erected by Psametik I after 616 B.C.E.[30] Megiddo Stratum II survived through the sixth century, and the citadel probably served the Babylonian government in this part of the country. At Tell Keisan in the valley of Acre a thriving city from this age maintained trade relations with Cyprus and Greece. This exemplifies what appears to have been the general situation along the coast, where the Phoenicians and other local population prospered under the aegis of the Babylonian and the following Persian empires. A comparable floruit seems to have existed in Transjordan, as far as can be judged from the few tombs and excavated sites there. The Babylonian period, which is not sufficiently known archaeologically, serves as a link with the following Persian period which lasted over two hundred years, and in which the country was part of the Persian empire. Under the Persians, the Jewish exiles returned from Babylon and the second temple in Jerusalem was erected. Historically and archaeologically, a new era began.

NOTES

1. B. Oded in *WHJP*, vol. 4, pp. 236–46.

2. M. Dothan, *Ashdod II–III. ʾAtiqot 9–10*, Jerusalem 1971; M. Dothan and Y. Porath, *Ashdod IV. ʾAtiqot 15*, Jerusalem 1982.

3. R. Gophna, *Bulletin of the Israel Exploration Society* 27 (1963), pp. 173–80 (Hebrew); idem, *ʾAtiqot* 3 (1966), pp. 41–51; ibid. 6 (1970), pp. 25–30 (Hebrew).

4. G. L. Kelm and A. Mazar, *BASOR* 248 (1982), pp. 1–36; idem, *BASOR Supplement* 23 (1985), pp. 108–16; idem, *BAR* 15:1 (1989), pp. 36–49. On Ekron (Tel Miqne), see S. Gitin and T. Dothan, *BA* 50 (1987), pp. 197–222.

5. E. D. Oren et al., *Qadmoniot* 19 (1986), pp. 83–91 (Hebrew).

6. D. Harden, *The Phoenicians*, Harmondsworth 1971; S. Moscati, *The World of the Phoenicians*, New York 1968; J. D. Muhly in: *BAT*, pp. 177–91.

7. Amiran (1969), pp. 272–75; S. Chapman, *Berytus* 21 (1972), pp. 55–194.

8. See the debate between J. D. Muhly and O. Negbi, E. Stern, and D. Stronach in: *BAT*, pp. 221–29.

9. Z. Gal, *ZDPV* 101 (1985), pp. 114–27.

10. For a historical outline, see Oded in: *WHJP*, vol. 4, pp. 247–75.

11. J. A. Sauer in: *BAT*, pp. 206–14; idem, *BASOR* 263 (1986), pp. 14–19 (with full bibliography); J. F. A. Sawyer and D. J. A. Clines (eds.), *Midian, Moab and Edom*, Sheffield 1983. See also L. Harding, *The Antiquities of Jordan*, New York 1967; R. H. Dorneman, *The Archaeology of the Transjordan*, Milwaukee 1983, pp. 65–164.

12. J. B. Pritchard, *Tell es-Saidiyeh: Excavations on the Tell, 1964–1966*, Philadelphia 1985, pp. 4–59, 75–80.

13. J. Hoftijzer and G. Van der Kooij, *Aramaic Texts from Deir Alla*, Leiden 1976; A. Lemaire, *BAR* 11:5 (1985), pp. 26–39; B. A. Levine in: *BAT*, pp. 326–39.

14. *ANET*, pp. 320–21.

15. A. D. Tushingham, *Excavations at Dibon (Dhiban) in Moab. AASOR* 40, Cabbridge 1972; R. S. Boraas and L. T. Geraty (eds.), *Heshbon 1973–1976*, Berrien Springs, Mich., 1975–78.

16. G. M. Landes, *BA* 24 (1961), pp. 66–86. For more recent discoveries, see H. O. Thompson, *ADAJ* 17 (1972), pp. 47–72; ibid. 18 (1973), pp. 5–14; idem, *BASOR* 227 (1977), pp. 27–34.

17. A. Abou-Assaf, *Ugarit Forschungen* 12 (1980), pp. 7–102.

18. C. M. Bennett, *Levant* 5 (1973), pp. 1–11; ibid. 6 (1974), pp. 1–24; ibid. 9 (1977), pp. 1–10; idem in: *Kenyon Festschrift*, pp. 165–71.

19. C. M. Bennett, *ADAJ* 12–13 (1967–68), pp. 53–55; idem, *Levant* 3 (1971), pp. v–vii; ibid. 16 (1984), pp. 1–23; idem in: Hadidi (1982), pp. 181–87. On Umm el-Biyara, see idem, *PEQ* 98 (1966), pp. 123–26. On Ghara see: S. Hart, *Levant* 20 (1988), pp. 89–100.

20. E. Mazar, *IEJ* 35 (1985), pp. 253–69.

21. Yadin (1963), pp. 291–461; P. Albenda, *BA* 43 (1980), pp. 222–29.

22. E. Stern, *BA* 38 (1975), pp. 26–53; on the Assyrian architecture in Palestine see I. Dunayevsky and R. Amiran, *BASOR* 149 (1958), pp. 25–32; R. Reich in *Architecture*, pp. 182–88.

23. R. Reich, *IEJ* 25 (1975), pp. 234–36.

24. B. Brandel and R. Reich, *PEQ* 117 (1985), pp. 41–54.

25. E. D. Oren, *BA* 45 (1982), pp. 159–60.

26. G. Van Beek, *Qadmoniot* 21 (1973), pp. 23–27 (Hebrew).

27. R. Reich, *IEJ* 34 (1984), pp. 32–38.

28. A. Malamat in: *WHJP*, vol. 4, pp. 205–21.

29. S. Weinberg, *The Israel Academy of Sciences and Humanities, Proceedings* 5:5, Jerusalem 1969.

30. A. Malamat, *Journal of the Ancient Near Eastern Society of Columbia University* 5 (1973), pp. 267–81.

APPENDIX:
RECENT DISCOVERIES AND STUDIES

This Appendix includes descriptions of some new discoveries and references to recent publications.

ADDITIONAL GENERAL BIBLIOGRAPHY

P. R. S. Moorey, *A Century of Biblical Archaeology*, Cambridge, 1991.
W. G. Dever, *Recent Archaeological Discoveries and Biblical Research*, Seattle and London 1990. A collection of four essays: on the general approach to archaeology and biblical research; on the Israelite settlement; on Israelite monumental architecture; and on the Israelite cult.
H. D. Lance, *The Old Testament and the Archaeologist*, Philadelphia 1981.

CHAPTER TWO

Excavations at Basta in southern Transjordan (the region of Petra) revealed a well-preserved Pre-Pottery Neolithic B village. Stone houses with rectangular rooms were preserved to a height of more than 1 m. This is additional proof, aside from Biedha, of the importance of southern Transjordan in the Neolithic period, a significance that is probably due to different environmental conditions in this region, which today is arid and harsh.[1] Continued excavations at Ain Ghazal near Amman revealed more statues and clay figurines of great artistic interest. One piece (dubbed "pietà") is one of the earliest expressions of emotion in ancient art.

A late phase of the Pre-Pottery Neolithic period has been dubbed "PPNC." It contains the earliest evidence for pottery production.[2]

An amazingly well preserved Pre-Pottery Neolithic village was discovered in underwater excavations off the shore near ᶜAtlit, south of Haifa. Stone buildings, a well, built-up graves, and organic materials were found in an area that had been covered by water due to changes in the seashore since the Neolithic period.[3]

Yarmukian sites of the Pottery Neolithic period are now known in Transjordan (in the region of Jerash [Jebel Abu Thawab]). And at the upper level at Ain Ghazal.[4] Yarmukian remains were also found in the remote Nahal Kanah Cave, in the western Samaria Hills. These discoveries demonstrate the spread of the Yarmukian culture over the entire northern part of Palestine, on both sides of the Jordan.

NOTES

1. H. Nissen et al., *ADAJ* 31 (1987), pp. 79–120.
2. G. O. Rollefson, *ADAJ* 28 (1984), pp. 13–30; 30 (1986), pp. 41–55.
3. Excavations carried out by U. Galili on behalf of the Israel Antiquities Authority.
4. Z. Kafafi, *ADAJ* 29 (1985), pp. 31–41.

CHAPTER THREE

At the remote karstic cave of Nahal Kanah in the western Samaria Hills, important Chalcolithic finds are probably related to burial of highly ranked people. The most elaborate discovery is eight gold ring-shaped objects, each weighing between 88 and 165 grams.[1] The gold may have originated in Egypt, though no proof is available. These are the earliest gold objects found in the Levant, though contemporary gold is known from other regions of the ancient world. The Nahal Kanah discovery demonstrates long-distance trade, as well as a high degree of wealth and social ranking in the Chalcolithic period. Other finds in the cave include copper objects similar to those found in the Cave of Treasure in the Judean Desert.

NOTES

1. A Gopher et al., *Current Anthropology* 31 (1990), pp. 436–42.

ADDITIONAL BIBLIOGRAPHY

On metal objects: P. R. S. Moorey, *World Archaeology* 20 (1988), pp. 171–89; T. E. Levy and S. Shalev, *World Archaeology* 20 (1989), pp. 352–72.

On Ghassulian wall paintings: D. O. Cameron, *The Ghassulian Wall Paintings*, Luton 1981.

On the Chalcolithic site Tel Tsaf in the Jordan Valley: R. Gophna et al., *TA* 15–16 (1988–89), pp. 3–55.

CHAPTER FOUR

At Zeirakun in northern Transjordan, a large fortified Early Bronze III city was revealed. It included a cluster of temples and a circular altar, recalling the ritual complex at Megiddo. The discovery illustrates the spread—and abrupt end—of urbanism in northern Transjordan during this period.[1]

Continuous excavations at Yarmuth have revealed new data concerning the development of the fortification system, as well as the existence of a huge square architectural complex, the nature of which is as yet unclear, in the last phase of EB III.[2]

Research on the megalithic monument of Rujm Hiri in the Golan Heights has shown that this unique site was probably constructed during the Early Bronze period. It consists of three concentric circles of large basalt boulders, with transverse walls and two gates. The outer diameter is 156 m. At the center, there is a cairn 20 m in diameter and 7 m high, in which a room was constructed. The room, perhaps a burial place, was reused in the Late Bronze period. The design recalls megalithic stone circles in Europe. Research concerning the function of this site as an "astronomical observatory," and its possible function as a cultic and perhaps as a burial site, is in progress.[3]

A related study of the dolmens in the Golan Heights may indicate that many of them were established during the Early Bronze Age.[4]

The southernmost EB III site in Israel is Tel ʿIra, in the Arad Valley.[5]

NOTES

1. Excavations directed by S. Mittmann and M. Ibrahim.
2. P. de Miroschedji, *Eretz Israel* 21 (1991), pp. 48*–61*. The volume, dedicated to R. Amiran, contains additional papers dealing with the Early Bronze period.
3. The study is part of the Land of Geshur project directed by M. Kochavi. The research on Rujm Hiri is directed by Y. Mizrahi. See M. Kochavi, *IEJ* 39 (1989), pp. 11–13; M. Zohar, *IEJ* 39 (1989), pp. 18–31.
4. L. Vinitsky, *Eretz Israel* 21 (1991), pp. 167–73 (in Hebrew).
5. I. Beit Arieh, *IEJ* 41 (1991), pp. 1–18.

CHAPTER FIVE

Study of the pattern of settlement in the ENBIV/MBI period in the central hills region of Palestine reveals a substantial number of settlements that can be related to the vast cemeteries in this region.[1]

NOTE

1. I. Finkelstein, *IEJ* 41 (1991), pp. 19–45. See also idem, *Levant* 21 (1989), pp. 129–40.

CHAPTER SIX

Tel Nami, a small port town south of Haifa, is an additional MB IIA site in the chain of sites from this period established along the northern coastal plain. Like some other MB IIA sites in this region, it was abandoned in the MB IIB period.

Discoveries at Ashkelon include a tremendous rampart and glacis defending the northern slope of the mound. It is perhaps the best example of an MB IIB fortification system. A massive mud-brick wall was found on top of the rampart, as well as remains of what appears to be a gate structure. Structures at the bottom of the rampart may have been related to an outer gate leading to a nearby harbor. On the rampart, perhaps along a roadway leading to the upper gate, a small sanctuary was found. Inside the sanctuary a statuette of a young bull (calf) made of bronze and plated with silver was discovered in a pottery vessel shaped like a shrine. This is an excellent demonstration of the role of the young bull in Canaanite iconography, providing the background for the use of the golden calves in the Israelite temples of Dan and Bethel.[1]

Several articles address the question of the reasons for the fall of some great MB IIB cities and the disappearance of the dense MB IIB settlements in the Central Hill Country. Hoffmeier, following Redford, denies that Egypt played a major role in this process. Dever continues to hold the view that Egyptian pharaohs of the New Kingdom were responsible for major destruction in the country.[2] His view that the Middle Bronze period should be ended by the time of Tuthmosis III is not accpetable in my view. It ignores a cultural horizon characterized by Bichrome Ware in the coast and inner valleys and Chocolate-on-White Ware in the Jordan Valley and Transjordan.

An MB II shrine excavated at Tel Haror in the northern Negev illustrates the importance and wealth of this large site, one of the chain of Canaanite cities in southern Palestine that provide the background for the emergence of the Hyksos rule in Egypt.

A large project of neutron-activation analysis carried out on pottery from Tell ed-Dabᶜa, Palestine, and Syria has shown that many of the pottery vessels at Tell ed-Dabᶜa originated from southern Palestine. This is further evidence for the strong connections between this area and the eastern Delta during the Second Intermediate period in Egypt.[3]

A demographic study based on an estimation of the area of all the MB IIB settlements known so far concluded that the population of the country (west of the Jordan) was about 140,000 people.[4]

NOTES

1. L. E. Stager, *BAR* XVII:2 (1991), pp. 24–31 and front page.
2. J. K. Hoffmeier, *Levant* 21 (1989), pp. 181–93; W. G. Dever, *Levant* 22 (1990), pp. 75–82; J. K. Hoffmeier, *Levant* 22 (1990), pp. 83–90; S. Bunimowitz in: N. Naᵓaman and I. Finkelstein (eds.), *From Nomadism to Kingship*, Jerusalem 1990, pp. 257–83 (Hebrew; English edition in press).
3. M. Bietak, *BASOR* 281 (1991), pp. 27–72, and W. G. Dever comments, op. cit., pp. 73–79.
4. M. Broshi and R. Gophna *BASOR* 261 (1986), pp. 73–90.

ADDITIONAL BIBLIOGRAPHY

On the painted floor in Minoan style from Kabri: A. Kempinski and W.-D. Niemeier, *Excavations at Kabri—Preliminary Report of 1989 Season*, Tel Aviv 1990, pp. XVI–XXVIII.

CHAPTER SEVEN

Excavations on the Upper Mound at Hazor have revealed what was probably the palace of the local ruler during the Late Bronze Age.[1] The excavation of this impressive, monumental building has only started.

Excavations at Tel Beth Shean have shown that the sanctuary of Stratum IX there had two phases, which probably date to the late fifteenth and fourteenth centuries B.C.E. In an earlier phase, but later than the MB IIB period, an additional small temple was found. It is the earliest example of a temple with an irregular plan, benches and raised platforms along the walls. It recalls the Fosse Temple at Lachish and the temple of Tel Mevorakh.[2]

The ongoing debate over the date of the Exodus and the archaeological background for the Israelite conquest continues. Recent suggestions date the Exodus in the mid–fifteenth century B.C.E. and identify a Late Bronze I destruction level at Jericho as reflecting the conquest of that city by Joshua. These suggestions appear to me naive and irrelevant, in spite of their being based on analysis of archeological finds.[3]

NOTES

1. Information based on a tour of the site by the excavator, Prof. A. Ben Tor.
2. A. Mazar, *Eretz Israel* 21 (1990), pp. 197–211 (Hebrew; English version in press).
3. J. J. Bimson, *Redating the Exodus and Conquest*, Sheffield 1981. On Jericho, see: B. G. Wood, *BAR* XVI: 2 (1990), pp. 44–59; XVI:5 (1990), pp. 45–49. Contra P. Bienkowski, *Jericho in the Late Bronze Age*, Warminster 1986; idem, *BAR* XVI:5 (1990), pp. 45–46.

CHAPTER EIGHT

F. J. Yurco has suggested that reliefs on one of the walls of the temple of Amun at Karnak, which had been dated to the time of Ramesses II, belong in fact to the time of Merneptah. The conquest of Ashkelon (see p. 235 in this book) and of two additional anonymous cities depicted on this relief may reflect the conquest of Ashkelon, Gezer, and Yenoam mentioned in "the Israel Stele" of Merneptah. Yurco has identified the Israelites with a group of surrendering people who look like Canaanites shown in this relief. E. F. Rainey has suggested that the Israelites should be identified with another group of people on this relief, who are shown in the usual Egyptian manner of depicting the nomadic Shasu. These suggestions may have important implications for the study of the origins of Israel and its status as a well-known group of nomadic tribes in the thirteenth century B.C.E.[1]

Philistine finds at Ashkelon are similar to those at Ashdod and Ekron. Locally produced Mycenaean IIIC pottery marks the arrival of the Philistines and is followed by the appearance of Philistine Bichrome Ware.[2]

At Dor, the Iron Age I city probably occupied by the *tkr* Sea Peoples, is buried under deep debris of later periods. However, the period was reached in a small area, which produced important data concerning the nature of the stratigraphy and the relations of the city with Cyprus.[3]

At Tel Hadar, on the eastern shore of the Lake of Galilee, a rounded, fortified town of the eleventh century B.C.E. was explored. A storehouse with two rows of pillars is one of the best preserved and earliest examples of such buildings in Israel. An attached building was a public granary. The site may have been an administrative center in the Land of Geshur. It was heavily burned, perhaps during the Israelite conquest by Saul or David.[4]

NOTES

1. F. J. Yurco, *BAR* XVI:5 (1990), pp. 20–38; A. F. Rainey, *BAR* XVII:6 (1991), pp. 54–60, and Yurco's response, op. cit., p. 61.
2. L. Stager, *BAR* XVII:2 (1991), pp. 32–43.
3. A. Gilboa, *IEJ* 39 (1989), pp. 204–18.
4. M. Kochavi, *IEJ* 39 (1989), pp. 9–11.

ADDITIONAL BIBLIOGRAPHY

On the Israelite settlement: W. G. Dever in: C. D. Miller, P. D. Hanson, and S. D. McBride (eds.), *Ancient Israelite Religion: Essays in Honor of Frank Moore Cross*, Philadelphia 1987, pp. 207–47. Also Dever (above, general bibliography).
On the discoveries at Giloh: A. Mazar, *IEJ* 40 (1990), pp. 77–101.
On the excavation of Khirbet ed-Dawwara (a small village site from the end of the Iron Age I in the Land of Benjamin): I. Finkelstein, *TA* 17 (1990), pp. 163–208.
On the survey of the Land of Manasseh: A. Zertal, *BAR* XVII:5 (1991), pp. 28–49.
On the Philistine culture: S. Bunimovitz, *TA* 17 (1990), pp. 210–22.
On the excavations at Ekron: T. Dothan, *BAR* Vol. XVI:1 (1990), pp. 20–36.
On Megiddo Stratum VIIA: I. Zinger, *TA* 15–16 (1988–89), pp. 101–12.

CHAPTER NINE

Controversy over basic problems of the archaeology of the United Kingdom grew to new dimensions in recent articles. See mainly: A. R. Millard, *BAR* XV:3 (1989), pp. 20–29; K. A. Kitchen, op. cit., pp. 30–34; G. J. Wightman, *BASOR* 277/278 (1990), pp. 5–22; D. Ussishkin, op. cit., pp. 73–91; J. S. Holladay, op. cit., pp. 23–65; W. E. Rast, *Eretz Israel* 20 (1989), pp. 166*–71*; J. M. Miller, *PEQ* 123 (1991), pp. 28–31;

A. R. Millard, op. cit., pp. 119–18. Some of the views in these articles appear unacceptable to me. Wightman, for example, leaves the time of Solomon with almost no archaeological evidence, while he glorifies the time of Ahab. Holladay's conclusions may cause confusion in the entire Iron Age pottery chronology of Palestine.

CHAPTER TEN

Excavations at Jezreel (directed by D. Ussishkin and J. Woodhead) after salvage operations at the site revealed fortifications and perhaps part of a monumental enclosure dating from the Israelite Kingdom (ninth to eighth centuries B.C.E.), when Jezreel served as a palace of the kings of the Northern Kingdom of Israel.

ADDITIONAL BIBLIOGRAPHY

On the Assyrian siege of Lachish: D. Ussishkin, *TA* 17 (1990), pp. 53–86.
On the development of Iron Age pottery at Lachish: O. Zimhoni, *TA* 19 (1990), pp. 3–50.
For a new historical evaluation, diminishing the kingdom of Josiah: N. Naᵓaman, *TA* 18 (1991), pp. 3–71.
On Dor and the development of Iron Age II city gates: E. Stern, *IEJ* 40 (1990), pp. 12–30.
For a final report on the excavations at Kinneret: F. Fritz, *Kinneret*, Wiesbaden 1990.

CHAPTER ELEVEN

ADDITIONAL BIBLIOGRAPHY

On small altars from Ekron and other sites: S. Gitin, *Eretz Israel* 20 (1989), pp. 52*–67*.

CHAPTER TWELVE

ADDITIONAL BIBLIOGRAPHY

On the shrine at Hurvat Qitmit: Y. Beit Arieh, *TA* 18 (1991), pp. 93–116.
On the excavations of the Iron Age II city at Ekron: S. Gitin, *BAR* XVI:2 (1990), pp. 32–43.

GENERAL INDEX

SCRIPTURES INDEX

CENTER FOR JUDAIC-CHRISTIAN STUDIES

The emergence in our time of the third commonwealth of Israel has been a boon to biblical studies, both for Jews and for Christians. The ever-enlarging research in Israel, by archaeologists, historians, linguists, and rabbinic and New Testament specialists, is increasing our knowledge and enriching our appreciation of our common spiritual heritage.

The interrelationships of Judaism and Christianity and the Hebraic foundations of both are subjects of considerable interest to the Center for Judaic-Christian Studies. Through a wide range of educational endeavors we are informing the Christian community about its biblical roots and its fertile Hebrew heritage. We do this through lectures, seminars, and national conferences; producing audio and video teaching tapes and a twelve-part television series; and publishing unique and outstanding books such as the present volume by Amihai Mazar.

The cornerstone of the Center's biblical interests is the innovative work in Israel of the Jerusalem School of Synoptic Research. This team of Jewish and Christian scholars, building upon twenty-five years of fruitful collaboration between Dr. Robert Lindsey and Professor David Flusser, is illuminating the life and times of Jesus within the Jewish cultural milieu of the first century.

You may learn more about the Center for Judaic-Christian Studies by writing to us at the address below. A complimentary copy of the *Jerusalem Perspective,* a bimonthly report from Israel on Gospel research, is available upon request, as is a copy of the Center's catalog of educational materials.

Dwight A. Pryor, President
Center for Judaic-Christian Studies
P.O. Box 293040
Dayton, OH 45429